MONEY, MORALITY, AND CULTURE IN LATE MEDIEVAL AND EARLY MODERN EUROPE

Money, Morality, and Culture in Late Medieval and Early Modern Europe

Edited by
JULIANN VITULLO and DIANE WOLFTHAL

ASHGATE

Published by
Ashgate Publishing Limited
Wey Court East
Union Road
Farnham
Surrey, GU9 7PT
England

Ashgate Publishing Company
Suite 420
101 Cherry Street
Burlington
VT 05401-4405

www.ashgate.com

British Library Cataloguing in Publication Data
Money, morality, and culture in late medieval and early modern Europe.
1. Europe--Economic conditions--To 1492. 2. Europe--Economic conditions--16th century. 3. Europe--Economic conditions--17th century. 4. Economics--Sociological aspects. 5. Money in literature. 6. Wealth--Moral and ethical aspects--Europe--History--To 1500. 7. Wealth--Moral and ethical aspects--Europe--History--16th century. 8. Wealth--Moral and ethical aspects--Europe--History--17th century.
I. Vitullo, Juliann M. II. Wolfthal, Diane.
306.3'094'09022-dc22

Library of Congress Cataloging-in-Publication Data
Vitullo, Juliann M.
Money, morality, and culture in late medieval and early modern Europe / Juliann Vitullo and Diane Wolfthal.
p. cm.
Includes bibliographical references and index.
ISBN 978-0-7546-6497-0 (hardback : alk. paper)
1. Money--Moral and ethical aspects--Europe--History. 2. Europe--Social conditions.
I. Wolfthal, Diane. II. Title.

HG220.3.V58 2009
306.3094'0903--dc22

2009035315

ISBN 9780754664970

Mixed Sources
Product group from well-managed forests and other controlled sources
www.fsc.org Cert no. SA-COC-1565
© 1996 Forest Stewardship Council
FSC

Printed and bound in Great Britain by
MPG Books Group, UK

Contents

List of Figures

Notes on the Contributors

Kathleen Ashley, Professor of English at the University of Southern Maine, has published widely on medieval cultural performance, hagiography, autobiography, conduct literature, and cultural history. She is the author of an edition of the morality play *Mankind* (forthcoming); *Being a Pilgrim: Art and Ritual on the Medieval Routes to Santiago* (2009); and *The Cults of Sainte Foy and the Cultural Work of Saints* (forthcoming). She has published several articles from her studies of late medieval and early modern Burgundy using a micro-historical approach to the bourgeoisie based in archival research, and is at work on a book about these "shapers of urban culture."

Michael Long is Associate Professor of Music at the University at Buffalo (SUNY). He has published several articles on fourteenth- and fifteenth-century music in the *Journal of the American Musicological Society*, most recently "Singing Through the Looking Glass: Child's Play and Learning in Medieval Italy" (Summer 2008). Other essays have appeared in *L'ars nova italiana del trecento*, *Early Music History*, *Music and Society: Antiquity and the Middle Ages*, and *Antoine Busnoys: Method, Meaning and Context in Late Medieval Music*. His book, *Beautiful Monsters: Imagining the Classic in Musical Media*, was published in 2008.

Julia I. Miller is Professor of Art History at California State University, Long Beach, specializing in late medieval and Renaissance art. She has published articles on Italian and Flemish art in journals including the *Art Bulletin* and *Studies in Iconography*, concentrating on patronage and context. Her current research has been in collaboration with Laurie Taylor-Mitchell, and has focused on the religious order of the Humiliati. They have jointly published three articles about specific works of art in the Humiliati church of Ognissanti in Florence, and they are working on a monograph about the church as a whole.

Ian Frederick Moulton, Head of Interdisciplinary Humanities and Communication in Arizona State University's School of Letters and Sciences, is a cultural historian and literary scholar who has published widely on the representation of gender and sexuality in early modern literature. He is the author of *Before Pornography: Erotic Writing in Early Modern England* (2000), and editor and translator of Antonio Vignali's *La Cazzaria*, an erotic and political dialogue from Renaissance Italy (2003). He is currently writing a book on the cultural dissemination of notions of romantic love in sixteenth-century Europe.

James M. Murray is Professor of History and Director of the Medieval Institute at Western Michigan University. He is the author of *Bruges, Cradle of Capitalism, 1280–1390* and *A History of Business in Medieval Europe*. His current research is devoted to the origins of money and commodities markets in the medieval Low Countries.

Bradley D. Ryner is Assistant Professor of English at Arizona State University. He has published articles on the representation of battle as a system of exchange in *The Battle of Maldon* (*English Studies*, 2006), commodity fetishism in Richard Brome's *A Mad Couple Well Watched* (*Early Modern Literary Studies*, 2008), and commercial metaphors in Shakespeare's *Cymbeline* (in *Global Traffic*, 2008). He is currently working on a book-length manuscript that examines the conventions used by mercantile writers and dramatists to represent economic systems c. 1600–1642.

Robert S. Sturges is Professor of English at Arizona State University, where he teaches late medieval literature, literary theory, and gender and sexuality studies. His research interests range from Middle English devotional literature to cultural constructions of the late medieval body and the representation of power relations in late medieval and early modern culture. His books include *Medieval Interpretation* (1990), *Chaucer's Pardoner and Gender Theory* (2000), *Dialogue and Deviance* (2005), and, as editor, *Law and Sovereignty in the Middle Ages and the Renaissance* (forthcoming). He is currently completing, with Elizabeth Urquhart, an edition of *The Middle English Pseudo-Augustinian Soliloquies and Its Anti-Lollard Commentary*.

Laurie Taylor-Mitchell teaches Art History at Hood College in Frederick, Maryland. She has written extensively on guild patronage in Florence at Orsanmichele, and is currently writing a book with Julia Miller on the patronage of the Humiliati order in the church of Ognissanti. They have co-authored an essay on Giotto's *Ognissanti Madonna* and the patronage of the Humiliati, published in *The Cambridge Companion to Giotto* (2003), "Donatello's 'S. Rossore', the Battle of San Romano and the church of Ognissanti" (*Burlington Magazine*, 2006), and "Humility and Piety: The *Annunciation* in the Church of Ognissanti in Florence" (*Studies in Iconography*, 2009).

Giacomo Todeschini is Professor of Medieval History at the University of Trieste. His research focuses on the development of medieval economic theory and languages, the Christian doctrine of infamy and exclusion from citizenship and the marketplace, and the political role of Jews inside of the Christian medieval-modern world. He has been a fellow at the École Normale Supérieure (Paris), the Oxford Centre for Hebrew and Jewish Studies, and the Institute for Advanced Study (Princeton). Among his main publications: *I mercanti e il Tempio. La società cristiana e il circolo virtuoso della ricchezza fra Medioevo* *ed Età Moderna* (2002); *Visibilmente crudeli. Malviventi, persone sospette e gente qualunque dal medioevo all'età moderna* (2007); *Franciscan Wealth. From Voluntary Poverty to Market Society* (2009).

Juliann Vitullo is Associate Professor of Italian and Associate Director of the School of International Letters and Culture at Arizona State University. She is the author of *The Chivalric Epic in Medieval Italy* (2000), and the co-editor of the volume *At the Table: Metaphorical and Material Cultures of Food in Medieval and Early Modern Europe* (2007). Her current research projects include *The Art of Fatherhood in Early Modern Italy*, which focuses on debates about fatherhood in the mercantile world of early modern Italy.

Diane Wolfthal, David and Caroline Minter Chair in the Humanities and Professor of Art History at Rice University, has authored *The Beginnings of Netherlandish Canvas Painting* (1989), *Images of Rape: The "Heroic" Tradition and its Alternatives* (1999), *Picturing Yiddish: Gender, Identity, and Memory in Illustrated Yiddish Books of Renaissance Italy* (2004), and *In and Out of the Marital Bed: Seeing Sex in Late Medieval and Early Modern Art* (forthcoming). She edited a book of peace and negotiation, and co-edited another on the family. She serves as Founding Co-editor of *Early Modern Women: An Interdisciplinary Journal*.

Acknowledgments

Since beginning this study five years ago, we have been helped by innumerable friends, colleagues, and institutions. We are grateful to Arizona State University (ASU) for permitting us to team-teach a seminar on "Merchants and Culture," in which we developed the ideas for this volume. We would also like to thank ASU's Institute for Humanities Research (IHR) for a Collaborative Fellowship, which we were awarded in 2006–2007, which funded a monthly seminar for faculty and students as well as a public symposium that grew out of that course. Deepest thanks are due Jennifer Pendergrass, our research assistant, for generously and expertly facilitating these activities. We would also like to thank the Institute's directors, Rachel Fuchs and Sally L. Kitch, as well as its staff member, Jennifer Petruzzella, for their support. We owe a special debt of gratitude to Carol Withers, the Assistant Director of IHR, whose kindness and competence we benefitted from on a daily basis. We are also grateful to the Phoenix Art Museum for hosting the symposium, and the School of International Letters and Cultures, the School of Art, and the Arizona Center for Medieval and Renaissance Studies, for their support of the symposium. We greatly appreciate the participation of Jim Murray, who first presented a paper at the symposium and then contributed an essay to this volume. Several members of the faculty seminar—Ian Moulton, Brad Ryner, Bob Sturges—not only gave presentations at the seminar, but also contributed essays to this volume. We would also like to express our gratitude to Giacomo Todeschini for presenting a talk at ASU and then contributing the essay that developed from that paper to this volume. We are further indebted to Kathleen Ashley, Michael Long, Julia Miller, and Laurie Taylor-Mitchell for contributing essays to this volume. One editor, Diane Wolfthal, would like to thank her present institution, Rice University, for granting her release time and research moneys to complete this volume. Finally, we greatly appreciate the efforts of our editor Erika Gaffney and the comments of an anonymous reader. We dedicate this book to our husbands, Taylor Corse and Maurice Wolfthal, with gratitude for the "wealth" of their companionship and support.

Introduction

As we prepare this volume for press, the entire global economy is at risk of recession. After years in which public debates about "values" have emphasized sexual practices, the economic crisis has changed that focus to monetary transactions and financial policy. The United States government is discouraging banks from "hoarding" money, the President speaks about "sharing" the wealth, and many editorial writers decry the "greed" of Wall Street. These discussions encourage us as scholars to study early debates that took place during the rise of the monetary economy, from the thirteenth through the seventeenth centuries, in which monetary practices were discussed as moral decisions, which affected both the soul of the individual and the greater Christian community. The invitation of these early thinkers to examine the fairness and communal benefit of even small everyday transactions offers us a remarkable challenge from the past, yet the inclination to scapegoat and persecute targeted groups during times of economic change and crisis is a historical tendency that we do not want to repeat.[1] We want to ensure that our culture does not resurrect Shylock. Finally, by rediscovering the joys and hopes that the fluidity and mobility of the monetary system represented, as well as the insecurities that the new abstract economy generated, we can better face some of our own ethical contradictions and financial fears.

The thirteenth-century philosopher, Thomas Aquinas, following 1 Timothy 6:10, declared:

> … we must say that covetousness, as denoting a special sin, is called the root of all sins, in likeness to the root of a tree, in furnishing sustenance to the whole tree. For we see that by riches man acquires the means of committing any sin whatever, and of sating his desire for any sin whatever, since money helps man to obtain all manner of temporal goods, according to Ecclesiastes 10:19: "All things obey money": so that in this desire for riches is the root of all sins.

This quotation is a good example of the kind of theological condemnation not only of usury, the lending of money for interest, but of money itself in the late Middle Ages.[2]

Whether pride or avarice should be established as the "root of all sins" was a debate that had existed for centuries.[3] Theologians could cite biblical passages to support either point of view. Although both vices remained important in religious writings as the origins of other sins, avarice gained ground during the commercial revolution. It even became more "visible" as iconographic depictions of a hideous man grasping tightly a bag of coins or weighed down by purses around his neck became as prolific as the images of a sumptuously dressed knight as the symbol of pride.[4] Specific social groups with different ways of gaining and maintaining power were associated with the two deadliest of sins: knights with pride and merchants with avarice. At the same time, however, both pride and avarice were still described as important elements of a vicious circular movement in which sinners at once distance themselves from God (pride) and instead focus on worldly goods (avarice): both, then, were seen acting in a symbiotic relationship as the genealogical origin of all sin.[5] It is more a question of emphasis; artists and writers of the late Middle Ages and early modern periods focus attention on the vice of avarice rather than of pride, just as new religious movements, such as the mendicants, concentrate more on the virtue of voluntary poverty than on obedience.[6]

It is not surprising, then, that out of the approximately 20 punishments that Dante depicts in his thirteenth-century *Hell*, at least ten deal with an excessive desire for riches.[7] He targets two groups of sinners when condemning monetary sins, high ecclesiastics, including recent Popes, and men from Italian mercantile cities such as Florence, Siena, Bologna, and Padua.[8] One of the earliest reflections on exchange and the marketplace in the writings of Church fathers was the notion that consecrated goods were priceless and could not be sold. Augustine was one of many Christian authors who unfairly condemned Jews for having confused a sacred good without a fixed value that cannot be sold with a non-sacred good with a fixed value that can be sold. The importance of separating sacred from non-sacred goods, and the great desire to exclude spiritual goods from the marketplace, placed simony at the heart of many philosophical and literary discussions as the monetary economy developed. It also falsely stereotyped the Jew as the avaricious sinner who placed the love of temporal goods, symbolized most often as money or a money bag, above spiritual commitments and divine truths.[9] The avaricious, especially the simonists, refuted the supremacy of the divine by selling spiritual goods, just as Judas had supposedly sold Christ for coins. His money sack became an emblematic depiction of money that is visualized throughout the early modern period, and that created a strong symbolic connection between money and heresy, since Jews were often lumped together with pagans and other groups who, according to some Christian theologians, also refused to honor the priceless nature of the Divine.[10] This great desire in early modern Christian thought to retain a sacred space, a pure identity beyond the material world of monetary negotiations and financial transactions, was one attempt to control the fluidity of the new marketplace, and it was a strategy that engendered endless contradictions and anxieties, which still challenge us today.

In search of this utopian identity, St Francis, the son of a wealthy cloth merchant from Assisi, made a very strong statement in the debate about money, men, and morality at the beginning of the thirteenth century when he renounced his family's possessions and wealth by stripping off his clothes in a public square and giving them back to his own biological father, whom he also renounced for the Heavenly one. This scene, which became part of the standard iconography of St Francis' life, was reproduced in images throughout the early modern period. His first biographer, Thomas Celano, emphasizes that even before his public conversion, the saint no longer wanted to even touch money.[11] Yet during the same period in which Thomas Aquinas and Francis of Assisi portrayed money as a spiritual contagion, the modern European monetary economy developed, quickly transforming every aspect of everyday life.

As the monetary economy emerged, new urban social groups of merchants, artisans, notaries, and lawyers also evolved and encouraged enormous social changes. For practical reasons of trade, they wrote documents and records in the languages that they spoke. While the Church continued to cultivate an ecclesiastical culture in Latin, the mercantile cities became centers of new vernacular literary cultures. These groups helped to break down the borders between the sacred and secular by forming their own lay religious groups, such as confraternities, in which they would express their spirituality in prayers written and sung in the vernacular, and through affective, physical forms of spirituality such as flagellation, in which the new city-dwellers tried to connect directly with Christ by imitating his suffering and revering his poverty.[12] While the monetary economy encouraged the development of new urban social groups, many members of the European mercantile cities had important questions about ethical uses of money: How could a man participate in the monetary economy and still follow the example of Christ or even St Francis? Was the decision of St Francis to voluntarily distance himself from both his family and the monetary economy the only model? Could Christians use the monetary economy for virtuous purposes? These questions, which centered on the role of a merchant in Christian culture, helped shape late medieval and early modern debates about what it meant to be a Christian in a society that both religious and secular writers increasingly depicted in terms of the marketplace.

Armando Sapori dates the origins of capitalism to this period when men started not only to work for pure sustenance or to create a more comfortable life, "but with the will to reinvest money earned in order to multiply it and that they use their means to proceed not empirically but rationally and systematically."[13] This new goal—to not only earn money but then make that money grow in a methodical fashion—challenged many traditional Christian and classical notions of how men were supposed to work. It also created a new class of men who, distanced from physical labor and manual tasks, learned to strategize and manipulate the abstract fictions of the monetary economy. While this volume explores the contradictions, fears, and anxieties that arose as capitalist values competed with traditional classical and Christian ethics, it also investigates the creative ways in which Europeans responded to the new moral challenges of a more fluid and global economic system.

Other scholars have paved the way for this interdisciplinary volume, focusing on how the development of the monetary economy changed both the cognitive and quotidian habits of Europeans. Jacques Le Goff suggests that the notion of Purgatory, the third realm of the afterlife, developed with the monetary economy, which encouraged a questioning of traditional binary oppositions such as Heaven and Hell or nobles and peasants.[14] Joel Kaye also explores how the rise of the monetary economy was tied to new forms of relativistic analysis in which one could determine the value of an object through negotiation and by context.[15] Anne Derbes and Mark Sandona have shown how the debate over usury encouraged reflection on charity and the creation of magnificent works of art.[16] Like the work of Le Goff, that of Derbes and Sandona implies that the ethical debates over usury might have provoked new ways of thinking and new forms of creativity.[17] Michael Baxandall suggests that mercantile skills, such as gauging, influenced formal aspects of early modern painting.[18] Evelyn Welch examines the consumerism of early modern culture; Simon Schama investigates the ambivalence the Dutch felt about their wealth; while Lisa Jardine explores how the trade in luxury goods affected Christians' relationships with Muslims.[19] These are just a few of the studies that encouraged us to examine how the medieval and early modern texts, images, and music that we research were influenced by new practices and ideals that developed with the rise of the monetary economy; in particular we decided to focus on the ways in which these same historical artifacts participated in debates about "trading values," or negotiating different sets of often conflicting moral principles.

* * *

This volume consists of nine essays that explore the negotiations between the rise of the monetary economy and the cultural values of late medieval and early modern culture. Our contributors specialize in a range of disciplines—art history, economic history, musicology, and English, Italian, and comparative literature—and explore a wide geographical area—Italy, the Netherlands, France, and England—as well as five centuries, from the thirteenth through the seventeenth. Furthermore, they focus on a broad range of topics—peasants, merchants, prostitutes, moneychangers, and philanthropists, as well as a religious movement and a madrigal. But these essays collectively demonstrate that the dramatic shift occasioned by the new mercantile economy crossed cultural and political boundaries.

The first group of three essays, "Defining the Players," examines the debates about the meaning of specific economic terms, which represented important concepts in the developing monetary economy. Robert Sturges, in his essay "'Nerehand nothyng to pay or to take': Poverty, Labor, and Money in Four Towneley Plays," focuses on the ideological conflict surrounding contrasting notions of poverty through the analysis of four medieval English mystery plays attributed to the Wakefield Master. Sturges notes that the Wakefield Master at times suggests that the source of the peasants' bitterness is their poverty, and even recognizes class "inequalities and abuses." However, the poet is consistently critical of any attempts by the peasants to improve their material condition through participation in the monetary economy. The poet opens a space for anti-manorial feeling through the words of Cain and Noah's wife, but these expressions go against sacred history. Sturges concludes that, especially in the *Second Peasant's Play*, class consciousness is sharper and the gentry are blamed in bitter language for the peasants' poverty. In the end, though, the apparent tension of conflicting views of poverty is resolved as the poet concludes by supporting the dominant Christian ideology, and depicting the peasants' attempts at betterment as foolish and sinful. Sturges' essay also suggests that many contemporary medievalists who continue to interpret the depiction of poverty in medieval texts in strictly theological terms not only avoid the tension between different notions of poverty that exists in the textual tradition, but also adopt the same idealized concept of poverty and "harmony models" as the Wakefield Master.

The next two essays in the section on defining economic terms both deal with the question of usury. While Giacomo Todeschini examines the definition of usury in late medieval religious texts, James Murray discusses the slippery distinction between usurer and moneychanger in the well-developed monetary economy of Flemish urban society. Todeschini's essay, "The Incivility of Judas: 'Manifest' Usury as a Metaphor for the 'Infamy of Fact' (*infamia facti*)," begins by exploring the association between the conceptions of usury and infamy, that is, the incapacity to participate in the life of the Christian community. Focusing on theological writings and canon law, he shows that a new definition of exclusion arose, which was termed the "infamy of fact." Those who fell into this category made visible their misdeeds. To better our understanding of this category, Todeschini turns to the role of Judas and Judaism as metaphors of otherness in theological and economic discourses. He then shows how authors contrasted Judas to the Magdalene, through contrasting styles of managing wealth. By tracing changes in how Judas and usury were conceived, he successfully demonstrates how the definition of *usura* was transformed from "a sign of evil" and "generic greediness" to "a specific economic transaction realized by the selling of money and the pledging of immobile goods." Todeschini concludes his discussion of the evolving definition of this term by suggesting that the prohibition against usury had more to do with its metaphoric connections to infamy and infidels (specifically Judas) than with the opposition to specific monetary transactions.

While Todeschini focuses on the metaphorical meanings of usury, James M. Murray, in his essay, "The Devil's Evangelists? Moneychangers in Flemish Urban Society," examines proverbs, paintings, archival evidence, biblical exegesis, and theological treatises in the Aristotelian tradition to investigate the ambivalent attitudes towards the role of moneychangers in the Low Countries from the thirteenth through the sixteenth centuries. The moneychangers' chief role was to ensure that underweight and damaged coins were removed from circulation, but they were also sometimes merchants, bankers, and entrepreneurs who borrowed and lent money at interest, and so became associated with usury. The target of riots, moneychangers were also largely absent from the inner circle that dominated Flemish finance and politics. They largely consisted of members of marginal groups, such as foreigners and women. Murray's essay demonstrates that while the moneychanger "was at the center of the urban economy in the late medieval Low Countries," the value of the profession remained ambivalent; a striking tension persisted between "the economic and social moral status of the profession."

The second group of three essays, "Questions of Value," examines how music and literature explore anxieties that arose around the new meaning of value that accompanied the rise of the monetary economy. All three essays investigate, to cite Ian Moulton's words, the concerns Europeans had about "the fluidity of money, and its capacity to undermine traditional social structures of value and identity." Moulton's essay, "Whores as Shopkeepers: Money and Sexuality in Aretino's *Ragionamenti*," argues that the Italian sixteenth-century writer Pietro Aretino employs the figure of the whore Nanna to offer a biting critique of the mercantile economy, in which it often seemed that "everything can be openly bought and sold." But Aretino also ironically implies that the prostitute is, in fact, "the last honest person," since she is candid about her commoditization. Aretino suggests through Nanna that whores are not women, but rather form a separate category of gender, since, like men, they compete in the marketplace and often against men. Moulton's essay suggests that early modern Italians judged the motivation of courtesans differently than their medieval counterparts; they viewed prostitutes as driven not by sexual pleasure, but rather by money. Moreover, unlike Aretino's chapters in the *Ragionamenti* that explore the life of the nun and the wife, the final chapter on the life of the prostitute thoroughly adopts the terms of the marketplace to describe Nanna's sexual activities. Not only is it filled with economic metaphors for sex, but Aretino shows how Nanna develops economic strategies to enrich herself: she diversifies her clients, invests for greater future gains, and acknowledges that the greatest power is financial. Moulton's essay then suggests that the picture of the whore Nanna is also a self-portrait of the writer Aretino, who had successfully marketed his writing, including erotica, in order to accumulate great wealth. In this essay, Moulton justly defines a key cause for anxiety in this period: "If everything can be changed into anything else, nothing has any real identity beyond an abstract (and fluctuating) exchange value. If anything has a price, nothing is unique; nothing has a fixed identity." He concludes with a sentence that succinctly summarizes one of the themes of this book: "market values confer social value, even moral value."

Unlike earlier publications that interpret the effect of the monetary economy on late medieval music, Michael Long's "The Sound of Money in Late Medieval Music" examines the ways in which this music is intimately linked to the proportional, material, and moral aspects of coinage. First, Long closely analyzes an Aristotelian treatise on the debasement of coinage, *De moneta*, which was written by the Frenchman Nicole Oresme in the 1350s. In this text, Oresme contends that political, financial, and musical matters, such as tenor-based polyphony, should reflect a "balance inherent to a fair and equitable system of currency and currency management under the watchful eye of a strong and well-advised prince." Long further argues that the dependence on coins as a "model and metaphor" for thinking about proportions influenced the development of the musical concept that a particular note is to be held for a particular length of time. The essay then examines "Dà a chi avaregia" by the Tuscan Lorenzo Masini, which draws on the sound of the clink of coins, the proportional system found in both music and currency, and the moral discourse surrounding the new monetary economy. Furthermore, in this madrigal, the rapidity of notes is designed to suggest the accumulation of wealth. Long further demonstrates that we are meant to hear in Masini's music the vicissitudes of the financial market. Niccolò Soldanieri's lyrics for this composition concern hoarding and interrogate the value of money. Long concludes that musical education was intimately tied to the function of money and the practice of merchants in an ethical society.

Like Long's essay, the last article in this section, Bradley D. Ryner's "Anxieties of Currency Exchange in Middleton and Rowley's *The Changeling*," is in large part concerned with the problem of the devaluation of currency. Ryner investigates how *The Changeling*, a play that was completed in 1622, expresses anxieties about the depreciation of English coins and its effects on that nation's precarious position in international trade. Written at the same time as the economic depression of 1620–24, *The Changeling* articulates the widespread uneasiness about the instability of the value of money and the vicissitudes of exchange. Ryner examines the play in the context of contemporary mercantile reports and treatises by Thomas Mun and Gerard Malynes, and explores the ways in which anxiety about the monetary economy is inscribed within the language, plot, and title of the play. Ryner investigates the playwrights' choice of such economically charged words as "venture," the failure of the attempt by one character, Beatrice-Joanna, at prudent investment, and the revelation that she and another character, De Flores, are changelings. Ryner justly concludes that both the financial treatises and the theatrical play were independent reactions to the same economic concerns, especially the problem of "how to correctly judge the relationship between an object's intrinsic and extrinsic (or ascribed) value, how to judge the commensurability of objects, and how to make sense of the obscure forces that cause value to fluctuate."

The final set of three essays explores the relationship between wealth and Christian ideals. It opens with Julia I. Miller and Laurie Taylor-Mitchell's "'To honor God and enrich Florence in things spiritual and temporal': Piety, Commerce, and Art in the Humiliati Order," which explores how the Humiliati adjusted to the rise of the mercantile economy. After summarizing the early history of the Humiliati, Miller and Taylor-Mitchell focus on the order's experience in Florence, from their beginnings in the thirteenth century to the suppression of their male branch in 1571. A religious order that initially believed in the ideal of the simple apostolic life, they were not mendicants, but instead supported themselves financially through manual labor. They became experts in textile manufacturing who specialized in the production of wool. Merchants and entrepreneurs, the Humiliati soon accumulated extraordinary wealth. But their affluence conflicted with their founding principles, and they soon abandoned labor as an ideal and instead promoted their identity and expressed their ideals through the commissioning of lavish art, especially for their Ognissanti church. By the end of the sixteenth century, the contradictions between their initial ideals of charity and humility, and their actual existence as wealthy landowners and art patrons, contributes to their demise.

In the next essay, "Trading Values: Negotiating Masculinity in Late Medieval and Early Modern Europe," Juliann Vitullo and Diane Wolfthal further explore the apparent conflict between the Christian ideals of poverty and charity, on the one hand, and the accumulation of wealth by merchants on the other. But unlike the Humiliati, lay merchants learned ways to reconcile their riches with their religious values. This essay returns to the gender issues raised earlier in the volume by James Murray and Ian Moulton. It explores how the rise of the monetary economy produced a new mercantile ideal of masculinity, how this new model produced anxiety concerning men's proper relationship to money, and how both wives and children played a critical role in easing that anxiety. By examining theological treatises, texts written by merchants, and paintings and prints produced both north and south of the Alps from the thirteenth through the sixteenth centuries, Vitullo and Wolfthal first explore how culture helped produce the new ideal of the merchant, which was based on ideas developed by mendicant theologians who discussed the proper use of money. When money produced money through investments or loans, practices common among merchants, this process was deemed sterile and usurious. But money also had "fruitful" functions: it could be used wisely to benefit the family, aid the needy, and help the Christian community. Texts written by merchants and portraits painted for them adopt strategies to ensure that they are portrayed as "fruitful" merchants rather than sterile usurers. After analyzing other images, which reveal a deep ambivalence concerning money and an anxiety concerning whether it can be earned and spent in a "fruitful" manner, the essay concludes by showing that merchants emphasized in art and literature their positive role as husbands, fathers, and benefactors of the community in order to reinforce the idea that they were "fruitful" contributors to Christian society

The last essay in this volume is Kathleen Ashley's "Abigail Mathieu's Civic Charity: Social Reform and the Search for Personal Immortality," the first case study of a little-known woman who generously shared her immense wealth through charitable donations that strengthened the spiritual renewal of seventeenth-century Chalon-sur-Saône. Through this study of Mathieu, Ashley demonstrates that it was not only men who used money to shape the spirituality and institutions of the past, but also women. Mathieu amassed a fortune through inheritance and a series of marriages, and her wealth enabled her to become one of the most important benefactors of Chalon. Donating to the local hospital, high school, an Ursuline convent that she was instrumental in founding, and to prisoners and the poor, she constructed an identity for herself as a donor who gave broadly and generously, but had a special interest in helping educate and marry women. Ashley concludes that through these donations, Abigail expressed an agenda in line with Catholic renewal, created substitute children for herself, and ensured that many in Chalon would remember her charitable deeds and the fact that she used her wealth towards the spiritual renewal of her city. This essay gestures towards what will become a more common reaction to the monetary economy in the modern era, since Mathieu expresses more concern for her legacy than for her soul, and her masses of wealth seem to cause her little anxiety.

This volume sheds light on the rich and complex web of connections between money, morality, and culture in an age that saw the entrenchment of the mercantile economy. We have traced how Europeans accommodated capitalism step by step, slowly adjusting to the idea that wealth could be acceptable to God, in fact, could benefit Christian society. Theologians and monks, artists and writers, musicians and merchants, all employed text or image to work through their ambivalence and anxiety concerning wealth, the vicissitudes of the marketplace, and the dramatic changes that capitalism brought to the social fabric of society. But while the articles in this volume trace the ethical struggles with the value of wealth of the past, where is the same struggle today?

Notes

1 Giacomo Todeschini writes about the ethical importance placed on "weights, prices, measures, commodities and coin's relative values" in his essay "Theological Roots of the Medieval/Modern Merchants' Self-Representation," in *The Self-Perception of Early Modern Capitalists*, ed. Margaret C. Jacob and Catherine Secretan (New York: Palgrave Macmillan, 2008), 17–46, 28; another recent work by Giacomo Todeschini treats the false conflation of avarice and Jewish identity: "Ebrei, avari, gente comune," in *Visibilmente crudeli: Malviventi, persone sospette e gente qualunque dal Medioevo all'età moderna* (Bologna: Il Mulino, 2007), 171–204.

2 Thomas Aquinas, *Summa theologica*, Iª-IIae q. 84 a. 1, <http://www.newadvent.org/summa>. See the original at <http://www.corpusthomisticum.org>.

3 Richard Newhauser reminds us that the history of the sin of avarice was at times analyzed as the "chief threat to the social order" even before the development of the monetary economy, particularly when the focus of the discussion was the practical consequences of the vices; see his "Towards modus in habendo: Transformations in the Idea of Avarice," in *Sin: Essays on the Moral Tradition in the Western Middle Ages* (Aldershot: Ashgate, 2007), II, 1–22, 2.

4 Lester K. Little, "Pride Goes before Avarice: Social Change and the Vices in Latin Christendom," *The American Historical Review* 76, no. 1 (February 1971): 16–49, 37.

5 For an analysis of both the competition and the relationship between pride and avarice, see Carla Casagrande and Silvana Vecchio, *I sette vizi capitali* (Turin: Einaudi, 2000) 96–100. For information about the "visibility" of avarice, see Little, "Pride Goes before Avarice," 16–49.

6 Little, "Pride Goes before Avarice," 48–9.

7 Peter Armour, "Gold, Silver, and True Treasure: Economic Imagery in Dante," *Romance Studies* 23 (1994): 7–30, 14.

8 For an analysis of the "convergence between avarice and papal authority" in Dante's *Inferno*, see chapter 2 of Nick Havely's *Dante and the Franciscans* (Cambridge: Cambridge University Press, 2004).

9 For an explanation of the sin of simony and of this sin's connection to the Jews, see Giacomo Todeschini, "La riflessione etica sulle attività economiche," in *Economie*

urbane ed etica economica nell'Italia medievale, ed. Roberto Greci, Giuliano Pinto, and Giacomo Todeschini (Rome: Laterza, 2005), 153–228, 167–72.

10 Janet Robson, "Judas and the Franciscans: Perfidy Pictured in Lorenzetti's Passion Cycle at Assisi," *Art Bulletin* 86, no. 1 (March 2004): 31–57.

11 Thomas Celano, "The First Life of Saint Francis," in *English Omnibus of the Sources for the Life of St Francis*, ed. Marion A. Habig (Chicago: Franciscan Herald Press, 1973) 225–334, 236.

12 John Henderson, *Piety and Charity in Late Medieval Florence* (Oxford: Clarendon Press, 1994); Lester K. Little, *Religious Poverty and the Profit Economy in Medieval Europe* (Ithaca: Cornell University Press, 1978).

13 Armando Sapori, *Studi di storia economica (secoli XIII-XIV-XV)* (Florence: Sansoni, 1955), vol. 2, 814.

14 Jacques Le Goff, *La naissance du Purgatoire* (Paris: Gallimard, 1981); and *La bourse et la vie: économie et religion au Moyen Age* (Paris: Hachette, 1986).

15 Joel Kaye, *Economy and Nature in the Fourteenth Century* (Cambridge: Cambridge University Press, 1998).

16 Anne Derbes and Mark Sandona, "Barren Metal and the Fruitful Womb: The Program of Giotto's Arena Chapel in Padua," *Art Bulletin* 80 (1998): 274–91. See their most recent book, which appeared as ours was going to press, *The Usurer's Heart: Giotto, Enrico Scrovegni, and the Arena Chapel in Padua* (University Park, PA: Pennsylvania State University Press, 2008).

17 For a recent summary of discussions about usury in different fields, see Lutz Kaelber, "Max Weber and Usury: Implications for Historical Research," in *Money, Markets and Trade in Late Medieval Europe*, ed. Lawrin Armstrong, Ivana Elbl, and Martin M. Ebl (Leiden: Brill, 1977), 59–85.

18 Michael Baxandall, *Painting and Experience in Fifteenth Century Italy: A Primer in the Social History of Pictorial Style* (Oxford: Oxford University Press, 1972).

19 Simon Schama, *The Embarrassment of Riches: An Interpretation of Culture in the Golden Age* (New York: Knopf, 1987); Evelyn Welch, *Shopping in the Renaissance: Consumer Culture in Italy 1400–1600* (New Haven: Yale University Press, 2005); Lisa Jardine, *Worldy Goods* (London: Macmillan, 1996). As our book neared completion, a new collection of essays appeared that explored the self-perception of merchants, *The Self-Perception of Early Modern Capitalists*, ed. Margaret C. Jacob and Catherine Secretan (New York: Palgrave Macmillan, 2008).

PART I
Defining the Players

Chapter 1

"Nerehand nothyng to pay or to take": Poverty, Labor, and Money in Four Towneley Plays

Robert S. Sturges

In 1987, David Aers published a polemical essay about what he then saw as the reactionary conduct of medieval studies as a discipline. He argued that medieval literary studies in particular "systematically occluded" the "interlocking histories of class and gender relations, of changing economic realities, [and] of conflicting ideologies" in favor of idealized "harmony-models," that is, visions of a Middle Ages characterized by "quiet hierarchies" rather than social conflict.[1] Aers also attempted a still-useful analysis of *Piers Plowman* based in precisely those histories of conflict and in the material conditions of agricultural labor in late medieval England. Twenty years later, however, as more and more medievalists have heeded Aers' call for a criticism of medieval culture that foregrounds the conflicts of classes and ideologies, the main polemical thrust of his essay may seem to have lost some of its immediacy.

Nevertheless, the late medieval English mystery plays generally, and the Towneley plays in particular, especially the six plays that have enough in common to have been attributed to a single author known as the "Wakefield Master," are still regularly, and indeed necessarily, interpreted as exemplifying the harmonizing tendency of medieval Christianity.[2] Their overt representations of class conflict are still habitually resolved, even by critics who focus on such representations, into a serene "harmony-model" by means of a reading in which typology functions either as the critic's grounding assumption in reading a given play, or as the critic's goal—most famously in the now universal and invariable understanding of the sheep-stealing episode in the *Second Shepherds' Play* as a typological forecast of the Nativity.[3] Rarely does such criticism go beyond the interpretation of a single play, or seek out the ideological patterns governing the Wakefield Master's works as a whole. This kind of criticism, which, if it recognizes the presence of class conflict in these plays, does so only to smoothe it out in a Christian reading, is, as I have already suggested, a necessary and even inevitable response to these plays, given their undeniably religious nature and function: the plays themselves insist on such a reading. Nevertheless, in this essay I will attempt to follow Aers and a few more recent critics in resisting this harmonizing Christian reading as long as possible, focusing instead on such issues as economics, class, money, and ideology in several of the plays attributed to the Wakefield Master; I will also, when the Christian reading can be resisted no longer, try to understand the plays' religious element in these ideological terms.[4]

The central portion of Aers' essay, on Langland's *Piers Plowman*, lays out some of the late medieval social conflicts that also inform the somewhat later Towneley plays; his findings are supported by historians of the medieval English economy.[5] The late medieval economy in England, according to most economic historians, was in a booming period for the laboring classes. The effects of the Black Death in the later fourteenth century, and of repeated outbreaks of the plague in the early fifteenth, meant that the labor supply was in decline, and that workers could therefore demand higher wages and better working conditions. The fact that they did make such demands is clear from such ordinances as the infamous 1351 Statute of Laborers, which attempted to control wages:

> Against the malice of servants who were idle and unwilling to serve after the pestilence without taking outrageous wages it was recently ordained by our lord the king, with the assent of the prelates, nobles and others of his council, that such servants, both men and women, should be obliged to serve in return for the salaries and wages which were customary (in those places where they ought to serve) during the twentieth year of the present king's reign (1347–48) or five or six years previously. … First, that carters, ploughmen, leaders of the plough, shepherds, swineherds, domestic and all other servants shall receive the liveries and wages accumstomed in the said twentieth year and four years previously.[6]

Agricultural laborers are here specified and singled out as the objects of this statute, and explicitly set against the prelates, nobles, and the king himself. The "customary" economic "quiet hierarchy" is no more than a past ideal to which the latter desire a return. The so-called Peasants' Revolt of 1381 has been partially attributed to workers' resistance to such ordinances.[7]

Additionally, economic historians like M.M. Postan point out that in the Wakefield Master's own period:

> the costs of demesne cultivation were rising, mainly as a result of higher wages. They began to rise in the first quarter of the fourteenth century, and continued on the ascent until some time in the second quarter of the fifteenth century. They stayed thereafter upon their high plateau until the end of the century. On the other hand … agricultural prices remained stationary, or perhaps even sagged somewhat.[8]

In most sectors of the economy, then, the condition of peasants greatly improved in the late fourteenth and early fifteenth centuries, and it was the landlords who suffered the most clear-cut reversals. While Postan's work has been controversial, it is largely supported by more recent historians such as Christopher Dyer, who finds evidence of larger peasant landholdings, improved diet, a higher grade of possessions, lower taxes, and other indicators of a higher standard of living in the period after 1350.[9] Dyer, indeed, even suggests that "the world was turned upside down because the aristocracy lost income, and the lower oders … prospered."[10] The West Riding of Yorkshire, in particular—where Wakefield is located—shows evidence of such increased prosperity among the laboring classes.[11]

In order to specify what is unique about the plays under consideration here, it is useful to note additionally that the Towneley plays are closely related to the cycle performed at York, the Towneley manuscript having derived several individual pageants from York.[12] Indeed, while the manuscript of the Towneley plays is now widely considered to be a compilation drawn from various areas in Yorkshire and Lancashire rather than a unified cycle, among the features shared by four of the six plays attributed to the Wakefield Master—the four I will be primarily considering in this essay—are their local topographical references to the Wakefield area as well as the Yorkshire dialect that they have in common with the rest of the Towneley plays.[13] This fact helps to account for the important differences between these plays and the York Cycle. In the mid-fifteenth century, Wakefield's economy was still primarily based on the manor, unlike the mercantile economy of York, which was a larger urban center. Thus the plays attributed to the Wakefield Master are concerned with issues of importance to Wakefield's specific manorial audience, which would have included peasants as well as townspeople and landowners:

> [W]hat the Wakefield Master did was to make his cycle indigenous to his setting and responsive to his image of the people who inhabited that setting. Economically, Wakefield was a manorial seat and the chief town in the riding during the time that the plays were collected and performed. But even as a commercial hub it was always under seigneurial control, and its government in no way resembled the trade oligarchy of York … Wakefield was very much a county seat, run by landed gentry.[14]

These facts about the Wakefield economy may also help explain another apparent anomaly in the six Wakefield Master plays. The usual thing to say about these plays is that, like other late medieval representations, they anachronistically represent biblical events as if they were taking place in the original audience's contemporary late medieval world; however, these plays seem anachronistic even as representations of the late Middle Ages in England. Despite the relative prosperity of agricultural laborers in late medieval England, in the contemporary works attributed to the Wakefield Master, we find bitter peasant complaints about their ongoing poverty and specifically about their sufferings at the hands of the landowning gentry and their liveried employees. I would suggest that this somewhat old-fashioned view may be partly attributable to Wakefield's ongoing manorial economy, in which the perception of class inequality among the peasants would have been more acute than in the mercantile economy of an urban center such as York.

This is not to suggest that York was necessarily more prosperous than Wakefield, or that poverty was in reality more acute in the latter town, but only that Wakefield had not fully undergone the changes wrought by the mercantile and monetary economy of a town like York, and that those changes may have been regarded with envy by those still implicated in the more traditional economy of Wakefield.

> Whereas feudal society was hierarchic, fairly static, and reasonably protective, the society which was beginning to emerge in fifteenth-century England put more stress on individuality and self-reliance. A man's possibilities were not as limited by the conditions of his birth as they had been. A certain amount of social mobility was possible … In rural society bondmen could become tenant farmers, or could leave their own districts and become wage laborers.

But

> [t]hose imbued with the more traditional notions of social theory … saw everywhere in contemporary society only extravagance, ambition, greed and self-interst, which they felt were destroying the set of values which they accepted and disrupting the stability of the social order they knew.[15]

The Wakefield Master represents both these points of view: the desire for social mobility among those left behind in these fifteenth-century developments (what J.A. Raftis calls "the bitter reaction against the vestiges of villeinage") and the fear of the social disruption this kind of mobility and class bitterness might be imagined to cause.[16] Barbara Hanawalt suggests that "[b]ehind the poets' concern for the commons was the fear that unless they were cared for, they would rise in revolt once again" as they had in 1381.[17] Aers, too, suggests that while the "demographic collapse" after 1348 "benefited the drives of larger peasants to accumulate holdings" and "strengthened the bargaining position of those who sold their labour-power" as well, these results also "increased the discontent of those forced to serve their lords rather than sell their labour-power on the market."[18] Indeed, the overall prosperity of the post-1350 period was hardly universal; as Dyer points out, "[d]eep strata of poverty existed in peasant society," including an underclass that survived by "casual labouring, gleaning, begging, prostitution, and sheaf-stealing"—an underworld represented by at least one character in the Wakefield Master's works.[19]

The Wakefield plays concern a class of workers who are aware of the existence of a money economy, and who may even fantasize about improving their economic status by participating in it, but for whom money is always elsewhere: their positive relation to the monetary economy is for the most part imaginary rather than participatory. Money, for the Wakefield Master, is almost always literally unreal, and his treatment of it reflects the widespread medieval anxiety about the substitution of symbolic monetary value for concrete use value.[20] The economic bitterness of the plays' characters is related to, though not fully explained by, this gap between the fantasy of economic improvement through money and a perceived reality (whether accurate or not) of ongoing exploitation.

Of the six complete plays usually attributed to the Wakefield Master, four are directly concerned with labor typical of fifteenth-century English manorial working classes; these four plays are also the ones in which direct references to Wakefield and its environs occur, which strengthens the case for considering the four together in terms of Wakefield's manorial economy.[21] If we turn to these plays themselves, we can find evidence both of the imaginary relation to money, and of the class resentment identified by Raftis and Hanawalt. They are presented both with a degree of sympathy and with an at least equal degree of criticism. The Wakefield Master, a poet of some learning, shows something like a modern sociological understanding that the roots of peasant crime lay in peasant poverty, and he is even able to identify the sources of their poverty in specific class inequalities and abuses.[22] At the same time, however, he is, like the Statute of Laborers, equally critical of peasant attempts to participate in the money economy to make a profit or even to conserve what little they have, representing their various attempts at profit-making as fantasy, as crime, as foolishness, as error, or as defiance of God's will. This ambivalence stems from an ideological impasse: the religious perspective that informs all these plays both enables the social criticism and in the long run co-opts it for a conservative ideology.

The mystery cycles represent universal history from a Christian perspective, from the Creation to the Last Judgment. In the Wakefield plays, the sympathetic and class-conscious portrayal of peasant poverty begins with the first play in the manuscript usually attributed to the Wakefield Master, the *Mactacio Abel*, or *The Killing of Abel*, in which Cain plays the leading role. Cain is a plowman, and enters driving his uncooperative plowteam. Although he is obviously not to be understood as heroic in any sense,[23] the author does suggest something of the plight of the tenant farmer in Cain's complaints about tithing in response to Abel's pious suggestion:

> We! wherof shuld I tend, leif brothere?
> For I am I ich yere wars than othere—
> Here my trouth it is none othere.
> My wynnyngys ar bot meyn:
> No wonder if that I be leyn. (ll. 110–14)
>
> [What? Why should I tithe, dear brother? / For every year I am worse off than before— / Here is my oath that it is not otherwise. / My profits are but small: / No wonder that I am lean.][24]

Tithes are here understood from the peasant point of view as an unjust tax imposed on the already overburdened manorial tenant farmer. Indeed, God himself appears to Cain's understanding as an unjust and unkind landlord: to Abel's suggestion that "al the good thou has in wone / Of Godys grace is bot a lone" (ll. 118–19) ["all the goods that you hold / Are merely a loan by the grace of God"], Cain replies that as far as he is concerned, God has never loaned him anything, but rather has been remarkably stingy:

> Lenys he me? As com thrift apon the so!
> For he has euer yit beyn my fo;

For had he my freynd ben,
Othergatys it it had beyn seyn.
When I should saw and wantyd seyde,
Then was myne not worth a neld.
When I should saw, and wanted seyde
And of corn had full gret neyde,
Then gaf he me none of his;
No more will I gif hym of this. (ll. 120–29)

[Does he give me a loan? May you receive similar prosperity! / For up to now he has always been my enemy; / For if he had been my friend, / Things would have appeared differently. / When I had to sow and needed seed, / Then mine was not worth a needle. / When I had to sow, and needed seed, / and had great need of grain, / Then he gave me none of his; / No more will I give him of this.]

Cain judges God to be an unfriendly neighbor, one unwilling to participate in the manorial economy of loans and barter documented by, for example, Christopher Dyer.[25] Far from being neighborly, in fact, God makes the unjust demands of the typical bad landlord familiar from English sermons, requiring payment even when he has failed to provide for his tenants.[26]

While the agricultural world presented in this play is primarily pre-monetary, its economic system based on the direct exchange of goods, Cain also speaks for the laborer's relation to money: when Abel suggests that God had provided Cain's "lifyng," Cain swears "Yit boroed I neyer a farthyng / Of hym" (ll. 100–102) ["I have never yet borrowed one farthing / Of him"], and indeed that "My farthyng is in the preest hand" (l. 106) ["My farthing is in the priest's hand"]. The farthing was the smallest denomination of silver coin in England, and even that amount is more money than Cain has ever received from God—indeed, the farthing he had has been pocketed by the priest.[27] Cain's desire, and frustrating inability, to participate in the monetary economy resurface at the end of the play, when he tells Garcio to try and collect money from the audience: "Byd euery man theym pleasse to pay" (l. 440) ["Bid every man that it may please them to pay"]. Having, in his opinion, received nothing from God, Cain turns to his neighbors in the audience, once again linking them to Cain, but now in specifically monetary terms.

Cain fails to recognize the qualitative difference between divine and human demands, and is obviously wrong; but it is easy to imagine that the manorial agricultural laborers in the play's audience might have also sympathized with his anti-manorial desire to keep what he produced for himself:

Wemay, man, I hold the mad!
Wenys thou now that I list gad
To gif away my warldys aght?
The dwill hym spede that me so taght!
What nede had I my trauell to lose,
To were my shoyn and ryfe my hose? (ll. 150–55)

[Oh, man, I think you are mad! / Now do you believe that I would be in a hurry / to give away my wordly property? / To the devil with anyone who taught me such behavior! / What good would it do me to waste my work, / To tear my stockings while wearing shoes?]

Similarly, Noah's wife, in the play of *Noah and His Sons*, is represented as engaged in spinning, the type of labor most typical of women's work in late medieval Yorkshire.[28] She complains about the plight in which Noah's work on the ark leaves his family:

Now, as euer myght I thryfe,
The wars I the see.
Do tell me belife,
Where has thou thus long be?
To dede may we dryfe,
Or lif, for the,
For want.
When we swete or swynk,
Thou dos what thou thynk;
Yit of mete and of drynk
Have we veray skant. (ll. 276–86)

[Now, as I wish to thrive, / I see you the worse. / Tell me on your life, / Where have you been so long? / We may be driven to death / Before life, because of you / For want. / While we sweat or labor, / You do as you please; / Yet of food and drink / We have very little.]

The audience knows that Noah is doing God's will in building the ark, but from his wife's point of view, in doing so he is neglecting his family responsibilities. For them, indeed, this is literally a matter of life and death, as she points out: without his productive labor on their behalf, the family goes hungry. (A spinster was unlikely to be able to support a family with her own labor.[29]) Like Cain, Noah's wife is wrong in the eyes of sacred history, but also like him, she speaks for the laborer who is barely making enough to survive; her fear for her own and her children's survival is again one that the laborers in the audience might share.[30]

Also like Cain, Noah's wife has an imaginary relation to money: expressed only in the subjunctive, it suggests a fantasized world of ease that might be brought about by her husband's death. Were he dead, she tells him, "For thi saull, without lese, / Shuld I dele penny doyll" (ll. 564–65) ["For your soul, without lying, / I would dole out a mass-penny"]. Although the penny was declining in value in the fifteenth century, it still represents a considerably larger sum than Cain's farthing.[31] Nevertheless, this mass-penny is equally out of her reach, and represents a fantasy of wealth that contrasts starkly with the life of bare subsistence suggested in her other speeches. As for Cain, positive participation in a money economy is for Noah's wife desired, but even more clearly unrealistic.

The two shepherds' plays are especially interesting in that they both initially separate questions of peasant poverty from questions of religion: Cain and Noah's resistant wife are in the long run shown to be wrong, no matter how much the audience may sympathize with them at first, but the shepherds of the Nativity are often idealized characters, and their sufferings at the hands of the Wakefield area gentry thus seem like more direct, and less questionable, social critiques, especially in the early speeches made by the shepherds in both the *First* and *Second Shepherds' Plays*. These plays are two versions of the same situation, the annunciation to the shepherds of the birth of Jesus, and if we, like several critics, understand the second play as a later revision of the first, we might go so far as to suggest that the Wakefield Master makes this play more radically class conscious in the revised version: the critique of the manorial economy and its exploitation of peasant labor is heightened in the second version, and directed more specifically against the gentry.[32]

In the *First Shepherds' Play*, the shepherds complain in general terms about their unhappiness, which is in part a result of poverty, as the first shepherd suggests:

> Fermes thyk ar comyng,
> My purs is bot wake,
> I haue nerehand nothyng
> To pay nor to take.
> I may syng
> With purs penneles,
> That makys this heuynes,
> "Wo is me this dystres!"
> And has no helpyng. (ll. 44–52)

> [Heavy rent payments are coming due, / My purse is but weak, / I have nearly nothing / To pay or to take. / I may sing / With a penniless purse, / Which causes this unhapiness, / "Woe is me, this distress!" / And there is no help for it.]

This speech is one of the few moments in this version that attribute the shepherds' distress directly to the manorial economy: it is his upcoming rent payment that threatens to reduce him to pennilessness. This worker has a more fully realized part in a monetary economy than either Cain or Noah's wife, but it does not bring about the ease imagined by the latter; instead, it brings just another form of deprivation. Even here, though, there is no direct accusation that such payments are attributable to the landlord's rapacity; they are simply an unfortunate, but unavoidable, aspect of the laborer's life, and the fault of no one in particular.

Typical of the *First Shepherds' Play* is the generalized commentary on poverty exemplified in a speech of the second shepherd:

> Poore men ar in the dyke
> And oft-time mars.
> The warld is slyke;

Also helpars
Is none here. (ll. 135–39)

[Poor men are in dire straights / And often fare ill. / That's how the world is. / And helpers / Are not to be found here.]

There may be an implicit comparison here between poor and rich, but the overall effect is one of resignation: the evils of poverty are simply the way of the world, and nothing can be done about them.

The *Second Shepherds' Play* introduces the trickster character Mak, also complaining about his own and his family's hunger:

Now, Lord, for thy naymes vii,
That made both moyn and starnes
Well mo then I can neuen,
Thi will, Lorde, of me tharnys.
I am all vneuen;
That moves oft my harnes.
Now wold God I were in heuen,
For the[r] wepe no barnes
So styll. (ll. 274–82)

[Now, Lord, for your seven names, / Who made both moon and stars / Far more than I can name, / Your will, Lord, is lacking to me. / I am all at odds; / This is wracking my brains. / Now I wish to God I were in heaven, / For there no children weep / So quietly.]

Mak, often understood merely as a comic villain, here takes on some characteristics of a more tragic hero, wracking his brains to understand how God's will can include his children weeping with hunger. Mak seems like one of the criminal underclass described by Dyer, and his extreme poverty actually makes him long for death and a heaven imagined as a place where there will be help for such weeping; indeed, like Noah's wife, he claims at certain points to be near death's door:

Full sore am I and yll.
If I stande stone-styll,
I ete not an nedyll
Thys moneth and more. (ll. 335–38)

[I am very sore and ill. / As I stand still as a stone, / I have eaten not a needle / For this month and longer.]

His own and his family's hunger is a clear-cut motive for his theft of the sheep that sets the play's plot in motion: in a parodic foreshadowing of the Nativity, Mak and his wife Gyll pretend that the stolen lamb is their newborn child.

Unlike the *First*, however, the *Second Shepherds' Play* attributes the financial misery of the peasants more directly to the gentry and their henchmen, as in the opening speech:

We ar so hamyd,
Fortaxed and ramyd,
We ar mayde handtamyd
With thyse gentlery-men …
Thus ar husbandys opprest,
In ponte to myscary
On lyfe.
Thus hold thay vs hunder,
Thus thay bryng vs in blonder;
It were greatte wonder
And euer shuld we thryfe. (ll. 23–26, 33–39)

[We are so hamstrung, / Overtaxed and beaten down, / We are hand-tamed / By these officers of the gentry … / Thus are farmers oppressed, / To the point of forfeiting / Our life. / Thus they hold us down, / Thus they bring us to trouble; / It would be a great wonder / If we should ever thrive.]

It is now the gentry and their representatives who are directly responsible for the oppression of peasant laborers, in particular for the conversion of farmers ("husbandys") into shepherds through the enclosure of arable land. The manorial peasant is not, in such speeches, merely the victim of unalterable circumstances that can only be accepted with resignation; instead, he is now victimized by an identifiable class, and expresses his class resentment directly.[33] Through such means as enclosure and taxation, the manorial peasant is harried almost to the point of death; his concerns, in other words, are similar to those of Cain and of Noah's wife. Now, however, it is not God's will being flouted by the peasant characters, but only the inhumane will of the landlords and their officers. The metaphorical divine landlord of *The Killing of Abel* is now a literal human landlord, and the laborer is therefore no longer inherently in the wrong, but is able instead to enunciate a coherent social critique.[34]

In this world, money is seen as a potential solution. The *Second Shepherds' Play* revisits the fantasized relation to money familiar from Noah's wife: like her, Mak imagines that he would give "all in my cofer / To-morne at next to offer / Hyr hed-maspenny" (ll. 362–64) ["everything in my coffer / Tomorrow morning as an offering / For her mass-penny"]. But money here is more than merely a fantasized offering in exchange for peace and quiet: as in the *First Shepherds' Play*, these characters also have a real-life relation with money, and, overtaxed as they are, are nevertheless prepared to offer some to Mak's and Gyll's supposed newborn. Says the third shepherd, "Let me gyf youre barne / Bot vi pence" (ll. 825–26) ["Let me give your child / But sixpence"]. This sixpence is the sole concrete, real-world money in the four plays under investigation, and suggests that money can be a real-world way to alleviate the poverty of Mak's family, a perception the audience might have shared.

Thus in all four of the Wakefield plays concerned with peasant labor, there is an at least somewhat sympathetic portrayal of their poverty, not as an ideal condition but as a form of unmerited suffering; and by the *Second Shepherds' Play* we have something like a sociological understanding of poverty as the root cause of crime (in Mak's case) and as the result of social injustice (in the case of the other shepherds).

Nevertheless, there is also an impulse in all four plays to criticize any attempt on the laborers' part to remove themselves from poverty: attempts to benefit from one's own labor or to get ahead financially are invariably understood as foolish at best or blasphemous at worst, regardless of how much sympathy is raised for the condition of poverty itself. Kellie Robertson has recently suggested that medieval Britain simultaneously held two separate but indivisible conceptions of the laborer's body, one "theological and idealized," the other "juridically regulated," and these simultaneous views are visible in the Wakefield Master's plays, which may be said to participate in this regulation of the laborer's body.[35] This is most obvious in Cain's case: he is, after all, the first murderer, and whatever sympathy the audience may feel for his plight is tempered by this knowledge. Thus his attempt to retain what he has earned for himself is both comical and blasphemous, as, in tithing, he cannot bring himself to give any but the worst grain to God:

> We! aght, aght, and neyn, and ten is this:
> We! this may we best mys.
> Gif hym that that ligys thore?
> It goyse agans myn hart ful sore. …
> Now and he get more, the dwill me spede!—
> As mych as oone reepe—
> For that cam hym full light chepe;
> Not as mekill, grete ne small,
> As he myght wipe his ars withall. …
> Thou wold I gaf hym this shefe? Or this sheyfe?
> Na, nawder of thise ii wil I leife.
> Bot take this. Now has he two,
> And for my saull now mot it go;
> Bot it gos sore agans my will,
> And shal he like full ill. (ll. 220–23, 236–40, 253–58)

> [Oh, eight, eight and nine, and this makes ten: / Yes, this we can do without. / Give him that one lying there? / It goes painfully against my heart. … / Now the devil take me if he gets more!— / Not even one handful— / For he got this as a bargain; / Not enough, great or small, / For him to wipe his ass with. … / You want me to give him this sheaf? Or that sheaf? / No, I won't part with either of these two. / But take this one. Now he has two, / And that's enough, by my soul, / But it goes sore against my will, / And he will like it very little.]

Although Cain's reluctance to part with the fruits of his labor are perfectly understandable, the inability, or deliberate refusal noted earlier, to understand the qualitative difference between God and a human landlord reaches comically shocking proportions with the declaration that God can wipe his ass with these tithes. Cain, indeed, recognizes that he is arousing God's wrath, and nevertheless chooses his own will—and his own comfort—over God's. The very characteristic that might arouse the laboring audience's sympathy—his resentment at having to give away the results of his labor to a powerful authority—is thus eventually revealed as sinful, on both his part and theirs. It is also revealed as foolish: Cain is a ridiculous as well as a sinful character. And Cain might also have been understood by contemporaries as the progenitor of the peasant class itself, which thus shares in his sin as it shared in his desire.[36]

Noah's wife, too, insists, against God's will, on performing her customary labor at the spindle—typical woman's work in the Yorkshire West Riding sheep-raising and cloth-making manorial economy imagined in these plays—even as the flood waters are rising, another simultaneously blasphemous and comical attempt to continue profit-making labor:

> Wheder I lose or I wyn,
> In fayth, thi felowship
> Set I not at a pyn.
> This spyndill will I slip
> Apon this hill
> Or I styr oone foote. (ll. 525–30)
>
> [Whether I lose or I win, / In faith, your fellowship / I value less than a pin. / This spindle will I work / Upon this hill / Before I move one foot.]

Noah's wife, like Cain, refuses to trust in God to provide, and insists on trying to provide for herself by means of her own work. The work that earns the peasants' living is thus itself understood as a blasphemous refusal to cooperate with divine grace, and the desire to provide for oneself as a refusal to accept God's will. Like Cain, Noah and his wife, through the curse on their son Ham, might also be perceived as the progenitors of peasants as a class—and thus as a sinful one.[37]

The two shepherds' plays, as I have suggested, are less critical of their peasant subjects. In the *First Shepherds' Play*, the first shepherd's desire to replace and increase his flock is not necessarily irreligious, but it is understood as a nonsensical fantasy: like Noah's wife, he has a merely imaginary relation to the money economy, and imagines it as providing, if not the life of ease she imagines, at least a flock of sheep that might be bought (ll. 58–65). The first and second shepherds argue over where the first will pasture his nonexistent sheep, and the third shepherd points out their folly: the first shepherd has no wherewithal to buy more sheep, and he is ridiculed for imagining the possibility, though his desire, unlike Cain's and Noah's wife's, is not actually presented as being opposed to God's will:

> *3 Pastor.* Yey, bot tell me, good,
> Where ar youre shepe, lo?
> *2 Pastor.* Now, syr, by my hode,
> Yet se I no mo,
> Not syn I here stode.

3 Pastor: God gyf you wo
And sorow!
Ye fysh before the nett,
And stryfe on this flett;
Sich folys neuer I mett
Evyn or at morow. (ll. 194–204)

[*Third Shepherd*: Yes, but tell me, good man, / Lo, where are your sheep? / *Second Shepherd*: Now, sir, by my hood, / I have seen none, / Not since I have been standing here. / *Third Shepherd*: May God give you woe / And sorrow! / You fish without a net, / And fight in this place; / Such fools I never met, / Morning or evening.]

The nonexistent flock is a pathetic, but ridiculous, fantasy of self-improvement: while the desire for profit is not sinful or blasphemous in this case, it is as foolish as Cain's or Noah's wife's desire to keep their own goods or to continue working in the teeth of divine wrath. The desire for profit, or for social mobility, is merely silly in the world of this play, and the first shepherd's desire to participate in the money economy ultimately reduces him to metaphorical monetary valuelessness: as the third shepherd suggests in exposing the others' fantasies as fantasies, "He were well qwytt / Had sold for a pownde / Sich two" (ll. 211–13) ["He would be well rewarded / Who sold for a pound / Such a pair"]. The pound represents a large sum of money, here worth considerably more than the shepherds who imagine their own participation in the money economy; the very largeness of the sum suggests the degree of unreality in the shepherds' imaginary relation with money.[38] Indeed, this play is a reflection of one medieval strain of stereotyping peasants, the one that classifies them as stupid: even the Third Shepherd, who exposes the foolishness of the first two, is himself a fool, as he pours his own grain on the ground to illustrate the pointlessness of his colleagues' quarrel (ll. 238–52).[39]

In the *Second Shepherds' Play*, the attempt to better one's financial status is presented as thievery, when Mak steals the sheep:

Now were tyme for a man
That lakkys what he wolde
To stalk preuely than
Vnto a fold,
And neemly to wyrk than
And be not to bold,
For he myght aby the bargan,
If it were told
At the endyng. (ll. 387–95)

[Now is the time for a man / Who lacks what he needs / To stalk quietly then / To a sheepfold, / And then nimbly to work / And be not over-bold, / For he might pay the consequences, / If it were revealed / In the end.]

Once again, Mak's crime has sociological underpinnings: he is a man characterized by want. But he inevitably sacrifices some of the sympathy he may have gained earlier in the play as his need results in the victimization of his equally needy fellow-peasants: his labor or "wyrk" here is sheep-stealing. More than merely a foolish fantasy as in the *First Shepherds' Play*, the desire for worldly goods is now characterized as criminal activity.

The link between profit and sinful resistance to God's will is also drawn in this play: Mak is represented as a comically demonic figure, as he engages in witchcraft to further his criminal intentions, casting a spell on the other shepherds to ensure that they remain asleep while he makes off with their stock:

Bot abowte yow a serkyll
As rownde as a moyn,
To I haue done that I wyll,
Tyll that it be noyn,
That ye lyg stone-styll
To that I haue done;
And I shall say thertyll
Of good wordys a foyne:
"On hight,
Ouer youre heydys, my hand I lyft.
Outt go youre een! Fordo youre syght!" (ll. 400–410)

[But around you a circle / As round as a moon, / Until I have done what I want, / Until it is noon, / That you lie stone-still / Until I have done; / And to that effect I shall say / A few good words: / "On high, / Above your heads I lift my hand. / Out go your eyes! Away with your sight!"]

By the fifteenth century, the casting of such spells or curses was sometimes linked to blasphemy as well as to rebellion by the lower orders.[40] As in the case of Cain, the very characteristic that initially arouses sympathy for Mak—his need—is now transformed into condemnation by way of blasphemy. Here again, the desire for betterment, initially understandable, is eventually revealed as both comical and sinful.

So far I have been trying to follow the suggestions Aers makes in his essay, by resisting the usual exclusively religious readings of these plays, focusing intead on the interplay between Christianity and social critique; but because the endings of the two shepherds' plays represent the Nativity, as the shepherds, impelled by the angel, seek out the newborn Jesus, the Christian reading becomes unavoidable. However, their two representations of the Nativity are radically different, and again seem to suggest that the Wakefield Master rethought the Nativity theme as he revised the *First Shepherds' Play* into the *Second*. The first version represents Jesus as a powerful king, duke, and knight as well as lord, and the gift offered by the first shepherd, a coffer, suggests the accumulation of monetary wealth as well:

Hayll, kyng I the call!
Hayll, most of myght!

Hayll, the worthyst of all!
Hayll, duke! Hayll, knyght!
Of greatt and small
Thou art Lorde by right.
Hayll, perpetuall!
Hayll, faryst wyght!
I pray the to take,
If thou wold, for my sake—
With this may thou lake—
This lytyll spruse cofer. (ll. 660–72)

[Hail, king I acknowledge thee! / Hail most powerful! / Hail, most worthy! / Hail, duke! Hail, knight! / Of great and small / Thou art rightfully Lord. / Hail, everlasting! / Hail, fairest one! / I pray thee to take, / If thou would, for my sake— / You can play with this— / This little spruce coffer.]

In this version of the play, Jesus is imagined in terms of the medieval political hierarchy—king, duke, knight, and rightful lord—which is thus naturalized and stabilized by means of the divine participation in it. And far from resisting tithes as Cain does, the first shepherd's gift implies the naturalization of financial contributions to the Church as well.

In the second version, though, the shepherds offer humbler gifts, and the infant Jesus seems to have taken the shepherds' sufferings onto himself:

1 Pastor: Fare well, lady,
So fare to beholde,
With thy childe on thi kne.
2 Pastor: Bot he lygys full cold.
Lord, well is me!
Now we go, thou behold.
3 Pastor: Forsothe, allredy
It semys to be told
Full oft.
1 Pastor: What grace we haue fun!
2 Pastor: Com furth; now ar we won!
3 Pastor: To syng ar we bun—
Let take on loft! (ll. 1076–88)

[*First Shepherd*: Farewell, lady, / So fair to behold, / With thy child on thy knee. / *Second Shepherd*: But he lies full cold. / Lord, well is me! / Now we go, you may see. / *Third Shepherd*: Forsooth, already / It seems to have been told / Very often. / *First Shepherd*: What grace we have found! / *Second Shepherd*: Come forth: now are we saved! / *Third Shepherd*: To sing are we bound— / Let it be taken on high!]

Whereas the shepherds suffered from the cruel weather at the beginning of the play, Jesus is now the one lying "full cold," while the shepherds themselves express a newfound physical comfort associated with divine grace and salvation. Nowhere to be found, however, are the specific social complaints directed against landlords and the unjust exercise of hierarchical power that also characterized the opening of this version of the play: the sociological underpinnings have disappeared by the end, as Jesus takes their poverty as well as the cold onto himself. Unlike the Christ-child at the end of the *First Shepherds' Play*, in this version he has an even smaller relation to the money economy than the shepherds themselves:

> My hart wold blede
> To se the sytt here
> In so poore wede,
> With no pennys. (ll. 1055–58)
>
> [My heart would bleed / To see thee sitting here / In such poor attire, / Penniless.]

Pennilessness is now the condition of Christ, and the shepherds' poverty brings them into contact with him. Unlike their counterparts in the *First Shepherds' Play*, these shepherds do not make an offering suggestive of wealth, but allow the identification of Christ's poverty with their own to remain in place. From this perspective, their earlier offering of sixpence to the false child—and by implication the involvement in the money economy desired in all these plays—however well intentioned, was not only a mistake, but a false solution to the problem of poverty, whose true solution lies in the acceptance of, and identification with, the poverty of Christ.

This suspicion of money as spiritually harmful is played out most thoroughly in another of the plays usually attributed to the Wakefield Master, *Herod the Great*, which concerns Herod's slaughter of the innocents. This is represented above all as a financial transaction between Herod and the soldiers who carry out the massacre: he offers them "markys, rentys, and powndys" (l. 387) ["marks, rents, and pounds"] in exchange for the killings.[41] The fanciful exchange of human life for a pound imagined in the *First Shepherds' Play* here becomes a horrifying reality as the first soldier makes a wager that substitutes money for a life: speaking of the mother of his next victim, he says "I hold here a grote / She lykys me not weyll / Be we parte" (ll. 475–77) ["I hold here a groat / That she is not pleased with me / By the time we part"].[42] The monetary economy, understood in the earlier plays as fantasy, foolishness, and error for those who wish to participate in it, here emerges as the very epitome of sin, in its indiscriminate exchange of life for coin. Far from a solution to the problem of poverty, money unleashes a terrifying substitution in which human life, and particularly the life of the least powerful, simply disappears.

In the *Second Shepherds' Play*, Christian ideology overwhelms and co-opts social critique—though it is perhaps the Christian ideology that makes the critique of social ideology possible to begin with: it was, at any rate, not uncommon in medieval Christian thought to suggest that if the peasant was oppressed on earth, "God would reward him in heaven," or even that "the poor will rule in heaven."[43] Not surprisingly, a social critique that might be produced under a variety of different circumstances takes on a specifically Christian coloring in medieval

Europe. Freedman cites an *exemplum* from the thirteenth-century theologian Jacques de Vitry's preaching handbook that suggests a specifically Christian matrix for fifteenth-century social critique. It describes a peasant, like those at the beginning of the *Second Shepherds' Play*, "shivering in the cold"; like them too, he finds comfort in the idea that "in heaven he will be able to warm his feet whenever he wishes by extending them a little over the pit of hell, where the rich will be burning."[44] Jacques de Vitry's story embodies social critique within an explicitly Christian ideology; the Wakefield Master, however, while he seems to be starting from a similarly Christian ideological position, eventually eliminates social critique from Christian comfort. The Master himself thus appears finally as a commentator like those Aers criticizes, imposing his own "harmony-model" on the class tensions that he himself has revealed.

Notes

1 David Aers, "The Good Shepherds of Medieval Criticism," *Southern Review* (University of Adelaide) 20 (1987): 168–85. Aers quotes the phrase "quiet hierarchies" from D.W. Robertson, Jr., *A Preface to Chaucer* (Princeton: Princeton University Press, 1963), 51.

2 Because of the pioneering work of Barbara Palmer, "Recycling 'The WakefieldCycle': The Records," *Research Opportunities in Renaissance Drama* 1 (2002): 88–130; and "'Towneley Plays' or 'Wakefield Cycle' Revisited," *Comparative Drama* 21 (1987): 318–48; and Garrett P.J. Epp, "The Towneley Plays and the Hazards of Cycling," *Research Opportunities in Renaissance Drama* 32 (1993): 121–50, the plays of the Towneley manuscript are now widely understood not as a unified mystery cycle perfomed at Wakefield, but rather as a compilation drawn from various Yorkshire and Lancashire locations, including Wakefield among others. Nevertheless, the attribution of six full plays and portions of several others to a single "Wakefield Master" has been seriously challenged only in one unpublished but oft-cited conference paper: see John T. Sebastian, "The Birth, Death, and Afterlife of the Wakefield Master," paper delivered at the International Congress on Medieval Studies, Western Michigan University, 2002, unpublished. While the Wakefield Master's existence cannot be proven, Peter Happé's recent book, *The Towneley Cycle: Unity and Diversity* (Cardiff: University of Wales Press, 2007), convincingly argues the stylistic case for continuing to see a single hand in the portions of the Towneley plays traditionally attributed to the Wakefield Master; see also the books by Purdon and Stevens cited in note 3. I thank Professor Sebastian for graciously providing me with a copy of his conference paper.

3 The most fully elaborated typological interpretation of the plays usually attributed to the Wakefield Master is Liam O. Purdon, *The Wakefield Master's Dramatic Art: A Drama of Spiritual Understanding* (Gainesville: University Press of Florida, 2003), and he provides a good example of the dominant Christian reading: the plays "afforded each viewer the possibility of the tropological cognitive experience fundamental to the religious metaphysics of the age—the tropological cognitive

experience, in other words, implicit in allegoresis …" (15). For typological criticism that also engages issues of politics, class, and power, see, on *The Killing of Abel*, Edith Hartnett, "Cain in the Medieval *Towneley Play*," *Annuale Mediaevale* 12 (1971): 21–9, which nevertheless suggests that "the counterpoint of type and anti-type … is the Christian purpose and structural principle of all the pageants and the cycle as a whole" (24). Edmund Reiss also suggests a typological reading in "The Symbolic Plow and Plowman and the Wakefield *Mactacio Abel*," *Studies in Iconography* 5 (1979): 3–30, quoted approvingly in James H. Morey, "Plows, Laws, and Sanctuary in Medieval England and in the Wakefield *Mactacio Abel*," *Studies in Philology* 95, no. 1 (Winter 1998): 41–55. Martin Stevens, *Four Middle English Mystery Cycles: Textual, Contextual, and Critical Interpretations* (Princeton: Princeton University Press, 1987), also finds that the play "must be read as a typological forecast" (128). Purdon and Stevens make the two major attempts at reading the Wakefield Master's works as a whole, but now see also Happé, *Towneley Cycle*. On the *Second Shepherds' Play*, see Erik Kooper, "Political Theory and Pastoral Care in the *Second Shepherds' Play*," in *This Noble Craft*, ed. Erik Kooper (Amsterdam: Rodopi, 1991), 142–51, 150; and Stevens, *Four Middle English Mystery Cycles*, 175–80. The other four plays attributed to the Wakefield Master have not received the same degree of attention, especially in terms of class and power relations, as these two.

4 See Norma Kroll, "The Towneley and Chester Plays of the Shepherds: The Dynamic Interweaving of Power, Conflict, and Destiny," *Studies in Philology* 100, no. 3 (2003): 315–45. Important work on medieval drama that resists the typological or allegorical impulse also includes Anthony Gash, "Carnival Againt Lent: The Ambivalence of Medieval Drama," in *Medieval Literature: Criticism, Ideology and History*, ed. David Aers (Southampton: Harvester Press, 1986), 74–98; and Kellie Robertson's *The Laborer's Two Bodies: Literary and Legal Productions in Britain, 1350–1500* (New York: Palgrave Macmillan, 2006), 153–82. While concerned primarily with the morality play *Mankind*, Gash's and Robertson's comments resonate interestingly with the works of the Wakefield Master as well. Robertson's point that contemporary audiences would have seen the drama's figures not merely as religious allegories but as characters with real-life counterparts posing ideological problems (167) is especially pertinent. See also Claire Sponsler, *Drama and Resistance: Bodies, Goods, and Theatricality in Late Medieval England* (Minneapolis: University of Minnesota Press, 1997), for a comparable argument.

5 Stevens, *Four Middle English Mystery Cycles*, 118, dates the Wakefield cycle in its final form to "the last third of the fifteenth century."

6 Translated as "The Statute of Laborers, 1351" in R.B. Dobson, ed., *The Peasants' Revolt of 1381*, 2nd edition (London: Macmillan, 1983), 62; his source is the statute 25 Edward III, Stat. 2, cc. 1–7, in *Statutes of the Realm*, vol. 1 (London, 1810), 311–13.

7 See, for example, Paul Freedman, *Images of the Medieval Peasant* (Stanford: Stanford University Press, 1999), 262. On fifteenth-century labor statutes and ongoing resistance to them, see Robertson, *Laborer's Two Bodies*, 157–61.

8 M.M. Postan, *The Medieval Economy and* Society (1972) (repr. Harmondsworth: Penguin, 1975), 117. The "demesne" was the land directly cultivated by the lord of the manor using hired labor, as distinct from the tenant farms.

9 Christopher Dyer, *Standards of Living in the Later Middle Ages: Social Change in England c. 1200–1520*, revised edition (Cambridge: Cambridge University Press, 1998), 140–50, 158–60, 176–7.

10 Christopher Dyer, *An Age of Transition?: Economy and Society in England in the Later Middle Ages* (Oxford: Clarendon Press, 2005), 32.

11 Dyer, *Standards of Living*, 183–4.

12 On the relationship between the York cycle and the Towneley plays, see Stevens, *Four Middle English Mystery Cycles*, 88–96 and 109–24. And now see also Palmer, "'Towneley Plays' or 'Wakefield Cycle'," 336.

13 On the localization of the Towneley plays, see Stevens, *Four Middle English Mystery Cycles*, 97–109; Palmer, "'Towneley Plays' or 'Wakefield Cycle'," 335–6.

14 Stevens, *Four Middle English Mystery Cycles*, 126.

15 V.J. Scattergood, *Politics and Poetry in the Fifteenth Century* (New York: Barnes and Noble, 1972), 347–8.

16 J.A. Raftis, "Social Change versus Revolution: New Interpretations of the Peasants' Revolt of 1381," in *Social Unrest in the Late Middle Ages*, ed. Francis X. Newman (Binghamton: Medieval and Renaissance Texts and Studies, 1986), 3–22, 15.

17 Barbara A. Hanawalt, "Peasant Resistance to Royal and Seigneurial Impositions," in *Social Unrest in the Late Middle Ages*, ed. Francis X. Newman (Binghamton: Medieval and Renaissance Texts and Studies, 1986), 23–47, 44. On peasant/landlord economic relations in this period, see also Freedman, *Images*, 262.

18 Aers, "Good Shepherds," 174.

19 Dyer, *Standards of Living*, 180–81.

20 This phenomenon has been widely remarked: see, for example, R.A. Shoaf, *Dante, Chaucer, and the Currency of the Word* (Norman, OK: Pilgrim Books, 1983); Andrew Cowell, "The Fall of the Oral Economy: Writing Economics on the Dead Body," *Exemplaria* 8 (1996): 145–68.

21 These references to Wakefield have regularly been noted in the criticism, and include an attribution to Wakefield at the beginning of *Noah and His Sons*, the reference to "Gudeboure," a Wakefield street, in *The Killing of Abel* (l. 369), the reference to "Hely," or Healey, a town four miles southwest of Wakefield, in the *First Shepherds' Play* (l. 352), and the famous reference to the "crokyd thorne" in the *Second Shepherds' Play* (l. 581). In addition to the works cited in note 12, see the notes on these lines in Martin Stevens and A.C. Cawley, eds., *The Towneley Plays*, 2 volumes, EETS s.s. 13–14 (Oxford: Oxford University Press, 1994) vol. 2, 445, 488, and 505; see also the note on the *Second Shepherds' Play*, l. 170–71, 498. These references are also discussed in Happé, *Towneley Cycle*, 15–16. Quotations from the Towneley plays follow the text in volume 1 of the Stevens–Cawley edition, and are cited by line numbers in the body of the text.

22 Recent speculation about the Wakefield Master has eschewed biography, but for a discussion of the learning evident in the plays themselves, see Stevens, *Four Middle English Mystery Cycles*, 162–3.

23 G.R. Owst, *Literature and Pulpit in Medieval England*, 2nd revised edition, 1961 (repr. New York: Barnes and Noble, 1966), points out that Cain would have been recognizable as the figure of the bad husbandman familiar from vernacular sermons, 491–2.

24 Modern English translations from the Wakefield plays are my own.

25 Dyer, *An Age of Transition?*, 66–85, offers a thorough consideration of cooperation among members of the peasant communities, as well as the landlords' occasional disruptions of traditional modes of cooperation. Landlords' borrowings come in for criticism in the *Second Shepherds' Play*; on this topic, see R.H. Hilton, *The English Peasantry in the Later Middle Ages* (Oxford: Clarendon Press, 1975), 48–9.

26 On sermon criticism of landlords who exploit laborers, see Owst, *Literature and Pulpit*, 298–303.

27 See Catherine Eagleton and Jonathan Williams, *Money: A History*, 2nd edition (London: British Museum Press, 2007), 80.

28 On spinning in the peasant cloth-making economy of Yorkshire, see, for example, Dyer, *Standards of Living*, 145. And c.f. P.J.P. Goldberg, *Women, Work, and Life Cycle in a Medieval Economy: Women in York and Yorkshire c. 1300–1520* (Oxford: Clarendon Press, 1992, repr. 1996), 118–21.

29 As Goldberg suggests, *Women, Work, and Life Cycle*, 119–20.

30 Owst, *Literature and Pulpit*, 492, points out that she, like Cain, is also a familiar figure from sermons; the "disobdient wife."

31 On the history of the English silver penny, see Peter Spufford, *Money and its Use in Medieval Europe* (Cambridge: Cambridge University Press, 1988), 402.

32 For a consideration of the debate over the relationship between the *First* and *Second Shepherds' Plays*, see Purdon, *Wakefield Master's Dramatic Art*, 251, note 2.

33 On medieval perceptions of the mistreatment of peasants as a class, see Freedman, *Images*, 40–55.

34 Owst, *Literature and Pulpit*, suggests the extent to which such critiques could have been inspired by contemporary preaching; see 287–312.

35 On the laborer's two bodies, see Robertson, *Laborer's Two Bodies*, 28. Robertson does not discuss the Wakefield plays.

36 See Reiss, "Symbolic Plow," 3–14; Freedman, *Images*, 91–3.

37 On the "curse of Noah," see Freedman, *Images*, 93–103.

38 On the medieval English pound, see Eagleton and Williams, *Money*, 78.

39 On stereotypical peasant stupidity, see Freedman, *Images*, 150–54.

40 This passage calls into question Freedman's assertion that peasants were not associated with irreligion; see *Images*, 137–9. Cf. Richard Kieckhefer, *Magic in the Middle Ages* (Cambridge: Cambridge University Press, 1989; repr. 2000), 80–82, 181–93; Jeffrey Burton Russell, *Witchcraft in the Middle Ages* (Ithaca, NY: Cornell University Press, 1972), 167–225.

41 On the medieval English mark, see Eagleton and Williams, *Money*, 78. Herod extravagantly makes good on his promise at ll. 638–50 and 664–75, referring to pounds, pennies, and marks.

42 On the groat, a coin of substantial value in late medieval England, see Spufford, *Money and its Use*, 406.

43 See Freedman, *Images*, 204, 218–23.

44 Freedman, *Images*, 220, referring to *The Exempla or Illustrative Stories from the "Sermones vulgares" of Jacques de Vitry*, ed. Thomas F. Crane (London: 1890), 50.

Chapter 2

The Incivility of Judas: "Manifest" Usury as a Metaphor for the "Infamy of Fact" (*infamia facti*)*

Giacomo Todeschini

Usurarius manifestus, namely someone who publicly and directly lends on interest, appears in the twelfth century as the clearest individual example of what canon law calls "infamy of fact."[1] From an economic and social point of view, the main legal characteristic of this person was shaped by the "fact" that his selling of money was openly visible and therefore proof of his shameless character, of his carelessness about his own reputation. In order to understand this correspondence between usury and infamy, namely to understand the metaphorical meaning at the origin of the notion and word *usura*, it is, however, crucial to keep in mind the close medieval textual relation which, before the twelfth century, links together infidelity as a basic typology of exclusion (defined by heresy, resistance to conversion, or misunderstanding of Christian notions) and avarice as a sign of the otherness, mainly connoting Jews and Jewish people, but also infidels and the so-called "pagans" or peasants (*rustici*).[2] Actually, the link between infidelity and public crime that defined a specific legal exclusion was developed by canon law, especially after the middle of the twelfth century. This connection, however, had its origin not only in the Roman law that was reshaped by Justinian's Code, but also in the redefinition of the notion of infamy (*infamia*) produced by canon law from the ninth to the twelfth century. The word *infames* designated in Roman law a well-defined range of dishonored social conditions derived on the whole from the sentence of a judge (the Roman "praetor").[3] Subsequently the textual stratification producing the canon law, beginning with the *Decretum Gratiani*, will reconsider the notion of "infamy" and shape a new definition of exclusion: the so-called "infamy of fact" (*infamia facti*). Canon law represented this new type of public dishonor as the openly visible shame[4] testified by the common opinion, the *vox publica*, and daily embodied by a multifarious range of criminals, heretics, infidels, or subjects of ill repute, whose common evil and aggressive nature was, on the whole, recapitulated through the expression "they, who fight against the fathers."[5] The idea at the basis of this new definition of incapacity to participate in the public life of the Christian community was that infidelity or moral deviations (that is visible behaviors assumed as vicious as condemned crimes) were the presumable starting point of an aggressive attitude against the ecclesiastical powers, or the beginning of a perverse will to desecrate and defame them: this hypothetical violent and "cruel," namely "savage," habit of infidels, criminals, and sinners was then perceived and described by ecclesiastical jurists as the reason for their untrustworthiness and unacceptability as witnesses. "Whoever is an infidel to God, cannot be trustworthy to people" ("Non potest erga homines esse fidelis, qui Deo extiterit infidus").[6]

It is actually possible to grasp more precisely the conceptual association between visible infamy (as the opposite of citizenship or belonging to a holy community) and usury (as shameful economic behavior or habit-shaping separation and exclusion) if we consider the role of Judas and Judaism as figures and metaphors of otherness, rudeness and incomprehension or misunderstanding of Scriptures in the formation of the western theological tradition, as well as the economic discourses on belonging to the Christian city and market (or, with the modern word, on "citizenship").[7] At the same time, it is necessary, to gain a deep understanding of the link connecting infamy, usury, Judas, and Judaism, to keep in mind the growing interplay between Roman and canon law from the ninth to the twelfth century.[8]

Indeed, the ancient theological representation of Judas' avarice and unfaithfulness, the theological association of these attributes with heretics, Jews, and outcasts, and the juridical idea that usury is a typical form of "infamy," became related even more closely from the middle of the twelfth century through the continuous textual collaboration of canonists and Romanists.[9] Nevertheless, the roots of these associations were ancient.

The Latin and Greek Fathers already[10] portrayed Judas' betrayal as the more visible manifestation of a vicious attitude toward money. In the words of Ambrose of Milan, a close but unclear relationship had existed between Judas, the Jews, and the usurers. Actually Ambrose, through intentionally obscure rhetoric, states that some usurers had lent the money acquired by the infidel apostle. Their remote and fabulous wickedness became the prototype and metaphor for the wickedness of the present usurers. Behind the past and present usurers, however, it is possible to recognize the black shadow of the usurer par excellence: the devil.

> … Wicked were the usurers who gave money that they might destroy the author of salvation; wicked also those who give that they might destroy an innocent man. And he also who receives money, like the betrayer Judas, hangs himself also with a halter. He [king David as author of the Psalms] considered that Judas himself also should be condemned with this curse, that the usurer should search his substance [Ps. 109, 11], because what proscription of tyrants or the violence of robbers is wont to do, this the wickedness alone of the usurer is accustomed to inflict. More learned men, indeed, think that the devil himself should be compared to a usurer, who destroys the things of the soul and the patrimony of our precious intellect by a kind of lending of iniquity at interest. Thus he catches with gain, he entices with gold, thus he involves us in crime, thus he demands our life in exchange for treasure. …[11]

The root of Judas' avarice, Ambrose notes, was his misunderstanding of the value of Christ. At the same time, this misunderstanding appeared also in Judas' notion of useful wealth: as declared in the episode of Magdalene's precious anointment jar:

> John the Evangelist tells that Judas Iscariot had estimated that anointment at three hundred denarii and declared that the anointment could be sold for three hundred denarii and the money given to the poor (John XII, 5). So he declared that the emblem of the cross was worth three hundred coins. The Lord in contrast does not require a previous exact knowledge of the mystery, rather He prefers that the believers' faith would be hidden inside. That was told to us by each Apostle. Judas then was condemned to be greedy: he actually preferred the money instead of the death of Christ; although he perceived the future Passion, he sinned because of the costly selling: Christ wants to be valued at a low price, so that everybody could buy him, so that no poor person would be frightened.[12]

The avarice of Judas was then embedded in his own incapacity to make a distinction between the visible or material value of the wealth, and its spiritual or hypothetical, that is, mysterious, value. The tradition beginning with Jerome and summed up by Isidore, established then that Judas' economic attitude was connected to the original and familiar identity of Judas, and was actually visible in Judas' name:

> The name of Judas Iscariot—Isidore says—derived from the village where he was born, or from the tribe named Issachar. That was a sort of prophecy regarding his future condemnation. Issachar actually means "merces" (a payment) so that it would indicate the price of the betrayer who sold the Lord …[13]

At the same time, the close association between Judas' betrayal and the untrustworthiness, infidelity, and misinterpretation of Christian truth typical of heretics and Jews made him in Augustinian texts, as well as in the canons of the post-Nicene Christianity, an intelligible prototype for the misconduct and final desperation of outsiders and aliens. Monastic culture emphasized the affinity between greedy and imperfect monks and Judas. A good example of this linguistic procedure is given by John Cassian who, in condemning the greedy habit of some monks, says that:

> because Judas wanted to recover the money which he had lost when he was a companion of Christ, not only did he become a traitor of the Lord and lost his position as apostle, he also was not worthy to conclude his life as everybody does, and so finished his life by killing himself …[14]

So Judas and the Jews began to appear, through the fourth and fifth centuries, as the main exemplars of the daily infidelity (and untrustworthiness) of the "common" uncultivated people. Through the name of the infidel apostle, the patristic and canonical sources hinted at many different social groups whose common characteristic was to be imperfectly Christianized and therefore contemptible, even though their specific identity was very blurred. Judas and the Jews as extra-temporal community could symbolize the ignorant, rude, and hostile or infamous people. Chromatius of Aquileia, a pupil of Ambrose, and Bede could then reorganize the representation of Judas' avarice in terms of a common contemptible identity, by commenting on the well-known passage of Matthew (5:13) representing the apostolic power through the metaphor of salt that makes the true believers rich in spirit and sense: "You are the salt of the world. But if the salt should lose its taste, how can it be made salty again? It's good for nothing but to be thrown out and trampled on by people" (*vos estis sal terrae quod si sal evanuerit in quo sallietur? ad nihilum valet ultra nisi ut mittatur foras et conculcetur ab hominibus*). Judas' story appeared as the paradigmatic story of a fall from an extraordinary role and situation to the vile and contemptible condition of a criminal or of an anonymous rascal:

> Judas Iscariot—Chromatius says—was part of [*literally*: belonged to] that salt, but after his refusal of the divine wisdom and after his transformation from apostle to apostate, he not only became useless to others, but also useless and disgraceful to himself. And so the Lord could add: he is unworthy, then he must be rejected outside and tread by people; actually who, like Judas, is no more faithful (trustworthy) or belonging to the family (to the house), and is consequently rejected from the Church, should be considered as an alien and an enemy …[15]

The textual history of the metaphor of salt losing its power ("if salt becomes tasteless," "vain, *foolish* salt": *si sal evanuerit, sal infatuatum*) to represent human corruption and then different forms of useless and bestialized humanity is very intriguing. It is possible to retrace this semantic path by analyzing the change of meaning and the interplay of Hebrew, Greek, and Latin words such as *ba'ar*, *morainein*, *evanuere*, and *infatuare* from the Bible to the Gospels and from the Gospels to the Vulgata and finally to the *Glossa Ordinaria*. Here, it will be enough to remember that since the eighth century to the standardization of the *Glossa Ordinaria*, and beyond, this metaphor had a very long life. Indeed, it was in the story of Judas that this image of devaluation first assumed its linguistic power.

In the words of a comment on Luke attributed to Bede:

> … Like salt which has become tasteless (vain) and then useless to dress the food and to desiccate the meat turns out to be totally worthless … so each one who comes back after he had been aware of the truth, neither will be apt to produce something good, nor will be useful to others. And so he should be cast away, namely excluded from the Church …[16]

This conceptualization was then reformulated and transmitted by Carolingian authors like Walafridus Strabo,[17] and finally since the ninth to the twelfth century codified by the *Glossa Ordinaria* and *interlinearis*, which could conclude that the individual, losing his spiritual power like the salt its taste, is sterile and useless, and can therefore be expelled from the community and despised: "… he who goes backward and no longer brings fruit, nor nurtures [others], is to be cast away."[18]

It is very easy to detect, in commentaries like this one, the connection between uselessness and infidelity, silliness and incapacity to believe Christian truths. The "machine-like repetitions, the repetitions at the core" of the formation of western "Christian-ness"[19] clearly incorporated ancient representations of Judas as an exemplar of human weakness or, even better, as a paradigm of the ease by which a condition of assured humanity (of probable holiness) can quickly transform into a form of dishonored and devalued disidentification: from salt, which gives name, meaning, and savor, to dust which everyone can ignore and tread. The paradoxical comparison between the apparent infamy of the good thief on the cross and the temporary apostolic role of Judas was used also to represent, from Patristic times to the late Middle Ages, the possibility of being recognized as a good Christian despite a dishonored appearance, and to emphasize the ease of falling from an honored situation to the notorious condition so typical of heretics, criminals, and "pagans." In the words of a Monastic Rule composed by the Spaniard Lupus de Olmeto in the fifteenth century, by means of words and phrases written many centuries earlier by Jerome:

> … Judas from the high condition of Apostle falls in the abyss of perdition, and neither his belonging to the company participating in the [last] supper, nor the partaking of the bread, nor the grace of the kiss can prevent him from betraying (selling out) Christ as He would be a man, although he was aware that Christ was the Son of God.[20]

Judas' (more or less innate) greed or avarice represented nevertheless the core of his degeneration, namely of his transformation from apostle to traitor/renegade/deserter (technically, an *infamis de jure* in Roman law) and, then, in a hanged corpse (that is, in an emblematically and *de facto* infamous "object": a hanged thief).[21] This economic and vicious character of Judas made him, in Gospels and in their patristic and then scholastic interpretation, especially apt to play the enigmatic and perturbing role of apostolic administrator (*oeconomus*, *boursier* in medieval French[22]). In other words, the economic infamy of Judas was constantly connected to his identity as an economically specialized individual. It is very important to keep in mind that it was not by chance that the economic role of the *oeconomus*, the ecclesiastic or lay administrator of the institutional goods of a church or monastery, could be represented as a particularly ambiguous economic role (mostly after the Gregorian reform). The traditional presence of the *oeconomus* was actually functional to the depiction of the spiritual danger that bishops or abbots could run as a consequence of their too close relation with the goods they managed. Bernard of Clairvaux summed up this warning when, in writing to Pope Eugene III, he reminded him that the *oeconomus* was a necessity for rulers (even if not a very pleasant one): Christ too, Bernard wrote, decided in fact to have his *oeconomus*.[23] Indeed, the paradoxical economic nature of Judas—*oeconomus* of Christ, thief of the apostolic money (as John's Gospel declared), and traitor because of his cupidity—made him not only the prototype of the infidel's and notorious person's treacherous nature, but also the metaphor of each carnal, greedy bureaucrat or manager. At the same time, Judas' role suggested that the economic ability of a good administrator, employee, or economic expert could be no more than his own presumably obtuse carnality; this represented something very different than the economic and political skillfulness that derived from the spiritual competence of rulers who, like kings, bishops, and abbots, managed the wealth of their religious communities or of their countries with the goal of producing or improving the so-called "common good."[24]

The well-known episode of Christ's visit to the house of Simon actually was the textual occasion to show, through the representation of the dialectic between Judas and the pious woman (the "Magdalene"[25]), the conflict between two different and opposite ways of understanding wealth and its use. There is first (in John's Gospel) an opposition between, on one hand, the ceremonial or honorific dispersion and spreading of wealth materialized in the precious anointment owned by the Magdalene, and, on the other, Judas' hypothesis of a possible monetary conversion of the anointment's value, of the pragmatic utility of that monetary value. This conflict (actually not having in the Gospel the shape of an explicit dialogue between the future traitor and the redeemed woman) becomes in patristic and scholastic exegesis the textual root of an opposition between a useful and thus Christian management of wealth and a useless and thus infidel management of wealth. At the same time, the theological identification of Magdalene, namely of the pious woman in the house of Simon the Pharisee, as repentant sinner makes this opposition a meaningful occasion to emphasize the contrast between two different types of notorious as well as wealthy persons: namely to represent two contrasting styles of owning and managing wealth. The double "infamy" of Judas and Magdalene becomes actually a different historical object in consequence of the dissimilar perspective from which the patristic (and scholastic) sources look at these two archetypical characters. On the one hand, Magdalene as an intellectual synthesis of different women represented by the Gospels (in the sense well explained by Katherine Jansen) represented infamy *after* repentance. The spread of wealth, in this case, showed that "she" recognized and understood the holy value embodied by Christ. Infamy (denoted as luxury) was her past; *largitio*, namely the spread of wealth (as manifestation of her *fides*) appeared the best way to negate her tainted reputation (*macula*) and to allow her to move toward the world of the *spirituales*. On the other hand, Judas represented infamy *before* the fall, namely before the betrayal. His decision to assign an exact monetary value to a spiritual and precious object (the anointment through which Christ is honored) was, from the point of view of the patristic and scholastic exegesis, the clearest sign of his carnal and bestial or uncivilized (that is unspiritual) "avarice." Judas' greed actually appeared to the Christian commentators on Scripture to be the prelude to many specific forms of economic infidelity, namely the failure (then represented as typical of the *symoniaci*) to understand the infinite value of Christ's body, or of the ecclesiastic community embodied by the Church and led by the bishops.

In the tenth century, Odo from Cluny, reconnecting to the Ambrosian interpretation of the Magdalene as figure of the Church, was even more explicit in assimilating to "Judas" each enemy of the Church, that is, each one whose infamy depended on a supposed hostility against Church and clergy: "the fact that Judas Iscariot was angry against this holy woman and said 'instead of wasting the anointment etc.', makes clear that the wicked and infidels daily assault the holy Church …"[26] It is important to bear in mind that since the ninth century, as I mentioned before, the pseudo-Isidorian canonical collections had produced and circulated a key-phrase, "they, who fight against the fathers," (*qui contra patres armantur*), which designated infidelity and civic infamy as habits intentionally and physically threatening the "fathers," that is to say, the Christian authorities.[27]

So, at the beginning of the so-called Gregorian Reform, in the first half of the eleventh century, Judas was the most common representation (the clearest textual example) of a civic infamy whose roots were greed and the bestial and obtuse misunderstanding of the value and spiritual meaning of Christ's body. This complex conceptualization was easily summed up by the legal terminology describing the hostility against the "fathers" as a form of aggression against the entire holy Christian community perceived as a community of elects. So, Judas was accurately depicted as the obvious archetype of the *symoniaci* or simonists, and more generally of those criminals whose shame, like in the case of manifest usurers, was evident and openly visible even *before* they would be formally accused and condemned.[28] The new legal culture so typical of the eleventh and twelfth centuries and so strictly connected to the Gregorian Reform could so very neatly describe the guilt and the obvious infamy of many not yet condemned *infames de facto* through the image of Judas. As Yves de Chartres declares in his *Decretum*, while writing about judicial forms of procedure: "… Our Lord Jesus Christ too did know that Judas was a thief, since nobody had formally charged him, so it was impossible to banish him …"[29]

At the same time, this new ecclesiastical legal consciousness made clear to the cultures of Roman and canon law that the brutish and shameful attitude of the infidels or fake Christians was equivalent to a misunderstanding of the plainest economic logic. Around 1140, Gratian, in his renowned *Decretum*, then observes through an astonishing theological/economic syllogism that the avarice of Judas matched with his incapacity to understand that an alienated value is no more fruitful: "… Judas sold the Redeemer and therefore, after his hanging, he could not obtain the grace of redemption. That was right, because nobody can keep what he has sold …"[30]

Judas' avarice[31] was in sum the main explanation of his transformation from apostle and elect to a pariah and notorious criminal, from meaningful man to a non-individuated subject whose perfidy was simply the way through which God had realized his own sacrifice and the salvation of mankind. Avarice as a synonym of carnality (*carnalitas*) and greed (*tenacia*) revealed Judas' nature as an anonymous, non-converted Jew; avarice as a synonym of hoarding made of him the prototype of the also anonymous manifest usurer and, moreover, the incarnation of each form of public and explicit money-selling, that is to say, of selling of what pertained to the holy community of the Christians. Nevertheless, the ordinary nature of Judas' abjection, his obtuse misunderstanding of the metaphysical value, as well as his Jewish identity, made of him a perfect representation of many forms of, so to say, "normal infamy" or daily untrustworthiness. Altogether his avarice, demonstrated by the selling of an infinite value for a small sum of coins, declared the possibility of representing otherness or incivility in a specific economic behavior or attitude.

The notion of infamy as ordinary roughness, that is vulgar incompetence on spiritual matters (*spiritualia*), eventually associated with the brutal or insidious threat embodied in heresy and Jewish literal exegesis of Scriptures, had also been defined by Augustine in terms of contemptible "inferiority" in his comment on Psalm 90. By commenting on the Gospel of Matthew (5:13), Augustine had then written that a person or thing that is considered "inferior," that is "bestial" or "carnal," is not (or is no longer) human and so can be trodden. Alternatively, he had added, that someone is not "inferior" who fixes his *inner* eye on the heavens.[32] This complex Augustinian definition had suggested the idea of a structural civic inadequacy embodied in people who—like imperfect Christians, heretics, or Jews—could not understand and therefore threatened the importance of superior and apparently illogical Christian truths.

Tertullian's paradoxical, contradictory and enigmatic definition of the way Christian rationality worked, rooted as it was in Paul's first letter to Corinthians—"The son of God was crucified; it is not shameful, because it must be shameful. And the son of God died; it is absolutely credible, because it is absurd. And the buried rose again; it is certain, because it is impossible" (*crucifixus est dei filius: non pudet, quia pudendum est. et mortuus est dei filius: prorsus credibile est, quia ineptum est. et sepultus resurrexit: certum est, quia impossibile*)—became, through the Augustinian interpretation, the more or less visible core of a spiritual as well as political identity inaccessible to the rough (*carnalis*) or illiterate people.[33] This inadequacy was revealed not only by attitudes of open defiance or manifest unfaithfulness but also by many forms of economic pragmatism or, so to say, economic literalism. The various metaphors organized by the Greek and Latin Fathers and renewed by Carolingian intellectuals about the word *bestia* (brute) as images portraying infidels, fake Christians, but also ignorant and carnal people, was moreover at the basis of this chain of reasoning.[34]

From this perspective too, the "avarice" of Judas was easily perceivable as a metaphor or symbol of the "infamy of fact" revealed by the quotidian amorality of ordinary Christian people, whose paradigmatic and allegorical representation was the infidelity and narrow-mindedness of Jews, pagans, or peasants (*rustici*). The loneliness, isolation, and despair that theological discourses and their pictorial translations attributed to Judas,[35] as well as his "perfidy," became, especially after the twelfth century, but more so at the end of the thirteenth, a good representation of the theological ignorance, common greed, bad renown, or, more simply, doubtful reputation and final perdition presumably characterizing the vulgar and abject people (the *vulgus* and the *viles et abiectae personae*). Judas and the Jews gradually turned out to be the shadow and the metaphor of a multifarious and wicked crowd, which was composed of historical Jews, simonists, heretics, criminals, as well as greedy and morally imperfect low people. *Usura*, namely "manifest usury," was supposed to be the obvious economic manifestation of different forms of infidelity or uncivilized habits, namely, the logical consequence of the incapacity to understand the holy value of goods especially when they belonged to the Christian community represented by churches, ecclesiastic institutions, or cities (*civitates*). "Usury" was thus perceived as the economic or social analogy of the literal, that is, non-spiritual, interpretation of Scriptures attributed to the Jews since the patristic age.[36]

With that established, we can turn now to consider more closely the way in which this linguistic and theological evolution affected the Christian institutional attitude about usury since Gratian and the third Lateran Council.[37] At the same time, we will examine how the economy managed by ecclesiastic or civic institutions since the twelfth century included all the previous discourses on infamy, infidelity, and avarice, altogether represented by the figure of Judas.

It is necessary to emphasize first that the Christian notion of "usury" (*usura*) was very vague and obscure until the middle of the twelfth century.[38] The notion of a specific contractual relation identifying usurious transactions appears first in the juridical and theological discourse after Gratian's *Decretum*. Only after further explanations in canon and Roman law will it become clear that usury was actually defined as the public and unequivocal selling of money. Before Gratian and the twelfth-century Lateran Councils (1123 and 1139), on the contrary, *usura* was the key word summarizing a multifarious range of economic relations indicating different forms of unequal or asymmetrical exchange; "usury happens when more is requested in restitution than was actually given" (*Usura est, ubi amplius requiritur quam quod datur*), as the 14th *quaestio* of Gratian's *Decretum* repeats.

This transition from a general meaning of iniquity deeply connected to the complex theological vocabulary defining carnality and infidelity, to a new and more specific meaning of economic abuse, occurred, on the other hand, in the aftermath of the so-called Gregorian Reform. That is to say it occurred during the conflict on simony as an economic crime, which directly menaced the organization of symbolic, mobile, and especially immobile ecclesiastic wealth. In other words, this semantic shift from *usura* as sign of evil and carnal attitude or generic greediness, to *usura* as a specific economic transaction realized by the selling of money and the pledging of immobile goods, happened during a very special political conflict. The theological as well as economic idea that monetary affairs in some cases could be a weapon that the enemies of Christianity used against the Church was a typical aspect of this conflict. The ideological roots of this notion of economic danger were ancient, and the Carolingian Episcopal culture had renewed them. Nevertheless, it was after the Investiture Conflict and the connected juridical elaborations that the idea of economic infamy as menacing spiritual authorities and desecrating wealth developed in a reflection on specific contractual forms. A direct consequence of this transformation of meaning was the adoption of canons on usury that, from the Third to the Fourth Lateran Council,[39] aimed at representing the manifest usurer and the explicit selling of money as alien realities very different from useful credit transactions intended to improve the welfare of Christian society. The Christian usurer and his obscure shadow and double, the Jewish usurer, could then be indicated as menacing outsiders or strangers who treacherously intruded on the Christian social body.

It was, then, in a situation described by theologians and canonists as a clash between *carnales* and *spirituales* that the word "usury" (*usura*) finally defined a specific contract of buying and selling money. Money, on the other hand, was now perceived as an object whose value infidels or doubtful Christians (that is *carnales*) could not correctly calculate and use. Usury actually came to appear the more evident historical and quotidian translation of the avarice traditionally attributed to infidels or fake Christians. Money managed by carnal people, and money managed by Jews, was then even more frequently represented as the outcome of larcenies and usuries. In this way, usury turned out to be an economic synonym and a metaphor for "infamy."[40] Judas, as a portrait of each notorious sinner and criminal whose corruption and infamy derived from a misunderstanding of the infinite value of divinity, namely from egotistical or individualistic conduct, obtained a new theological attention and became the "modern" representation of outsiders' or outcasts' suspicious anonymity.

The usurer, like Judas, was only interested in his own private wealth and wellbeing. When, at the beginning of the thirteenth century, Vincent de Beauvais represented Judas' greed as a form of familiar selfishness, he was actually representing and circulating a model of economic crime whose notorious protagonists were normally recognized as fake Christians, as Jews or as judaizing ones (*judaizantes*):

> … So Mary [Magdalene] opened the alabaster jar and spread the anointment on Jesus' head … but Judas Iscariot became angry, as if he had lost the [price of the] anointment, because he was a thief and, as he kept the Lord's satchels, he was accustomed to give to his wife and children what he had stolen …[41]

From this perspective, it is possible to have a deeper understanding of the late medieval symbolic versatility of Judas' image (in miniatures, paintings, and written sources). The ambiguous economic and symbolic role played by Judas and Jews since the ninth century actually became in the twelfth and thirteenth centuries a more specific rhetorical and visual image. It is important to remember that this conceptual and iconographic development took place during the gradual growth of a new complicated credit economy, whose core was the distinction between the legitimacy of credit transactions performed by institutional powers and the legal and moral ambiguity of credit transactions performed by private entrepreneurs of dubious reputation and unknown social or familial origin. Definitions of credit in Roman and canon law, as well as theological representations of the market, incessantly emphasized, since the end of the twelfth century, the difference between the economic and institutional meaning of credit carried out by kings, ecclesiastical institutions, or their lay agents, and the lending and borrowing managed by "common people." An abyss of meaning separated the credit and banking done by the Church from the selling of money performed by "those who—as Peter the Chanter says—publicly declare to be usurers or show it through some well-known sign."[42]

In this light, usury and manifest usurer (*usura* and *usurarius manifestus*) could appear, since the end of the twelfth century, less a specific economic definition in the modern sense than a metaphorical or civic representation of infidel, or uncivilized economic behaviors, hinting at a whole galaxy of dubious economic and social habits. Judaizing (*judaizare*) as well as being similar to Judas or being recognized as *usurarius manifestus* (as a public usurer) definitely came to signify being or looking suspect of moving outside of the sacred/institutional space of bargaining: the city, the Church, or the Christian society (*civitas*, *ecclesia*, or *societas christianorum*).

Actually, Judas as a type of carnal Jew hinting at the infidelity of pagans and imperfect Christians was replaced in large part in the thirteenth century by Judas as a figure of an unworthy and therefore untrustworthy people (*viles et abiectae personae* in the legal language of the canonists and glossators). Greed and lack of spiritual intelligence, defined by canonists and jurists since 1180 as the main characteristic of "ordinary people," were perfectly summed up by Judas' incapacity to maintain his apostolic and authoritative condition. Peter the Chanter in his *Verbum abbreviatum* could therefore define the Christian usurers through the expression *Judaei nostri* ("our Jews").[43] The phrase did not signify, as historians mainly interpret, that Peter (even in the Paris of the beginning of the thirteenth century) considered usury as a typical Jewish profession. Instead, Peter affirmed the way that Jewish civic infamy, depicted by theologians as a visible and daily allusion to Judas' and Jewish spiritual greed and incomprehension of Christian values, was the specific attribute of Christians, who earned their living by usurious transactions, that is by economic transactions beyond the control of landlords and ecclesiastical powers and therefore perceived as menacing the body of Christian society as *ecclesia*. In other words, from the twelfth to the thirteenth century the infamy of Judas and the Jews became a clear representation of manifold types of civic irregularity.

Indeed, the new thinking on the reasons and forms of social identity that determined the exclusion from civic interplay was a specific characteristic of Italian, French, and English juridical development in this period. This growing legal consciousness also empowered the above-mentioned equation between Judas' and Jewish infamy and more common features of notoriety. Thomas of Chobham, around 1215, could therefore clearly connect the legal or Roman notion of public infamy to the religious or canonistic notion of untrustworthiness through the renewed category of *irregularitas*: "Irregularity is the word defining somebody's indignity: it determines the expulsion from holy Orders and from liturgy or the impossibility to act legally namely to testify or charge …"[44]

Irregularity can have, Thomas argued, many origins, and derives from both innocent and guilty identities, attitudes, and behaviors. Its source can be servitude and physical handicap, like crime and common infamy, namely well-known shameful conduct. Usury as a patent example and metaphor of common visible crime and heresy is the more obvious case of irregularity, dependent both on a civic infamy and a mental or intellectual deviation. Alternatively, as the Romanist Baldus de Ubaldis will say a century later, irregularity defined by notorious behaviors like manifest usury proscribes from participating in civic rituals because of the indelible "scar in the state of nature" it produces. "…infamy actually is a scar in the state of nature and there are two types of infamy … an inner infamy contextually produced by a legal sentence, and an outer infamy deriving from a common and widespread defamation …"[45]

The use by the Franciscans of Judas to warn, at the beginning of the Trecento, the friars who wished to abandon strict poverty rules—as Janet Robson properly showed[46]—is a good example of a more general process rooted in the described semantic amplification of the meanings implied by "Judas" as the main example of *carnalitas* and avarice, namely of vicious opposition to voluntary and evangelical poverty.

It is not by chance that the mystical Franciscan economist Peter John Olivi, in commenting on the Gospel of Matthew, utilizes again the figure of Judas to emphasize the condemnation of a carnal use of spiritual things. At the same time, Olivi, employing the typical Franciscan psychological approach, transforms avarice as public shame embodied by Judas and Jews or infidels into an inner, not necessarily evident, emotion or feeling. In this way Judas, Jews, and patent usurers now become a dark mirror that reflects the latent economic or social infamy of the so-called *viles et abiectae personae*, the common, uncultivated, and poor or non-Christian people:

> … like Judas, by selling Christ, could not make Him an object of profit without having an awful feeling and plunging his heart in a deep and gloomy abyss of evil which is not possible to express, so not even the spiritual things can be intended to produce a material profit without an awful feeling and a fall of the heart …[47]

From the thirteenth to the fifteenth centuries, the growing multiplication of portraits and writings representing Judas, like an isolated, excluded, and haunted ordinary man (at the Last Supper, in the house of Simon the Pharisee, and as a hanged body), circulated the notion that Jewish greed (*avaritia*, *tenacia*) was a form of infamy that menaced every Christian. Since Judas' failure continued to be represented as depending on his incapacity to appreciate and understand both the value of Christ and his own apostolic role, the lack of understanding and practice in Christian rules and way of life could be then described as the gate leading to an abyss of infamy and bad reputation, namely, to a desperate civic anonymity. The late medieval and early modern increase of theological and juridical texts showing the hopeless condition of the usurer, prescribing his separation and mandatory expulsion from the civic body, displays, from this point of view, the spread of the notion of economic infamy as a synonym for common infidelity derived from ordinary economic habits. The prohibition and detestation of usury appear finally to be more a metaphor of economic and civic exclusion rather than the result of a specific ecclesiastic or civic opposition to Christian credit transactions.

Notes

* I began to write this paper during my stay at the Institute for Advanced Study (Princeton, January–April 2008). I want to express my gratitude to the colleagues and staff I had the chance to meet there. I am especially grateful to Caroline Bynum and Bill Caferro who helped me by discussing some aspects of my work.

1 Frank J. Rodimer, *The Canonical Effects of Infamy of Fact: A Historical Synopsis and a Commentary* (*Washington*: Catholic University of America Press, 1954); Georg May, "Die Bedeutung der pseudo-isidorischen Sammlung für die Infamie im kanonischen Recht," *Österreichisches Archiv für Kirchenrecht* 12 (1961): 87–113, 191–207; Idem, "Die Anfänge der Infamie im kanonischen Recht," *Zeitschrift für Rechtsgeschichte—Kanonische Abteilung* 47 (1961): 77–94; Peter Landau, *Die Entstehung des kanonischen Infamienbegriffs von Gratian zur Glossa Ordinaria* (Köln-Graz: Böhlau Verlag, 1966); Francesco Migliorino, *Fama e infamia. Problemi della società medievale nel pensiero giuridico nei secoli XII e XIII* (Catania: Giannotta, 1985); Julien Théry, "Fama: l'opinion publique comme preuve judiciaire. Aperçu sur la révolution médiévale de l'inquisitoire (XIIe–Xve siècle)," in *La preuve en justice de l'Antiquité à nos jours*, ed. B. Lemesle (Rennes: Presses Universitaires de Rennes, 2003), 119–47; Thelma Fenster and Daniel L. Smail, eds, *Fama: The Politics of Talk and Reputation in Medieval Europe* (Ithaca and London: Cornell University Press, 2003).

2 Wolfram Drews, "Jews as Pagans? Polemical Definitions of Identity in Visigothic Spain," *Early Medieval Europe* 11, no. 2 (2002): 189–207; Paul Freedman, *Images of the Medieval Peasant* (Stanford: Stanford University Press, 1999). See Giacomo Todeschini, *Visibilmente crudeli. Malviventi, persone sospette e gente qualunque dal Medioevo all'età moderna* (Bologna: Il Mulino, 2007).

3 Or from the *nota* of a *praetor*; Abel H.J. Greenidge, *Infamia: Its Place in Roman Public and Private Law* (Oxford: Oxford University Press, 1894); Alberto Maffi, "La costruzione giuridica dell'infamia nell'ordinamento romano," in *La fiducia secondo i linguaggi del potere*, ed. Paolo Prodi (Bologna: Il Mulino, 2007), 41–51.

4 Public shame and dishonor were produced by the so-called *vox publica* as it was accepted and recognized by the ecclesiastical *auctoritas*. See the quoted works of Migliorino, Théry, Fenster and Smail.

5 Pseudo-Stephanus I, *Epistola Decretalis Stephani Papae Hilario Episcopo Directa*, in *Decretales pseudoisidorianae et Capitula Angilramni*, ed. Paul Hinschius (Leipzig: Tauchnitz, 1863): "Infames autem esse eas personas dicimus, qui pro aliqua culpa notantur infamia, id est, omnes, qui christianae legis normam abiciunt et statuta

ecclesiastica contemnunt, similiter fures, sacrilegos et omnes capitalibus criminibus irretitos, sepulchrorum quoque violatores et apostolorum atque successorum eorum reliquorumque sanctorum patrum statuta libenter violatores et omnes qui adversus patres armantur, qui in omni mundo infamia notantur" (http://www.pseudoisidor.mgh.de/html/047.htm); *Decretum Gratiani* C. III q. V 13, ed. Emil Friedberg (Leipzig: Tauchnitz, 1879), 517: "Omnes, qui aduersus Patres armantur, ut patrum inuasores infames esse censemus." See Todeschini, *Visibilmente crudeli*, 58–61.

6 Fourth Council of Toledo (633), c. 64: see Walter Pakter, *Medieval Canon Law and the Jews* (Ebelsbach: Rolf Gremer, 1988), 161; Amnon Linder, *The Jews in the Legal Sources of the Early Middle Ages* (Detroit: Wayne State University Press, 1997), 490.

7 Bernhard Blumenkranz, *Juifs et chrétiens dans le monde occidental, 430–1096* (Paris-La Haye: Mouton, 1960); Idem, *Juifs et Chretiens. Patristique et Moyen Age* (London: Variorum Reprints, 1977); Leah Dasberg, *Untersuchungen über die Entwertung des Judenstatus im 11. Jahrhundert* (Den Haag: Mouton, 1965); Gilbert Dahan, *Les intellectuels chrétiens et les juifs au moyen âge* (Paris: Cerf, 1990); Anna Sapir Abulafia, *Christians and Jews in the Twelfth Century Renaissance* (London: Routledge, 1995); Stephen R. Haynes, *Reluctant Witness: Jews and Christian Imagination* (Westminster: John Knox Press, 1995); Robert Chazan, *Medieval Stereotypes and Modern Antisemitism* (Berkeley and Los Angeles: University of California Press, 1997); Jeremy Cohen, *Living Letters of the Law: Ideas of the Jew in Medieval Christianity* (Berkeley: University of California Press, 1999); Miri Rubin, *Gentile Tales: The Narrative Assault on Late-Medieval Jews* (Yale: Yale University Press, 1999); Sarah Lipton, *Images of Intolerance: The Representation of Jews and Judaism in the Bible moralisée* (Berkeley: University of California Press, 1999); Eva Frojmovic, ed., *Imagining the Self, Imagining the Other: Visual Representation and Jewish–Christian Dynamics in the Middle Ages and Early Modern Period* (Leiden: Brill, 2002); Cristopher Cluse, ed., *The Jews of Europe in the Middle Ages (Tenth to Fifteenth Centuries): Proceedings of the International Symposium Held at Speyer, 20–25 October 2002* (Turnhout: Brepols, 2004); Carolyn Walker Bynum, *Wonderful Blood: Theology and Practice in Late Medieval Northern Germany and Beyond* (Philadelphia: University of Pennsylvania Press, 2007).

8 Mordechai Rabello, *Giustiniano, Ebrei e Samaritani alla luce delle fonti storico-letterarie, ecclesiastiche e giuridiche* (Milan: Giuffré, 1987–88); Idem, *The Jews in the Roman Empire. Legal Problems: From Herod to Justinian* (London: Ashgate, 2000); John Gilchrist, "The Canonistic Treatment of Jews in the Latin West in the Eleventh and Early Twelfth Centuries," *Zeitschrift der Savigny Stiftung für Rechtsgeschichte—Kanonische Abteilung* 106, no. 75 (1989): 70–106; Pakter, *Medieval Canon Law and the Jews*; Linder, *The Jews in the Legal Sources of the Early Middle Ages*.

9 Giacomo Todeschini, *I mercanti e il tempio. La società cristiana e il circolo virtuoso della ricchezza dal Medioevo all'Età Moderna* (Bologna: Il Mulino, 2002); Idem, *Visibilmente crudeli*; Diego Quaglioni, Giacomo Todeschini, and Gian Maria Varanini, eds, *Credito e usura fra teologia, diritto e amministrazione. Linguaggi a confronto (sec. XII–XVI)* (Rome: Ecole Française de Rome, 2005).

10 Hans-Josef Klauck, *Judas. Ein Jünger des Herrn* (Freiburg: Herder, 1987); Idem, *Judas, un disciple de Jésus. Exégèse et répercussions historiques* (Paris: Cerf, 2006); Pierre-Emmanuel Dauzat, *Judas: de l'Évangile à l'Holocauste* (Paris: Bayard, 2006).

11 Lois Miles Zucker, ed., *S. Ambrosii De Tobia : A Commentary, with an Introduction and Translation* (Washington, DC: The Catholic University of America, 1933), 32–3; Ambrosius Mediolanensis, *De Tobia* 4, 12, in *Opere* VI (Milan and Rome: Città Nuova, 1983): "Mali faeneratores, qui dederunt pecuniam, ut interficerent salutis auctorem, mali et isti qui dant, ut interficiant innocentem. Et iste quoque qui pecuniam acceperit ut proditor Iudas laqueo se et ipse suspendit. Ipsum quoque Iudam hoc maledicto putauit esse damnandum, ut scrutaretur faenerator eius substantiam [Ps. 109, 11], quia quod proscriptio tyrannorum, aut latronum manus operari solet, hoc sola faeneratoris nequitia consueuit inferre. Doctiores autem ipsum faeneratori putant diabolum conparatum, qui res animae et pretiosae mentis patrimonium faenore quodam usurariae iniquitatis euertit. Sic sumptu capit, sic auro inlicit, sic reatu inuoluit, sic caput pro thensauro reposcit."

12 Ambrosius Mediolanensis, *Super Lucam* VI, 29–31, in *Patrologia latina* 15, 4; CC sl 14 (Turnhout: Brepols, 1957): "Denique Joannes Evangelista inducit sermone Judae Iscariotis aestimatum trecentis denariis illud unguentum, sicut habes: Potuit enim venumdari trecentis denariis, et dari pauperibus (John, XII, 5). Trecentorum autem aera crucis insigne declarat: sed Dominus non perfunctoriam mysterii praescientiam quaerit, sed consepeliri in se fidem credentium mavult. Id tamen de caeterorum apostolorum vocibus intelligimus: Judas autem condemnatur avaritiae, qui pecuniam Dominicae praetulit sepulturae, qui etiamsi de passione sensit, erravit tam cara auctione: vili vult aestimari se Christus, ut ab omnibus ematur, ne quis pauper deterreatur. Gratis, inquit, accepistis, gratis date (Matth. X, 8). Pecuniam non quaerit divitiarum altitudo, sed gratiam. Ipse nos pretioso sanguine redemit, non vendidit. De quo plenius diceremus, nisi a nobis ipsis tractatum alibi recordaremur [*Lib. III de Spiritu sancto*, cap. 18]."

13 Isidorus, *Etymologiae*, VII 9, 20 (VII C.), ed. Wallace Martin Lindsay (Oxford: Oxford University Press, 1911); ed. Manuel C. Diaz y Diaz (Madrid: BAC, 1983): "*Judas Iscariotes*, vel a vico, in quo ortus est, vel ex tribu Issachar vocabulum sumpsit, quodam praesagio futuri in condemnationem sui. *Issachar* enim interpretatur *merces*, ut significaretur pretium proditoris, quo vendidit Dominum, sicut scriptum est: *Et acceperunt mercedem meam, triginta argenteos, pretium quo appretiatus sum ab eis* (Matth. XXVII, 9)."

14 Iohannes Cassianus, *De institutis coenobiorum et de octo principalium vitiorum remediis* (a. 420–24) = Jean Cassien, *Institutions cénobitiques*, ed. Jean-Claude Guy (Paris: Cerf, 2001), VII: "Iudas autem volens resumere pecunias, quas antea Christum secutus abiecerat, non solum ad proditionem Domini lapsus apostolatus gradum perdidit, sed etiam vitam ipsam communi exitu finire non meruit eamque biothanati morte conclusit."

15 Chromatius Aquileiensis (second half of fourth century), *Tractatus XVIII in Evangelium S. Matthaei*, in *Patrologia latina* 106, 337, in *Chromatii Aquileiensis Opera*, ed. Raymond Etaix and Joseph Lemarié (CC sl, IXA, Turnhout: Brepols, 1974), 282–3:

"Denique Judas Scariothes de hujusmodi salibus fuerat: sed postea quam divinam sapientiam reprobavit, et de Apostolo apostata factus est, non solum aliis prodesse non potuit, sed et sibi miser et inutilis factus est. Et ideo addidit Dominus dicens: *Ad nihilum valet, nisi ut projiciatur foras, et conculcetur ab hominibus* [Mt 27:3–5]: quia hujusmodi, jam non fideles ac domestici, sed proiecti ab Ecclesia, ut extranei et fidei hostes habendi sunt. Unde et Judas de domestico fidei, inimicus factus est veritatis. Proiecti itaque hujusmodi extra Ecclesiam, necesse est ut diversis vitiis carnis et variis voluptatibus saeculi conculcentur; et hoc est quod ait: *Ad nihilum valet, nisi ut projiciatur foras, et conculcetur ab hominibus*."

16 Beda (?), *In Lucam* IV 14 (seventh/eighth century) in *Patrologia latina* 91, 519: "*Bonum est sal: Si autem sal quoque evanuerit, in quo condietur?* Ad superiora respicit, ubi turrem virtutum non solum inchoandam, sed etiam praeceperat esse consummandam. Bonum quippe est Dei verbum audire, frequentius sale sapientiae spiritalis cordis arcana condire, imo ipsum cum apostolis sal terrae fieri, id est, eorum quoque qui adhuc terrena sapiunt imbuendis mentibus sufficere. At si quis semel condimento veritatis illuminatus ad apostasiam redierit, quo alio doctore corrigitur, qui eam quam ipse gustavit sapientiae dulcedinem, vel adversis saeculi perterritus, vel illecebris allectus abjecit? Juxta hoc quod quidam sapiens ait: *Quis medebitur incantatori a serpente percusso* (Eccli. XII)? Qua sententia Judae Iscariot socios ipsumque designari non immerito credatur qui philargyria victus et gradum apostolatus prodere et Dominum tradere non dubitavit. *Neque in terram, neque in sterquilinium utile est, sed foras mittetur. Sicut sal infatuatum cum ad condiendos cibos carnesque siccandas valere desierit, nullo jam usui aptum erit* (neque enim in terram utile est, cujus injectu germinare prohibetur, neque in sterquilinium agriculturae profuturum, quod vivacibus licet glebis immistum non fetare semina frugum, sed exstinguere solet), *sic omnis qui post agnitionem veritatis retro redit, neque ipse fructum boni operis ferre, neque alios excolere valet, sed foras mittendus, hoc est ab Ecclesiae est unitate secernendus*, ut, juxta praemissam parabolam, irridentes eum inimici, dicant quia hic homo coepit aedificare, et non potuit consummare."

17 Walafridus Strabo (ninth century), *In Matthaeum* 5, 13 in *Patrologia latina* 114, 91: "Quod si sal, etc. Id est, si vos, per quos alii condiendi sunt, adversis vel prosperis cesseritis: per quos a vobis error auferetur, cum vos Deus tollere aliis elegerit? Ad nihilum valet: quia (ut alius evangelista ait) nec terrae utilis est quam suo injectu germinare prohibet, nec sterquilinio quod non fecundare sinit. Sic qui retro vadit, nec ipse fructum fert, nec alios valet excolere, sed ab Ecclesia ejicitur, et in haec verba ridetur: Hic homo coepit aedificare, et non potuit consummare. Si sal evanuerit (Luc. IV). Id est, si timore vel cupidine doctor saporem sapientiae omiserit, per quem fatuitas ejus emendabitur? Hoc solis apostolis convenit: Quod sequitur, omnibus magistris: Ad nihilum valet ultra, etc. In fine de omnibus concludit sic: Nisi abundaverit justitia, etc."

18 *Glossa Ordinaria, ad Mt. 5, 13* (*Biblia Latina cum Glossa Ordinaria*, Strassburg: A. Rusch, 1480; reprinted with introductions by Karlfried Froehlich and Margaret T. Gibson, Turnhout: Brepols 1992, vol. 4): "… Si autem sal evanuerit etc. Id est si apostoli per quos alii condiendi sunt prosperis vel adversis cesserint per quos eis error auferetur, cum eos deus elegit tollere aliis, neque in terra neque in sterquilinio, quia

qui retro vadit neque ipsum fructum ferre, neque excolere valet, sed eijcitur." *Glossa interlinearis* (ibidem): "Sal infatuatum, tribulationi cedentes."

19 Kathleen Biddick, *The Theological Imaginary: Circumcision, Technology, History* (Philadelphia: University of Pennsylvania Press, 2003), 12.

20 Lupus de Olmeto (d. 1433), *Regula monachorum ex scriptis Hieronymi per Lupum de Olmeto collecta. Prologus* in *Patrologia latina* 219 (see Cambridge, Harvard University, Houghton Library, ms Lat 189 = Monastic Rule, compiled from the writings of St Jerome for the Observants of the Order of St Jerome by Lupus de Olmedo and approved by Pope Martin V in 1428): "Latro credit in cruce, et statim meretur audire: *Amen dico tibi: hodie mecum eris in paradiso.* Judas vero de apostolatus fastigio in perditionis tartarum labitur, et nec familiaritate convivii, nec intinctione bucellae, nec osculi gratia frangitur, ne quasi hominem tradat, quem Filium Dei noverat."

21 It should be noted that in fourteenth- and fifteenth-century Italy, as well as France or England, hanging was the typical and ignominious punishment for theft. The representation of Judas as a thief in the Gospel of John, and, then, as a hanged thief in a wide range of medieval texts and images, is a historigraphical (and anthropological) problem not yet investigated. See Maria Pia Di Bella, ed., *Vol et sanctions en Meditérranée* (Amsterdam: Éditions des Archives Contemporaines, 1998); Alexander Murray, *Suicide in the Middle Ages* I (Oxford: Oxford University Press, 1998), 154, 299; II (Oxford: Oxford University Press, 2000), 323; Mitchell B. Merback, *The Thief, the Cross and the Wheel: Pain and the Spectacle of Punishment in Medieval and Renaissance Europe* (Chicago: University of Chicago Press, 1999); Robert Mills, *Suspended Animation: Pain, Pleasure and Punishment in Medieval Culture* (London: Reaktion Books, 2005).

22 Omer Jodogne, ed., *Le mystère de la passion d'Arnoul Gréban* I (Bruxelles: Academie Royale de Belgique, 1965), 11073.

23 Bernhard of Clairvaux, *De Consideratione ad Eugenium papam*, IV VI 19, in *Opere di San Bernardo* I, ed. F. Gastaldelli (Milan: Città Nuova, 1984), 887. See Giacomo Todeschini, *Il prezzo della salvezza. Lessici medievali del pensiero economico* (Rome: NIS, 1994); Idem, "Judas mercator pessimus. Ebrei e simoniaci dall'XI al XIII secolo," *Zakhor. Rivista di storia degli ebrei in Italia* I (1997): 11–23; Idem, "Franciscan Economics and Jews in the Middle Ages: From a Theological to an Economic Lexicon," in *Friars and Jews in the Middle Ages and Renaissance*, ed. Stephen McMichael and Susan Myers (Leiden and Boston: Brill 2004), 99–117.

24 Matthew S. Kempshall, *The Common Good in Late Medieval Political Thought* (Oxford: Oxford University Press, 1999); Peter von Moos, "'Public' et 'privé' à la fin du moyen âge. Le 'bien commun' et la 'loi de la conscience'," *Studi Medievali* s. 3a, XLI/2 (2000): 505–48; Giacomo Todeschini, *Le "bien commun" de la civitas christiana dans la tradition textuelle franciscaine (XIIIe–XVe siècle)*, in *Politique et religion en Méditerranée. Moyen âge et époque contemporaine*, ed. Henri Bresc, Georges Dagher, and Christiane Veauvy (Paris: Bouchène, 2008), 265–303.

25 Katherine L. Jansen, *The Making of the Magdalen: Preaching and Popular Devotion in the Later Middle Ages* (Princeton: Princeton University Press, 2000); Pierre-Emmanuel Dauzat, *L'Invention de Marie-Madeleine* (Paris: Bayard, 2001).

26 Odo Cluniacensis (?), *Sermo. In veneratione Sanctae Mariae Magdalenae* (tenth century) in *Patrologia latina* 133, 716: "... Quod vero Judas Iscariot contra hanc sanctissimam mulierem indignatus dicitur: pro effusione tanti unguenti, datur aperte intelligi, quia reprobi et infideles contra sanctam Ecclesiam quotidie saeviunt (...)"

27 Pseudo-Stephanus I, *Epistola decretalis Stephani papae Hilario episcopo directa*, in *Decretales pseudoisidorianae et Capitula Angilramni*, ed. Paul Hinschius (Leipzig: Tauchnitz, 1863), 182; Pseudo-Stephanus I, *Epistola* II, ibidem: "Scimus, dilectissimi, quia semper carnales spiritales solent persequi et malivoli benevolos infamari et lacerari. Idcirco apostoli et successores eorum ac reliqui sancti patres noluerunt fieri facilem episcoporum accusationem, quoniam, si facilis esset, aut nullus aut vix aliquis modo inveniretur. Throni enim dei vocantur, ideo non debent moveri aut affligi vel perturbari. De ipsis ergo ait propheta: Caeli enarrant gloriam dei, et opera manuum eius annuntiat firmamentum. Hi vero, qui non sunt bonae conversationis et quorum vita est accusabilis, aut quorum fides, vita et libertas nescitur, non possunt eos accusare"; see Todeschini, *Visibilmente crudeli*, ch. 2.

28 Humbertus de Silvacandida, *Adversus simoniacos libri tres*, ed. Friedrich Thaner, Monumenta Germaniae Historica, "Libelli de lite" I (Hannover: Hahn 1891), 162–3.

29 Yvo Carnotensis, *Decretum* VI c. 317 (1090 c.), <http://project.knowledgeforge.net/ivo/decretum/ivodec_6_1p0.pdf>: "... Nihil tamen absque legitimo et idoneo accusatore fiat. Nam et Dominus noster Iesus Christus Iudam esse sciebat furem, sed quia non est accusatus, ideo non est eiectus; et quicquid inter apostolos egit, pro dignitate ministerii, ratum mansit. ..."

30 *Decretum Gratiani* C. I q. 1 c.11 (text from the Council of Nicaea II, a. 787 *cum additionibus saeculi XI*), ed. Emil Friedberg (Leipzig: Tauchnitz, 1879), 361: "... Spiritus sancti donum precio conparari quid aliud est quam capitale crimen et symoniaca heresis ? ... Iudas omnium redemptorem vendidit, mox laqueo suspensus eandem redemptionis gratiam non obtinuit, et merito, quia nemo potest retinere quod vendidit. (...)"

31 Richard Newhauser, *The Early History of Greed: The Sin of Avarice in Early Medieval Thought and Literature* (Cambridge: Cambridge University Press, 2000, 2006).

32 Augustinus, *Enarratio in Ps. 90*, 9, 13, in *Opere di S. Agostino* (Rome: Città Nuova, 1976); Idem, *De sermone domini in monte I*, 6, 16 in *Opere di S. Agostino* (Rome: Città Nuova, 1976): "Rectissime itaque sequitur: *Vos estis sal terrae*, ostendens fatuos esse iudicandos, qui temporalium bonorum vel copiam sectantes vel inopiam metuentes amittunt aeterna, quae nec dari possunt ab hominibus nec auferri. Itaque: *Si sal infatuatum fuerit, in quo salietur?*, id est si vos per quos condiendi sunt quodammodo populi, metu persecutionum temporalium amiseritis regna caelorum, qui erunt homines per quos vobis error auferatur, cum vos elegerit Deus, per quos errorem auferat ceterorum? Ergo: *Ad nihilum valet sal infatuatum, nisi ut mittatur foras et calcetur ab hominibus*. Non itaque calcatur ab hominibus qui patitur persecutionem, sed qui persecutionem timendo infatuatur. Calcari enim non potest nisi inferior; sed inferior non est qui, quamvis corpore multa in terra sustineat, corde tamen fixus in caelo est." See Celia Chazelle, *The Crucified God in the Carolingian Era: Theology and Art of Christ's Passion* (Cambridge: Cambridge University Press, 2001), 77–8.

33 Tertullianus, *De carne Christi*, V 23–25 in *La Chair du Christ*, ed. Jean-Pierre Mahé (Paris: Cerf, "Sources Chrétiennes" 216, 1975), ed. Ernest Evans, <http://www.tertullian.org/articles/evans_carn/evans_carn_03latin.htm>. See Avril Cameron, *Christianity and the Rhetoric of the Empire: The Development of Christian Discourse* (Berkeley: University of California Press, 1991); Guy G. Stroumsa, *Barbarian Philosophy: The Religious Revolution of Early Christianity* (Tübingen: Mohr Siebeck, 1995).

34 Giacomo Todeschini, "Licet in maxima parte adhuc bestiales: la raffigurazione degli Ebrei come non umani in alcuni testi altomedievali," *Studi Medievali* XLIV 3 (2003), 1135–49.

35 Ruth Mellinkoff, *Outcasts: Signs of Otherness in Northern European Art of the Late Middle Ages* (Berkeley: University of California Press, 1993); Brigitte Monstadt, *Judas beim Abendmahl:Figurenkonstellation und Bedeutung in Darstellungen von Giotto bis Andrea del Sarto* (Muenchen: Scaneg, 1995); Ingrid Westerhoff, "Der moralisierte Judas: mittelalterliche Legende, Typologie, Allegorie im Bild," *Aachener Kunstblätter des Museumsverein* 61 (1995–97), 85–156; Lee R. Sullivan, "The Hanging of Judas: Medieval Iconography and the German Peasants' War," *Proceedings of the Illinois Medieval Association—Essays in Medieval Studies* 15 (1998): 93–101; Janet Robson, "Judas and the Franciscans: Perfidy Pictured in Lorenzetti's Passion Cycle at Assisi," *Art Bulletin*, 86, no. 1 (March 2004): 31–57.

36 Blumenkranz, *Juifs et Chrétiens*; Todeschini, "Franciscan Economics and Jews in the Middle Ages"; Cohen, *Living Letters of the Law.*

37 See, in this volume, the essay by James M. Murray: "The Devil's Evangelists? Moneychangers in Flemish Urban Society."

38 Harald Siems, *Handel und Wucher im Spiegel hochmittelalterlichen Rechtsquellen* (Hannover, Schriften der Monumenta Germaniae Historica, 35: Hahnsche Buchhandlung, 1992); Todeschini, *Il prezzo della salvezza*; Idem, *I mercanti e il tempio.*

39 *Conciliorum Oecumenicorum Decreta*, ed. J. Alberigo, P.P. Joannou, C. Leonardi and P. Prodi, consultante H. Jedin (Bologna: EDB, 1973, 1991), *Concilium Lateranense* III (1179), c. 25; *Concilium Lateranense* IV (1215), c. 67.

40 Todeschini, *Visibilmente crudeli*, chapter 4; Idem, "Christian Perceptions of Jewish Economic Activity in the Middle Ages," in *Wirtschaftsgeschichte der mittelalterlichen Juden. Fragen und Einschätzungen*, ed. Michael Toch (Munich, Schriften des Historischen Kollegs, Bd. 71: Oldenbourg, 2008), 1–16.

41 Vincent de Beauvais, *Speculum Historiale* (1220 c.) VIII 31 (from *Petri Comestoris Historia scholastica, Historia evangelica*, 1160 c.) c. 116 (Nuernberg: Anton Koberger, 1483), in <http://www.cs.uu.nl/groups/IK/archives/vincent/bibl/subj/sh.htm#sh>: "… Maria ergo aperuit alabastrum et effundebat unguentum super caput Ihesu, et etiam unxit pedes eius, et extersit, capillis suis. In memoriam huius rei, eodem sabbato dominus papa debet erogare pauperibus. Hi enim sunt pedes domini sedentis in celo, adhuc ambulantes in terra. Cuius largitionis occupatione eadem die non egreditur ad aliquam ecclesiam, cum ceteris diebus XLe stationem faciat ad celebrandum missam. Indignabatur autem Iudas Scariotes, quasi de perdito unguento, quia fur erat et loculos domini habens, uxori et filiis dabat, que furabatur."

42 Peter the Chanter, *Verbum abbreviatum. Textus conflatus*, I 48, ed. Monique Boutry (Turnhout: Brepols, 2004), 325: "Et cum quereretur qui essent notorii, dictum est: 'Qui publice fatentur se esse usurarios vel aliquot noto signo hoc indicant', ut quasi capistra venalia in summitate haste vel virge fenerandam pecuniam circumferant …"

43 Peter the Chanter, *Verbum abbreviatum. Textus conflatus*, ibidem.

44 Thomas of Chobham, *Summa confessorum* (1215/16) q. III, Ia, *De irregularitatibus*, ed. F. Broomfield (Louvain and Paris: Éditions Nauwelaerts, 1968) 61: "Est autem irregularitas indignitas alicuius persone propter quam repellitur ab ordinibus et ab officiis divinis vel a legitimis actibus, ut a testimonio vel ab accusatione. Et contrahitur talis irregularitas quandoque a statu corporis; ut si fuerit aliquis corpore vitiatus per diminutionem membrorum vel deformitatem eorum. Similiter quando aliquis nascitur servus ex origine irregularis est nisi redigatur in libertatem. Quandoque contrahitur ex ipso genere facti sine omni peccato ; ut ex eo quod iudex occidit furem irregularis est, licet non peccet. Similiter si quis contrahat cum vidua vel duas habuerit uxores, quod dicitur bigamia, irregularis est quantum ad ordines suscipiendos. Contrahitur etiam irregularitas ex infamia."

45 Baldus de Ubaldis, *In Decretalium volumen commentaria* (1360 c.) (Venezia: Giunta, 1595), f. 234rb: "… infamia enim est cicatrix naturalis status, et est duplex infamia scilicet interior, quae constat legis dispositione, et exterior ex vulgi diffamatione … Ulterius nota quod in causa criminali infamia facti repellitur testem et est ratio, quia testificari est honor, a quo repelluntur infames …"; see Migliorino, *Fama e infamia*; Idem, *Corpo, scrittura, identità*, in Francesco Migliorino, *Il corpo come testo. Storie del diritto* (Turin: Bollati Boringhieri, 2008), 62–83.

46 Robson, *Judas and the Franciscans.*

47 Petrus Johanni Olivi, *In Matthaeum* (1280 c.): Padua: Biblioteca Antoniana, ms. 336, f. 121v: "… sicut Iudas non potuit vendendo ordinare Christum ad temporale lucrum nisi cum orrendo affectu et cum ineffabili precipitio cordis in quandam tetram et profundissimam voraginem iniquitatis, sic nec spiritualia possunt studiose ordinari ad temporalia lucra sine orrendo affectu et precipitio cordis …"

Chapter 3

The Devil's Evangelists? Moneychangers in Flemish Urban Society

James M. Murray

Two pictures and a proverb together pose the question addressed in this chapter. The two paintings are the familiar *The Moneychanger and his Wife* by Quenten Massys (Figure 8.13) and *The Banker and His Client*, a frequently copied painting of Massys, now lost, but perhaps best known in the version by Marinus van Reymerswaele. Both issue from early sixteenth-century Antwerp, even though the subjects are clad in fashions of the mid-fifteenth century, harking back perhaps to an earlier composition.[1] In each painting, a scene from the business life of a banker/moneychanger is depicted: in one the moneychanger is picking and culling coins, while his wife looks on over the folios of a book of hours.[2] In the other, a banker and his customer are interrupted as an entry is being made in the ledger: as in the former painting, coins are prominently displayed. There is a remarkable shift in tone from the first painting to the second; where the first represents moral choice and ambiguity, where good is still a possibility, the second is "aggressively ugly," satirical and condemnatory. "Secular satire has become the new form of *sermonizing*, where instruction in the good emerges from the hostile presentation of the vicious."[3] In other words, both paintings depict the profession of banking as morally ambiguous at best, and as evil and corrupting at worst.

The proverb reads:

> Een woekeraar, een molenaar,
> Een wisselaar, een tollenaar,
> zijn de vier evangelisten van Lucifaar.
>
> (Translation: "a usurer, a miller, a moneychanger, a toll-collector, are the four evangelists of Lucifer.")

Like the paintings, the proverb can only be traced back to the sixteenth century, and judging from the dialect, it probably also originated in Antwerp.[4] But this too is a genre piece whose sentiments express hostilities latent in late medieval urban society, so conceivably the proverb also has roots in the fourteenth or fifteenth century. Three of the figures, of course, are familiar "villains" in the struggle between the "money" and the "moral" economy. The "usurer" ("woekeraar") was either a public or private moneylender who profited from the cash shortages of the later Middle Ages by making either secured or unsecured loans at high interest rates. Public usurers, or pawnbrokers, in the cities of the medieval Low Countries purchased the privilege to conduct their business through payment of an annual fee. They usually lent small sums for consumption purposes, securing the loans by receiving personal property as pledge.[5] Modern Dutch still retains the phrase "tegen woeker prijzen" (at usurer's prices) as a surviving echo of customer outrage. Little need be said about the miller, who alone among the four was deemed a scoundrel in both city and country. Toll collectors were viewed with particular disfavor by the subjects of the Burgundian dukes, judging from the number and insistence of the complaints made against them in the fifteenth century.[6]

The moneychanger is the surprise member of this diabolical foursome, for in modern scholarship, the moneychanger has cut a decidedly more dashing and less infernal figure. Particularly as depicted in my work and that of Raymond de Roover, the moneychanger was a major player in the financial success of Flemish business and trade in the fourteenth and fifteenth centuries. Not only was he (and sometimes she) a banker, but moneychangers were also entrepreneurs in the classic sense, in that they provided both financial services and investment capital to businessmen and their customers. Their interests also extended to real estate, urban finance, import–export, and even, on occasion, to state finance. There seems to be little in our current historical literature that could account for the singling out of moneychangers, among all merchants, as objects of popular hostility.[7]

Have we missed something? Is there confirming evidence of popular ambivalence about moneychangers in the Low Countries in other sources? I believe we have and there is, and by briefly presenting that evidence, another face of the moneychanging business becomes apparent, which explains some of the smoldering tensions embedded in late medieval urban society.

There is abundant evidence of governmental ambivalence and hostility towards moneychangers. This was due in part to the anomalous position of the changer as a public official, usually holding his office as a fief of the count or duke, as well as a private businessman (or woman) seeking to make a profit.[8] As an official, the moneychanger was to be the guardian of the coinage, removing underweight or damaged coins from circulation, thereby insuring a steady flow of bullion to the mint, as well as enforcing decrees setting exchange rates and coins acceptable as legal tender. A moneychanger's business interests could frequently conflict with official policy, especially when market prices of coins and bullion bore little relation to official prices. Governmental suspicion of moneychangers led to unannounced inspections by comital and ducal officials, with fines and confiscations for the transgressors, as well as attempts to reduce the number of moneychangers in all the cities of the Burgundian Low Countries.[9]

Evidence of overt popular hostility towards moneychangers is much more difficult to obtain. We know that moneychangers, along with moneylenders and pawnbrokers, were the targets of riots in Ghent as a result of ducal monetary policies in 1432.[10] Philip van Artevelde was also giving vent to popular mistrust of moneychangers when he decreed, in January 1382, that from that date there would be only one exchange in Ghent and it would "value each penny according to its worth."[11] An earlier ordinance in Bruges also enjoined the moneychanger to "judge each penny according to its worth, either good or bad."[12] By the fifteenth century, Burgundian policy had reduced the number of money exchanges in Ghent to two, and these were kept under close surveillance and supervision by ducal authorities.[13]

There is some additional evidence in Bruges, which had many more moneychangers than Ghent in the fourteenth and fifteenth centuries. It is likely that they fell victim with their close allies, the brokers/hostellers, to the targeted violence of the victorious Ghent militia in May 1382.[14] In the early fourteenth century, two "keuren," or edicts, sought to ban moneychangers from the office of alderman, along with usurers, clerics, tax farmers, grain and wine dealers, and again the hapless toll collectors.[15] Although this edict never became law, moneychangers are largely absent from aldermen and other positions of power in the city even though they were numerous there, averaging at least sixteen for most of the fourteenth century, declining to six to eight in the fifteenth. It was in Bruges, too, that moneychangers were most prominent in the urban economy, which may explain the incidence of a popular nickname preserved in the city accounts for 1305. Here fines were recorded received from "changers who are called ghukellaers."[16]

In all Middle Dutch, this term, applied to moneychangers, occurs only in Bruges in the year 1305–1306. Given that this was a period once labeled by Henri Pirenne, with some exaggeration, as one of "democratic revolution," this may very well give us some insight into popular attitudes about the profession of moneychanger.[17] The name was anything but complimentary, for it is etymologically related to the word for gambler or magician, as in the Middle Dutch translation of the New Testament, where Simon Magus is called a "gokelare."[18] The intended meaning was probably akin to the like-sounding "woekeraar," or usurer.[19]

What were the origins of such attitudes? Despite the sparseness of direct proof, there are little noticed sources which, taken together, can give some idea about the roots of popular opinion regarding moneychangers. These consist of moral philosophical teachings about the relationship of usury and moneychanging, as well as archival data about the labor status of the profession of moneychanging within Flemish cities.[20]

One place to start is with the writings of moral theologians, whose works furnished the raw material both for penitentials and for sermons. Much has been written about their attitudes toward usury and merchants in general, particularly in the thirteenth century, but little attention has been devoted to moneychangers in particular.[21] Not surprisingly, scholars from the southern Low Countries played a leading role in defining the place of moneychanging in the moral order of Christian society.

There were two major streams of influence on the writing of moral theology from the mid-thirteenth century: the Bible, with the exegetical tradition of western Christianity, and the recently recovered corpus of Greek philosophy, especially the writing of Aristotle. These traditions have something to say about moneychanging, and in neither case is it flattering, particularly in the form in which the traditions reached medieval theologians.

Matthew 21:12–13 and its exegesis form the basis of one tradition. This is the famous *Christ's cleansing of the temple*:

> And Jesus entered the temple of God and drove out all who sold and bought in the temple, and he overturned the tables of the moneychangers and the seats of those who sold pigeons. He said to them, "It is written, 'My house shall be called a house of prayer'; but you make it a den of robbers."[22]

It was the misfortune of moneychangers to be one of the two professions named here and to be grouped among the "you" who had made the house of God a "speluncam latronum." But the medieval tradition moved from this source in two directions: the first found in the story a symbol of clerical corruption, of allowing the marketplace to rule the institutions of the Church. The second saw in the story a sweeping condemnation of merchants of all kinds, especially the usurer, and it inspired a decretum that became know as *Eiciens*, borrowing the verb from the Vulgate description of Christ's actions.[23] By the end of the thirteenth century, scholastic moral theologians had considerably softened the harsh tone of *Eiciens*, pointing out that Christ was not condemning merchants universally, only *ratione loci*, that they were profaning a sacred place. Whatever the eventual conclusion of the exegetical tradition, moneychangers certainly suffered by association with a famous event in Christ's ministry, described in all four gospels. One example of the fallout is John of Salisbury's sarcastic remark about the Pope's shortcomings: "Peter has gone traveling, leaving his house to the moneychangers."[24]

The acquisition in the west of the entire corpus of Aristotle's work brought another strand of authoritative thinking about moneychanging. Of course the vehicle for the introduction of Aristotle's works was Latin translations of Greek or Arabic, and one of the most important translators of the thirteenth century was a Fleming, William of Moerbeke. His translation of the *Politics* became the standard for schoolmen throughout the later Middle Ages. In that text, chapter 1, Aristotle condemns a form of economic activity which modern translations call trading.[25] In a crucial error, Moerbeke translates the Greek with the Latin *campsoria*, a word that his medieval readers would understand as moneychanging.[26] Aristotle brackets this together with usury as activities which cause great moral sickness in their practitioners.

The theologian who did the most to make sense of these traditions in light of contemporary practice was another Fleming, Henry of Ghent, who died in 1293. He was unusual in devoting an entire *quaestio* to "Whether the business of exchange is lawful?" which may betray his origins in a thriving commercial city and his residence in another, Paris.[27] Henry brought tremendous intelligence and subtlety to the question of whether moneychanging was licit, making the conceptual breakthrough that recognized the distinction between nominal and intrinsic value of money, that is to say, what the "official" value and "market" value of a coin might be. Thus there were two ways that the profession of moneychanger could be practiced without sin, Henry wrote. First, in the exchange of one current coin for another current coin, which must follow the legal exchange rates, to which the moneychanger may only add a fee for "his labor in counting and keeping the coins."[28] Secondly, if a foreign, or non-current, coin is to be exchanged for a current coin, the moneychanger may take into account the intrinsic value of the bullion in the coin and the market demand for the coin in setting the price.[29] Henry in no way endorsed a free market in coin valuation, however, for the end of all money, in his view, and by extension the end of moneychanging, is as a means of exchange: Money must never be an end in itself.[30]

Even in Henry of Ghent's rather favorable view, moneychanging put its practitioners on a tightrope between the licit and the illicit, and he was referring to just the manual exchange of coins. By the time of Henry's death, moneychangers in Flanders had already evolved into bankers who accepted deposits from customers, made investments with customers' money, and lived—and some grew rich—from the profit. No fourteenth-century theologian took up the problem of deposit banking as an adjunct of moneychanging, but there are several clues as to how customers viewed the moneychanger as banker.[31]

The uncertain boundary between the changer and the usurer was further complicated by the development of deposit banking. The very terminology used by contemporaries to describe this new function reflects this. In Lille in 1294 some moneychangers were granted a comital privilege to not only exchange one type of coin for another, but also to accept deposits (literally "to receive money") and to make payments from these deposits.[32] Raymond de Roover commented that this went far beyond the simple safekeeping of valuables on the part of the moneychanger, creating in fact a debtor–creditor relationship between banker and depositor. In other words, the banker/moneychanger "borrowed" money from his customers at least as they probably understood their relationship.[33]

This business relationship of customer–moneychanger is even clearer in Flemish. In a little noticed Bruges town account of 1305, there is a record of the receipts of a forced loan from "wiselaars in gheleenden gheld," literally "changers in lent or borrowed money."[34] What does this mean? On the one hand, it signifies that moneychangers had become bankers in Bruges before 1305; on the other it implies that in popular understanding, bank deposits were "borrowed money," again underlining the relationship of moneychanger and depositor as that of debtor–creditor. A document of 1309 sets another *terminus ante quem*, when it describes moneychangers' activities in Bruges beyond exchange of coins, as "to make payments through exchange," thus proving the existence of a system of book transfers by this date.[35]

Was the moneychanger then conducting a business as simultaneously lender and borrower, accepting deposits and disbursing that money through investments and payments? And were these "disbursements" loans by another name, disguising illegal interest payments and thereby drawing the moneychanger over the line into usury? Some contemporaries thought so. In the English adaptation of a fourteenth-century Flemish–French conversation manual published in 1483 by William Caxton, the description of a moneychanger reads:

Randolf, the changer
Hath seten in the change 30 yere
The moneys ben well desired,
so that folke put him in peryll
to be damned.
It is grete folye
For to gyve the eternalite
For the temporalte.[36]

The nature of Randolf's temptation seems to be yielding to market pressures in establishing coin values, echoing Philip van Artevelde's prohibition of 1382. This is quite comprehensible if we accept the reality of a bullion famine in Western Europe in the fifteenth century.[37] But lending at interest is also a possible interpretation of the passage, for there would have been considerable opportunity for a capital-laden banker to loan money. Corroborating evidence of moneychangers practicing usury is scarce, but there are examples from Bruges. Collard de Marke, one of the Bruges moneychangers whose ledgers survive, rarely mentions loans in his accounts, which is understandable given that usury was illegal and his accounts were public documents in case of his bankruptcy. But loans are mentioned in the accounts, and are more frequently described in the more hurriedly composed journals, from which the definitive entries in the ledgers were drawn. These suggest that de Marke supplied on occasion the type of small consumption credit usually extended by pawnbrokers and other moneylenders.[38] We cannot know if, and at what rate, interest was assessed on these loans, but the taint of usury seems quite close.

The line between moneychangers and pawnbrokers was also sometimes overstepped. Pawnbrokers were those who made loans on the pledge of personal property, and were the sole licensed usurers in the urban communities of the Low Countries. Notwithstanding the implied monopoly of these licenses, there are examples of changers lending on pledge. In 1366–68, Jehan Moreel of Tournai, called "le cangeur" in the account he kept with de Marke, was fined for pawnbroking in Bruges without a license.[39] In Bruges and Tournai in the fifteenth century, moneychangers made loans to Burgundian dukes in return for silver plate and jewels kept as pledges. The Tournai changer charged 20 percent interest on the loan, about half of the customary rate for a pawnbroker.[40] In the Bruges case, the jewels were never redeemed and were later sold to Henry VII, king of England. Conversely, in an ordinance of 1441, Philip the Good, duke of Burgundy, guaranteed the lombards (that is to say, licensed pawnbrokers) of Ghent the right to buy, sell, and exchange both goods and coins.[41] In other words, the distinction between the two professions was far from clear.

If usury and moneychanging were not quite synonymous in the cities of the late medieval Low Countries, they were close neighbors both in fact and popular opinion. The distinction, of course, made all the difference, for even "licensed" usurers were social and religious outcasts, and the even more numerous "unlicensed" moneylenders were committing a crime as well as imperiling their souls.[42] Given this close professional proximity, is there any evidence that moneychangers suffered any kind of social stigma or ostracism?

The traditional answer is no, for, unlike pawnbrokers, changers had to be "poorters"—by definition members of the most privileged group of urban residents who formed the economic and political elite. But this distinction can be easily exaggerated, for upon closer examination of the social and gender background of moneychangers in Bruges (for which we have the most evidence) the picture is much more ambiguous.[43]

Pawnbrokers (sometimes called Cahorsins or lombards) in Flemish cities were most often foreigners. In Bruges, many came from northern France or Walloon Flanders; in Ghent the preponderance came from Italy.[44] Sometimes they purchased the right to be a "porter" in order to enjoy full rights as a merchant of the city. A striking number of unlicensed, or illegal, moneylenders in both Bruges and Ghent were women; some issued from families of considerable wealth and influence in their respective cities; most were of humbler status.[45] Thus the social profile of the moneylender was a more or less naturalized foreigner in many cases, with a significant minority of women and other natives.

Turning to moneychangers in Bruges, their social origins were more mixed than the pawnbrokers, but particularly from the mid-fourteenth century to the end of the century, more and more practicing moneychangers were of foreign origin. Many came from the same cities of Walloon Flanders and northern France as did the pawnbrokers.[46] Willem Ruweel, for example, was most likely from the francophone south.[47] Women were also a prominent minority of moneychangers in both Ghent and Bruges, particularly in the fourteenth century. Women sometimes ran money exchanges themselves or in partnership with husbands or male relatives. Two impressive examples were Celie Amelakens in Ghent and Margaret Ruweel in Bruges.[48] Elsewhere in northern Europe, women were also represented among moneychangers.[49]

In short, the social profile of moneychangers does not diverge too sharply from that of pawnbrokers and other moneylenders: significant representation of foreigners and women, often the most marginal of urban groups. Thus it is likely that the social status of moneychangers, like moneylenders, was lower than their economic position as investors and entrepreneurs.[50] Are there other indications of this disjunction between the economic and social?

One area of social discrimination that seems to have grown in importance through the late Middle Ages was the exclusion of moneychangers from the office of alderman. This has already been referred to above in the case of Bruges during the revolutionary years of the first decade of the fourteenth century. Even though this restriction was never adopted into law, it is striking that only one fourteenth-century moneychanger held high urban office.[51] Bruges was not alone in this exclusion of moneychangers, especially during times of social and political upheaval. In Leuven during the troubled accession of Mary of Burgundy in 1477, the popular party asked that moneychangers, innkeepers, bastards, and foreigners all be excluded from urban office.[52] Already in 1373 in Leuven, moneychangers were bracketed with tavern and innkeepers as ineligible for election to dean of the merchant guild of the city.[53] The case of Cologne shows that this was not a phenomenon confined to the Low Countries. There, moneychangers were disqualified for election to the ruling urban council in the course of the fifteenth century.[54]

The second area of social discrimination was in urban finance. Anyone who has looked into the history of urban finance in the medieval Low Countries knows the importance of excise taxes as a source of revenue. Paid by the consumers of beer, mead, and wine, these taxes often provided the majority of income for city governments, and of the three, the assize on wine was often the most lucrative, particularly in affluent Bruges. Given that these taxes were almost invariably farmed out to the highest bidder on a quarterly basis, the holder of the right to collect the wine assize was likely to be among the most powerful financiers in the city. The successful bidder for this and other assizes, in both Bruges and Ghent, was most often a member of an old and socially prominent family. Such membership conferred political position and probably access to inside information that might be useful in bidding for the assize. Marc Boone noted this "osmosis between the politically and financially powerful" in the case of Ghent: in effect, those who governed the city as aldermen were drawn from the same group that profited from the city's finance.[55] Strikingly rare in their ranks were moneychangers.

In Bruges, moneychangers were often the successful bidders for the right to collect the lesser assizes, those for beer and mead, but very seldom for wine. Usually members of the van der Buerze, Metten Eye, and Scuetelare clans carried off this prize. It was no coincidence that these clans dominated much of Bruges' economic and political life in the fourteenth century. The two exceptions to this rule were the moneychangers Jacob Ruebs and Willem Ruweel, but these seem rather to confirm than contradict the rule. Ruebs was probably the richest and most successful changer in Bruges from 1360 to 1380, yet he rarely bid on the wine assize in this period.[56] Ruweel was probably gambling in his bids for the assize, for his changing business was already in decline, and his bankruptcy shortly after his terms as a tax farmer suggests that his gamble was a financial failure. The conclusion is that moneychangers did not quite belong to the inner circle of those who dominated urban finance and politics in Bruges.[57]

Conclusion

The contrast between the economic and social moral status of the profession of moneychanger is striking. There is little doubt that the changer was at the center of the urban economy in the late medieval Low Countries, as merchant, banker, and entrepreneur. But that does not seem to have brought the profession any great measure of social esteem or freedom from the suspicion of usury. Admittedly, part of this may have been the prejudice attached to those who manipulated money for a living and thereby worked a kind of magic in the estimation of the uninitiated. However, moneychangers themselves contributed to popular prejudice through their activities as moneylenders and as the figureheads and enforcers of sometimes unpopular monetary policies. Bankruptcies should also not be overlooked as a source of popular outrage, for our own recent history shows the depths of rage and incomprehension caused when bank deposits disappear into the ether. Taken together with medieval society's deep ambivalence about money and its use, it is no wonder that moneychangers became a lightning rod of popular suspicion and discontent. If money could be the root of evil, what did that make its professional proselytizers?

Notes

1 Larry Silver, *The Paintings of Quinten Massys* (Montclair, NJ: Allanheld and Schram, 1984), 138, citing the sixteenth-century description of such a *Banker and His Client* by Jan van Eyck in an Italian collection, which must have dated from before 1440.

2 Picking and culling was an operation to separate heavier, presumably newer, coins from older, underweight ones. It was strongly condemned by public officials and it was a charge frequently leveled at moneychangers. See Raymond de Roover, *Money, Banking and Credit in Mediaeval Bruges: Italian Merchant Bankers, Lombards and Money Changers* (Cambridge, MA: Medieval Academy of America, 1948).

3 Silver, *Paintings*, 136–8 and plates 118 and 121. *The Moneychanger and his Wife* dates from 1514; *The Banker and His Client* survives only in copies and is probably later than *Moneychanger*.

4 K. Ter Laan, *Nederlandse Spreekwoorden, Spreuken en Zegswijzen* (Amsterdam: Elsevier, 1986), 371. The expression is of uncertain age but was certainly current by the sixteenth century as it was included in the work of J. Gruterius, *Florilegium ethico-politicum nunquam antehac editum* (Frankfurt: Rhodius, 1610–12), 3 volumes. In the opinion of the dialectologist Jacques van Keymeulen of the University of Ghent, the word endings and rhyme scheme are consistent with the dialect of East Flanders or Western Brabant, putting Antwerp right at the center. Antwerp's urban milieu could have been conducive to the social tensions expressed in the rhyme. Silver also cites the rhyme (138), arguing that it well represents some of the didactic poetry composed by members of the guild of St Luke in Antwerp, a guild of rhetoricians, of which Massys the painter was a member.

5 On moneylending in Bruges, see James M. Murray, *Bruges, Cradle of Capitalism* (Cambridge: Cambridge University Press, 2005), 134–48; de Roover, *Money, Banking*, 99–108; and J. Marechal, *Bijdrage tot de geschiedenis van het bankwezen te Brugge* (Bruges: De Tempel, 1955). For France, see Christopher Vornefeld, "Einheimische und lombardische Wucherer im Frankreich von Charles VI. Eine neue Quelle zur Sozialgeschichte des Wuchers," *Journal of Medieval History* 15 (1980): 269–87; and more recently for the Low Countries, see David Kusman, "Une couronne anglaise pour le Duc de Brabant: L'engagement de joyaux du roi d'Angleterre à Bruxelles et à Liège (1297–1298)," *Annales de la société royale d'archeologie de Bruxelles* 67 (2006): 12–49.

6 Walter Prevenier and Wim Blockmans, *In de Ban van Bourgondië* (Houten: Fibula, 1988), 151. Dozens of complaints drawn from all over the Burgundian Netherlands were lodged against corrupt toll collectors upon Mary of Burgundy's accession in 1477.

7 De Roover, *Money, Banking*, 171–90, gives no hint about suspicions of usury among moneychangers. I remark on the moneychangers' ambiguous image in *Bruges, Cradle*, 163–5. Art historians have called attention to artistic expressions of this hostility, but they have failed to explain why moneychangers were singled out, instead of lumping them together with merchants as the objects of ridicule. Giacomo Todeschini's essay in this collection explores the association of usury with Judas and his descendants, the Jews. Interesting to note in this context is that in the towns and cities of late medieval Flanders, there were no Jewish communities practicing moneylending.

8 The practice of licensing moneychangers varied slightly from area to area in the Low Countries, but usually remained the prerogative of the prince. See de Roover, *Money, Banking*, 181–2.

9 De Roover believed that Burgundian hostility was largely responsible for the virtual disappearance of moneychangers in the cities of the Low Countries by the mid-fifteenth century. He was criticized for this, however, by a number of other historians. The controversy is ably summarized by Erik Aerts, "Middeleeuwse bankgeschiedenis volgens Professor Raymond de Roover," *Bijdragen tot de Geschiedenis der Nederlanden* 63 (1980): 49–86, especially 60. A more subtle analysis of the role of the Burgundian dukes in the money market of Ghent by Marc Boone reveals the effects of the contest between duke and city that resulted in a steep decline in the number of changers and moneylenders. See Marc Boone, "Geldhandel en pandbedrijf in Gent tijdens de Bourgondische periode: politieke, fiscale en sociale aspecten," *Revue belge de Philologie et d'Histoire* 66 (1988): 767–91, 790. Even if the reasons for the virtual disappearance of changers are disputed, there is agreement about governmental hostility towards them.

10 Boone, "Geldhandel," 775.

11 Boone, "Geldhandel," 770, fn. 12: "Voordt, dat maar eene wissele in Ghent ne zoude ghehouden zijn, ende die zoude elken penninc valuweren near zijne weerde." The complete text is publised in N. de Pauw, ed., *De voorgeboden der stad Gent in de XIVe eeuw (1337–1382)* (Ghent: C. Annoot-Braeckman, 1885), 158. For the historical context, see David Nicholas, *The Van Arteveldes of Ghent* (Ithaca: Cornell University Press, 1988), 164–5.

12 "Ende hierbi zo zal elc wisselare jugieren den penninc na zire waerd, iof goed iof quaed ..." Stadsarchief, Brugge (hereafter SAB) politieke oorkonden, 1e reeks, #237. The ordinance dates from 1309.

13 Boone, "Geldhandel," 771–2.

14 In the lists of victims mentioned by most chroniclers, butchers, fishmongers, and brokers are prominent. Given that these guilds worked closely with moneychangers (indeed, some hostellers/brokers were also moneychangers), it is quite likely that the money exchanges also fell victim to the Ghentenars and their allies. For the historical background, see J.A. van Houtte, *De Geschiedenis van Brugge* (Tielt: Lannoo, 1982), 120–21, and Nicholas, *Van Arteveldes*, 173.

15 The two "keuren" were intended to regulate the production of cloth within the city. Thus one was for the fullers, entitled "De Cuerbrief van den Vulres"; the other was for the shearers, called "De Cuere van den Scerres." That each went beyond guild regulation to include urban politics is a symptom of the political turbulence of the time. With the victory of the Flemish militias over the French at the battle of Courtrai in 1302, groups formerly excluded from power demanded their voice be heard on urban aldermanic councils. On this political turn, see David Nicholas, *Medieval Flanders* (London: Longman, 1992), 197–203. The texts are printed in full by G. Espinas and H. Pirenne, eds, *Recueil de documents relatifs à l'histoire de l'industrie drapière en Flandre*, 4 volumes (Brussels: P. Imbreghts, 1906), pt. 1, vol. 1, 532–52.

16 "Boeten van wisselaers, die men heet ghukellaers ..." SAB, stadsrekeningen, 1305–06, pt. 1, f. 64; published in L. Gilliodts-van Severen, *Coutumes des pays et comtés de Flandre. Quartier de Bruges*, 2 volumes (Bruges: F. Gobbaerts, 1874), vol. 1, 518.

17 See Nicholas, *Medieval Flanders*, 201–3.

18 E. Verdam and E. Verwijs, *Middelnederlansche Woordenboek*, 12 volumes (Den Haag: Martinus Nijhof, 1889), vol. 2, columns 2052–2053: "Daer hi van een gokelare ... die gokelare hiet Symon Magis ..."

19 But another entry from the same city account proves that they were not synonymous: "Item, Pelskine, up sinene dienst van der stede, als dat hie die huse verhurde ende woukerars ende ghukelars toe brochte, 20 lb." Quoted in Marechal, *Bijdrage tot de geschiedenis*, 29, n. 58.

20 A methodological overview of this question, with an anthropological emphasis, can be found in Jacques le Goff, "Licit and Illicit Trades in the Medieval West," in *Time, Work and Culture in the Middle Ages* (Chicago: University of Chicago Press, 1980), 58–70. Le Goff mentions "exchange brokers," that is to say, moneychangers, in passing without further elaboration. Useful and more recent is Diana Wood, *Medieval Economic Thought* (Cambridge: Cambridge University Press, 2002), especially 198–201. Once again this seems a distinct departure from Giacomo Todeschini's findings about the identification of Judas as the arch simoniac, not Simon Magus.

21 There is a voluminous literature on the relationship of medieval merchants and usury doctrines, ably summarized in the bibliography of Odd Langholm, *Wealth, Exchange, Value, Money and Usury According to the Paris Theological Tradition, 1200–1350* (Leiden: Brill, 1992), 605–20.

22 Taken from the Revised Standard Version. The Vulgate reads: "Et intravit Jesus in templum Dei; et ejicieat omnes vendentes et ementes in templo, et mensas numulariorum et cathedras vendentium columbas evertit; et dicit eis: Scriptum est: Domus mea domus orationis vocabitur; vos autem fecistis illam speluncam latronum."

23 Langholm, *Wealth, Exchange*, 101–3.

24 Quoted from L.K. Little, *Religious Poverty and the Profit Economy in Medieval Europe* (Ithaca: Cornell University Press, 1978), 39. This line of criticism was revived and amplified by religious reformers of the Reformation, which may account for the much greater popularity of this biblical episode in the art of the sixteenth century. To my knowledge, only one artist of the medieval Low Countries, Hans Memling, depicted it in his "Scenes from the Passion of Christ."

25 Langholm, *Wealth, Exchange*, 264.

26 Langholm, *Wealth, Exchange*, 178.

27 Henry's *Opera Omnia* are gradually being edited (under the aegis of the University of Leuven's De Wulf-Mansion Center, Leuven, Leiden: Brill, 1979–). A biographical sketch of Henry by R. Macken is found in the introduction to volume 5 of the series, vii–xii.

28 "Pro labore computandi et custodiendi numismata ..." Langholm, *Wealth, Exchange*, 269.

29 *Opera Omnia, Quodlibet VI*, ed. G.A. Wilson (Leiden and Leuven: Brill, 1987), 207–8.

30 "And to make the medium a terminus for greater profit is usury, which is entirely unlawful ...," Henry concludes; Langholm, *Wealth, Exchange*, 271.

31 According to John T. Noonan, Jr., *The Scholastic Analysis of Usury* (Cambridge: Harvard University Press, 1957), 336: "The astonishing truth is that Dominic Soto is the first scholastic writer specifically to describe and to evaluate morally the credit creation of the banks, though this had been an economic activity which had prevailed for over three hundred years; and even as he approaches the subject, he confesses the scant knowledge in his own day of the essential characteristics of lending operations: 'For, beyond the businessmen, we are rare, even among the scholastics, who understand these facts.' What he goes on to describe is the changer's practice of crediting extra money to a customer's account so that he may draw on it during fair time to pay loans, draft letters of exchange, etc. This Soto approves as non-usurious; but other thinkers of the sixteenth and seventeenth century do not"; see 337–8. Soto lived from 1495–1560.

32 The text is edited in Georges Bigwood, *Le régime juridique et économique du commerce de l'argent dans la Belgique du moyen âge*, 2 volumes (Brussels: M. Lamertin, 1921), vol. 2, 304–5; for commentary, see de Roover, *Money, Banking*, 202.

33 De Roover, *Money, Banking*, 203.

34 Marechal, *Bijdrage tot de geschiedenis*, 54, n. 59, 65, 68. The verb, "lenen," in Middle Dutch can mean either to borrow or to lend. The appellation is not without ambiguity, however, for the mention of "loaned money" could refer to the forced loan to which the moneychangers were contributing. This ambiguity is removed by a contemporary

of the scribe who copied the accounts and added "prest," the more typical word used in this account to indicate a loan. Also given that this list of changers has no members in common with that of the "changers called gukelaers," it is clear that it was a type of moneychanger being indicated and not the forced loan.

35 "Het es ghecuerd ende gheordenerd … dat niemene en moet wisselen no doen wisselen, no paiement doen van wisselne binden scependoeme van Brucghe het en zi in dopenbare wissele van Brucghe …" SAB, politieke oork., 1e reeks, #237; though de Roover mentions this document (*Money, Banking*, 180), he apparently relied solely on the description in the inventory and missed this passage as a result.

36 Jean Gessler, ed., *Le livre des mestiers de Bruges et ses dérivés, quatre anciens manuels de conversation* (Bruges: Fondation universitaire, 1931), 48; see Philip Grierson, "The Dates of the 'Livre des Mestiers' and its Derivatives," *Revue belge de philologie et d'histoire* 35 (1957): 783, who proves that it dates from 1465–66 when Caxton was governor of the English nation in Bruges. For corrections and disagreements, see Alison Hanham, "Who Made William Caxton's Phrase-Book?" *The Review of English Studies* 56, no. 227 (2005): 712–29.

37 The locus classicus of the bullion famine theory remains John Day, "The Great Bullion Famine of the Fifteenth Century," *Past and Present* 79 (1978): 3–54.

38 SAB, 305. Koopmansboeken, de Marke, Journal 1, 10 November 1368: "item, prestet a Copin le varlet sire Jehan Bonin dou Dam par li contet, 5s. gro." Other examples from de Marke: 5, 34v, Jak. De Gerart owes de Marke "que je avoie oublyet aconter a lui lesquels je li prestay 21 mart si quil apert ou fuelt 110 de men autre papier 30 nobles de 65 groten." It is very rare that de Marke mentions a loan of any size. An exception is in register 5, f. 44v in an account of Jakop Doupuchiel where a loan was made to Jehan de Velaine of Tournai for 40 lb. gro at Antwerp.

39 Marechal, *Bijdrage tot de geschiedenis*, 117; de Roover, *Money, Banking*, 306. De Roover labeled Moreel a "shady money-changer" who had embraced usury after failing to earn a living by more honorable means.

40 O. Mus, "De Brugse companie Despars," *Annales de la Société d'émulation de Bruges* 101 (1964): 34, n 134.

41 Boone, "Geldhandel," 777: "Y tenir ou faire tenir en leur nom table ou plusieur et seurement y acheter, vendre, changier, marchander et gaignier de leurs deniers et biends en toutes les manieres qu'ilz cuidront et sauront faire venir prouffit et avantaige." In this Philip was merely renewing what had probably been the case since the late thirteenth century, that lombards also changed money; see Bigwood, *Le régime*, vol. 1, 391–2.

42 An interesting case of absolution gained posthumously by one usurer in Bruges is given in J. Marechal, "De Houding van de Deken van de Christenheid tegenover een Woekeraar en Voorkoper te Brugge in 1344," *Annales de la Société d'émulation de Bruges* 97 (1954): 73–81. John Noonan noted this question in *Scholastic Analysis*, 191–2, and concluded that the distinction between bankers and usurers was not at all clear, and that many medieval people seemed to be in a state of confusion about just what constituted usury.

43 De Roover made much of the fact of the poorter status of moneychangers in general and the social status of the former moneychanger, Evrard Goederic, in particular. He

is mistaken in equating the honorific "Der" to patrician status in Bruges (189). It was a title reserved for aldermen or former aldermen, which does indicate elite status, but not necessarily membership in the oldest and most influential families.

44 Marechal, *Bijdrage tot de geschiedenis*, 14; for Ghent, see Boone, "Geldhandel," 788; after 1441 in particular, the Italian Boba family had a near monopoly on pawnbroking in the city.

45 David Nicholas, *The Domestic Life of a Medieval City: Women, Children, and the Family in Fourteenth-Century Ghent* (Lincoln and London: University of Nebraska Press, 1985), 84–94; and Boone, "Geldhandel," 789, who notes that women practically disappear from the lists of moneylenders after 1431. For Bruges, see Marechal, *Bijdrage tot de geschiedenis*, 12 and 93–119.

46 Marechal, *Bijdrage tot de geschiedenis*, 49.

47 For Ruweel, see James M. Murray, "Family, Marriage, and Moneychanging in Medieval Bruges," *Journal of Medieval History* 14 (1988): 116.

48 Nicholas, *Domestic Life*, 91–3; for Margaret Ruweel, see Murray, "Family, Marriage," 118.

49 De Roover, *Money, Banking*, 174; for France, see Robert Favreau, "Les changeurs du royaume sous le règne de Louis XI," *Bibliothèque de l'école des chartes* 122 (1964): 229.

50 This is true even in Leuven, among whose moneychangers were members of some of the oldest and most prominent families, and yet there was still some stigma attached to the profession as well; see Raymond van Uytven, *Stadsfinanciën en Stadsekonomie te Leuven van de XIIe tot het einde der XVIe eeuw* (Brussels: Paleis der Academiën, 1961), 456.

51 De Roover made much of the fact that at least Evrard Goederic was an alderman in Bruges in the fourteenth century. But it should be noted that this occurred after he had given up the business, and it is not at all true that moneychangers served often as aldermen either in Bruges or Ghent. From 1362, the published list of the two bodies of aldermen in Bruges mentions only Goederic and Pieter Adornes as moneychangers who were also aldermen. But they also prove the rule, since Adornes was an alderman before he purchased the exchange and thereafter served as city treasurer, never again as an alderman. Two changers had fathers who were aldermen, but they themselves never held the office. These were Willem van Wulfsberghe and Jan van Curtericke. For sources, see Marechal, *Bijdrage tot de geschiedenis*, 120–37.

52 On the other hand, several moneychangers served as members of the city council of Leuven, and some also attained the important office of "rentemeester" in the late Middle Ages; see van Uytven, *Stadsfinanciën en Stadsekonomie*, 456.

53 Van Uytven, *Stadsfinanciën en Stadsekonomie*, p. 457.

54 In Cologne they were lumped together with barbers, innkeepers, and real estate agents! See Sigrun Haude, "The Rule of Fear: The Impact of Anabaptist 'Terror' 1534–1535" (PhD diss., University of Arizona, 1993), 72.

55 Boone, "Geldhandel," 788–9: "Een systematisch onderzoek van de Gentse stadsfinanciën tijdens dezelfde (1389–1432) periode bracht een opmerkelijke osmose tussen enerzijds het politieke personeel en anderzijds de milieus van de

pachters der indirecte belastingen van de stad en van de stedelijke leveranciers aan het licht." See also, Boone, *Geld en Macht. De Gentse stadsfinanciën en de Bourgondische staatsvorming (1384–1453)* (Ghent: Maatschappij voor Geschiedenis en Oudheidkunde, 1990), 130.

56 On Ruebs, or Reubs, see Murray, "Family, Marriage," 120; and *Bruges, Cradle*, 161, 173, 176.

57 For a fuller consideration of this conclusion, see Murray, *Bruges, Cradle*, 172–7.

PART II
Questions of Value

Chapter 4

Whores as Shopkeepers: Money and Sexuality in Aretino's *Ragionamenti*

Ian Frederick Moulton

> The nun betrays her sacred vows and the married woman murders the holy bond of matrimony, but the whore violates neither her monastery nor her husband; indeed she acts like the soldier who is paid to do evil, and when doing it, she does not realize that she is, for her shop sells what it has to sell. The first day that a tavern keeper opens his tavern, he does not have to put up a sign, for everyone knows that there one drinks, one eats, one gambles, one screws, betrays, and cheats, and anyone who would go there to say his prayers or start a fast would find neither altars nor Lent. Gardeners sell vegetables, druggists sell drugs, and the bordellos sell curses, lies, sluttish behavior, scandals, dishonesty, thievery, filth, hatred, cruelty, deaths, the French pox, betrayals, a bad name and poverty; but since the confessor is like a doctor who would rather cure the disease he can see on the palm of your hand rather than the one which is hidden from him, go there freely with Pippa and make a whore of her right off; and afterward, with the petition of a little penance and two drops of holy water, all whorishness will leave her soul.
>
> Aretino, *Dialogues*, 158.[1]

This remarkable passage comes at the conclusion of Pietro Aretino's *Ragionamenti* (Dialogues), published in Venice in 1534. The *Ragionamenti* consists of three days of fictional discussions between two Roman prostitutes, the older and more experienced Nanna, and the somewhat younger Antonia. The object of their deliberations is to choose the best way of life for Nanna's young daughter Pippa. Nanna and Antonia see only three options for a young woman in early modern Italy—all three defined by her sexuality: she can become a nun, who vows to abstain from sex in favor of a spiritual life; a wife, who vows to limit her sexual availability to her husband; or a whore who, rather than vowing to restrict her sexuality, sells her sexual availability for profit. Conveniently, Nanna has experienced all three conditions, so she and Antonia decide to base their decision on her experiences. On each day of the dialogue Nanna tells Antonia about her life, first as a nun, then as a wife, then as a whore. When Antonia has heard all Nanna has to say, she concludes the volume by deciding, in the passage quoted above, that Pippa should be brought up to be a whore.

By giving this advice, Antonia chooses the market—and market values—over traditional forms of social identity and exchange. Prostitution may or may not be "the oldest profession," and it certainly predates modern capitalism.[2] Nonetheless, from early modern satire to postmodern film,[3] prostitution has served as a powerful metaphor for capitalist exchange. In a society that considers sexuality to be private and intimate, selling sexual activity comes very close to selling one's very identity. If sex can be sold, what is beyond the reach of the market?

Sexuality may well have been less "private" in the early modern period than it is now,[4] but all the same, Aretino's *Ragionamenti* effectively uses the figure of the whore to provide a devastating critique of the emerging commercial society of early modern Italy—a society where it often seems that everything can be openly bought and sold. He provocatively compares prostitution to more honorable forms of service, equating courtiers with courtesans, and whores with soldiers. But he also ironically suggests that in the changing society of early modern Europe, the prostitute is the last honest person, for she is the only one who understands and admits to her own commodification.

Furthermore, there is a strong metaphorical correlation between the fictional prostitutes represented in the text and Aretino's own identity as a servant, a courtier, and a literary entrepreneur. A man of humble birth, Aretino amassed enormous wealth and social power through the shrewd marketing of his writing—including erotic writing and personal letters. Thus the author, like a prostitute, becomes a merchant of intimacy, who blurs the line between self-fashioning and selling oneself.

How good is this analogy? Is Antonia serious in her choice for Pippa? And how is the reader meant to respond? It is unclear how ironic Antonia's advice is meant to be, but leaving aside for a moment questions of tone and authorial intention, the rhetoric of the passage bears close attention. Antonia's defense of whores and the market is not necessarily logical, or coherent; rather it shifts from one ground to another, making a series of provocative arguments that are worth examining in some detail.

First, Antonia argues that whores are preferable to nuns and wives because they are more honest. Unlike nuns and wives, whores have taken no vows governing their sexual behavior, so even if their sexual behavior is sinful, it is not hypocritical. Being aware of her sin, a whore can confess it and "with the petition of a little penance and two drops of holy water, all whorishness will leave her soul." Of course (as the fictional Antonia may not know) in Catholic theology forgiveness of sin is contingent not only on simple confession of guilt but on sincere contrition and penance.[5] But (as Aretino the author certainly knew) in this world the outward forms often sufficed. In any case, excessive indulgence in a natural appetite was often considered a less serious sin than the breaking of a vow.[6] Thus, while Antonia's argument is theologically flawed, it does have a certain practical logic.

Antonia takes for granted that nuns and wives do not follow their vows—a cynical attitude that permeates Aretino's text. The nuns that Nanna describes in Book I live an orgiastic life of gluttony and sexual indulgence. The wives in Book II want nothing more than to dupe their impotent and often elderly husbands in favor of more energetic sexual partners. The implication in Nanna's account of both nuns and wives is that women are fundamentally sexual beings who cannot possibly abstain from satisfying their desires. This is a common view in early modern culture,[7] memorably articulated by Montaigne, who plainly states that "women have an incomparably greater capacity for the act of love than [men] do and desire it more ardently."[8]

So it might seem that in promiscuously selling their sexual activities, whores are honestly accepting their sexual nature as women. But this is not the case. The whores that Nanna describes care little for sex (and have no illusions about romance). As Nanna says:

> If anyone ever tells you: "Such a whore died for so-and-so," you can tell him that it's not true. Every once in a while we may get a yen for a big prick, wanting to taste it two or three times, but these whims last as long as the sun in the winter and rain in the summer. The truth is, it is impossible for a woman who submits to everyone to fall in love with anyone (119).[9]

The whores want something far more powerful and abstract than sex: they want money.

This focus on money and power rather than sexual pleasure makes whores different than other women. It is this rejection of supposedly feminine sexual insatiability that lies behind Nanna's memorable remark: "Whores are not women; they are whores" (135).[10] The paradoxical implication is that whoredom allows women to transcend biology—freed from a feminine addiction to sexual pleasure, whores can control their desires and enter into a market economy where they can compete with men, often (at least, to hear Nanna tell it) on favorable terms. In Book III, it is the clients, not the whores, who are in thrall to their desires, gazing at the youthful Nanna "as prisoners gaze at a ray of sunlight" (107).[11] Selling sex to desperate customers, whores can buy power and prestige. Nanna lives a life of luxury, manages her own finances, and occasionally employs small bands of armed men to protect her interests (115–16).

In the third book of the *Ragionamenti*, sex is thoroughly commodified. Nanna's description of the life of whores is crammed full of economic metaphors for sex: Aretino slyly mentions that Nanna's mother worked as a prostitute "in a house behind Via dei Banchi" (Bank Street)—a street in Rome frequented by prostitutes that, as its name suggests, was also home to financial institutions (17). As Nanna enters the trade posing as a virgin of noble stock, she is "pure French wool" (109).[12] Her mother puts her "on display" in a window of their rented house (107). Frustrated clients are "like a gambler who had lost all his money" (110–11)[13] or "as frenzied as a spendthrift who has nothing to spend" (130).[14] Nanna is "stingy" with herself, withholding her favors like "a Jew [unwilling] to lend money to a person without collateral" (112).[15] Yet she also sells her virginity "more times than one of these miserly priests sells his first Mass" (114).[16] By comparing sexual activity to financial transactions, and sexual desire to prodigality, Aretino connects sexuality with a wide range of economic exchange, from legitimate trade, to gambling, to religious ceremony. Spiritual values, traditional social values, personal values—all are superseded by monetary value. As Nanna has learned, "Every little thing can be turned into cash" (127).[17] Masses are bought and sold just like orgasms and wool.

The economic discourse in Book III is not only ubiquitous, it is detailed and shrewdly insightful: for example, Nanna not only sells her body to clients, she also gets clients to buy things for her from neighborhood merchants, thus making them her commercial allies (127). She makes small initial investments to get larger returns, buying "a pair of partridges and a pheasant" that she pretends are a gift from a suitor, in order to get another client to buy more lavish things for her (119). And she discourses at length on the need to diversify one's clientele. It is not enough to rely on a few very wealthy patrons; better to sell to many middle income people: "a thousand men who are not great lords will eventually fill your hands to overflowing" (117).[18] After all, social appearances can be deceiving: "She who disdains those who do not wear velvet is weak in the head, because grand ducats hide under rough clothes, and I know quite well that the best fees are paid by tavern keepers, cooks, chicken-pickers, water-carriers, middlemen and Jews" (117).[19] Courtiers are often impoverished, despite their fine clothes and great lineage: "those silken clothes are lined with corroding debts. The majority of courtiers are like snails; they carry their houses on their backs and have nothing else to their names" (117).[20] In all his writings, Aretino was finely attuned to the gap between social status and economic power, and nowhere is this focus stronger than in his depiction of Nanna. She insists throughout that real power is ultimately economic—it is better to be a wealthy merchant than an impoverished aristocrat.

This commercial and economic discourse of sexuality is all the more striking in that it is almost completely absent from the first two books of the *Ragionamenti*. There is almost no reference to sex as a commodity in the life of nuns[21]—sex in the first book is entirely a matter of pleasure and desire. The nuns live a cloistered existence outside commerce, in an uneconomic world of luxurious indulgence. Hearing Nanna's description of a gorgeous dinner table in the convent, Antonia remarks, "the diligence they'd brought to adorning the table could only be the work of nuns, who have plenty of time on their hands" (39).[22] This world may seem orgiastically utopian, but by the end of the book it is revealed as sterile, confining, violent, and abusive. Nanna eventually leaves the convent after a beating from her clerical lover that "stripped half a foot of skin off [her] buttocks" (56).[23]

Similarly, the second book uses almost no economic metaphors to describe the adulterous sex of its unsatisfied wives.[24] For the wives, sex is personal, not commercial: one person is not satisfying, so another is found. No cash and few gifts are exchanged; what is exchanged is sex. The book opens with Nanna speaking to the wife of a wealthy merchant who complains that his money does her no good, for he is utterly sexually unsatisfying: "He looks good on the piazza," she laments, "but all he's really good for is to fill me with fandangles. One needs something else, the Bible says in plain Italian, because man doesn't live on bread alone" (62).

She goes on to have a passionate affair with a man who "was long on muscle and short on bread" (62),[25] prioritizing sexual satisfaction over economic gain.

Thus in each book, sex not only defines women's social identity; it also represents what they desire most—the thing most forbidden to them. In Book I, for nuns, sex is physical indulgence; in Book II, for wives, sex is freedom of choice and of movement; in Book III, for whores, sex is money, and the social power that money can buy. As Antonia says in her defense of the whore's profession: "It is a fine thing to be called a lady, even by gentlemen, eating and dressing always like a lady, and continually attending banquets and wedding feasts" (158).[26] Such a life may be precarious, but how else could someone like Antonia ever participate in it? In a market-driven world, how could she resist marketing her most valuable asset? Moreover, in the *Ragionamenti* sex is *only* productive in an economic sense. Neither the nuns, wives or whores want children. The whores are selling pleasure, not fertility.

Though Antonia delights at the prospect of purchasing a luxurious life, many writers in the early modern period were alarmed at the fluidity of money, and its capacity to undermine traditional social structures of value and identity. Ben Jonson's parasitic trickster Volpone worships:

> Riches, the dumb god, that giv'st all men tongues:
> That canst do naught, and yet mak'st men do all things;
> The price of souls; even hell, with thee to boot,
> Is made worth heaven! Thou art virtue, fame,
> Honor, and all things else! Who can get thee,
> He shall be noble, valiant, honest, wise
> (*Volpone* 1.1.22–27)

As Volpone realizes, money does not just purchase goods—it can buy social or spiritual qualities: nobility, courage, honor, wisdom, even salvation—everything has a price. And so Volpone, a man with no visible means of financial support, uses the illusion of wealth to attract wealth. Living in a Venetian palazzo, he feigns perpetual illness to attract an endless stream of priceless gifts from greedy clients, each hoping to buy his affection and thus become heir to his fortune. Through Volpone, Jonson makes the point that money is generated not by services or goods but by desire—and desires can be stimulated by fictions as much as by reality. Although he is finally unmasked and punished, Volpone's stunning success is much more resonant than his eventual failure. (There is some reason to think that Jonson modeled Volpone—the big fox—on Aretino.)[27]

A similar concern about the transformative power of money comes in the description of gold in Shakespeare's *Timon of Athens*—lines that made a strong impression on the young Karl Marx over 200 years later:[28]

> This yellow slave
> Will knit and break religions, bless the accursed;
> Make the hoar leprosy adored, place thieves

And give them title, knee and approbation
With senators on the bench: This is it
That makes the wappen'd widow wed again;
She, whom the spital-house and ulcerous sores
Would cast the gorge at, this embalms and spices
To the April day again. … Damned earth,
Thou common whore of mankind, that putt'st odds
Among the rout of nations.
…
Thou bright defiler
Of Hymen's purest bed! Thou valiant Mars!
Thou ever young, fresh, loved and delicate wooer,
Whose blush doth thaw the consecrated snow
That lies on Dian's lap! Thou visible God!
That solder'st close impossibilities,
And makes them kiss!

(*Timon of Athens* 4.3.34–44; 387–393)

Marx exclaimed that in these passages Shakespeare had grasped the "real nature of money."[29] He saw that Shakespeare had made two key observations: first, by enabling the exchange of one thing for another, money turns the world upside down, erasing traditional categories of hierarchy and status. Second, money is like a pimp; it facilitates the satisfaction of all human desires. But although Marx noted that Shakespeare relates money to prostitution, he did not remark on the consistently erotic language Shakespeare uses to describe money. In *Timon of Athens*, gold is not just a "whore," but the force of sexual desire itself: it is the "young, fresh, loved and delicate wooer" who can melt Diana, goddess of chastity; make post-menopausal widows remarry; insert itself into the bed of Hymen, goddess of marriage; and make impossibilities kiss.

Shakespeare's sexualization of money is not new in itself: as we have seen, it is central to the *Ragionamenti*, written some 70 years earlier. Indeed, money and sexuality had long been related in medieval thought. Condemnations of usury made much of the notion that interest on loans was a perverse parody of sexual fertility, making barren metal increase as if it were a living being; Dante famously placed the usurers with the sodomites in the *Inferno*, on the grounds that both perverted natural processes of generation, and were thus violent against God.[30] In *Timon of Athens* money is not merely a medium of exchange; it is a source of desire and pleasure, fertility far beyond the bounds of natural sexuality. Similarly, in Jonson's play, Volpone's financial trickery is matched by his sexual unorthodoxy: he is lecherous, unmarried, kisses his male servant, and is surrounded by dwarves and hermaphrodites, who are rumored to be his misshapen illegitimate children.[31]

Aretino had particular reasons for linking commercial power and sexuality. After being driven from Papal Rome in the mid 1520s, Aretino found it increasingly difficult to make his living as a writer in the traditional way, by securing the patronage of powerful members of the nobility. Settling in Venice in the early 1530s, he became increasingly dependent on the book market for his living.[32] Venice was at the time the greatest printing center in Europe, with several hundred presses operating in the city, accounting for 73.7 percent of Italian book production.[33] Collaborating with Venetian printers, primarily Francesco Marcolini, Aretino achieved enormous financial success, especially with the publication of his letters beginning in 1538. But although Aretino later bragged that the press freed him from servile dependence on the aristocracy,[34] the move was fraught. Selling writing had long been equated with prostitution: Raymond Waddington cites a striking phrase by Fillipo da Strata, a late fifteenth-century monk and scribe who urged the Doge to ban printing from Venice: *Est virgo haec penna: meretrix est stampificata*: Writing is a virgin with a pen, a whore in print.[35] Though Waddington's study of Aretino's public image has relatively little to say specifically about the *Ragionamenti*, he is right to suggest that Aretino's genius was not to reject the relation between print and prostitution, but rather to make a virtue of necessity, rhetorically embracing both.

Not that Aretino earned money the way a successful author does today. Instead of profiting directly from royalties on sales, he used the press to stimulate more income from patrons. He did this by traditional means of dedications and presentation copies, but also by mentioning patrons positively in the body of his texts, especially in his letters, but also in plays, dialogues, and elsewhere, even mentioning specific gifts they had given him.[36] He thus used the press to make private patronage a public matter—brilliantly anticipating the role print media would come to have in the creation of the public sphere. And yet, at moments, Aretino could also be disdainful of mere commerce: in a published letter to his printer Marcolini, he wrote: "if someone wants to make profits, let him learn to be a merchant; he can become a bookseller and give up the name of poet."[37] (Perhaps this was too candid; in any case, the letter was suppressed in later editions.)

The *Ragionamenti*'s portrayal of prostitution is similarly complex and contradictory. On the one hand, Aretino sees prostitutes as the ultimate product of a market-driven economy: this makes them, ironically, an intriguing role model for the market-driven author, who makes his living by manipulating the desires of his readers in order to increase sales of his books. On the other hand, Aretino sees prostitutes as analogous, not to writers dependent on the print market, but to the old-fashioned courtier poets—courtiers who are no better than courtesans, striving only to pleasure their powerful masters until they are worn out and discarded: as Nanna remarks: "whores and courtiers can be put in the same scales; in fact you see most of them looking like defaced silver coins rather than bright gold pieces" (136).[38]

In both cases, these analogies elide important material distinctions; they work better as metaphor than as precise social analysis. As Margaret Rosenthal has pointed out, Aretino's satiric equation of courtiers and courtesans may be useful to express the frustration of male courtiers, but it is ultimately false: courtiers may "prostitute" themselves to their masters, but they are not actual prostitutes, forced to sell their bodies to anyone with enough cash to buy them.[39] Building on her insight, one may note that the same is true of the rhetorical equivalence between selling one's writing and selling one's body. The press may be a whore, but a whore does not have the social power of the press. As Aretino has Nanna observe in the second part of the *Ragionamenti*:

> If you set on one side all the men ruined by whores, and on the other side all the whores shattered by men, you will see who bears the greater blame, we or they. I could tell of tens, dozens, scores of whores who ended up under carts, in hospitals, kitchens, or on the streets, or sleeping under counters in the fairs; and just as many who went back to slaving as laundresses, landladies, bawds, beggars, bread-vendors, and candle-peddlers, thanks to having whored for this man or that; but nobody will ever show me the man who, due to the whores, became an innkeeper, coachman, horse-currier, lackey, quack, cop, middleman, or mendicant bum (269).[40]

Of course, it would be a mistake to look to a satirical work like the *Ragionamenti* for a realistic account of the actual condition of women's lives in sixteenth-century Italy. Aretino's trickster whores are no more reflective of actual social realities than his insatiable nuns and nymphomaniac wives. At times the text gestures towards the harsh conditions of prostitutes' lives, as when Nanna admits that:

> a whore always has a thorn in her heart which makes her uneasy and troubled: and it is the fear of begging on those church steps and selling those candles … I must confess that for one Nanna who knows how to have her land bathed by the fructifying sun, there are thousands of whores who end their days in the poorhouse (135–6).[41]

But Nanna's account of the dangers inherent in prostitution understates the situation considerably. Even prominent courtesans like Veronica Franco and Angela Zaffetta suffered prosecutions, persecution, and rape.[42] The lot of ordinary prostitutes was much harder.[43] They were abused by clients and pimps, never in control of their lives or finances, and very likely to contract syphilis—an incurable and thus often fatal disease.[44]

In fact, the *Ragionamenti* offers a relatively narrow vision of early modern women's social roles and opportunities. Given the three options that the *Ragionamenti* outlines for women—nuns, wives, and whores—whoring is the only way that women can enter the market. In actuality early modern women were involved in a wide range of commercial activities.[45] If anything, women's role as wage-laborers in trades was increasing in the sixteenth century.[46] Most women who worked for wages were spinners, weavers, or servants, but there were exceptions. In fifteenth-century Florence, 15 percent of female heads of households were involved in the minor guilds, including goldsmiths, butchers, grain dealers, and cobblers. A few were even in major guild professions: merchants in wool or silk, bankers, moneychangers.[47] Such women were not "normative," but neither are characters like Nanna and Antonia. It is telling that Aretino's account of women's options has no place for widows, who tended to be the women who had the most control over their finances.

But then in some sense Book III of the *Ragionamenti* is not about whores or women—it is about economics, specifically the consequences of living in a world where everything is for sale and market values trump all other considerations. Nanna functions best not as a realistic character or a sociological study, but as a metaphor. As several critics have pointed out, she bears more than a passing resemblance to the image that Aretino cultivated for himself—a shrewd operator who amasses social capital by separating powerful fools from their money; a clear-sighted observer who speaks frankly and sees the world as a naked struggle for power—a struggle she intends to win through her wits and cunning.[48] When Nanna describes her tactics, she provides an excellent portrait of Aretino the satirist, the low-born "scourge of princes":

> I behaved according to the habits of all good whores and took great delight in causing scandals, kindling feuds, breaking up friendships, rousing hatreds, goading men to curse each other and brawl. I was always dropping the names of princes and passing judgment on the Turks, the Emperor, the King, the famine of foodstuffs, the wealth of the Duke of Milan, and the future Pope. … I skipped from dukes to duchesses and talked about them as if I had trampled over them like doormats with my feet (143).[49]

Through Nanna, Aretino embraces whoredom, and fantasizes about the power one could have if one fully accepted the logic of a market-driven world where everything is for sale and money can buy anything.

The supremacy of market values brings us to Antonia's second justification of whores: they cannot be blamed, for they are simply responding to the market demand for their services; they sell what their shops have to sell. Everyone knows what a brothel is, and what is sold there, and yet people seek it out, like they do a tavern. In a society based on money, market value confers social value, even moral value. Money blinds the whore to the harm she is doing—because people pay her, she knows her work is valuable. We are back to the supposed "honesty" of the whore's trade; now she is an honest merchant, who openly displays her wares for all to see. In a world where everyone is corrupt, the most openly corrupt person is the most virtuous.

Let us return to those questions of authorial tone and intention: one might be tempted to read Antonia's advice to make Pippa a prostitute as entirely ironic, an indictment of the systematic corruption of early modern society. After all, Nanna's account shows whores to be utterly dishonest and manipulative. In fact, according to Antonia, whores do not sell sex at all; what brothels offer for sale is "curses, lies, sluttish behavior, scandals, dishonesty, thievery, filth, hatred, cruelty, deaths, the French pox, betrayals, a bad name and poverty" (158). Thus by the time Antonia makes her judgment, the notion of an honest whore has become laughably oxymoronic. Indeed, between 1548 and 1658, Book III of the *Ragionamenti* was published independently of the rest of the text (and without Aretino's permission) in Spanish, French, Latin, and English editions as a warning to young men about the evils of prostitution.[50]

And yet, Aretino excused his lascivious writings in much the same way that Antonia excuses whores—there is a market demand for such products, and everyone has to earn a living. In a letter to Vittoria Colonna, he explained:

> I confess too that I have made myself less useful to the world and less acceptable to Christ when I spend my time on lying trifles and not on eternal truths. But the root of all the evil is the lewdness of others and my own needs. … Look at my friend Brucciolo. Five years ago he dedicated his translation of the Bible to that King who calls himself most Christian, yet so far he has not had an answer. Perhaps the book wasn't well translated or well bound. At any rate, my *Cortegiana*, which was rewarded with a chain of gold, will not laugh at his *Old Testament*, for that would not be decent. So you see my scribblings have at least this excuse. They were composed to make a living and not from wickedness.[51]

It may still be a bad argument, but it is one that Aretino offered in all seriousness.

In arguing that whores are blameless because they simply respond to market forces, Antonia makes a series of provocative analogies, comparing prostitution to other, more reputable professions. The first is particularly shocking—whores are like soldiers, "paid to do evil." What could be further from the whore than the soldier? Military activity was commonly seen as the highest calling in early modern society—"the principal and true profession" of Castiglione's ideal courtier "must be that of arms" (1.17).[52] Aristocratic masculinity, in particular, was founded on the notion that military ability was crucial to masculine honor. If soldiers are honorable men, whores, on the other hand, were at the opposite extreme of the scale: women without honor. So what do whores have in common with soldiers? The answer, of course, is that they fulfill a vital and sometimes unsavoury social service in exchange for pay. Moreover, both represent extreme positions on the spectrum of early modern gender identity. Early modern gender ideology tended to see sexual activity as fundamentally feminine, violence as fundamentally masculine.[53] Whores are women paid to be hyper-feminine; soldiers are men paid to be hyper-masculine.

In early modern Italy, no states kept standing armies of citizens; almost all professional soldiers were mercenaries, and most mercenaries were foreigners. Though idealized rhetoric still saw military skill as a noble attribute, most soldiers in the Italian wars were fighting for pay, not for honor or duty or country. All sixteenth-century Italian states relied on mercenary troops for defense,[54] and yet the evils of mercenary soldiers were painfully apparent. The cruelties of the German mercenaries during the Sack of Rome in 1527 were particularly infamous.[55] But more worrisome was the question of whether or not mercenary troops had the interests of their employers at heart. You can buy troops, but you cannot buy loyalty. Machiavelli, a strong advocate of citizen-soldiers, was particularly dubious about mercenaries: "they have no love or other motive to keep them in the field save a small stipend, and this is not sufficient to make them want to die for you."[56] Rightly or wrongly, Machiavelli saw military force as more powerful than economics: "the sinews of war are not gold, but good soldiers; for gold alone will not procure good soldiers, but good soldiers will always procure gold."[57] As Aretino himself found out later in life in his unsuccessful bid to become a cardinal, money cannot quite buy everything. Sex and violence can be bought; affection and loyalty cannot.

In the case of both whores and mercenaries, the danger is integrally related to the fluidity of money. A soldier paid to defend you one day can be paid to kill you the next. Similarly, a whore you pay for pleasure may repay you with violence, theft, or (more likely) syphilis. The most frightening thing about money, after all, is its fungibility. If everything can be changed into anything else, nothing has any real identity beyond an abstract (and fluctuating) exchange value. If everything has a price, nothing is unique; nothing has a fixed identity.

Nanna is particularly perceptive on this account. The commodification of sexuality turns women's bodies themselves into cash, a fluid medium of exchange, an abstract marker of value. In the world of the whore, "a pair of luscious buttocks … has as much power as money" (130).[58] And thus women themselves become a fungible medium of exchange, stripped of individual identity, valuable not for their families, their skills, or their labor, but for their pure interchangeability. Nanna recounts how older prostitutes will adopt young girls:

> so that the girl will begin to bloom just when they whither and fade. And they give her the loveliest names you can hope to discover and keep changing them every day, so that a stranger can never be sure which name is her right one. Today they're called Giulia, the next day Laura, Lucrezia, Cassandra, Portia, Virginia, Pantasilia, Prudenzia, or Cornelia.… Besides, there is the difficulty of guessing who is the father of those children we actually give birth to, though we always claim they are the daughters of noblemen and great monsignors. For so varied and diverse are the seeds sown in our gardens that it is well-nigh impossible to determine who planted the seed that actually impregnated our soil (136).[59]

Most of the names given the girls are those of literary and historical figures renowned for their chastity: Petrarch's Laura, chaste Roman wives Lucrezia, Portia, and Cornelia, the virginal daughters Virginia and Cassandra, and Penthesilia the Queen of the Amazons. That many of these women ended up raped or murdered makes the list even more sinister,[60] but the main point is that the names no longer signify anything. In a society where identity is still very much a function of parentage, and more specifically paternity, these young girls have no identity whatsoever: no father, no family, and no name. Ultimately, this is the future that Antonia recommends for Pippa. And despite his imaginative flirtation with prostitution as a model for the author under capitalism, this is a future that, needless to say, Aretino did not wish for himself and did everything to save his own daughters from.[61]

Notes

1 All English quotations from the *Ragionamenti* are from Pietro Aretino, *Aretino's Dialogues*, trans. Raymond Rosenthal (New York: Marsilio, 1994). Subsequent

references are by page number in the text. Original language for all translated citations will be found in the notes. All Italian quotes from the *Ragionamenti* are from Pietro Aretino, *Ragionamento. Dialogo*, ed. Giorgio Bàrberi Squarotti and Carla Forno (Milan: Rizzoli, 1988). "La monica tradisce il suo consagramento, e la maritata assassina il santo matrimonio ma la puttana non attacca né al monistero né al marito: anzi fa come un soldato che è pagato per far male, e faccendolo non si tiene che lo faccia, perché la sua bottega vendo quello che ella ha a vendere; e il primo dì che uno oste apre la taverna, sanza metterci scritta s'intende che ivi si beve, si mangia, si giuoca, si chiava, si rinega e si inganna: e chi ci andasse per dire orazioni o per digiunare, non ci troveria né altere né quaresima. Gli ortolani vendono gli erbaggi, gli speziali le spezarie, e I bordelli bestemmie, menzogne, ciance, scandoli, dishonestà, ladrarie, isporcizie, odi, crudeltade, morti, mal franciosi, tradimenti, cattiva fama e povertà; ma perché il confessore è come il medico, che guarisce più tosto il male che si gli mostra in su la palma che quello che si gli appiatta, vientene seco alla libera con la Pippa, e falla puttana di primo volo: che a petizione di una penitenzietta, con due gocciole di acqua benedetta, ogni puttanamento andrà via dell'anima" (275).

2 On prostitution in antiquity, see Thomas A.J. McGuinn, *The Economy of Prostitution in the Roman World: A Study of the Social History of the Brothel* (Ann Arbor: University of Michigan Press, 2004). He argues that based on material evidence, prostitution was ubiquitous in Roman cities and "their aim was to make as much money from the practice of prostitution as they could, both for the individual and for the state … Instead of keeping prostitution hidden in their cities the Romans preferred to have it out in the open as much as possible" (4). On prostitution in the medieval period, see Leah Lydia Otis, *Prostitution in Medieval Society: The History of an Urban Institution in Languedoc* (Chicago: University of Chicago Press, 1985). She stresses that prostitution is essentially an urban phenomenon, relying on circulation of money goods, and traveling or unmarried men (2).

3 Jean-Luc Godard's *Vivre sa vie* (1962) is perhaps the most striking example.

4 Roger Chartier, introduction to *A History of Private Life, vol. 3, Passions of the Renaissance*, ed. Philippe Ariès and Georges Duby, trans. Arthur Goldhammer (Cambridge, MA: Harvard University Press, 1989); and Ian Frederick Moulton, *Before Pornography: Erotic Writing in Early Modern England* (New York: Oxford University Press, 2000), 14–15.

5 See Thomas Aquinas, *Summa Theologica*, trans. Fathers of the English Dominican Province, 2nd and revised edition (New York: Benziger Brothers, 1947–48), Part IIIa, question 90: "Penance is composed of several things, viz. contrition, confession, and satisfaction."

6 In Dante's *Commedia*, lust is punished in the second circle of Hell and expiated at the highest level of Purgatory, indicating that it is the least grave fault in both systems. Hypocrisy, on the other hand, is punished in the eighth circle of Hell. See Dante Alighieri, *The Divine Comedy*, trans. Allen Mandelbaum (New York: Bantam, 1995), *Inferno*, cantos 5 and 23, *Purgatorio* cantos 25–27.

7 Moulton, *Before Pornography*, 74–9.

8 Michel de Montaigne, *The Complete Essays*, trans. M.A. Screech (New York: Penguin, 1987), Essay 3.5, 964: "Elles sont, sans comparaison, plus capables et ardentes aux effects de l'amour que nous." Michel de Montaigne, *Essais, Livre 3*, ed. Alexandre Micha (Paris: Flammarion, 1979), 69.

9 "E dì a chi dice 'La tale cortigiana è morta del tale,' che non è vero, perché son capricci che ci entrano a dosso per beccar due o tre volte di un grosso manipolo; i quali ci durano quanto il sole di verno e la pioggia di state; ed è impossible che chi si sottomette a ognuno ami niuno" (241).

10 "Le puttane non son donne, ma sono puttane" (256).

11 "come i furanti allo spicchio del sole" (231).

12 "lane francesche" (233).

13 "che parea un giuocatore che avesse perduto i denari" (234).

14 "come un liberale che non ha da spendere" (251).

15 "come un giudeo a chi non ha pegno" (235).

16 "I più volte … che non vende un di questi pretacci la messa novella" (237).

17 "ogni cosa è robba" (249).

18 "mille di quelli che non son gran maestri che ti empieno la mana" (240).

19 "E chi non degna se non ai velluti è pazza; perché i panni hanno sotto di gran ducati, e so bene io che buona mancia fanno osti, pollaiuoli, acquaruoli, spenditori e Giudei" (240).

20 "la maggior parte dei cortegiani simigliano lumache che si portano la casa a dosso; e non hanno fiato" (240).

21 There are a few exceptions: Nanna compares the chatter at the convent table to "the gabble of some customers haggling with some Jews" in the market of the Piazza Navona (20–21), though the reference is more to the liveliness of the conversation than to any specific financial transaction.

22 "la diligenza usato nello imbellettare il tavolino non volea essere opra se non di suore, le quali gettano il tempo dietro al tempo" (100).

23 "mi s'alzò la carne per le natiche una spanna" (117).

24 Again, there are exceptions: Nanna sympathizes with the sexual frustration of one of the wives, saying "she had so much right on her side she could set up in business and sell it" (62).

25 "Egli è un bello-in-campo, e buono solamente a pascermi di fogge; altro ci bisogna, dice il Vangelo in volgare, perché solo del pane non vive l'uomo"; "che hanno più carne che pane" (160).

26 "è bella cosa a essere chiamata signora fino dai signori, mangiando e vestendo sempre da signora, stando continuamente in feste e in nozze" (275).

27 Mario Praz, *The Flaming Heart* (New York: Doubleday, 1958), 181–5; Moulton, *Before Pornography*, 207.

28 Karl Marx, "The Power of Money in Bourgeois Society," in *The Marx-Engels Reader*, ed. Robert C. Tucker, 2nd edition (New York: Norton, 1978), 101–5.

29 Marx, "The Power of Money," 103.

30 Dante, *Inferno*, canto 17.

31 Volpone twice kisses his servant Mosca (1.3.79; 1.4.137). On his "family" of freaks, see 1.2.1–81 and 1.5, 42–48. See also Moulton, *Before Pornography*, 208–9.

32 Raymond B. Waddington, *Aretino's Satyr: Sexuality, Satire, and Self-Projection in Sixteenth-Century Literature and Art* (Toronto: University of Toronto Press, 2004), 33–55; Brian Richardson, *Printing, Writers, and Readers in Renaissance Italy* (New York: Cambridge University Press, 1999), 91–5.

33 Richardson, *Printing, Writers, and Readers*, 5–6.

34 Aretino's "Dream of Parnassus" letter to Gianiacopo Lionardi, Book I, letter 280.

35 Waddington, *Aretino's Satyr*, 40. Similar rhetoric, metaphorically linking printed texts to public women, was common in sixteenth-century English texts as well. See Wendy Wall, *The Imprint of Gender: Authorship and Publication in the English Renaissance* (Ithaca, NY: Cornell University Press, 1993), 169–88; and Moulton, *Before Pornography*, 51–2.

36 Richardson, *Printing, Writers, and Readers*, 92–3.

37 Letter 1.336—suppressed after the third edition of 1542. See Pietro Aretino, *Lettere: Il primo e il secondo libro*, ed. Francesco Flora (Verona: Mondadori, 1960), 429: "Impari a esser mercatante chi vole i vantaggi de l'utile, e facendo l'essercizio di libraio sbattezzisi del nome di poeta."

38 "le puttane e i cortegiani stanno in un medesima bilanca, e però ne vedi molti più di carlini che d'oro" (256). See also Moulton, *Before Pornography*, 134–5.

39 Margaret Rosenthal, "Epilogue," in Pietro Aretino, *Aretino's Dialogues*, trans. Raymond Rosenthal (New York: Marsilio, 1994), 387–402, especially 400–402.

40 "Ma ponghinsi da un canto tutti gli uomini rovinati da le puttane, e da l'altro lato tutte le puttane sfracassate dagli uomini: e vedrassi chi ha più colpa, o noi o loro. Io potria anoverarti le dicine, le dozzine e le trentine de le cortigiane finite ne le carrette, negli spedali, ne le cocine, ne la strada e sotto le banche, e altrettante tornate lavandaie, camere-locande, roffiane, accatta-pane e vende-candele, bontà de lo aver sempre puttanato col favor di colui e di costui; ma non sarà niuno che mi mostri a lo incontro persone che per puttane sien diventati osti, staffieri, stregghiatori di cavalli, ceretani, birri, spenditori e arlotti" (443).

41 "una puttana sempre ha nel core un pongolo che la fa star malcontenta: e questo è il dubitare di quelle scale e di quelle candele … e ti confesso che, per una Nanna che si sappia porre dei campi al sole, ce ne sono mille che si muoiono nello spedale" (256).

42 Margaret Rosenthal, *The Honest Courtesan: Veronica Franco, Citizen and Writer in Sixteenth-Century Venice* (Chicago: University of Chicago Press, 1992), especially 153–203 on Franco's trial before the Inquisition and 37–41 on poems written attacking Zaffetta.

43 On the hierarchy of prostitution, see Guido Ruggiero, *Binding Passions: Tales of Magic, Marriage, and Power at the End of the Renaissance* (New York: Oxford University Press, 1993), 35–7.

44 Paul Larivaille, *La vie quotidienne des courtesanes en Italie au temps de la Renaissance* (Paris: Hachette, 1975), especially chapter 6 on the economic and personal exploitation of whores and chapter 7 on syphilis.

45 Parts one and two of Angela Groppi, ed., *Il Lavoro delle donne* (Bari: Laterza, 1996) collect essays dealing with the wide range of female labor in medieval and early modern Italy, including the role of women in guilds, the role of dowries in the medieval economy, and slavery.

46 Angela Groppi, "Lavoro e proprietà delle donne in età moderna," in *Il Lavoro delle donne*, ed. Angela Groppi (Bari: Laterza, 1996), 119–63, especially 121–5.

47 Samuel K. Cohn, Jr., "Women and Work in Renaissance Italy," in *Gender and Society in Renaissance Italy*, eds. Judith C. Brown and Robert C. Davis (New York: Longman, 1998), 107–26, especially 115.

48 Moulton, *Before Pornography*, 134–5; Waddington, *Aretino's Satyr*, 45.

49 "a usanza di buona puttana avea gran piacere di seminare scandoli di ordire garbugli, di turbare le amicizie, di indurre odio, di udire dirsi villani e di mettere ognuno alle mani; sempre pondendo la bocca nei prencipi, facendo giudicio del Turco, dello imperadore, del re, della carestia, della dovizia, del duca di Milano, e del papa avvenire. … saltando dai duci alle duchesse, ne parlava come io le avessi fatte co'piedi" (262).

50 Ian Frederick Moulton, "Crafty Whores: The Moralizing of Aretino's *Dialogues*," in 'Reading in Early Modern England,' ed. Sasha Roberts, *Critical Survey* 12, no. 2 (Spring 2000): 88–105.

51 Aretino, *Lettere*, vol. 2, no. 7: "Confesso che mi faccio meno utile al mondo e men grato a Cristo, consumando lo studio in ciance bugiarde non in opere vere. Ma d'ogni male è cagione la voluptà d'altrui e la necessità mia. … Ecco: il mio compar Bruciolo intitola la Bibbia al re, che è pur christianissimo, e in cinque anni non ha avuto risposta. E forse che il libro non era ben tradutto e ben legato? Onde la mia *Cortigiana*, che ritrasse da lui la gran catena, non si rise del suo *Testamento vecchio* perché non è onesto. Sì che merito scusa de le ciancie, da me composte per vivere e non per malizia" (449–50). English translation quoted from Thomas Caldecot Chubb, ed. and trans., *The Letters of Pietro Aretino* (New Haven, CT: Shoe String Press, 1967), 131–2. See also Waddington, *Aretino's Satyr*, 7.

52 All English quotations from the *Courtier* are from Baldassar Castiglione, *The Courtier*, ed. Daniel Javitch, trans. Charles Singleton (New York: Norton, 2002). Because of the multiplicity of editions, references to the text of the *Courtier* are to book and section number. Baldassar Castiglione, *Il Libro del cortegiano*, ed. Giulio Carnazzi and Salvatore Battaglia (Milan: Rizzoli, 1987): "La principale e vera profession del cortegiano debba esser quella dell'arme."

53 Moulton, *Before Pornography*, 70–79.

54 Michael Mallett, *Mercenaries and Their Masters: Warfare in Renaissance Italy* (Totowa, NJ: Rowman and Littlefield, 1974), 13–21, 208–9.

55 Aretino himself describes the Sack of Rome at some length in book 5 of the *Ragionamenti* (242–4), published in 1536.

56 Niccolò Machiavelli, *The Prince*, chapter 12, trans. William J. Connell (New York: Bedford, 2005), 76. "Le non hanno altro amore né altra cagione che le tenga in campo, che un poco di stipendio, il quale non è sufficiente a fare che voglino morire per te." Niccolò Machiavelli, *Il Principe e altre opere politiche*, eds. Delio Cantimori and Stefano Andretta (Milan: Garzanti, 1979), 50.

57 Niccolò Machiavelli, *Discourses on the First Ten Books of Titus Livius*, Book 2, chapter 10, in *The Prince and the Discourses*, trans. Christian E. Detmold (New York: Random House, 1950), 310. "Dico pertanto non l'oro … essere il nervo della guerra, ma i buoni soldati, perché l'oro non è sufficiente a trovare i buoni soldati, ma i buoni

soldati sono bene sufficienti a trovare l'oro." Machiavelli, *Il Principe e altre opere*, 271.

58 "due meluzze … ha tanto forza quanto ne hanno i denari" (251).

59 "e la tolgano di una età che appunto fiorisce nello sfiorire della loro, e gli pongono un dei più belli nomi che si trovino, il quale mutando tuttodì; né mai un forestiere può sapere qual sia il suo nome dritto: ora si fanno chiamare Giulie, ora Laure, ora Lucrezie, or Cassandre, or Portie, or Virginie, or Pantasilee, or Prudenzie, or Cornelie.… E c'è dei guai a indovinare il padre di quelle che facciamo noi, se bene diamo il nome che son figliuole de signori e di monsignori: perché son tanti vari I semi che si spargono nei nostri orti, che è quasi impossiblile di appostare chi sia quello che ci piantò quello impregnativo" (256).

60 Lucretia committed suicide after being raped (Livy, 1.57–59); Virginia was killed by her father to prevent her being raped (Livy, 3.46–48); Cassandra was raped at the fall of Troy (*Aeneid* 2.403–408); and Penthesilia was killed in battle by Achilles (Pseudo-Apollodorus, *Epitome of the Bibliotheke* 5.1).

61 See Waddington, *Aretino's Satyr*, 83–90 on Aretino's attempts to ensure a secure and respectable future for his illegitimate daughter, Adria.

Chapter 5

The Sound of Money in Late Medieval Music

Michael Long

On the rare occasions when scholars of late medieval music have invoked money in their historical conversations, its primary role has been to corroborate arguments concerning the cultural or political status of institutions and individuals, of patrons and artists. We have gained some sense of how medieval and early modern musical production was evaluated in its time by the interests it served by means of archival notations recording payments to musicians (including performers, composers, and teachers) in the forms of currency, real estate, ecclesiastical benefices, or even wine and clothing. Beginning with the relatively well-documented musical artists of the fifteenth century who have served musicology for more than a century as organizing nodes on the historiographical timeline of late medieval musical styles (for example, Guillaume Du Fay, Johannes Ockeghem, Antoine Busnoys, Josquin Desprez), such traces of the money trail have enriched our understanding of musical transmission and reception, along with music's supporting role in specific institutional or dynastic enterprises.[1] That late medieval composers themselves were cognizant of the mundane financial parameters of their craft is revealed by the popularity of songs referring to money (and specifically to the musician's lack of it) such as "Adieu mes amours."[2]

Taking musical activity as an economic system in an even broader and more abstract sense, polyphonic music's transition to modernity must surely be located within the century c. 1410–1510, which witnessed a number of sea changes. Among them was the turn to paper rather than parchment for the notation of non-deluxe or non-liturgical music manuscripts. This more economical means of preserving a "literate" (that is to say, written-down and thus reperformable) repertory, was facilitated by the expansion of the paper-making industry throughout Europe, a process begun in the thirteenth century. Whatever its end use, the rapid proliferation of paper, especially in Italy, was likely connected with a rising demand for economical writing materials that could be used in the writing-intensive practices of double-entry commercial accounting (a subject to which I will return).[3] Paper gave rise to unexpected shifts in the technology of musical writing itself, notably the replacement of black noteheads with white (void) noteheads for all but the shortest rhythmic durations (still a feature of western music notation today), thus reducing the practical problems of bleed-through and disintegration caused by the application of acidic ink to the porous writing surface. Coincidentally, it likely also had a deleterious effect on the general survival rate for non-deluxe musical manuscripts of the transitional period.[4] The commercial possibilities of a paper music culture were expanded by the introduction of mechanical music printing in the first years of the sixteenth century. At that point, monetary concerns began to intersect with other sorts of intriguing cultural dynamics, including those involving the intellectual and artistic ownership of musical texts. In this environment, new issues (some of which remain contested in the digital world) gained immediacy: questions of accuracy, authenticity, and copyright were all generated by the production and dissemination of notated music outside the institutional environments of officially patronized manuscripts. The question, "Who owns music?" thereafter took on new and more flexible implications than it might have in the time when all musical production was governed by traditional principles of dynastic or ecclesiastical patronage.[5]

While these kinds of inquiry open out to rich cultural and historical landscapes, this essay approaches money's conjunctions with late medieval music from a particularly concrete and circumscribed perspective. It addresses not a general historical topography wherein music and musicians—at least in the European arena—were first commodified, nor the moral aesthetics often invoked in critiques of these sorts of cultural commodifications, but rather a few unusual historical landmarks. Each marks a moment in which essential aspects of money and currency systems were literally identified with the practical or theoretical elements of contemporaneous musical practice. In considering how "the sound of money" may have been constituted in the cultural imagination of late medieval Europeans—including musicians, writers on music, and musical auditors—I will suggest that the noise of medieval currency was "audible" in both philosophical and acoustical senses, and that it resonated with the most familiar tenets of European political and theological moral systems.

Balancing the Scale

Even if the "Pythagorean model" has been overemphasized by modern scholars "as a means to interpret what medieval authors habitually say about the technical, aesthetic, and moral aspects of music," as Christopher Page has suggested, it nevertheless formed one of the most fundamental metaphorical and technical strains in medieval writings on music, especially those linked to institutional pedagogy, and thus to basic training in music.[6] Pythagoreanism, in a general sense as "the belief that all reality—including music—inheres in numbers and their relationships," lay behind medieval canonics and the study of the monochord, crucial to the intellection of medieval pitch space.[7] Boethius' use of the single plucked string of the monochord in the *De institutione musica* (typically abbreviated *De musica*) to derive the double octave (the pitch series or *scala* that would be invoked by later medieval pedagogues in teaching singers the melodies of liturgical plainchant) supplied a straightforward demonstration of neo-Pythagorean concepts. It placed the relationship between musical sounds and the realm of number at the theoretical heart of Christendom's only official musical repertory. This linkage, after the Boethian model, would be re-enacted in texts and in classrooms for almost a millennium afterwards.[8] In the background of all medieval musical number "theory" lay broader understandings of the "truth" inherent in pure numbers, of conceptual (non-sounding) harmonies of the cosmos, and of social ethics regulated by individual souls operating in harmonic balance with larger societies and universal forces. These concepts—distilled from a range of Greek sources, including Ptolemy, Plato's *Republic* and Aristotle's *Politics* and *Nicomachean Ethics*—form the core material presented by Boethius at the outset of the first book of *De musica*.[9] In later medieval music, these same numerical relationships were projected at a variety of levels, extending beyond the generating numbers of individual pitches to vertical intervals and temporal relationships, especially in the genre of the polyphonic motet. This tendency was particularly evident in the isorhythmic motets of the fourteenth century, a genre whose construction was grounded in arithmetic relationships governing both texts and music, and linked in its early Parisian phase with one of the most influential musicians (and mathematicians) of the day, Philippe de Vitry.[10]

Against this traditional and widespread intellectual background emerges a rare and explicit link between medieval understandings of real (sounding) music and of real money, forged in an unusual treatise written in the 1350s by Nicole Oresme. Oresme is best known to medievalists for his activities as a chaplain and counselor to King Charles V of France, for whom he eventually undertook a series of glossed vernacular translations of the principal works of Aristotle in the 1370s.[11] Oresme was clearly well-read in music and regularly drew upon Boethius as his musical *auctoritas* when glossing Aristotle for a French courtly audience (royal and ecclesiastical) in the fourteenth century.[12] Glosses in which Oresme attempted to update Aristotle's remarks about ancient Greek music so that they might be understood within the contexts not just of Christian plainchant but, even more unusually, the polyphonic musical practice of Charles' elite musical court, are particularly interesting.[13] Well before he undertook the Aristotle translations, Oresme had already produced some interesting original academic works. Whether as an act of straightforward homage or with an eye towards future professional advancement, he dedicated one of them, *Algorismus proportionum* (*The Algorithm of Ratios*), to Philippe de Vitry. At the time of the treatise's composition, Vitry was Bishop of Meaux, and he might well have served Nicole as a role model for a particular variety of politically charged and academically active ecclesiastical career path.[14]

Based on a single, unusually specific phrase occurring in a unique and significant fourteenth-century treatise on mensural music (that is, music which, unlike plainchant, possesses meter and rhythm in the modern sense of those terms), I suspect that Nicole and Philippe may have become acquainted, perhaps as pupil and master, at the Collège de Navarre. The anonymous writer declares that the minim (a note shape whose introduction into musical practice is regularly linked to Vitry and to Paris) was invented "in Navarina."[15] Despite its suggestiveness in this context, I know of no specific corroborating evidence linking Vitry to the College during his time in Paris. In the fourteenth century, when—scandal and factionalism notwithstanding—the Church was one of the most powerful multinational corporations in existence, an ambitious young academic might enroll in the new and richly endowed Collège de Navarre at the University of Paris, a particularly effective conduit into the fast-track of courtly ecclesiastical culture, and the intellectual, artistic, and financial fringe benefits such a career could entail. In its combination of a strong academic program with significant contacts among the upper echelons of Church and court, we might appropriately compare the College's position among future "évêques de cour" to something like the MBA track at Harvard, especially as it flourished during the period of the Reagan presidency in the United States. Among the distinguished products of the College in the fourteenth century was Oresme, who became a master of the College in 1356, a canon of Rouen a few years later, and dean of the cathedral in 1364, and eventually, with the king's favorable intervention, Bishop of Lisieux.[16]

Oresme's original treatise on currency, *De moneta*, survives in academic manuscript anthologies, most likely produced for university students in Paris, dating from the late fourteenth and the fifteenth centuries, but the work probably dates from before 1360, having been inspired by recent monetary crises involving the debasement of coinage in the reigns of Philip VI and John II, in whose court Oresme may have tutored the Dauphin Charles.[17] It serves as both a philosophical tract on the nature of money, and as a primer for princes and prelates as they contemplate their specific responsibilities with respect to the material, the minting, and the valuation of coinage. Most of the speculative material in the work is based on Aristotle, who provided the answer to the question that generates the sixth chapter of the treatise: "who owns the money?" (*cuius sit ipsa moneta*). Following the Philosopher, Nicole explains that "while it is the duty of the prince to put his stamp on the money for the common good, he is not the lord or owner of the money current in his principality. For money is a *balancing* instrument for the exchange of natural wealth." Citing both Aristotle and Cicero as authorities, he maintains that "money belongs to the community and to individuals."[18] These individuals are, of course, the individual members of the body politic who, through their work, support the natural balance of community life in exchange for equitable pay in the form of coinage, the *medium* of exchange.

By the mid-fourteenth century, credit and bills of exchange were in use in Italy (and I will return to these later), but like the paper currency of the modern era, these virtual representations of the exchange of material lacked the allure and pedigree of coinage. Coins, after all, bore weight, texture, shine, and indeed produced pitched sound if two pieces collided. In the French Kingdom, currency theory derived from the *Politics* and *Ethics* of Aristotle, who had emphasized the significance of coinage as the primary marker of wealth, and the prime object of those who seek wealth, in part because of its quantifiable aspects (such as weight), and—once stamped—readily identifiable value.[19] Of the three types of coinage discussed in currency theory—white (silver), yellow (gold), and black (alloy)—silver and gold were of greatest intellectual interest, not only by virtue of their significance to a wide range of symbolic and iconic cultural systems ranging from the liturgical to the alchemical, but also because their values could be expressed in terms of a simple and direct mathematical proportion, one to the other, a proportion that essentially defined the economies of medieval states. Throughout Europe, these proportions derived from the Carolingian monetary system. Relying on Cassiodorus as his source, Oresme lays out the principal values of the Roman monetary system.[20] He does not describe the smaller values (like the Roman *dragma*), since their names are not "proper," which is to say, they do not derive etymologically from their identification with some essential aspect of the coin (for instance, the *solidus*, named for its resemblance to the gleaming, golden sun), and such etymologies, or pseudo-etymologies, were of particular significance in the time of Cassiodorus.

Both the proportional and material aspects of coinage make their way into music theoretical discourse in the late Middle Ages. Commentaries on Aristotle's *De anima* describe the relative sonorousness of particular metals and the implications for the creation of musical instruments. In these and other music treatises dealing with sonority from a physical perspective, gold, silver, and copper are ranked highest, with tin and lead (the metals of debased alloy coinage) at the bottom of the scale.[21] Additionally, the manner in which Oresme lays out the arithmetic parameters of the Roman system, from the format in which the interlocked proportions are developed, to the specific terminology employed, is very much in keeping with late medieval musical notation theory. Indeed, even though Oresme does not proceed to the smallest values in his exposition on the subject, among the divisions of the *uncia* (ounce) is the division into eight parts, each called *dragma*. Anna Maria Busse Berger's discovery of this detail of Roman coinage at last shed light on one of the oddest elements of late medieval notation, the bizarre note shape called (inexplicably, prior to Berger) *dragma* by late fourteenth-century music theorists.[22] It was introduced to effect sesquialteral proportions at the level of the semibreve (in most cases, the musical pulse or beat, represented by the shape of a simple rhombus and equally divisible into three shorter parts, or minims). The same amount of musical time accommodated three such *dragmas*, each worth two minims. They were drawn as semibreves with ascending stems and descending tails attached, replacing two normal (three-minim) semibreves.

Figure 5.1 The fourteenth-century *dragma*

So, for instance, in the following excerpt from a ballata, "Nessun ponga sperança," by the late fourteenth-century Italian composer Francesco Landini, the manuscript source represents the rhythms of the second bar by the figures: semibreve (half of a breve, and the basic pulse of what moderns would term compound duple meter), minim (the shortest note), dragma (two-thirds of a regular semibreve).[23]

Figure 5.2 Francesco Landini, "Nessun ponga sperança" (mm. 46–7)

This small detail of practice (for notation was terminologically part of the practical *ars* of making music and not the Boethian *scientia* of music, that is to say, speculative theory) underscores the significance of commercial arithmetic to the medieval understanding of the proportional values of the notation system, and I will expand upon that connection in the next section of this essay.

But if, as Oresme teaches, the prince does not *own* the currency of his realm, what is his role? As overseer, the prince must not accrue wealth, or encourage or allow others to do so, through such means as price-fixing or alteration of the material content of coins. Most important, the prince must maintain the integrity of the proportional system in which the various coin types are embedded. Oresme's notion that currency—properly maintained as a nested system of proportional values—reflects the social balance of a kingdom reveals his classic, Boethian approach to the philosophy of number, and its manifestation in sounds. Since coins are tactile, or sensible, representations of human acts of exchange, consistency in matters of weight, composition, and valuation are paramount, and so is the coherence and stability of the nested structure of the system as a whole. If there is a revaluing, it must be carried out at all levels of the system, and not merely one, or the coins will lose their essential meaning. Significantly perhaps, Nicole employs the term "mutation" for revaluing, the same word commonly used by medieval musicians to refer to a shift in the systematic conceptualization of musical pitches, relocations from one to another segment of the 20-pitch *scala* (or *gamut*), for instance from the "natural" hexachord C-D-E-F-G-A to the "soft" or "hard" hexachords on F and G respectively (or vice versa).[24] Mutations enabled singers to accommodate pitches that extended beyond the six notes of the natural hexachord by reconceiving the pitch environment wholesale (even if only for a few notes at a time). Oresme's concern for systematic integrity with respect to quantity is also reminiscent of the arguments concerning the relationship between the *figura* (the notational symbol, a simple quadrangle) of the breve and the value of the tempus, the musical measure it indicated, that rippled through notation treatises early in the fourteenth century at a time when the breve was undergoing a devaluation in an inflated notational context brought on by the innovations of Vitry and his contemporaries.[25]

After citing Aristotle's analogy between music and the "harmonious state" from the fifth book of the *Politics*, Oresme modernizes Aristotelian political ethics for the French courtly audience accustomed to polyphonic motets. Mingling a Boethian sense of numerical harmony with the sounds of polyphonic music that Oresme clearly prefers to unison chant, he addresses the dangers of royal debasement of metal coins (of the sort practiced by the recent French kings Philip and John). He first sketches his foundational analogy, which relies upon the image of a choir of singers:

> In a chorus unison (*equalitas*) has no power to please [that is to say, unison is insufficient to constitute polyphonic music] and excessive or improper dissonance destroys and spoils the whole harmony … A proportional and measured difference of tone is needed to produce the sweet melody of a joyous choir.[26]

Suggesting that a kingdom cannot survive if the prince draws excess riches to himself through alteration of the coinage, he extends his polyphonic metaphor: "if the prince, who is, as it were, *tenor et vox principalis in cantu*, stands out greatly and is discordant with the rest of the community, the sweet music of the kingdom's constitution will be disturbed." The word "tenor" in the context of medieval polyphonic music did not refer, of course, to a specific male vocal range as it does today. Derived from the Latin, *tenere*, the tenor was the voice bearing the *cantus prius factus*, the later medieval version of the older ninth- and tenth-century pedagogical term, *vox principalis*. Both referred to the pre-existent melody that served as the foundation for the rest of the polyphonic complex (which in the fourteenth-century motet repertory usually consisted of three or four voice parts). Tenors, even in motets that were more political or polemical than devotional, were still often chant-derived, as they had been when the genre came into existence around the turn of the thirteenth century; tenors possessed, therefore, a certain implication of timeless stability and cultural renewal of the past that was not lost on Oresme when he constructed this royal analogy.

Moreover, in the specific repertory of motets associated with the French royal court (and indeed of the Vitry-era compositions of Oresme's youth in Paris), the tenor was the first—and at times the only—strand in the composition to be subject to the rigorous arithmetic and proportional structuring of isorhythmic techniques. It moved in the longest rhythmic values, and from the perspective of a standard listener's attention and interest, took a back seat to the rhythmically active, text-bearing triplum and motetus voices. It glued the whole together, allowing the active voices free rhythmic play at the local level, while subtly maintaining their adherence to certain global aspects of periodicity through its inexorable melodic and rhythmic repetitions (*color* and *talea*). The tenor's musical organization in larger units that stood in fixed proportions to the smaller bars of the triplum and motetus (3:1 or 2:1) provided an especially appropriate sounding analogy to the fixed proportions of the Roman monetary system that lay behind the French. This was a connection that could only be drawn by a reader familiar with the structure of rather high-level polyphonic music composition of the fourteenth century. Indeed, one cannot help but wonder whether Nicole had in mind some reminiscence of the well-known isorhythmic motet found in the satirical *Roman de Fauvel*, usually attributed to his mentor, Vitry: *Garrit gallus / In nova fert animus mutatas / Tenor*.[27]

The work's triplum and motetus texts took aim at Philip IV's court and particularly Enguerran de Marigny (his chief counselor and, according to the triplum text, "a traitorous fox"), part of the wider indictment of state and church that characterize the *Fauvel* project. Making a musical play on the motetus' citation of the first phrase of Ovid's *Metamorphoses* and specifically its reference to mutation, Vitry subjects the tenor voice part to a constant and unprecedented alternation between triple ("perfect") and duple ("imperfect") units of organization, as if to paint an acoustical portrait of an unstable kingdom facing inevitable decay. For Nicole and his educated readers, as much concerned with political and financial matters as with matters liturgical, the structure of tenor-based polyphony might be heard, then, not just in the general way—as a reflection or reminder of a harmonious Aristotelian cosmos—but more specifically as an acoustical realization of the balance inherent to a fair and equitable system of currency and currency management under the watchful eye of a strong and well-advised prince.[28]

The Value of Music

Modern musicians give little thought to the pedigrees of their nuts-and-bolts vocabulary. Those trained in the traditional British system have learned the terms "semibreve" and "minim" to identify the same note shapes that Americans call "whole note" and "half note." But they are not likely to reflect upon the origins of those quaint terms during a time of tremendous and conflicted innovation in the writing down of composed music that took place, mainly in Paris among academic circles, in the period spanned by the years c. 1240–1325. When the art of measurable music (*ars cantus mensurabilis*, as it was named in the title of Franco of Cologne's famous treatise of c. 1280) was first promulgated in thirteenth-century Paris, the avant-gardists had to reflect upon the discursive models they could draw upon to express in their pedagogical texts the proportional aspects of rhythmicized, metrical music as it would be represented in their new, highly systematized form of rhythmic notation. For the first time in musical history, individual graphical objects (geometrical figures composed of squares, rhomboids, and lines) were to be used to signify as unambiguously as possible the individual durations of musical sounds in written music (what we now call rhythm). Longer durations were related to shorter ones proportionally, in ratios based on the numbers two and three, and those proportions were embodied in the new network of rhythmic symbols.

The first generation, as it came to be represented in the burgeoning historiography of musical practice found in the introductions to medieval pedagogical volumes (with Franco's name invoked as conceptual figurehead), would be called retrospectively *ars antiqua* by those of Vitry's generation, the *ars nova* practitioners, beginning in the second decade of the fourteenth century. As I have already indicated, we are now beginning to understand that commercial, as opposed to just "quadrivial" or Boethian, arithmetic shared a good deal of conceptual and practical ground with late medieval music. I would suggest that there is a rather remarkable shift discernible in the linguistic nuances of mensural notation theory at the juncture between those two practices that may well reflect concurrent developments in quantitative thinking in general, and in the increased teaching and proliferation of commercial models for arithmetic, including the reliance upon currency as a model and metaphor for systematic proportions (especially in France and Italy) after the turn of the fourteenth century.[29] This transformation of the terms in which musical time was imagined remains with us today. To any musician, the notion of the "rhythmic value" of a note shape, that a long note is "worth" *n* number of smaller notes, is fundamental and part of our training. That this metaphorical turn in all European languages took root, rather than any number of other possibilities, is likely linked to a shift in the language of proportional quantity itself, grounded in the economic discourse of the late Middle Ages.

While the details of mensural notation practice are irrelevant to my essay, a particular detail of its written promulgation, one that has been overlooked in discussions of theoretical treatises of the period, is especially significant. Late thirteenth-century mensural theory characterized the relationships between longer and shorter notes by positing relationships of "equivalence," relying upon forms of the classical Latin *valeo*. In the first wave of mensural treatises, writers explained the durations of note shapes in terms of a simple standard: a long note (*longa*), signified by a quadrangle with a descending tail on the right side, was the temporal equivalent of two of the short notes (*brevis*), signified by the simple quadrangle. In certain cases, however, the long note might be as long as both combined. Thus, the possible values of the principal note shapes were 1, 2, or 3 (derived from the sum of 2+1). John of Garland, a Parisian academic of both music and Latin poetry (whose long and short values were in some ways related to those of contemporaneous music), was among the earliest to describe the features of the system. For example, in one specific situation, that of a *longa* followed immediately by another *longa*, the first was to be counted not just as 2, but as 2+1: "longa ante longam *valet* longam et brevem."[30] Virtually all thirteenth-century treatises on mensural notation repeat the dictum precisely. This notion of worth is more general than numerical. It is, like the classical Latin term it relies upon, based on the notion of a balanced equivalence of worth (*pretium*), not upon any sense of a system of numbers or of nested proportions. In the fourteenth century, the language is subtly but fundamentally different. Notes are no longer related by simple equivalence of the temporal space they fill. Rather each note shape in the new, expanded spectrum of shapes possesses a discrete "value," each related to longer and shorter notes by duple or triple proportions. A search of the admirably complete database of Latin music-theoretical writings housed at the

University of Indiana, the *Thesaurus Musicarum Latinarum* (*TML*), reveals that use of the medieval Latin *valor*, insignificant in treatises of the thirteenth century (26 occurrences, all very late in the century, all in mensural treatises) and not a classical Latin word at all, increases in the fourteenth century by 200 percent (73 occurrences), after which time the word begins to recede from prominence (67 instances in the fifteenth century).

The Latin *valor* appears to be a medieval neologism, related to vernacular terms like the old French *value* (which makes its way into vernacular English early in the fourteenth century), increasingly used in European legal documents in the latter centuries of the Middle Ages.[31] Value in this legal sense is the precise and "actual" value of something (like property)—in vernaculars, its "vroie value" or "verraye value"—as distinct from the conceptual equivalency implied in the old Roman notion of *pretium*, and expressed by *valeo*-words.[32] Note shapes in the new systems of fourteenth-century France and Italy were, like coins, markers of discrete mathematical value in a system wherein all units were related to one another by proportional operations (which by the end of the century, in the florid musical style of the so-called *ars subtilior*, had grown quite complex in its options). In the terms employed by fourteenth-century mensural theory, a note shape could be replaced by anything adding up to the same "valor," and the ultimate calculation of its value in performance was based on the unit of exchange, as in a standard formulation like: "a *longa* before a *longa*, or before its [numerical] equivalent ('ante valorum') is worth ('valet') three tempora (the time-value of the breve)," essentially a currency-based reformulation of John of Garland's earlier teaching. Emblematic of the new trend is one of the only late medieval treatises written in the vernacular, an Italian anonymous primer written at the turn of the fifteenth century that bears the straightforward rubric: "Notitia del valore delle note" ("Information about the value of note-shapes").[33]

Fortunes and Fortuna

It is perhaps not surprising that Italy, and specifically Tuscany, would be the environment in which music pedagogy would emerge within the domain of the literate vernacular. As a means of transmitting the content of Latinity, especially the principal works of classical authors, to an educated bourgeois citizenry, *volgarizzamenti* were fundamental to the late medieval classroom enterprise, above all in Florence.[34] Tuscan classrooms were also models of "moral" education. The best-documented elements in medieval Italian classroom culture are those related to the teaching of grammars: those of the vernacular and of elementary Latin.[35] Recently, scholars have drawn the teaching of singing and basic musical training into the same pedagogical frame.[36] But another strand of the curriculum, particularly in northern Italy, was basic arithmetic, or abacus training. While evidence suggests that this was often carried out in special *botteghe*, or *scuole d'abbaco*, it seems unlikely that other institutional spaces (for example, conventual schools or even in-home tutoring) would have failed to incorporate some basic counting or reckoning exercises as part of a general (moral) education.[37] Conceptual intersections between the increasingly quantitative (and philosophically harmonious) notation system, often represented in treatises in the form of number charts, and the "times tables" that appear in late medieval abacus books suggest that simultaneous learning of these basics would have made good pedagogical sense. Indeed, one of the most intriguing aspects of this conjunction is the appearance of arabic numerals in the notation of metrical proportions in Tuscan music manuscripts around the turn of the fifteenth century. I have described elsewhere a musical unicum contained in what appears to be a primarily pedagogical collection which may even have served as a child's counting song.[38]

One of the best-known music pedagogues of trecento Florence was Lorenzo Masini (aka Lorenzo da Firenze).[39] Among his surviving works—some of which were clearly designed for classroom use or for the entertainment of his pedagogical peers—is a madrigal setting that unites several of the themes of this essay. The acoustical clink of hard coinage, the proportional divisions of the musical and monetary systems, and the moral thread that runs through them both, all come together in Lorenzo's "Dà a chi avaregia." The appearance of colloquial proverbs in musical dress is characteristic of the trecento madrigal, in which they usually operate at didactic (often moralistic) and humorous levels. Indeed, the extent to which these idiomatic phrases are woven into madrigal poetry often lends to even the best "translation" an aura of inscrutability. An interesting case is a work composed by Lorenzo on a text by Niccolò Soldanieri preserved in the deluxe Squarcialupi codex (Florence, Biblioteca Laurenziana, MS Med. Palat. 87).[40]

Da a chi avaregia pur per se
Se'l tempo gli si volge a scherzo d'orsa
Che non si trov' amico fuor di borsa.

Tu o tu che ai stato ascolta me:
Quegli a il destro a fare a se amico
Ch'a il pie nell' acqua, il panico.

Ritornello:
De, pensa che tardi si rincoccha
Chi scende risalir Ara'a chui toccha.

In Richard Hoppin's translation:

> Give, give, even to him who hoards for himself, If (bad) times come his way at the whim of a she-bear, Because without a purse one does not find a friend. You, O you who have a (good) position, listen to me: He has a chance to make a friend for himself Who has his foot in the water, his beak in the millet. *Ritornello:* Think now, think that he who falls, slowly refits the arrow to the bow to rise again (slowly helps himself to rise again). Woe to him whose turn it is.

Figure 5.3 Lorenzo Masini, “Dà a chi avaregia” (opening)

For an auditor hearing the song in performance (the intended mode of reception), the ear is immediately hooked by the rapid-fire reiterations in both voice parts of the first word, a short and hard musical phoneme.

There is a sense of musical theatre here, however a listener might "envision" the virtual scenario. The musical iterations suggest greed as it is treated in moralistic discourse related to wealth (for instance, those of Oresme and his authority Aristotle), tempered by Florentine pragmatism. We might think of Silas Marner and his box of gold, Ebenezer Scrooge in his counting house, King Midas and similar examples for whom the sensory aspects of coin symbolize an "unnatural" system of ethical priorities, representations grounded in Aristotle's description of "a man with wealth in the form of coined money [who] will not have enough to eat."[41] Each palatal attack might be taken literally as the clink of coins, or more generally as an image of interminable repetitive acts of paying out from the perspective of the one who is doing the giving. Those who deal in the gathering of coin as a profession run the risk of being perceived as usurers; the unnatural multiplication of coins is suggested in the song's ritornello.

Figure 5.4 Lorenzo Masini, "Dà a chi avaregia" (ritornello)

Lorenzo has fractured the note durations, incrementally, throughout this passage, providing an acoustical portrayal of an arithmetical increase—in this case, an increase in individual (and thus asocial) wealth. As in the opening moments of the piece, the consistent passing of material back and forth from the top to the lower voice emphasizes the sensation of numerical magnitude with respect to individual musical sounds, rendering them especially concrete and, in a way, anti-melodic. As engaging as the acoustical surface of this unusual song may be, there is more to its aphoristic intentions. The poem unites its theme of greed with the image of the proverbial bear who tricks the trapper into allowing it to escape before it has been caught, an image fraught with medieval and modern economic associations.

Whether or not the trades of bankers and dealers in bullion were, as Oresme characterized them in *De moneta*, "disgraceful," the churches and states of Europe, including the Kingdom of France, needed their expertise. And many practitioners were to be found in Italy, whose own ancient currency Nicole eventually derides as an example of the perils of monetary mutation. The bad coins of the *Ytalici* that still turn up in France, he suggests, is "why their noble empire came to nothing."[42] The debasement of Roman coinage notwithstanding, by the middle of the fourteenth century some of the new *Ytalici*—those operating within the "golden triangle" of Genoa, Venice, and Florence—had developed economic systems that relied heavily on written representations of acts of exchange and monetary quantity.[43] Indeed, the spread of bills of exchange, credit, and the new double-entry accounting system drove the expansion of paper production and technology (which, as I pointed out above, left its own imprint on the later history of European music transmission). But even the earliest Genoese account books of the 1340s reveal a way of doing business that is fundamentally modern, and to most of us, thoroughly familiar (sometimes painfully so). An example is what we now term "selling short," involving a contract to buy some commodity prior to delivery at a price the buyer believes to lie below that of the price at which they will eventually sell it. If, however, the market price falls, or the goods are not delivered, a loss is sustained, which is what befell the Genoese government in the early 1340s, when they paid for 8,000 pounds of pepper, the value of which fell by around 10 percent by the time of delivery and resale. This sort of financial failure provides the economic context for the cultural icon whose presence within colloquial American discourse surrounding the economy has been especially notable since the turn of the new millennium: the bear. When this forest denizen found its way into the language of English financial markets in the first decade of the eighteenth century, the Genoese pepper deal would have been classified as a disastrous "bear job," a bear-jobber being the capitalist engaged in the short-selling endeavor. But the notion goes back much farther, and pre-dates that other creature, the bull (also an eighteenth-century symbol) by several centuries.[44]

Proverbial expressions throughout Europe warn of "selling the bearskin before the bear is caught," and this is clearly the origin of the bear in financial argot. In Italian literature, I have found it as early as the sixteenth century in the *Commedie* of Giovanni Maria Cecchi: "Bisogna prima pigliare l'orso e poi vender la pelle" (you need to first catch the bear, and *then* sell the skin).[45] It is also found in a fifteenth-century redaction of Aesop, and so I think it safe to assume that the phrase existed in mainstream, oral traditions for centuries before. The ritornello speaks of the one who descends and rises again, and that the arrow will be recocked and fired again.[46] And so, when the melody traces its contours of descent followed by ascent (see Figure 5.4), I think the vicissitudes of financial fortune are what we are meant to hear. By the end of the passage, our "bear-jobber" has been given, or paid, enough in sound to reconstitute himself, or at least his pile of coins.

I would also draw attention to the extraordinarily balanced imitative structure of this eccentric piece. Throughout, Lorenzo maintains imitative equilibrium between the voices. The composer's father was a second-hand dealer, engaged in the sort of trade that Aristotle identifies as the primary impetus behind the community's need for coinage, and Lorenzo (a local *prete*, rather than a globe-hopping courtly ecclesiastic) must have possessed first-hand knowledge of the most mundane aspects of the Florentine economy. In addition, his charges in the classroom must have been drawn primarily from the Florentine business community, students whose educations would involve more than practice in elementary music theory. Tuscan bankers and accountants were among those engaged in the development of new procedures for accounting in the decades after 1350, the time of Lorenzo's activities in Florence, likely at the church of San Lorenzo. Even prior to the fully fledged double-entry system of the end of the century, in which credits are listed in one column and debits in an adjacent column, non-columnar account books display a sort of balanced alternation (hence the term *bilancio* for such an account record). Consider these excerpts from a Datini company ledger:

> Gli asti nostri della chasa e della bottegha che tengnamo da lloro in Vignone *deono dare* dì xxiiii di diciembre 1366 etc.
>
> (*Debit* on December 24, 1366, the landlords of our Avignon branch etc.)
>
> Gli osti nostri della chasa a della bottegha che tengniamo da lloro in Vignone *deono avere* dì xxxi di diciembre 1366 etc.
>
> (*Credit* the landlords of our Avignon branch on December 31, 1366 etc.)

Such ledgers possessed their own conventional style and jargon. In Tuscany, as a rule, debit entries begin with the formula *dee dare* or *deono dare*, and credits with *dee avere* or *deono avere*. These formulas are even clearer in side-by-side columnar double-entry items, as in a Pisan account book of 1382:[47]

> *Bartolomeo Chatanelli* de'dare *a dì 13 di dicembre etc. Bartolomeo Chatanelli* de'avere *a dì 14 di dicembre etc.*
>
> Debit Bartolomeo Chatanelli on December 13 etc. Credit Bartolomeo Chatanelli on December 14, etc.

To me, the unusual contrapuntal texture of Lorenzo's madrigal, and the way in which the setting foregrounds the text formulas of debit and credit that reside in the first line of Soldanieri's poem, sounds for all the world like a Florentine ledger come to life. The extraordinary degree of fractionalization of note values adds to this a dimensional acoustic associated with the "real" money that drives even paper-based exchange: "Debit/Credit … Debit/Credit … clink, clink, clink …"

The soundscape of the early twenty-first century has taken on certain aspects we typically associate with that of the late fourteenth, even if today our senses are fed (or bombarded) by the details of political, ecclesiastical, and economic argument and scandal through mass electronic media, rather than Latin isorhythmic motets or Italian madrigals. Increasingly, news-writing has taken on a moralistic inflection, sometimes ornamented by improvised newsreader glosses. Grand words like "greed," "corruption," "fraud," and "hypocrisy" are now regularly woven into mini-sermons that invoke (without naming her) the goddess Fortuna's power to effect miraculous rises and spectacular falls. These melodramatic and moralized reports, like the texts of the fourteenth century, tell cautionary tales of a world, with money sitting at the fulcrum, that has gone "out of balance." Lorenzo's madrigal, recording in sound the economics of gain and loss, was surely composed just about a decade after the spectacular bankruptcy of the Bardi in the 1340s. How far of a leap is it from the Bardi and Peruzzi crises to the collapses of Enron, Arthur Andersen, and IndyMac? Whether reviled (like the sons of John Rigas) or beloved (like Martha Stewart), those corporate princes, whose wealth or power seem to increase with no apparent relation to work or services rendered to the rest of the community, those for whom money is therefore not part of a balanced and equitable exchange, are impaled on Fortune's wheel and particularly prone to its rotations. In the western tradition, economics and ethics are integrated at the deepest level. Music's potentially ethical capacities, because of associations with ancient Greek philosophical notions of musical *ethos*, have been addressed mainly within the context of the speculative Boethian tradition taught within the quadrivial disciplines at medieval universities. In light of recent research concerning the nature of medieval education, especially at more elementary levels, it seems abundantly clear that music was by no means an outsider to the more mundane (and for us moderns, more familiar) cultural conversation surrounding matters of money in a moral society.

Notes

1 The scholarly literature on the subject is too extensive to survey here. Ockeghem, for example, was rewarded for his perceived musical "quality" over his years of service in the royal chapel of King Charles VII with fine cloth, an annuity, and nomination to the position of treasurer at the important church of St Martin of Tours. See Leeman L. Perkins, "Musical Patronage at the Royal Court of France under Charles VII and Louis XI (1422–83)," *Journal of the American Musicological Society* 37 (1984): 522–4. Compare also Paula Higgins' account of Busnoys' promotion to a position at the same church, in "'In hydraulis' Revisited: New Light on the Career of Antoine Busnois,"

Journal of the American Musicological Society 39 (1986): 71–4. Giulio Ongaro, "Sixteenth-Century Patronage at St Mark's, Venice," *Early Music History* 8 (1988), notes that patronage of singers at that institution was intended "not only to maintain the musical standards of the chapel, but also to reward its singers for faithful service and for a morally acceptable lifestyle" (114). Josquin's later career provides the most famous documentary record linking cultural evaluation to material compensation: the letters sent by Gian de Artiganova to Ercole d'Este, Duke of Ferrara, regarding the recruitment of a new chapel master in the first years of the sixteenth century. There, Gian laid out the aesthetic and economic cases for "crowning" the ducal music establishment by appointing Josquin (at a 200-ducat salary) or opting instead for the more "good-natured and companionable" Heinrich Isaac (at 120 ducats). See Lewis Lockwood, *Music in Renaissance Ferrara, 1400–1505* (Cambridge, MA: Harvard University Press, 1984), 203–4.

2 Josquin's setting of the text is the best known. The song concludes: "Je n'ay plus d'argent, vivray je du vent / Se l'argent du roy ne vient plus souvent" (I have no more money; shall I live on air, if the king's money does not come more often?).

3 See the discussion of the early fifteenth-century manuscript, Florence, Biblioteca nazionale centrale, Panciatichi 26 in my dissertation, *Musical Tastes in Fourteenth-Century Italy: Notational Styles, Scholarly Traditions, and Historical Circumstances* (PhD diss., Princeton University, 1981), 185–6. The codex is undoubtedly one of the earliest paper music manuscripts to survive in something close to complete form. Concerning the growth of the European paper industry, see Jonathan M. Bloom, *Paper Before Print: The History and Impact of Paper in the Islamic World* (New Haven: Yale University Press, 2001), 203–13.

4 One of the earliest paper sources to be written in mainly white (void) notation is the collection, Oxford, Bodleian Library, Canon. misc. 213, especially important for its transmission of early songs by the composer Guillaume Du Fay, and likely copied in northern Italy in the first quarter of the fifteenth century. The manuscript is available in a facsimile edition: *Oxford, Bodleian Library, Canon misc. 213, with an Introduction and Inventory by David Fallows* (Chicago: University of Chicago Press, 1995).

5 Jane A. Bernstein addressed the new situation from a number of perspectives in "Financial Arrangements and the Role of Printer and Composer in Sixteenth-Century Italian Music Printing," *Acta musicologica* 63 (1991): 47–55. The question of musical "ownership" in the late medieval and early modern period was contemplated in a session of the International Musicological Society Congress in Leuven, Belgium (August, 2002). I am grateful to John Kmetz for inviting me to participate in that session, where a portion of the material contained in this essay was first presented.

6 Christopher Page, *Discarding Images: Reflections on Music and Culture in Medieval France* (Oxford: Oxford University Press, 1993), 12–13.

7 The representation is drawn from Jan Herlinger's excellent introduction to the subject, "Medieval Canonics," in *The Cambridge History of Western Music Theory*, ed. Thomas Christensen (Cambridge: Cambridge University Press, 2002), 169.

8 For Boethius' division of the monochord (canon) in the diatonic genus, see *Anicius Manlius Severinus Boethius: Fundamentals of Music*, trans. with introduction and notes by Calvin M. Bower (New Haven: Yale University Press, 1989), 126–31.

Herlinger (168–9) points out that approximately 150 texts on music surviving from the period c. 1000–1500 deal explicitly with canonics, while many others assume some familiarity with the subject.

9 Herlinger, 170; *Fundamentals of Music*, 1–10. Concerning the ethical aspects of the Greek *tonoi* (scale types), see also Thomas J. Mathiesen, "Greek Music Theory," in *The Cambridge History of Western Music Theory*, op. cit., 125–8.

10 The tendency to use number relationships as the basis for musical and symbological analyses of these artful and academic compositions came to the foreground in the 1960s and 1970s. An approach to musical structures by way of "modular numbers" was a crucial feature of Ernest Sanders' important article, "The Medieval Motet," in *Gattungen der Musik in Einzeldarstellungen: Gedenkschrift Leo Schrade* I, ed. Wulf Arlt, Ernst Lichtenhahn, and Hans Oesch (Berne and Munich: Francke Verlag, 1973), 497–573. Sanders and those who followed were influenced by what Page has termed "cathedralism," associated with an emphasis on proportions that scholars outside the discipline of musicology (such as Otto von Simson) had brought to the discourse of art criticism and history in the previous decades, as well as by the principles of numerical text composition familiarized by Ernst Curtius. See Page, *Discarding Images*, 1–42. Page's critique notwithstanding, the fundamental arithmetic behind the basic construction of isorhythmic works has been lucidly and compellingly demonstrated by Daniel Leech-Wilkinson, *Compositional Techniques in the Four-Part Isorhythmic Motets of Philippe de Vitry and his Contemporaries*, 2 volumes (New York: Garland, 1989).

11 For an overview of the association with Charles and the production of the translations, see Nicole Oresme, *Le Livre du Ciel et du Monde*, ed. Albert D. Menut and Alexander J. Denomy (Madison: University of Wisconsin Press, 1968), 3–9.

12 See, for example, Oresme, *Le Livre du Ciel et du Monde*, 482–6, and Albert Douglas Menut, "Maistre Nicole Oresme: Le Livre de Politiques d'Aristote," *Transactions of the American Philosophical Society*, n.s. 60, pt. 6 (1970): 347–50.

13 Plainchant (or "plainsong" in England) is the anglicized form of the Latin *cantus planus* (known today more colloquially as "Gregorian" chant). *Cantus planus* lay at the core of all music-theoretical writings from the ninth through the eleventh centuries, gradually yielding some of its ground as a pedagogical focus to its polyphonic elaborations (organum) and eventually the subjects of meter and rhythm in the twelfth and thirteenth centuries. The late fourteenth-century Latin- and French-texted motet repertory which Oresme would likely have encountered in the academic and royal circles in which he moved, and which clearly flavored his musical thinking as evidenced by his own treatises, is available in a number of modern editions with commentary. From the perspective of musical mathematics, the most significant (and very much a product of its musicological time) is Ursula Günther, ed., *The Motets of the Manuscripts Chantilly, Musée condé, 564 (olim 1047) and Modena, Biblioteca estense, a. M. 5, 24 (olim lat. 568)* (n.p.: American Institute of Musicology, 1965). Günther's isorhythmic analyses—which encapsulate the metrical and rhythmic profiles of these works in complex fractions containing numbers, mensuration signs, and a range of arithmetical operators (+, >, <)—resemble mathematical or chemical formulas.

14 Edward Grant, trans. and annotator, "Part I of Nicole Oresme's *Algorismus proportionum*," *Isis* 56 (1965): 327–41. Oresme's dedication indicates that he expected Vitry to read the work, the first to deal with multiplication and division of ratios involving fractional exponents. Referring to the composer as Phillipe "of Meaux" (and thus dating the work to the period 1351–61), and as a reincarnation of Pythagoras, he expresses his hope that "if it is agreeable to your Excellency you may correct that which I put before you," further hinting at a master and pupil relationship between the two mathematicians. Testimony to Philippe's active participation in mathematical research in Paris in the early decades of the century is also found in the writings of Levi ben Gerson, who furnished a mathematical proof at Vitry's request of the special qualities inherent in the Pythagorean ratios (*dupla*, *sesquialtera*, *sesquitertia*, and *sesquioctava*), which in terms of the Boethian monochord yield the three consonant intervals of the octave (2:1), perfect fifth (3:2), perfect fourth (4:3), along with the whole tone (9:8). See Joseph Carlebach, *Lewi ben Gerson als mathematiker* (Berlin: L. Lamm, 1910), 62–4.

15 An account by the author of the anonymous *Quatuor principalia* places the note shapes that indicate the rhythmic values of mensural music in "historical" perspective, beginning with the thirteenth-century author of the *Ars cantus mensurabilis*, Franco of Cologne (also active in Paris), who taught only of the long, breve, and semibreve. The new short value of the minim was an introduction of the Parisian *ars nova*, emerging in the second decade of the fourteenth century, and documented in many treatises of the next several decades, some of which are ascribed to Philippe de Vitry, although none are likely his original works. The *Quatuor principalia*'s unique treatment of the subject refers to "Navarre": "De minima autem magister Franco mentionem in sua arte non facit, sed tantum de longis et brevibus ac semibrevibus. Minima autem in Navarina inventa erat, et a Philippo de Vitriaco."

16 On the characterization of Oresme, and his time at the College, see Menut, "Le Livre de Politiques," 13–14. Evidence that musical discourse enlivened the academic activities of the College of Navarre in the following century is provided by Don Harrán, *In Defense of Music: The Case for Music as Argued by a Singer and Scholar of the Late Fifteenth Century* (Lincoln: University of Nebraska Press, 1989).

17 Charles Johnson, ed., *The De Moneta of Nicholas Oresme and English Mint Documents* (Edinburgh and London: Thomas Nelson and Sons Ltd., 1956), x. Menut, Le Livre de Politiques," 15, cites a reference to Oresme as *precepteur* to Charles.

18 Johnson, *De Moneta*, 11.

19 See, for example, *Politics*: I, 9.

20 Johnson, *De Moneta*, 17–18.

21 See Gabriela Ilnitchi, "*Musica mundana*, Aristotelian Natural Philosophy, and Ptolemaic Astronomy," *Early Music History* 21 (2002), who cites Albertus Magnus' commentary on *De anima* (48) and an anonymous Italian treatise, *Epistola cum tractatu de musica* of the thirteenth century (47). The latter is particularly interesting in its drawing this material into the context of Boethian musical philosophy.

22 Anna Maria Busse Berger, *Mensuration and Proportion Signs: Origins and Evolution* (Oxford: Clarendon Press, 1993), 38–9.

23 Busse Berger (44) qualifies her linkage between the note shape and the monetary system: "One could argue that since the *dragma* in music is not always worth one-eighth of the breve, it is unlikely that musicians derived the name from the fraction. But perhaps the precise correspondence of fractions is not what they were after. Everybody knew that a *dragma* was one of the subdivisions of the *uncia*, and it was therefore readily adapted as one of the subdivisions of the breve." I am not sure we need to take the notion of proportion as one related entirely to "division" of larger into smaller units, and that there may in fact have been a specific reason for the terminological correspondence. All of the principal divisions of the Carolingian monetary system are by twelve. The *uncia*, however, has its first "regular" division by 24 at the level of the *scrupulus*. Thinking from the bottom up, the *dragma* divides the *uncia* by eight, that is 3/24, standing—in a general sense—in a sesquialteral proportion to all the other standard divisions of the currency system, which prior to this level have been divisions by twelve, that is 2/24. Thus, even if the musical dragma was in practice two-thirds rather than three halves the normal semibreve (as in the example), it was a figure that—as perhaps revealed by its special, borrowed Attic name (*drachma*)—possessed an inherent quality outside the norm, specifically one related to the proportion of sesquialtera.

24 Oresme's attention to music throughout his written works suggests that he took the study of singing (a requirement for all churchmen of his day) more seriously than most, and engaged more deeply with the language of medieval music theory. It would be tempting to speculate that he invoked the term "mutation" precisely because of the primacy of the "natural" hexachord as the generating collection for the pitch system, as it was taught to musicians from the time of Guido of Arezzo (eleventh century) onwards. The F and G hexachords each contained a variety of the pitch B, problematic in chant performance because it possessed the capacity to produce the unallowable interval of the tritone (*diabolus in musica*) if the wrong B (in modern terms, B-flat versus B-natural) were sung, especially by novice singers. Hexachordal mutations, of course, could take place in any direction among the three collections.

25 See, for example, the discussion in my *Musical Tastes*, 48–53.

26 Johnson, *De Moneta*, 44.

27 This work, and other polyphonic music found in the *Fauvel* manuscript, are edited in Leo Schrade, *The Roman de Fauvel. The Works of Philippe de Vitry. French Cycles of the Ordinarium Missae*, Polyphonic Music of the Fourteenth Century I (Monaco: Éditions de l'Oiseau-Lyre, 1956).

28 Indeed, Charles, as king, implemented the advice of Oresme's treatise, tenaciously maintaining a stable metallic content in the coin of the realm. See Menut, "Le Livre de Politiques," 15.

29 Alfred W. Crosby, in *The Measure of Reality: Quantification and Western Society, 1250–1600* (Cambridge: Cambridge University Press, 1997) seems to sense something similar, in a highly generalized fashion, arguing for "the West's shift from qualitative perception to, or at least toward, quantificational perception" (49). He rightly includes mentions of Hindu–Arabic numerals and abacus reckoning as parts of the tapestry, and even of Oresme's *Algorismus* and Vitry's isorhythm, but the discussions of medieval music (to which he devotes an entire chapter) are highly unsystematic, and based on

a collection of almost random details drawn from many periods, places, genres, and practices that lie well outside the author's field of expertise.

30 Erich Reimer, ed., *Johannes de Garlandia: De mensurabili musica*, 2 volumes (Wiesbaden: Steiner, 1972), I, 38 (emphasis added).

31 On medieval appearances of the word in a variety of languages, see Nathan Matthews, "The Valuation of Property in the Early Common Law," *Harvard Law Review* 35 (1921): 18–23. See also the entry "Valor" (2) in Charles Du Fresne Du Cange, *Glossarium mediae et infimae latinitatis*, 5 volumes (reprint, Graz: Akademische Druck-U. Verlagsanstalt, 1954), 5: 240.

32 Matthews, "The Valuation of Property,"18.

33 Armen Carapetyan, ed., *Anonimi: Notitia del valore delle note del canto misurato* (Nijmegen: American Institute of Musicology, 1957).

34 Alison Cornish, "*Volgarizzamenti*: To Remember and to Forget," forthcoming in *The Art of Memory: Between Archive and Invention from the Middle Ages to the Late Renaissance; Acts of an International Conference, Florence, Villa I Tatti, May 11, 2006* (Florence: Olschki, 2008).

35 See especially Paul F. Gehl, *A Moral Art: Grammar, Society, and Culture in Trecento Florence* (Ithaca: Cornell University Press, 1993); also Robert Black, *Humanism and Education in Medieval and Renaissance Italy: Tradition and Innovation in Latin Schools from the Twelfth to the Fifteenth Century* (Cambridge and New York: Cambridge University Press, 2001).

36 Katherine Zieman, *Singing the New Song: Literacy and Learning in Late Medieval England* (Philadelphia: University of Pennsylvania Press, 2007), refers to the subjects of grammar and singing as classroom "twins" (8–10). Anna Maria Busse Berger, *Medieval Music and the Art of Memory* (Berkeley and Los Angeles: University of California Press, 2005), demonstrates the extent to which music pedagogy—particularly as it has been recorded in medieval treatises—is firmly grounded in the practices of *ars memorativa* and *ars grammatica*. I have explored these matters further in "Singing Through the Looking Glass: Child's Play and Learning in Medieval Italy," *Journal of the American Musicological Society* 61 (2008): 253–306.

37 On medieval reckoning schools, see Frank Swetz, *Capitalism and Arithmetic* (La Salle, IL: Open Court Publishing, 1987), 20–24. Compare also Gehl, *A Moral Art*, 21. Busse Berger pointed to the relevance of abacus training for musical practice in *Medieval Music and the Art of Memory*, 116–18, and the significance of commercial arithmetic in general in *Mensuration and Proportion Signs*, 199–200.

38 See my discussion of "Lamantacha" in Long, "Singing Through the Looking Glass," 294–5.

39 On this aspect of Lorenzo's profile, see Long, "Singing Through the Looking Glass," 262–4.

40 Text after Richard Hoppin, ed., *Anthology of Medieval Music* (New York: W.W. Norton, 1978), 148–51. The work appears on folios 50v–51r of the codex. I am grateful to Trevor C. Bjorklund, who prepared the musical examples for this article.

41 *Politics* I, ix.

42 Johnson, *De Moneta*, 30.

43 For a useful overview of scholarship pertaining to the development of double-entry bookkeeping, see Geoffrey T. Mills, "Early Accounting in Northern Italy: The Role of Commercial Development and the Printing Press in the Expansion of Double Entry from Genoa, Florence and Venice," *Accounting Historians Journal* 21(1994): 81–96.

44 The earliest appearance of the bull in literature according to the *Oxford English Dictionary* is Charles Johnson, *Country Lasses* (I, i; 1714): "Instead of changing honest staple for gold and silver, you deal in Bears and Bulls."

45 Salvatore Battaglia, ed., *Grande Dizionario della lingua italiana* (Torino: Unione tipografico-editrice torinese, 1961–99), xii, 160.

46 While a late twentieth-century musicologist may likely gravitate toward a sexual reading of such images (and some others: the "purse," the gender of the bear ("orsa"), and, in the second strophe, of a bird's beak), I think this highly unlikely within the context of Lorenzo's apparent seriousness as a pedagogue responsible for preparing young Florentines for the musical aspects of their future roles as productive and moral citizens of the *patria*. See Long, "Singing Through the Looking Glass," 296–300.

47 For a detailed account of these practices, see Edward Peragallo, *Origin and Evolution of Double Entry Bookkeeping: A Study of Italian Practice from the Fourteenth Century* (New York: American Institute Publishing Company, 1938). Peragallo (23) published several examples of account ledgers, including those cited in my text.

Chapter 6

Anxieties of Currency Exchange in Middleton and Rowley's *The Changeling*

Bradley D. Ryner

Throughout the early modern period, English merchants' activity in international commerce lagged conspicuously behind their Italian, Spanish, Portuguese, and Dutch counterparts. At the start of the sixteenth century, at least half of England's exports (consisting mainly of wool, unfinished cloth, and tin) were shipped and marketed by foreign merchants, primarily German members of the Hanseatic League and Italians.[1] English merchants who did trade abroad mostly trafficked through the exchange at Antwerp, rather than attempting direct trade with more distant regions.[2] By the early seventeenth century, English merchants had gained control over the majority of English exports and had significantly increased their presence in global commerce with trading ventures to the Mediterranean, the Baltic, the Indian Ocean, North Africa, and America.[3] This period of commercial expansion was far from painless, however, and, for merchants and non-merchants alike, it was a period of uncertainty and anxiety about England's place in the global economy.

The theater was one place where widespread concerns about economic changes could be explored. Literary scholars have shown sophisticated engagement with economic concerns by a range of plays featuring characters who explicitly participate in international commerce, such as Christopher Marlowe's *The Jew of Malta* (1589), William Shakespeare's *The Merchant of Venice* (1596), and Philip Massinger's *The Renegado* (1623).[4] The engagement of the early modern English playhouse with the expanding commercial world, however, was not limited to such plays. The following essay focuses on Thomas Middleton and William Rowley's *The Changeling* (1622), a play that does not stage international trade mimetically but, nonetheless, powerfully articulates anxieties about the instability of value arising from England's precarious place in the international market economy.

There is a long and well-justified scholarly tradition of reading *The Changeling* topically. Most topical readings focus on the play's references to the scandals surrounding Frances Howard, who was released from the Tower of London four months before the play's debut. Both Howard's sensational divorce from the Earl of Essex in 1613 and her involvement in the murder of Thomas Overbury, which cleared the way for her marriage to Robert Carr, are clearly alluded to in the text.[5] The presence of these allusions has prompted some scholars to read the play pseudo-allegorically. Annabel Patterson incisively notes the limits of such readings when she faults "narrowly historical" interpretations of the play for failing to account for "the play's capacity to make us believe in its characters and their predicament—the quality for which it continues to be successfully revived."[6]

In some ways, the essay that follows is a mediation between character-focused and context-focused readings of the play.[7] It is important to bear in mind that the play's power derives from the characters' apparent psychology, from their struggles to recognize and understand the erotic desires of themselves and others. An uneasiness about proper valuation and perhaps even a terror about the vicissitudes of exchange underlies the interactions of these characters. My fundamental argument is that the anxiety about value articulated in the play as a psychological problem in erotic relationships is part of a larger anxiety about valuation made pressing by the period's economic conditions.[8] At the time *The Changeling* was written, England was experiencing a trade depression that occasioned both emotional unease and intellectual uncertainty. In what follows, I examine *The Changeling* alongside reports by two committees convened by King James I to investigate the causes of this depression. I read the committees' reports and *The Changeling* as independent responses to the same set of economic concerns prevalent in England circa 1622. Despite obvious similarities, my model here is not the New Historicist one of circulation between distinct cultural spheres, which might suggest economic ideas originating in mercantile works before being appropriated by the stage. Instead, my approach is influenced by Michel Serres, who insists upon the ability of "literary" texts to explain the material and social world as insightfully as "scientific" texts, but to do so using a different vocabulary.[9] I suggest that both the committee members and the playwrights that I examine independently wrestled with the same fundamental questions raised by the trade depression: how and why does value fluctuate, and to what degree can one hope to be insulated from such fluctuations? The former did so in the emergent language of mercantile treatises while the latter did so in the established theatrical language of the London playhouses.

Economic Crisis

A number of factors contributed to the economic depression most palpably felt between roughly 1620 and 1624. One was the disastrously ill-conceived Cockayne project of 1614.[10] Observing that undyed cloth exported from England to the Netherlands was being dyed, finished, and re-exported for a profit, Alderman Cockayne proposed prohibiting the exportation of unfinished cloth. Not only did the project fail to foster a profitable finishing industry in England, but it also opened the door for foreign competitors to seize the share of the unfinished cloth market formerly held by the English.[11] By the time the project was abandoned in 1617, the English cloth industry had been thoroughly dislocated. Weakened by the diminished cloth trade, the English economy was pushed into acute crisis by the short-term currency manipulations known as *der Kipper- und Wipper-zeit* (the "tilting and wagging time").[12] Taking advantage of the disparity between coins' material value and their denomination, Germany and Poland systematically adjusted their currency to maximize their profit, with the result of discouraging English trade on the continent.

In the face of worsening economic conditions, the English populace was left to anxiously contemplate the rules that governed its commercial relationship with the larger world. It is hard to overstate the sense of crisis felt by all members of society who experienced the depression's wide-reaching effects. Barry Supple argues that "if we measure an economic depression by the depth and extent of *the reaction* to it," then that of England in the early 1620s "was unrivalled."[13] This reaction included the formation of several committees. I will be focusing on two sub-committees created by the Privy Council, one of the Stuart monarchy's principal administrative bodies. The first committee was charged with investigating the role that exchanges played in the depression, and the second was charged with evaluating the findings of the first.

The first committee, which met during the spring of 1622, had as one of its key members Gerard Malynes. Malynes had entered the public eye in 1601 by publishing a pair of treatises in which he argued that devious foreign bankers were siphoning off England's supply of bullion by setting inequitable exchange rates.[14] Malynes and his supporters argued that merchants usurped royal authority by setting currency prices because the power to establish the value of a coin rested solely with the monarch. In order to ensure equitable trade, he argued, the monarch needed to establish and enforce an international exchange rate based on coins' metal content. Malynes worried that, in the absence of any such internationally recognized par of exchange, foreign bankers were revaluing English coins to the detriment of the English economy.

In 1622, the formation of the committee to investigate currency exchange gave Malynes a chance to reiterate and refine his earlier arguments, and the committee's report shows his strong influence. On May 1, the committee issued its report to King James.[15] It maintained that in "elder, and evener tymes" the exchange rate between English and Flemish coins had corresponded to their metal content. Now, they argued, the English were giving coins with a greater silver content in exchange for coins that were worth less in account. Their proposed solution was that "a just price by edicte [edict] should be set vpon all currant coynes, accordinge to the [coins'] intrinsicke valewe [value] in fine silver & gould." They claimed that such an arrangement had historical precedent because it had been "accorded by auncient contracts."[16]

This committee's report was sent to the second committee for review. The most prominent member of the second committee was Thomas Mun, and this committee's reports outline concepts anticipated by Mun's *Discourse of Trade* (1621) and elaborated in his later writing.[17] Mun's committee issued its first report to King James on May 31, 1622.[18] They began by disputing the earlier committee's claim that currency exchange had ever been governed by intrinsic value. They argued—probably correctly—that currency had always been traded by merchants using bills of exchange that "varied in the rate accordinge to the plenty or scarsitie of monyes and the occasions of the parties takeinge & deliuerigne the same respectiuely."[19] The committee went on to argue that any legislation aimed at establishing a par of exchange would be ineffective at stopping the flow of money out of the kingdom because the movement of money is governed by a "balance of trade." They stated:

> we finde that as longe as we spend in this kingedom a greater valewe of forraine comodities, then forraine parts doe of ours, soe longe there must be of necessity exported as much of our monyes, as will ballance & levell that difference, and this is soe necessarilie and vniuersallie [universally] true, as that noe lawe, noe treaty noe losse to the marchant, nor par vpon the exchange, nor danger to the exporter can prevent it.[20]

Thus, the committee raised the frightening prospect that national laws might be overridden by what later generations would call "economic laws," but which the committee ominously termed "a necessitie of nature beyond all resistance."[21]

The same anxieties about proper valuation, national sovereignty, and abstract economic laws that emerge in the committees' reports are also legible in *The Changeling*, which was composed while the first committee was meeting and was licensed for performance a week after this committee issued its report.[22] I emphasize the proximity between the first committee's report and the play, not to suggest that the former was in any way a source for the latter. Middleton and Rowley certainly would not have known of the committee's work, which would have been available only to the committee members, the Privy Council, and James I himself. Although they might have read the published works by Malynes and Mun that strongly foreshadowed the findings of the committees, I find such speculation unnecessary. My argument is not that the ideas of mercantile writers somehow influenced the playwrights, but that both the mercantile writers and the playwrights, writing at a time when exchange rates were (in the words of one committee member) "in public agitation,"[23] were drawn to the same fundamental questions about valuation.

Change, Exchange, and Venturing

As many literary scholars have demonstrated, the various possible meanings of the play's title resonate significantly with the play's content, and many characters merit the name.[24] According to the *Oxford English Dictionary* (OED), a "changeling" could be "a fickle or inconstant person,"[25] and the play deals with the erratic nature of erotic desire. Most obviously, Beatrice-Joanna finds herself inexplicably attracted to DeFlores, the man she had only intended to use to kill her fiancé so that she could be with her real love Alsemero. Because a "changeling" was also a deformed child left by fairies in place of a healthy one,[26] the title additionally suggests DeFlores's physical deformities. The fabled imperfections of changeling children accounts for the use of the term to designate an "idiot" or "imbecile,"[27] a definition that obviously corresponds to Antonio, who—in the subplot—disguises himself as a madman to seduce the wife of the overseer of the madhouse. All of these meanings depend on the basic definition of a "changeling" as "A person or thing (surreptitiously) put in exchange for another."[28] This meaning, in turn, depends on the fact that, at the time, "change" and "exchange" were synonymous.[29] Indeed, mercantile bourses (such as England's Royal Exchange) were referred to both as "exchanges" and "changes."[30] To fully understand the play's fascination with (ex)change, we must consider the period's concern with exchange as an economic concept.[31]

In the context of anxieties about exchange, the play's Spanish setting takes on a special significance. Given the uneasy state of Anglo–Spanish diplomacy and the proposed match between Prince Charles and the Spanish Infanta, it is easy to see why Middleton and Rowley might have been drawn to a story with a Spanish setting.[32] It is worth emphasizing, though, that England's desire to maintain diplomatic relationships with Spain was due in large part to the latter's prominence in international commerce. Moreover, during the debates about exchange of the 1620s, Spanish currency took on a unique aura that bears directly on *The Changeling*.

In the mid-sixteenth century, an undervaluing of Spanish silver coins had prompted an influx of reales, the currency in which most international commerce was transacted.[33] Many of these coins were melted down and reminted as English currency; however, the role of the Spanish real in international commerce exceeded the value of its composite metal. The English learned this fact after a 1601 attempt to mint coins modeled on the Spanish real for use in East Indian trade. The same size, weight, and purity as Spanish reales, the new coins were, nonetheless, rejected by merchants in the East Indies who did not have the same faith in the English stamp that they had in the Spanish.[34] In 1606, James I gave the English East India Company permission to stop attempting to use the new coins and to rely instead on Spanish reales. Thus, Malynes' philosophical point that "the denominacoin [denomination] of a thinge doth not alter the substance"[35] was undercut in practice by the ability of coins with a Spanish stamp to purchase more commodities than the same amount of metal with an English stamp.

Over the next two decades, the English East India Company's practice of exporting silver continued to be the subject of polemical attacks, such as Robert Kayll's *The Trade's Increase* (1615). In *A Discourse of Trade* (1621), Thomas Mun defended the company by arguing that the re-exportation of goods purchased with the Spanish reales actually resulted in a net increase in the country's supply of silver. Mun claimed that, between 1601 and 1620, the company had "shipped away" £548,090 in Spanish reales.[36] However, he made a distinction between "consumption of the Kingdomes stock" and "transmutations" of value.[37] Rather than being lost, Mun argued, the Spanish reales were being transmuted into wares in the East Indies, which could be transmuted back into silver in European markets for a net gain. According to Mun's calculations, Spanish silver purchased five times its value in East Indian wares. Thus, through the magic of trade, he claimed, £100,000 in Spanish reales was being converted into £500,000 in Spanish reales every year.[38]

In many ways, Beatrice-Joanna embodies the same anxieties associated with the Spanish real, which was ambivalently perceived as both a prized treasure and a sign of foreign dominance, whose transmutable value seemed to defy rationality. This is not to suggest that Beatrice-Joanna is simply an allegorical figure for currency. Indeed, one of the things that the play skillfully accomplishes is to invoke horror at the notion that people could be equated with money. Most memorably, DeFlores is disgusted that Beatrice-Joanna should "Offer gold" for "The life-blood of a man" (3.3.67–8).[39] Most audience members likely feel similar revulsion when Beatrice-Joanna, planning to pay Diaphanta to sleep with Alsemero on their wedding night so that her own lost virginity will not be detected, remarks: "'Tis a nice piece / Gold cannot purchase" (4.1.55–6). At the same time that the play insists on the manifest wrongness of conflating people and currency, it achieves much of its emotional effect by attaching the same anxieties surrounding the objects and practices of international trade to Beatrice-Joanna and her erotic relationships.

We see this overlapping of the commercial and the erotic in the play's repeated references to venturing.[40] The play begins with Alsemero abruptly canceling his planned trip to Malta because he has fallen in love with Beatrice-Joanna (1.1.1–57). In Middleton and Rowley's prose source, Alsemero wants revenge on the Dutch for killing his father in battle, and he is traveling to Malta in hopes of fighting in the Maltese navy.[41] Although mention is made of Alsemero's dead father in *The Changeling* as well, his reasons for traveling to Malta are not made explicit. There is a suggestion, however, that the voyage might be a commercial one. Left with nothing to do in lieu of the voyage, Jasperino signals his intention to court Beatrice-Joanna's waiting woman by saying: "I meant to be a venturer in this voyage. Yonder's another vessel; I'll board her: if she be lawful prize, down goes her topsail" (1.1.89–92). Although the word "venturer" could mean any type of risk-taker, it predominantly referred to someone who had invested in a commercial undertaking.[42] Additionally, an English audience would have associated the Mediterranean island with commerce, not least because of Marlowe's *Jew of Malta*. If Middleton and Rowley did think of this voyage as commercial, they may have been conflating it with two earlier voyages mentioned in their source, according to which Alsemero, "[made] two viages to the West-Indies, from which he return[ed] flourishing and rich."[43]

Regardless of whether or not one thinks of a literal commercial venture being abandoned in the opening scene, the dynamic of "venturing" becomes one of the play's chief concerns. Forms of the word "venture" occur eight subsequent times—five more times in the main plot and three in the subplot.[44] I will examine these instances in greater detail below, but to grasp their full significance, it is worth first considering a similar repetition in an earlier Middleton play, *A Chaste Maid in Cheapside* (1611), where the word appears five times, each at a moment when the domain of erotic desire converges with that of economic calculation.[45] In that play, Touchwood Junior plans to elope with Moll Yellowhammer, defeating her goldsmith father's plans of marrying her to a wealthy gentleman. In the opening scene, Touchwood Junior asks Yellowhammer to make a wedding ring that will fit Moll's finger, proclaiming that he is sure it is the same size as that of the woman he intends to marry. Yellowhammer says that he will make the ring if Touchwood Junior "dare[s] venture by her finger," to which Touchwood Junior responds: "Ay, and I'll 'bide all loss, sir" (1.1.195–6), conflating his economic and emotional investment in Moll. Likewise, later in the play, the Wench who has successfully managed to extort money from the father of her illegitimate child in exchange for abandoning it tells the audience that she has similarly disposed of four previous children but promises: "if e'er I venture more, / Where I now go for a maid, may I ride for a whore" (2.1.105–6). Here, the word "venture' reminds us that, for the Wench, illegitimate children pose not only potential risk, but also potential profit. In a city comedy, such as *A Chaste Maid in Cheapside*, which is overtly concerned with the economic aspects of sex and marriage, the simultaneously economic and emotional aspects of "venture" are clear. The word functions similarly in *The Changeling*, but its economic dimension is only clear in light of concerns about the role of currency exchange in international commerce.

Before entering Vermandero's castle, Alsemero wonders: "How shall I dare to venture in his castle / When he discharges murderers at the gate?" (1.2.226–7). It is routinely noted that the reference to "discharg[ing] murderers," which literally means firing cannons, may allude to James I's release of Frances Howard and her husband from the Tower earlier that year. But I would like to focus attention on the first clause of the sentence, in which the word "venture" on its surface means "dare to advance upon," but also suggests that the castle is a place in which risk-taking akin to financial investment will take place.[46] The venturing that takes place in *The Changeling* is qualitatively different from that which takes place in *A Chaste Maid in Cheapside*. The challenge faced by characters in the earlier play is to follow one's sexual desires without ending up with more children than can be supported (Touchwood Senior and his wife) or too few to ensure that familial wealth will continue into the next generation (the Kixes). Their problems are those of the retail merchant, who must wisely proportion expenses to likely gains. By contrast, the problems faced by venturers in *The Changeling* are conceptually closer to those posed by international currency exchange: how to correctly judge the relationship between an object's intrinsic and extrinsic (or ascribed) value, how to judge the commensurability of objects, and how to make sense of the obscure forces that cause value to fluctuate.

At first, Alsemero's courtship of Beatrice-Joanna is represented as a perfectly equitable exchange. During their first meeting in the castle, Alsemero responds to her vows of love by claiming: "We're so like / In our expressions, lady, that unless I borrow / The same words, I shall never find their equals" (2.2.12–14). His love for her can only be equated to her love for him. In order to free Beatrice-Joanna to marry him, Alsemero proposes challenging her fiancé to a duel. She objects, saying: "Are not you ventured in the action, / That's all my joys and comforts?" (2.2.31–2). Her unwillingness to "venture" Alsemero in the hopes of gaining Alsemero marks the limits of equal exchange. Instead, she hatches a secret plan to hire DeFlores to kill her fiancé, thereby following a sound logic of economic investment by giving less than she hopes to gain. She signals this logic by telling Alsemero only: "The present times are not so sure of our side / As those hereafter may be. We must use 'em, then, / As thrifty folks their weatlh: sparingly, now, / Till the time opens" (2.2.49–52). Her attempt at a frugal investment, however, goes awry because of her failure to understand what was truly required in exchange for DeFlores' services.

Upon returning from the murder, DeFlores rejects money, exclaiming: "Offer gold / For the life-blood of man? Is any thing / Valued too precious for my recompense?" (3.4.67–9). He then demands that she give up her virginity to him. In response to her revulsion, he promises: "Thou'lt love anon / What thou so fear'st and faint'st to venture on" (3.4.174).[47] Indeed, Beatrice-Joanna is transformed in precisely the way DeFlores suggests. Her experience can be seen as a nightmarish analogue to the experience of English commercial venturers. According to Malynes' committee, English merchants who expected money to be purely instrumental—"a publike measure" of goods—were taken advantage of by countries who altered the relationship between a coin's denomination and its substance.[48] In the nightmare logic of the play, Beatrice-Joanna resembles Malynes' merchants in her failure to recognize the true cost of her exchange. Whereas she believed that she was exchanging gold for the ability to marry Alsemero, she was actually exchanging DeFlores for Alsemero as the murderer of Piracquo. Through an obscure process, the perverse irrationality of which continues to fascinate readers and audience members, the play validates this exchange, making DeFlores as highly valued to Beatrice-Joanna as Alsemero was. After having sex with DeFlores, she admits: "I'm forc'd to love thee now, / 'Cause thou provid'st so carefully for my honour" (5.1.46–7). Shortly thereafter, she goes further, saying: "Here's a man worth loving" (5.1.75). We might correlate this loss of Beatrice-Joanna's individual will in the forced re-valuation of DeFlores with Thomas Mun's assertion that abstract economic processes constitute "a necessitie of nature beyond all resistance."[49] As Malynes feared was happening to English merchants, Beatrice-Joanna's intention is mysteriously subverted by the very process of exchange, and—like England itself, losing its supply of precious metals—she undergoes a physical alteration as the result of this exchange in the loss of her virginity.[50] While Beatrice-Joanna is not reducible to an analogue for Spanish currency, or English merchants, or national wealth, she becomes the locus for the same sort of anxieties that surround these entities.

Out of fear that Alsemero will discover her lost virginity on their wedding night, she proclaims: "There's no venturing / Into his bed" (4.1.11–12). But "venturing," in the economic sense, is precisely what she does by paying the virginal

Diaphanta to take her place in bed. In order to successfully fool Alsemero in the exchange, Beatrice-Joanna takes advantage of a virginity test that she discovers in Alsemero's closet. The test consists of a phial of liquid that causes virgins to yawn, sneeze, and laugh. By observing Diaphanta's reaction to drinking the liquid, Beatrice-Joanna is not only able to verify Diaphanta's virginity, but is also able to mimic her reactions when Alsemero asks her to drink the liquid on their wedding night. Various scholars have linked this strange plot element to the virginity test that Frances Howard underwent when securing her divorce from the Earl of Essex.[51] In order to prove her claims that the marriage had never been consummated, Howard agreed to be examined by a group of women, provided that she was able to keep her face veiled to preserve her modesty, leading to speculation that a true virgin had been examined in Howard's place. Although *The Changeling* clearly glances at the Howard case, I argue that the virginity test scenes were theatrically compelling largely because of the anxieties they activated about determining value. Like merchants of the period assessing a coin, Alsemero looks to material substance to verify ascribed value. Handing the drink to Beatrice-Joanna, he reassures her of its wholesomeness, saying: "this, upon my warrant, you shall venture on" (4.2.136). The dramatic irony of this line arises from the audience's awareness that Beatrice-Joanna understands what is ventured on her part far more fully than Alsemero does. Beatrice-Joanna proves herself to be a consummate venturer, and—as Malynes feared was the fate of unwary merchants—Alsemero is duped by his lack of knowledge and his inability to measure intrinsic qualities accurately.

Stamping, Naming, and Hypallage

Even more unsettling than the failure of individuals to gain accurate knowledge about the intrinsic qualities of an object or a person, though, is the apparent power of extrinsic valuation to trump material reality. As was the case with the quantity of silver that was worth more with a Spanish stamp than an English, the value of people and objects in the play is driven not by their material being but by their ascribed value. Moreover, ascribed value actually seems to alter material being.[52] This mysterious power of ascribed value is epitomized by a distinctly odd metaphor early in the play when Vermandero speaks of knowing Alsemero's father "Before our chins were worth Iulan down," referring to Iülus Ascanius in *The Aeneid*, "whose name may have come from the Greek word for 'first growth of the beard'" (1.1.178, n.). He says that their friendship "continued till the stamp of time / Had coin'd us into silver" (1.1.172–3). This metaphor is unusual because of the transformative power that it attributes to the stamp. Normally, the stamp simply validates the material into which it is pressed. For example, Shakespeare uses a similar metaphor in *Measure for Measure* when Angelo worries that he is being placed in office before he has proven himself worthy: "Let there be some more test made of my metal / Before so noble and so great a figure / Be stamped upon it" (1.1.47–9). In *The Changeling*, by contrast, the "stamp of time" actually alters the material into which it is stamped, converting it from "down" to "silver."

Likewise, throughout the play material worth is determined and altered by ascribed value. In trying to explain Beatrice-Joanna's aversion to DeFlores, whom everyone else seems to prize, Alsemero draws attention to the failure of any material item to be consistently valued by everyone, which he calls "a frequent frailty in our nature" (1.1.116). Observing that even things generally thought to be pleasing, such as roses, oil, and wine, are despised by some people, he concludes that: "There's scarce a thing but is both lov'd and loath'd" (1.1.122). Roberta Baker and David Nicol have observed that Freudian readings of the play frequently wrest this line from its context to suggest that Beatrice-Joanna simultaneously experiences desire and repulsion for DeFlores from the beginning of the play.[53] Though these lines can be read beyond their contextual meaning to suggest that some objects are simultaneously loved and loathed by the same person, their primary suggestion that the same object could be valued differently by different people resonates more powerfully with the play's other examples of the importance of ascribed value. By the same logic, DeFlores—acutely aware that he is physically unattractive to most people—holds out hope that Beatrice-Joanna will love him "Because there's daily precedents of bad faces / Beloved beyond all reason" (2.1.84–5). Of course, if ascribed value differs from person to person, the problem becomes deciding whose concept of value triumphs.

The ability of one ascription of value not only to override all others but also to alter the physical essence of the thing being valued is unsettlingly demonstrated in DeFlores' revaluation of Beatrice-Joanna after Piracquo's murder. He tells her:

> settle you
> In what the act has made you. You're no more now;
> You must forget your parentage to me.
> You're the deed's creature; by that name
> You lost your first condition, and I challenge you,
> As peace and innocency has turned you out
> And made you one with me. (3.4.137–43)

One of the most striking features of this speech is the unusual attention it draws to the word "name," which appears jarringly in line 140 without its referent—"the deed's creature"—being immediately apparent. In this speech, to rename is to recreate: by being named the deed's creature, Beatrice-Joanna has been materially transformed into something identical to DeFlores. Additionally, the effect of these lines depends on their reversal of the normal distribution of agency. Rather than subjects doing actions and creating deeds, acts and deeds create subjects. Being accustomed to thinking of deeds as the creations of subjects, we more easily accept as a logically formulated sentence: "the deed is your creature." "You're the deed's creature" is the play's most crucial instance of hypallage, the rhetorical figure also known as "the changeling" that consists of switching words from a more logical to a less logical order.[54]

Throughout the play, hypallage stands in opposition to chiasmus. Both chiasmus and hypallage are figures of *commutatio* (change, or exchange). In chiasmus, key words in a sentence follow an "ABBA pattern of mirror inversion."[55] A well-known example is John F. Kennedy's call for Americans to "ask not what your country can do for you—ask what you can do for your country." Whereas the chiasmic inversion produces two logical, complementary statements, hypallage "[changes] the natural order of the elements of a sentence" or "[reverses] the relations of two elements of a sentence" to produce an illogical sentence.[56] The effects of hypallage can be poetic, as in the example from a Tudor list of rhetorical figures: "Darksome wandering by the solitary night," in which the night's darkness is attributed to the wanderer, and the wanderer's solitariness to the night.[57] They can also be comic, as when Shakespeare's Bottom proclaims: "The eye of man hath not heard, the ear of man hath not seen …"[58] Whereas a chiasmic exchange "seems to set up a natural internal dynamic that draws the parts closer together," a hypallagic exchange threatens to reduce a statement to nonsense.[59]

This opposition is put to comic effect in the subplot when Antonio, disguised as a fool, is tested by Lollio, who presents him with questions that, in Lois E. Bueler's words, "pretend to be matters of arithmetic" but "are all 'solved' by means of verbal quibbles involving rhetorical figures of change."[60]

> LOLLIO: Tony: how many is five times six?
>
> ANTONIO: Five times six is six times five.
>
> LOLLIO: What arithmetician could have answered better? How many is one hundred and seven?
>
> ANTONIO: One hundred and seven is seven hundred and one, cousin. (3.3.171–7)

Antonio's first reply, which reverses the sequence of elements in the sentence while still forming a logically correct statement, is a clear example of chiasmus. In his second reply, though, the chiasmic switch veers into hypallage because the statement fails to make sense, logically or mathematically. Bueler argues that these questions are intended to show that the fools' world consists either of "mindless, specious equivalency" or "pointless repetition."[61] The equivalence of (5×6) and (6×5) may seem trivial to us, but we should remember that Malynes was scandalized by the fact that 4 oz. of silver is not necessarily equivalent to 4 oz. of silver. To adumbrate Malynes' argument: 4 oz. of silver equals £1 (English); 4 oz. of silver also equals 38s. (Flemish); however, £1 (English) buys only 33s. 4d. (Flemish).[62] In Malynes' view, currency exchangers selling Flemish money were profiting by making 33s. 4d. seem to equal 38s. Malynes' fears are the counterpoint to Mun's enthusiastic claim that £1 of Spanish silver equals £5 worth of East Indian commodities. In both cases, the arithmetic that governs international commerce seems akin to that used by Antonio, for whom 107 equals 701. If, as Mun promised, commerce made £1 equal £5, then England literally had a money-making machine. If, however, as Malynes warned, international merchants made 38s equal to 33s. 4d., then each transaction generated loss.

Antonio's fanciful math recalls the earlier mathematical fantasy in which DeFlores reasoned that Beatrice-Joanna may shift her affections to him because she had already shifted them from Piracquo to Alsemero:

> for if a woman
> Fly from one point, from him she makes a husband,
> She spreads and mounts then like arithmetic:
> One, ten, a hundred, a thousand, ten thousand. (2.2.60–63)

Antonio's fallacious math, by which 107 is transformed into 701 through a process of verbal exchange, at first seems to parody the "arithmetic" of DeFlores' fantasy, in which Beatrice-Joanna's sexual desire is multiplied exponentially. The parody turns serious, however, when Beatrice-Joanna becomes DeFlores' paramour through his hypallagic creation of her as "the deed's creature." Beatrice-Joanna's desire suddenly seems governed by rules that defy rationality, logic, and arithmetic.

Taking Account

With Alsemero's sudden discovery of Beatrice-Joanna's and DeFlores' crimes in the final act, the play gives the impression that rationality has miraculously triumphed. Alsemero's revelation of the truth to Vermandero is accompanied by a striking moment of chiasmus. Believing Antonio and Franciscus to be guilty, Vermandero proclaims: "I have suspicion near as proof itself / For Piracquo's murder," to which Alsemero responds: "Sir, I have proof / Beyond suspicion for Piracquo's murder" (5.3.123–5). The chiasmic switching of "proof" and "suspicion" in these lines, which are more obtrusively patterned than any of the lines immediately proceeding them, signals the re-establishment of balanced, equitable exchange. The horror of the confessions that accompany Beatrice-Joanna's and DeFlores' murder-suicide gives way to a somber assessment of the changes that have occurred during the play. Alsemero exclaims: "What an opacous body had that moon / That last changed on us" (5.3.196–7). But, with the moon's opaqueness lifted, he can clearly see in Beatrice-Joanna "beauty changed / To ugly whoredom" and in DeFlores "servant-obedience" changed "To a master-sin: imperious murder" (5.3.197–9). The other characters then systematically catalogue the changes that they have undergone. In the world of the play, it seems, even the irrationality and horror of the preceding events can be rationalized and reduced to a series of exchanges.

As much as the participants in the 1620s trade committees might have loved arriving at a similarly clear-sighted and rational assessment of exchange, there was no comparably reassuring ending outside of the playhouse. A little over a month after *The Changeling*'s debut, the debate once more spilled into print. Edward Misselden's *Free Trade* sparked an angry rejoinder by Gerard Malynes, titled *The Maintenance of Free Trade*.[63] Misselden concurred with Malynes that Spanish reales were flowing to Holland because they would fetch more there than they would in England.[64] However, like Mun, he rejected the notion that the par of exchange advocated by Malynes could rectify the problem, because exchange rates did not determine the value of coins; rather, "the plenty or scarcity of monies" relative to demand for them did.[65] Malynes responded by insisting that there is a fundamental difference between money (the public measure of all things) and commodities (the things being measured). Whereas the latter could fluctuate in value without affecting the parity of trade, the former could not. He stated his case most memorably in these words: "the yard doth measure the Cloth, but the Cloth doth not measure the yard."[66] Malynes had made this comparison in several earlier treatises, but he had not previously given it the pithy expression resulting from the chiasmic switching of *yard* and *cloth*. In Malynes' well-turned phrase, as in *The Changeling*, a hypallagic threat to order (cloth measuring the yard; commodities determining the value of money) is contained within a reassuring chiasmic structure. Like Middleton and Rowley, Malynes seems to have intuited that "the changeling" is the ideal figure for voicing an anxiety that inequitable systems of exchange were perverting rational valuation and subordinating individual will to mysterious economic laws.

Notes

1 C.G.A. Clay, *Economic Expansion and Social Change: England 1500–1700*, 2 volumes (Cambridge: Cambridge University Press, 1984), 2: 106.

2 Ibid., 2: 106.

3 Ibid., 2: 126; 2: 184.

4 See, for example, Douglas Bruster, *Drama and the Market in the Age of Shakespeare* (Cambridge: Cambridge University Press, 1992); Jonathan Gil Harris, *Sick Economies: Drama, Mercantilism, and Disease in Shakespeare's England* (Philadelphia: University of Pennsylvania Press, 2004); Theodore B. Leinwand, *Theatre, Finance and Society in Early Modern England* (Cambridge: Cambridge University Press, 1999); Daniel Vitkus, *Turning Turk: English Theater and the Multicultural Mediterranean, 1570–1630* (New York: Palgrave Macmillan, 2003); and Valerie Forman, *Tragicomic Redemptions: Global Economics and the Early Modern English Stage* (Philadelphia: University of Pennsylvania Press, 2008).

5 See J.L. Simmons, "Diabolical Realism in Middleton and Rowley's *The Changeling*," *Renaissance Drama* 11 (1980): 135–70; Margot Heinemann, *Puritanism and Theatre: Thomas Middleton and Opposition Drama under the Early Stuarts* (Cambridge: Cambridge University Press, 1982), 178–9; and Lisa Hopkins, "Beguiling the Master of the Mystery: Form and Power in *The Changeling*," *Medieval and Renaissance Drama in England* 9 (1997): 149–61. Judith Haber, "'I(t) Could Not Choose but

Follow': Erotic Logic in *The Changeling*," *Representations* 81 (2003): 79–98, deftly situates both the Howard scandal and Middleton's invocation of it in the context of seventeenth-century "fears and fantasies about women, sexuality, and marriage" (80).

6 Annabel Patterson, "Introduction" to *The Changeling*, ed. Douglas Bruster, in *Thomas Middleton: The Collected Works*, ed. Gary Taylor and John Lavagnino (Oxford: Oxford University Press, 2008), 1632. The object of Patterson's criticism is A.A. Bromham and Zara Bruzzi's *The Changeling and the Years of Crisis, 1619–1624* (New York: Pinter Publishing, 1990), which, she rightly argues, starts from a "reasonable hypothesis" about Middleton's political sympathies and "stretch[es] it beyond plausibility" to "[construct] a huge allegorical edifice, in which almost every detail of the play text is pressed into service" (1634).

7 For other recent examples of character-focused readings of *The Changeling*, see Roberta Baker and David Nicol, "Does Beatrice Joanna Have a Subtext?: *The Changeling* on the London Stage," *Early Modern Literary Studies* 10, no. 1 (2004); Joost Daalder and Antony Telford Moore, "'There's Scarce a Thing But is Both Loved and Loathed': *The Changeling* I.i.91–129," *English Studies* 80, no. 6 (1999): 499–508; and Charles W. Crupi, "The Transformation of De Flores in *The Changeling*," *Neophilologus* 68, no. 1 (1984): 142–8.

8 I use the—admittedly nebulous—term "anxiety" here, not in its technical psychoanalytic sense, but more loosely to refer to the simultaneously affective and intellectual experience of uncertainty about economic circumstances.

9 Michel Serres, *Hermes: Literature, Science, Philosophy*, ed. Josué V. Harari and David F. Bell (Baltimore: Johns Hopkins University Press, 1982), especially 1–62. See also Bradley D. Ryner, "The Panoramic View in Mercantile Thought: Or, A Merchant's Map of Cymbeline," in *Global Traffic: Discourses and Practices of Trade in English Literature 1550 to 1700*, ed. Barbara Sebek and Stephen Deng (New York: Palgrave Macmillan, 2008), 77–94, 86.

10 B.E. Supple, *Commercial Crisis and Change in England 1600–1642* (Cambridge: Cambridge University Press, 1964), 33–51.

11 Clay, *Economic Expansion*, 2: 120.

12 Supple, *Commercial Crisis*, 73–98. Charles P. Kindleberger, "The Economic Crisis of 1619 to 1623," *The Journal of Economic History* 51, no. 1 (1991): 149–75, corrects earlier historians who had translated *Kipper* as "clipping" and argues that "tilting and wagging" refers to the irregular movement of exchangers' scales during the period.

13 Supple, *Commercial Crisis*, 52 (italics mine).

14 For an overview of Malynes's ideas, see Andrea Finkelstein, *Harmony and Balance: An Intellectual History of Seventeenth-Century English Economic Thought* (Ann Arbor: University of Michigan Press, 2000), 26–53. Harris, *Sick Economies*, insightfully reads the concept of value in Malynes' 1601 treatises against that of Shakespeare's *Troilus and Cressida*, which was likely produced the following year (83–107).

15 British Library (BL), Additional Manuscripts (Add. MSS.) 34324: 153–4.

16 Ibid., 153.

17 See Finkelstein, *Harmony and Balance*, 74–88.

18 BL, Add. MSS. 34324: 155–7.

19 Ibid., 155.

20 Ibid., 156v.

21 Ibid., 157.

22 On the dating of *The Changeling*, see Michael Neill, ed., *The Changeling by Thomas Middleton and William Rowley* (New York: A&C Black Publishers, 2006), xi.

23 Ralph Maddison, quoted in Supple, *Commercial Crisis*, 268.

24 See Lois E. Bueler, "The Rhetoric of Change in *The Changeling*," *English Literary Renaissance* 14, no. 1 (1984): 95–113; Catherine A. Hébert, "A Note on the Significance of the Title of Middleton's *The Changeling*," *College Language Association Journal* 12 (1968): 66–99; Dale B.J. Randall, "Observations on the Theme of Chastity in *The Changeling*," *English Literary Renaissance* 14, no. 3 (1984): 347–66; Ann Pasternak Slater, "Hypallage, Barley-Break, and *The Changeling*," *The Review of English Studies* 34, no. 136 (1983): 429–40; N.K. Sugimura, "Changelings and *The Changeling*," *Essays in Criticism* 56, no. 3 (2006): 241–63.

25 OED, "Changeling," *n.* 1.

26 OED, "Changeling," *n.* 3.

27 OED, "Changeling," *n.* 4.

28 OED, "Changeling," *n.* 2.

29 OED, "Change," *v.* 1.

30 OED, "Change," *n.* 3.

31 Although no one has examined exchange as an economic concept *per se* in the play, excellent work has been done on economic underpinnings of the play's master–servant and husband–wife relationships. See Mark Thornton Burnett, "*The Changeling* and Masters and Servants," in *Early Modern English Drama: A Critical Companion*, ed. Garrett A. Sullivan, Jr., Patrick Cheney, and Andrew Hadfield (Oxford: Oxford University Press, 2006), 298–308; Swapan Chakravorty, *Society and Politics in the Plays of Thomas Middleton* (Oxford: Oxford University Press, 1996); Deborah G. Burks, "'I'll Want my Will Else': *The Changeling* and Women's Complicity with their Rapists," *ELH* 62, no. 4 (1995): 759–90; Anthony B. Dawson, "Giving the Finger: Puns and Transgression in *The Changeling*," *The Elizabethan Theatre* 12 (1993): 93–112; and Scott Wilson, "General Economy and The Changeling," in *Cultural Materialism: Theory and Practice* (Oxford: Blackwell Publishers, 1995).

32 Both Christina Malcolmson, "'As Tame as Ladies': Politics and Gender in *The Changeling*," *English Literary Renaissance* 20 (1990): 320–39, and Bromham and Bruzzi, *The Changeling and the Years of Crisis* (37–78) argue for reading the tragic marriage between Beatrice-Joanna and Alsemero in the context of the proposed marriage between Prince Charles and the Spanish Infanta. See also Dale B.J. Randall, "Some New Perspectives on the Spanish Setting of *The Changeling* and Its Source," *Medieval and Renaissance Drama in England* 3 (1986): 189–216, which discusses the play's place realism.

33 C.E. Challis, *The Tudor Coinage* (Manchester: Manchester University Press, 1978), 193–6.

34 Ibid., 146.

35 BL, Add. MSS. 34324: 160.

36 Thomas Mun, *A Discourse of Trade, from England vnto the East-Indies*. London: John Pyper, 1621, Sig. D2v.

37 Mun, *A Discourse of Trade*, Sig. (d). Valerie Forman, "Transformations of Value and the Production of 'Investment' in the Early History of the English East India Company," *Journal of Medieval and Early Modern Studies* 34, no. 3 (2004): 611–41, examines the key role of Mun's notion of "transmutation" in forming modern notions of "investment" and cogently critiques the occlusion of labor that accompanied it. In *Tragicomic Redemptions*, she connects this notion of investment to the rise of tragicomedy.

38 Mun, *A Discourse of Trade*, Sig. (d2).

39 All references are to Taylor and Lavagnino, eds, *Thomas Middleton: The Collected Works*, op. cit.

40 On the affective nature of venturing as a practice, see Leinwand, *Theatre, Finance and Society*, 110–39.

41 John Reynolds, *The Triumphs of Gods Revenege, against the Crying, and Execrable Sinne of Murther* (London: Felix Kyngston, 1621), Sig. Q1v–Q2v.

42 OED, 1 and 2.

43 Reynolds, *The Triumphs of Gods Revenege*, Sig. Q2.

44 These occurrences are: 1.1.226; 2.2.31; 3.3.193; 3.3.259; 3.4.174; 4.1.11; 4.2.136; and 4.3.43.

45 1.1.195; 2.1.105; 2.1.188; 3.3.32; and 4.3.375.

46 OED, 9.a.

47 Haber, "Erotic Logic in *The Changeling*," notes that variations on these lines, which echo those in Ben Jonson's *Hymenaei* ("Shrink not, soft Virgin, you will love / Anon what you so fear to prove"), also appear in Middleton's *Women Beware Women* and *A Game at Chess* (79, 82–3). Only in *The Changeling*'s version, however, does Middleton use the word "venture."

48 BL, Add. MSS. 34342: 161v.

49 For examinations of the play's depictions of the loss of agency, see Burks, "*The Changeling* and Women's Complicity"; Haber, "Erotic Logic in *The Changeling*"; and Sugimura, "Changelings and *The Changeling*."

50 The play's representation of value is inextricably linked to its representation of gender. In what follows, I will only gesture broadly to the play's gendered power dynamic, which has been more thoroughly analyzed by others, including: Baker and Nicol, "*The Changeling* on the London Stage"; Burks, "*The Changeling* and Women's Complicity"; Haber, "Erotic Logic in *The Changeling*"; and Malcolmson, "Politics and Gender in *The Changeling*."

51 See note 5 above.

52 This subordination of the material to the ideological is part and parcel of the rise of the autonomous sign that David Hawkes argues developed alongside the capitalist economy. See David Hawkes, *The Faust Myth: Religion and the Rise of Representation* (New York: Palgrave Macmillan, 2007); and idem, *Idols of the Marketplace: Idolatry and Commodity Fetishism in English Literature 1580–1680* (New York: Palgrave Macmillan, 2001).

53 Baker and Nicol, "Does Beatrice Joanna Have a Subtext?," para. 31.

54 Several scholars have examined the significance of the figure of hypallage in *The Changeling*. Sugimura, "Changelings and *The Changeling*," artfully demonstrates the slippage "between objective percepts and subjective perceptions" that the play achieves through hypallage, but does not note "the deed's creature" as an example, singling out, instead, the unusual placement of "parentage" in the lines above (246). Slater, "Hypallage, Barley-Break, and *The Changeling*," argues that the play enacts a "moral hypallage, whereby vice and virtue exchange places, so that vices are committed in the name of virtue, and virtues themselves become vicious" (431).

55 Richard A. Lanham, *A Handlist of Rhetorical Terms*, 2nd edition (Berkeley: University of California Press, 1991), 33. Following the customary usage of scholars of English (rather than scholars of Latin), I am treating "chiasmus" as a synonym for "antimetabole." As Lanham notes: "Chiasmus and commutatio sometimes imply a more precise balance and reversal, antimetabole a looser, but they are virtual synonyms" (14).

56 Warren Taylor, *Tudor Figures of Rhetoric* (Whitewater, WI: The Language Press, 1972), 102–3.

57 Ibid., 103.

58 William Shakespeare, *A Midsummer Night's Dream* 4.1.204–5.

59 Lanham, *Handlist of Rhetorical Terms*, 33.

60 Bueler, "The Rhetoric of Change," 101.

61 Ibid., 102–3, 104.

62 BL, Add. MSS. 34324: 153, 165.

63 *Free Trade* was entered into the Stationers' Register on June 15, 1622. *The Maintenance of Free Trade* was entered on October 20, 1622. Two subsequent treatises in the debate, Misselden's *The Circle of Commerce* and Malynes' *The Center of the Circle of Commerce*, were entered on May 20, 1623 and November 20, 1623 respectively.

64 Misselden, *Free Trade*, Sig. B4v.

65 Ibid., Sig. H4v.

66 Malynes, *The Maintenance of Free Trade*, Sig. E7v.

PART III
Wealth and Christian Ideals

Chapter 7

"To honor God and enrich Florence in things spiritual and temporal": Piety, Commerce, and Art in the Humiliati Order

Julia I. Miller and Laurie Taylor-Mitchell

Although they were a recognized religious order for some 370 years (1201–1571), the Humiliati ("Humbled Ones") produced a paltry number of holy figures, a handful of beati, and only one, probably apocryphal, saint, Giovanni de Meda.[1] Venerated by the order from the fifteenth century onwards, Giovanni de Meda was commemorated as their twelfth-century founder. A legend recounted how the penniless saint was visited by the archangel Gabriel, who gave him a sack of gold to feed himself and his brethren, and one of these coins was later treasured as a relic.[2] Repeating this story, the historian John Wickstrom dryly noted: "[i]t is difficult to imagine a gold coin serving as a remembrance of Dominic."[3] Wickstrom's comment perfectly characterizes the singular position of the Humiliati within later medieval Italian society, especially in its contrast to other religious orders, such as the mendicants, who had their origins at precisely the same time. The early Humiliati shared ideals with the Franciscans and Dominicans, namely the rejection of the lavish materialism enjoyed by secular clergy and the return to a life of apostolic simplicity. While they embraced the virtues of charity and humility, the Humiliati did not take a vow of poverty, and were not averse to handling and earning money. Indeed, during the first century of their existence, they were a lively part of the dynamic, proto-capitalist activities in Italian cities, even acting as merchants and entrepreneurs. This situation enhanced the wealth of this order, and they attempted to resolve the contradictory impulses of humble simplicity and material success by embracing biblical passages such as Luke 14:11—"he who humbles himself will be exalted" (as in the text illustrated in Figure 7.4). Ultimately the Humiliati were unable to reconcile their religious ideals and a precarious monastic identity with their financial success. By the fifteenth century, their disengagement from commerce resulted in their decline and eventual suppression.

This essay will present the main outline of Humiliati history, and some of the intersections between their religious piety and their commercial enterprises.

Most historical studies of this order have concentrated on northern Italy, as the origins of the Humiliati were in Lombardy and Piedmont, and they were always most numerous in these areas.[4] We will instead deal with the specific situation of the order in Florence, where—surprisingly—there has been relatively little focus on their activities.[5] Although much of the documentation for the Humiliati in Florence has been lost, the surviving evidence demonstrates that the order was welcomed in the city because of their expertise in the field of woolworking, and through the thirteenth century they continued to be valued for their contributions to growing commercial ventures. We will also address briefly the artistic patronage of the order, as exemplified in their principal Florentine establishment, the Ognissanti or "All Saints" Church. Unlike the mendicant orders, whose vows of poverty meant that the building and decoration usually depended on wealthy lay contributors, the Florentine Humiliati seem to have been active as patrons themselves, employing, among other prominent artists, Giotto, Bernardo Daddi, Donatello, and Domenico Ghirlandaio.[6]

During the twelfth century, certain parts of Europe, particularly Italy, began to experience a rapid re-urbanization, with the growth of trade and manufacturing leading to expansions in both the numbers of inhabitants and the physical size of cities. The disruptions caused by growing urban populations also led to the rise of heretical groups, who often appealed more directly to the displaced populace than the conventional church.[7] The Humiliati began in the later twelfth century in northern Italy as small groups of lay people and clerics; men and women lived together chastely, and they embraced the apostolic ideal of a simple life, devoted to work and prayer. Some of the laymen engaged in preaching—an action that usurped Church prerogative. Their disobedience of Church law led to their condemnation as heretics by Pope Lucius III in 1184, who grouped the Humiliati with other, even more unorthodox, sects such as the Cathars.[8] When Innocent III was elected Pope in 1198, he instituted a policy of embracing the exponents of new religious experience, such as the mendicants, in part to turn them into effective agents against heresy. Under Innocent, the Humiliati were successful in moving from an outcast group to an accepted religious order. In 1201, the Pope recognized the Humiliati in the form of three different units, a First Order of clerics (although in communities that included women), a Second Order of religious men and women who lived communally—essentially as monks and nuns—and mostly in joint monasteries. A Third Order of lay people remained in their own homes, but followed the spiritual aims of the order, anticipating the later tertiaries among the mendicants.[9]

The Humiliati rule, derived in part from the Benedictine and Augustinian rules, applied to the First and Second Orders.[10] An unusual aspect of their rule was the provision of extra hours designated for work as a key principle of the order.[11] Another striking difference from the mendicants was that the Humiliati refused alms, and supported themselves by their own labor.[12] Beyond self-sufficiency, any profits were to be given as contributions to the poor, and the rule included the verse from Acts (20:35) that "it is more blessed to give than to receive," honoring the virtue of charity.[13] The standard vows for profession to the order were the usual ones for monks or nuns: obedience, stability, and conversion. Brothers and sisters were to relinquish most personal property upon entering the order, but a specific vow for poverty was not added until 1374.[14]

While the Humiliati were initially (and somewhat ironically) active as preachers against heresy, they were soon overtaken in this practice by the vigorous new order of the Dominicans.[15] Instead, they became most memorable for their work activities. Although some Humiliati communities were in rural areas, most were urban, and it appears that the bulk of the work they performed was in the largest (and most lucrative) industry of this period: textile manufacturing, especially of wool cloth.[16] The order was best known for producing a simple, rather coarse cloth ("panno degli Umiliati") used for their own habits. Indeed, early observers noted that members of the incipient order distinguished themselves by garments of rough, unbleached wool (*berettino*), mostly of a pale grayish color. As the Laôn chronicler put it, "[t]hey called themselves Humiliati, because they did not use colored cloth for clothing, but restricted themselves to plain dress."[17]

Although based partly on legend, an illustrated chronicle of the Humiliati written in the early fifteenth century by one of their brethren, Giovanni di Brera, emphasized the importance of woolworking for the order from their beginnings, and it is probable that this part of Giovanni's history was largely accurate.[18] The chronicle suggests a division of labor based on the separate units within the Humiliati; the brothers and sisters of the Second Order manufactured wool cloth (Figure 7.1), while clerics of the First Order acted as merchants (Figure 7.2). While in practice the distinctions between the orders were often blurred, the images do emphasize the prominence of women, since many of the initial steps in creating wool cloth, such as spinning the fibers, were traditionally "women's work," and many weavers were also women.[19] The "panno degli Umiliati" was presumably sold cheaply to the poor, but some documentation shows that the Humiliati also produced a higher-quality cloth, and a few of their monasteries apparently owned dyeworks.[20] In the illustrated chronicle (Figure 7.2), the First Order clerics sell bolts of white and colored (blue) cloth to their secular counterparts. The setting for this transaction is a secular building; the Humiliati are identified by their tonsures and by their plain garments. They are also given greater status than the secular merchants through their higher placement in the room; the merchants bend almost protectively over the cloth, while the clerics stand upright. Moreover, the Humiliati gesture towards the cloth but do not actively touch or fold it as the merchants do, perhaps indicating a distance from the economics of the transaction.[21]

The Humiliati were markedly successful in the first decades following their recognition. A measure of this success may be judged by references to the

Figure 7.1 Chronicle, Giovanni di Brera, *Humiliati (Second Order) Manufacturing Cloth*, c. 1421. Milan, Biblioteca Ambrosiana, G 301 inf., fol. 4 verso. Photo: Biblioteca Ambrosiana

Figure 7.2 Chronicle, Giovanni di Brera, *Humiliati Clerics (First Order) Selling Cloth to Merchants*, c. 1421. Milan, Biblioteca Ambrosiana, G 301 inf., fol. 5 verso.
Photo: Biblioteca Ambrosiana

numbers of communities that emerged during the thirteenth century. Jacques de Vitry claimed that by 1216, there were already 150 "conventual" Humiliati houses in Milan alone (excluding the tertiaries), and by 1278, the Milanese Humiliati tertiary Bonvesin della Riva proudly asserted that there were no fewer than 220 establishments of the Second Order in Milan, along with seven canonial (or First Order) houses.[22] A "census" from 1298 of the Humiliati throughout Italy cites 389 houses in total; it has been estimated that this figure would have included about 4,000 brothers and sisters, again excluding unknown numbers of tertiaries.[23]

While almost all Humiliati churches were initially in the north of Italy, by the mid-thirteenth century there were smaller numbers of churches and monasteries in other regions, including Tuscany. The earliest Tuscan community was in Florence, and in 1239 the order was specifically invited by the Archbishop to establish a presence in the city. A group of Humiliati from the First Order monastery of San Michele in Alessandria (near Turin) was ceded the small church and monastery of San Donato in Polverosa. San Donato had been an Augustinian establishment in a rural area west of Florence, about two and one-third kilometers beyond the city's walls, and over a kilometer inland from the Arno.[24] The initial invitation was for both men and women from San Michele to take up residence in San Donato, yet subsequent records for the Florentine house account only for men, and the segregation of men and women into separate monasteries and convents seems to have been the norm for all subsequent Tuscan establishments.

Although it cannot be proven conclusively that Humiliati expertise in woolworking was the only reason the order was initially invited to Florence, it has been reasonably proposed as a primary motivation. The Humiliati had received similar invitations from other cities, including Perugia, Rimini, Parma, and Bologna—all places where the cloth industry was being established in the mid-thirteenth century.[25] In Florence, a document from 1251 is particularly interesting in portraying the commercial activities of the Humiliati. Issued by Archbishop Giovanni dei Mangiadori, it confirmed an arrangement made in the previous year, 1250, that gave the order a different church, Santa Lucia sul Prato, in place of San Donato.[26] The document specifies that the transfer was crucial for the order to be able to carry out their "art," that is *lanificium*, or woolworking.[27] It also makes clear the advantages of Santa Lucia over San Donato; closer by about two kilometers to the center of the city, it facilitated commerce between the Humiliati and secular merchants in the city. Furthermore, Santa Lucia was only a few blocks from the Arno, and access to a convenient source of flowing water was essential to many of the processes in cloth manufacturing, from the initial cleaning of the wool to the fulling that felted and compressed the fibers of the woven cloth.[28] The document includes the pleasing phrase that the order had "grown to honor God and enrich Florence in things spiritual and temporal so that the city could flower with great abundance," a metaphor redolent of the city's name, derived from the Roman *Florentia* or flowering.[29] The phrase also recalls a later expression linking commerce with piety, the wording at the top of the ledgers kept by Francesco Datini of Prato (1335–1410): "In the name of God and profit."[30] Although there is no record of guild membership for the Humiliati in Florence, the reference to dealings with merchants supports the idea that the order was not excluded from selling their products, either to guild members, or in limited trade outside of the wool guild.[31]

In 1250, when the Florentine Humiliati initially exchanged San Donato for Santa Lucia, they also purchased an adjacent parcel of land from the Tornaquinci family, and they began building a large new church, the Ognissanti, which was completed in 1256.[32] The Ognissanti church was built on the eastern edge of the tract, closer to the old city walls, and the land purchase included the water rights to the Arno along with a smaller stream in the area, the Mugnone—again demonstrating the importance of running water for cloth production.[33] The order continued buying land in the western area of Florence over the next few decades, and by 1278, when the Signoria resolved to build a new, much larger circle of city walls, the Humiliati brothers sold a portion of their land for the construction of the new wall. In addition, they ensured a guarantee of passage to their land beyond the walls by means of city gates (including the still-extant Porta al Prato), and secured the right to carve out a large piazza in front of their new church, fronting on the Arno river.[34]

The Humiliati also built or purchased pieces of industrial infrastructure, including *tiratoi*, large sheds used to stretch or dry lengths of fabric; they also controlled *gualchiere*, or fulling mills—water-driven machines that cleaned the woven cloth and softened the fibers to create a smoother texture.[35] It has been suggested that the Humiliati were partners with the Florentine government in developing this area of the city, helping to promote new settlement, construction, and commercial activity.[36] This partnership was manifested as well by the Humiliati functioning as treasurers for the city, often rotating in these responsibilities with other monks, especially the Cistercians.[37] The Humiliati and Cistercians held similar positions in several other cities, most notably in Siena, where the covers of some government account books (*biccherne*) show members of these orders serving as treasurers.[38] For example, on a cover dating from 1324 (Figure 7.3), the monk is identified in the lower inscription as "Frate Grigorio," and as belonging to the Humiliati ("Umiliati"). His white garments are clearly linked to the full, white money bag displayed on the bench. The monk holds the bag partially closed with his left hand, as he is about to insert additional money with his right hand, actions emblematic of his fiscal supervision.[39] Richard Trexler suggested that the reliance on clerics as treasurers and for tax assessments was predicated on their ability to operate in secret, and to be honest and impartial.[40] Furthermore, the special dependence on Cistercians and Humiliati for these fiscal responsibilities might have been an acknowledgement that both orders were accustomed to commerce and the handling of money, as Cistercian monasteries often included large agricultural estates. These positions even gained the Humiliati and Cistercians certain tax exemptions from the city.[41] In view of their role in both the commercial and financial lives of Italian cities, Robert Davidsohn, the great historian of Florence, aptly described the Humiliati as "businessmen in monastic habits."[42]

Figure 7.3 Biccherna Cover, *Humiliati Monk as Treasurer of Commune of Siena*, 1324. Siena, Archivio di Stato. Photo: Archivio di Stato, Siena

In Florence, the Ognissanti church grew to become not only the largest Humiliati church and monastery in Tuscany, but also one of the largest and most important in the entire order.[43] By 1335, the Florentine Humiliati were supplying the chaplain and a small chapter to Santa Maria in Cigoli, near San Miniato al Tedesco, which housed a miracle-working image of the Virgin.[44] And by the mid-Trecento, the Humiliati in Ognissanti, while continuing to run the parish church of Santa Lucia, had expanded their jurisdiction to two institutions just north of Florence, the nun's church of Santa Marta in Montughi, and the nearby church of San Martino.[45]

Despite their initial record of success and expansion, problems in the Humiliati order as a whole became apparent early on in their history. For example, misbehavior in their double monasteries brought forth condemnations by a series of Popes, and resulted in ever more restrictive barriers being erected between the living quarters of monks and nuns, ultimately leading to the establishment of separate convents for female Humiliati.[46] The vigorous growth experienced by the Humiliati in the Duecento had stopped by the middle of the next century. While the order accounted for 389 houses in 1289, by 1344 this number had fallen to 261, as many smaller institutions merged with larger ones or disappeared entirely.[47]

Perhaps more significant for their distinctiveness as an order, by the mid-fourteenth century the Humiliati started to abandon their involvement in the textile industry, especially by moving away from manual labor. Humiliati brothers and sisters began to assume more typical religious lives, and in particular the friars began to imitate the Dominicans in a turn towards clericization and scholarship.[48] The order's disengagement from the textile industry during the course of the fourteenth century may have reflected the general downturn in Italian production of wool cloth.[49] Yet perhaps the change among the Humiliati towards a more conventional and scholarly mode of monastic life resulted from some embarrassment at the very success that helped them flourish at their peak. Another possible motive for abandoning manual labor was the fact that many Humiliati communities had become very rich. Gene Brucker has shown that the Ognissanti and its Humiliati brothers were among the wealthiest monasteries in Florence in the 1420s, and the wealth of other Humiliati churches can be demonstrated as well.[50] There has been some attempt to show that certain financial dealings of the order, such as the purchase of real estate, or the lending of money, may have reflected the charitable intentions of their rule. Maria Pia Alberzoni, for example, has examined some transactions in Milan, and has found a few cases where the Humiliati purchased buildings to relieve the inhabitants of debt, or similarly loaned money as a benevolent act.[51] Nevertheless, there is little doubt that the initial idea for the Humiliati to donate all profits from their labors to the poor quite quickly fell by the wayside. Indeed, the wealth of the order became legendary, as the eighteenth-century historian Giuseppe Richa, while confessing not to know much about the Humiliati, could still describe them as "industriosi, e ricchi"—industrious and rich.[52]

As in Florence, many Humiliati establishments had invested in real estate to secure a comfortable patrimony, and when members of the order did continue in business, it was as landlords and entrepreneurs rather than as workers. A few documents that touch on the Ognissanti church later in its history offer tantalizing glimpses into the continuing—if diminishing—commercial activities of the Humiliati. For example, the order owned fulling mills as late as the end of the fifteenth century, although they were increasingly selling this kind of equipment to private owners. The prominent humanist Giorgio Antonio Vespucci—a patron of artworks in the Ognissanti church—returned fulling mills to the Humiliati that he had previously bought from them when he entered the Dominican order in 1497.[53] And in about 1518, Michelangelo briefly negotiated with the Ognissanti to lease a structure to use as a workshop for his sculptural projects, probably one of their drying sheds which was no longer being used in cloth production.[54]

The arc of Humiliati history can be seen in part as a reflection of the larger tensions in later medieval society, as the growth of prosperity and of their commercial activities conflicted with the traditional church teachings that condemned wealth and its accumulation. The gradual changes in the order, including the shift away from manual labor, and a disengagement with the textile industry, may not have been a specific response to outside pressure or opinion; in the surviving documentary record, for example, the reasons for criticisms of the Humiliati were for such faults as unchaste behavior, and for failing to carry out monastic obligations, such as reciting the Divine Office.[55] Nevertheless, the early business success of the order might have seemed an uncomfortable manifestation of piety in an era that idolized the voluntary poverty of St Francis. And despite the affluence of many Humiliati houses, troubles within the order accelerated in the later Trecento. While other religious organizations faced similar crises in this period, the great mendicant orders were revitalized by Observant movements, which established reformed communities based on the ideals of the order's founders. There were no Observant Humiliati, however; their original ethos—simple communities of men and women, pursuing humble lives of work and prayer—was too much at odds with the developed state of the order, which had mostly abandoned modest labor.[56]

Moreover, the Humiliati had no charismatic founder whom members of the order could identify with or revere. This led the Humiliati to "appropriate" saints as their own—some prominent, like the Cistercian St Bernard, and others more obscure, such as Homobonus, the patron saint of Cremona. Bernard was already being promoted as the founder of the order by the fourteenth century, while the fifteenth century saw the development of the legend of Giovanni de Meda.[57] Their lack of a clearly defined identity was further demonstrated in 1436 when, under the jurisdiction of Pope Eugenius IV, the order rejected their cumbersome old rule and adopted the Benedictine rule.[58] By that time, the order was clearly gripped by an inexorable, if slow, decline. We will return to their final deterioration and suppression at the end of this essay.

If the accumulation of wealth by Humiliati monasteries was ultimately destructive to their initial way of life, it did allow them to attempt to construct and promote their identity through the commissioning of works of art. While no paintings or sculptures from the first century of the order's existence can be securely identified, by the early fourteenth century they were actively embellishing their churches with altarpieces, frescoes, and other works.[59] Perhaps the thirteenth-century Humiliati—successful, expanding, but still close to their initial "humble" roots—saw little need for elaborate artistic commissions to promote their ideas. But by the early Trecento they were compelled to vie with other orders, particularly the mendicants, for lay support, and for their own membership. By this time, works of art may have taken on a greater importance as a means of representing Humiliati ideals.

A number of works can be shown to have been commissioned by members of the order. In Florence, for example, an inscription on a triptych by Bernardo Daddi painted for Ognissanti in 1328 identifies the donor of the work as a Brother Nicholas, almost certainly a member of the order, and a century later Donatello was hired by the Florentine Humiliati to craft a reliquary bust for their newly acquired relic of Saint Rossore.[60] Although the patronage of art can also be found among the mendicants, even among the Franciscans who held to the idea of absolute poverty, the direct involvement of the Humiliati in the commissioning and funding of works may have led to a special desire for their images to function as the expression of Humiliati ideals.

But just as the changes in the order mirror larger tensions, so too the works of art made for Humiliati churches contain an essential contradiction, as their founding principles of charity and humility are often expressed in images that are conspicuously rich and lavish. Two examples illustrate the manifestation of these apparent inconsistencies. A glittering polyptych by Luca di Tommè and Niccolò di Ser Sozzo from 1362 (Figure 7.4), almost certainly made for the Humiliati church of San Tommaso in Siena, shows St Benedict as one of the saints adjoining the central panel of the seated Virgin and Child, whose garments and throne are extravagantly tooled and gilded. Benedict, dressed in the white habit of the Humiliati, holds a book displaying his rule opened to the beginning of Chapter VII—passages that extol the virtue of humility.[61] Similarly, a now-dismembered polyptych of the *Coronation of the Virgin* with saints, dating probably from 1363, and painted by Giovanni da Milano for the high altar of Ognissanti in Florence, shows St Gregory the Great among the saints venerating the central *Coronation* (Figure 7.5). As in the San Tommaso altarpiece, the surface of the painting is richly tooled with gold; also similar to the contemporary Sienese polyptych, St Gregory in the Ognissanti painting holds a book with a legible text, this time an excerpt from his *Moralia in Job* praising the virtue of charity.[62]

Again, such a paradox was not limited to the Humiliati; in the vaults over the tomb of St Francis in the lower church of San Francesco in Assisi, for example, the great exponent of poverty is shown transfigured in sparkling gold.[63] While

Figure 7.4 Luca di Tommè and Niccolò di Ser Sozzo, *Madonna and Child with Saints*, Polyptych, 1362. Siena, Pinacoteca Nazionale. Photo: Alinari/Art Resource, NY

Figure 7.5 Giovanni da Milano, *Coronation of the Virgin*, detail of St Gregory the Great, c. 1363. Florence, Uffizi. Photo: Soprintendenza Speciale per il Polo Museale Fiorentino, Gabinetto Fotografico

such contradictions did trouble certain medieval observers, what strikes many modern viewers as hypocritical was probably seen by most as a sincere depiction of divine glory, and an appropriate expenditure to celebrate the church and its importance.[64] The Franciscans, however, had an advantage in being able to manipulate the images of their sanctified founder, St Francis. For the Humiliati, it was necessary to resort to the depiction of surrogates, or "borrowed" saints, in their art. Even before the adoption of the Benedictine rule in the fifteenth century, there are several examples of Benedict shown prominently in Humiliati art, wearing the order's white habit as in the Sienese polyptych (Figure 7.4).[65] Similarly, portrayals of Church Fathers such as Gregory the Great became increasingly popular among the Humiliati, probably as they helped to project the new scholarly image of their membership.[66]

Two other examples reveal similar ideas. One of the first artists who can be documented as working in the Ognissanti church, the great painter Giotto, probably produced at least four significant works for the church—three panel paintings that survive, plus a frescoed chapel, since destroyed.[67] The most famous of the panel paintings, the large Virgin and Child altarpiece known as the *Ognissanti Madonna* (Figure 7.6), was probably made for the high altar of the church in around 1310.[68] Giotto was already a famous artist by the time he painted for the Humiliati, and he had a pattern of working for the richest patrons in Italy, including the wealthy Paduan, Enrico Scrovegni. It is likely that the wealthy Humiliati hired Giotto in part because of his reputation and fame. Yet the *Ognissanti Madonna* contains references to the founding virtues of the order.

The angels kneeling at the base of the painting wear the same grayish-white cloth of the Humiliati habit, and even the Virgin's white tunic under her blue mantle reflects the order's garb, as it visibly differs from her traditional red garment. Moreover, the order's eponymous virtue of humility would have been conveyed by the position of the angels. In an inversion of the traditional spiritual hierarchy, Giotto places four large angels below the other figures near the central throne. Located below the saints, their spiritual inferiors, the angels visualize exaltation through humility, a contradiction of the usual visual pattern in which a greater spiritual status is defined by a higher location in space. Indeed, most artists after Giotto, including many of his followers, continued to place their angels above the saints in the space flanking the throne. The subsequent resistance to Giotto's spatial inversion of angels and saints in the early Trecento, when many other aspects of the *Ognissanti Madonna* were imitated, suggests that this inversion was related to the commission for the Humiliati. Furthermore, within the pyramidal structure created by the white garments of Mary and those of the kneeling angels, the color worn by the lowest figures in the panel is repeated in the highest one. Giotto thereby inverts the traditional celestial hierarchy by uniting the Madonna, the highest figure, with the lowest angels, and conveys her exaltation through her humility. This understanding of humility is the same idea found in the text of the Benedictine rule, as shown in Luca di Tommè's

Figure 7.6 Giotto, *Ognissanti Madonna*, c. 1310. Florence, Uffizi.
Photo: Scala/Art Resource, NY

polyptych (Figure 7.4). The text, taken from the beginning of Chapter VII, reads: "For he who exalts himself will be humbled, and he who humbles himself will be exalted" (Luke 14:11). The kneeling angels of the *Ognissanti Madonna*, representing the humility of the order's brethren, also give thanks to Mary and the Christ Child, whose charity is reciprocated by the offering of flowers and other objects in the painting.[69]

A final example is from a fresco cycle painted in 1368 for the Humiliati church of San Michele in Paganico, which particularly emphasizes the virtue of charity.[70] Attributed to Biagio di Goro, the lower register on the south wall of the choir includes figures kneeling and offering gifts to St Michael as he weighs souls (Figure 7.7). The woman to the left of St Michael holds a spindle and presents a tunic made of white cloth, most likely the type manufactured by the Humiliati.[71] Clothed in red garments suggesting charity, her actions are described in the inscription on the scroll in front of her, stating that by means of the thread she has produced, she has been charitable to the poor.[72] The content of the Paganico frescoes hearkens back to the origins of the Humiliati order, when men and women worked humbly and demonstrated their charity by donating the fruits of their labors. Even by the 1360s, however, such manifestations were part of the order's distant, and even legendary, past, and increasingly irrelevant to their mature concerns.[73]

Works of art continued to be commissioned for the Ognissanti church well into the sixteenth century, but there is an emerging pattern of patronage beginning in the later fourteenth century that seems to differ from the earlier period. That is, as the Humiliati retreated from their founding impulses, along with their work activities, they also withdrew from their direct control of chapels and altars in the church.[74] These spaces were ceded to the more conventional control of private families, who also became largely responsible for the commissioning of art.[75] Thus although no family patronage in Ognissanti can be documented until the middle of the fourteenth century—quite unlike the usual model in mendicant churches—over the next century private families had built new chapels, or taken over old spaces in most of the church. By the later fifteenth century, an important local merchant family, the Vespucci, had established no fewer than three family chapels in Ognissanti.[76]

In the sixteenth century, as the Humiliati declined in numbers and influence throughout Italy, they were driven from their churches by more powerful orders, whose increasing numbers must have made the taking over of Humiliati establishments highly desirable. In 1561, with only six brothers still residing in the Ognissanti monastery in Florence, the ruling Medici were instrumental in having the Humiliati expelled in favor of Observant Franciscans; the remaining brethren were transferred to the smaller church of Santa Caterina.[77] Meanwhile, the vigorous young Archbishop of Milan and future saint, Carlo Borromeo, had also been appointed as the Cardinal-Protector of the Humiliati.[78] In that position, he was actively engaged in reforming what had become, by the 1560s, a notoriously corrupt order. Resisting these reforms, a cabal of Humiliati leaders

Figure 7.7 Attributed to Biagio di Goro, *Woman Offering Tunic to St Michael*, 1368. Paganico, Church of San Michele. Photo: By permission of the Ministero per i Beni e le attività culturali, Soprintendenza P.S.A.E. di Siena e Grosseto

recruited a disgruntled brother to assassinate the saintly Archbishop. The attempt on Borromeo's life (October 26, 1569) was unsuccessful, the conspiracy quickly uncovered, and the culprits executed. In 1571, the entire male branch of the Humiliati was suppressed.[79]

When the Observant Franciscans took control of Ognissanti in 1561, they began carrying out renovations to virtually all areas of the church. The transformation into a "Franciscan" church was no doubt accelerated by the disgrace and suppression of the Humiliati a decade later. From the later sixteenth century through the eighteenth century, the vast majority of the early decoration at Ognissanti was destroyed. Altars were rebuilt and rededicated, paintings were moved or discarded, and little of the earlier appearance of the church remained.[80] In its prime, however, the Ognissanti church, like other churches of the Humiliati order, was adorned with numerous works of art that promoted their founding ideals of charity and humility. The irony that these virtues appeared within costly images is a fitting reflection of the sometimes intractable contradictions of late medieval society, contradictions manifested as well in the larger history of the Humiliati order.

Notes

We are especially grateful to Don Gianantonio Borgonovo and Valerio Brambilla of the Biblioteca Ambrosiana for their assistance with obtaining illustrations from the Humiliati chronicle.

1 Lists appear in sixteenth-century missals of the Humiliati, as in a printed one from 1504: Girolamo Tiraboschi, *Vetera Humiliatorum Monumenta annotationibus, ac dissertationibus prodromis illustrata*, 3 volumes (Milan: J. Galeatius, 1766–68), 1: 193.

2 The legend appears in a chronicle from about 1420 written by a Humiliati brother, Giovanni di Brera; the text appears in Luigi Zanoni, *Gli Umiliati nei loro rapporti con l'eresia, l'industria della lana ed i comuni nei secoli XII e XIII*, Biblioteca di storia economica, 2nd series, vol. 2 (Milan: Hoepli, 1911; reprint Rome: Multigrafia, 1970), 336–44.

3 John Wickstrom, "The Humiliati: Liturgy and Identity," *Archivum Fratrum Praedicatorum* 62 (1992): 215.

4 With a few notable exceptions—especially the most comprehensive recent study, Frances Andrews, *The Early Humiliati* (Cambridge: Cambridge University Press, 1999)—historical writings on the Humiliati have been in Italian, and most of these have focused on their origins and early years. A classic source is Zanoni, *Gli Umiliati* (as cited in note 2). For a useful bibliography, see Annamaria Ambrosioni, "Umiliate/Umiliati," in *Dizionario degli istituti di perfezione* (Rome: Edizioni paoline, 1997), 9: 1506.

5 Among the few writings devoted to the Humiliati in Florence is the essay by Anna Benvenuti Papi, "Vangelo e tiratoi. Gli Umiliati ed il loro insediamento fiorentino,"

in *La "Madonna d'Ognissanti" di Giotto restaurata*, Gli Uffizi, Studi e Ricerche, 8 (Florence: Centro Di, 1992), 75–84. See also Franek Sznura, *L'espansione urbana di Firenze nel Dugento* (Florence: La Nuova Italia, 1975), 77–83; and Julia Miller and Laurie Taylor-Mitchell, "The *Ognissanti Madonna* and the Humiliati Order in Florence," in *The Cambridge Companion to Giotto*, ed. A. Derbes and M. Sandona (Cambridge: Cambridge University Press, 2004), 157–75.

6 We are currently working on a book about Humiliati art in Ognissanti and other Tuscan churches.

7 See Malcolm Lambert, *Medieval Heresy. Popular Movements from the Gregorian Reform to the Reformation*, 2nd edition (Oxford: Blackwell, 1992); and Gordon Leff, *Heresy in the Later Middle Ages: The Relation of Heterodoxy to Dissent c. 1250–c. 1450* (Manchester: Manchester University Press, 1967).

8 Andrews, *Early Humiliati*, 38–50.

9 The lay element was one of the most original aspects of the Humiliati. See Andrews, *Early Humiliati*, 80–98, and 249–50, where she assumed that the tripartite structure recognized the related but distinct units already existing within the Humiliati; this opinion has been challenged by Sally Mayall Brasher, *Women of the Humiliati: A Lay Religious Order in Medieval Civic Life* (New York: Routledge, 2003), 30–31, who suggested the structure was imposed upon the order.

10 The text of the rule is in Zanoni, *Gli Umiliati*, 352–70; for analysis, see Andrews, *Early Humiliati*, 109–20; and Daniela Castagnetti, "La regola del primo e secondo ordine dall'approvazione alla 'Regula Benedicti'," in *Sulle tracce degli Umiliati*, ed. M.P. Alberzoni, A. Ambrosioni, and A. Lucioni (Milan: Vita e Pensiero, 1997), 179–87.

11 The Humiliati Rule integrates manual labor with prayers, and the importance of manual labor is reinforced with Biblical passages in Chapter XVI of their rule, citing Paul's dictum "If you do not labor, you shall not eat" (Thessalonians 2, 3:8), as well as a passage from Psalm 128 praising the good of manual labor; see Zanoni, *Gli Umiliati*, 360. Indeed, the emphasis upon labor during the day, after vespers, and possibly after compline, has led to an estimate that both men and women in the order may have worked up to twelve hours a day in the summer; see Andrews, *Early Humiliati*, 115–16 and n. 91, citing various chapters of the Humiliati Rule; and Lorenzo Paolini, "Le Umiliate al lavoro: appunti fra storiografia e storia," *Bullettino dell'Istituto storico italiano per il Medio Evo e archivio muratoriano* 97 (1991): 262–3.

12 See especially Andrews, *Early Humiliati*, 109–27, 178–81 and Zanoni, *Gli Umiliati*, 92–104.

13 Andrews, *Early Humiliati*, 121. The setting aside of profits for charity was also practiced by Italian companies in the fourteenth and fifteenth centuries, with the reserved funds described as those given to "the Lord God," who represented the poor; see Raymond de Roover, *San Bernardino of Siena and Sant'Antonino of Florence*, Kress Library of Business and Economics Series, no. 19 (Cambridge: Harvard University Press, 1967), 15 and n. 60.

14 Andrews, *Early Humiliati*, 118–26. On the vow of poverty, see Tiraboschi, *Humiliatorum Monumenta*, 3: 113, 183; and Wickstrom, "Liturgy and Identity," 215.

15 Jacques de Vitry (c. 1160–1240), an Augustinian canon and bishop, praised the Humiliati (in a letter of 1216, as well as in his *Historia Occidentalis* of about 1220) for their anti-heretical activities in Milan: see J. Hinnebusch, *The Historia Occidentalis of Jacques de Vitry* (Fribourg: University Press, 1972), 144–6; and Brenda Bolton, "Sources for the Early History of the Humiliati," in *The Materials, Sources and Methods of Ecclesiastical History*, ed. Derek Baker (New York: Barnes and Noble Books, 1975), 129. The Ursulines from the late sixteenth century can be seen as a parallel to the Humiliati, especially in their use of lay people to combat heresy: see Kathleen Ashley, "Abigail Mathieu's Civic Charity: Social Reform and the Search for Personal Immortality," in this volume.

16 In a mid-thirteenth century sermon, the Dominican preacher Humbert of Romans specified that both men and women of the order worked in cloth: Paolini, "Le Umiliate al lavoro," 236–7. Documentation for work in the earliest years of the order, however, is scarce; see Andrews, *Early Humiliati*, 54.

17 The *Chronicon universale anonymi Laudunensis*, by an anonymous Praemonstratensian Canon of Laôn, goes up to the year 1219, and deals with the Humiliati in the period c. 1178–84: Walter L. Wakefield and Austin P. Evans, *Heresies of the High Middle Ages, Selected Sources Translated and Annotated* (New York: Columbia University Press, 1969), 158–9; and Andrews, *Early Humiliati*, 24. On *berettino* as grey or ashen-colored, undyed wool, see Paolini, "Le Umiliate al lavoro," 232.

18 The chronicle, originally written by Giovanni di Brera in 1419, survives in an illustrated, excerpted version from c. 1421 (Biblioteca Ambrosiana G 301 inf) and in two more extensive, seventeenth-century copies (Biblioteca Ambrosiana G 302 inf., fondo Trotti, 41). For the text, see Zanoni, *Gli Umiliati*, 336–44; also Carlo Castiglioni, "L'Ordine degli Umiliati in tre codici illustrati dell'Ambrosiana," *Memorie storiche della Diocesi di Milano* 7 (1960): 7–11; Marco Lunari, "Alla ricerca di un'identità. La cronaca di Giovanni di Brera," in *Un Monastero alle porte della città, Atti del convegno per i 650 anni dell'Abbazia di Viboldone* (Milan: Vita e Pensiero, 1999), 143–63. The church of S. Maria di Brera, where this author lived, was one of the oldest and most important Humiliati churches in Milan; it was partly demolished in 1808 and incorporated within the palace which bears its name and houses the famous Pinacoteca.

19 See Paolini, "Le Umiliate al lavoro," 256–9. On the unclear distinctions between the First and Second Orders, see also Andrews, *Early Humiliati*, 145–6; and Ambrosioni, "Umiliate/Umiliati," 1493–4. Giovanni di Brera's chronicle has several pages illustrating women of the order.

20 On their simple cloth, see Raoul Manselli, "Gli Umiliati, lavoratori di lana," in *Produzione, commercio e consumo dei panni di lana (nei secoli XII–XVIII)*, ed. Marco Spallanzani (Florence: L.S. Olschki, 1976), 233. On the evidence for dyeworks, see, for example, Maria Teresa Brolis, *Gli Umiliati a Bergamo nei secoli XIII e XIV* (Milan: Vita e Pensiero, 1991), 64; and Ambrosioni, "Umiliate/Umiliati," 1499.

21 This detachment from the cloth manufacturing process is reserved for the clerics; in Figure 7.1, men and women of the Second Order carry and stretch cloth. For medieval views on the virtues of merchant trade, especially in connection with charity, see

Juliann Vitullo and Diane Wolfthal, "Trading Values: Negotiating Masculinity in Late Medieval and Early Modern Europe," in this volume.

22 Andrews, *Early Humiliati*, 136–45, who discusses the use of the term "domus" in connection with the Humiliati; the word may not have always referred to a church or traditional monastery, but perhaps to more "ephemeral" or only quasi-monastic congregations.

23 For the list, see Tiraboschi, *Humiliatorum Monumenta*, 3: 264–85; see also Paolini, "Le Umiliate al lavoro," 249–50, for the estimate of 4,000 brothers and sisters, with perhaps double that number of tertiaries.

24 For the document, see Giovanni Lami, *Sanctae Ecclesiae Florentinae Monumenta* (Florence: Angelo Salutati, 1758), 2: 1035–6; and Benvenuti Papi, "Vangelo e tiratoi," 77–8.

25 Paolini, "Le Umiliate al lavoro," 251, and Tiraboschi, *Humiliatorum Monumenta*, 1: 162–6. For specialized studies, see, for example, Ilaria Francica, "Gli Umiliati a Bologna nel '200: Forme e significato di una *religio* attiva," *Atti e Memorie: Deputazione di Storia Patria per la Province di Romagna* 45 (1994): 280–81; and Caterina Bruschi, "Gli Umiliati a Parma (XIII–XIV secolo). Instaurazione e sviluppo di rapporti molteplici," *Rivista di Storia e Letteratura Religiosa* 36 (2000): 224–5.

26 The original charter was issued by Archbishop Filippo Fontana in 1250, and then reconfirmed the following year: Lami, *Florentinae Monumenta*, 2: 948–9; the text of the charter also appears in Giuseppe Richa, *Notizie istoriche delle chiese fiorentine* (Florence: P.G. Viviani, 1754–62), 4: 207, and is reprinted (with the original Latin and an Italian translation) in Alberto Busignani and Raffaello Bencini, *Le Chiese di Firenze: Quartiere di Santa Maria Novella* (Florence: Sansoni, 1979), 197–8. Santa Lucia was a small church adjacent to a hospital, and that association may have been favorable to the charitable aims of the Humiliati; it remained under Humiliati control until 1547: Busignani and Bencini, *Chiese di Firenze*, 197–202.

27 "… exercere non possint commode artem suam, videlicet lanificium, texere pannos, & vendere": Lami, *Florentinae Monumenta*, 2: 948–9.

28 On the processes of wool production, see Iris Origo, *The Merchant of Prato. Francesco di Marco Datini 1335–1410* (New York: Alfred A. Knopf, 1957), 35–46; and Walter Reininger, "The Florentine Textile Industry in the Middle Ages," *Ciba Review* 27 (1939): 961–3.

29 "Sicut Fratrem Humiliatorum S. Michaelis de Alexandria laudibus, & probata Religio, plantata nuper in Diocesi Florentina, grande satis, & placidum Deo & gentibus Civitatis Florentiae in Spiritualibus & temporalibus attulit incrementum per quod & Civitas ipsa floret uberius": Lami, *Florentinae Monumenta*, 2: 948.

30 See Origo, *Merchant of Prato*, xiv. The link between religion and commerce in Florence was also exemplified in its currency through the image of John the Baptist on the florin, and a book cover of the coiner's guild from the early fourteenth century which shows the Baptist with six florins flanking his halo; see Gene Brucker, *Florence, The Golden Age, 1138–1737* (Berkeley: University of California Press, 1998), 70–71.

31 While it appears that the Humiliati were either excluded or exempted from joining the guild in certain Tuscan cities such as Florence, Siena, and Pisa, it seems likely

that they did join the guild or were subject to its rules in other Italian cities, as is documented for Genoa, Padua, Parma, and Bologna. For this evidence, see Steven A. Epstein, *Wage Labor and Guilds in Medieval Europe* (Chapel Hill, NC: University of North Carolina Press, 1991), 97–8; Bruschi, "Gli Umiliati a Parma," 225–6; and Francica, "Gli Umiliati a Bologna," 283.

32 Robert Davidsohn, *Storia di Firenze*, trans. G.B. Klein from *Geschichte von Florenz*, 1896–1927 (Florence: Sansoni, 1956–68), 2: 501–2. See also Walter Paatz and Elisabeth Paatz, *Die Kirchen von Florenz* (Frankfurt: Vittorio Klostermann, 1952) 4: 407–8. The dedication to All Saints for the new church appears in the 1251 charter ("et Ecclesia, quam edificare intenditis ad honorem Sanctorum omnium sicut dicitis"): Lami, *Florentinae Monumenta*, 2: 949.

33 Sznura, *L'espansione urbana*, 78.

34 See Richa, *Notizie istoriche*, 4: 254–5; and Davidsohn, *Storia di Firenze*, 3: 336, 682, and 6: 146.

35 Benvenuti Papi, "Vangelo e tiratoi," 79–83. Fulling mills were introduced in Europe at the end of the tenth century, and were used in Florence by 1164: R.Van Uytven, "The Fulling Mill: Dynamic of the Revolution in Industrial Attitudes," *Acta Historiae Neerlandica* 5 (1971): 1–3.

36 See especially Sznura, *L'espansione urbana*, 79–82.

37 Richard C. Trexler, "Honor Among Thieves. The Trust Function of the Urban Clergy in the Florentine Republic," in *Essays Presented to Myron P. Gilmore*, ed. Sergio Bertelli and Gloria Ramakus (Florence: La Nuova Italia Editrice, 1978), 321–2, cites a friar from Ognissanti acting as *camerarius comunis florentini* as early as 1259.

38 Cities where the Humiliati served as treasurers included Alessandria, Bergamo, Brescia, Como, Cremona, Novara, Parma, and Pavia, while in Milan they seem to have held many governmental positions. See Andrews, *Early Humiliati*, 34, 210, 241–2; and Zanoni, *Gli Umiliati*, 225–33. See also Alessandro Tomei, ed., *Le Biccherne di Siena, Arte e Finanza all'alba dell'economia moderna* (Rome: Retablo, 2002); and William Bowsky, *The Finance of the Commune of Siena, 1287-1355* (Oxford: Clarendon Press, 1970), 7–14.

39 The cover is discussed in Tomei, *Le Biccherne di Siena*, 140–41. The gilding applied to the coinage has largely disappeared.

40 Trexler, "Honor Among Thieves," 328–30.

41 Lami, *Florentinae Monumenta*, 2: 1053. Similar exemptions applied in Siena: Tomei, *Le Biccherne di Siena*, 246.

42 "… gli uomini d'affari in abito monachale": Davidsohn, *Storia di Firenze*, 2: 502. Davidsohn's description echoes the illustration in Giovanni di Brera's chronicle depicting the Humiliati visiting cities in Lombardy, and opening the city gates with keys, designating their fiscal roles as treasurers. However, the text accompanying this illustration emphasizes the religious aspect of their service in relation to charity, as they were not compensated for it; see chronicle (Ambrosiana, G 301 inf), 12 verso.

43 The Humiliati also had churches in Pistoia, Pisa, and Siena, which established a further outpost in Paganico. In 1344, Ognissanti is listed as containing 41 brothers, larger than all but two other Humiliati monasteries: Tiraboschi, *Humiliatorum Monumenta*, 3: 271–84.

44 Paolo Morelli, "Per una storia delle istituzioni parrocchiali nel basso Medioevo: la prepositura di S. Maria e S. Michele di Cigoli e la pieve di S. Giovanni di Fabbrica," *Bollettino storico pisano* 51 (1982): 36–56.

45 See Luigi Santoni, *Raccolta di notizie storiche riguardanti le chiese dell'arcidiogesi di Firenze* (Florence: G. Mazzoni, 1847), 125–6; and Ferdinando Batazzi and Annamaria Giusti, *Ognissanti* (Rome: Fratelli Palombi, 1992), 7.

46 See, for example, letters from Popes John XXII (1327), Gregory XI (1373), and Boniface IX (1401): Tiraboschi, *Humiliatorum Monumenta*, 2: 378–80, 3: 28–9, 35–7. On reforms to their practices, see also Ibid., 3: 127–30.

47 Ibid., 3: 273–84; and Paolini, "Le Umiliate al lavoro," 249–50. The fourteenth century did, however, see some notable additions to the order, including S. Cristoforo ("Madonna dell'Orto") in Venice, and the venerable church of S. Cecilia in Trastevere in Rome.

48 The Humiliati had already adopted forms of worship from the Dominicans in the thirteenth century, and some of the earliest histories of the order were written by Dominicans: see Andrews, *Early Humiliati*, 8, and Wickstrom, "Liturgy and Identity."

49 Anthony Molho, "Masaccio's Florence in Perspective: Crisis and Discipline in a Medieval Society," in *The Cambridge Companion to Masaccio*, ed. D. Ahl (Cambridge: Cambridge University Press, 2002), 22–3; whereas Florence produced about 90,000 bolts of wool cloth in the 1330s, this was reduced to only about 20,000 by the 1380s, and to only 10,000 by the early fifteenth century.

50 Gene Brucker, "Monasteries, Friaries, and Nunneries in Quattrocento Florence," in *Christianity and the Renaissance: Image and Religious Imagination in the Quattrocento*, ed. T. Verdon and J. Henderson (Syracuse: Syracuse University Press, 1990), 45–51. Only the Badia within the city walls, and the ex-urban Certosa, were wealthier, and the Humiliati nun's church, Santa Marta, was the fourth richest convent. For the comparable wealth of S. Tommaso, the Humiliati church in Siena, see Patrizia Angelucci, "Gli Umiliati di Siena e la chiesa del borgo franco di Paganico," in *Chiesa e società dal secolo IV ai nostri giorni: studi storici in onore del p. Ilarino da Milano* (Rome: Herder, 1979), 267.

51 Maria Pia Alberzoni, "L'esperienza caritativa presso gli Umiliati: Il caso di Brera (secolo XIII)," in *La Caritá a Milano nei secoli XII–XV* (Milan: Jaca Book, 1989), 201–23. See also Brasher, *Women of the Humiliati*, 91–105, who stresses the charitable acts involved in the administration of hospitals, especially by Humiliati tertiaries.

52 Richa, *Notizie istoriche*, 4: 252. Regarding the obscurity of the order, he observed that "questi Frati, le quali o incognito, o poco sapute sono state fin ora" ("these brothers are currently either unknown, or little known.")

53 Ronald Lightbown, *Sandro Botticelli* (Berkeley: University of California Press, 1978), 1: 129–30. On fulling mills, see above, note 35.

54 Michelangelo ultimately found a studio closer to San Lorenzo; see William E. Wallace, *Michelangelo at San Lorenzo: The Genius as Entrepreneur* (Cambridge: Cambridge University Press, 1994), 66; and *The Letters of Michelangelo*, trans. E.H. Ramsden (Stanford: Stanford University Press, 1963) 1: 136–7, 278–9. Our thanks to Professor Wallace for bringing this letter to our attention.

55 See the letters cited in note 46 above; for a later condemnation, see Simona Schenone, "Frate Mario Pizzi e la decadenza degli Umiliati," in *Sulle tracce degli Umiliati*, ed. M.P. Alberzoni, A. Ambrosioni, and A. Lucioni (Milan: Vita e Pensiero, 1997), 67–100.

56 Marco Lunari, "Appunti per una storiografia sugli Umiliati tra Quattro e Cinquecento," in *Sulle tracce degli Umiliati*, ed. M.P. Alberzoni, A. Ambrosioni, and A. Lucioni (Milan: Vita e Pensiero, 1997), 53–4.

57 Zanoni, *Gli Umiliati*, 14–17.

58 Castagnetti, "La regola," 220.

59 Numerous works remain from the fourteenth century, including impressive fresco cycles in S. Pietro in Viboldone, near Milan, and S. Michele in Paganico.

60 The inscription reads: ANO DNI MCCCXXVIII FR. NICHOLAUS DE MAZINGHIS DE CAMPI ME FIERI FECIT PRO REMEDIO ANIME MATRIS ET FRATRUM BERNARDUS DE FLORENTIA ME PINXIT. See Luisa Marcucci, *Gallerie Nazionali di Firenze: I Dipinti Toscani del secolo XIV* (Rome: Istituto Poligrafico dello Stato, 1965), 27–8. For Donatello, see Julia Miller and Laurie Taylor-Mitchell, "Donatello's '*S. Rossore*,' the Battle of San Romano, and the Church of Ognissanti," *Burlington Magazine* 148 (2006): 685–8.

61 Sherwood A. Fehm, *Luca di Tommè: A Sienese Fourteenth-Century Painter* (Carbondale: Southern Illinois University Press, 1986), 18–20, 80–83.

62 Mina Gregori, "Giovanni da Milano: Storia di un polittico," *Paragone* 265 (1972): 3–35; and Daniela Parenti, ed., *Giovanni da Milano: Capolavori del gotico fra Lombardia e Toscana* (Florence: Giunti Editore, 2008), 220–31.

63 Illustrated in Elvio Lunghi, *The Basilica of St Francis in Assisi* (Florence: Scala, 1996), 108.

64 Although no contracts for Giotto's works at Ognissanti are known to survive, some contracts connect praise for the subject with the beauty of its depiction, as in the contract of 1285 for Duccio's *Rucellai Madonna*: "… the painting of a most beautiful picture to the honor of the blessed and glorious Virgin Mary"; see Jane Immler Satkowski, *Duccio di Buoninsegna*, ed. Hayden B.J. Maginnis (Athens: University of Georgia Press, 2000), 52. Dale Kent's cautionary remark regarding the imposition of modern social concepts of class on the past also seems applicable to understanding the large sums spent by religious orders on imagery rather than charity: "the modern class consciousness often assumed to exist in this period may well have been inhibited by universally held religious beliefs …"; see Dale Kent, *Cosimo de' Medici and the Florentine Renaissance: The Patron's Oeuvre* (New Haven: Yale University Press, 2000), xii.

65 In the Ognissanti church, for example, Benedict appears in Giotto's *Ognissanti Madonna*, in a fresco of the *Crucifixion* in the sacristy by Taddeo Gaddi of about 1350, and in Giovanni da Milano's Polyptych; in all he is dressed in the grayish-white of the Humiliati habit.

66 Best known are the frescoes of *St Augustine* by Botticelli, and *St Jerome* by Ghirlandaio, which were once on the choir screen of Ognissanti, flanking an opening that allowed a view of Giovanni da Milano's polyptych on the high altar.

67 In his *Commentarii* of about 1450, Lorenzo Ghiberti described the *Ognissanti Madonna* and mentioned a chapel, a large crucifix, and three other *tavole*, or panel paintings; see S.U. Baldassarri and A. Saiber, eds, *Images of Quattrocento Florence* (New Haven: Yale University Press, 2000), 190.

68 See Miller and Taylor-Mitchell, "The *Ognissanti Madonna*," 163–6.

69 Ibid., 171–2.

70 Gaudenz Freuler, *Biagio di Goro Ghezzi a Paganico. L'affresco nell'abside della Chiesa di San Michele* (Florence: Electa, 1986), 77–94.

71 Ibid., 89–92. Cordelia Warr demonstrated the close connection between manual labor, charity, and salvation in the frescoes at Paganico; see "Women, Weaving and Salvation: The Allegory of the Afterlife in San Michele, Paganico," in her book *Dressing for Heaven: Religious Clothing in Italy, 1215–1545* (Manchester: Manchester University Press, forthcoming). We are grateful to Professor Warr for making her paper available to us prior to publication.

72 "Del mio filato lamosina feci quaggiu al povaro che chiese in tua vecie" (translated by Warr as "From my spinning, I gave alms in this world to the poor man who asked in your place"); see Freuler, *Biagio di Goro*, 90. The connection of red with charity was made by Bernard, who had likened the Virgin to a red rose for her charity: "Maria autem rosa fuit … rubicunda per charitatem," quoted by Margrit Lisner, "Significati e iconografia del colore nella 'Madonna d'Ognissanti'," *La Madonna d'Ognissanti di Giotto* (Florence: Centro Di, 1992), 57 and n. 3. For additional associations of red with charity in texts and imagery of the thirteenth and fourteenth centuries, see Anne Derbes and Mark Sandona, *The Usurer's Heart: Giotto, Enrico Scrovegni, and the Arena Chapel in Padua* (University Park, PA: Pennsylvania State University Press, 2008), 74.

73 Humiliati tertiaries declined along with the rest of the order in the fourteenth century, and by the end of the Trecento they had substantially disappeared: Andrews, *Early Humiliati*, 11.

74 This pattern may apply throughout the order, but there are as yet no thorough studies of patronage in other churches to confirm whether this is the case.

75 The order transferred an altar on the choir screen to a private family in 1418, and similarly ceded a chapel to a lay donor in 1518; for the altar, which had a now-disputed painting by Giotto, see Richa, *Notizie istoriche*, 4: 258–9, and Miller and Taylor-Mitchell, "The *Ognissanti Madonna*," 165–6; for the chapel, see David Franklin, "Rosso, Leonardo Buonafé and the Francesca de Ripoi altar-piece," *Burlington Magazine* 129 (1987): 652–62.

76 Batazzi and Giusti, *Ognissanti*, 46–56.

77 Richa, *Notizie istoriche*, 4: 261.

78 Carlo (1538–84), the nephew of Pope Pius IV, was named Cardinal-Protector of not only the Humiliati (1560), but also the Franciscans, the Carmelites, and the Knights of Malta. He was appointed Archbishop of Milan in 1564: Armando Guidetti, *San Carlo Borromeo: La Vita nell'iconografia e nei documenti* (Milan: Rusconi Libri, 1984), 6–24.

79 On the assassination attempt, see Tiraboschi, *Humiliatorum Monumenta*, 1: 408–31; and Castiglioni, "L'Ordine degli Umiliati," 27–35. Only the male branch of

the order was suppressed, and separate congregations of Humiliati nuns continued until about 1810: Wickstrom, "Liturgy and Identity," 217.

80 The Franciscans initially found Ognissanti to be probably the ugliest church in Florence: "una Chiesa forse la più brutta di Firenze," cited in Richa, *Notizie istoriche*, 4: 291. On the transformations of the Franciscans, see also Paatz and Paatz, *Die Kirchen von Florenz*, 4: 411–27; and Gabriella di Cagno and Donatella Pegazzano, "San Salvatore in Ognissanti: gli altari del Cinquecento (1561–1582) e il loro arredo nel contesto della Riforma Cattolica," in *Altari e Committenza: Episodi nell'età della Controriforma*, ed. C. de Benedictis (Florence: Angelo Pontecorboli editore, 1996), 93–104.

Chapter 8

Trading Values: Negotiating Masculinity in Late Medieval and Early Modern Europe

Juliann Vitullo and Diane Wolfthal

With the rise of the monetary economy in the late thirteenth century, Europe underwent a radical transformation as the new symbolic system of money restructured every aspect of life, from urban space and religious practices to gender roles and the production of art and literature. Over the next 300 years Europeans struggled with complex ethical issues, which were rooted in the apparent contradiction between the Christian ideals of poverty and charity, on the one hand, and the pervasive role of money and the desire to accumulate wealth, on the other. Definitions of avarice, usury, charity, and poverty were fiercely debated in both text and image, revealing the tensions inherent in a culture that was both Christian and capitalist. This essay will explore late medieval and early modern texts and images that suggest that the rise of the monetary economy produced a new ideal of masculinity, that this ideal engendered anxiety concerning men's proper relationship to money, and that both women and children played a role in easing that anxiety. This essay rests on the assumption, well supported by recent research, that economic and theological ideas circulated throughout western Europe, spread by mendicant preachers, humanist writers, and international merchants, and that these ideas affected the values, art, and literature of the time.[1]

The Emergence of a New Masculine Ideal

Odd Inge Langholm has traced the development of economic theory by Aristotelian scholars who were active in northern Europe,[2] but theologians of the mendicant or poor orders, primarily Franciscans and Dominicans, were also among the first economic theorists of the new monetary economy, and among the first writers to create symbolic bridges between the culture of voluntary poverty and contemporary monetary practices.[3] From the thirteenth through the sixteenth centuries, religious and secular writers strove to distinguish merchants from usurers and to delineate the skills that allowed a merchant to earn a legitimate profit. Both Franciscan and Dominican theologians recycled the Aristotelian critique of money as sterile since it could not reproduce naturally like the land or livestock. They therefore condemned usurers who tried to make money multiply "against nature" and then hoarded their earnings rather than recirculating them in the Christian community. At the same time, however, thirteenth-century mendicant writers, such as Thomas Aquinas and Peter Olivi, also defined "fruitful" ways of using money that included meeting the needs of one's family, the poor, and the greater good or the "bonum commune." Although the marriage of St Francis to poverty remained a model for ecclesiastics, certain theologians realized that it was not tenable for most lay people, and thus developed ideas about how those involved in the monetary economy might adopt a "usus pauper" or "poor use" of money, which shared the same intention as the perfect poverty of the observant or spiritual Franciscans.[4] From this point of view, even merchants involved in everyday economic transactions could imitate in their own way the perfection of apostolic poverty. According to Dominicans like Thomas Aquinas or Franciscans like Peter Olivi, what matters is the civic utility of the merchants' labors, that is, if their use of money contributes to the prosperity of a fruitful Christian community or instead encourages sterile, selfish acts of usury and hoarding. These mendicant writers first enumerated the talents and resources necessary to be a successful merchant, such as the skill of measuring and pricing goods or the ability to provide a variety of products from different countries to one's own community, and then concluded that merchants should earn a profit in compensation for those acts of labor.[5]

Thomas Aquinas states that what matters is the merchant's intention for gaining a profit, whether he plans to use it for the good of his family or his community:

> … gain which is the end of trading, though not implying, by its nature, anything virtuous or necessary, does not, in itself, connote anything sinful or contrary to virtue: wherefore nothing prevents gain from being directed to some necessary or even virtuous end, and thus trading becomes lawful. Thus, for instance, a man may intend the moderate gain which he seeks to acquire by trading for the upkeep of his household, or for the assistance of the needy: or again, a man may take to trade for some public advantage, for instance, lest his country lack the necessaries of life, and seek gain, not as an end, but as payment for his labor.[6]

Following Aquinas and Olivi, fourteenth- and fifteenth-century popular mendicant preachers, such as Bernardino of Siena, translated the theological tradition for lay people by describing in the vernacular both fruitful and sterile forms of mercantile activities.[7] In one of his many vernacular sermons on merchants and business, San Bernardino begins by praising the "fruitful merchants": "There are many reasons that the Doctors teach that mercantile activity is of great necessity for human generation. And among other reasons, the first is that it is fruitful and useful for the common good."[8] In describing the "splendor" of fruitful mercantile activity, San Bernardino lists seven requirements for the merchant. These include performing his profession in order to provide the necessities for his family; giving alms for a hospital, or other pious work; being fair by selling his goods in the same fashion to all customers; and ensuring that his profession promotes the welfare of his own soul, of his neighbor, and of his community (105–6). San Bernardino also states that fruitful business is legitimate because it fulfills the real needs of communities; virtuous merchants travel from country to country providing different communities with the goods that they lack (99).

Merchants and humanists in fifteenth-century Florence, such as Giovanni Morelli and Leon Battista Alberti, adopted many of the same arguments. They focused on the importance of using money and household possessions (*masserizia*) wisely and of teaching their sons a profession rather than simply how to make money. They understood the importance of depicting themselves and their offspring as fruitful, industrious citizens whose labor and investments benefited the entire community, rather than as sterile, avaricious usurers who hoarded the wealth for themselves. In the family memoir, or *ricordi*, of the early fifteenth-century merchant Giovanni di Pagolo Morelli, the Florentine writer explains that he is recording the history of his *nazione*, or people, for posterity. In discussing the glory of his clan, Morelli stresses how hard most of his ancestors worked and how their family and the *comune* benefited from that labor. Morelli also explains that his father made money through the production and trade of wool and in investments as well as loans, yet everything he developed was due to his own *fatica* or labor. Besides his abilities as a merchant, Morelli also underlines his father's ability to produce and maintain a family:

> He knew how to wisely govern all his things, saving himself for all the noble and virtuous activities; and if God had wanted to loan him even ten more years of life, he would have had more wealth than 50,000 florins, and his family would have become large, since he had at least one child every year.[9]

In this quotation, Morelli clearly juxtaposes his father's economic and biological fertility; he produces both florins and children at an extraordinary rate. With the word *prestare*, or the loaning of time, Morelli suggests that God might not have realized what a good investment he had embodied in his father. He then explains that his father had done so well for himself that he was the first member of the family to become eligible to serve the state as an elected official. It was at the time of his "flowering [*fiorire*] in all great feats" that his father died (159). Morelli completes the ideal merchant's portrait by emphasizing his father's generosity: "Pagolo [Morelli's father] was of good character, loving and a great almsgiver; he never rejected the request of a poor man or a rich man and he was especially generous with money …"[10]

Later in his *ricordi* Morelli will offer clear advice about how to follow his father's example as a fruitful merchant. Morelli wants men to build reputations as good merchants rather than as usurers primarily for the wellbeing of their children; he claims that men feel free to cheat and trick others who have the reputation of being usurers and he advises merchants not to place that burden on their children (249). This recommendation appears in a long section in the book in which Morelli writes about the advice that children miss when they lose their father. Morelli views the death of a father not only as a loss to the child, but also to the whole community, who would have profited from a citizen who had been taught how to be a good merchant, a devoted member of the Guelph party, and a loyal Florentine.

Humanists like Matteo Palmieri in his *Vita civile*, Leon Battista Alberti in his *La famiglia*, and Poggio Bracciolini in his *De avaritia* address directly the social value of money and of merchants by suggesting, like earlier theologians, that they play an important role for families and the state as long as they remain fruitful and not sterile. Palmieri advises that money must be acquired virtuously and then used in a proper manner. He explains that money serves a specific purpose, which is to facilitate trade among unequal things, and to thus help meet the needs of all citizens.[11] In a similar way, Palmieri also approves of the merchant's labor as long as the profits are eventually used for real needs, and here he is referring above all to the needs of the city: "When [mercantile activity] is great and copious, diffused and conducted in many places, with abundance of a variety of things, which one then sells freely without avarice, certainly it merits praise …"[12] Here again the emphasis is on the fertility of mercantile activity that brings variety and abundance to the city. While Palmieri follows classical models and praises the ideal of the citizen farmer and agriculture as the most natural and useful art, he recognizes the importance of certain "mercenary" professions, such as the kind of "great" trade he describes above. Only large-scale, international commerce that provides the local community with goods that it lacks deserves praise. Like other fifteenth-century Italian writers, Palmieri tries to distinguish "copious" mercantile activity, which sustains families and cities, from lesser forms of trade.

In a similar fashion, Alberti's *La famiglia* also labels trade as a "mercenary" activity, yet explains its value for both the status of his family and of his city. He first makes clear that the merchant is receiving a profit for his labor: "For the commodity you receive the equivalent in money, and for your work you receive the profit."[13] He realizes that some people believe that mercantile activities "are never quite clean, never untainted by considerable fraud," but the position put forward in the text is that although trading is a mercenary activity, it can be noble and even necessary.[14]

Alberti's dialogue also suggests that wealth is "necessary to bring about and to preserve contentment in a family."[15] Later he adds to that argument by discussing the importance of wealth and trade for the city:

> Here everyone admits he [the merchant] is very useful to the republic and still more to his own family. Wealth, if it is used to help the needy, can gain a man esteem

> and praise. With wealth, if it is used to do great and noble things and to show a fine magnanimity and splendor, fame and dignity can be attained. In emergencies and time of need we see every day how useful is the wealth of private citizens to the country itself.[16]

The text goes on to praise the Alberti family for their role as honest merchants whose trading has not only increased the wealth of the city, but also strengthened its reputation:

> No man who ever played a role in our affairs—this is a fact of our history—has permitted any kind of dishonest dealing. In every contract our agents have acted with justice, with perfect simplicity, and with purest honesty. Thus have we gained our fame as great merchants, a fame we enjoy inside and outside Italy, in Spain, in the East, in Syria, in Greece and in all ports.[17]

Thus, Alberti's description of his family's mercantile activity meets all the criteria described first by Peter Olivi and later by San Bernardino for a "fruitful" merchant. Their profit derives from real labor, thus is a natural activity; they bring necessities for their republic from all over the world; and they use profits from their work to strengthen their family and the greater community, even to attend to the needs of the poor.

Poggio Bracciolini's dialogue on avarice, *De avaritia*, provides more oppositional attitudes toward money and mercantile activities, yet through the voice of one interlocutor presents the radical opinion that avarice is actually a virtue rather than a vice. Although Bracciolini creates a character who pushes notions of the utility of commerce to an extreme, many of the arguments have commonalities with Alberti's and Palmieri's texts. Questioning the Augustinian mandate that Christians should only possess what is necessary, Bracciolini's character expresses the viewpoint that if men were not avaricious and did not collect excess profits, it would be a great detriment to their cities:

> Consider what disorder would result for all things, if we were to want nothing more than what is sufficient; the practice of the most popular virtues, mercy and charity, would disappear; there would be no one generous or liberal: what, in fact, will he give to others who has nothing to give? In what way will he be able to show his munificence he who possesses only what he needs? The magnificence of the city will be lost; every beauty and decoration will be suppressed; churches, porticos, palaces will not be built; and the arts will all be neglected. It will cause, therefore, an upheaval of our life and of governments, if every person will be content with what he needs.[18]

This passage reiterates, albeit in an exaggerated form, the idea that money and profit not only offer real civic benefits but can also help men to embody Christian virtues.

The fifteenth-century text that perhaps best summarizes the arguments about the necessity and virtue of mercantile activity is *Il libro dell'arte di mercatura* by Benedetto Cotrugli. It is an advice manual for merchants, which also includes arguments from the humanist tradition. Cotrugli was a merchant from the Republic of Ragusa on the Dalmatian coast. He worked in several Italian cities including Genoa and Florence, and lived for many years in Naples where he wrote his manual. In the third book of his manual he states that "the utility, the comfort, and the health of the Republic proceed greatly from the merchant, not plebian or vulgar merchants, but glorious ones."[19] It is thanks to these "glorious" merchants that "sterile" homelands possess food and defenses:

> The usefulness, the tranquility, and the health of the Republic proceed greatly from the merchant, not plebian or vulgar merchants, but glorious ones ... It is in this respect that mercantile activities and operations provide sterile homelands with food and munitions. They accommodate various needs by having merchandise come from places where it is abundant to places where it is lacking, making these lands abundant with money, jewels, gold, silver and every sort of metal; [merchants] also make abundant the arts of different professions. Thus the cities and countries are able to cultivate the lands and raise herds, count earnings and incomes, help the poor survive with their business operations ... and by consequence they increase the public and communal treasury.[20]

Cotrugli deliberately contrasts the sterility of the homelands to the abundance and fertility that the merchants provide.

In the same chapter Cotrugli also describes the value of mercantile activities for a family and particularly for children. He begins by quoting a proverb: "It is a sad house that knows nothing of trade."[21] Cotrugli then contrasts a merchant to a "gentleman" who just lives off the revenue from his land and argues that the merchant is a better provider for his family because he can "cultivate" the earnings or "fruits" of his industry while the nobleman, "due to impotence," often has to sell off land in order to provide for the needs of his children, such as dowries for daughters.[22] Reversing a metaphor that had existed since classical times, Cotrugli associates money and merchants not with sterility but with the abundance and life traditionally conferred to agriculture. According to Cotrugli, money could and should grow in order to support the needs of cities and families, especially children. Like Palmieri and Alberti, Cotrugli distinguishes great merchants from other men engaged in commerce and suggests that they embody a new masculine ideal because their mercantile activities include real labor, and make the entire community more "fertile."

Around 1430 Donatello created an enormous allegorical statue of *dovizia*, or wealth, which was placed on top of a column in Florence's Mercato Vecchio, the city's open-air market. Although the statue is now lost, we know from early modern descriptions that the figure showed a standing female who balanced a basket of fruit on her head and carried a cornucopia with her left arm.[23] Surviving enameled terracotta statuettes of *dovizia* from the della Robbia workshop probably echoed the Donatello statue on a smaller scale for the domestic market. Several of the statuettes include male children and two display an inscription: "May honor and wealth [*divitie*] be in your home."[24] With figures in both the public marketplace and in the home, Florentines visualized the connection between commerce and fertility, and promoted the concept that merchants could be virtuous men who provide new life for the city.

The New Masculine Ideal in Northern European Art

The new masculine ideal of the merchant also developed in northern Europe. In this volume James M. Murray has outlined many criticisms that Flemish authors leveled at moneychangers, and concluded that the Low Countries were instrumental in defining the moral dimension of the new mercantile economy in Christian Europe.[25] Langholm's book on the economic thought of Aristotelian scholars in northern Europe makes clear that the ideas of German, French, and Flemish writers agree with those expressed in Italy, and confirms the many points of exchange between northern and Italian economic thinkers. In the fourteenth century the Frenchman Nicolas Oresme discussed the purposes served by money, and concluded that money "belongs to the community and was instituted for the common good."[26] Parisian writers affirmed that "human need" was the true measure of goods.[27] For that reason Oresme and others condemned usury and "speculative" moneychanging.[28] But like the Italians, Oresme also praised merchants' usefulness, citing, for example, their travel over long distances to obtain goods that would benefit the community. He also justified their earning a profit so long as it was spent on necessities for themselves or their families, or for the benefit of the community.[29] Henry of Ghent, who was active in Bruges, Tournai, and Paris, argued that merchants could be paid for "counting and custody of money," but any profit beyond this level is to be considered usury and prohibited. Merchants should not gain any profit beyond that needed for themselves and their family; nor should they hoard money, but rather donate any excess profit to the church and to charity.[30]

By the fifteenth and sixteenth centuries the new masculine ideal was portrayed in Netherlandish painting. The international trading centers of Bruges and Antwerp, in particular, shared many ideas about the new monetary economy with Florence and other Italian mercantile cities. A comparison of the portrait of Duke Charles of Burgundy, the future Holy Roman Emperor, which was painted by the Brussels artist Bernard van Orley in 1516, and the portrait of a merchant, painted by the Antwerp artist Jan Gossart around 14 years later, reveals the emergence of the new masculine ideal (Figures 8.1 and 8.2).[31] Whereas Charles' aristocratic hand is idle, the merchant is busy writing in a ledger. Whereas Charles' eyes are unfocused and his mouth slightly ajar, creating a dreamy expression, the merchant gazes intently at the viewer, and his lips and jaws are tightly clenched.

Figure 8.1 Bernard van Orley, *Charles V*, 1516. Paris, Louvre. Photo: Hervé Lewandowski. Photo Credit: Réunion des Musées Nationaux/Art Resource, NY

Figure 8.2 Jan Gossart, *A Merchant*, c. 1530. Washington, DC, National Gallery of Art. Alisa Mellon Bruce Fund. Image courtesy of the Board of Trustees

Whereas Charles sits in an unspecified space and his main attribute is his huge collar of the chivalric Order of the Golden Fleece, the merchant is portrayed at his place of business, surrounded by the tools of his trade. On the back wall are two batches of papers (labeled ledgers and letters), balls of twine, and a Hispano-Moresque dagger. Portrayed in the foreground are a sand shaker for blotting ink, a magnifying glass, scissors, an ink well, coins, a leather-bound book, a pair of scales with a Spanish coin in one pan, and a metal container for sealing wax, paper, and quill pens.

Both portraits make clear that their sitters are wealthy, and both encourage the viewer to enjoy the splendor of the objects portrayed, but only the merchant is shown as the new masculine ideal. Alert and busy, he can read and write, and he knows how to successfully engage the viewer, and presumably his customers. He has lots of business, and that business is international in nature, to judge by the Spanish coin and Hispano-Moresque dagger. In short, this portrait visualizes the qualities of the successful businessman. Presumably commissioned by a merchant, the painting idealizes his trade, and this is but one of a group of similar portraits produced at this time, including Maerten van Heemskerck's *Portrait of a Mintmaster and his Wife* of 1529 (Figure 8.14) and Hans Holbein's *Portrait of the Merchant Georg Gisze* of 1532 (Figure 8.3).[32]

In all three portraits only a few coins are discreetly shown, and in Gossart's painting they are placed next to the merchant's scale, to suggest that he is fair and honest. These men are merchants, but as John Hand justly observes: "In the sixteenth century … merchants who dealt in commodities or in wholesale trade were likely to be financiers and to deal with money in some manner as money-changers, issuers of bills of exchange, or lenders of money."[33] For this reason, such merchants were considered usurers, since they lent money for profit, either directly or through bills of exchange, and in this way reproduced money unnaturally, according to the Aristotelian view.[34] By including only a few coins, Gossart, Holbein, and Heemskerck downplay the merchants' involvement in practices that were viewed negatively, such as lending, exchanging, or investing money. But such financiers also needed to show that they earned their livelihoods through labor. Labor, the legacy of Adam's disobedience, was deemed the proper way to earn a living, and the many objects that surround the merchants serve to emphasize that they work for their money, rather than having their money reproduce unnaturally. In these ways, artists counteract the negative aspects of their sitters' trade.

Similarly, in the *Goldsmith's Shop*, painted in 1449 by the Bruges artist Petrus Christus, coins are visible on the counter in the foreground but off to the side (Figure 8.4).[35] Once again they lie near the merchant's scales, which serves to suggest his honesty. The goldsmith does not touch the money; in fact, he turns away from it to look towards the betrothed couple at his side. He weighs their wedding ring, a socially useful practice that contributes to the holy sacrament of matrimony. Furthermore, he is surrounded by objects that he has made with his hands, some of which are adorned with such christological motifs as the pelican

Figure 8.3 Hans Holbein, *Portrait of the Merchant Georg Gisze*, 1532. Berlin, Gemäldegalerie, Staatliche Museen zu Berlin. Photo Credit: © Bildarchiv Preussischer Kulturbesitz/Art Resource, NY

and its young. In this way Christus simultaneously draws attention away from the profit that the goldsmith makes, while emphasizing that he works for his livelihood and that this labor contributes to the common good.

Changes in the compositions of two paintings further suggest that care was taken to construct men's proper relationship to money. Jan van Eyck, who was active in Bruges, initially planned his *Rolin Madonna* to include a large purse hanging from the Chancellor's belt, as infrared reflectograms reveal. Jan later

Figure 8.4 Petrus Christus, *Goldsmith's Shop*, 1449. New York, The Metropolitan Museum of Art, Robert Lehman Collection, 1975 (1975.1.110). Image © The Metropolitan Museum of Art

eliminated the purse by painting over it. Craig Harbison, following Elisabeth Dhanens, justly asks whether "a sense of propriety … kept this purse out of the finished work."[36] Similarly, the portrait of a man weighing gold, painted by Adriaen Isenbrandt of Bruges, did not originally show him holding a scale for weighing money, according to the X-radiography and underdrawing. Perhaps this adjustment was made in the painted stage, because the patron, a merchant, wanted to emphasize his fairness and honesty.[37]

The Critique of Wealth

Writers concerned with the morality of the rise of the mercantile economic system made clear that the new masculine ideal was not only concerned with how merchants made their money, but also with how they spent it. It was understood that few financiers were going to adopt the Christian ideal of poverty, which is visualized in numerous Italian and Netherlandish paintings.[38] But the new masculine ideal promoted the idea of reinvesting wealth in the community. Using profits to benefit one's family, one's church, or the genuinely needy dovetailed with traditional criticisms of uncharitable hoarding and prodigality. The justification of certain limited roles for money, together with the development of a new masculine ideal that emphasized the merchant's charity and "fertility," were explored in both theological and more secular debates. But although many authors and artists described a new ideal of mercantile masculinity that included certain monetary transactions, others continued to depict money in strictly negative terms. If portraits of merchants portray their positive traits and make clear that they earned their money through proper financial practices, then other texts and images condemn men who use their money improperly by hoarding it or spending it on frivolous things.[39]

The constant fear that money itself is a danger to the soul, especially for merchants, is commonly expressed in didactic writings. For Palmieri money that is hoarded is a grave risk: "wealth is vain and of no value when we hide it away, dead, without using it for our comfort and welfare."[40] It is better to use money moderately rather than to hoard it and become "servi delle richeze," or slaves of wealth (173). Although Cotrugli praises "glorious" mercantile activity, he also warns fellow merchants that men "who have made gold and silver their god" and "direct and give themselves to collecting money" should be "chased away from the human consortium" for their avarice.[41] In his view, working with money still carried the risk of losing one's humanity and transforming one into an insatiable, brutish animal (219).

These criticisms are repeated in German prints, especially those in satirical books. Jost Amman's *The Money Fool*, an illustration in Hans Sachs' *Ständebuch*, or *Book of Trades*, published in Nuremberg in 1568, depicts a rich man grasping a large money bag close to his body and away from a pauper, whose poverty is suggested by his servile pose, patched bag, torn sleeve, and one bare leg (Figure 8.5).[42] The rich man snarls at the beggar, and the accompanying poem similarly portrays him as animal-like through the use of the word "friss," which means to eat like an animal. It also associates the rich man with usurious Jews through his long nose, and marks him as a fool not simply by the title of the page, "Der Geltnarr," or "Money Fool," but also by his fool's cap, identifiable by its donkey ears, which rests on his shoulders. The accompanying poem notes that the rich man is a fool because he thinks only of acquiring money through shameless and cunning practices, such as usury. He is criticized as close-fisted, even denying

Figure 8.5 Jost Amman, *The Money Fool* in Hans Sachs' *Ständebuch* (Nuremberg, 1568). Photo Credit: Brown University Library

himself good things. But the image focuses on his refusal to help the poor. By declining a just request for charity, the money fool demonstrates that his desire for wealth is stronger than his concern for the state of his soul. Images such as this continue an earlier tradition that associates men who have money with the

Figure 8.6 Albrecht Dürer (?), *Of Greed* in Sebastian Brant, *Ship of Fools*, 1494. Berlin, Staatsbibliothek zu Berlin—Preussischer Kulturbesitz

Christian sin of avarice. In particular, Judas, the epitome of greed, was termed a merchant.[43]

Sebastian Brant's *Ship of Fools*, dated 1494, includes an illustration conceived in a similar vein (Figure 8.6). A fool fingers a pile of coins on the table, while he puts his other hand in his purse. Another pile of money lies nearby, while a large chest behind him further suggests his wealth. Two men approach carrying a shepherd's crook. One, like the man at the table, wears a fool's cap. The other lifts his hat and says, "gnad her," that is, "Noble lord," a greeting. The woodcut is reproduced twice. It accompanies a poem titled "Of Greed" ("von gytikeit"), which criticizes frivolous spending, sharing one's wealth with foolish friends, but especially hoarding money.[44] But the woodcut focuses only on this last problem. This print also accompanies a poem titled

Figure 8.7 Hans Holbein, *The Rich Man*, from *Dance of Death*, 1523–26. London, British Museum. Photo: © British Museum/ Art Resource, NY

"Contempt of Poverty" ("von verachtung armut"), which categorizes usury as a crime akin to murder and treason, argues that poverty is a gift of God, and praises those who need "neither goods nor gain" ("Der nit wolt haben gut noch gelt").[45] The improper use of money is a recurrent theme in the text and images of this book, which repeatedly portray the rich man as greedy and uncharitable.

Hans Holbein's *Dance of Death*, which was designed in 1523–26, also includes an image of a man who improperly uses money (Figure 8.7).[46] Double metal bars on the window are meant to protect the locked money chests, sacks of cash, and piles of coins that fill the room. Here, too, the rich man is denigrated by giving him a stereotypical Jewish nose and foreign-looking headdress. And he is condemned for his greed. Although he seems unconcerned about the hourglass on the table, which indicates that his death is imminent, the rich man is outraged as death eagerly grabs a large fistful of coins to add to his bowl, which is already brimming with money.

Petrarch's popular Latin dialogue, *De remediis utrius que fortunae* (*Remedies for Fortune Fair and Foul*), completed in 1360, was well known in Italy and the north. He depicts a debate about wealth between the allegorical figures of Reason and Joy that demonstrates the kind of interior conflict that many theologians and moralists hoped would occur in the minds of men who worked with money. In Dialogue 53, Petrarch raises another issue that created an obstacle for obtaining the new masculine ideal of the successful and fruitful merchant. It suggests that money can become a fetish or idol that might control those who desire it. When Joy states: "I have enormous wealth," Reason replies:

> Beware lest you be the one who is possessed, and in fact, do not hold your riches but are held by them … Thus your greed and mind bent on profit makes servants out of you who should be masters. Everyone knows that the use of money is to purchase the necessities of life … Anything beyond these is burdensome—not so much wealth as shackles and chains.[47]

Here Petrarch combines the Augustinian notion that avarice is the selfish desire for more than one needs with the idea that love of money is a form of idolatry, which forces men to relinquish control of themselves.[48] Thomas Aquinas, for example, compares idolaters to the avaricious as they both adopt servile positions when they subjugate themselves to a false divinity.[49] This common analogy depicted love of money as a very dangerous sin because it juxtaposed men who sought to gain unnecessary profits with infidels. In Augsburg in 1532, Hans Weiditz illustrated the passage from Petrarch's dialogue by showing a rich man as a prisoner of the devil (Figure 8.8).[50] His neck and feet are chained as the devil offers him even more sacks of money along with another chain. The gesture of the rich man reveals his inner conflict: whether or not to follow his greedy urges. But his avarice has already enslaved his soul.

Figure 8.8 Hans Weiditz, *Devil Offering More Gold* in Francesco Petrarch, *Von der Artzney Bayder Glück/des Guten und Widerwertigen* (Augsburg, 1532). Sydney, Mitchell Library, State Library of NSW, MRB/Q851.18, opp. p. LXX

The Shower of Coins and Anxiety about the Proper Uses of Money

Figure 8.9 Robinet Testard, *Avarice*, from a Book of Hours, c. 1475, Poitiers, France. New York, The Pierpont Morgan Library, M. Ms. 1001, fol. 86. Photo Credit: The Pierpont Morgan Library, New York

Money, especially shiny metal coins, was seen as incredibly seductive. Petrarch, in his *De remediis utrius que fortunae*, linked the attractiveness of money to its dangers to the soul: "For the shape of money is noxious, its glitter poisonous and destructive. Like a golden serpent it delights with shiny scales, pleases the eye and strikes your soul."[51] These words carried great resonance in fifteenth- and sixteenth-century northern Europe, where the motif of a shower of glittering, golden coins became popular in art in a variety of contexts. Collectively this group of images demonstrates an ambivalence towards money. An illumination by Robinet Testard in a Book of Hours produced at Poitiers around 1475 shows a man seated on a ferocious, snarling beast, the wolf, which had long been associated with greed (Figure 8.9).[52] The man holds a banner identifying himself as Avarice, while a horned devil with golden wings, crouching on the floor beside him and identified by a scroll as Mammon, makes clear that greed is a mortal sin. A large purse hangs from the rider's belt, while he empties a second purse filled with shiny golden coins wastefully onto the ground.

Men become violent because of greed, in a second image of the shower of coins. Another print by Weiditz from the Augsburg version of *De remediis utrius que fortunae* shows a man being robbed (Figure 8.10).[53] Coins rain down from his purse and from a large sack over which men fight. The accompanying text characterizes money as meaningless. Later prints employ the motif of a cascade of coins to condemn man's prodigality. In Jan Wierix's *The Prodigals*, which illustrates a 1585 version of Dirck V. Coornhert's *Recht ghebruyck ende misbruyck van tijdelijke have* (*The Use and Abuse of Worldly Good*), a young man wastes his money on unsuitable company in a tavern.[54] He pours coins on a table, which are gathered up by a gambler, a musician, and two loose women. Behind him weeps an old woman, labeled Poverty, who serves to foreshadow the prodigal's future. Pushed to the sidelines, no one notices her.[55] Another print from the same volume shows a fool emptying his purse full of coins for the benefit of Venus and Bacchus, that is, women and wine.[56]

Figure 8.10 Hans Weiditz, *Man Being Robbed* in Francesco Petrarch, *Von der Artzney Bayder Glück/des Guten und Widerwertigen* (Augsburg, 1532). Sydney, Mitchell Library, State Library of NSW, MRB/Q851.18, opp. p. XVIII

But if some images associate the shower of coins with avarice, violence, and prodigality, others employ it as a positive motif. Boccaccio's *Decameron* relates the story of a rich but greedy merchant named Ermino de' Grimaldi who asks a gentleman to suggest the subject for a painting that could adorn his magnificent house. The gentleman replies "Paint courtesy here" ("Fateci dipignere la Cortesia"), by which he means nobility in the sense of such virtues as generosity or largesse, which are expected of a man of the court ("la corte").[57] A French version of the *Decameron*, translated by Laurent de Premierfait, was illuminated for the Duke of Burgundy, John the Fearless, in 1411–13.[58] Folio 27v shows at the left the rich man conversing with the gentleman, on the right, who holds a rolled parchment scroll in his hand. He displays the image, which represents generosity as a crowned woman who raises a golden beaker in her right hand and empties a sack full of coins with her left hand. A miniature once attributed to Jean Pichore, which was painted in the first quarter of the sixteenth century for Louise de Savoie, Duchess of Angoulême, depicts Generosity riding a rooster and holding a platter, while spilling coins from her purse (Figure 8.11). The virtue of generosity is once again associated with the shower of coins and opposed to the sin that it conquers, avarice, who here rides a monkey.[59]

Figure 8.11 French, *Generosity Against Avarice*, from *Rondeaux des Vertus*, created for Louise de Savoie, sixteenth century. Ecouen, Musée National de la Renaissance, E. Cl. 22718b. Giraudon/The Bridgeman Art Library

These images and their accompanying texts make clear that the merchant had to toe a fine line. Money was viewed both positively and negatively, depending on how it was earned and how it was spent. This must have caused merchants a considerable amount of anxiety. Several late fifteenth- and early sixteenth-century illuminations from the so-called Ghent–Bruges school of manuscripts confirm this. Their four-sided border portrays one or two men tossing coins from on high, while figures below scramble to collect them. This composition appears in varied contexts: surrounding St Roch, St Mark in his Study, or Mary on the Crescent Moon, or facing the Adoration of the Magi (Figure 8.12).[60] Other examples show the same general composition, but

Figure 8.12 The Hastings Hours, “Memorial of the Three Kings” and “Shower of Coins.” London, British Library, Add Ms. 54782, fols 42v–43r. © British Library Board

Memoria de tribus regibus
Ab oriente ve
nerunt ma
gi in bethle
em adorare
dominum.
et apertis
thezauris suis preciosa mu
nera obtulerunt aurum si
cut regi magno thus sicut
deo mirram sepulture
Reges tharsis
et in munera offerent.
Reges arrabium et sabba do
na adducent. Oremus
Deus qui tres magos

with the coins transformed into jewels, flowers, or manna. Anja Grebe justly cautions that the meaning of this marginal composition varies with context, and is, in fact, not always clearly related to the central text or miniature.[61]

The earliest example appears in the Hastings Hours, dated around 1480, where it is set before a cathedral, surrounds the text of a Memorial for the Magi, and faces a full-page miniature of the Adoration of the Magi (Figure 8.12). Several interpretations of this scene have been proposed. Some scholars have suggested that the text and the two illuminations are all linked by the theme of donation.[62] Just as the Magi present the Christ child with golden gifts, so men distribute golden coins in the border decoration. But what sort of donation is this? The border scene is generally interpreted as a representation of munificence, because a border in a later manuscript in Brussels, which shows a similar composition, is labeled "largesse," that is, the distribution of coins by a ruler on the occasion of a special entry, festival, or other exceptional event.[63] But the miniature in the Hastings Hours is not labeled largesse, and related compositions appear in a wide range of contexts, not all of which refer to munificence. Janet Backhouse, following Derek Turner, suggests a third theory: that the spark for this composition came from the original owner of the manuscript, William Lord Hastings, Master of the Royal Mint.[64]

Since the image of coins was commissioned by a mintmaster, does it articulate a positive interpretation of money? Pamela Tudor-Gray justly notes that the men at the top are "openhanded to the point of recklessness." Similarly, the figures below scramble to collect the coins in an undignified manner.[65] Two men greedily snatch up the money on their hands and knees, the figure at the far right is portly, the man at the far left stands in an unsteady pose as if tipsy, and the sole woman raises her skirt in an unseemly manner.[66] Furthermore, the image forms a striking contrast to the Adoration on the facing folio. The Madonna of Humility sits on a cloth spread on the straw-strewn ground, and she wears a simple blue gown and plain white veil. This contrasts with the fashionable dress of the figures who collect the coins. Moreover the quiet, peaceful devotion of the Adoration scene differs radically from the lively worldly activity on the facing folio. Finally, by confining the distribution of coins to the margins, the artist clearly differentiates it from the holy sphere of the central miniatures. Although this border makes clear the seductiveness of money, it also suggests its negative aspects, even in a manuscript commissioned by a mintmaster.

Only a handful of manuscripts show the shower of coins, and of these two patrons are known.[67] Besides Hastings, the other known patron is Cardinal Albrecht van Brandenburg, whose Book of Hours, dated 1522–23, includes 14 references to another troublesome monetary issue, the sale of indulgences.[68] The images and texts that we have discussed thus far collectively reflect and reinforce an anxiety about the proper uses of money, as early modern society questioned whether money had become a seductive fetish, and whether merchants were selling their souls for a golden, glittering shower of coins.

Merchants and Fertility

One way in which early modern European culture dealt with the increasing importance of mercantile activity in the lives of powerful men who represented a new masculine ideal was to emphasize their role as husbands and fathers. Thus both women and children played a critical function in easing the anxiety that this new ideal generated. The new mercantile model could apply equally well to women, some of whom could read and write. Whereas the primary economic responsibility of women in Italy was to preserve the possessions that their men acquired,[69] French language manuals and archival documents make clear that Flemish women were not confined to the private sphere, but rather were active in the marketplace, in such trades as agriculture, manufacturing, and exchange.[70] James M. Murray observes that since men with power wanted to avoid the stigma that was associated with the position of moneychanger, "women as managers and owners of exchanges and other businesses were an almost common sight in Bruges."[71] Yet they are rarely shown alone in conjunction with money.[72] But since the ill-gotten wealth of merchants was linked to unnatural reproduction and sterility, one way to counteract this association was to insert women as motifs of piety or fertility. Anne Derbes and Mark Sandona have shown how Giotto's frescoes in the Arena Chapel, which were painted around 1305 for the usurer Enrico Scrovegni, portray "(female) fecundity as [the antithesis and] antidote to (male) usury," and link "the redemptive power of Mary's womb" to "the sterility of ill-gotten gains."[73] Likewise Margaret Carroll has shown that the *Arnolfini Portrait* includes a bed, fruit, and the "swelling figure" of Arnolfini's wife in order to counteract the association between merchants and sterile money.[74]

Similarly, in images of merchants who are shown counting or fingering money, their wives are sometimes included to show that the family is virtuous and devout. The presence of pious or fertile women served to counteract any negative associations that are linked to their husbands' trade. The frame of the *Moneychanger and his Wife*, painted by the Antwerp artist Quentin Massys in 1514, is reported to have originally been inscribed with a quote from Leviticus: "Let the balance be just and the weights equal" (Figure 8.13).[75] Scholars generally agree that the work portrays the moneychanger in a positive light. Unlike the satirical paintings of Massys, this couple is handsome. Furthermore, Massys envisions the moneychanger as capable of righteous conduct, since he carefully weighs the coins lying before him. If any doubts about his profession were to arise in the viewer's mind, they would be quashed by the image of his wife, who is shown looking up momentarily from her devotions to see what her husband is doing. Her book is clearly a holy one, since it is adorned with images of the Madonna and Child and the Lamb of God. Behind the couple, shelves display a crystal vase, crystal beads, and a piece of fruit, which in earlier paintings would have had sacred connotations. But now these are mixed with scraps of paper, a pen, and account books, that is, signs of the earthly

Figure 8.13 Quentin Massys, *The Moneychanger and his Wife*, 1514. Paris, Louvre, inv. 1444. Photo: Gérard Blot. Photo Credit: © Réunion des Musées Nationaux/Art Resource, NY

world of the merchant. Here the active life of commerce and the contemplative life of prayer are intermingled and gendered.

A similar example is the *Portrait of a Mintmaster and his Wife*, painted in 1529 by the Dutch artist Maerten van Heemskerck, in which the husband holds open an account book with his left hand while fingering coins in his right hand (Figure 8.14).[76] Additional coins lie on the table before him. Objects of his trade complete the picture: an inkwell, pen, knife (perhaps for sharpening the pen), sand shaker, sealing wax, a seal, and a ball of yarn. His wife, on the accompanying panel, sits before a prominently displayed spinning wheel, holding thread in her left hand as she spins, an act often associated with the virtue of hard work.[77] Her virtue serves to counterbalance any negative associations raised by the coins in her

Figure 8.14 Maerten van Heemskerck, *Portrait of a Mintmaster and his Wife*, 1529. Amsterdam, Rijksmuseum

Figure 8.15 Joos van Cleve, *Portrait of a Mercantile Couple*, c. 1530. Enschede, Collection Rijksmuseum Twenthe. Photography: R. Klein Gotink

husband's hands, and her actions, like the objects that surround her husband, serve to emphasize that their money was gained through labor rather than through the unnatural reproduction of money.

A portrait diptych, painted by the Antwerp artist Joos van Cleve in 1530, also sharply differentiates the gender roles of a mercantile couple while intermingling religion and money (Figure 8.15).[78] The husband wears a pin of the Virgin and Child on his hat, the wife one of St Sebastian on her bodice, and both wear crosses.[79] But just below his cross, the counter is filled with signs of trade. The husband fingers a silver coin, and other coins lie nearby, as does an illegible hand-written note and a quill pen, which rests against the frame. By contrast, his wife holds a cluster of grapes, and grape leaves lie on the sill before her, a visual counterpart to her husband's money. Jan Baptist Bedaux observes that this may well refer to her fertility, since Psalm 128 reads: "The wife shall be as a fruitful vine."[80] It is possible that the grapes allude to their hopes for future children, but Eddy de Jongh has proposed an opposing theory, that the grapes refer to the "second virginity" that is granted to married couples whose love remains pure.[81] Van Cleve may also have employed the fruit to counteract the negative view of money as sterile by balancing the husband's barren coins with the wife's fertile grapes.[82] Furthermore, as Ingvar Bergström has suggested, the portrait of the wife would have recalled images of the pure and pious Virgin with grapes, such as those by Massys and van Cleve.[83]

Similar strategies appear in German portraits. As early as 1501 a double portrait of a mintmaster and his wife, painted by an artist from Nuremberg, shows a bust-length likeness of a well-dressed man wearing a fur hat, rings, and necklace, who turns to the right.[84] His wife, also shown in bust length and well dressed, turns to the left. Whereas the mintmaster holds the iron used to stamp coins, apparently a sign of his position, his wife displays a carnation. The sterility of the man and his metal coins are in this way contrasted with the fertility and fruitfulness of the woman and her flower.

Artists in Italy had earlier adopted similar strategies to counteract the stigma of merchants' association with money and avarice. Some chose to reinforce men's "fertility" by emphasizing their role as community fathers who accepted their nurturing responsibility with children. A fresco, dated 1386, which was originally displayed on the external wall of a confraternity's residence, shows the captains or leaders of Florence's Compagnia di Santa Maria della Misericordia connecting homeless children with natural or adoptive mothers in the loggia of their own headquarters (Figure 8.16). The captains of the confraternity included merchants; for instance, Cosimo dei Medici served as a captain in 1425.[85] In addition, there is archival evidence that the confraternity did run a hospice for abandoned children, and one of the principal painters of the fresco, Ambrogio di Baldese, was paid by the Misericordia to maintain it.[86] Performing and advertising their charitable acts on a loggia clearly shows that members of the confraternity wanted others to be aware of the service that they were offering the community, particularly women and children.[87]

Figure 8.16 N. di Pietro Gerini and A. Di Baldese, *Consignment of the Abandoned Children*, c. 1386. Florence, Museo del Bigallo. Image courtesy of the Museo del Bigallo

In a series of late fifteenth-century frescoes from the workshop of Domenico Ghirlandaio, members of the Buonomini di San Martino, a fifteenth-century confraternity dedicated to helping the *poveri vergognosi*, or shame-faced poor, are actively involved in performing the seven acts of mercy: feeding the hungry, giving drink to the thirsty, clothing the poor, nursing the sick, providing lodging for pilgrims, visiting prisoners, and burying the dead. As they perform these traditional acts of charity, they are wearing the traditional garments of Florentine citizens.[88] In one fresco, men behind a *banco*, or counter, distribute clothes to the poor, including a boy, even though such counters were often used for transactions with money, including exchanging currencies (Figure 8.17). In another fresco, Buonomini bring food and drink—a chicken and a flask of wine—as well as supplies such as swaddling bandages to a mother who has just given birth to the baby who lies next to her in bed (Figure 8.18).

The connection between merchants and the nurturing of children is also evident in Domenico Ghirlandaio's *Adoration of the Magi*, which was commissioned for the high altar of the church of Florence's foundling hospital in 1485 (Figure 8.19). The hospital was founded with the bequest of a famous merchant, Francesco Datini, and supervised by the Silk Guild whose patron saint, John the Evangelist, kneels on the right and presents one of the two innocents.[89] Together with the three Magi, a large entourage of elaborately dressed men in fine costumes, which might include portraits of merchants belonging to the Silk Guild, present gifts to the Christ child.[90] Several of the men in the painting display shimmering silk garments decorated with golden thread; silk was the luxury product that was quickly becoming the most important commodity in the fifteenth-century Florentine economy.[91] At the same time Ghirlandaio elevates other forms of work: he depicts himself and the hospital's prior in the crowd to the left of the Christ child, and bricklayers directly behind the holy family.[92] Like the gifts of the Magi, the hospital's construction is depicted as an offering to Christ and his community. In contrast, in the left background the Massacre of the Innocents is shown. The message is clear: that the members of the Silk Guild are fruitful merchants whose profits contribute to the common good. Rather than hoarding their earnings from the selling of luxury goods, they reinvest them into the community, and in particular use their money to protect orphaned and abandoned children. Both of these were considered essential qualities of a fruitful merchant rather than a sterile usurer. In the farthest background of this painting appear a city and an active port with ships. This altarpiece, then, participates in the debate about the nature of commerce by suggesting that merchants can be good Christians who not only help to make their cities thrive but also protect the poorest and most vulnerable members of their community.

The texts and images that we have discussed collectively demonstrate the rich and complex web of ideas surrounding the new mercantile ideal of masculinity that developed with the rise of the monetary economy. Whereas some depict the new traits demanded of the successful merchant or explore the proper uses of

Figure 8.17 Domenico Ghirlandaio (School of), *Clothing the Naked*, from the *Works of Mercy*, c. 1478–79. Florence, S. Martino dei Buonomini. Credit: Scala/Art Resource, NY

Figure 8.18 Domenico Ghirlandaio (School of), *Visiting the Sick*, from the *Works of Mercy*, c. 1478–79. Florence, S. Martino dei Buonomini. Photo Credit: Scala/Art Resource, NY

Figure 8.19 Domenico Ghirlandaio, *Adoration of the Magi*, 1485. Florence, Ospedale degli Innocenti. Photo Credit: Scala/Art Resource, NY

the money that they earned, others continue to warn against hoarding money or spending it on frivolous things. The ambivalence towards money is explored in images of the shower of coins, which could denote either generosity or avarice. Besides idealizing the positive personal characteristics in portraits of individual merchants, other texts and images emphasize the fruitfulness of a merchant's labor and how his trade benefits his family and his community, an important part of the new ideal of masculinity. Furthermore, they often assign women and children the role of assuaging the anxieties that this new ideal produced. This new model of masculinity also brought into question the boundary between the domestic and the public, and between feminine and masculine social spaces, creating yet another source of anxiety, as men stressed the importance of skills such as reading and measuring, which women could also clearly master, and at the same time, sought to portray themselves with qualities that were traditionally associated with women.

Notes

1 We would like to thank Anne Derbes, Alison Kettering, and James Murray for their careful reading of an earlier version of this essay and for their many helpful and generous suggestions. See, among others, Paula Nuttall, *From Flanders to Florence: The Impact of Netherlandish Painting, 1400–1500* (New Haven and London: Yale University Press, 2004); and Ingrid Alexander-Skipnes, ed., *Cultural Exchange between the Low Countries and Italy (1400–1600)* (Turnhout: Brepols, 2007) for cultural exchange between Italy and the Netherlands. For the interrelationship between art, economics, and morality, see Margaret Carroll, "'In the Name of God and Profit': Jan van Eyck's *Arnolfini Portrait*," *Representations* 44 (Fall 1993): 96–132; Anne Derbes and Mark Sandona, "Barren Metal and the Fruitful Womb: The Program of Giotto's Arena Chapel in Padua," *Art Bulletin* 80 (1998): 274–91; Anne Derbes and Marc Sandona, *The Usurer's Heart: Giotto, Enrico Scrovegni, and the Arena Chapel in Padua* (University Park, PA: Pennsylvania State University Press, 2008); Diane Wolfthal, "Florentine Bankers and Flemish Friars: New Light on the Patronage of the Portinari Altarpiece," in *Cultural Exchange between the Netherlands and Italy*, ed. Ingrid Alexander-Skipnes (Turnhout: Brepols, 2007), 1–21. For an analysis of how the monetary economy affected ethics, see Jacques Le Goff, *Your Money or Your Life: Economy and Religion in the Middle Ages*, trans. Patricia Ranum (New York: Zone Books, 1988); and Joel Kaye, *Economy and Nature in the Fourteenth Century: Money, Market Exchange, and the Emergence of Scientific Thought* (Cambridge: Cambridge University Press, 1998). For examples of the influence of merchants on literature, see Vittore Branca, ed., *Merchant Writers of the Italian Renaissance*, trans. Murtha Baca (New York: Marsilio, 1999).

2 Odd Inge Langholm, *Wealth and Money in the Aristotelian Tradition: A Study in Scholastic Economic Sources* (Bergen: Universitetsforlagen, 1983).

3 Giacomo Todeschini, "La riflessione etica sulle attività economiche," in *Economie urbane ed etica economica nell'Italia medievale*, ed. R. Greci, G. Pinto, and G. Todeschini (Rome: Laterza, 2005), 153–228, especially 175–6. Todeschini labels the mendicants "the most active economists of the thirteenth and fourteenth centuries." Also see Giacomo Todeschini, *Ricchezza francescana: dalla povertà volontaria alla società di mercato* (Bologna: Il Mulino, 2004).

4 Todeschini, *Ricchezza francescana*, 122.

5 Todeschini, "La riflessione," 205–6.

6 Ibid., 203–4; Thomas Aquinas, *Summa Theologiae*, II, II q. 77, a. 4, 1, <http://www.corpusthomisticum.org>. "Lucrum tamen, quod est negotiationis finis, etsi in sui

ratione non importet aliquid honestum vel necessarium, nihil tamen importat in sui ratione vitiosum vel virtuti contrarium. Unde nihil prohibet lucrum ordinari ad aliquem finem necessarium, vel etiam honestum. Et sic negotiatio licita reddetur. Sicut cum aliquis lucrum moderatum, quod negotiando quaerit, ordinat ad domus suae sustentationem, vel etiam ad subveniendum indigentibus, vel etiam cum aliquis negotiationi intendit propter publicam utilitatem, ne scilicet res necessariae ad vitam patriae desint, et lucrum expetit non quasi finem, sed quasi stipendium laboris."

7 Ibid., 215.

8 Bernardino da Siena, *Le prediche volgari*, ed. Ciro Cannarozzi (Pistoia: Alberto Pacinotti, 1934), vol. I, 98. "E molte ragioni s'assegnano pe' dottori che è di grande necessità all'umana generazione la mercatanzia. E, fra l'altre ragioni, la prima si è che l'è fruttuosa e utile per la per la comune utilità."

9 Giovanni di Pagolo Morelli, *Ricordi*, ed. Vittore Branca (Florence: Le Monnier, 1956), 157. "Seppesi bene e saviamente governare in tutte le sue cose, ritraendosi a tutte cose nobili e vertudiose; e se a Dio fusse piaciuto prestagli pure dieci anni più di vita, e veniva grande di ricchezza di più di cinquantamila fiorini, e veniva grande di famiglia, però che egli aveva ogni anno il meno un figliuolo."

10 Ibid., 159. "Fu Pagolo di buona condizione, molto amorevole e gran limosiniere; mai disdisse né a povero né a ricco nulla di che e' fusse richiesto, e spezialmente di danari molto ne fu largo …"

11 Matteo Palmieri, *Vita civile*, ed. Gino Belloni (Florence: Sansoni, 1982), 175.

12 Ibid., 187. "Quando [la mercatantìa] fusse grande et copiosa, mandante et conducente di molti luoghi, con abbondanza di varie cose, le quali poi sanza avaritia liberalmente venda, certo merita loda …"

13 Leon Battista Alberti, *I libri della famiglia*, ed. Ruggiero Romano and Alberto Tenenti (Turin: Einaudi, 1980), 171. "… per la roba rimane a te commutato el danaio; per la fatica ricevi il soprapagato."

14 Leon Battista Alberti, *The Family in Renaissance Florence*, trans. Renée Neu Watkins (Long Grove, IL: Waveland Press, 2004), 142; Alberti, *I libri*, 171. "Né pare ad alcuni questi essercizii, come gli chiameremo, pecuniarii mai stieno netti …"

15 Alberti, *The Family*, 141; Alberti, *I libri*, 170. "[Le ricchezze] … dicemmo essere necessarie a rendere e mantenere felice una famiglia."

16 Ibid., 171. "… e quale per tutti si confessa alle republice essere molto e alle famiglie ultilissimo. Sono atte le ricchezze ad acquistare amistà a lodo, servendo a chi ha bisogno. Puossi colle ricchezze conseguire fama e autorità adoperandole in cose amplissime e nobilissime con molta larghezza e magnificenza. E sono negli ultimi casi e bisogni alla patria le ricchezze de' privati cittadini, come tutto el dí si truova, molto utilissime."

17 Alberti, *The Family*, 143; Alberti, *I libri*, 172. "Imperoché mai ne' traffichi nostri di noi si trovò chi ammettesse bruttezza alcuna. Sempre in ogni contratto volsono i nostri osservare somma simplicità, somma verità, e in questo modo siamo in Italia e fuor d'Italia, in Ispagna, in Ponente, in Soria, in Grecia, e a tutti e porti conosciuti grandissimi mercatanti."

18 Poggio Bracciolini, *De avaritia*, ed. Giuseppe Germano (Livorno: Belforte, 1994), 77. "Vide quanta rerum omnium sequatur confusio, si nihil habere velimus praeterquam

quod sit nobis satis: tolletur usus gratissimarum populo virtutum, misericordiae videlicet et caritatis; nullus erit neque beneficus neque liberalis: quid enim dabit alteri cui nihil ad dandum superest? Quomodo munificum se praestare poterit qui[d] tantum possidet quantum sibi soli sufficiat? Auferetur magnificentia civitatum, tolletur cultus atque ornatus omnis, nulla aedificabuntur templa, nullae porticus, nulla palatia, artes cessabunt omnes; perturbatio denique vitae nostrae et rerum publicarum sequetur, si quilibet eo quod sibi satis erit acquiescet."

19 Benedetto Cotrugli Raguseo, *Il libro dell'arte di mercatura*, ed. Ugo Tucci (Venice: Arsenale, 1990), 206. "La utilità, il commodo et salute della repubblica procede grandissimamente dalo mercante, non da mercanti plebei et vulgari, ma da gloriosi …"

20 Ibid., 206–7. "La utilità, il commodo et salute della repubblica procede grandissimamente dalo mercante, non da mercanti plebei et vulgari, ma da gloriosi … Et questo rispecto delle facciende et exercitationi mercantili mediante le quali si munisceno le patrie sterili de victo et de munitione. Acomodanxi etiamdio diverse cose facciendo venire de luoghi onde habunda ne luoghi dove mancano le mercie, fanno etiamdio abundare di pecunie, gioie, oro, argento et ogni sorta di metallo, fanno habundare arti di diversi mestieri, inde le ciptà et patrie, fanno cultivare le terre, habundare li armenti, valere l'intrate et rendite, fanno campare li poveri mediante li loro exercitii … et per consequens acrescono l'erario publico et commune."

21 Ibid., 207. "Trista la casa che non sente di mercantia."

22 Ibid., 207. "Et come lo mercante megliora di conditione alli figli et alle figlie nello aparentare, così il massaro et gentile homo *per inpotentia* bisogna che 'l dia in piggior grado sempre disgradando a vilissime conditioni, et il mercante per contrario" (our emphasis).

23 We would like to thank Anne Derbes for making us aware of Donatello's lost statue; Sarah Blake Wilk, "Donatello's *Dovizia* as an Image of Florentine Political Propaganda," *Artibus et Historiae* 7, no. 14 (1986): 9–28, especially 11.

24 "Gloria et divitie in domo tua." For information about the relationship of Donatello's statue to the statuettes and an analysis of how these figures depict wealth, see David G. Wilkins, "Donatello's Lost *Dovizia* for the Mercato Vecchio: Wealth and Charity as Florentine Civic Virtues," *Art Bulletin* 65, no. 3 (September 1983): 401–23.

25 See James M. Murray, "The Devil's Evangelists? Moneychangers in Flemish Urban Society," Chapter 3, this volume.

26 Langholm, *Wealth and Money*, 12.

27 Ibid., 28.

28 Kevin B. Bales, "Nicole Oresme and Medieval Social Science: The Fourteenth Century Debunker of Astrology Wrote an Early Monetary Treatise," *American Journal of Economics and Sociology* 42 (1983): 101–11, 106.

29 Langholm, *Wealth and Money*, 54

30 Ibid., 53; Peter Coffey, "Henry of Ghent," *The Catholic Encyclopedia* VII (New York: Robert Appleton Company, 1910), August 9, 2008 <http://www.newadvent.org/cathen/07235b.htm>.

31 For the portrait by Gossart, see John Oliver Hand and Martha Wolf, *Early Netherlandish Painting* (Washington: National Gallery of Art, 1986), 103–7. For van

Orley's painting, see Edouard Michel, *Musée National du Louvre. Catalogue raisonné des peintures du moyen-âge, de la renaissance et des temps modernes. Peintures flamandes du XVe et du XVIe siècles* (Paris: Musées nationaux, 1953), 233–4.

32 Although some scholars had earlier identified Gossart's merchant as a tax collector, Hand justly is cautious about this identification. See Hand and Wolf, *Early Netherlandish Painting*, 104.

33 Hand and Wolf, *Early Netherlandish Painting*, 104.

34 Derbes and Sandona, "Barren Metal and the Fruitful Womb," 277.

35 For this painting, see Maryan W. Ainsworth and Keith Christiansen, eds, *From Van Eyck to Bruegel: Early Netherlandish Painting in the Metropoltian Museum of Art* (New York: Metropolitan Museum of Art, 1998), 150–53; and Diane Wolfthal, "Picturing Same-Sex Love: Images by Petrus Christus and the Housebook Master," in *Troubled Vision: Gender, Sexuality and Sight in Medieval Text and Image*, ed. Robert Mills and Emma Barker (Hampshire: Palgrave Macmillan, 2004), 17–46.

36 Craig Harbison, *Jan van Eyck: The Play of Realism* (London: Reaktion Books, 1991), 109; and Elisabeth Dhanens, *Hubert and Jan van Eyck* (New York: Alpine Fine Arts Collection, 1980), 279 (photograph on 276).

37 Ainsworth and Christiansen, *From Van Eyck to Bruegel*, 194. I would like to thank Maryan Ainsworth of the Metropolitan Museum of Art for generously discussing this painting with me and sharing with me its X-ray.

38 See, for Sassetta's *St Francis Marrying Poverty* and *St Francis Renouncing his Heritage*, John Pope-Hennessy, *Sassetta* (London, Chatto and Windus, 1939), Pls. XX and XVIII; and for van Orley's *St Anthony Abbot Distributing his Goods*, and his *St Roche Distributing his Goods*, c. 1515–25, Jos Koldeweij, *Geloof en Geluk: Sieraad en Devotie in Middeleeuws Vlaanderen* (Bruges: Gruuthuse, 2006), 64, 80.

39 Illustrated books could cost as much as painted portraits, so their viewers did not necessarily come from a different income bracket. For example, the cost of an unbound and uncolored copy of the *Nuremberg Chronicle* sold for 2 gulden, the same price paid by Albrecht Dürer for a portrait of a king. I would like to thank Jeffrey Chipps Smith for this information. See Adrian Wilson, *The Making of the Nuremberg Chronicle* (Amsterdam: Nico Israel, 1976), 237; Albrecht Dürer, *Albrecht Dürer: Sketchbook of His Journey to the Netherlands (1520–21)*, ed. Philip Troutman (New York and Washington: Praeger), 46.

40 Palmieri, *Vita civile*, 173. "Vane et di niuno valore sono le richeze che, morte, si nascondono sanza usarle per commodità et bene di nostro vivere."

41 Cotrugli, *Il libro*, 218. "Però che sono alcuni che hanno facto lo dio loro oro et argento … solo in congregare pecunia si sono rivolti et det dati. Quaesti tali sono per la loro avaritia da essere cacciati dallo humano consortio …"

42 For this, see Jost Amman and Hans Sachs, *The Book of Trades [Ständebuch]*, intro. Benjamin A. Rifkin (New York: Dover, 1973), 119.

43 See especially Janet Robson, "*Speculum imperfectionis:* The Image of Judas in Late Medieval Italy," (PhD diss., The Courtauld Institute, 2001); and Derbes and Sandona, *The Usurer's Heart*. For the original German, see Amman and Sachs, *The Book of Trades*, 119.

44 See Sebastian Brant, *The Ship of Fools*, trans. Edwin Zeydel (New York: Dover, 1962), 66–7. It is interesting to note the poem's mercantile language: "Some day accounting he must make" ("Und dar umb rechnung geben müß" and "They'd not redeem him for a sou" ("Sie lößten inn kum mit eym pfundt").

45 Ibid., 271–5.

46 For Holbein's *Dance of Death*, see Linda C. Hults, *The Print in the Western World: An Introductory History* (Madison: University of Wisconsin Press, 1996), 113–14. The prints were cut by Hans Lützelburger, designed in 1523–26, and published in 1538.

47 Francesco Petrarch, *Petrarch's Remedies for Fortune Fair and Foul*, ed. Conrad H. Rawski (Bloomington and Indianapolis: Indiana University Press, 1991), I, 164–5. Petrarch, *Liborum Francisci Petrarche impressorum annotation* (Venice: Simonem de Luere, 1501), n.p (Dialogue 53): "Sparse si fuerint decrescent: servate non te divitem sed occupatum: non dominu facient sed custode … Vide ne potius habeare: hoc est ne non divitie tue sint sed tu illarum: negille serviant sed tu ipsis … Usus quidem pecunie notus est: ut nature necessaria comparentur … quicquid excesserit grave est … nec la corporis ornamenta: sed impedimenta animi et sollicitudinum atq; formidinum acervi."

48 For St Augustine's definition of avarice, see St Augustine, *The Literal Meaning of Genesis*, trans. John Hammond Taylor (New York: Newman Press, 1982) vol. II, 146. For a discussion of the theological tradition that compared love of money to idolatry, see Richard Newhauser, *The Early History of Greed: The Sin of Avarice in Early Medieval Thought and Literature* (New York: Cambridge University Press, 2006), 77–9; and Carla Casagrande and Silvana Vecchio, *I setti vizi capitali: storia dei peccati nel medioevo* (Turin: Einaudi, 2000), 103–8.

49 Thomas Aquinas, *Summa Theologiae*, II, II, 118, a. 5, 4, <http://www.corpusthomisticum.org>. "Ad quartum dicendum quod avaritia comparatur idololatriae per quandam similitudinem quam habet ad ipsam, quia sicut idololatra subiicit se creaturae exteriori, ita etiam et avarus. Non tamen eodem modo, sed idololatra quidem subiicit se creaturae exteriori ut exhibeat ei cultum divinum; avarus autem subiicit se creaturae exteriori immoderate ipsam concupiscendo ad usum, non ad cultum. Et ideo non oportet quod avaritia habeat tantam gravitatem quantam habet idololatria."

50 See Walther Scheidig, *Die Holzschnitte des Petrarca-Meisters* (Berlin: Senschelverlag, 1955), 104; Franciscus Petrarcha, Francesco Petrarch, *Von der Artzney Bayder Glück/ des Guten und Widerwertigen* (Hamburg: Friedrich Wittig, 1984), I, 49v; Petrarch, *De remediis utrius que fortunae*, ed. Rudolf Schottländer (Munich: W. Fink, 1975).

51 Petrarch, *Petrarch's Remedies*, III, 48. Petrarch, *Liborum Francisci Petrarche* (Dialogue 13): "Noxia enim pecunie forma est: venenosus fulgor ac pestifer: Itaqz velut serpens squamis aureis: mulcendo oculos: aiam ferit." We would like to thank Erik Drigsdahl and Roger Wieck for their generous help with this section of the chapter.

52 For this illumination (Morgan Ms. 1001, fol. 91r), which illustrates Psalm 51 (Vulg. 50), see William M. Voelkle, "Morgan Manuscript M. 1001: The Seven Deadly Sins and the Seven Evil Ones," in *Monsters and Demons in the Ancient and Medieval Worlds: Papers Presented in Honor of Edith Porada*, ed. Anne E. Farkas, Prudence

O. Harper, and Evelyn B. Harrison (Mainz: Philipp von Zabern, 1987), 101–14, 105; and Suzanne Blöcker, *Studien zur Ikonographie der Sieben Todsünden in der Niederländischen und Deutschen Malerei und Graphik von 1450–1560* (Münster: Lit, 1993), 294. For the association of the wolf and greed, see also Cesare Ripa, *Baroque and Rococo Pictorial Imagery*, ed. Edward A. Maser (New York: Dover, 1971), 115.

53 Scheidig, *Die Holzschnitte des Petrarca-Meisters*, 207; Petrarch, *Von der Artzney Bayder*, II, 17v.

54 For these illustrations, see Nanette Salomon, *Shifting Priorities: Gender and Genre in Seventeenth-Century Dutch Painting* (Stanford: Stanford University Press, 2004), 47.

55 This woman is labeled *Egestas*.

56 Salomon, *Shifting Priorities*, 47.

57 Day 1, novella 8. Giovanni Boccaccio, *Decameron*, ed. Vittore Branca (Turin: Einaudi, 1984), 110–12, 112.

58 Vatican City, Biblioteca Apostolica Vaticana, Pal. Lat. 1989. See Eberhard König, *Boccaccio Decameron* (Stuttgart: Belser, 1989), 57–8.

59 Encouen, Musée national de la Renaissance, E. Cl. 22718b. The poem is attributed to André de la Vigne. See A. Boinet, "Choix de miniatures détachées conservées au Musée de Cluny à Paris," *Bulletin de la Société française de reproduction de manuscrits à peintures* 6 (1922), 5–30, especially 20. For Pichore, see Caroline Zöhl, *Jean Pichore Buchmaler, Graphiker und Verleger in Paris um 1500* (Turnhout: Brepols, 2004).

60 Those showing the motif of the shower of coins include the Hasting Hours; the Book of Hours of Cardinal Albrecht of Brandenburg, for which see below; a border surrounding St Mark in his Study, in the Brooklyn Museum, inv. no. II. 503, for which see Frauke Steenbock, "Largesse—Münzen, Blüten, und Mannaregen. Eine Motivstudie," in *Festschrift für Peter Bloch*, ed. Hartmut Krohm and Christian Theuerkauff (Mainz am Rhein: Philipp von Zabern, 1990), 135–42, 137, figure 4; and an illumination surrounding Mary on the Crescent Moon in the Croy-Arenberg Hours, for which see Anne Margreet W. As-Vijvers, "More than Marginal Meaning? The Interpretation of Ghent–Bruges Border Decoration," *Oud Holland* 116 (2003): 3–33, 6, figure 4. See ibid., 7 and note 17 for possible additional examples. For an illumination that includes pearls and jewelry as well as coins, see Anja Grebe, "The Art of the Edge: Frames and Page-Design in Manuscripts of the Ghent–Bruges School," in *The Metamorphosis of Marginal Images*, ed. Nurith Kenaan-Kedar and Asher Ovadiah (Tel Aviv: Tel Aviv University, 2001), 93–102, 95, figure 2.

61 Grebe, "The Art of the Edge."

62 Ibid., 95 and 100, note 9 is ambivalent concerning this theory. James H. Marrow, "Simon Bening in 1521: A Group of Dated Miniatures," in *Liber Amicorum Herman Liebaers*, ed. Frans Vanwijngaerden (Brussels: Crédit Communal de Belgique, 1984), 537–59, 549.

63 For Brussels, Bibl. Roy. Albert Ier, Ms. IV 280, fol. 205r, see Grebe, "The Art of the Edge," 95, figure 2. Those supporting the theme of largesse include Derek H. Turner, *The Hastings Hours* (London: Thames and Hudson, 1983), 116, 132; Thomas Kren,

ed., *Renaissance Painting in Manuscripts: Treasures from the British Library* (New York: Hudson Hills Press, 1983), 22; Marrow, "Simon Bening," 549; Steenbock, "Largesse," 135 and 140; Grebe, "The Art of the Edge," 95.

64 Turner, *The Hastings Hours*, 116; Janet Backhouse, *The Hastings Hours* (London: British Library, 1996), 49. This theory is doubted by Grebe, "The Art of the Edge," 100, note 9. Hastings' extensive contacts with the Burgundian Netherlands, mostly diplomatic, might have led to his commissioning of an artist from Ghent, who moved in court circles, the Master of the First Prayer Book of Maximilian, who is sometimes identified with Alexander Bening.

65 Pamela Tudor-Gray, "The Hours of Edward V and William Lord Hastings: British Library Manuscript Additional 54782," in *England in the Fifteenth Century. Proceedings of the 1986 Harlaxton Symposium,* ed. Daniel Williams (Woodbridge: The Boydell Press, 1987), 351–69, 365.

66 See images of Danaë for the sexual connotations of this pose, as, for example, in Madlyn Millner Kahr, "Danaë: Virtuous, Voluptuous, Venal Woman," *Art Bulletin* LX (1978): 43–55.

67 See note 60.

68 Christopher De Hamel, *The Hours of Albrecht of Brandenburg, Illuminated Manuscript by Simon Bening*, Sotheby's London, June 19, 2001, 27, 58. The manuscript is dated 1522–23 (vol. II, fol. 63v).

69 Evelyn Welch, *Shopping in the Renaissance: Consumer Culture in Italy 1400–1600* (New Haven: Yale University Press, 2005), 221–2.

70 Peter Stabel, "Women at the Market: Gender and Retail in the Towns of Late Medieval Flanders,"*Secretum Scriptorum: Liber Alumnorum Walter Prevenier* (Louvain: Garant, 1999), 259–76.

71 James M. Murray, "Family, Marriage and Moneychanging in Medieval Bruges," *Journal of Medieval History* 14 (1988): 115–25; see also his essay in this volume.

72 Elizabeth A. Honig, *Painting and the Market in Early Modern Antwerp* (New Haven: Yale University Press, 1998), discusses images of women buying and selling in the marketplace, but they are never shown touching money. Prostitutes, however, are shown taking money.

73 Derbes and Sandona, "Barren Metal and the Fruitful Womb," 274, 287.

74 Carroll, "'In the Name of God and Profit'," 96–132, especially 107.

75 Larry Silver, *The Paintings of Quinten Massys* (Montclair: Allanheld and Schram, 1984), 210. See also 136–8, 211; and Martha Howell, "The Properties of Marriage in Late Medieval Europe: Commercial Wealth and the Creation of Modern Marriage," in *Love, Marriage and Family Ties in the Later Middle Ages*, ed. Isabel Davis, Miriam Müller and Sarah Rees Jones (Turnhout: Brepols, 2003), 17–61. For this painting, see also James M. Murray's article in this volume.

76 This couple was traditionally identified as Gerritsz Bicker, the mintmaster of Amsterdam, and his wife, Anna Codde. See Rainald Grosshans, *Maerten van Heemskerck: die Gemälde* (Berlin: Bottcher, 1980), 91–3.

77 Grosshans, *Heemskerck*, 92.

78 This couple was formerly identified as Anthonis van Hilten, a tax collector and financial administrator, and Agniete van den Rijne, his wife. See Koldeweij, *Geloof*

en Geluk, 59. For the problem with this identification, see John Oliver Hand, *Joos van Cleve* (New Haven and London: Yale University Press, 2004), 64, 67, 130.

79 Koldeweij, *Geloof en Geluk*, 58–9.

80 Jan Baptist Bedaux, "Fruit Symbolism in Netherlandish Portraiture of the Sixteenth and Seventeenth Centuries," *Simiolus* 17 (1987): 150–68, especially 158–9, 162–4.

81 Hand, *Joos van Cleve*, 31; Eddy de Jongh, "Grape Symbolism in Paintings of the 16th and 17th Centuries," *Simiolus* 7 (1974): 166–87, 187.

82 For grapes as a reference to Agniete's fertility, see Bedaux, "Fruit Symbolism," 162.

83 Ingvar Bergström, "Disguised Symbolism in 'Madonna' Pictures and Still Life," *Burlington Magazine* 97 (October 1955): 342–9, 349. For an example by Massys, see figure 28 in de Jongh, "Grape Symbolism," 166–87.

84 Alfred Schädler, *Die Frankische Galerie: Zweigmuseum des Bayerischen Nationalmuseums* (Munich: Deutscher Kunstverlag, 1987), 61, cat. nos. 69–70. For the profession of mintmaster, see Ludwig Veit, *Das Liebe Geld: Zei Jahrtausende Geld- und Münzgeschichte* (Munich: Prestel, 1969). I would like to thank Matthias Weniger for generously sending me bibliography on these paintings.

85 John Henderson, *Piety and Charity in Late Medieval Florence* (Oxford: Clarendon Press, 1994), 407.

86 William R. Levin, *The 'Allegory of Mercy' at the Misericorida in Florence* (Dallas: University Press of America, 2004), 67; William R. Levin, "Advertising Charity in the Trecento: The Public Decorations of the Misericordia in Florence," *Studies in Iconography* 17 (1996), 215–309; William R. Levin, "'Lost Children', a Working Mother, and the Progress of an Artist at the Florentine Misericordia in the Trecento," *Publications of the Medieval Association of the Midwest* 6 (1999): 34–84.

87 Henderson, *Piety and Charity*, 345; Levin, "Advertising Charity," 221–33.

88 Jean K. Cadogan, *Domenico Ghirlandaio* (New Haven: Yale University Press, 2000), 210.

89 Richard A. Goldthwaite, "La fondazione e il consenso della città," in *Gli Innocenti e Firenze nei secoli*, ed. Lucia Sandri (Florence: Istituto degli Innocenti, 2005), 15–20, 20; Cadogan, *Domenico Ghirlandaio*, 261.

90 Attilio Piccini, "The Innocenti: Art and History," in *Spedale degli Innocenti*, ed. Francesco Papafava (Florence: Beccocci/Scala, 1977), 5–16, especially 7.

91 Goldthwaite, "La fondazione," 10.

92 Cadogan, *Domenico Ghirlandaio*, 261.

Chapter 9

Abigail Mathieu's Civic Charity: Social Reform and the Search for Personal Immortality[1]

Kathleen Ashley

"Do We Still Need Women's History?" the historian Alice Kessler-Harris recently asked, acknowledging the productive shift in the 1990s to the history of gender and gender relations.[2] In response to her own query, Kessler-Harris argues that "the history of women constitutes the original database for gendered interpretation," and she worries that focusing solely on the concept of gender may express "a resistance to the idea that women's activities, interests and ideas constituted a significant portion of the motivation for organizing societies, waging wars, [and] constructing particular kinds of economic systems," especially "in areas where the history of women is still being excavated."[3]

One example of this reluctance to give women their due as historical agents may be found in accounts of the Catholic Reformation. As Barbara Diefendorf comments in her study *From Penitence to Charity*: "Traditional histories have obscured women's active part in shaping the institutions, spirituality, and value system that characterized the Catholic Reformation in France by concentrating too narrowly on the achievements of a handful of great men."[4] Diefendorf's study of the role played by pious women in the early seventeenth-century Catholic revival marks an intervention into the dominant masculinist interpretations of religious history. She stresses the importance of individual laywomen donors with initiative, organizational skills, and money who built innumerable convents and who were "leaders in the spiritual revival that lay at the heart of the Catholic Reformation."[5] Her focus is the women of Paris, but she ends her study with the implicit plea for research into the roles that pious women may have played in the Catholic Reformation elsewhere in France.[6] This essay, which makes a case for the importance of the immensely wealthy Abigail Mathieu to the early modern history of Chalon, takes up Diefendorf's challenge to document female leadership in building the social institutions and religious values of their place and time.

Abigail Mathieu (1563–1638) was perhaps the most notable female benefactor of early seventeenth-century Burgundy. Her fortune was based on inheritances from her affluent merchant father and increased through a succession of marriages to rich husbands. Despite Abigail's well-documented charity—contained within two lengthy wills, a major donation and an even longer codicil preserved in the Chalon archives[7]—she has never been the subject of serious study by modern historians.[8] This essay is therefore a preliminary attempt to assess the life and legacy of the richest woman in early modern Chalon-sur-Saône. Given the massive documentation provided by Abigail's wills and the relatively meager information about her personal life, the focus here must fall primarily on her public role and charitable legacy; however, I would suggest that, read closely, the documents reveal much about her character and her commitments. The wills portray a bourgeois woman using her wealth to meet the pressing needs of her urban society; more than that, I will argue that they illuminate her vision for the city of Chalon, documenting her bold blueprint for spiritual renewal of the city after decades of religious conflict. The bequests made with Abigail Mathieu's immense fortune transcend conventional pious goals to imagine a city reconstituted by a reformed Catholicism, with her own body as a sacred relic at its ritual center, and it is also clear that her wealth was meant to establish her permanent identity as the premier benefactor of Chalon.

We know very little about the family from which such a rich and influential person as Abigail Mathieu originated, a fact that has puzzled local historians. The Mathieu name is rare in the Chalon records; a merchant named Jean or Jehan Mathieu is mentioned in contracts of the 1520s, and there are two Mathieu women (Laurence and Jehanne) whose names appear in contracts of the 1540s,[9] but their relation to Abigail or her brother Nicolas Mathieu, who were alive in the later sixteenth and early seventeenth century, is unclear. In her 1619 donation, Abigail mentions her father "honeste Etienne Mathieu"; however, the absence of prayers for her parents' souls in the many foundations made by this pious donor is especially striking and suggests that Abigail has shaped an identity independent of family affiliation.

The mystery of Abigail's parents is explained by a file in the town criminal records, documenting the January 1594 case against the merchant Etienne Mathieu for his Protestant views and activities, made public while guarding the town gate at the bridge with his neighborhood watch.[10] His was a "cas de crime et scandalle publicq et de plusieurs propos tenuz contre les sanctions des sacrez concilles de l'eglise catholique apostolique et romane" ("a case of crime and public scandal, and of several propositions held against the sanctions of the sacred councils of the catholic, apostolic and roman church"). Specifically, he had defended his right and those of other Huguenots to sing the psalms in the French translations by Clément Marot and Théodore de Bèze in their own homes. Told that such singing was forbidden by the Church authorities, and that singing loudly would "scandalize" the neighbors, Etienne stubbornly maintained that he could do what he wanted in his own home. As a result of these accusations, Etienne—who was in his sixties and in ill health—was sent to the episcopal prison. He was released after a few days on an "indemnity" of 50 écus and the case dragged on until August 1594. In the final documents, Etienne was ordered to abjure, to follow the Catholic rituals including the sacrament at Easter, and to pay a sizeable fine of 20 écus. Etienne's religious sympathy with the Huguenots would certainly account for Abigail's minimal acknowledgment of her parents as she became a significant force for the Catholic Reformation in Chalon. This case against Etienne nevertheless reveals how much Abigail was, in fact, her father's daughter despite their confessional differences, inheriting both his vigorous commitment to his beliefs and his reforming spirit.

For Chalon's local historians, the most salient fact about Abigail Mathieu's personal life is her multiple marriages. Abigail was born in 1563 and first married a member of the large and influential Beuverand family of Chalon.[11] However, we have no information about when the marriage occurred or when the first husband died. Moreover, he is never commemorated in Abigail's later acts where she acknowledges her other husbands.

In 1608, at the age of 45, Abigail married Edme Vadot, her senior by 30 years. He was, in other words, her father's peer and, apparently, his friend. Edme's signature appears under Etienne's as a witness to the proceeding at the end of the January 26, 1594 document by which Etienne is allowed out of prison.[12] Even more significantly, Edme Vadot was a relative of Abigail's mother, Jehanne Vadot, although the exact relationship is unclear. Edme was the eldest of at least four siblings in this well-established bourgeois family of Chalon. Pierre Vadot, the father, was a prosperous merchant draper and, by the time Abigail married him, the aging Edme himself was one of the leading citizens of Chalon. When he died eleven years later in 1619, Abigail married in quick succession Louis de Rymon, baron of La Rochette (1622), and Pierre de Pize, a counselor in the royal bailliage of Macon[13]—however, those marriages were short-lived.[14] In 1630 Abigail married her fifth husband, the Baron of Traves, who was living when she died at age 76 in 1638.[15]

The evidence we have strongly suggests that Edme Vadot was her favorite husband, as we shall see, but what seems to have brought them together was social conscience and a mutual commitment to direct their wealth to the public good. As the other essays in this volume have shown, the productive and spiritually beneficial use of wealth was a major topic of debate in late medieval and early modern culture. Members of the affluent bourgeoisie like Edme Vadot and Abigail Mathieu became the symbolic test cases for an emerging ideology that could reconcile Christianity and capitalism. The essay "Trading Values" traces the arguments of social thinkers from the fraternal orders, merchant, and humanist settings that money could be used "fruitfully" if it met the legitimate needs of the family or the poor and contributed to "the prosperity of a fruitful Christian community." Such an ideology of civic responsibility provides both the implicit structure and the explicit rationale for the charitable activity of Abigail Mathieu and her second husband.

Moreover, the focus of this joint benevolence was the city of Chalon. Many upwardly mobile sixteenth-century bourgeois families acquired country properties and titles that went with them—to which, by the seventeenth century, they had typically relocated, shifting their allegiances from urban to rural estates and their identities from bourgeois to noble. Abigail's various documents may itemize her titles,[16] but they are always written in her residence on the Grand Rue of Chalon and, with some exceptions,[17] the major donations are for institutions and people in the city. In her husband's documents, too, the long list of lands to which he owns title is usually preceded by the epithet "citoyen" ("citizen") of Chalon.

Chalon during the early seventeenth century was, and still is, a prosperous commercial city strategically located on the river Saône.[18] Since Roman times it has been an important city on major north–south trade routes, and its winter and summer fairs were famous across medieval Europe. After 1477, Chalon was on the frontier between the Duchy and the County of Burgundy, which led to a rebuilding of its walls and increased fortification in the centuries that followed. Less associated with regional government than Beaune under the Dukes of Burgundy in the later Middle Ages, or Dijon, site of the Burgundian Parlement in the fifteenth through eighteenth centuries, Chalon had a strong municipal government and well-developed identity as a city.

By the beginning of the sixteenth century, the bourgeois "notables" of Chalon had taken complete charge not just of town government but also of the social institutions that provided education, welfare, and health services to the citizens of the town. Edme Vadot was one of those civic leaders,[19] and he and Abigail were no doubt considered the "power couple" of their time. During their eleven years of marriage, they devoted their considerable wealth and influence to improving life for their fellow citizens of Chalon by donations to the "collège," the hospital, and various categories of poor and needy people.

In this pattern of charitable activity, the couple was not atypical of other affluent urban bourgeois of late medieval and early modern Europe—including Abigail's parents, whose 1583 donation to the town of 233 1/3 "escus" to support the teacher at the "collège," to feed the poor at the hospital, to distribute to poor prisoners, and to teach two poor orphan children a craft may be found in the archives.[20] In Abigail's case the extant documents also invite a personal interpretation. Reading between the lines of Abigail's known biography, we might come to the conclusion that, in a sense, Abigail only found her identity—became fully the person she wanted to be—by centering her life on spiritually motivated public charity. The decision to focus her activism on Chalon, with its sizeable population and well-established institutional infrastructure, reveals the intensity of her desire and the reach of her ambition to reform society.

Abigail's 1619 donation, in which she gives a major portion of the land she owns to the hospital, was written with the full participation of Edme Vadot—although perhaps with awareness of his imminent death at age 86.[21] Acknowledging God who has blessed her with goods, Abigail says she believes she can best employ them by giving "charite par almones au pauvres en presence et du bon avis et conseil dudict sieur vadot son mari"(f. 1: "charity through almsgiving to the poor in the presence and with the good counsel of the said M. Vadot her husband"). The elaborately described donation of her vines, house, and land at Poncey[22] and another property ("meix, maison, vignes, terres, preyes"—"enclosed plot, house, vines, land and fields") at Saint Martin des Champs "pour le soulagement et nourriture des dicts pauvres" (f. 6v: "for the comfort and feeding of the said poor") thus functions as her testament to the marriage with Vadot and to their unity of charitable purpose to alleviate the suffering of the poor. Significantly, this land donation is the only place Abigail mentions her father; he is referred to as "feue honeste Etienne Mathieu, cytoyen dudict Chalon, son pere" (" deceased honest Etienne Mathieu, citizen of the said Chalon, her father") from whom she has the property at Saint Martin des Champs (f. 7). The intimate detail in the description of the house, the garden, and the fields suggests that this might have been her childhood home.

As an expression of the couple's values, the 1619 document stresses the importance of inclusiveness in the distribution of charity. For example, each week money for bread should be given "indifferente a tous les prisonniers qui seront aux prisons Royalles du Chatelet dudict Chalon, soit criminel ou debteuriers" (f. 10v: "without discrimination to all the prisoners who are in the royal prisons of the Chatelet of the said Chalon, whether criminals or debtors"). All, "indifferente," are to receive this assistance. In addition, those who are debtors of good reputation, but without the means of leaving prison, shall be given money for their release (f. 11v). For students at the "collège," money will be allocated so that the doors of education can be open regardless ("indifferent") of socio-economic status: "cent quatrevingt livres qui seront annuellement payes au principal dudict college par ayder a render la porte dudict college libre indifferent a tous escoliers pauvres et riches" (f. 12: "one hundred and eighty livres which will be annually paid to the principal of the said college to aid in making the door of the said college free to all students, poor and rich alike"). While responding to the traditional Christian mandate to minister to the poor and disadvantaged, Abigail reveals a sophisticated understanding of the connection between material deprivation and social misfortune. Only when the most basic needs of all people are met will the community as a whole thrive, the document suggests.

One of the first recipients of the couple's charity was the Chalon "collège," a high school created for sons of the town's governing class, although Abigail and Edme also seem intent upon broadening access to education. They gave 3,000 livres to build a new chapel dedicated to Saint Nicolas to the left of the main portal of the school, citing the rationale that having a church so close to the school would enable the teachers to better "faire leur prieres et leur devotions"("say their prayers and their devotions").[23] In the 1619 donation, Abigail concerns herself with the curriculum by funding a prize for students in both the third and the fourth years who shall be judged to have written the best essays. A prize also goes to the student in the fifth year who is able to talk about assigned books (f. 13), and another for writing (f. 13v). Officials from the town government and the "collège" will select and distribute the prizes, and she includes small sums of between five and thirty solz to repay them for their efforts (ff. 13v–14).[24] She also gives money for the wages of a writing instructor. Of the 200 livres left to the "collège," 20 were to buy silver medals with the inscription "don d'Abigail Mathieu" ("gift of Abigail Mathieu") and on the other side her coat of arms and insignia; these were to be distributed as prizes to the students (ff. 12v–13). Even after Edme's death, Abigail continued to invest in the school. On June 26, 1634, the town made an agreement with the Jesuits about using college money to pay students to recite the requisite prayers in the cathedral on the feasts of Christmas, Saint-Vincent's Day, and Holy Thursday; Abigail was present at the meeting and gave her consent for the Jesuits to use the annual rent of 180 livres that she had willed the college in 1619, as long as they continued to maintain a writing teacher![25]

As a couple, Abigail and Edme Vadot are especially remembered for their outstanding generosity toward the charity hospital located on an island in the Saône River across from the city. At the end of the sixteenth century, the hospital was fairly new, having been built on open land there in 1530, and both Abigail and Edme contributed significantly to its expansion.[26] In 1596 there was a severe plague in Chalon; the regular hospital for plague sufferers (the Maladière) was full, and the town council pronounced it a crisis situation. The town registers record the offer from Edme Vadot to buy some empty grange buildings from the Carmes and donate them as an annex to the hospital to house plague victims, since the main hospital buildings were reserved for those who had not been infected.[27] For her part, in 1626 Abigail gave the sum of 1,000 livres toward the construction of an infirmary building and was consequently given the honor of laying the foundation stone.[28] The 1638 will further allocates 200 livres of "rente" on a principal of 3,200 livres for the hospital (f. 7v).

In her 1638 will, Abigail describes portraits in oil of herself and her second and third husbands, Edme Vadot and La Rochette, that are at her house but upon her death should be given to the hospital. She specifies that gold lettering on each portrait should give the name and age of each person and their date of death (ff. 9–9v). The portraits still hang in the hospital, providing a continuing reminder of the eminent seventeenth-century benefactors.[29] Evidently, Abigail's directives about the information to be inscribed in gold were not followed; according to an inscription on her painting, Abigail was 46 years old in 1609; her husband Edme was 76 in the year his portrait was painted. Abigail is dressed in black with an elaborate lace collar and cuffs. She wears a long rope of pearls—later bequeathed to the hospital to adorn the altar. Edme, looking slightly older with a white-tinged beard, is also dressed in black. Both wear black caps. These are portraits of urban "notables," the affluent but sober bourgeois who expressed their power by generous giving to the needy of their community and through support of the institutions of public welfare.

The fact that Abigail Mathieu and her husband Edme Vadot arranged to be buried by the altar of the hospital chapel also speaks to their privileged relationship with the institution. After their deaths, an epitaph memorializing the couple as major benefactors of the charity hospital, as well as of other institutions and categories of poor assistance, was inscribed on a copper plaque and put on the wall of the hospital chapel. It reads:

> Ci gisent le sieur Edme Vadot sgr des Montots, Noiry, Frontenard, Navilly la ville, Charette, Mervins etc. et qui décéda le 15 sept 1619 et âgé de 86 ans, et dame Abigail Mathieu sa femme qui décéda le 20 janvier 1638 et agée de 75 ans lesquels ont fait de grands dons et foundations même pendant leur vie pour le soulagement des pauvres de cet hôpital pour la construction de l'infirmairie pour l'établissement des Ursules pour la nourriture des prisonniers et pour l'instruction des enfants au Collège. ("Here lies Sir Edme Vadot, lord of Montots, Noiry, Frontenard, Navilly the town, Charette, Mervins, etc., who died the 15th of September 1619 at 86 years of age and Dame Abigail Mathieu his wife who died the 20th of January 1638 at the age of 75 years, who made great gifts and foundations both during their life for the comfort of the poor of this hospital, for the construction of the infirmary, for the establishment of the Ursulines, for the feeding of prisoners, and for the instruction of the children of the college.")

The epitaph then singles out Abigail for her "liberalités" ("generosity") toward many poor people, especially her establishment of dowries to enable poor girls to marry, and her help for other poor children to aid them in learning a "métier" or trade.

Individual copper plaques on the hospital wall give more detail about each of the spouses' benefactions. In her 1619 donation, Abigail had specified that four copper plaques should be engraved with her benefactions and put in the town hall, the choir of the hospital, the college and the prison chapel (ff. 16v–17); however, only the hospital plaque survives.[30] Her 1624 will calls for the purchase of good fustian (f. 11: "bure") to make robes for hospital patients and slippers of wool (f. 11v: "pantouffles doubles de frize"), while the 1638 will gives even more detail about the outfits for the sick in the hospital—specifying bonnets of wool and bed shirts of cotton in addition to the robes and slippers (f. 7). Abigail also leaves ten livres to buy "craquelins feulletez" (a type of crunchy pastry) to be distributed at lunch each day throughout Carnival to the poor patients (1624, f. 11 and 1638, f. 7). Likewise in the 1638 will, 50 bushels of grain ("boiseault de froment") were dedicated to feeding poor wives and widows at her death and another 50 bushels to the same women a year later (ff. 5v–6), while 200 livres was dedicated to buying charcoal for the heating needs of poor prisoners (f. 11v). Although Abigail's 1638 will was dictated from her sickbed three days before her death on January 20, it typifies her lifelong effort to direct her wealth to the diverse needs of the poor in the Chalon community.

In his will, Edme articulated his philosophy of charity as one of recompense for the prosperity he had been blessed with—a philosophy Abigail may well have shared:

> Dieu lui ayant fait la grâce de bénir son labeur, et ne ouvant mieux employer ces dits biens que pour quelques ausmones et charités envers les pauvres, a donné et donne par ces présentes, par irrévocable donation entre-vifs au grand hospital ou Hôtel-Dieu de Chalon, et pour la nourriture des pauvres icelluy … Grandes granges sises au lieu des Chavannes, de la paroisse Saint-Laurent, vis-à-vis le couvent des Cordeliers, la rivière de Genise entre deux; claustres, murailles, bastiments, pavillons; jardins, terres, montant a 101 journaux, y compris le grand vergier et 54

> soitures de pré … ("God through his grace having blessed his labor, and not having a better way of employing the said goods but by alms-giving and charity to the poor, he has given and gives by these, by irrevocable donation between the living, to the great hospital or Hotel-Dieu of Chalon and for the feeding of its poor … Great barns located in the place of Chavannes, in the parish of Saint-Laurent, opposite the convent of the Franciscans, the river Genise between the two; enclosures, walls, buildings, pavilions; gardens, lands amounting to 101 'journaux' and including the great orchard and 54 'soitures' of meadow … ")[31]

Edme Vadot appears to have made a few major charitable gifts, mostly centered on the "collège" and on the hospital that, as a town official, he had been responsible for supervising. Compared to his focused almsgiving, Abigail's much broader vision of Chalon's social and spiritual needs—as well as her special interest in alleviating the plight of women—is clearly discernible. For Abigail, the "reformation" implies a reform of Catholic practices in response to urban culture's neediest members: the poor, the sick, the homeless, those in need of education and jobs, and women.

Also discernible is Abigail Mathieu's desire to form strong family bonds with all the people in her life, and thus to create communities bound by the values of loyalty and affection. After Edme Vadot, her closest relation was her brother Nicolas Mathieu, whom she names as her heir and the executor of her various wills and other legal documents. The sparse documentary evidence suggests that Nicolas was at least 20 years younger than Abigail and perhaps her half-brother, since we know her mother Jehanne Vadot was dead in 1585.[32] It is possible that Etienne Mathieu, her father, remarried shortly thereafter and that Nicolas was a product of this second marriage, born when Abigail was already in her twenties. Certainly, the references to her brother in all her legal documents are deeply affectionate and convey absolute trust in his judgment and integrity. He is always her "treschere et bien ayme frere" ("very dear and well loved brother"), a phrase which may be formulaic, but her reliance on him is clear from the many decisions she delegated to him both in life and in her will. She is also explicit in her 1624 will about her emotional connection to Nicolas' wife, Elisabeth Bernard, "her dear sister," "qu'elle ayme, et a tousjours aymee comme si c'estoit sa proper fille" (f. 25v: "that she loves and has always loved as if she was her own daughter"). At the time Nicolas is already a lieutenant "particulier" ("private") at the "bailliage" (the local administrative unit of the central government) and a "conseiller du roy" ("counselor of the king"), but the couple have no children yet; Abigail gives Elisabeth rings and jewels that she hopes will be given to their first daughter, to whom they will also give Abigail's name (f. 26).[33]

Her wills also testify to Abigail's strong ties to the children of her various husbands and to others she included in her extended family. The 1624 will gives 16,000 livres to her husband Pierre de Pize; it can take the form of cash or of rents, whichever he chooses (f. 23v). Pierre's son Anthoine will receive a ruby, a diamond, and two gold rings from among her jewels (f. 24–24v), while his sister Crestienne gets her choice of pearls and gold bracelets (f. 24v). Her sister-in-law Jehanne de Pize will get another of her diamonds, while Pize's sister-in-law Estienette Grillet will get a diamond as well. Elisabeth Bernard's relatives also get 2,000 livres and gold rings decorated with diamonds (f. 25). The 1638 will adds 4,000 livres for Jean Bernard, who is named as one of the executors, and substantial sums for various Pontoux family members (Jeanne Pontoux was married to Jean Bernard) (f. 15). Her best diamond now goes to Jeanne Vadot, daughter of Edme, her second husband (f. 14v).

Tradespeople, estate workers, and servants are all remembered in her 1624 will and rewarded for loyalty. Jehan Muguet, the son of Philibert Muguet, the surgeon, will receive 100 livres when he marries—if he continues to work for Nicolas Mathieu and Elisabeth Bernard (f. 31). Barb Goy and her husband Andrez Testu, a carter, are given 25 livres for each daughter when they marry (f. 31v). Esme Niece, a "vigneron" ("wine grower") at Poncey, will get 30 livres for his daughter Abigaye when she marries (f. 32). Claude Girard, the tile-maker at her brother's tile factory in Saint Jehan des Vignes, will receive 50 livres (f. 35v). The 1624 will lists all the "grangiers" ("estate managers") of her country properties at Fontaines, Saint Martin des Champs, Verdenet, Chavanes, Mortieres, Cortiambles, and La Chault des Bordes (ff. 34v–36). Her personal servants will receive 20 livres, and those who have worked for more than a year for her then-husband Pierre de Pize's family and for her brother's family also receive a legacy (ff. 37–37v). The four nursing sisters at the hospital, whom she calls her "daughters" ("filles"), will each receive a white dress (of the kind they customarily wear) for Abigail's funeral ceremonies (ff. 32–32v). She also sets aside 50 livres annually for the support of a young man and a young woman of Chalon to learn a craft, whatever "leur nature se trouvera plus proper et enclin" (f. 22: "their nature finds most suitable and apt"). She instructs Nicolas as the executor to choose if possible the children of those who have been their servants living in Chalon, but above all that the candidates must be products of "loyal marriage de peres et meres pauvres et gens de bien" (f. 22: "loyal marriage of fathers and mothers, both poor and wealthy"). Abigail's individual gifts recognize personal relationships and devoted service, of course, but a surprising number of them are explicitly tied to marriage—either rewarding good marriages or enabling young women to marry. For this much-married woman, marriage represents the fundamental bond on which the stability of society is founded, and she clearly intends through her wealth to alleviate the vulnerability of females who need a dowry.

Her favorite cause was the Ursuline convent that she founded after the death of Edme Vadot. For the last 18 years of her life it was her most sustained and deeply felt charitable activity, which was connected to her aim of reforming Chalon as well as her search for a place in the community's "memoria." In the Ursuline foundation, Abigail's public and personal goals were inextricably intertwined—and gendered. In nurturing women, Abigail created her own identity and contributed to the spiritual health of her community.

On the 100th anniversary of the founding of the Ursuline convent in Chalon, one of the sisters produced a history of the house, a handwritten narrative of 75 folio pages dated 1726.[34] In a preface, the author says she read all the founding documents from the 1620s, some of which are still preserved in the Chalon municipal archives.[35] What emerges from her account is a vivid picture of Abigail's determination to bring the Ursulines to Chalon beginning in 1620, as well as her central role as "fondatrice" ("founder") in managing the initial years of the convent in tandem with the mother superior.

The Ursulines were a new female order that had begun in Italy in the 1530s with an educational mission directed at young women of urban families; Pope Paul III gave official sanction to the Company of Saint Ursula in 1544.[36] From the beginning, the Ursuline houses shared a "catechizing goal which understood the abandonment of the traditional monastic model in favor of the adoption of a 'mixed' way of life."[37] Its "spiritual devotion" was considered "a third way of life between the convent and marriage."[38] Although the Ursulines entered France as communal but uncloistered foundations, throughout the early seventeenth century there was pressure for claustration. "The idea of lay associations of women dedicated to an active apostolate or communities of uncloistered women flew in the face of political, ecclesiastical, and social pressure and the implementation of the Tridentine decrees."[39]

The Ursulines saw their vocation as part of the Catholic Reformation, a female counterpart to the Jesuits.[40] In the words of an early chronicler, Parayre, the Ursuline houses answered a need in the Church at a time when "heresy was multiplying its efforts to corrupt, pervert all young women and steep them in error … God inspired diverse people, particularly the French, to address the Company of St Ursula, whose principal end is to teach girls in their houses in order to give them safeguards against heresy."[41]

Louis XIII of France only authorized Ursuline foundations in the kingdom in 1608,[42] and a house was founded in Dijon soon after, which was cloistered in 1619.[43] We do not know when Abigail Mathieu first began to take an interest in this new women's movement, but its goals coincided perfectly with her own predilections. Around 1619, the year of Edme's death, Abigail turned her charitable focus toward the Ursulines. She gained the support of Chalon bishop Jacques de Neuchèze and promised an endowment of 10,000 livres to bring Ursulines from the Dijon convent to start a house in Chalon. The contract for the 10,000-livre endowment was drawn up in 1621; also in 1621, Abigail obtained authorization from the king for her female establishment, which was to provide free education for the town's children and young women. The unarticulated counter-reformation agenda was to ensure that Huguenot beliefs would not spread again, and therefore the female students were to be instructed in proper conduct, with the Catholic faith as religious foundation. The language of the founding documents specifies "the instruction of little girls in piety, good manners, and honest exercises appropriate to their sex."[44] Like other Ursuline houses, this one would have a threefold mission: to train its own members, to welcome a number of boarders, and to give lessons to day students.[45]

Ironically, despite Abigail's lofty goals and efficient planning, the Chalon mayor and councilmen—most of them Abigail's acquaintances, professional councilors, and even her own brother—demanded a larger endowment of 25,000 livres for the new establishment.[46] As the eighteenth-century Ursuline historian comments: "the difficulty of finding the funds did not slow the 'fondatrice' down one bit" (f. 12). She wrote to the Dijon house, which recognized "the zeal of that pious woman," and then Abigail went up to Dijon to confer with the mother superior. It was finally decided that a certain Catherine Valon, who wanted to retire to a convent, would give the remainder of the money in return for spending her final years being cared for by the Ursuline sisters of Chalon. A contract to that effect was drawn up in 1626, and Abigail then obtained a second "brevet" from King Louis XIII authorizing the establishment of the Ursuline convent in Chalon, a document that praised the "zeal and piety" of Abigail (f. 17). Abigail, who understood the power of written records to the functioning of urban institutions, had all of these documents inscribed in the town registers of Chalon. The whole process of bringing the Ursulines to Chalon reveals not just her persistence but also Abigail Mathieu's considerable political skills. Although as a woman she could not be an elected official of the city, Abigail nevertheless assumed a civic role and responsibilities comparable to those of her male peers.

She was nothing if not a "hands-on" benefactor; according to the hour-by-hour account in the eighteenth-century history, as the first five sisters from Dijon prepared to move to Chalon, Abigail busied herself finding a place for them to stay. She also organized the bishop, his retinue, and other dignitaries to greet the women's carriage on its arrival in Chalon, and then accompanied them to the bishop's palace, where they ate dinner that night and the next. There Abigail made a ceremonial presentation of the contract for her 10,000 livres, the only stipulation of which was that she could put four girls into the convent on a one-time basis; the sisters retained the power to accept or reject them with "les voix deliberatives" (f. 19: "voice vote"). Her brother Nicolas Mathieu was asked to take charge of the temporal administration of the convent.

Abigail had at first rented lodgings for the Ursulines in the cloister of St Vincent church, and there she fitted out one room as a place to celebrate mass, which she took with the sisters at the hand of the bishop. When the sisters searched for more permanent buildings, Abigail went with them in a carriage furnished by the bishop. A building was purchased across from the church of the Carmes and the Saint Pierre monastery church on the Place Saint Pierre, one of the ritual centers of the city. Eventually, one side of the square was lined with handsome convent buildings that, although architecturally somewhat modified and serving new purposes, still exist. Abigail's involvement with the Ursulines continued even after they were established in the city. She accompanied the mother superior to a meeting in Dijon with other Ursuline mothers superior in July 1628 (f. 23), and the convent historian says that Abigail often ate with the sisters in their convent.[47]

The counter-reformation agenda of the Ursulines emerges explicitly in this history when we are told that a Huguenot girl, Magdalaine Goujon, was put into the convent to be instructed in the Catholic faith. The sisters were so successful that the girl abjured her heresy before the bishop, made first confession and communion, and was sent home to her parents, where she died shortly—a "tres bonne catholique" (f. 22: "a very good Catholic")!

The history of the Chalon Ursulines' first 100 years ends with the statement that the author would like to provide an "eloge" ("panegyric") of Madame de Traves, their founder, but that she has found no memoir with other details about her other than those she has already included. According to the writer, when Abigail died in January 1638, she left a black velour ceremonial cloth (a "parement"). We know, she adds, that the founder was not just a woman of singular piety who gave us 10,000 livres. The good she did us was worth more than the dowry ("dot") and she did not impose either charges or prayers on the sisters in return for her gifts. The writer speculates that Abigail must have led a life full of adventure since she was married seven times [sic] and had no surviving children. Her husbands left her all their goods so that she found herself immensely rich ("puissamment riche"). The interpretation offered by the convent historian is that Abigail wanted to assure her salvation ("salut") by her good works ("bonnes oeuvres") and her infinite numbers of charities.

As we have noted, the surviving records of Abigail Mathieu's life emphasize her public roles; however, we can read between the lines to draw some deductions about her personal motivations. The investment of money and energy Abigail made in the Ursulines had deeply personal implications, for the convent clearly became a substitute for the family she never had. The establishment eventually numbered 30 women religious and had a school for 60 children.[48]As the eighteenth-century writer says, Abigail may have been childless, but she became a mother to a great number of virgins (f. 65). Abigail, who led the sisters in processions to ceremonial occasions alongside the mother superior, considered the Ursulines as daughters—"leur filles" (f. 28).

The childless Abigail also invested her wealth by creating endowments to literally perpetuate her name. Imagining a generation of infants who would bear her name, Abigail's 1638 will identified 13 young couples with the stipulation that they would receive 50 or 100 livres when they named their first female child "Abigail" (ff. 18–21v). There were no generally accepted "naming rules" in this early period, but eldest children were often named for relatives. Abigail's importance to the families with which she was intermarried is indicated by the presence of several "Abigayes" among the children of her brother Nicolas and the nieces or grandchildren of her various husbands, as well as children of friends.[49] However, her "naming" bequests are not directed just to those relatives, but rather are designed to ensure her memory among a broader population of young Chalon families. The will also lists an enormous number of young women who are to receive 50 or 100 livres with, evidently, no strings attached. In some cases where she is obviously enabling a marriage by her donation, she says that if there are no children from the marriage to inherit, then her money should return to the poor at the hospital. The importance of marriage in Abigail's vision of a stable and purified Chalon thus emerges in these documents.

The two Chalon institutions for which Abigail was the prime benefactor, as we have seen, were the hospital and the Ursuline convent. Her intimate connection with both foundations is signaled at the beginning of her 1638 will where she gives directions for her burial. She wants her body to be buried before the main altar of the chapel in the Chalon hospital where her beloved second husband Monsieur Vadot is buried, and her heart with the body of her beloved third husband, Louis de Rymon, the Baron of La Rochette, in the chapel built on his estate during their marriage (f. 1v). However, her entrails should be carried to the convent of the Ursulines that she had founded, to be buried before the main altar of that church.[50] She gives permission to embalm her in case all these arrangements take a long time (f. 2)! At the convent, her entrails are to be displayed in a room draped in black velvet, the container surrounded by burning candles (a "chapelle ardante," f. 3–3v). A cloth of black velvet will also adorn the altar of the St Ursula chapel. The cloth over her tomb will have a cross in white satin embroidered with her coat of arms in the center, which will adorn the convent chapel for a year and then be returned to the hospital for safe-keeping (ff. 2–2v). Subsequently, the velvet cloth will be put on her tomb on the first of May, Saint Barnabe's feast, since she founded two high masses to be said on that day "in perpetuity." Other ornaments are to remain in the possession of her spiritual lineage, her "daughters the religious" at the Ursuline convent (f. 2v).

Abigail's funeral arrangements, fully described in her final will, are of an elaboration and detail I have never encountered in my study of Burgundian wills, and we can read them for insight not just into her public persona but also into her personal goals. Significantly, she makes little explicit reference to the fate of her soul; her focus is on ensuring her place in Chalon's urban "memoria."[51] In addition to the adornment of the black cloths ("draps"), her funeral scenario includes processions with 50 poor people in white clothing marching two by two before her body with white candles, and 25 poor people in black marching after her body carrying black candles (f. 4). She authorizes payment of a sol for each poor person—up to 600—who wants to carry a candle or torch in her funeral procession (f. 4v). The spectacle of her final rites is conceived in theatrical terms clearly designed to ensure that Chalon would not forget Abigail Mathieu.

That her funeral ceremonies are not just one-time events is also clear from her plan that the decorative black velvet cloths should be re-used for subsequent funerals of her brother and his wife and their successors, or for executors at the hospital and their wives and children—all of whom may use the "drap" until the 40-day mourning period ends. In addition, the velvet cloth will be available to "honorable" persons of the city of Chalon for their funerals, at the discretion of her brother who is her heir and executor (f. 2v). In other words, Abigail intends that her presence should continue to be visible and appreciated "in perpetuity" by the various communities of which she was such a charitable part.

The phrase "in perpetuity" is repeated at least four dozen times in her 1638 will as she provides the resources for innumerable foundations and charities. At the cathedral of Saint Vincent, for example, she founds a daily mass to be sung between 6 and 7pm "in perpetuity." Then there are masses in her memory founded at every other church in Chalon "in perpetuity." She also reserves ten livres to be disbursed to 200 poor people every year "in perpetuity" (f. 3v). For Abigail, this massive outpouring of charity was to be a form of immortality. What emerges from a reading of this final document is Abigail's conviction that she could, practically single-handedly, restore Chalon to physical and spiritual health—and that in so doing she would also guarantee that her memory would remain alive "in perpetuity" for her fellow citizens.[52]

It is often difficult to assess the impact of such documents or of a life at the remove of several centuries, but with regard to the cultural work in Chalon achieved by Abigail Mathieu, we can be less tentative. The portraits Abigail ordered of herself and her husbands still hang in the hospital as visible signs of their patronage. The plaques she had inscribed also remain there in the chapel. Evidently Abigail has achieved her deep desire to be known to posterity, for when the still-thriving hospital (now known as the Centre Hospitalier William Morey) decided in 1987 to formally promote its historical and architectural heritage, the resulting association took the name of Abigail Mathieu!

In making a case for the importance of pious women in the religious politics of the late sixteenth and seventeenth centuries, Barbara Diefendorf offers a paradigm in which an initial penitential asceticism gave way after the 1630s to a more socially focused activism. She associates the first with the wars of the Catholic League and the second with the "battles of the Fronde half a century later."[53] The charitable career of Abigail Mathieu is not an exact fit with Diefendorf's paradigm, since Chalon's chief benefactress died in 1638; however, it is clear that Abigail's passion was social reform and not ascetic mysticism.

Inspired by the ideals of Catholic charity, with the city of Chalon as her geographical focus, Abigail poured her increasing wealth into the established institutions, providing education and medical services for all citizens, and also worked to expand access to the truly needy in society. She founded an innovative community of women dedicated to female education, which would provide the basis for the city's spiritual renewal. Finally, she used her economic, political, and affective leadership informally to enable marriages, support families, and build friendships—strengthening the social fabric of Chalon through which her charitable legacy would be forever remembered.

Notes

1 I would like to acknowledge the invaluable assistance of John Reuter in doing the archival research for this essay as well as in discussing the implications of Abigail's wills. I am also grateful to Henri Huet, who has generously shared his wide knowledge of Chalon history over the years. The busy staff of the Bibliothèque Municipale graciously photocopied the extensive documents of Abigail Mathieu when the town archives were located in their building. More recently, Estelle François and her

colleagues at the Archives de Chalon have provided access to the vital documents, including facilitating the use of the Hospital Archives. For all their help, I am most grateful.

2 Alice Kessler-Harris, "Do We Still Need Women's History?" *The Chronicle of Higher Education* (December 7, 2007): Section B, 6–7.

3 Kessler-Harris, "Do We Still Need Women's History?" B, 7.

4 Barbara B. Diefendorf, *From Penitence to Charity: Pious Women and the Catholic Reformation in Paris* (Oxford: Oxford University Press, 2004), 245.

5 Diefendorf, *From Penitence to Charity*, 247.

6 Diefendorf, *From Penitence to Charity*, 251.

7 These documents, including a 1619 donation of 44 pages, a 1638 will of 72 pages, and an enormous codicil of 183 pages, are GG 60 in the municipal archives of Chalon. Also in Chalon, documents collected under the rubric GG49 include Abigail's 1624 will of 84 pages and various donations to institutions and individuals in the city, the majority involving the Collège. See also FF99 for her donations to the Collège.

8 Local historians of the nineteenth century were the main ones to take an interest in her life and achievements. See, for example, Henri Batault, the secretary of the Chalon historical society, in his study, *Notice historique sur l'association des Dames de la Miséricorde de Chalon-s.-Saône (1638–1877)* (Chalon-sur-Saône: Jules Dejussieu, 1878). He dedicates his first appendix to "Madame Abigail Mathieu, Baronne de Traves, Bienfaitrice des pauvres de la ville de Chalon" (276–309). These early notices, however, do not incorporate all the documents available in town and departmental archives or in the historical society.

9 The source for the contracts is real estate transactions described by the compiler of a two-volume study of Chalon houses, Raoul Violot, *Histoire des Maisons de Chalon*, 2 T (Paris: Éditions F.E.R.N., 1969).

10 Archives de Chalon, FF 8. This file contains 13 documents dated from January 22, 1594 to August 20, 1594 concerning the case against Etienne Mathieu for his claim that singing the psalms in their Protestant translations—even "a haulte voix" ("in a loud voice"), as long as it was in his own home—was permissible. There are several detailed depositions from his neighbors and fellow guards who heard him make the pro-Protestant comments, as well as reports of two interrogations of Etienne. The file also contains a long and theologically erudite analysis of the problem of using the vernacular versus Latin as the language for public worship, "pour exprimer plus nettement avec moins d'ambiguitez les divins et sacre misteres" ("to express more clearly with less ambiguity the divine and sacred mysteries"). In private worship, it concludes that since God can understand all languages you could say your prayers in any language—nevertheless, the psalms as translated by Marot and Bèze were forbidden by the Church and therefore to individuals!

11 Nineteenth-century histories put the number of husbands at five, although they do not offer documentation for the first marriage to a Beuverand and I have not been able to find any sixteenth-century records to support the claim.

12 Archives de Chalon, FF8.

13 For Pierre de Pize, see Adrien Arcelin, *Indicateur héraldique et généalogique du Maconnais* (Marseille: Laffitte Reprints, 1976, from the 1865 edition).

14 In her 1638 will (f. 9v), May 17, 1623 is given as the death date of Louis de Rymon, Baron of La Rochette, and his age as 71.

15 The Baron of Traves was from the Choiseul family; see Henri Beaune and Jules d'Arbaumont, *La Noblesse aux Etats de Bourgogne de 1350 à 1789* (Genève: Mégariotis Reprints, 1977, from Dijon edition of 1864).

16 The 1619 will of Edme Vadot identifies him with the following titles and locations: "citoien de Chalon, seigneur de Montots, Navilly, Lavileneuve, Monts, Charette, Varenne-sur-Doubs, Frontenay, Mervane, la Cuilliere et Noiry." Note that "citoien de Chalon" is first in the list. Abigail Mathieu's 1638 will names her "Dame de Varennes-sur-Doubs, Frontenard, Labergement, Merran, La Cuilliere, La Groye, Epouse de Messire Philippe de Traves, Chevalier Seigneur de Vatheau."

17 In her 1638 will, she gives money for a commemorative mass and alms at the churches of her various domains, including La Rochette, Frontenard-sur-le-Doubs, Varennes-sur-le-Doubs and Simandre.

18 For the classic description of Chalon, see Claude Courtépée and Edme Beguillet, *Description générale et particulière du Duché de Bougogne*, ed. Pierre Gras and Jean Richard, 3rd edition, 3 T (Avallon: Éditions F.E.R.N.; distr. Paris: Librairie Guénégaud, 1967). The original "Description de Chalon-sur-Saône" (198–266), with a 1573 Rancourel map of the city, was written in the eighteenth century. A recent general introduction is *Histoire de Chalon-sur-Saône*, ed. Pierre Lévêque (Dijon: Éditions Universitaires de Dijon, 2005).

19 In the nineteenth century, a bust of white gypsum was uncovered in a niche of the "Granges Vadot", an annex of the Chalon hospital. The statue was of a dignified male dressed in magistrate's clothing of the end of the sixteenth century and was eventually identified as that of Edme Vadot, who had given the buildings to the hospital in 1597 to house plague sufferers. The process of identification, which provides considerable information about Vadot, has been described by Henri Batault in an article, "Edme Vadot: Eschevin de Chalon et Bienfaiteur de l'Hôpital, 1603," in *MSHAC* T. VI (1872): 334–45. Batault records Vadot's will (340–41).

20 3 1/3 "escus" went to the teacher, 3 1/3 "escus" for "nourriture des pauvres malades" ("feeding of the indigent sick") of the hospital, 5 solz to be distributed to poor prisoners at the castle each Monday, and 8 1/3 "escus" each year was dedicated to teaching a craft to two poor orphan children, boys or girls (Archives de Chalon GG 49). The archives of the hospital contain a document from August 4, 1585, that refers to 1583 donations, but makes clear that Etienne Mathieu's wife Jehanne is now dead (B I, 151).

21 Archives de Chalon GG 60. The document in this file was written by the notary Benoist Monnet on May 27, 1619, and signed by Abigail Mathieu, her brother Nicolas Mathieu, Edme Vadot, and 13 other witnesses (f. 18v). The "bien fait and liberalite de ladicte damoiselle" ("good deed and liberality of the said lady") was then acknowledged by an assembly in the "maison de la ville"("town hall") including town officials and the directors of the "collège" and hospital, who decided to celebrate her generosity "perpetually" by ordering a high mass at the hospital each first Sunday in June at eight in the morning, with another at five in the evening

at which Psalm 120, "Beatus vir," would be sung as well as a "de profundis" with prayers and suffrages (19–19v). All the foregoing officials should be in attendance at the masses. Furthermore, "to perpetuate her memory," each year for an hour in the morning and evening the bells of the town clock should be rung ("treselee et carillonnes" f. 20). The document was then judicially ratified by the chancellerie court in Chalon on June 1, 1619 (f. 20v) and acknowledged again by the same authority on June 12, 1731. The 1624 will calls the document a "donation entre vifs" (f. 21v. "a donation between the living").

22 For files containing the Poncey and other donations, see also the Hospital Archives B II/III, 401, which contains copies of the 1619 and 1638 testaments, as well as letters from her descendant in 1711 taking the hospital to task for not following the mandates of Abigail's will with regard to the annual high mass and singing. On the hospital's Poncey holdings in the later seventeenth and eighteenth centuries, see the Hospital Archives B II/III, 402 and B II/III, 404.

23 Batault, "Edme Vadot," 339. The Chalon *Registre* for May 30, 1616 notes that the couple gave the 3,000 livres to build the new chapel, and Batault says that it survived until 1762. See also Archives de Chalon DD28 for a document of September 3, 1618 negotiating an "indemnity" of 150 livres for the new chapel in case it blocked the light of a neighboring building.

24 The final part of her 1619 donation carefully spells out how her brother Nicolas Mathieu and his successors, as well as the town officials, may use her 3,200 livres donation (ff. 15–16v); Abigail clearly knew how to manage her money. After the death of Vadot, Abigail's contracts are hers alone, "constitue en sa personne," ("constituted in my own person"), although she may be identified as the wife of someone (see contacts for 1625 and 1626 in AD Saone-et-Loire 3E 34739). In the 1620s and 1630s she had total financial independence.

25 Archives de Chalon FF 99.

26 Chalon had missed having the Hôtel-Dieu that Chancellor Rolin wanted to build there in 1436 when the canons of the Cathedral Saint-Vincent objected to his plans, so he began to construct the hospital in Beaune a few years later (1453). See Marie-Thérèse Berthier and John-Thomas Sweeney, *Le Chancelier Rolin, 1376–1462* (Precy-sur-Thil: Éditions de l'Armancon, 1998).

27 See Registre des délibérations de la ville de Chalon, February 3, 1597, BB 11, f. 307v.

28 See Hospital Archives B II/III, 401 for an October 28, 1626 document.

29 See L. Armand-Calliat, *L'Hôpital de Chalon-sur-Saône et ses anciens objets d'art* (Chalon-sur-Saône: n.p., 1965), 64–6.

30 There is a three-page copy of the donations list from the plaque in the town hall in a file of college donations (Archives de Chalon GG49).

31 Batault, "Edme Vadot," 340. An extract from the testament of Edme Vadot listing his charities to town institutions may be found in the Archives de Chalon D 13, dated September 20, 1619.

32 A document in the Chalon Hospital Archives (B I, 151), dated August 4, 1585, refers to an earlier donation by Etienne Mathieu and "feu de lors vivant dame Jehanne Vadot" ("now deceased, then living Dame Jehanne Vadot").

33 The 1624 will further gives Elisabeth Bernard 1,500 livres, noting that they are in addition to the 2,500 livres given as a donation "entre vifz," May 2, 1620—perhaps at the time of her marriage with Nicolas. According to Batault, *Notice Historique*, 282, Nicolas did name his daughter Jehanne-Abigail.

34 The manuscript is preserved at the Société d'Histoire in Chalon as H31. It is entitled "Histoire de la Maison de Saincte Ursule de Chalon."

35 Archives de Chalon GG2 contains documents about the founding of the Ursuline convent by Abigail. See also EE 12, with a 1644 document of September 12, 1644 about the building of the new Ursuline church on grounds that the "arbaletiers" ("cross-bowmen") had traditionally used for their practice.

36 On the Ursulines, see Charmarie J. Blaisdell, "Angela Merici and the Ursulines," in *Religious Orders of the Catholic Reformation*, ed. Richard L. DeMolen (New York: Fordham University Press, 1994), 99–136, with a focus on Italian sixteenth-century foundations. Laurence Lux-Sterritt, *Redefining Female Religious Life: French Ursulines and English Ladies in Seventeenth Century Catholicism* (Aldershot: Ashgate, 2005), 3.

37 Lux-Sterritt, *Redefining Female Religious Life*, 22.

38 Daniel Culpepper, "'Our Particular Cloister': Ursulines and Female Education in Seventeenth-Century Parma and Piacenza," *Sixteenth Century Journal* XXXVI, no. 4 (2005):1017–37. As Culpepper points out, Ursulines enjoyed the honor that fully enclosed nuns had, "while also serving the interests of their well-connected families" (1018).

39 Blaisdell, "Angela Merici," 121.

40 Lux-Sterritt, *Redefining Female Religious Life*, 28–31.

41 Lux-Sterritt, *Redefining Female Religious Life*, 19.

42 There were Ursuline foundations in Avignon as early as 1598 and Aix in 1600, 1604 in Toulouse, and 1607 in Paris; see Robert Bireley, *The Refashioning of Catholicism, 1450–1700: A Reassessment of the Counter Reformation* (Washington, DC: Catholic University of America, 1999), 40, 133. According to Bireley: "Of all the women's congregations the Ursulines were undoubtedly the most numerous and probably the most influential" (38). See also Marie de Chantal Gueudré, *Histoire de l'ordre des Ursulines en France*, 2 T (Paris: Éditions Saint-Paul, 1958–63).

43 Diefendorf, *From Penitence to Charity*, 132–3.

44 The contracts drawn up in 1626 and registered with the town spell out these social and religious goals, as well as the financial arrangements for the new foundation (Archives de Chalon GG2).

45 Lux-Sterritt, *Redefining Female Religious Life*, 4.

46 The objections may not have been completely financial, as the Ursulines in many locations—including Dijon—encountered hostility during their first century of operation. Resistance came from urban elites who thought that their daughters should not be devoting themselves to such a service organization instead of getting married. In Dijon, Françoise de Xaintonge faced considerable suspicion: "why would young ladies of high social status decide to bring shame on their families and deny themselves good repute by casting off respectable society and abasing themselves by being school teachers for poor children?" (Lux-Sterritt, *Redefining Female Religious*

Life, 39). I have found no direct evidence that Abigail Mathieu faced that kind of hostility, but clearly her patronage of the order was not greeted with universal acclaim in Chalon. There was also sustained pressure by the religious authorities in France to remake Ursuline houses into cloistered convents.

47 Barbara Diefendorf, *From Penitence to Charity*, describes similar engagement on the part of Madame Luillier, patron of a new Ursuline foundation in Paris ca. 1610 (125 7).

48 According to Batault, *Notice Historique*, 293.

49 Her 1638 will specifies the two daughters of her third husband Louis de Rymon, giving them each 300 livres when they marry, on condition that they name their first daughter Abigail. The two children of Pierre de Pize, her fourth husband, are each to get 100 livres if they will name their first-born girl Abigail, and she refers to the 6,000 livres she gave in 1626 as the "dot" to marry off Pize's daughter Chrestianne. She also gives 100 livres to Abigail Vadot, of her second husband's family, and names several "Abigayes" who are getting 100 livres at marriage: Abigaye Clerguet, Abigaye Colmont, Abigaye Dupray, and so on (ff. 18–21).

50 In the 1624 will, Abigail had requested that her heart be buried in the sepulcher of her then-husband Pierre de Pize in St Pierre church, Macon (Archives de Chalon GG 49, f. 2); however, in her final will of 1638 she substituted another husband, Louis de Rymon, the Baron of La Rochette, asking that her heart be buried in the church at La Rochette that they had built during their marriage (Archives de Chalon GG 60, f. 1v).

51 The 1638 will is based on the 1624 will, but extends the donations that alleviate the plight of the poor and emphasizes her concern for women, in particular including the Ursulines, which she had established in Chalon after the first will was written. The earlier will contains elaborate descriptions of church furnishings she donates, while the 1638 will expresses a much more direct desire to improve the lives of her fellow citizens and to be remembered by them.

52 On behalf of the community, the Chalon town council acknowledged receipt of the revenues from "Madame de Traves" in a meeting on June 2, 1638 at which her will's executor Nicolas Mathieu was present (*Registre* BB 14, ff. 461v–462v.)

53 Diefendorf, *From Penitence to Charity*, 203.

Bibliography

Aers, David. "The Good Shepherds of Medieval Criticism." *Southern Review* (University of Adelaide) 20 (1987): 168–85.

Aerts, Erik. "Middeleeuwse bankgeschiedenis volgens Professor Raymond de Roover." *Bijdragen tot de Geschiedenis der Nederlanden* 63 (1980): 49–86.

Ainsworth, Maryan W. and Keith Christiansen, eds. *From Van Eyck to Bruegel: Early Netherlandish Painting in the Metropoltian Museum of Art*. New York: Metropolitan Museum of Art, 1998.

Alberti, Leon Battista. *I libri della famiglia*, edited by Ruggiero Romano and Alberto Tenenti. Turin: Einaudi, 1980.

——. *The Family in Renaissance Florence*, translated by Renée Neu Watkins. Long Grove, IL: Waveland Press, 2004.

Alberzoni, Maria Pia. "L'esperienza caritativa presso gli Umiliati: Il caso di Brera (secolo XIII)." In *La Caritá a Milano nei secoli XII–XV*, 201–23. Milan: Jaca Book, 1989.

—— and Annamaria Ambrosioni, eds. *Sulle tracce degli Umiliati*. Milan: Vita e Pensiero, 1997.

Alexander-Skipnes, Ingrid, ed. *Cultural Exchange between the Low Countries and Italy (1400–1600)*. Turnhout: Brepols, 2007.

Ambrosioni, Annamaria. "Umiliate/Umiliati." In *Dizionario degli istituti di perfezione*. Rome: Edizioni paoline, 1997.

Ambrosius Mediolanensis. *De Tobia*. In *Opere* VI. Milan and Rome: Città Nuova, 1983.

——. *Super Lucam*. In *Patrologia latina* 15; in Corpus Christianorum series latina 14. Turnhout: Brepols, 1957.

Amman, Jost and Hans Sachs. *The Book of Trades [Ständebuch]*, introduction by Benjamin A. Rifkin. New York: Dover, 1973.

Amster, Mara. "Frances Howard and Middleton and Rowley's *The Changeling*: Trials, Tests, and the Legibility of the Virgin Body." In *The Single Woman in Medieval and Early Modern England: Her Life and Representation*, edited by Laurel Amtower and Dorothea Kehler, 211–32. Tempe, AZ: Arizona Center for Medieval and Renaissance Studies, 2003.

Andrews, Frances. *The Early Humiliati*. Cambridge: Cambridge University Press, 1999.

Angelucci, Patrizia. "Gli Umiliati di Siena e la chiesa del borgo franco di Paganico." In *Chiesa e società dal secolo IV ai nostri giorni: studi storici in onore del p. Ilarino da Milano*. Rome: Herder, 1979.

Anicius Manlius Severinus Boethius: Fundamentals of Music, translated with introduction and notes by Calvin M. Bower. New Haven: Yale University Press, 1989.

Anonymous of Laon. *Chronicon universale*, edited by G. Waitz. In *Monumenta Germaniae Historica, Scriptores*. Hanover: Hahn, 1826.

Apollodorus. *The Library*. 2 volumes, Loeb Classical Library, translated by Sir James George Frazer. Cambridge, MA: Harvard University Press, 1961.

Aquinas, Thomas. *Summa Theologica*, translated by Fathers of the English Dominican Province. 2nd and revised edition. New York: Benziger Brothers, 1947–48.

——. *Summa Theologiae*, II, <http://www.corpusthomisticum.org>.

——. *Summa theologica*, I^{a}-IIae q. 84 a. 1, <http://www.newadvent.org/summa>.

Archivio di Stato di Milano (ASMi).Archivio Diplomatico, pergamene per fondi, cart. 632[A], 640, 707.

Archivio di Stato di Palermo (contains document collection for the Humiliati of Cremona). Colloc. dal pergamene, 1146.

Arcelin, Adrien. *Indicateur héraldique et généalogique du Maconnais*. Marseille: Laffitte Reprints, 1976, from the 1865 edition.

Aretino, Pietro. *Aretino's Dialogues*, translated by Raymond Rosenthal. New York: Marsilio, 1994.

——. *Lettere: Il primo e il secondo libro*, edited by Francesco Flora. Verona: Mondadori, 1960.

——. *The Letters of Pietro Aretino*, edited and translated by Thomas Caldecot Chubb. New Haven, CT: Shoe String Press, 1967.

——. *Ragionamento. Dialogo*, edited by Giorgio Bàrberi Squarotti and Carla Forno. Milan: Rizzoli, 1988.

Armand-Calliat, L. *L'Hôpital de Chalon-sur-Saône et ses anciens objets d'art*. Chalon-sur-Saône: n.p., 1965.

Armour, Peter. "Gold, Silver, and True Treasure: Economic Imagery in Dante." *Romance Studies* 23 (1994): 7–30.

As-Vijvers, Anne-Margreet W. "More than Marginal Meaning? The Interpretation of Ghent–Bruges Border Decoration." *Oud Holland* 116 (2003): 3–33.

St Augustine. *The Literal Meaning of Genesis*, translated by John Hammond Taylor. New York: Newman Press, 1982.

——. *De sermone domini in monte*. In *Opere di S. Agostino*. Rome: Città Nuova, 1976.

——. *Enarratio in Ps. 90*. In *Opere di S. Agostino*. Rome: Città Nuova, 1976.

Backhouse, Janet. *The Hastings Hours*. London: British Library, 1996.

Baker, Roberta and David Nicol. "Does Beatrice Joanna Have a Subtext?: *The Changeling* on the London Stage." *Early Modern Literary Studies* 10, no. 1 (2004).

Baldassarri, S.U. and A. Saiber, eds. *Images of Quattrocento Florence*. New Haven: Yale University Press, 2000.

Baldus de Ubaldis. *In Decretalium volumen commentaria*. Venice: Giunta, 1595.

Bales, Kevin B. "Nicole Oresme and Medieval Social Science: The Fourteenth Century Debunker of Astrology Wrote an Early Monetary Treatise." *American Journal of Economics and Sociology* 42 (1983): 101–11.

Barbieri, Gino. "La funzione economica degli Umiliati." In *Produzione, commercio e consumo dei pani di lana (nei secoli XII–XVII.) Atti della seconda settimana di studio, Prato 1970*, edited by M. Sallanzani, 145–52. Florence: Olschki, 1976.

Batault, Henri. "Edme Vadot: Eschevin de Chalon et Bienfaiteur de l'Hôpital, 1603." *MSHAC* T. VI (1872): 334–45.

——. *Notice historique sur l'association des Dames de la Miséricorde de Chalon-s.-Saône (1638–1877)*. Chalon-sur-Saône: Jules Dejussieu, 1878.

Batazzi, Ferdinando and Annamaria Giusti. *Ognissanti*. Rome: Fratelli Palombi, 1992.

Battaglia, Salvatore, ed. *Grande Dizionario della lingua italiana*. Torino: Unione tipografico-editrice torinese, 1961–99.

Baxandall, Michael. *Painting and Experience in Fifteenth-Century Italy: A Primer in the Social History of Pictorial Style.* Oxford: Oxford University Press, 1972.

Beaune, Henri and Jules d'Arbaumont. *La Noblesse aux Etats de Bourgogne de 1350 à 1789*. Geneva: Mégariotis Reprints, 1977, from Dijon edition of 1864.

Beda. *In Lucam.* In *Patrologia Latina* 91.

Bedaux, Jan Baptist. "Fruit Symbolism in Netherlandish Portraiture of the Sixteenth and Seventeenth Centuries." *Simiolus* 17 (1987): 150–68.

Benvenuti Papi, Anna. "Vangelo e tiratoi. Gli Umiliati ed il loro insediamento fiorentino." In *La "Madonna d'Ognissanti" di Giotto restaurata*, Gli Uffizi, Studi e Ricerche, 8, 75–84. Florence: Centro Di, 1992.

Bergström, Ingvar. "Disguised Symbolism in 'Madonna' Pictures and Still Life." *Burlington Magazine* 97 (October 1955): 342–9.

Bernardino da Siena. *Le prediche volgari*, edited by Ciro Cannarozzi. Pistoia: Alberto Pacinotti, 1934.

Bernhard of Clairvaux. *De Consideratione ad Eugenium papam*. In *Opere di San Bernardo* I, edited by Ferruccio Gastaldelli. Milan: Città Nuova, 1984.

Bernstein, Jane A. "Financial Arrangements and the Role of Printer and Composer in Sixteenth-Century Italian Music Printing." *Acta musicologica* 63 (1991): 39–56.

Berthier, Marie-Therèse and John-Thomas Sweeney. *Le Chancelier Rolin, 1376–1462*. Precy-sur-Thil: Éditions de l'Armançon, 1998.

Biblia Latina cum Glossa Ordinaria. Strassburg: A. Rusch, 1480; reprinted with introductions by Karlfried Froehlich and Margaret T. Gibson. Turnhout: Brepols 1992.

Biddick, Kathleen. *The Theological Imaginary. Circumcision, Technology, History*. Philadelphia: University of Pennsylvania Press, 2003.

Bigwood, Georges. *Le régime juridique et économique du commerce de l'argent dans la Belgique du moyen âge*. 2 volumes. Brussels: M. Lamertin, 1921.

Bireley, Robert. *The Refashioning of Catholicism, 1450–1700: A Reassessment of the Counter Reformation*. Washington, DC: Catholic University of America, 1999.

Black, Robert. *Humanism and Education in Medieval and Renaissance Italy: Tradition and Innovation in Latin Schools from the Twelfth to the Fifteenth Century*. Cambridge and New York: Cambridge University Press, 2001.

Blaisdell, Charmarie J. "Angela Merici and the Ursulines." In *Religious Orders of the Catholic Reformation*, edited by Richard L. DeMolen, 99–136. New York: Fordham University Press, 1994.

Blöcker, Suzanne. *Studien zur Ikonographie der Sieben Todsünden in der Niederländischen und Deutschen Malerei und Graphik von 1450–1560*. Münster: Lit, 1993.

Bloom, Jonathan M. *Paper Before Print: The History and Impact of Paper in the Islamic World*. New Haven: Yale University Press, 2001.

Blumenkranz, Bernhard. *Juifs et Chrétiens dans le monde occidental, 430–1096*. Paris-La Haye: Mouton, 1960.

———. *Juifs et Chrétiens. Patristique et Moyen Age*. London: Variorum Reprints, 1977.

Boccaccio, Giovanni. *Decameron*, edited by Vittore Branca. Turin: Einaudi, 1984.

Boinet, A. "Choix de miniatures détachées conservées au Musée de Cluny à Paris." *Bulletin de la Société française de reproduction de manuscrits à peintures* 6 (1922): 5–30.

Bolton, Brenda. "Innocent III's Treatment of the Humiliati." In *Popular Belief and Practice: Papers Read at the Ninth Summer Meeting and the Tenth Winter Meeting of the Ecclesiastical History Society*, edited by G.J. Cuming and D. Baker, 73–82. Cambridge: Cambridge University Press, 1972.

———. "The Poverty of the Humiliati." In *Poverty in the Middle Ages*, edited by David Flood, 52–9. Werl/Westfalen: Dietrich-Coelde-Verlag, 1975.

———. "Sources for the Early History of the Humiliati." In *The Materials, Sources and Methods of Ecclesiastical History*, edited by Derek Baker. New York: Barnes and Noble Books, 1975.

Boone, Marc. "Geldhandel en pandbedrijf in Gent tijdens de Bourgondische periode: politieke, fiscale en sociale aspecten." *Revue belge de Philologie et d'Histoire* 66 (1988): 767–91.

———. *Geld en Macht. De Gentse stadsfinanciën en de Bourgondische staatsvorming (1384–1453)*. Ghent: Maatschappij voor Geschiedenis en Oudheidkunde, 1990.

Bowsky, William. *The Finance of the Commune of Siena, 1287-1355*. Oxford: Clarendon Press, 1970.

Bracciolini, Poggio. *De avaritia*, edited by Giuseppe Germano. Livorno: Belforte, 1994.

Branca, Vittore, ed. *Merchant Writers of the Italian Renaissance*, translated by Murtha Baca. New York: Marsilio, 1999.

Brant, Sebastian. *The Ship of Fools*, translated by Edwin Zeydel. New York: Dover, 1962.

Brasher, Sally Mayall. "Toward a New Understanding of Women's Medieval Religiosity. The Humiliati and Beguine Movements Compared." In *Magistra: A Journal of Women's Spirituality in the Middle Ages*. Winter 2005.

——. *Women of the Humiliati. A Lay Religious Order in Medieval Civic Life*. New York: Routledge Press, 2003.

Brodman, James William. *Charity and Welfare: Hospitals and the Poor in Medieval Catalonia*. Philadelphia: University of Pennsylvania Press, 1998.

Broggi, Maria Motta. "Il Catalogo del 1298." In *Sulle tracce degli Umiliati*, edited by M.P. Alberzoni and Annamaria Ambrosioni, 3–44. Milan: Vita e Pensiero, 1997.

Brolis, Maria Teresa. *Gli Umiliati a Bergamo nei secoli XIII e XIV*. Milan: Vita e Pensiero, 1991.

Bromham, A.A. and Zara Bruzzi. *The Changeling and the Years of Crisis, 1619–1624*. New York: Pinter Publishing, 1990.

Brucker, Gene. "Monasteries, Friaries, and Nunneries in Quattrocento Florence." In *Christianity and the Renaissance: Image and Religious Imagination in the Quattrocento*, edited by T. Verdon and J. Henderson. Syracuse: Syracuse University Press, 1990.

——. *Florence, The Golden Age, 1138–1737*. Berkeley: University of California Press, 1998.

Bruschi, Caterina. "Gli Umiliati a Parma (XIII–XIV secolo). Instaurazione e sviluppo di rapporti molteplici." *Rivista di Storia e Letteratura Religiosa* 36 (2000).

Bruster, Douglas. *Drama and the Market in the Age of Shakespeare*. Cambridge: Cambridge University Press, 1992.

Bueler, Lois E. "The Rhetoric of Change in *The Changeling*." *English Literary Renaissance* 14, no. 1 (1984): 95–113.

Burks, Deborah G. "'I'll Want my Will Else': *The Changeling* and Women's Complicity with their Rapists." *ELH* 62, no. 4 (1995): 759–90.

Burnett, Mark Thornton. "*The Changeling* and Masters and Servants." In *Early Modern English Drama: A Critical Companion*, edited by Garrett A. Sullivan, Jr., Patrick Cheney, and Andrew Hadfield, 298–308. Oxford: Oxford University Press, 2006.

Busignani, Alberto and Raffaello Bencini. *Le Chiese di Firenze: Quartiere di Santa Maria Novella*. Florence: Sansoni, 1979.

Busse Berger, Anna Maria. *Medieval Music and the Art of Memory*. Berkeley and Los Angeles: University of California Press, 2005.

——. *Mensuration and Proportion Signs: Origins and Evolution*. Oxford: Clarendon Press, 1993.

Bynum, Carolyn Walker. *Wonderful Blood. Theology and Practice in Late Medieval Northern Germany and Beyond*. Philadelphia: University of Pennsylvania Press, 2007.

Cadogan, Jean K. *Domenico Ghirlandaio.* New Haven: Yale University Press, 2000.
Cameron, Avril. *Christianity and the Rhetoric of the Empire: The Development of Christian Discourse*. Berkeley: University of California Press, 1991.
Carapetyan, Arman, ed. *Anonimi: Notitia del valore delle note del canto misurato.* Nijmegen: American Institute of Musicology, 1957.
Carlebach, Joseph. *Lewi ben Gerson als mathematiker*. Berlin: L. Lamm, 1910.
Carroll, Margaret. "'In the Name of God and Profit': Jan van Eyck's *Arnolfini Portrait*." *Representations* 44 (Fall 1993): 96–132.
Casagrande, Carla and Silvana Vecchio. *I setti vizi capitali: storia dei peccati nel medioevo.* Turin: Einaudi, 2000.
Castagnetti, Daniela. "La regola del primo e secondo ordine dall'approvazione alla 'Regula Benedicti'." In *Sulle tracce degli Umiliati*, edited by M.P. Alberzoni, A. Ambrosioni, and A. Lucioni. Milan: Vita e Pensiero, 1997.
Castiglione, Baldassar. *The Courtier*, edited by Daniel Javitch, translated by Charles Singleton. New York: Norton, 2002.
——. *Il Libro del cortegiano*, edited by Giulio Carnazzi and Salvatore Battaglia. Milan: Rizzoli, 1987.
Castiglioni, Carlo. "L'Ordine degli Umiliati in tre codici illustrati dell'Ambrosiana." *Memorie storiche della Diocesi di Milano* 7 (1960).
Celano, Thomas. "The First Life of Saint Francis." In *English Omnibus of the Sources for the Life of St Francis*, edited by Marion A. Habig, 225–334. Chicago: Franciscan Herald Press, 1973.
Chakravorty, Swapan. *Society and Politics in the Plays of Thomas Middleton*. Oxford: Oxford University Press, 1996.
Challis, C.E. *The Tudor Coinage*. Manchester: Manchester University Press, 1978.
Chartier, Roger. Introduction to *A History of Private Life, Vol. 3, Passions of the Renaissance*, edited by Philippe Ariès and Georges Duby, translated by Arthur Goldhammer. Cambridge, MA: Harvard University Press, 1989.
Chazan, Robert. *Medieval Stereotypes and Modern Antisemitism.* Berkeley and Los Angeles: University of California Press, 1997.
Chazelle, Celia. *The Crucified God in the Carolingian Era. Theology and Art of Christ's Passion*. Cambridge: Cambridge University Press, 2001.
Christiansen, Keith. *From Van Eyck to Bruegel: Early Netherlandish Painting in the Metropolitan Museum of Art.* New York: Metropolitan Museum of Art, 1998.
Chromatius Aquileiensis. *Tractatus XVIII in Evangelium S. Matthaei*. In *Patrologia latina* 106; in *Chromatii Aquileiensis Opera*, edited by Raymond Etaix and Joseph Lemarié. Turnhout: Brepols, 1974.
Clay, C.G.A. *Economic Expansion and Social Change: England 1500–1700*. 2 volumes. Cambridge: Cambridge University Press, 1984.
Cluse, Cristopher, ed. *The Jews of Europe in the Middle Ages (Tenth to Fifteenth Centuries): Proceedings of the International Symposium held at Speyer, 20–25 October 2002*. Turnhout: Brepols, 2004.

Coffey, Peter. "Henry of Ghent." In *The Catholic Encyclopedia* VII. New York: Robert Appleton Company, 1910. August 9, 2008 <http://www.newadvent.org/cathen/07235b.htm>.

Cohen, Jeremy. *Living Letters of the Law: Ideas of the Jew in Medieval Christianity*. Berkeley: University of California Press, 1999.

Cohn, Samuel K. *The Laboring Classes in Renaissance Florence.* New York: Academic Press, 1980.

———. "Women and Work in Renaissance Italy." In *Gender and Society in Renaissance Italy*, edited by Judith C. Brown and Robert C. Davis. New York: Longman, 1998.

Conciliorum Oecumenicorum Decreta, edited by J. Alberigo, P.P. Joannou, C. Leonardi and P. Prodi, consultant H. Jedin. Bologna: EDB, 1973.

Cornish, Alison. "*Volgarizzamenti*: To Remember and to Forget." Forthcoming in *The Art of Memory: Between Archive and Invention from the Middle Ages to the Late Renaissance; Acts of an International Conference, Florence, Villa I Tatti, May 11, 2006*. Florence: Olschki, 2008.

Cotrugli, Benedetto (Raguseo). *Il libro dell'arte di mercatura*, edited by Ugo Tucci. Venice: Arsenale, 1990.

Courtépée, Claude and Edme Beguillet. *Description générale et particulière du Duché de Bourgogne*, edited by Pierre Gras and Jean Richard. 3rd edition. Avallon: Éditions F.E.R.N.; distr. Paris: Librairie Guénégaud, 1967.

Cowell, Andrew. "The Fall of the Oral Economy: Writing Economics on the Dead Body." *Exemplaria* 8 (1996): 145–68.

Crosby, Alfred W. *The Measure of Reality: Quantification and Western Society, 1250–1600*. Cambridge: Cambridge University Press, 1997.

Crupi, Charles W. "The Transformation of De Flores in *The Changeling*." *Neophilologus* 68, no. 1 (1984): 142–8.

Culpepper, Daniel. "'Our Particular Cloister': Ursulines and Female Education in Seventeenth-Century Parma and Piacenza." *Sixteenth Century Journal* XXXVI, no. 4 (2005): 1017–37.

Daalder, Joost and Antony Telford Moore. "'There's Scarce a Thing But is Both Loved and Loathed': *The Changeling* I.i.91–129." *English Studies* 80, no. 6 (1999): 499–508.

Dahan, Gilbert. *Les intellectuels chrétiens et les juifs au moyen âge*. Paris: Cerf, 1990.

Dante Alighieri. *The Divine Comedy*, translated by Allen Mandelbaum. New York: Bantam, 1995, Doubleday, 1958.

Dasberg, Leah. *Untersuchungen über die Entwertung des Judenstatus im 11. Jahrhundert*. Den Haag: Mouton, 1965.

Dauzat, Pierre-Emmanuel. *Judas: de l'Évangile à l'Holocauste.* Paris: Bayard, 2006.

———. *L'Invention de Marie-Madeleine.* Paris: Bayard, 2001.

Davidsohn, Robert. *Storia di Firenze*, translated by G.B. Klein from *Geschichte von Florenz*, 1896–1927. Florence: Sansoni, 1956–68.

Dawson, Anthony B. "Giving the Finger: Puns and Transgression in *The Changeling*." *The Elizabethan Theatre* 12 (1993): 93–112.

Day, John. "The Great Bullion Famine of the Fifteenth Century." *Past and Present* 79 (1978): 3–54.

Decretales pseudoisidorianae et Capitula Angilramni, edited by Paul Hinschius. Leipzig: Tauchnitz, 1863.

Decretum Gratiani, edited by Emil Friedberg. Leipzig: Tauchnitz, 1879.

De Hamel, Christopher. *The Hours of Albrecht of Brandenburg, Illuminated Manuscript by Simon Bening*. Sotheby's London, June 19, 2001.

De Jongh, Eddy. "Grape Symbolism in Paintings of the 16th and 17th Centuries." *Simiolus* 7 (1974): 166–87.

De Pauw, N., ed. *De voorgeboden der stad Gent in de XIVe eeuw (1337–1382)*. Ghent: C. Annoot-Braeckman, 1885.

Derbes, Anne and Mark Sandona. "Barren Metal and the Fruitful Womb: The Program of Giotto's Arena Chapel in Padua." *Art Bulletin* 80 (1998): 274–91.

——. *The Usurer's Heart: Giotto, Enrico Scrovegni, and the Arena Chapel in Padua*. University Park, PA: Pennsylvania State University Press, 2008.

De Roover, Raymond. *Money, Banking and Credit in Mediaeval Bruges: Italian Merchant Bankers, Lombards and Money Changers*. Cambridge, MA: Medieval Academy of America, 1948.

——. *San Bernardino of Siena and Sant'Antonino of Florence*. Kress Library of Business and Economics Series, no. 19. Cambridge: Harvard University Press, 1967.

Dhanens, Elisabeth. *Hubert and Jan van Eyck*. New York: Alpine Fine Arts Collection, 1980.

Di Bella, Maria Pia, ed. *Vol et sanctions en Meditérranée*. Amsterdam: Éditions des Archives Contemporaines, 1998.

Di Cagno, Gabriella and Donatella Pegazzano. "San Salvatore in Ognissanti: gli altari del Cinquecento (1561–1582) e il loro arredo nel contesto della Riforma Cattolica." In *Altari e Committenza: Episodi nell'età della Controriforma*, edited by C. de Benedictis, 93–104. Florence: Angelo Pontecorboli editore, 1996.

Diefendorf, Barbara B. *From Penitence to Charity: Pious Women and the Catholic Reformation in Paris*. Oxford: Oxford University Press, 2004.

Dobson, R.B., ed. *The Peasants' Revolt of 1381*. 2nd edition. London: Macmillan, 1983.

Drews, Wolfram. "Jews as Pagans? Polemical Definitions of Identity in Visigothic Spain." *Early Medieval Europe* 11, no. 2 (2002): 189–207.

Du Cange, Charles Du Fresne. *Glossarium mediae et infimae latinitatis*. 5 volumes. Reprint, Graz: Akademische Druck-U. Verlagsanstalt, 1954.

Dürer, Albrecht. *Albrecht Dürer: Sketchbook of His Journey to the Netherlands (1520–21)*, edited by Philip Troutman. New York and Washington: Praeger, 1971.

Dyer, Christopher. *An Age of Transition?: Economy and Society in England in the Later Middle Ages*. Oxford: Clarendon Press, 2005.

——. *Standards of Living in the Later Middle Ages: Social Change in England c. 1200–1520*. Revised edition. Cambridge: Cambridge University Press, 1998.

Eagleton, Catherine and Jonathan Williams. *Money: A History*. 2nd edition. London: British Museum Press, 2007.

Epp, Garrett P.J. "The Towneley Plays and the Hazards of Cycling." *Research Opportunities in Renaissance Drama* 32 (1993): 121–50.

Epstein, Steven A. *Wage Labor and Guilds in Medieval Europe*. Chapel Hill, NC: University of North Carolina Press, 1991.

Espinas, G. and H. Pirenne, eds. *Recueil de documents relatifs à l'histoire de l'industrie drapière en Flandre*. 4 volumes. Brussels: P. Imbreghts, 1906, pt. 1, vol. 1, pp. 532–52.

Favreau, Robert. "Les changeurs du royaume sous le règne de Louis XI." *Bibliothèque de l'école des chartes* 122 (1964): 229.

Fehm, Sherwood A. *Luca di Tommè: A Sienese Fourteenth-Century Painter*. Carbondale: Southern Illinois University Press, 1986.

Fenster, Thelma and Daniel L. Smail, eds. *Fama: The Politics of Talk and Reputation in Medieval Europe*. Ithaca, London: Cornell University Press, 2003.

Finkelstein, Andrea. *Harmony and Balance: An Intellectual History of Seventeenth-Century English Economic Thought*. Ann Arbor: University of Michigan Press, 2000.

Forman, Valerie. *Tragicomic Redemptions: Global Economics and the Early Modern English Stage*. Philadelphia: University of Pennsylvania Press, 2008.

——. "Transformations of Value and the Production of 'Investment' in the Early History of the English East India Company." *Journal of Medieval and Early Modern Studies* 34, no. 3 (2004): 611–41.

Francica, Ilaria. "Gli Umiliati a Bologna nel '200: Forme e significato di una *religio* attiva." *Atti e Memorie: Deputazione di Storia Patria per la Province di Romagna* 45 (1994).

Franklin, David. "Rosso, Leonardo Buonafé and the Francesca de Ripoi altarpiece." *Burlington Magazine* 129 (1987): 652–62.

Freedman, Paul. *Images of the Medieval Peasant*. Stanford: Stanford University Press, 1999.

Freuler, Gaudenz. *Biagio di Goro Ghezzi a Paganico. L'affresco nell'abside della Chiesa di San Michele*. Florence: Electa, 1986.

Frojmovic, Eva, ed. *Imagining the Self, Imagining the Other: Visual Representation and Jewish–Christian Dynamics in the Middle Ages and Early Modern Period*. Leiden: Brill, 2002.

Gash, Anthony. "Carnival Against Lent: The Ambivalence of Medieval Drama." In *Medieval Literature: Criticism, Ideology and History*, edited by David Aers. Southampton: Harvester Press, 1986.

Gehl, Paul F. *A Moral Art: Grammar, Society, and Culture in Trecento Florence*. Ithaca: Cornell University Press, 1993.

Gessler, Jean, ed. *Le livre des mestiers de Bruges et ses dérivés, quatre anciens manuels de conversation*. Bruges: Fondation universitaire, 1931.

Gilchrist, John. "The Canonistic Treatment of Jews in the Latin West in the Eleventh and Early Twelfth Centuries." *Zeitschrift der Savigny Stiftung für Rechtsgeschichte—Kanonische Abteilung* 106, no. 75 (1989): 70–106.

Gilliodts-van Severen, L. *Coutumes des pays et comtés de Flandre. Quartier de Bruges*. 2 volumes. Bruges: F. Gobbaerts, 1874.

Goldberg, P.J.P. *Women, Work, and Life Cycle in a Medieval Economy: Women in York and Yorkshire c. 1300–1520.* Oxford: Clarendon Press, 1992, repr. 1996.

Goldthwaite, Richard A. "La fondazione e il consenso della città." In *Gli Innocenti e Firenze nei secoli*, edited by Lucia Sandri. Florence: Istituto degli Innocenti, 2005.

Grant, Edward, translator and annotator. "Part I of Nicole Oresme's *Algorismus proportionum*." *Isis* 56 (1965): 327–41.

Grebe, Anja. "The Art of the Edge: Frames and Page-Design in Manuscripts of the Ghent–Bruges School." In *The Metamorphosis of Marginal Images*, edited by Nurith Kenaan-Kedar and Asher Ovadiah, 93–102. Tel Aviv: Tel Aviv University, 2001.

Greenidge, Abel H.J., *Infamia: Its Place in Roman Public and Private Law*. Oxford: Oxford University Press, 1894.

Gregori, Mina. "Giovanni da Milano: Storia di un politico." *Paragone* 265 (1972): 3–35.

Grierson, Philip. "The Dates of the 'Livre des Mestiers' and its Derivatives." *Revue belge de philologie et d'histoire* 35 (1957): 778–83.

Groppi, Angela. "Lavoro e proprietà delle donne in età moderna." In *Il Lavoro delle donne*, edited by Angela Groppi, 119–63. Bari: Laterza, 1996.

Grosshans, Rainald. *Maerten van Heemskerck: die Gemälde.* Berlin: Bottcher, 1980.

Grundmann, Herbert. *Religiöse Bewegungen im Mittelalter.* Berlin: E. Ebering: 1935; 2nd revised edition, Darmstadt: Wissenschaftliche Buchgesellschaft, 1961.

——. *Religious Movements of the Middle Ages*, translated by Steven Rowan, edited by Robert Lerner. Notre Dame: University of Notre Dame Press, 1995.

Gruterius, J. *Florilegium ethico-politicum nunquam antehac editum.* Frankfurt: Rhodius, 1610–12.

Guerrini, P. "Gli Umiliati a Brescia." In *Miscellanea Pio Paschini. Studi di storia ecclesiastica I.* Rome: Facultas theologica pontificii athenaei lateranensis, 1948.

Gueudré, Marie de Chantal. *Histoire de l'ordre des Ursulines en France.* 2 T. Paris: Éditions Saint-Paul, 1958–63.

Guidetti, Armando. *San Carlo Borromeo: La Vita nell'iconografia e nei documenti*. Milan: Rusconi Libri, 1984.

Günther, Ursula, ed. *The Motets of the Manuscripts Chantilly, Musée condé, 564 (olim 1047) and Modena, Biblioteca estense, a. M. 5, 24 (olim lat. 568)*. N.p.: American Institute of Musicology, 1965.

Haber, Judith. "'I(t) Could Not Choose but Follow': Erotic Logic in *The Changeling*." *Representations* 81 (2003): 79–98.

Hanawalt, Barbara A. "Peasant Resistance to Royal and Seigneurial Impositions." In *Social Unrest in the Late Middle Ages*, edited by Francis X. Newman, 23–47. Binghamton: Medieval and Renaissance Texts and Studies, 1986.

Hand, John Oliver. *Joos van Cleve*. New Haven and London: Yale University Press, 2004.

—— and Martha Wolf. *Early Netherlandish Painting*. Washington: National Gallery of Art, 1986.

Hanham, Alison. "Who Made William Caxton's Phrase-Book?" *The Review of English Studies* 56, no. 227 (2005): 712–29.

Happé, Peter. *The Towneley Cycle: Unity and Diversity*. Cardiff: University of Wales Press, 2007.

Harbison, Craig. *Jan van Eyck: The Play of Realism*. London: Reaktion Books, 1991.

Harrán, Don. *In Defense of Music: The Case for Music as Argued by a Singer and Scholar of the Late Fifteenth Century*. Lincoln: University of Nebraska Press, 1989.

Harris, Jonathan Gil. *Sick Economies: Drama, Mercantilism, and Disease in Shakespeare's England*. Philadelphia: University of Pennsylvania Press, 2004.

Hartnett, Edith. "Cain in the Medieval *Towneley Play*." *Annuale Mediaevale* 12 (1971): 21–9.

Haude, Sigrun."The Rule of Fear: The Impact of Anabaptist 'Terror' 1534–1535." PhD dissertation, University of Arizona, 1993.

Havely, Nick. *Dante and the Franciscans*. Cambridge: Cambridge University Press, 2004.

Hawkes, David. *The Faust Myth: Religion and the Rise of Representation*. New York: Palgrave Macmillan, 2007.

——. *Idols of the Marketplace: Idolatry and Commodity Fetishism in English Literature 1580–1680*. New York: Palgrave Macmillan, 2001.

Haynes, Stephen R. *Reluctant Witness: Jews and Christian Imagination*. Westminster: John Knox Press, 1995.

Hébert, Catherine A. "A Note on the Significance of the Title of Middleton's *The Changeling*." *College Language Association Journal* 12 (1968): 66–99.

Hedrick, Donald and Bryan Reynolds. "I Might Like You Better if We Slept Together: The Historical Drift of Place in *The Changeling*." In *Transversal Enterprises in the Drama of Shakespeare and his Contemporaries*, edited by Bryan Reynolds, 112–23. New York: Palgrave Macmillan, 2006.

Heinemann, Margot. *Puritanism and Theatre: Thomas Middleton and Opposition Drama under the Early Stuarts*. Cambridge: Cambridge University Press, 1982.

Henderson, John. *Piety and Charity in Late Medieval Florence*. Oxford: Clarendon Press, 1994; Chicago: University of Chicago Press, 1997.

Henry of Ghent. *Opera Omnia*. Leiden: Brill, 1979.

Herlinger, Jan. "Medieval Canonics." In *The Cambridge History of Western Music Theory*, edited by Thomas Christensen, 168–92. Cambridge: Cambridge University Press, 2002.

Higgins, Paula. "'In hydraulis' Revisited: New Light on the Career of Antoine Busnois." *Journal of the American Musicological Society* 39 (1986): 36–86.

Hilton, R.H. *The English Peasantry in the Later Middle Ages*. Oxford: Clarendon Press, 1975.

Hinnebusch, J. *The Historia Occidentalis of Jacques de Vitry*. Fribourg: University Press, 1972.

Histoire de Chalon-sur-Saône, edited by Pierre Lévêque. Dijon: Éditions Universitaires de Dijon, 2005.

Honig, Elizabeth A. *Painting and the Market in Early Modern Antwerp*. New Haven: Yale University Press, 1998.

Hopkins, Lisa. "Beguiling the Master of the Mystery: Form and Power in *The Changeling*." *Medieval and Renaissance Drama in England* 9 (1997): 149–61.

Hoppin, Richard, ed. *Anthology of Medieval Music*. New York: W.W. Norton, 1978.

Howell, Martha. "The Properties of Marriage in Late Medieval Europe: Commercial Wealth and the Creation of Modern Marriage." In *Love, Marriage and Family Ties in the Later Middle Ages*, edited by Isabel Davis, Miriam Müller, and Sarah Rees Jones, 17–61. Turnhout: Brepols, 2003.

Hughes, Diane Owen. "Kinsmen and Neighbors in Medieval Genoa." In *The Medieval City*, edited by Harry A. Miskimin, David Herlihy, and A.L. Udovitch, 95–111. New Haven: Yale University Press, 1977.

Hults, Linda C. *The Print in the Western World: An Introductory History*. Madison: University of Wisconsin Press, 1996.

Humbertus de Silvacandida. *Adversus simoniacos libri tres*, edited by Friedrich Thaner, Monumenta Germaniae Historica, "Libelli de lite" I. Hannover: Hahn 1891.

Ilnitchi, Gabriela. "*Musica mundana*, Aristotelian Natural Philosophy, and Ptolemaic Astronomy." *Early Music History* 21 (2002): 37–74.

Iohannes Cassianus. *De institutis coenobiorum et de octo principalium vitiorum remediis*. In Jean Cassien, *Institutions cénobitiques*, edited by Jean-Claude Guy. Paris: Cerf, 2001.

Isidorus. *Etymologiae*, edited by Wallace Martin Lindsay. Oxford: Oxford University Press, 1911; edited by Manuel C. Diaz y Diaz. Madrid: BAC, 1983.

Jacob, Margaret C. and Catherine Secretan, eds. *The Self-Perception of Early Modern Capitalists*. New York: Palgrave Macmillan, 2008.

Jacobs, Henry E. "The Constancy of Change: Character and Perspective in *The Changeling*." *Texas Studies in Literature and Language* 16, no. 4 (1975): 651–74.

Jansen, Katherine L. *The Making of the Magdalen: Preaching and Popular Devotion in the Later Middle Ages*. Princeton: Princeton University Press, 2000.

Jardine, Lisa. *Worldy Goods*. London: Macmillan, 1996.

Jodogne, Omer, ed. *Le mystère de la passion d'Arnoul Gréban*. Bruxelles: Academie Royale de Belgique, 1965.

Johnson, Charles, ed. *The De Moneta of Nicholas Oresme and English Mint Documents*. Edinburgh and London: Thomas Nelson and Sons Ltd., 1956.

Jonson, Ben. *Volpone*. In *The Alchemist and Other Plays*, edited by Gordon Campbell. New York: Oxford University Press, 1995.

Kaelber, Lutz. "Max Weber and Usury: Implications for Historical Research." In *Money, Markets and Trade in Late Medieval Europe*, edited by Lawrin Armstrong, Ivana Elbl, and Martin M. Ebl, 59–85. Leiden: Brill, 1977.

Kahr, Madlyn Millner. "Danaë: Virtuous, Voluptuous, Venal Woman." *Art Bulletin* LX (1978): 43–55.

Kaye, Joel. *Economy and Nature in the Fourteenth Century: Money, Market Exchange, and the Emergence of Scientific Thought*. Cambridge: Cambridge University Press, 1998.

Kayll, Robert. *The Trade's Increase*. London: Walter Barre, 1615.

Kempshall, Matthew S. *The Common Good in Late Medieval Political Thought*. Oxford: Oxford University Press, 1999.

Kent, Dale. *Cosimo de' Medici and the Florentine Renaissance: The Patron's Oeuvre*. New Haven: Yale University Press, 2000.

Kessler-Harris, Alice. "Do We Still Need Women's History?" *The Chronicle of Higher Education* (December 7, 2007): Section B, 6–7.

Kieckhefer, Richard. *Magic in the Middle Ages*. Cambridge: Cambridge University Press, 1989. Reprinted, 2000.

Kindleberger, Charles P. "The Economic Crisis of 1619 to 1623." *The Journal of Economic History* 51, no. 1 (1991): 149–75.

Klauck, Hans-Josef. *Judas. Ein Jünger des Herrn*. Freiburg: Herder, 1987.

———. *Judas, un disciple de Jésus. Exégèse et répercussions historiques*. Paris: Cerf, 2006.

Koldeweij, Jos. *Geloof en Geluk: Sieraad en Devotie in Middeleeuws Vlaanderen*. Bruges: Gruuthuse, 2006.

König, Eberhard. *Boccaccio Decameron*. Stuttgart: Belser, 1989.

Kooper, Erik. "Political Theory and Pastoral Care in the *Second Shepherds' Play*." In *This Noble Craft*, edited by Erik Kooper, 142–51. Amsterdam: Rodopi, 1991.

Kren, Thomas, ed. *Renaissance Painting in Manuscripts: Treasures from the British Library*. New York: Hudson Hills Press, 1983.

Kroll, Norma. "The Towneley and Chester Plays of the Shepherds: The Dynamic Interweaving of Power, Conflict, and Destiny." *Studies in Philology* 100, no. 3 (2003): 315–45.

Kusman, David. "Une couronne anglaise pour le Duc de Brabant: L'engagement de joyaux du roi d'Angleterre à Bruxelles et à Liège (1297–1298)." *Annales de la société royale d'archéologie de Bruxelles* 67 (2006): 12–49.

Lambert, Malcolm. *Medieval Heresy. Popular Movements from the Gregorian Reform to the Reformation*. 2nd edition. Oxford: Blackwell, 1992.

Lami, Giovanni. *Sanctae Ecclesiae Florentinae Monumenta*. Florence: Angelo Salutati, 1758.

Landau, Peter. *Die Entstehung des kanonischen Infamienbegriffs von Gratian zur Glossa Ordinaria*. Köln-Graz: Böhlau Verlag, 1966.

Langholm, Odd Inge. *Wealth and Money in the Aristotelian Tradition: A Study in Scholastic Economic Sources*. Bergen: Universitetsforlagen, 1983.

——. *Wealth, Exchange, Value, Money and Usury According to the Paris Theological Tradition, 1200–1350*. Leiden: Brill, 1992.

Lanham, Richard A. *A Handlist of Rhetorical Terms*. 2nd edition. Berkeley: University of California Press, 1991.

Larivaille, Paul. *La vie quotidienne des courtisanes en Italie au temps de la Renaissance*. Paris: Hachette, 1975.

Leech-Wilkinson, Daniel. *Compositional Techniques in the Four-Part Isorhythmic Motets of Philippe de Vitry and his Contemporaries*. 2 volumes. New York: Garland, 1989.

Leff, Gordon. *Heresy in the Later Middle Ages: The Relation of Heterodoxy to Dissent c. 1250–c. 145*0. Manchester: Manchester University Press, 1967.

Le Goff, Jacques. *La bourse et la vie: économie et religion au Moyen Age*. Paris: Hachette, 1986.

——. *La naissance du Purgatoire*. Paris: Gallimard, 1981.

——. "Licit and Illicit Trades in the Medieval West." In *Time, Work and Culture in the Middle Ages*, translated byArthur Goldhammer, 58–70. Chicago: University of Chicago Press, 1980.

——. *Your Money or Your Life: Economy and Religion in the Middle Ages*, translated by Patricia Ranum. New York: Zone Books, 1988.

Leinwand, Theodore B. *Theatre, Finance and Society in Early Modern England*. Cambridge: Cambridge University Press, 1999.

The Letters of Michelangelo, translated by E.H. Ramsden. Stanford: Stanford University Press, 1963.

Levin, William R. "Advertising Charity in the Trecento: The Public Decorations of the Misericordia in Florence." *Studies in Iconography* 17 (1996): 215–309.

——. *The 'Allegory of Mercy' at the Misericorida in Florence*. Dallas: University Press of America, 2004.

——. "'Lost Children', a Working Mother, and the Progress of an Artist at the Florentine Misericordia in the Trecento." *Publications of the Medieval Association of the Midwest* 6 (1999): 34–84.

Lightbown, Ronald. *Sandro Botticelli*. Berkeley: University of California Press, 1978.

Linder, Amnon. *The Jews in the Legal Sources of the Early Middle Ages*. Detroit : Wayne State University Press, 1997.
Lipton, Sarah. *Images of Intolerance: The Representation of Jews and Judaism in the Bible moralisée*. Berkeley: University of California Press, 1999.
Lisner, Margrit. "Significati e iconografia del colore nella 'Madonna d'Ognissanti'." In *La Madonna d'Ognissanti di Giotto*. Florence: Centro Di, 1992.
Little, Lester K. *Liberty, Charity, Fraternity: Lay Religious Confraternities in Bergamo in the Age of the Commune*. Northampton, MA: Smith College Library, 1988.
——. "Pride Goes before Avarice: Social Change and the Vices in Latin Christendom." *The American Historical Review* 76, no. 1 (February 1971): 16–49.
——. *Religious Poverty and the Profit Economy in Medieval Europe*. Ithaca: Cornell University Press, 1978.
Livy. *History of Rome*. 14 volumes, Loeb Classical Library, translated by B.O. Foster. Cambridge, MA: Harvard University Press, 1969.
Lockwood, Lewis. *Music in Renaissance Ferrara, 1400–1505*. Cambridge, MA: Harvard University Press, 1984.
Long, Michael P. *Musical Tastes in Fourteenth-Century Italy: Notational Styles, Scholarly Traditions, and Historical Circumstances*. PhD dissertation, Princeton University, 1981.
——. "Singing Through the Looking Glass: Child's Play and Learning in Medieval Italy." *Journal of the American Musicological Society* 61 (2008): 253–306.
Lunari, Marco. "Alla ricerca di un'identità. La cronaca di Giovanni di Brera." In *Un Monastero alle porte della città, Atti del convegno per i 650 anni dell'Abbazia di Viboldone*, 143–63. Milan: Vita e Pensiero, 1999.
——. "Appunti per una storiografia sugli Umiliati tra Quattro e Cinquecento." In *Sulle tracce degli Umiliati*, edited by M.P. Alberzoni, A. Ambrosioni, and A. Lucioni. Milan: Vita e Pensiero, 1997.
Lunghi, Elvio. *The Basilica of St Francis in Assisi*. Florence: Scala, 1996.
Lupus de Olmeto. *Regula monachorum ex scriptis Hieronymi per Lupum de Olmeto collecta*. In *Patrologia latina* 219.
Lux-Sterritt, Laurence. *Redefining Female Religious Life: French Ursulines and English Ladies in Seventeenth Century Catholicism*. Aldershot: Ashgate, 2005.
McDonnell, Ernest William. *The Beguines and Beghards in Medieval Culture with an Emphasis on the Belgian Scene*. New Brunswick: Octagon, 1986.
McGuinn, Thomas A.J. *The Economy of Prostitution in the Roman World: A Study of the Social History of the Brothel*. Ann Arbor: University of Michigan Press, 2004.
Machiavelli, Niccolò. *Discourses on the First Ten Books of Titus Livius*, in *The Prince and the Discourses*, translated by Christian E. Detmold. New York: Random House, 1950.
——. *The Prince*, translated by William J. Connell. New York: Bedford, 2005.

——. *Il Principe e altre opere politiche*, edited by Delio Cantimori and Stefano Andretta. Milan: Garzanti, 1979.

Maffi, Alberto. "La costruzione giuridica dell'infamia nell'ordinamento romano." In *La fiducia secondo i linguaggi del potere*, edited by Paolo Prodi, 41–51. Bologna: Il Mulino 2007.

Malcolmson, Christina. "'As Tame as Ladies': Politics and Gender in *The Changeling*." *English Literary Renaissance* 20 (1990): 320–39.

Mallett, Michael. *Mercenaries and Their Masters: Warfare in Renaissance Italy*. Totowa, NJ: Rowman and Littlefield, 1974.

Malynes, Gerard. *The Center of the Circle of Commerce*. London: Nicholas Bourne, 1623.

——. *The Maintenance of Free Trade*. London: William Sheffard, 1622.

Manselli, Raoul. "Gli Umiliati, lavoratori di lana." In *Produzione, commercio e consumo dei panni di lana (nei secoli XII e XIII.) Atti della seconda settimana di studio, Prato 1970*, edited by Marco Spallanzani, 231–6. Florence: L.S. Olschki, 1976.

Marcucci, Luisa. *Gallerie Nazionali di Firenze: I Dipinti Toscani del secolo XIV*. Rome: Istituto Poligrafico dello Stato, 1965.

Marechal, J. *Bijdrage tot de geschiedenis van het bankwezen te Brugge*. Bruges: De Tempel, 1955.

——. "De Houding van de Deken van de Christenheid tegenover een Woekeraar en Voorkoper te Brugge in 1344." *Annales de la Société d'émulation de Bruges* 97 (1954): 73–81.

Marrow, James M. "Simon Bening in 1521: A Group of Dated Miniatures." In *Liber Amicorum Herman Liebaers*, edited by Frans Vanwijngaerden, 537–59. Brussels: Crédit Communal de Belgique, 1984.

Marx, Karl. "The Power of Money in Bourgeois Society." In *The Marx–Engels Reader*, edited by Robert C. Tucker, 101–5. 2nd edition. New York: Norton, 1978.

Mathiesen, Thomas J. "Greek Music Theory." In *The Cambridge History of Western Music Theory*, edited by Thomas Christensen, 109–35. Cambridge: Cambridge University Press, 2002.

Matthews, Nathan. "The Valuation of Property in the Early Common Law." *Harvard Law Review* 35 (1921): 15–29.

May, Georg. "Die Anfänge der Infamie im kanonischen Recht." *Zeitschrift für Rechtsgeschichte—Kanonische Abteilung* 47 (1961): 77–94.

——. "Die Bedeutung der pseudo-isidorischen Sammlung für die Infamie im kanonischen Recht." *Österreichisches Archiv für Kirchenrecht* 12 (1961): 87–113, 191–207.

Mellinkoff, Ruth. *Outcasts: Signs of Otherness in Northern European Art of the Late Middle Ages*. Berkeley: University of California Press, 1993.

Menut, Albert Douglas. "Maistre Nicole Oresme: Le Livre de Politiques d'Aristote." *Transactions of the American Philosophical Society*, n.s. 60, pt. 6, 1970.

Merback, Mitchell B. *The Thief, the Cross and the Wheel. Pain and the Spectacle of Punishment in Medieval and Renaissance Europe*. Chicago: University of Chicago Press, 1999.

Michel, Edouard. *Musée National du Louvre. Catalogue raisonné des peintures du moyen-âge, de la renaissance et des temps modernes. Peintures flamandes du XVe et du XVIe siècles*. Paris: Musées nationaux, 1953.

Migliorino, Francesco. *Fama e infamia. Problemi della società medievale nel pensiero giuridico nei secoli XII e XIII*. Catania: Giannotta, 1985.

——. *Il corpo come testo. Storie del diritto*. Torino: Bollati Boringhieri, 2008.

Miller, Julia and Laurie Taylor-Mitchell. "Donatello's '*S. Rossore*,' the Battle of San Romano, and the Church of Ognissanti." *Burlington Magazine* 148 (2006).

——. "The *Ognissanti Madonna* and the Humiliati Order in Florence." In *The Cambridge Companion to Giotto*, edited by A. Derbes and M. Sandona, 157–75. Cambridge: Cambridge University Press, 2004.

Mills, Geoffrey T. "Early Accounting in Northern Italy: The Role of Commercial Development and the Printing Press in the Expansion of Double Entry from Genoa, Florence and Venice." *Accounting Historians Journal* 21(1994): 81–96.

Mills, Robert. *Suspended Animation. Pain, Pleasure and Punishment in Medieval Culture*. London: Reaktion Books, 2005.

Miskimin, Harry A., David Herlihy, and A.L. Udovitch, eds. *The Medieval Cities*. New Haven: Yale University Press, 1977.

Misselden, Edward. *The Circle of Commerce*. London: Nicholas Bourne, 1623.

——. *Free Trade*. London: Simon Waterson, 1622.

Molho, Anthony. "Masaccio's Florence in Perspective: Crisis and Discipline in a Medieval Society." In *The Cambridge Companion to Masaccio*, edited by D. Ahl. Cambridge: Cambridge University Press, 2002.

Monstadt, Brigitte. *Judas beim Abendmahl: Figurenkonstellation und Bedeutung in Darstellungen von Giotto bis Andrea del Sarto*. Muenchen: Scaneg, 1995.

Montaigne, Michel de. *The Complete Essays*, translated by M.A. Screech. New York: Penguin, 1987.

——. *Essais, Livre 3*, edited by Alexandre Micha. Paris: Flammarion, 1979.

Morelli, Giovanni di Pagolo. *Ricordi*, edited by Vittore Branca. Florence: Le Monnier, 1956.

Morelli, Paolo. "Per una storia delle istituzioni parrocchiali nel basso Medioevo: la prepositura di S. Maria e S. Michele di Cigoli e la pieve di S. Giovanni di Fabbrica." *Bollettino storico pisano* 51 (1982): 36–56.

Morey, James H. "Plows, Laws, and Sanctuary in Medieval England and in the Wakefield *Mactacio Abel*." *Studies in Philology* 95, no. 1 (Winter 1998): 41–55.

Moulton, Ian Frederick. *Before Pornography: Erotic Writing in Early Modern England*. New York: Oxford University Press, 2000.

——. "Crafty Whores: The Moralizing of Aretino's *Dialogues*." In "Reading in Early Modern England," edited by Sasha Roberts. *Critical Survey* 12, no. 2 (Spring 2000): 88–105.
Mun, Thomas. *A Discourse of Trade, from England vnto the East-Indies*. London: John Pyper, 1621.
Murray, Alexander. *Suicide in the Middle Ages*. Oxford: Oxford University Press, 1998–2000.
Murray, James M. *Bruges, Cradle of Capitalism.* Cambridge: Cambridge University Press, 2005.
——. "Family, Marriage, and Moneychanging in Medieval Bruges." *Journal of Medieval History* 14 (1988): 115–25.
Mus, O. "De Brugse companie Despars." *Annales de la Société d'émulation de Bruges* 101 (1964): 5–118.
Neill, Michael, ed. *The Changeling by Thomas Middleton and William Rowley.* New York: A&C Black Publishers, 2006.
Newhauser, Richard. *The Early History of Greed: The Sin of Avarice in Early Medieval Thought and Literature.* New York: Cambridge University Press, 2006.
——. "Towards modus in habendo: Transformations in the Idea of Avarice." In Richard Newhauser, *Sin: Essays on the Moral Tradition in the Western Middle Ages*, II, 1–22. Aldershot: Ashgate, 2007.
Nicholas, David. *The Domestic Life of a Medieval City: Women, Children, and the Family in Fourteenth-Century Ghent.* Lincoln and London: University of Nebraska Press, 1985.
——. *Medieval Flanders.* London: Longman, 1992.
——. *The Van Arteveldes of Ghent.* Ithaca: Cornell University Press, 1988.
Noonan, John T. Jr. *The Scholastic Analysis of Usury*. Cambridge: Harvard University Press, 1957.
Nuttall, Paula. *From Flanders to Florence: The Impact of Netherlandish Painting, 1400–1500.* New Haven and London: Yale University Press, 2004.
Odo Cluniacensis. *Sermo. In veneratione Sanctae Mariae Magdalenae.* In *Patrologia latina* 133.
Ongaro, Giulio. "Sixteenth-Century Patronage at St Mark's, Venice." *Early Music History* 8 (1988): 81–115.
Oresme, Nicole. *Le Livre du Ciel et du Monde*, edited by Albert D. Menut and Alexander J. Denomy. Madison: University of Wisconsin Press, 1968.
Origo, Iris. *The Merchant of Prato. Francesco di Marco Datini 1335–1410.* New York: Alfred A. Knopf, 1957.
Otis, Leah Lydia. *Prostitution in Medieval Society: The History of an Urban Institution in Languedoc.* Chicago: University of Chicago Press, 1985.
Owst, G.R. *Literature and Pulpit in Medieval England.* 2nd revised edition, 1961. Reprinted, New York: Barnes and Noble, 1966.
Oxford. Bodleian Library. Canon misc. 213. With an Introduction and Inventory by David Fallows. Chicago: University of Chicago Press, 1995.

Paatz, Walter and Elisabeth Paatz. *Die Kirchen von Florenz.* Frankfurt: Vittorio Klostermann, 1952.

Page, Christopher. *Discarding Images: Reflections on Music and Culture in Medieval France*. Oxford: Oxford University Press, 1993.

Pakter, Walter. *Medieval Canon Law and the Jews*. Ebelsbach: Rolf Gremer, 1988.

Palmer, Barbara D. "Recycling 'The Wakefield Cycle': The Records." *Research Opportunities in Renaissance Drama* 1 (2002): 88–130.

——. "'Towneley Plays' or 'Wakefield Cycle' Revisited." *Comparative Drama* 21 (1987): 318–48.

Palmieri, Matteo. *Vita civile*, edited by Gino Belloni. Florence: Sansoni, 1982.

Paolini, Lorenzo. "Le Umiliate al lavoro: appunti fra storiografia e storia." *Bullettino dell'Istituto storico italiano per il Medio Evo e archivio muratoriano* 97 (1991).

Parenti, Daniela, ed. *Giovanni da Milano: Capolavori del gotico fra Lombardia e Toscana*. Florence: Giunti Editore, 2008.

Patterson, Annabel. "Introduction" to *The Changeling*, edited by Douglas Bruster. In *Thomas Middleton: The Collected Works*, edited by Gary Taylor and John Lavagnino. Oxford: Oxford University Press, 2008.

Peragallo, Edward. *Origin and Evolution of Double Entry Bookkeeping: A Study of Italian Practice from the Fourteenth Century*. New York: American Institute Publishing Company, 1938.

Perkins, Leeman L. "Musical Patronage at the Royal Court of France under Charles VII and Louis XI (1422–83)." *Journal of the American Musicological Society* 37 (1984): 507–66.

Petrarch, Francesco. *De remediis utrius que fortunae*, edited by Rudolf Schottländer. Munich: W. Fink, 1975.

——. *Petrarch's Remedies for Fortune Fair and Foul*, edited by Conrad H. Rawski. Bloomington and Indianapolis: Indiana University Press, 1991.

——. *Von der Artzney Bayder Glück/des Guten und Widerwertigen.* Hamburg: Friedrich Wittig, 1984.

Peter the Chanter. *Verbum abbreviatum. Textus conflatus*, edited by Monique Boutry. Turnhout: Brepols, 2004.

Petrus Johanni Olivi. *In Matthaeum*. Padua: Biblioteca Antoniana, ms. 336.

Piccini, Attilio. "The Innocenti: Art and History." In *Spedale degli Innocenti*, edited by Francesco Papafava. Florence: Beccocci/Scala, 1977.

Pope-Hennessy, John. *Sassetta.* London: Chatto and Windus, 1939.

Postan, M.M. *The Medieval Economy and Society: An Economic History of Britain in the Middle Ages*. 1972. Reprinted, Harmondsworth: Penguin, 1975.

Praz, Mario. *The Flaming Heart*. New York: Doubleday, 1958; New York: Norton, 1973.

Prevenier, Walter and Wim Blockmans. *In de Ban van Bourgondië.* Houten: Fibula, 1988.

Purdon, Liam O. *The Wakefield Master's Dramatic Art: A Drama of Spiritual Understanding*. Gainesville: University Press of Florida, 2003.

Quaglioni, Diego, Giacomo Todeschini, and Gian Maria Varanini, eds. *Credito e usura fra teologia, diritto e amministrazione. Linguaggi a confronto (sec. XII–XVI)*. Rome: École Française de Rome, 2005.

Rabello, Mordechai. *Giustiniano, Ebrei e Samaritani alla luce delle fonti storico-letterarie, ecclesiastiche e giuridiche*. Milan: Giuffré, 1987–88.

——. *The Jews in the Roman Empire. Legal Problems: From Herod to Justinian*. London: Ashgate 2000.

Raftis, J.A. "Social Change versus Revolution: New Interpretations of the Peasants' Revolt of 1381." In *Social Unrest in the Late Middle Ages*, edited by Francis X. Newman, 3–22. Binghamton: Medieval and Renaissance Texts and Studies, 1986.

Randall, Dale B.J. "Observations on the Theme of Chastity in *The Changeling*." *English Literary Renaissance* 14, no. 3 (1984): 347–66.

——. "Some New Perspectives on the Spanish Setting of *The Changeling* and Its Source." *Medieval and Renaissance Drama in England* 3 (1986): 189–216.

Reimer, Erich, ed. *Johannes de Garlandia: De mensurabili musica*. 2 volumes. Wiesbaden: Steiner, 1972.

Reininger, Walter. "The Florentine Textile Industry in the Middle Ages." *Ciba Review* 27 (1939).

Reiss, Edmund. "The Symbolic Plow and Plowman and the Wakefield *Mactacio Abel*." *Studies in Iconography* 5 (1979): 3–30.

Reynolds, John. *The Triumphs of Gods Revenege, against the Crying, and Execrable Sinne of Murther*. London: Felix Kyngston, 1621.

Richa, Giuseppe. *Notizie istoriche delle chiese fiorentine*. Florence: P.G. Viviani, 1754–62.

Richardson, Brian. *Printing, Writers, and Readers in Renaissance Italy*. New York: Cambridge University Press, 1999.

Ricks, Christopher. "The Moral and Poetic Structure of *The Changeling*." *Essays in Criticism* 10, no. 3 (1960): 290–306.

Ripa, Cesare. *Baroque and Rococo Pictorial Imagery*, edited by Edward A. Maser. New York: Dover, 1971.

Robertson, D.W., Jr. *A Preface to Chaucer*. Princeton: Princeton University Press, 1963.

Robertson, Kellie. *The Laborer's Two Bodies: Literary and Legal Productions in Britain, 1350–1500*. New York: Palgrave Macmillan, 2006.

Robson, Janet. "Judas and the Franciscans: Perfidy Pictured in Lorenzetti's Passion Cycle at Assisi." *Art Bulletin* 86, no. 1 (March 2004): 31–57.

——. "*Speculum imperfectionis:* The Image of Judas in Late Medieval Italy." Unpublished PhD dissertation, The Courtauld Institute, 2001.

Rodimer, Frank J. *The Canonical Effects of Infamy of Fact: A Historical Synopsis and a Commentary. Washington*: Catholic University of America Press, 1954.

Rosenthal, Margaret. "Epilogue" in Pietro Aretino, *Aretino's Dialogues*, translated by Raymond Rosenthal. New York: Marsilio, 1994.

____. *The Honest Courtesan: Veronica Franco, Citizen and Writer in Sixteenth-Century Venice.* Chicago: University of Chicago Press, 1992.

Rubin, Miri. *Charity and Community in Medieval Cambridge.* Cambrige: Cambridge University Press, 1987.

____. *Gentile Tales: The Narrative Assault on Late-Medieval Jews*. Yale: Yale University Press, 1999.

____. "Imagining Medieval Hospitals." In *Medicine and Charity Before the Welfare State*, edited by Jonathan Barry and Colin Jones, 14–25. London: Routledge, 1991.

Ruggiero, Guido. *Binding Passions: Tales of Magic, Marriage, and Power at the End of the Renaissance.* New York: Oxford University Press, 1993.

Russell, Jeffrey Burton. *Witchcraft in the Middle Ages*. Ithaca, NY: Cornell University Press, 1972.

Russell, J.C. *Medieval Regions and their Cities.* Bloomington: University of Indiana Press, 1972.

Ryner, Bradley D. "The Panoramic View in Mercantile Thought: Or, A Merchant's Map of Cymbeline." In *Global Traffic: Discourses and Practices of Trade in English Literature 1550 to 1700*, edited by Barbara Sebek and Stephen Deng, 77–94. New York: Palgrave Macmillan, 2008.

Sallazani, M., ed. *Produzione, commercio e consumo dei panni di lana (nei secoli XII–XVII. Atti della seconda settimana di studio, Prato 1970.* Florence: Olschki, 1976.

Salomon, Nanette. *Shifting Priorities: Gender and Genre in Seventeenth-Century Dutch Painting.* Stanford: Stanford University Press, 2004.

Sanders, Ernest. "The Medieval Motet." In *Gattungen der Musik in Einzeldarstellungen: Gedenkschrift Leo Schrade*, edited by Wulf Arlt, Ernst Lichtenhahn, and Hans Oesch, I, 497–573. Berne and Munich: Francke Verlag, 1973.

Santoni, Luigi. *Raccolta di notizie storiche riguardanti le chiese dell'arci-diogesi di Firenze*. Florence: G. Mazzoni, 1847.

Sapir Abulafia, Anna. *Christians and Jews in the Twelfth Century Renaissance.* London: Routledge, 1995.

Sapori, Armando. *Studi di storia economica (secoli XIII–XIV–XV).* Florence: Sansoni, 1955.

Satkowski, Jane Immler. *Duccio di Buoninsegna*. Edited by Hayden B.J. Maginnis. Athens: University of Georgia Press, 2000.

Scattergood, V.J. *Politics and Poetry in the Fifteenth Century*. New York: Barnes and Noble, 1972.

Schädler, Alfred. *Die Frankische Galerie: Zweigmuseum des Bayerischen Nationalmuseums*. Munich: Deutscher Kunstverlag, 1987.

Schama, Simon. *The Embarrassment of Riches: An Interpretation of Culture in the Golden Age.* New York: Knopf, 1987.

Scheidig, Walter. *Die Holzschnitte des Petrarca-Meisters.* Berlin: Senschelverlag, 1955.

Schenone, Simona. "Frate Mario Pizzi e la decadenza degli Umiliati." In *Sulle tracce degli Umiliati*, edited by M.P. Alberzoni, A. Ambrosioni, and A. Lucioni, 67–100. Milan: Vita e Pensiero, 1997.

Schrade, Leo. *The Roman de Fauvel. The Works of Philippe de Vitry. French Cycles of the Ordinarium Missae*. Polyphonic Music of the Fourteenth Century, I. Monaco: Éditions de l'Oiseau-Lyre, 1956.

Sebastian, John T. "The Birth, Death, and Afterlife of the Wakefield Master." Unpublished paper delivered at the International Congress on Medieval Studies, Western Michigan University, 2002.

Serres, Michel. *Hermes: Literature, Science, Philosophy*, edited by Josué V. Harari and David F. Bell. Baltimore: Johns Hopkins University Press, 1982.

Shakespeare, William. *The Norton Shakespeare*, edited by Stephen Greenblatt, Walter Cohen, Jean E. Howard, Katherine Eisaman Maus and Andrew Gurr. 2nd edition. New York: W.W. Norton, 2008.

——. *Timon of Athens*, in *The Complete Works of Shakespeare*, edited by David Bevington. 6th edition. New York: Longman, 2008.

Shoaf, R.A. *Dante, Chaucer, and the Currency of the Word*. Norman, OK: Pilgrim Books, 1983.

Siems, Harald. *Handel und Wucher im Spiegel hochmittelalterlichen Rechtsquellen*. Hannover, Schriften der Monumenta Germaniae Historica, 35: Hahnsche Buchhandlung, 1992.

Silver, Larry. *The Paintings of Quinten Massys*. Montclair, NJ: Allanheld and Schram, 1984.

Simmons, J.L. "Diabolical Realism in Middleton and Rowley's *The Changeling*." *Renaissance Drama* 11 (1980): 135–70.

Simons, Walter. *Cities of Ladies: Beguine Communities in the Low Countries, 1200–1565*. Philadelphia: University of Pennsylvania Press, 2003.

Slater, Ann Pasternak. "Hypallage, Barley-Break, and *The Changeling*." *The Review of English Studies* 34, no. 136 (1983): 429–40.

Sponsler, Claire. *Drama and Resistance: Bodies, Goods, and Theatricality in Late Medieval England*. Minneapolis: University of Minnesota Press, 1997.

Spufford, Peter. *Money and its Use in Medieval Europe*. Cambridge: Cambridge University Press, 1988.

Stabel, Peter. "Women at the Market: Gender and Retail in the Towns of Late Medieval Flanders." In *Secretum Scriptorum: Liber Alumnorum Walter Prevenier*, 259–76. Louvain: Garant, 1999.

Stevens, Martin. *Four Middle English Mystery Cycles: Textual, Contextual, and Critical Interpretations*. Princeton: Princeton University Press, 1987.

—— and A.C. Cawley, eds. *The Towneley Plays*. 2 volumes. EETS s.s. 13–14. Oxford: Oxford University Press, 1994.

Stroumsa, Guy G. *Barbarian Philosophy. The Religious Revolution of Early Christianity*. Tübingen: Mohr Siebeck, 1995.

Sugimura, N.K. "Changelings and *The Changeling*." *Essays in Criticism* 56, no. 3 (2006): 241–63.

Sullivan, Lee R. "The Hanging of Judas: Medieval Iconography and the German Peasants' War." *Proceedings of the Illinois Medieval Association—Essays in Medieval Studies* 15 (1998): 93–101.

Supple, B.E. *Commercial Crisis and Change in England 1600–1642*. Cambridge: Cambridge University Press, 1964.

Swetz, Frank. *Capitalism and Arithmetic*. La Salle, IL: Open Court Publishing, 1987.

Sznura, Franek, *L'espansione urbana di Firenze nel Dugento*. Florence: La Nuova Italia, 1975.

Taylor, Warren. *Tudor Figures of Rhetoric*. Whitewater, WI: The Language Press, 1972.

Ter Laan, K. *Nederlandse Spreekwoorden, Spreuken en Zegswijzen*. Amsterdam: Elsevier, 1986.

Tertullianus. *De carne Christi*. In *La Chair du Christ*, edited by Jean-Pierre Mahé. Paris: Cerf, 1975. Edited by Ernest Evans: <http://www.tertullian.org/articles/evans_carn/evans_carn_03latin.htm>.

Théry, Julien. "Fama: l'opinion publique comme preuve judiciaire. Aperçu sur la révolution médiévale de l'inquisitoire (XIIe–XVe siècle)." In *La preuve en justice de l'Antiquité à nos jours*, edited by B. Lemesle, 119–47. Rennes: Presses Universitaires de Rennes, 2003.

Thomas of Chobham. *Summa confessorum*, edited by F. Broomfield. Louvain, Paris: Éditions Nauwelaerts, 1968.

Tiraboschi, Girolamo. *Vetera Humiliatorum Monumenta annotationibus, ac dissertationibus prodromis illustrata*. 3 volumes. Milan: J. Galeatius, 1766–68.

Todeschini, Giacomo. "Christian Perceptions of Jewish Economic Activity in the Middle Ages." In *Wirtschaftsgeschichte der mittelalterlichen Juden. Fragen und Einschätzungen*, edited by Michael Toch, 1–16. Munich, Schriften des Historischen Kollegs, Bd. 71: Oldenbourg, 2008.

——. "Franciscan Economics and Jews in the Middle Ages: From a Theological to an Economic Lexicon." In *Friars and Jews in the Middle Ages and Renaissance*, edited by Stephen McMichael and Susan Myers, 99–117. Leiden, Boston: Brill 2004.

——. *Il prezzo della salvezza. Lessici medievali del pensiero economico*. Rome: NIS 1994.

——. *I mercanti e il tempio. La società cristiana e il circolo virtuoso della ricchezza dal Medioevo all'Età Moderna*. Bologna: Il Mulino, 2002.

——. "Judas mercator pessimus. Ebrei e simoniaci dall'XI al XIII secolo." *Zakhor. Rivista di storia degli ebrei in Italia* I (1997): 11–23.

——. "La riflessione etica sulle attività economiche." In *Economie urbane ed etica economica nell'Italia medievale*, edited by Roberto Greci, Giuliano Pinto, and Giacomo Todeschini, 153–228. Rome: Laterza, 2005.

——. *Le "bien commun" de la civitas christiana dans la tradition textuelle franciscaine (XIIIe–XVe siècle)*, in *Politique et religion en Méditerranée.*

Moyen âge et époque contemporaine, edited by Henri Bresc, Georges Dagher, and Christiane Veauvy, 265–303. Paris: Bouchène, 2008.

——. "Licet in maxima parte adhuc bestiales: la raffigurazione degli Ebrei come non umani in alcuni testi altomedievali." *Studi Medievali* XLIV, no. 3 (2003): 1135–49.

——. *Ricchezza francescana: dalla povertà volontaria alla società di mercato.* Bologna: Il Mulino, 2004.

——. "Theological Roots of the Medieval/Modern Merchants' Self-Representation." In *The Self-Perception of Early Modern Capitalists*, edited by Margaret C. Jacob and Catherine Secretan, 17–46. New York: Palgrave Macmillan, 2008.

——. *Visibilmente crudeli. Malviventi, persone sospette e gente qualunque dal Medioevo all'età moderna.* Bologna: Il Mulino, 2007.

Tomei, Alessandro, ed. *Le Biccherne di Siena, Arte e Finanza all'alba dell'economia moderna.* Rome: Retablo, 2002.

Trexler, Richard C. "Honor Among Thieves. The Trust Function of the Urban Clergy in the Florentine Republic." In *Essays Presented to Myron P. Gilmore*, edited by Sergio Bertelli and Gloria Ramakus. Florence: La Nuova Italia Editrice, 1978.

Tudor-Gray, Pamela. "The Hours of Edward V and William Lord Hastings: British Library Manuscript Additional 54782." In *England in the Fifteenth Century. Proceedings of the 1986 Harlaxton Symposium*, edited by Daniel Williams, 351–69. Woodbridge: The Boydell Press, 1987.

Turner, Derek H. *The Hastings Hours.* London: Thames and Hudson, 1983.

Van Houtte, J.A. *De Geschiedenis van Brugge.* Tielt: Lannoo, 1982.

Van Uytven, Raymond. *Stadsfinanciën en Stadsekonomie te Leuven van de XIIe tot het einde der XVIe eeuw.* Brussels: Paleis der Academiën, 1961.

——. "The Fulling Mill: Dynamic of the Revolution in Industrial Attitudes." *Acta Historiae Neerlandica* 5 (1971).

Veit, Ludwig. *Das Liebe Geld: Zwei Jahrtausende Geld- und Münzgeschichte.* Munich: Prestel, 1969.

Verdam, E. and E. Verwijs. *Middelnederlansche Woordenboek.* 12 volumes. Den Haag: Martinus Nijhof, 1889.

Vincent de Beauvais. *Speculum Historiale.* Nuremberg: Anton Koberger, 1483.

Violot, Raoul. *Histoire des Maisons de Chalon.* 2 T. Paris: Éditions F.E.R.N., 1969.

Vitkus, Daniel. *Turning Turk: English Theater and the Multicultural Mediterranean, 1570–1630.* New York: Palgrave Macmillan, 2003.

Voelkle, William M. "Morgan Manuscript M. 1001: The Seven Deadly Sins and the Seven Evil Ones." In *Monsters and Demons in the Ancient and Medieval Worlds: Papers Presented in Honor of Edith Porada*, edited by Anne E. Farkas, Prudence O. Harper, and Evelyn B. Harrison, 101–14. Mainz: Philipp von Zabern, 1987.

Von Moos, Peter. "'Public' et 'privé' à la fin du moyen âge. Le 'bien commun' et la 'loi de la conscience'." *Studi Medievali* s. 3a, XLI, no. 2 (2000): 505–48.

Vornefeld, Christopher. "Einheimische und lombardische Wucherer im Frankreich von Charles VI. Eine neue Quelle zur Sozialgeschichte des Wuchers." *Journal of Medieval History* 15 (1980): 269–87.

Waddington, Raymond B. *Aretino's Satyr: Sexuality, Satire, and Self-Projection in Sixteenth-Century Literature and Art.* Toronto: University of Toronto Press, 2004.

Wakefield, Walter L. and Austin P. Evans. *Heresies of the High Middle Ages, Selected Sources Translated and Annotated.* New York: Columbia University Press, 1969.

Walafridus, Strabo. *In Matthaeum*. In *Patrologia latina* 114.

Wall, Wendy. *The Imprint of Gender: Authorship and Publication in the English Renaissance.* Ithaca, NY: Cornell University Press, 1993.

Wallace, William E. *Michelangelo at San Lorenzo: The Genius as Entrepreneur.* Cambridge: Cambridge University Press, 1994.

Warr, Cordelia. "Women, Weaving and Salvation: The Allegory of the Afterlife in San Michele, Paganico." In *Dressing for Heaven: Religious Clothing in Italy, 1215–1545.* Manchester: Manchester University Press, forthcoming.

Welch, Evelyn. *Shopping in the Renaissance: Consumer Culture in Italy 1400–1600.* New Haven: Yale University Press, 2005.

Westerhoff, Ingrid. "Der moralisierte Judas: mittelalterliche Legende, Typologie, Allegorie im Bild." *Aachener Kunstblätter des Museumsverein* 61 (1995–97): 85–156.

Wickstrom, John. "The Humiliati: Liturgy and Identity." *Archivum Fratrum Praedicatorum* 62 (1992): 215.

Wilk, Sarah Blake. "Donatello's *Dovizia* as an Image of Florentine Political Propaganda." *Artibus et Historiae* 7, no. 14 (1986): 9–28.

Wilkins, David G. "Donatello's Lost *Dovizia* for the Mercato Vecchio: Wealth and Charity as Florentine Civic Virtues." *Art Bulletin* 65, no. 3 (September 1983): 401–23.

Wilson, Adrian. *The Making of the Nuremberg Chronicle.* Amsterdam: Nico Israel, 1976.

Wilson, Scott. "General Economy and *The Changeling*." In *Cultural Materialism: Theory and Practice*. Oxford: Blackwell Publishers, 1995.

Wolfthal, Diane. "Florentine Bankers and Flemish Friars: New Light on the Patronage of the Portinari Altarpiece." In *Cultural Exchange between the Netherlands and Italy*, edited by Ingrid Alexander-Skipnes, 1–21. Turnhout: Brepols, 2007.

———. "Picturing Same-Sex Love: Images by Petrus Christus and the Housebook Master." In *Troubled Vision: Gender, Sexuality and Sight in Medieval Text and Image*, edited by Robert Mills and Emma Barker, 17–46. Hampshire: Palgrave Macmillan, 2004.

Wood, Diana. *Medieval Economic Thought.* Cambridge: Cambridge University Press, 2002.

Yvo Carnotensis, *Decretum* VI. <http://project.knowledgeforge.net/ivo/decretum/ivodec_6_1p0.pdf>.

Zanoni, Luigi. *Gli Umiliati nei loro rapporti con l'eresia, l'industria della lana ed i comuni nei secoli XII e XIII.* Biblioteca di storia economica, 2nd series, volume 2. Milan: Hoepli, 1911; reprinted, Rome: Multigrafica, 1970.

Zieman, Katherine. *Singing the New Song: Literacy and Learning in Late Medieval England.* Philadelphia: University of Pennsylvania Press, 2007.

Zöhl, Caroline. *Jean Pichore Buchmaler, Graphiker und Verleger in Paris um 1500.* Turnhout: Brepols, 2004.

Zucker, Lois Miles, ed. *S. Ambrosii De Tobia: A Commentary with an Introduction and Translation.* Washington, DC: The Catholic University of America, 1933.

Index

(References to illustrations are in *italic*)

The Criminal Law Library—No. 3

FORENSIC MEDICINE

EVAN STONE, QC, MA(Oxon)
Recorder of the Crown Courts,
Bencher of the Inner Temple; and
of the South-Eastern Circuit

and

HUGH JOHNSON, FRCPath, DMJ,
Late Professor of Forensic Medicine,
St Thomas's Hospital Medical School, London

WATERLOW PUBLISHERS

First Edition 1987

Waterlow Publishers
Oyez House, PO Box 55
27 Crimscott Street
London SE1 5TS
A division of Hollis Professional Services PLC

ISBN 0 08 039219 9

British Library Cataloguing in Publication Data

Stone, Evan
Forensic medicine.—(The Criminal law library; no. 3)
1. Medical jurisprudence
I. Title II. Johnson, Hugh III. Series
614′.1 RA1051

Printed in Great Britain by
A. Wheaton & Co Ltd, Exeter, Devon

Hugh Johnson: A Tribute

Hugh Johnson died suddenly and unexpectedly on 16 September 1986, at the height of his powers, at the early age of 57. Not only did he hold the Chair of Forensic Medicine at St. Thomas's Hospital, but he was also, amongst his many other distinctions, President of the Medico-Legal Society.

His qualities as a forensic pathologist and as a teacher were second to none, but I remember him in particular as a supreme expert witness. His quiet authority and grasp of his subject made him a very difficult man to cross-examine effectively, and his fairness was disarming and could reduce his challengers to zero. This is not to suggest that he was dogmatic or insensitive and I can remember with great clarity a case in which I had the great privilege of calling him as a pathologist for the Crown in a particularly gruesome murder, which had involved, *inter alia*, dismemberment of the victim while he was initially still alive. At an earlier consultation, he had demonstrated with great skill and authority his expert view of the events that must have led up to the death of the victim, and he gave evidence in No. 1 Court at the Central Criminal Court in a way which graphically demonstrated his great skill and learning, but also in a way which all could understand.

He will be greatly missed by all who had the privilege to know and admire him; above all he was a great friend and colleague.

This book owes so much to Hugh Johnson that it should always remain, if only in a small measure, as his memorial.

E.S.

Foreword

BY THE RT. HON. LORD JUSTICE LAWTON

When reading this book in proof memories of cases with which I had been connected during my fifty-two years in the law, either as a barrister or as a judge, came back time and time again. With them came the thought that had I known what this book tells me my conduct of many cases would have been different. I remember the humiliation I suffered in the St. Pancras Coroner's Court when, after two years in practice, I tried in cross-examination to persuade Sir Bernard Spilsbury that he was mistaken in his opinion that my client's husband had collapsed in front of a bus because of a cerebral haemorrhage whereas in fact he had been knocked down by it. I remember too the favourable and sympathetic summing up for a defendant which I delivered in the early 1960's in a case in which a young father was charged with the manslaughter of his baby daughter. His defence had been that she had slipped out of his hands whilst lifting her out of the bath. The consequent fall was the cause of her fractured skull, ribs and left leg. Now that this book is available others whose babies suffer these kinds of injuries would be wise to change their explanations for them or, better still, plead guilty.

When I started in the law, books on forensic medicine were available but my recollection is that they were written for doctors, not lawyers. Although I consulted them from time to time, they seldom provided the help which I wanted. This book does because it relates the pathology being discussed to the relevant crimes. Both the doctor and the advocate are directed to what has to be proved and what medical evidence may, or may not, provide the proof. Much time is wasted in court as a result of pathologists writing reports containing from a forensic standpoint irrelevant detail which the advocate does not recognise as being irrelevant. Both would benefit from reading this book and having it available for reference.

A lesson which many advocates are slow to learn is that the way to support or destroy an expert witness is to find out what facts he has relied upon to support his opinion. Once such a witness has committed himself to an opinion he is unlikely to change it because an advocate suggests to him that it is wrong. The advocate, however, often does not know what facts a medical witness is likely to have regarded, or should have regarded, as relevant. In my day in practice at the Bar I had to learn from experience. I must have missed, for example, many important factors relevant to a medical opinion about the time of death about which this book would have told me. By the time it is published I shall have retired from the practice of the law. If I could live my professional life in the criminal courts again, I would always have it with me.

Frederick Lawton

November 1986

Introduction

This book has been designed for use by legal practitioners and judges in the field of criminal law. We believe and hope that students, academics and others interested in the criminal law will also find the book helpful and instructive. We have included a bibliography at the end of this book for those who we feel that they would like to do some more extended reading.

We have sought to keep the legal part of the book to a minimum, basically only dealing with those parts of the criminal law which have direct forensic medicine implications. There are other areas which we have chosen not to cover, such as forensic psychiatry and toxicology, which, while we regard them as important, are not within the ambit of the authors of this particular book.

It is envisaged that many readers will wish to consult the book on particular topics with which they are concerned, rather than read it through. It is hoped that the presence of the glossary, photographs and diagrams, will assist lawyers to understand the medical terms used in the text, which we have endeavoured to set out in clear and comprehensible layman's language. Parts of the book and indeed some of the photographs may seem to be somewhat shocking, but it is felt that only a straightforward description of the topics under discussion will prove helpful and useful.

In literature, there are many descriptions of death, one of the most notable being in *Henry VI Part II,* Act III, Scene ii, where Gloucester says:

> "See how the blood is settled in his face.
> Oft have I seen a timely-parted ghost,
> Of ashy semblance, meagre, pale and bloodless
> Being all descended to the labouring heart;
> Who, in the conflict that it holds with death,
> Attracts the same for aidance 'gainst the enemy;
> Which with the heart there cools and ne'er returneth
> To blush and beautify the cheek again.
> But see, his face is black and full of blood,
> His eye-balls further out than when he lived,
> Staring full ghastly like a strangled man;
> His hair uprear'd, his nostrils stretch'd with struggling,

His hands abroad display'd, as one that grasp'd
And tugg'd for life and was by strength subdued:
Look, on the sheets his hair, you see, is sticking;
His well-proportion'd beard made rough and rugged,
Like to the summer's corn by tempest lodged.
It cannot be but he was murder'd here;
The least of all these signs were probable."

Our descriptions are more prosaic, but they were never intended to be literature in the first place.

If readers have any constructive suggestions to make for any future edition we would be very grateful to receive them, but if the busy lawyer, having consulted our book, finds that we have helped to clarify any matters which had been unclear beforehand, then we feel that the main purpose in writing the book will have been achieved.

We have endeavoured to state the law as at 31 July, 1986.

We have received much help from several sources which we gladly acknowledge below, but the final responsibility remains ours.

E.S.
H.J.

Acknowledgements

We are grateful to Sir Kenneth Newman, Commissioner of Police for the Metropolis, for permission to reproduce Metropolitan Police photographs taken in criminal cases in which Professor Johnson was involved, to Mr. Victor Gregory of the Department of Audio-Visual Services (Photography), St. Thomas's Hospital Medical School, for processing all the photographs in this book, and to Mr. Robert Lockheart of the Department of Medical Illustration, St. Thomas's Hospital for the diagrams. Our particular thanks are due to Miss Pam Darby and Mrs. Dawn Hancock of the Forensic Medicine Unit, St. Thomas's Hospital Medical School, for typing and retyping the manuscript so many times so willingly.

Professor G. Slavin of St. Bartholomew's Hospital kindly helped with the proof-reading after the untimely death of Hugh Johnson.

E.S.

Contents

List of Coloured Plates

List of Black and White Photographs and Diagrams

Table of Cases

Prosecutions brought by the Crown are listed under the name of the defendant.

Table of Statutes

CHAPTER 1

Offences Resulting in Death

LAW

Murder: Definition; Elements of the Offence

1.01 The common law definition, following Sir Edward Coke, is: "Murder is the unlawful killing of any reasonable creature in being and under the Queen's Peace, with malice aforethought either expressed or implied, the death following within a year and a day."[1] A more modern definition, taking into account statutes and judicial precedent, would be: "Murder is committed where a person of sound mind and discretion unlawfully kills any reasonable creature in being and under the Queen's Peace with intent to kill or cause grievous bodily harm, death following within a year and a day, subject to three exceptions, namely:

(i) provocation
(ii) suffering from diminished responsibility
(iii) acting in pursuance of a suicide pact."

If any person is charged with murder and the accused was (i) provoked or (ii) suffering from diminished responsibility or (iii) was acting in pursuance of a suicide pact, then the offence is reduced to manslaughter (see para. 1.04 *infra*).

Any act except perjury which is a substantial cause of the death renders the doer responsible for that death if the other elements of murder are proved. The act need not be the principal cause of death: see *R. v. Hennigan*[2] and para. 4.02 *infra*, where the Court of Appeal held that a proper direction on a charge of causing death by dangerous driving (now reckless driving) would be that the driving if dangerous must be "a substantial cause" of death, indicating that there must be something more than *de minimis*. Similar principles apply both in the case of murder and manslaughter.

Medical treatment of an injury

1.02 Where a person has received a wound and dies after an interval of

1 Coke's *Institutes* vol. 3, 47.
2 (1971) 55 Cr.App.R. 262 C.A.; [1971] 3 All E.R. 133.

time and the occurrence of intervening incidents and unsatisfactory treatment,

> "at the time of the death the wound is still an operating or substantial cause of death, albeit that some other cause is also operating. Only if it can be said that the original wounding is merely the setting in which another cause operates can it be said that death does not result from the wound. Putting it another way, only if the second cause is so overwhelming as to make the original wound merely part of the history can it be said that death does not flow from the wound."[3]

In *R. v. Malcherek* and *R. v. Steel*[4], the Court of Appeal, Criminal Division, ruled that where competent and careful medical treatment given to a victim of an injury inflicted by an assailant included putting the victim on a life support machine, the decision by the medical practitioners concerned to disconnect the machine because, by generally accepted medical criteria, the victim was dead, could not exonerate the assailant from responsibility for the death, if at the time of death the original injury was a continuing or operating cause of the death, for then this disconnection of the machine did not break the chain of causation between the infliction of the original injury and the death. Since on the facts in these two cases there was no evidence that the original injury inflicted on each victim had ceased to be a continuing or operating cause of death, following disconnection of the life support machine, it followed that the issue of causation was in each case properly withdrawn from the jury, applying *R. v. Smith* (*supra*). The Court of Appeal also decided that in the ordinary case, where treatment by life support machine was given in good faith by competent and careful medical practitioners, evidence was not admissible to show that treatment would have been administered differently by other medical practitioners.

Moment of Birth

1.03 To be a "reasonable creature in being" a person must have been born and be still alive. The common law defines the moments of birth and death; the cases to some extent are in conflict. In *Poulton*[5] it was decided that a child becomes a reasonable creature in being when it has been wholly expelled from its mother's body and is alive, but there is some lack of clarity as to whether the child's life must be independent of its mother. In *Crutchley*[6] it was decided that a child should have a circulation independent of its mother, e.g. as soon as the foetal heart begins to function, while in the same case and in the case of *Brain*[7] it was said that it

3 *R. v. Smith* [1959] 2 Q.B. 35; (1959) 43 Cr.App.R. 121.
4 [1981] 2 All E.R. 422.
5 (1832) 5 C. & P. 329.
6 (1837) 7 C. & P. 874.
7 (1834) 6 C. & P. 349.

is not necessary to establish that the umbilical cord has been severed as the child has breathed.[8] To kill a foetus as an unborn child is not murder but constitutes the offence under section 58 of the Offences against the Person Act 1861 of administering drugs or using instruments to procure an abortion (see para. 5.30 *infra*). The killing of a child in the process of being born is not murder as the birth process is not complete. It may be difficult to prove whether a child was killed in the process of birth or immediately after birth and if a jury were not sure that the killing occurred after birth, they could not return a verdict of murder; once the birth process has started section 58 of the Offences against the Person Act 1861 has no application. See, however, concealment of birth under section 60 of the Offences Against the Person Act 1861, and also the Infant Life (Preservation) Act 1929, which created the offence of child destruction.[9]

Manslaughter: Elements of the Offence

1.04 There are two categories of manslaughter:

(1) *Voluntary manslaughter*, which describes those killings where the defendant lacks the mental element necessary to convict him of murder, but which include an element of unlawfulness which renders the homicide criminal. Examples of voluntary manslaughter are where all the elements of murder are present, including an intent to kill or to cause grievous bodily harm, but the crime of murder is reduced to manslaughter by reason of (i) provocation, or (ii) diminished responsibility, or (iii) where death is caused in pursuance of a suicide pact.

(2) *Involuntary manslaughter*, which describes those unlawful killings without intent to kill or cause grievous bodily harm, but which include an element of unlawfulness which renders the homicide criminal.

The principles relating to causation and death following treatment, discussed in para. 1.02 *supra* under murder, apply equally to cases of manslaughter, and also to cases of causing death by reckless driving (see para. 4.02 *infra*).

Arson leading to Death: Definition; Elements of the Offence

1.05 By section 1(2) of the Criminal Damage Act 1971,

> "a person who without lawful excuse destroys or damages any property, whether belonging to himself or another:
> (i) intending to destroy or damage any property or being reckless as to whether any property would be destroyed or damaged, and

8 See also *Enoch* (1833) 5 C. & P. 539.
9 See also para. 3.01 *infra* and discussion of the Abortion Act 1967 at para. 5.30 *infra*.

(ii) intending by the destruction or damage to endanger the life of another or being reckless as to whether the life of another would be thereby endangered,

shall be guilty of an offence."

By section 1(3),

"An offence committed under this section by destroying or damaging property by fire shall be charged as arson."

If death in fact results from such an act or acts of criminal damage or arson, then depending on the facts and circumstances of the particular case, the defendent may be also charged either with murder or manslaughter.

Medico-Legal Aspects of Arson

1.06 The victims of arson are often innocent parties who frequently die from the inhalation of smoke and fire fumes or from burns when a conflagration spreads to involve upper parts of buildings or adjacent premises. This is particularly likely if they are asleep in upstairs rooms without ready means of escape. The bodies of such victims are often found by firemen putting out a fire or searching the premises after the blaze has been extinguished. The pathological investigation of death due to burns and fires is studied in more detail in paras. 1.107ff below.

TIME OF DEATH

1.07 Estimating the time of death of a dead person is one of the most difficult tasks a doctor is asked to undertake. Despite what larger textbooks of forensic medicine have to say with their formulae and other methods of determination of the time interval between death and examination of the body, an opinion as to time of death can only be an educated guess based on knowledge and experience. This is because the methods used to estimate time of death are imprecise and there are so many variables affecting each individual death that no common formula can be applied to all cases. The three methods commonly used are:

(1) loss of body temperature by cooling,
(2) the development of rigor mortis, and
(3) the extent of hypostasis or post mortem lividity.

Body temperature

1.08 This must be taken rectally with a low-reading thermometer such as one used for photography or taking the temperature of water in the kitchen or bathroom, with a range from 0–100°C. It is absolutely pointless trying to use a clinical thermometer which only goes down to

35°C on a site such as the mouth or axilla where totally false readings will be obtained. Firstly the ambient temperature of the surroundings must be taken with the thermometer placed beside the dead body and left for several minutes until the temperature reading stabilises, and this temperature should be noted. The rectal temperature of the body should then be taken, again allowing several minutes for equilibration to occur, and this temperature should be similarly noted. Ideally these two readings should be repeated in an hour in order to ascertain if there is any change in the ambient temperature of any significance and assess the fall in body temperature over the period of time that has elapsed between the two readings. Unfortunately there is no linear relationship between the drop in body temperature and the passage of time. Rather the graph of the relationship between the two is represented by a sigmoid curve of the pattern shown in Fig. 1.1

During the first two or three hours after death the rectal temperature of the body remains almost static at a figure of approximately 37°C. There is then a steep drop for several hours until the curve begins to flatten out as the body temperature approaches that of its surroundings. The curve becomes almost flat after about twelve hours, at which time the external surfaces of the body will usually feel cold to the touch. The rectal temperature of the body and the drop in temperature between two

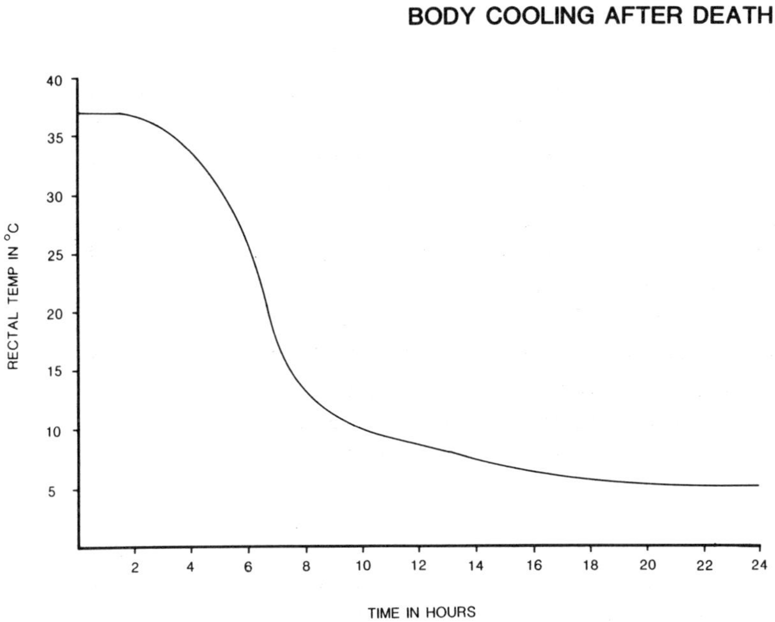

Fig. 1.1.

readings should enable the doctor to give some approximate idea of the time interval between death and his examination.

Obviously many factors will affect the temperature, both of the surroundings and the body itself, such as weather conditions, whether the body is inside premises or outside, whether it is clothed or unclothed, whether there is heating in the room or not, whether the body is in bed, whether there are draughts or other abnormal cooling conditions, and whether the body is fat or thin, all of which the doctor must take into account when he gives his estimate. It is said that clothing reduces the drop of body temperature to only two thirds of that reached when the body is unclothed.

If a person has died from a cerebral haemorrhage, particularly in the heat-regulating centre in the pons in the mid-brain, then the body temperature at death may be abnormally raised to as much as 40°C. Similarly a person dying with a high fever from an overwhelming infection may have a rectal temperature at death above the average figure and this will influence the doctor's calculations. Asphyxial modes of death such as strangulation may also raise body temperature.

All these factors having been taken into account, it should be possible to give some rough estimate of the time lapse following death, particularly if the body temperature has not fallen so much as to be approaching that of the ambient temperature surrounding the body. In severe winter weather the possibility that death may be due to hypothermia must be borne in mind, as in this case any assessment of the time of death may be wildly inaccurate.

Where a body is immersed in water at the time of or after death, the temperature changes will obviously depend on the temperature of the water itself. Warm water such as a domestic bath will slow the fall of body temperature, whereas cold sea water will hasten it. River water may vary enormously in temperature; warm sewage or other chemical effluent may warm up the water, particularly if it is stagnant. Conversely tidal rivers can often be extremely cold. A knowledge of the temperature of the water in which the body has been immersed is of vital importance to the pathologist attempting to estimate the time of death from body temperature.

Rigor Mortis

1.09 This is a chemical change wrought in the muscles by the breakdown of glycogen by enzyme activity, with lactic acid formation resulting in shortening and stiffening of muscle fibres. Immediately after death the body is completely flaccid. Under average conditions rigor mortis comes on in four to six hours, starting classically in the facial muscles, particularly those of the lower jaw, spreading to the arms, then to the trunk and legs, becoming fully established in twelve to eighteen hours and then passing off, taking another twelve to eighteen hours to disappear. It is quicker in onset and disappearance in infants and young children. It is speeded up by violent exercise prior to death, e.g. a fight or flight, and by heat, as in summer weather or feverish illness, and slowed by freezing. Once rigor mortis is broken down, say by straightening out a limb, it does not recur.

A body that is frozen by climatic conditions or refrigeration immediately after death has to thaw out before the process of development and disappearance of rigor mortis can take place. Heat stiffening of muscles, as may occur in bodies recovered from fires, may mimic rigor mortis but the presence of burning and other heat changes and the circumstances surrounding the finding of the body should alert the doctor to this possibility. Rigor mortis may also be mimicked by cadaveric spasm but this is so rare in actual practice and in any case only involves one limb that it can for all practical purposes be discounted.

Cadaveric Spasm

1.10 Under the influence of very strong emotion at the time of death a person may so fiercely grip an object in his or her hand that it may become locked in position after death and remain so until the body begins to decompose. A razor blade may be found between the fingers and thumb of someone who has cut his throat, or a button torn by a victim from the clothing of an assailant may be similarly so fixed. The condition cannot be reproduced after death and is not the same as rigor mortis in that it affects only one hand and occurs instantaneously at the time of death and remains unchanged, unlike rigor.

Hypostasis

1.11 This post mortem staining of the body is due to the sedimentation of blood in the dependent parts by gravity except for those areas where there is pressure on the tissues of the body over bony points. For example, the shoulder blades and buttocks and calves of a person lying on his back will be white when the post mortem lividity is distributed over the back of the body. This hypostasis commences in one to two hours and becomes marked in about six hours, following which it is said to be "fixed". If the body is turned over following death prior to the six hours elapsing, the blood resediments in the new dependent parts; for example, if the body was turned face down, the hypostasis would move to the front of the body. After hypostasis has become "fixed" there is no such redistribution of the lividity. Similar changes occur within the body and involve the internal organs. Unfortunately these time figures are so variable as to be very unreliable. Hypostasis, though, has its uses. It may be abnormal in colour, for example the cherry pink colouration of carbon monoxide poisoning, cyanide poisoning and hypothermia, or it may be useful in assessing position. The presence of pressure whitening around the nose and mouth may indicate the possibility of suffocation, particularly in infants.

Having examined the body and taken all these three methods of assessment into account, the doctor can but hazard an intelligent guess as to the time of death. He would be well advised before offering an opinion to find out from the police or others present when the deceased person was definitely last seen alive and exactly when the person was first found dead. This will give him two parameters into which the time of death must be fitted and it may be that, knowing these two times and taking his observations into account, he may be able to give an opinion as to the time of death, but he should always allow himself a margin of error on either side. If he does not know or cannot form an opinion, he should say so and not mislead those investigating the death.

Time of Assault

1.12 The doctor asked to assess the time of death should bear in mind that this is not necessarily the same as the time of an assault. A person receiving a fatal head injury may survive several hours unconscious or in coma prior to dying, or a victim of an assault with a knife may continue to bleed if unattended for a considerable period of time before succumbing. A freshly dead body may bleed from superficial post mortem injuries, especially if the tissues are engorged with blood. Such injuries are often seen in a person who has drowned and whose body has been attacked by predators such as fish or crabs, and such superficial injuries may arouse suspicion of foul play prior to death when in fact death has already occurred before the attack.

Eye Changes

1.13 Certain changes seen in the blood vessels of the back of the eye may be useful for the doctor in confirming the fact of death, but changes in the chemistry of the fluid within the eye as a means of estimating the time of death have been shown to be totally unreliable. A great deal of work has been done in this field in recent years, particularly in the United States, relating to the potassium content of fluid in the eye, but such investigations have proved to be unhelpful in timing death.

CHANGES AFTER DEATH

Decomposition

1.14 After the first twenty-four or thirty-six hours following death the changes of decomposition commence. They are usually visible to the naked eye at about forty-eight hours under average temperate conditions, when green staining of the lower abdomen and flanks of the trunk becomes apparent followed by a purplish pattern of the veins in the neck and chest becoming apparent. This is known as "marbling" because it is said that the discolouration of the veins resembles the markings in marble. Gas bubbles of decomposition form and the blood pigment stains the vessel walls. The skin begins to blister and the tissues swell up over the succeeding days so that by the end of a week the body is swollen with bloated and unrecognisable features, shedding of the skin and hair and bubbles of decomposition in all the tissues. The distension of the abdomen may force bloody fluid out of the lungs so that it may appear at the nose and mouth arousing suspicions of assault prior to death (see Plate 1). Similarly predators such as rats and foxes may attack the body causing injury (see Plate 2).

Blue-bottles and other insects may lay eggs on the body, particularly around body orifices and larvae and maggots will rapidly hatch out. They in turn will add to the destruction particularly of the head and neck. In hot weather or artifically warm conditions such as a centrally heated room, all these processes of decomposition may occur extremely rapidly. Over succeeding weeks the body tends to disintegrate further until after three months or more it may be reduced almost to the status of a skeleton. Cold weather will retard the decomposition process, as will burial. Various tissues resist decomposition more than others, particularly the uterus in a woman, which may assist in the sexing of human remains. The big muscle bulk of the back and limbs may similarly be recognised when other tissues have disintergrated. If the body is immersed in water, heat is lost more quickly but decomposition retarded unless the water is warm or contaminated by sewage when decomposition is hastened. Septicaemia, peritontis or jaundice prior to death all speed up the process.

Mummification

1.15 In dry warm surroundings such as the desert or in places in dwelling houses such as chimneys and airing cupboards, a body becomes mummified. This is not the same process as the preservation of the dead by the ancient Egyptians. The tissues are desiccated, the skin becomes leathery and is covered with powdery mould, and the soft tissues tend to disintegrate (see Fig. 1.2).

Often multiple small holes are found on the surface of the body. These are made by the larvae of the brown house moth which penetrate the tissues and destroy them so that a mummified body may prove to be nothing more than empty carcase when a post mortem examination is carried out. Mummification is particularly seen in new born infants

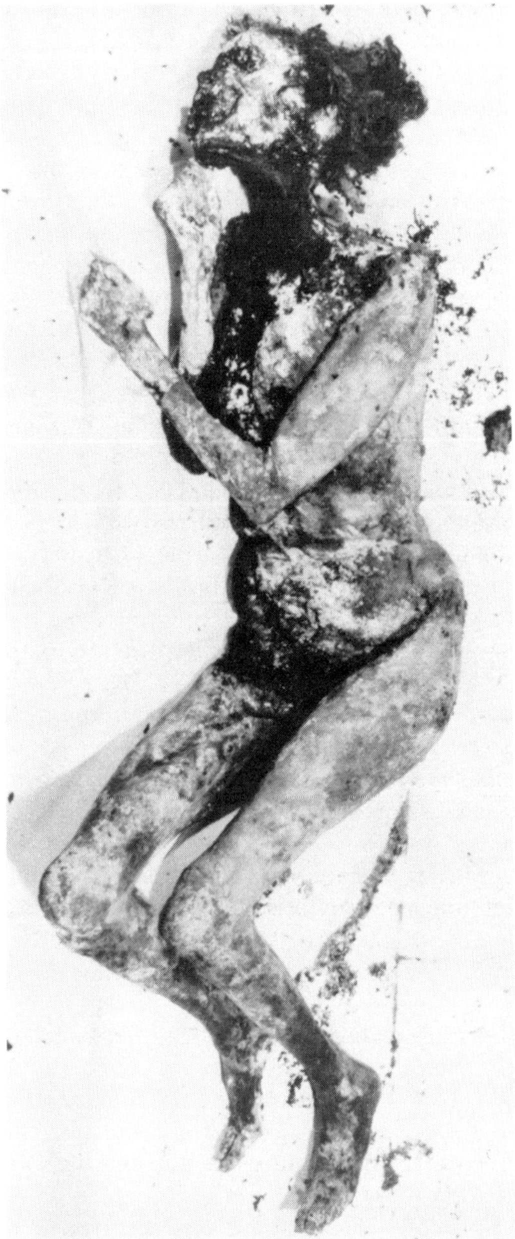

Fig. 1.2. Mummification and mould deposition

whose bodies are free from bacteria and hence are less likely to decompose.

Adipocere

1.16 Where a body is interred in warm moist surroundings, adipocere formation takes place, the unsaturated fatty acids of the body undergoing chemical changes so that they become suet-like with stiffening, hardening and swelling of the fat over a period of many months. This may preserve the form of the body and the internal organs, but their cellular detail is lost. Such changes may be found in exhumations or disturbances of old burial grounds.

1.17 Where a body is severely decomposed estimation of the time of death can be almost totally impossible on purely medical grounds and circumstantial evidence must be brought in as an adjunct to the scientific process. Such mundane details as the dates of newspapers and mail found inside the front door of premises and contact with relatives, officials and others which can establish date and time may assist the doctor not a little. Occasionally entymological examination of the insect life on the body may be used and in the hands of an expert it may be surprisingly exact, but the number of such experts is extremely small and the opportunity for use of their skills limited.

1.18 Too much importance should not be attached to the stomach contents and their state of digestion. While it is true that following a meal in an average person it takes between two and four hours to empty the stomach into the small intestine, digestion may be delayed by severe emotional stress or by unconsciousness either due to natural causes or to trauma or poisoning. Where the state of consciousness has been reduced to the level of very deep coma all digestive processes come to a halt for practical purposes and a person who dies following say a week in coma may be found at post mortem to have a stomach full of undigested food which can be immediately recognised and identified as a meal taken prior to a fatal head injury.

THE MEDICO-LEGAL AUTOPSY

1.19 (1) The medico-legal autopsy is done at the behest of the Coroner in England and Wales or the Procurator-Fiscal in Scotland and not on the instructions of the police. The Coroners' Rules allow for the police to make application to the Coroner for a named pathologist to carry out the autopsy but the decision as to who does the examination is entirely that of the Coroner and it is to him the pathologist will supply his report. There is a misconception in the public mind, particularly perpetuated by the media, that such post mortem examinations are done for the "establishment" or the Crown or the police and are not truly independent. This is far from the truth because the Coroner's autopsy *is* carried out by an independent pathologist. While the Coroner will take into consideration the feelings of the relatives of a deceased person and especially their religious beliefs, he may often override their objections to an autopsy in the interests of justice. The relatives can apply to the Divisional Court to have the Coroner's decision set aside, but in practice this is seldom done and when such an application is made it is very rarely successful. The police can ask the Coroner to name a pathologist of their choice to perform an autopsy on a case of suspected homicide and he will usually accede to their request but this is not invariably so. The ultimate choice of pathologist is the Coroner's.

(2) Many pathologists labelled "Home Office Pathologists" by the media do not in fact hold such appointments, there being only some twenty-nine named Home Office Pathologists in England and Wales. Many autopsies carried out in cases of murder or other serious crime are performed by university-based or National Health Service consultant pathologists not in any way involved with the Home Office or the police.

1.20 (1) The pathologist invited to carry out a medico-legal autopsy should always satisfy himself that he has the Coroner's authority to carry out the post mortem examination and if he is in doubt the pathologist should satisfy himself upon this point before doing anything else. If he does not feel competent to carry out the examination he should say so and suggest that a more experienced pathologist be called to do the autopsy. There is no shame in this. It is merely a matter of common sense. Nothing is worse for the conduct of a medico-legal examination than for the pathologist to find half way through that things are beyond him, or worse, that he has completed the examination without finding a definite cause of death and irretrievably damaged the body and obliterated post mortem features for anyone asked to do a second examination.

(2) The pathologist should have skilled assistance in the mortuary. While this is often available in a large hospital or public mortuary, it is not necessarily so and if the pathologist has no confidence in the mortuary staff he should do everthing himself rather than run the risk of a botched procedure ruining vital evidence. The pathologist himself should be able to do all the tasks that the mortuary staff can do, at least as well if not better.

(3) The pathologist must carry out every post mortem thoroughly and

carefully and leave nothing to chance, as no case is ever easy or straightforward. He must be very suspicious always and be on the look out for features suggesting death from unnatural causes, particularly in those under the age of 40 where unnatural death is much commoner than death from natural causes.

(4) Forensic autopsies are quite different from hospital autopsies. In the latter the bulk of attention is paid to the internal examination of the organs. In the forensic autopsy the external examination of the body can often be more important than the internal.

(5) Prior to autopsy the body should be left exactly as it arrived in the mortuary until the pathologist is ready to begin his examination. He must have a proper history of the case before he begins and if this is not available he should delay his examination until adequate information is forthcoming.

(6) The examination in the mortuary should begin by the pathologist appointing someone to take notes during the procedure and this person should make a list of everyone present, noting against each name his or her particular role, such as identifier, exhibits officer, scenes of crime officer, photographer etc. The list should include any doctor present who has been responsible for treatment, operation or anaesthesia. This is particularly important where somebody who has been the victim of a criminal assault dies subsequently in hospital. Unauthorised spectators must be excluded. In cases of difficulty where, for example, relatives or representatives of pressure groups demand to be present, the Coroner must be consulted, as he has the ultimate say. Where there is a conflict of interest, the Coroner usually suggests that a doctor, for example a general practitioner, should represent the interested party and this is often an acceptable compromise.

(7) The date, time and place of the examination must be noted and the deceased formally identified to the pathologist, the name of the identifying person being recorded by the scribe. If no one reliable or experiencced is present to take notes, the pathologist should make his own notes or dictate direct to a tape recorder.

(8) The body should be photographed as it has arrived in the mortuary, an overall view being taken of the front and back. Then the external surface of the body must be carefully examined, particularly as regards injury. All immediately apparent injuries should be photographed with a scale of measurement alongside each. Clothing should be removed, examined and labelled item by item, each garment being thoroughly searched and examined for stab wounds or other marks of injury or for material of evidential value such as blood stains. It is important to avoid cutting clothing, as sometimes it may be necessary to re-examine the clothing at a later date and if it has been badly cut about it may be

impossible to reassemble accurately. Each item of clothing should be placed separately in a labelled paper sack and sealed. Clothing, particularly wet clothing, should not be placed in plastic bags as this encourages mould formation. Wet clothing should be hung out to dry before being packaged insofar as this is practicable.

(9) The value of the examination of clothing is seriously underestimated by many pathologists, as the amount of clothing, the material, the layers and so on may influence the effects of weapons on the underlying body, absorbing force or deflecting penetrating objects such as knives or bullets. At every stage the co-operation of the scientific personnel should be engaged so that no foreign material such as glass, fibres, paint, hair and the like are lost and every facility should be given to the scientific officer for the collection of such material. On occasion it may be possible to examine the body with a laser which makes fibres fluoresce and bruising more obvious.

(10) Once the body has been unclothed its height, weight and build should be noted together with an account of the state of rigor mortis, the presence or absence of post mortem lividity and its colour; a careful note should be made of any scars, tattoos or other external abnormality. If the body has not been refrigerated, having just been brought to the mortuary from the scene of death, it is a useful precaution to take the body temperature if this has not already been done at the scene. If fingernail scrapings are to be taken, this is a good time to do them, otherwise the hands should be encased in plastic bags and sealed at the wrists with adhesive tape. This will prevent loss of material from beneath the fingernails or soiling of the pads of the fingers prior to fingerprinting, which can be carried out later. Before the bags are put on the hands it is vitally important that the pathologist should examine the hands carefully for the presence of defence wounds, particularly where there is evidence of assault, and there may be bruising on the back of the hand from warding off blows, or cuts on the palm or fingers from grasping or turning aside a knife. If there is bleeding from the nose, mouth or ears, all suggestive of head injury, this should be noted.

(11) A full systematic examination of the body externally should then be undertaken. All wounds found should be photographed with a scale beside them except in respect of stab wounds (see paras. 1.69ff). Photographs should be taken in duplicate with the wound as it was and the wound cleaned up. Injuries to the scalp are difficult to find and it may be necessary for the pathologist to shave the hair around such injuries prior to photography in order to reveal details of the injuries. It is better to take too many photographs rather than too few and the pathologist should not hesitate to explain to the photographer exactly how he wants photographs to be taken and assist him, for example in photographing

mouth injuries, by holding open the lips to reveal injuries within the mouth itself. Accurate notes should be kept of the photographs taken, especially details of those taken to show internal injuries, as these may not be readily recognisable by non-medical viewers.

(12) Each wound should be carefully examined in the company of the scientific officer to see if there is foreign material in it, such as metal or paint fragments. Nowadays tiny particles under sophisticated scientific examination can reveal an enormous amount of information and it is important that slovenly technique and a casual approach to the body should not be permitted, thus missing vital evidence. Agreement with the investigating officer and the scientific representatives should be reached as to what samples are going to be collected throughout the examination. Routinely in a case of homicide it is usual to collect head hair and pubic hair samples, duplicate swabs from mouth, anus, vagina or penis, stomach contents and blood and urine samples, all of which should be placed in proper containers, sealed, labelled and handed to the exhibits officer, a list being kept by the scribe the while. All hair samples should be plucked so as to include the roots and never cut. Further material can be collected during the examination according to the needs of the individual case. It is much better to collect too much, as unwanted material can always be discarded but omissions can seldom be made good.

(13) Throughout the examination it is important to retain the services of the photographer, as good photographs can supplement a report and are a record not only for the court but for any subsequent pathologist asked by the defence to carry out a second post mortem examination or any other doctor asked to give an opinion. It may be that during the examination further injuries will come to light which will need photography and such photographs are worth more than many pages of description.

(14) All wounds must be carefully described as to their nature, position, particularly as regards fixed anatomical points, direction and depth if penetrative, with associated underlying injury such as wound tracks or fractures or organ damage. Wounds relating to the cause of death on the surface of the body, for example stab wounds, should be excised and retained by the pathologist in case they are required for subsequent examination.

(15) The pathologist should not omit the examination of the eyes, the inside of the mouth, the neck, particularly the back of the body, the axillae, the groins, the perineal region and the arms. He should be alert for the possibility of finding needle puncture marks and other evidence suggestive of drug addiction and for defence injuries. He should also re-examine the body twenty-four hours after he has completed his examination, as wounds tend to become more apparent after post

mortem and refrigeration. When the superficial tissues are drained of blood, bruises may become much more apparent and appear to be more extensive than was originally appreciated. If this is the case, further photographs should be taken. When rigor mortis has passed off it may be easier to open the hands and check for defence wounds such as cuts and this should always be done.

(16) In all cases of bombing or shooting the body should be X-rayed prior to internal examination (see paras. 1.54ff). The same must be done in cases of infant deaths where the possibility of non-accidental injury exists (see paras. 3.14ff).

(17) The internal examination must be comprehensive and not be confined just to the internal organs. It must also extend to the internal aspects of the skeleton, including the spine, sternum, ribs and pelvis.

(18) After the pathologist has examined all the interior of the body he should retain portions of all the major organs for microscopic examination. It may be that if poisoning is suspected he may be asked to collect further samples such as stomach contents, liver, kidney, hair, nail, skin, bones, and muscle. The pathologist should also retain any organ which has been injured and led to death, such as the brain in fatal head injuries or the heart or lungs in the case of a fatal stab wound of the chest.

(19) At the conclusion of the examination the pathologist should inform the Coroner of his findings personally, unless he completes his examination at some anti-social hour, when it is customary and indeed sensible to wait until the Coroner is available.

(20) It is usual for the pathologist to tell the investigating officers of his findings, with an explanation of how he thinks injuries may have been caused, and he may be asked to examine a weapon or weapons which are allegedly responsible for the injuries he has described. He should include all the details of such weapons in his notes, supplemented by sketches.

(21) He should sign all the exhibit labels in conjunction with the scene of crime and exhibits officers and he should ensure that his list of exhibits and the exhibits officer's list are identical as regards the numbering and details of each specimen. It is usual for the pathologist to use his initials for all the material he himself collects and retains, numbering each in turn from one to whatever the final number turns out to be.

(22) The pathologist must retain all the notes he has taken or dictated to his scribe because he may be asked to produce them in court. They must never be discarded. Using them as a basis, he should provide a report for the Coroner and with the latter's consent, one for the police. Such a report should be set out clearly in an orderly manner, avoiding too many complex descriptions and abstruse medical terminology.

1.21 It is usual for the police report to be typed on special headed paper, in the form of a witness statement, incorporating the caution required by the Criminal Justice Act[10] at the beginning, following the name, address and personal details of the pathologist concerned. The report will describe the time and place of the examination, the list of those present, the formal identification of the body, the external examination and internal findings, and contain a list of specimens collected with their appropriate exhibit numbers, the whole ending with a set of conclusions, including the cause or causes of death, which are, as far as possible, clear, concise and unequivocal. Each page must be signed by the pathologist and his signature witnessed. The pathologist must retain a carbon copy of his report. This report will be used by the Crown as the pathologist's witness statement for the purposes of committal proceedings and the subsequent trial. It may be necessary for the pathologist to provide a preliminary report while he is awaiting results of an analysis for poisons or drugs, since this examination may take days or weeks. Such results can be incorporated into his final report.

1.22 The subject of second and subsequent autopsies is dealt with in Chapter 7. Such autopsies are usually carried out on behalf of accused persons as part of their defence or on behalf of aggrieved parties contemplating civil litigation. The Coroner has power to retain a body where it is likely that a second autopsy will be carried out and this may delay the funeral and disposal of the body, with consequent distress to relatives. The Coroner will usually put pressure on those requesting and carrying out the second examination to expedite matters. In cases of unreasonable delay the Coroner may release the body for disposal by the family.

1.23 The routine hospital post mortem examination may from time to time reveal unexpected injuries which may lead to the possibility of criminal proceedings. Any pathologist confronted by this situation should cease his examination at once, inform the Coroner and ask for skilled assistance if the pathologist himself has not the requisite experience to deal with such matters.

1.24 The forensic autopsy should be carried out as soon as reasonably possible after discovery of a dead body and before decomposition sets in, as obviously such changes make an examination more difficult to the extent that in a certain number of cases it may become impossible to determine a cause of death.

1.25 All the material the pathologist has retained at his examination should either be preserved in formalin or kept in the deep freeze until

10 Criminal Justice Act 1967 s. 2(2); now Magistrates' Courts Act 1980 s. 102(2).

such time as it is required for further inspection, for example by a pathologist on behalf of the defence, or until the case is concluded, when it should be discarded.

SUDDEN DEATH DUE TO NATURAL CAUSES MIMICKING CRIME

1.26 Many cases of sudden collapse, such as a heart attack, may result in the patient falling on to a hard surface like the roadway or pavement without making any attempt to save himself. In these circumstances there may be facial injuries suggestive of an assault, or a severe head injury with splitting of the scalp and possibly an underlying fracture of the skull, again raising the possibility of an attack by an assailant. Injuries occurring under such circumstances at or about the time of death are usually indistinguishable from those freshly inflicted in life, there having been no time for obvious lack of vital reaction or for post mortem changes to occur.

1.27 Examination of the injuries may give a clue as to their causation from their distribution. Injuries may be all on one side of the face or there may be no surrounding massive bleeding from severe injuries because the circulation has stopped and blood loss will therefore be minimal or only small, for in life scalp and facial wounds usually bleed profusely.

1.28 A careful external examination of the body should be carried out to exclude defence wounds and other external signs of assault. The injuries in post mortem collapses should be confined to one area only on one side of the body and deep-seated injuries to internal organs should be minimal. A full autopsy should reveal an underlying natural cause of death such as a coronary thrombosis or a ruptured aneurysm to account for the sudden collapse.

1.29 Persons having a cerebral haemorrhage may stumble about, knocking furniture and ornaments aside, breaking china and glass and causing a scene of disorder suggestive of a break-in, before collapsing and dying. Such persons may also injure themselves, for example an old person may break the neck or a femur. Careful autopsy techniques should demonstrate the extent of the natural disease and the limited results of injury.

1.30 (1) Massive haemorrhage from the oesophagus, stomach or bowel may present with the victim being found dead surrounded by large quantities of blood over the face and clothing. Such haemorrhage may follow ruptured varicose veins in the oesophagus in liver disease, or be due to gastric or duodenal ulcers or cancer. Lower down in the large intestine there may be ulceration or cancer in the colon or rectum and this may also bleed with massive haemorrhage rectally, the victim again being found dead surrounded by a large quantity of blood. If the victim is a woman there may be suggestions of a sexual assault. The only way to distinguish such cases from genuine assault is for the pathologist to examine the body *in situ* if there is doubt and clean up the body as far as possible to determine whether there are external injuries present or not. The source of the haemorrhage will be confirmed at autopsy.

(2) Similar massive haemorrhage may occur from the nose and mouth, usually due to cancer of the lung eroding one of the major blood vessels in the chest, the air passages filling with blood which then pours out externally. Less commonly similar haemorrhage may occur in cases of untreated or undiagnosed pulmonary tuberculosis.

(3) Vaginal haemorrhage may occur uncommonly with cancer in the pelvic organs usually involving the vagina or uterus. Again careful examination at autopsy should establish the true cause of the haemorrhage.

1.31 (1) One of the features of advanced liver disease is disorder of the blood-clotting mechanisms in the body with resultant spontaneous bruising. This is particularly seen in alcoholics, who tend to fall and injure themselves with the extent of the bruising being disproportionate to the trauma involved. Even without trauma there may be extensive spontaneous skin haemorrhages on the trunk or limbs and this again may mimic assault or provoke allegations of it, particularly where a drunken alcoholic has been taken into police custody and subsequently dies of alcoholic poisoning or inhalation of vomit.

(2) Other causes of spontaneous bruising are blood disorders such as leukaemia, where it is due to the relative absence of blood platelets from the underlying bone marrow disorder, or in haemophilia, where clotting factors are congenitally absent. Such haemorrhages are usually fairly easy to differentiate from bruising due to trama as in the latter there is nearly always some swelling or superficial damage to the epidermis of the overlying skin, both features being absent in spontaneous haemorrhages.

1.32 The epileptic who dies following a major seizure may cause considerable damage both to himself and to his surroundings if he has a fit in a confined space, a similar picture to that described above in a patient with a fatal cerebral haemorrhage. The presence of a bitten tongue, wet underclothing and an empty bladder at post mortem should give the clue in the absence of a definitive history of previous epileptic seizures. The suspicion of epilepsy may be confirmed by analysis for anticonvulsant drugs which may be found in low or therapeutic levels in the blood in such patients.

1.33 Reference is made elsewhere to neglect in the elderly, either self-neglect or deliberate neglect (see para. 1.111 *post*). The demented elderly may behave in many bizarre ways, particularly if they suffer from delusions or hallucinations. They may live in a state of total squalor and disarray, leaving doors and windows open, and if afflicted with hypothermia they may show paradoxical undressing as described at para. 1.110(5) below. When they are found dead, the whole scene may resemble a burglary or break-in. If in addition the dead person has injuries and sores which have not been attended to and allowed to fester and which may be extensive these may be mistaken for injury. The experienced doctor should be able to interpret these findings correctly and thus allay false suspicion.

PATHOLOGICAL ASPECTS OF HOMICIDE

1.34 Victims of homicide may die at once or extremely rapidly from dstruction of the vital centres such as the brain or heart or from torrential haemorrhage from the aorta. However, most victims survive for minutes or hours and some for days and weeks.

1.35 (1) They may die of shock and primary haemorrhage from wounds to any part of the body involving major blood vessels or vital organs. Severed arteries usually bleed copiously under pressure, with jets of blood causing exsanguination in a very few minutes either into body cavities or externally. Venous bleeding may be considerable, particularly if jugular veins in the neck are penetrated or cut across.

(2) Such injuries may be complicated by air embolism. Air enters the circulation by being sucked in through a partially severed major vein, causing cardiac arrest when the heart chambers are full of frothy blood and air, a process that usually takes two to three minutes in the vast majority of cases.

1.36 People who have been stabbed in the chest, injuring the heart, lungs or aorta, may survive longer than the ordinary lay person might imagine and be able to carry out complicated manoeuvres such as going upstairs to fetch a weapon, chasing an assailant, or running away a considerable distance before finally collapsing.

1.37 Head injury victims may survive for days, weeks or even months. When victims with head injuries are found dead it is worth remembering that the time of assault is not the same as the time of death and they may be separated by minutes or hours.

1.38 (1) When injured persons are brought alive to hospital, modern intensive care should ensure that the majority survive and the resulting charge may be one of grievous bodily harm and not of murder. However, some assault victims die despite the best treatment available, commonly from chest infections such as bronchopneumonia, or from thrombosis of the leg veins with resultant detachment of a blood clot which enters the circulation obstructing it in the lungs, so-called pulmonary embolism. This is particularly sccn in cases of prolonged immobility as in coma from head injury or following leg fractures.

(2) Others may die from wound infection, particularly when there are retained foreign bodies such as portions of clothing driven in by explosions or firearm missiles. Such infected wounds may cause secondary haemorrhage particularly if the wall of a major vessel is involved.

(3) Bladder and kidney infections often complicate unconsciousness, especially where there is incontinence or it is necessary to use a catheter to drain the bladder, as this procedure may allow infection to enter the bladder and track upwards into the kidneys.

(4) Pressure sores (commonly called bed sores) will occur over the buttocks, back and heels unless an unconscious person is moved regularly every two to three hours into a fresh position to relieve the pressure, particularly over bony parts such as the base of the spine, the hips and heels.

1.39 The pathologist should always consider the effects of the treatment received by the victim and be alert to the possibility that mistaken diagnosis or treatment has led to complications and death. This outcome would not normally have been expected, and may allow a defence of *novus actus interveniens*.[11] Such circumstances may arise where operations have been perfcrmed to treat injuries where there have been massive blood transfusions and other fluid replacement and where numerous drugs have been administered to the patient to treat or prevent infection or other complications.

11 But see the cases discussed in para. 1.02 *supra*.

ASPHYXIA

Definition

1.40 Asphyxia means different things to different people. It implies the cutting off of the oxygen supply to the brain. This may be due to an inadequate oxygen intake in the presence of irrespirable gases such as carbon monoxide, cyanide and methane, or obstruction to respiration either at the nose and mouth or in the mouth, the throat, the main air passages or in the lungs. It may be the consequence of natural disease such as inflammation or tumour or from haemorrhage. In this section the discussion of asphyxia will be limited to mechanical obstruction of respiration leading to death. Such obstruction may be deliberate or accidental. Mechanical obstruction to respiration is marked by congestion of the features with cyanosis, that is dark blue discolouration of the blood due to lack of oxygen, showing as pin-point or petechial haemorrhages in the eyes, skin of the face and mucous membranes of the mouth and throat, serous membranes of the lungs and heart (see Plate 3).

Obstruction of Air Passages

1.41 (1) In babies this may be deliberate or accidental where an infant is smothered in bedding either by an assailant pressing the head into a pillow or accidentally when the child is too immature to be able to raise its head from the pillow. In such cases, and indeed in all infant asphyxias, petechial haemorrhages are few in number. The post mortem findings are usually confined to pressure whitening around the nose and mouth with surrounding cyanosis of the post mortem lividity on the remainder of the face, with saliva, blood and tissue cells on the pillow where they may be detected in the forensic laboratory. The diagnosis of death by suffocation or smothering at post mortem is not easy, as the child may succumb very quickly and die before the classical changes associated with asphyxia in older children and adults have become established. There is no doubt that a small proportion (less than 10%) of so called "cot deaths" are in fact cases of deliberate suffocation (see paras. 3.05 and 3.24 below). In the absence of a confession on the part of the mother of the dead infant or clear-cut pathological findings, it may be difficult to found a successful criminal prosecution in a case of infanticide. If there is abundant convincing circumstantial evidence, it may be possible. However there is often a deep-seated reluctance to prosecute the mother concerned, particularly if she is young, immature or mentally ill. In such cases the placing of the woman concerned under medical or social care is more rewarding than punishment.

(2) Alcoholics and epileptics are also liable to suffocate from

obstruction of the air passages if they lie face down in bedding or on a carpeted floor or in other positions where the nose and mouth are occluded by material or fabrics. Rarely a person may be asphyxiated during natural or anal sexual intercourse from behind.

(3) Plastic bags placed over the head and neck may result in rapid fatal asphyxia. Such asphyxia may occur accidentally among children at play imitating space men, or more commonly as a form of suicide. In such latter cases drugs may also be taken by the victim and these may be detected on analysis following post mortem. As in suffocation in children, death results very quickly and petechial haemorrhages may not develop. The paucity of findings at autopsy if the bag has been removed and the pathologist is unaware that it had been present may result in his failing to diagnose the true manner of death. A helpful finding at autopsy if the bag has not been removed for very long is that condensation within the bag may lead to dampness of the hair and a characteristic sheen on the skin of the face. Occasionally the victim will place a pad soaked in some toxic material such as cleaning fluid over the face prior to putting on the plastic bag and securing it around the neck with string or a scarf. Such cases can be confused with people sniffing solvents who soak a pad in some volatile or aromatic fluid, place it over the nose and mouth and enclose the head and neck in a plastic bag to confine the vapour and prevent its dissipation. Under these circumstances the lack of oxygen within the bag and the build-up of carbon dioxide, quite apart from the volatile agent on the pad, will lead to rapid death before the victim is able to remove the bag. It may be difficult for the pathologist to differentiate between suicide or accidental death in such cases. Toxicological analysis may help to resolve the problem.

(4) Another form of obstruction of the airway at the nose and mouth is gagging. Intruders sometimes tie up and gag persons they find in the premises when they break in or who disturb them during their activities; night watchmen in work premises and factories are particularly at risk. If the gag is too tightly applied across the mouth, the tongue is forced into the back of the throat, obstructing the airway through the nose, and the victim suffocates, showing the classical symptons of congestion, cyanosis and petechial haemorrhages. The pathologist should examine inside the mouth because the pressure of the gag may well force the lips against the teeth, injuring the inner aspect of the lip with bruising and abrasion or laceration. Even if the gag is subsequently removed by the assailant, it should be possible for the pathologist to identify that a gag had been in position. Sometimes handkerchiefs or other portions of fabric, torn clothing and the like may be stuffed into the victim's mouth prior to the gag being applied and such material greatly increases the risk of fatal suffocation in the victim. It is imperative if the gag is in position when the

Fig. 1.3. Gagging and binding

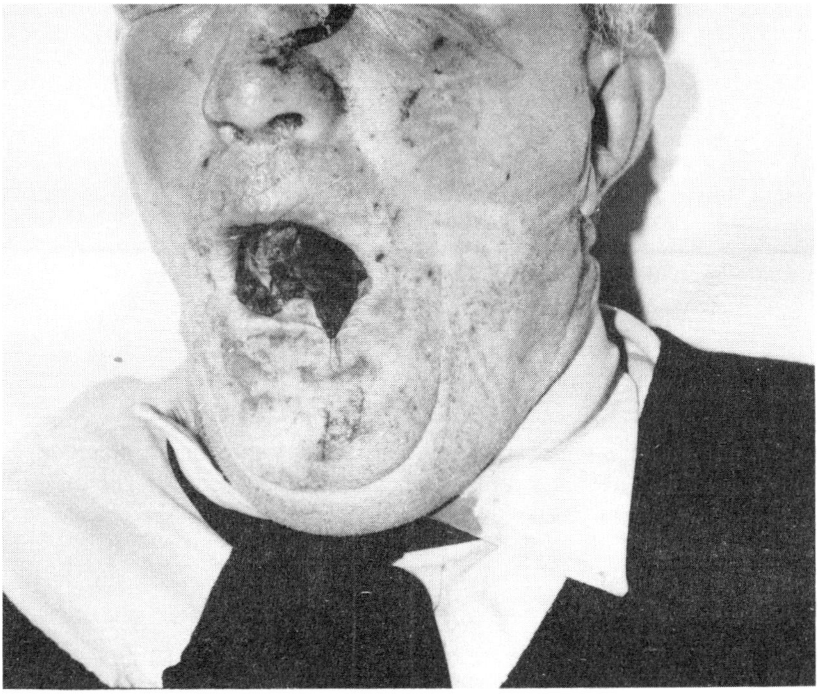

Fig. 1.4. Same case as Fig. 1.3. On removal of gag a handkerchief was found stuffed in the mouth

victim is found dead that photographs are taken before the gag is removed as once it is removed the post mortem appearances rapidly become less striking, as do the injuries inside the mouth already referred to.

(5) Obstruction of the air passages can also occur as a result of inhalation of blood from facial injuries such as a broken nose or dislodged teeth and tearing of the lips and gums received during a fight

where the victim has been worsted and left unconscious on his back, allowing blood to run backwards and downwards into the back of his throat and trachea. Similar injuries may contribute to death in alcoholics who fall or are knocked to the ground during fights and asphyxiate. Alcoholics also have a tendency to vomit and such vomit may be inhaled into the air passages, causing fatal obstruction.

(6) The air passages can be suddenly obstructed by foreign bodies such as toys in the case of children, unmasticated portions of food in the insane, dentures in the elderly and foodstuffs in the disabled whose swallowing mechanisms are severely impaired by, for example, multiple sclerosis or old poliomyelitis. The presence of a foreign body in the back of the throat may cause the patient to 'gag' and retch and vomit and inhale vomit, again with fatal results.

Compression of the neck

1.42 Compression of the neck may take the form of stamping on the neck with crushing of the neck structures, mugging with the arm around the neck with the assailant standing behind the victim, and compressing the neck by manual or ligature strangulation.

(1) Street fights, particularly among young people under the influence of alcohol, often result in multiple blows and kicks being exchanged and sometimes the victim while lying incapacitated on the ground has his neck stamped on repeatedly, crushing the laryngeal structures and causing bleeding and swelling of the soft tissues, compressing the trachea and larynx from without and obstructing the airway within with collapse of the integrity of the larynx itself. There may be patterned abrasions on the skin of the head and neck which may be identifiable as being caused by a particular shoe or boot and the pathologist must take care to ensure the preservation of such information by photography including measurement scales set at right angles to marks which may be due to footwear.

(2) Encircling the neck from behind with the forearm often leaves little evidence internally for the pathologist, although there will be signs of asphyxia on the face. If the victim is older and the hyoid bone and larynx more brittle with age, then there may be fractures found, but in a young person whose neck structures are elastic compression may not result in any significant injury and the only findings may well be bruising between the back of the larynx and the front of the spine, and some bleeding into the strap muscles of the neck.

(3)(i) *Manual strangulation*, while not as common as in previous decades, is found not infrequently in female homicide victims, particularly prostitutes, in whom it might be thought to be an occupational hazard. There may be few marks externally from the hand of the assailant but

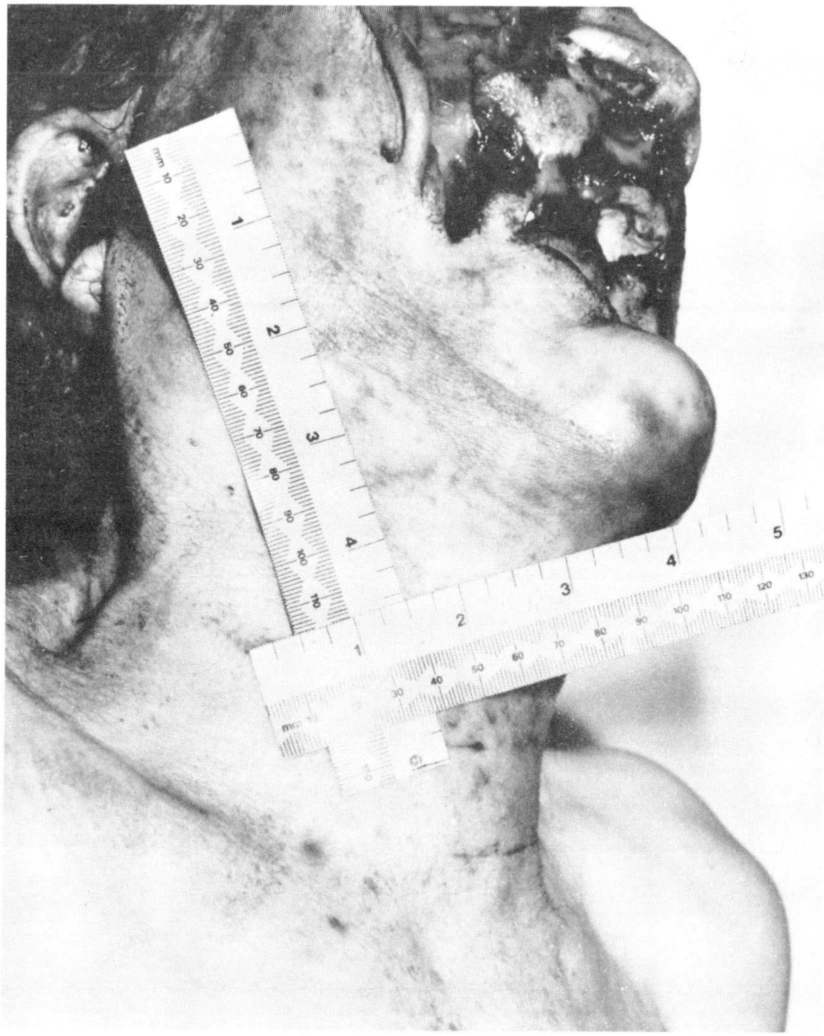

Fig. 1.5. Deliberate stamping on face and neck with tread marks from sole of shoe

there may well be multiple scratch marks caused by the victim herself trying to claw away the compressing hand. There will be congestion and cyanosis of the features with petechial haemorrhages in the eyes. Dissection will reveal bruising in the strap muscles of the neck and fractures of the hyoid bone and of the superior horns of the thyroid cartilages but, as explained above, these are not always found, particularly in young people. Such fractures should have fresh bleeding around them indicating that they occurred in life.

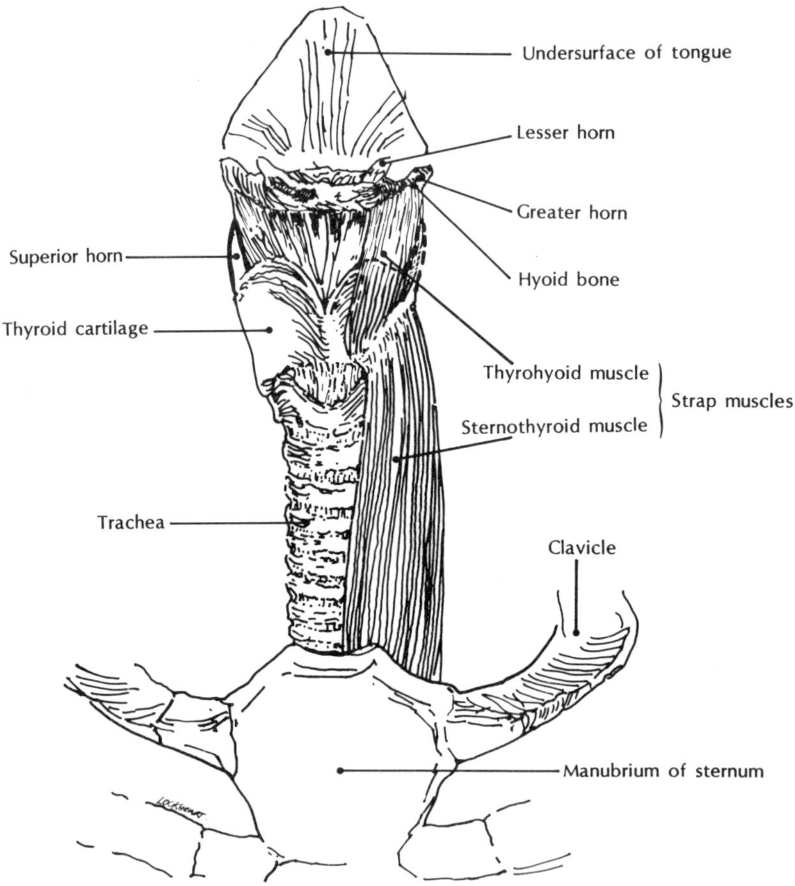

Diagram of front of neck to show hyoid bone, larynx and strap muscles

Fig. 1.6.

(ii) There may be some discrepancy in the marks on the neck of the victim and of the bruising in the muscles and other structures beneath the skin. This is because the skin is free to move over the neck structures and the assailant may well have pushed the neck skin upwards during his assault or changed his grip during the attack, so there may well be many more internal injuries than might be expected.

(iii) There may be bruising around the junctions of the carotid arteries on both sides of the neck. This must be sought for by the pathologist because there are many cases on record where an assailant has seized his victim by the throat and where the victim to his dismay has collapsed and died almost immediately. This is probably due to reflex cardiac arrest or vagal inhibition from pressure on the nervous plexuses which are found adjacent to the junctions of the carotid arteries. Comparatively brief but violent pressure on such sensitive nerve points may lead to sudden death with a minimal amount of external and internal injury.

(iv) It is impossible to know how long it takes for manual strangulation to cause death. It is probably of the order of 15 to 30 seconds, but obviously the time must vary with the violence and completeness of the compresssion and the extent of the struggle put up by the victim and his or her age and state of health.

(4)(i) *Ligature strangulation* is nearly always homicidal. If the ligature is still in position, all the signs of asphyxia will usually be obvious above it. If it has been removed, at may be possible to detect the pattern of it on the skin and clear adhesive tapings of the skin of the neck should be taken in order to detect fibres from rope, string or cloth that may help to identify the material used. Laser examination may be helpful. If the ligature is still in position, the pathologist should cut it away from the knot, reconstitute it with adhesive tape, and preserve it for examination by the forensic science laboratory.

(ii) Internally there may be bruising beneath the ligature but little other damage. Once the ligature has been removed, the elasticity of the tissues allows them to resume their normal configuration and apart from a few linear marks on muscle, there may be nothing to see internally.

(iii) However, if the victim, who is often a woman, has put up much of a struggle before being overcome, externally there may be scratch marks on the neck where she has attempted to claw away the ligature and she may well have inflicted injuries upon her attacker, particularly with her fingernails.

(iv) Marks on the neck may prove to be artefacts due to constriction by jewellery or clothing, particularly where there has been post mortem change with swelling of the tissues; skin folds may resembe ligature marks particularly to the inexperienced. Internal injuries may be caused by rough handling during dissection. Examination of the neck in a case of

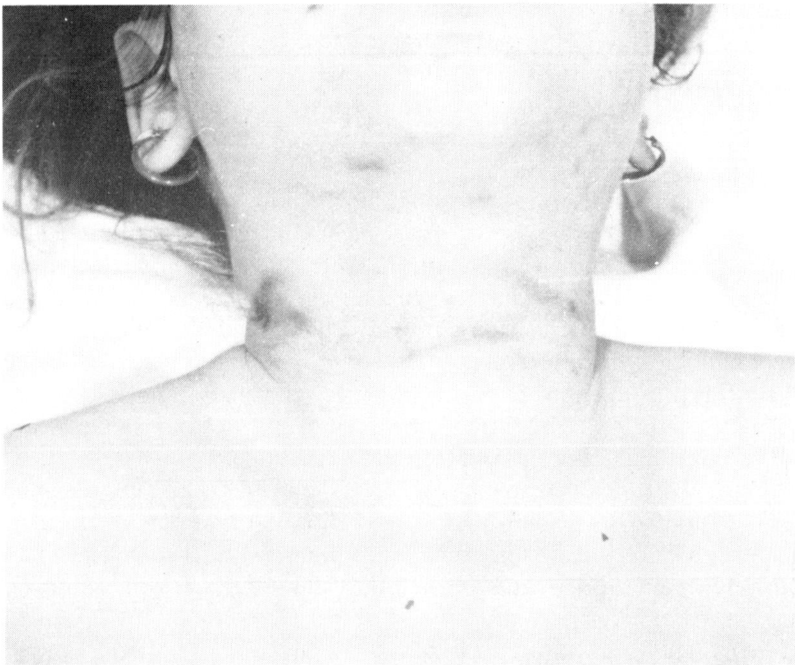

Fig. 1.7. Ligature strangling with skin abrasions made by victim's fingernails

suspected asphyxia requires skill, experience, patience and scrupulous technique.

(5) Occasionally cases of self-strangulation are encountered. Obviously they must all be due to ligatures as no one can compress his or her neck manually without loss of consciousness supervening and the hand compressing the neck relaxing, thus allowing the victim to recover. Self-strangulation may be difficult to differentiate from homicidal strangulation, as the material must be quickly and tightly tied prior to unconsciousness supervening and to prevent slippage of the ligature. The pathologist may well have to rely on circumstantial evidence such as the reported mental state of the deceased, the circumstances of the finding of the body, the suicide note if any, the door locked from within and so on, as well as the absence of scratch marks or other self-injury on the neck that are usually found in homicidal strangulations as described above. There may be marks of self-injury at the wrists or elsewhere which will help to confirm the assumption of suicide.

Hanging

1.43 Hanging is usually suicidal and is rarely found in a woman.

(1) Hanging may occur accidentally in babies who become entangled in pram harness or other forms of restraint, in children playing games and in young men indulging in aberrant sexual practices. Hanging is used as a form of judicial execution in certain parts of the world but there has been no case of judicial hanging in the United Kingdom since 1964.

(2) The usual scene of a suicidal hanging is a person suspended from a beam, hook, handle or projection with a noose around the neck deeply grooving it on one side and rising to a suspension point on the other with an overturned chair or some other piece of furniture from which the deceased has stepped or jumped. There may be other forms of suicidal preparation such as empty tablet containers or incised wounds on the wrists, and a door locked from within.

(3) Post mortem examination usually shows the deep grooving of the neck, bruising of the underlying tissues, quite frequently fractures of the hyoid bone or thyroid cartilage on the side of the deep grooving and signs of asphyxia above the ligature mark. If the body has been hanging for any length of time, then all the post mortem lividity will settle in the legs, feet, hands and forearms. If the ligature has been removed prior to the pathologist seeing the body, the pattern of the suspending agent may be recognisable on the neck.

(4) The body does not need to be totally suspended. Many victims are found slumped down with buckled knees and feet on the ground, the body weight being enough to stretch and tighten the ligature around the neck. If the victim has fallen a long way, for example down a whole stairwell at the end of a long length of rope, the sudden jerk when his fall is arrested may fracture the upper cervical spine or dislocate the head upon the top of the spine but such injuries are not common.

(5) Auto-erotic hanging is almost exclusively found in youths and young men. It is said that a degree of anoxia heightens sexual excitement. Such victims are usually found naked or dressed in female attire, often with rope, chain, straps or other forms of bondage about their person and a ligature around the neck from which they are suspended. The ligature is very often padded with a scarf, shirt or other material to prevent the ligature itself chafing the neck. There may be other impedimenta with sexual overtones around the body such as pornographic literature and there may be evidence of seminal emission. To the uninitiated such cases often are mistaken for homicidal tying-up and hangings.

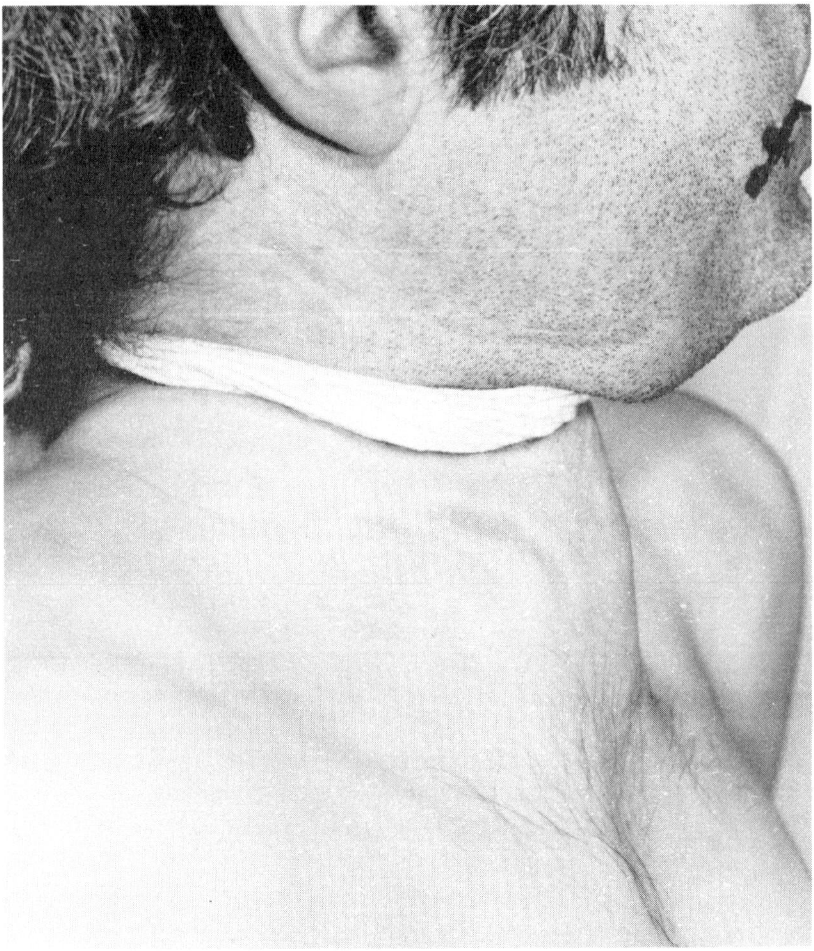

Fig. 1.8. Hanging: ligature grooving neck with congestion above it

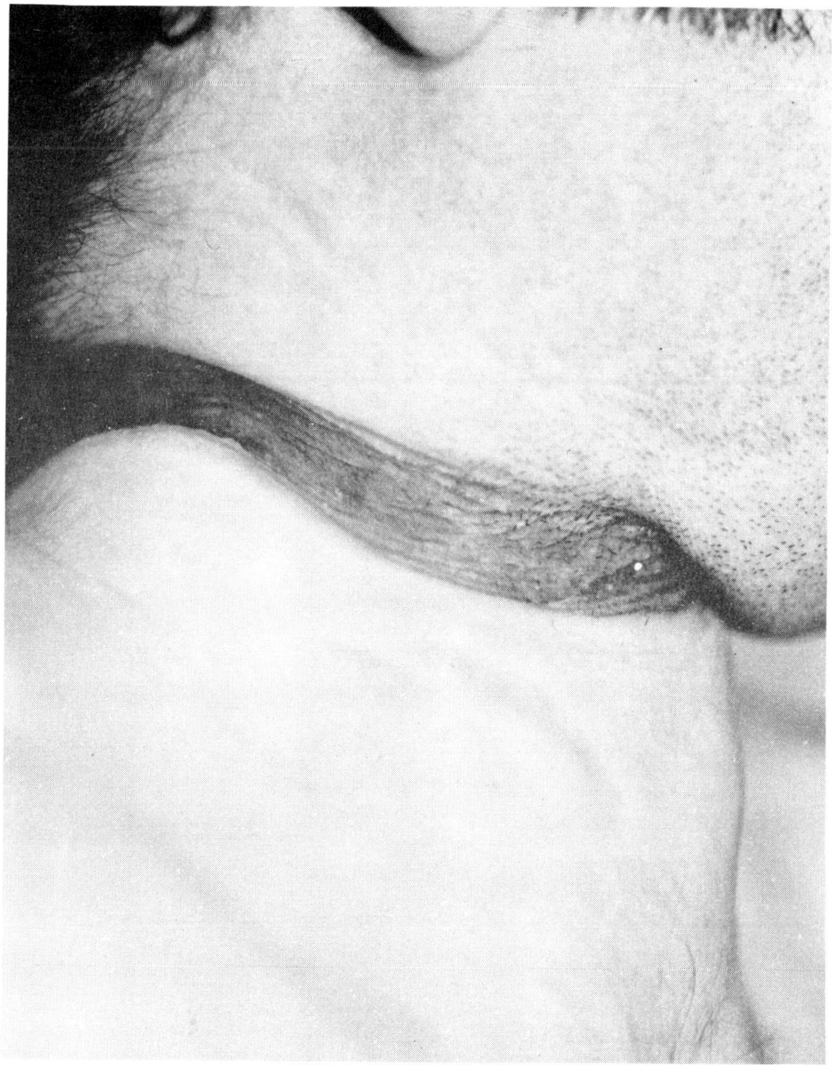

Fig. 1.9. Same case as Fig. 1.8. Hanging: pattern of ligature imprinted on skin

Fig. 1.10. Auto-erotic death with chains and bondage

Traumatic Asphyxia

1.44 Traumatic asphyxia occurs when the chest is crushed, preventing the victim from breathing and causing his death from asphyxia. It is classically found in persons buried in trenches they are excavating when the sides fall in or in children who are buried digging caves in sand dunes. It is also seen in homicidal circumstances where a terrorist bomb has caused great destruction and collapsing masonry has pinned and crushed victims in the rubble. It may be found in assault cases where the victim is jumped or stamped upon and crushed by one or more assailants. Often many ribs are fractured, thus totally disorganising the mechanics of respiration and leading to fatal asphyxia. In such cases asphyxia changes are often very pronounced and are associated with the other injuries caused by the trauma.

DROWNING AND IMMERSION

1.45 (1) Deaths in water are some of the most difficult cases that the doctor or forensic pathologist is called upon to examine and interpret. The majority are due to accidents or suicide. Homicidal drowning is rare. While anyone may drown, young children, the elderly, epileptics, the drunk and inebriated, the disabled and non-swimmers are particularly at risk. Death in water may be due to classical drowning, hypothermia, sudden cardiac arrest, so called vasovagal attacks, or from injury, for example striking the bottom of a swimming pool in the shallow end and fracturing or dislocating the neck.

(2) The mechanisms are different in salt and fresh water drowning. In what might be called classical drowning where the air passages and lungs become filled with water one does not see the changes described above in asphyxia deaths of congestion, cyanosis and petechial haemorrhages. The latter are particularly rare in drowning cases. There may be froth foaming from the lips and mouth when the body is freshly recovered from water and the lungs are overdistended and full of frothy fluid which fills the air passages. If there is gravel or mud or foreign material in the water in which the person drowns, then that material may well be found in the air passages and in swallowed fluid in the stomach. Grass or vegetation may be clutched in the hand by cadaveric spasm.

(3) In salt water drowning, where the salt content of the water is higher than the salt content of the blood and tissue fluids, water will be drawn from the body into the salt water inhaled into the lungs and cause even more flooding of the lungs and air passages. In fresh water drowning water is removed from the lungs into the blood stream and may cause destruction (haemolysis) of red cells, leading to release of potassium into the circulation and cardiac arrest.

(4) In both salt water and fresh water drowning, death occurs within a very few minutes, particularly in fresh water drowning. The mechanism is probably a combination of anoxia and a disturbed potassium–sodium relationship in the blood and tissue fluids leading to a rapid irregular beating of the heart known as ventricular fibrillation which characteristically causes death in fresh water drowning.

(5) In the past attempts have been made to estimate the salt or chloride level of the blood going to the lungs from the right side of the heart and coming back from the lungs into the left side of the heart, samples being

taken from the right and left ventricles for this purpose. If the person dies in salt water then increased salt levels should theoretically be found in the blood in the left side of the heart coming from the lungs as compared with that on the right. Contrariwise in fresh water drowning the chloride level in the blood on the right side of the heart should be higher than that coming from the lungs into the left side where the blood has been diluted by the fresh water. However, unless these tests are done within an hour or two of death and recovery of the body, the results are meaningless.

1.46 The majority of people who die in boating accidents or shipwreck die of hypothermia as demonstrated by the work of Keatinge.[12] The colder the water the more rapidly the victim dies. The classical story is of the sailing dinghy overturning and one of the crew swimming to the shore is seen by the others suddenly to throw up his hands and disappear from view. When his body is recovered it does not show the classical signs of drowning as described above nor conversely does it show the classical signs at post mortem of hypothermia which take time to develop. Keatinge's work showed that the body temperature in cold water drops slowly for a short time but then measurement of the core temperature of the centre of the body shows a sudden catastrophic fall with complete disorganisation of respiration and co-ordination leading to rapid death unless the subject is immediately rescued and resuscitated.

1.47 Occasionally someone is seen to dive into a swimming pool and not surface. When the body is rescued there is no injury and no sign of drowning and the temperature of the water usually precludes hypothermia as a diagnosis. It is postulated that these such people die of cardiac arrest or vagal inhibition from the impact of cold water on the larynx at the back of the throat causing reflex stoppage of the heart. This can only be a diagnosis of exclusion, based on witnesses' statements and the absence of pathological findings of drowning or injury.

1.48 (1) Unfortunately many bodies that are recovered from water have undergone putrefactive changes and decomposition in them is well established. There may be supra-added injury from fish, birds, river craft or other sources of trauma causing mutilation of the body.

(2) Post mortem examination of such cases is an unpleasant experience even for those used to it. A careful search must be made for evidence of ante mortem injury to differentiate it from post mortem damage. The presence of vital reaction such as reddening or inflammatory change around wounds is indicative that they were caused in life and

12 Keatinge, W.R. (1969) *Survival in Cold Water*. Blackwell: Oxford and Edinburgh.

differentiates them from post mortem trauma. Natural disease such as coronary thrombosis must be searched for to explain why somebody has fallen into water and been recovered dead. Evidence of drowning itself in a decomposing body must be difficult to detect unless one is fortunate enough to find foreign material such as sand and gravel or grass in the air passages and in the stomach.

(3) Alcohol determinations should be carried out if possible as even allowing for decomposition it may well indicate whether the subject was severely intoxicated at the time of death. A very large number of people dying in water are under the influence of alcohol at the time, as has been borne out by the work of Giersten[13] in Norway.

(4) It is often suggested that decomposition will result in high levels of alcohol accumulating in the dead body. This is not necessarily so, as it depends on the bacteria or yeasts complicating decomposition as to whether they ferment or destroy alcohol. Providing decomposition is not too advanced such changes are usually of the order of tens of milligrams and if for example a figure of 250 milligrams of alcohol per 100 millilitres of blood is found on analysis such a figure should be regarded as being due to alcoholic intoxication and not to post mortem fermentation. Blood alcohol estimations should be complemented if possible by urine alcohol determination as the bladder is relatively immune to decomposition and the urine as long as it is not obviously infected may well yield useful information as to levels of alcohol.

1.49 It must always be remembered that bodies can be victims of homicide which have been disposed of by their being weighed down and thrown into water. Occasionally one sees a case of suicide where a person fills the pockets of his clothing with stones and ties weights around his waist and legs prior to jumping into water. It may not be easy to differentiate the homicidal victim from the suicide and careful attention to the distribution of the weights and their attachments to the body may be all important.

1.50 If the body is severely decomposed and it is not possible to make a diagnosis of drowning with certainty with the naked eye, then tests for diatoms will have to be undertaken. Diatoms are unicellular algae with silica shells found in water. There are several thousand varieties with characteristic microscopic appearances, different species being found in cold water, warm water, salt water, fresh water, running water, stagnant water and so on. The principle is this: if a person dies from drowning,

13 Giersten, J.C. (1970) *Med. Sci. and Law, 10*, 216–19, "Drowning while under the influence of alcohol".

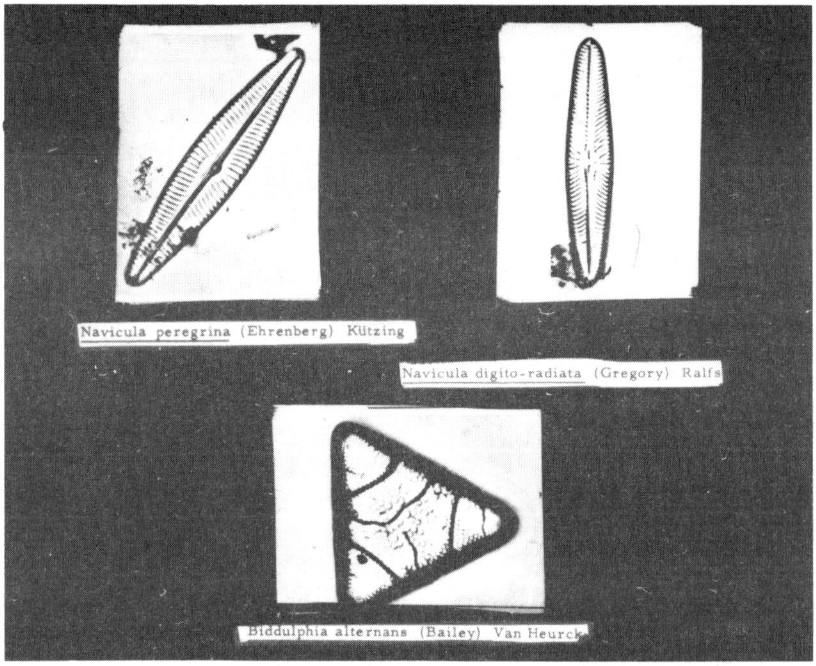

Fig. 1.11.

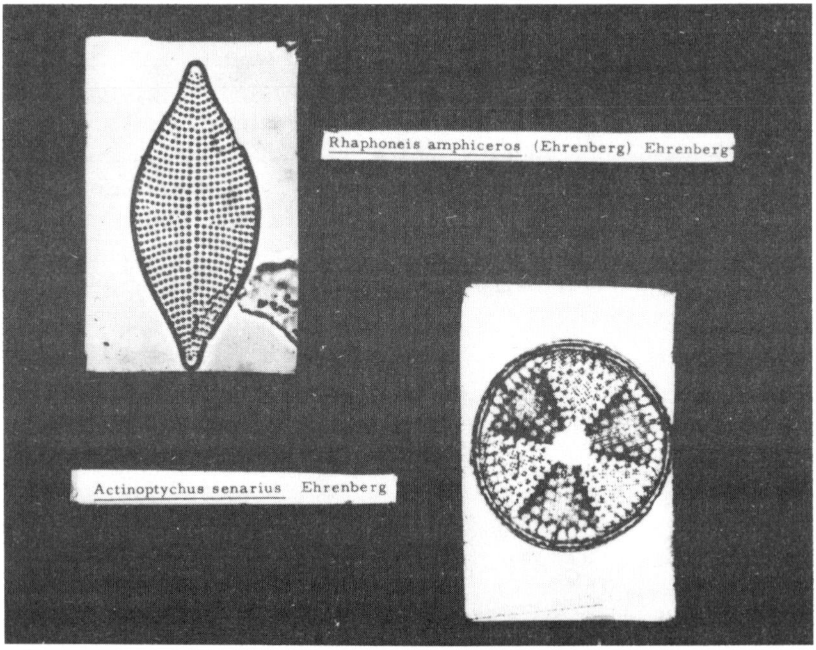

Fig. 1.12.
Various species of diatoms

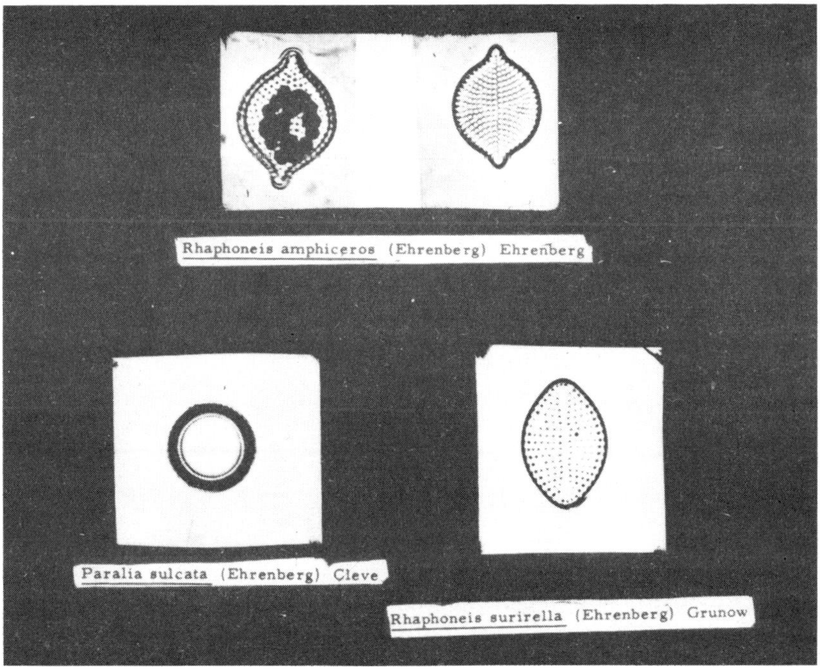

Fig. 1.13.

Further species of diatoms

during the few minutes it takes for the person to drown water passes into the circulation from the lungs taking with it the diatoms which are thus distributed throughout the body. Diatoms will be found in tissues remote from the air passages, for example the kidney and bone marrow. Samples of such tissues are taken together with portions of lung and a sample of the water in which the person has allegedly drowned and all are treated with strong acid by boiling for many hours. This effectively destroys all the organic material in each of the samples leaving only the silica shells of the diatoms. After neutralisation of the acid in the samples the deposits are examined under the microscope for the presence of diatoms. To make a positive diagnosis of drowning a significant number of diatoms of the same species must be found in all the samples including the water from which the body was recovered. Contrariwise, if the person was dead prior to going into the water, following, say, a coronary thrombosis, the circulation will have stopped and while water may pass into the lungs down the trachea, there will be no distribution of diatoms throughout the body tissues and tests carried out as described above will not demonstrate diatoms in the tissues but merely in the water sample. Scrupulous attention to detail is required in this test, in particular avoidance of contamination of the tissue samples with water.

1.51 *Death in the bathroom* is seldom due to drowning on its own. Many people who are found dead in the bath submerged beneath the water have not drowned. Many of them may have died of carbon monoxide poisoning from faulty water heaters and gas appliances with inadequate ventilation. Some will have died following injury such as slipping and striking the head on the taps or the side of the bath. Others may have taken excessive alcohol or a deliberate overdose of alcohol and drugs, or have cut their wrists or inflicted some other form of self injury. It is difficult for a fit healthy adult to drown in the bath, as the basic instincts for self-preservation tend to override the intention to drown oneself. Children, however, do drown in the bath, especially an infant who may be left in the bath by a mother who returns only to find the child submerged and dead. Some of these cases may be homicide and it may be impossible for the pathologist to differentiate the accidental from the deliberate drowning in such cases in the absence of any injuries such as grip marks or other signs of restraint or pressure. These are very rarely seen. New-born infants delivered precipitantly into the lavatory pan may die of drowning as described elsewhere (see para. 3.04).

Bodies recovered from water often show wrinkling of the skin of the hands and forearms, so called 'washerwoman's hands'. These are merely a sign of immersion in water for a long period and are not diagnostic of drowning.

1.52 From time to time cases are reported where the victim has been drugged or poisoned or otherwise attacked and the body later disposed of in a river or lake or in the sea to simulate drowning and thus avoid suspicion. A careful post mortem examination including examination for diatoms should establish whether the victim has drowned or not and toxicological analysis may reveal the presence of toxic or lethal levels of poison or drugs. The presence of injuries, particularly associated with vital signs such as reddening of the tissues or internal bruising or bleeding, should serve to differentiate such injuries from post mortem trauma.

1.53 *Deep sea diving*, for example in the North Sea in connection with oil rigs, carries a significant mortality. The common causes of death are hypothermia and drowning but in addition there is the risk of caisson disease and nitrogen narcosis. When divers work at great depth with a high ambient pressure the nitrogen in the atmosphere may dissolve in the bloodstream and when pressure is reduced too quickly by an over-rapid ascent to the surface by the diver, the nitrogen may come out of solution as bubbles, giving rise to agonising pains in the joints known as the "bends", necessitating rapid recompression and slow decompression under controlled conditions. Repeated episodes of such nitrogen escape into the bloodstream may cause death of bone, particularly in the upper end of the humerus, which may be detected radiologically. This is due to bubbles of nitrogen cutting off the blood supply to the bone. Tunnel workers and others working in increased atmospheric pressure may also suffer from the "bends".

Bodies that have drowned are sometimes found at post mortem to have haemorrhages into their middle ears. This is thought to be due to barotrauma.

WOUNDS FROM FIREARMS

1.54 No pathologist should ever carry out an autopsy on a case of fatal shooting suspected of being criminal without the assistance of a ballistics expert from a forensic science laboratory. Preferably the scientist should be present at the autopsy and consult with the pathologist during it. If this is not a practical exercise, then the pathologist should consult by phone with a suitable expert and discuss the case with him, particularly as to the retention and preservation of material for examination in the laboratory subsequently. The variety of present-day firearms is so wide and so extensive that no pathologist can hope to have more than a superficial knowledge of them and the injuries that they cause. Fortunately shooting in the United Kingdom is a relatively rare form of homicide, although regrettably in recent years the upsurge of urban terrorism and armed robberies and burglaries has produced an increase in such cases.

1.55 In outline, firearms are divided into long-barrelled weapons such as rifles or shot-guns, and hand guns such as pistols, revolvers and automatics. Occasionally home-made guns or antique weapons may be used. Firearm barrels are either smooth-bored or rifled, that is they have a spiral ridge and groove pattern running along the interior of the barrel causing the projectile to spin at high speed and imparting a gyroscopic stability to it, thus increasing its range. Such ridges or lands leave characteristic scratches on each bullet. The range of the weapon is also a result of the muzzle velocity; the bigger the charge the faster the bullet is fired from the gun and the further it will travel.

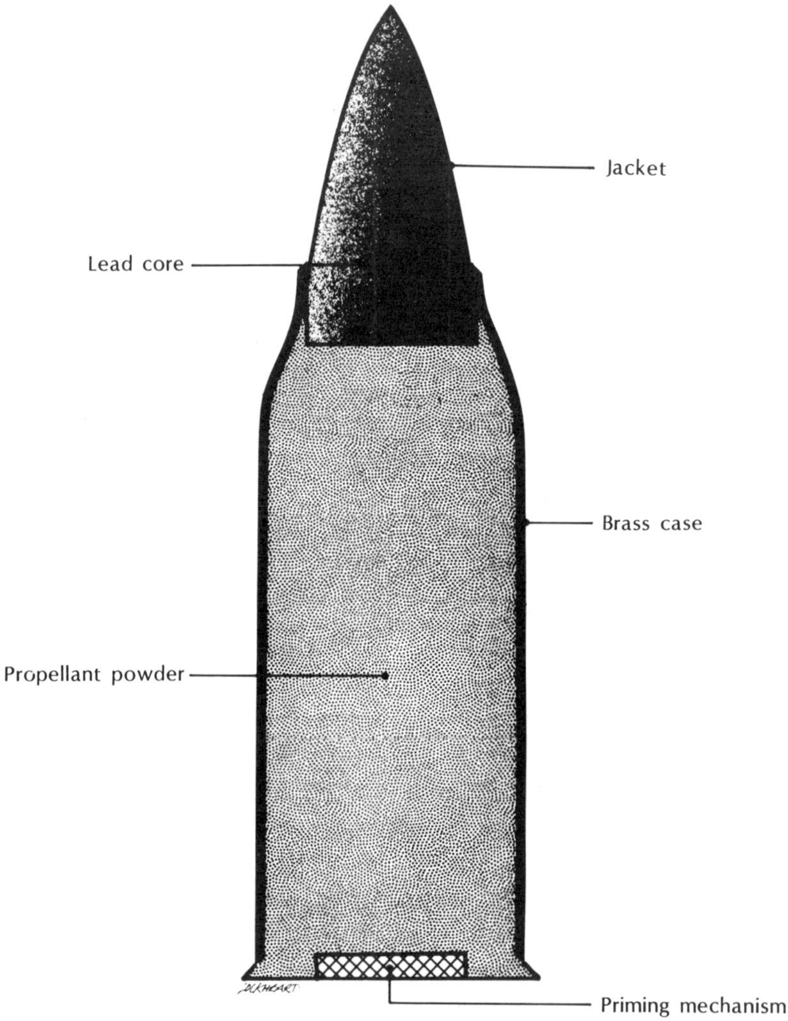

CROSS SECTION OF RIFLE BULLET

Fig. 1.14.

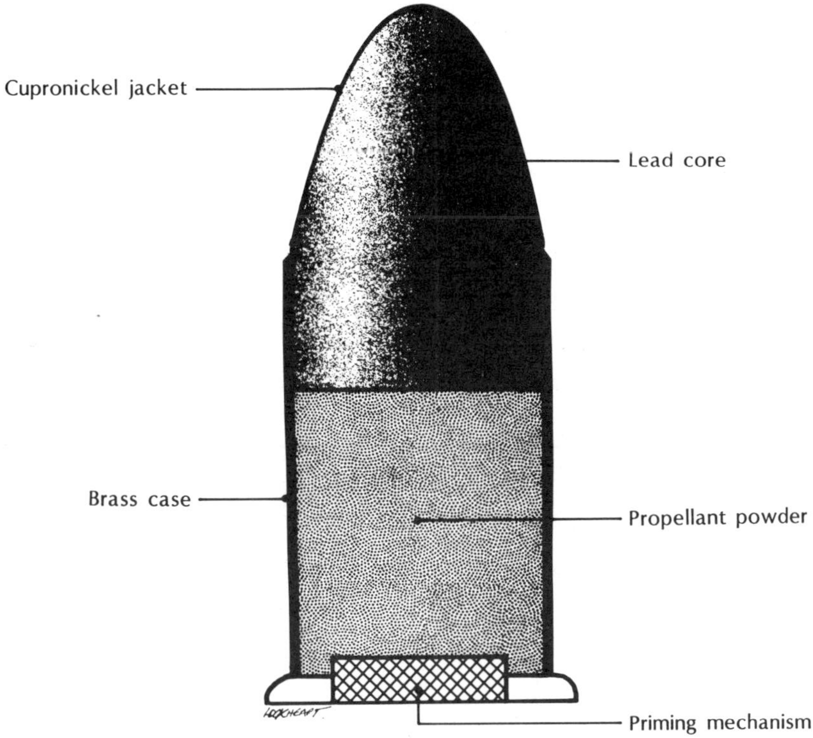

CROSS SECTION OF REVOLVER BULLET

Fig. 1.15.

1.56 The firing pin which detonates the charge is individual to every gun and the mark that the pin will make on the base of a cartridge case will be peculiar to the gun from which it was fired. In this way the markings on a cartridge case retained in a weapon and the marks on the bullet fired through its barrel will be individual to each particular weapon and it is these facts that make identification by the expert possible. To this end any surgeon or pathologist who is retrieving bullets or parts of them from a living patient or a corpse must take the greatest possible care when recovering the missile not to mark it in any way with the tips of forceps or other instruments thus scratching it and distorting the ballistic pattern. Nowadays guns are often modified by shortening the barrel and this may enormously alter the characteristcis of such a weapon.

Entry and Exit Wounds

1.57 There are two sorts of wounds that the pathologist or clinician may be called upon to examine, entry wounds and exit wounds.

(1) *Entry wounds*, as the name suggests, are made by the projectile or shot entering the body. If the weapon is fired at close range, that is less than three feet or arm's length, there will be burning of the margins of the

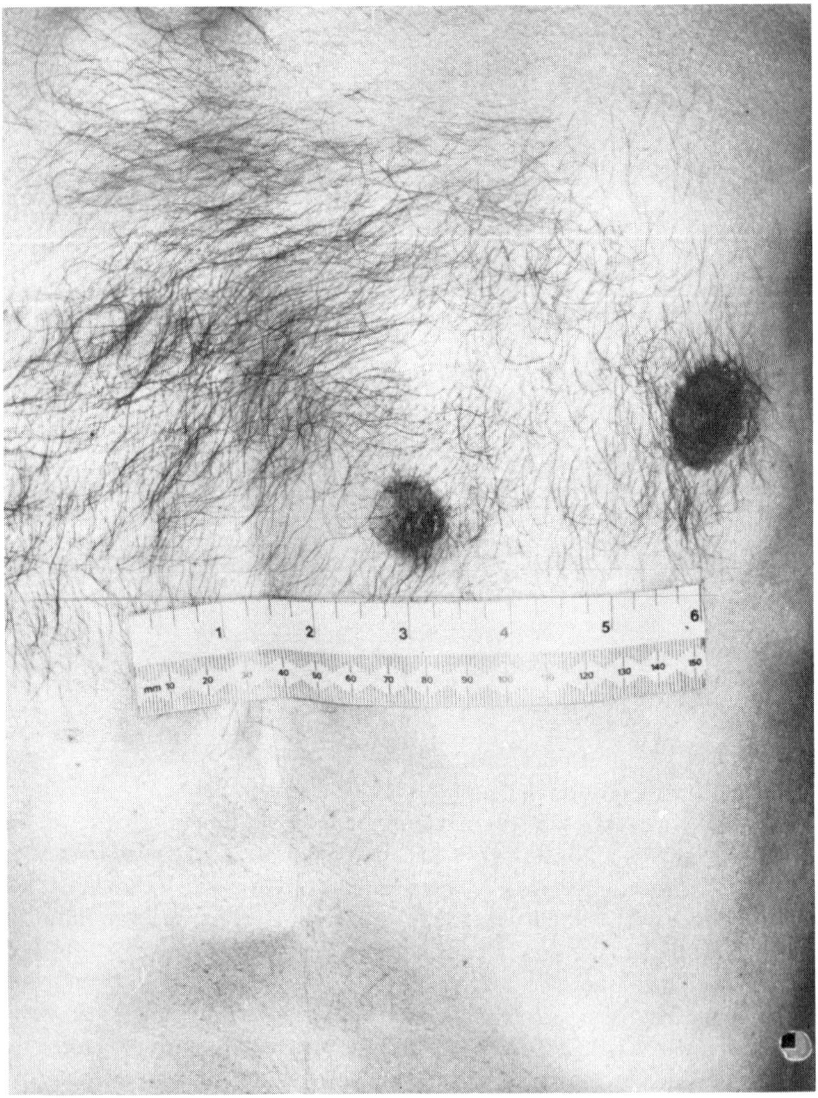

Fig. 1.16. Near-contact suicidal firearm wound in chest from 0.38 revolver. See Fig. 1.18 for exit wound in the back in same case

wound and possibly powder tattooing around the wound itself (see Fig. 1.16). If it is fired really close or in actual contact, then the wound itself will not have a round margin but be split and lifted up by the gases discharged, with the projectile erupting under the skin splitting and lifting it (see Fig. 1.17). This may also result in pink colouration of the

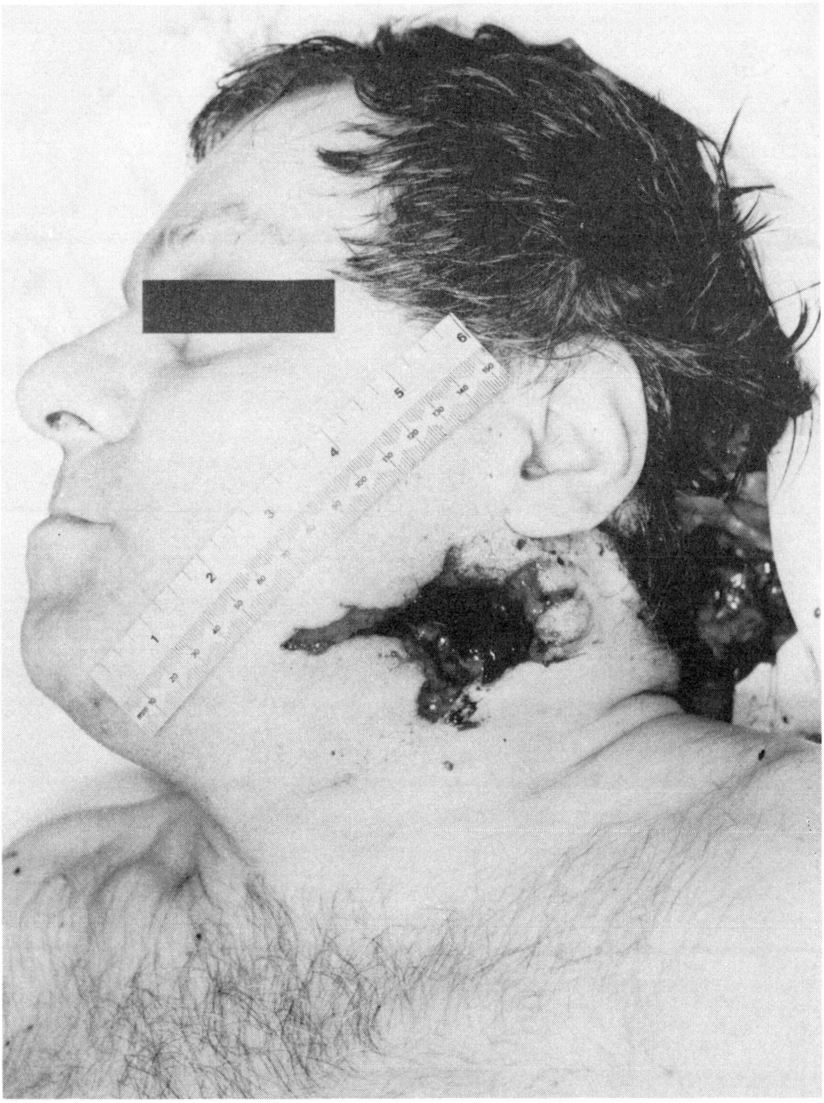

Fig. 1.17. Contact wound from 12-bore shotgun with radial splitting of skin margins

underlying soft tissues such as muscle from carbon monoxide contained in the gases. There may be lead soiling from the bullet on bony margins of wounds in the skull.

(2) *Exit wounds* are different in that they are often cruciate or irregular without, naturally, any burning or tattooing. They may be in very unexpected places. They may be very large if portions of bone or other

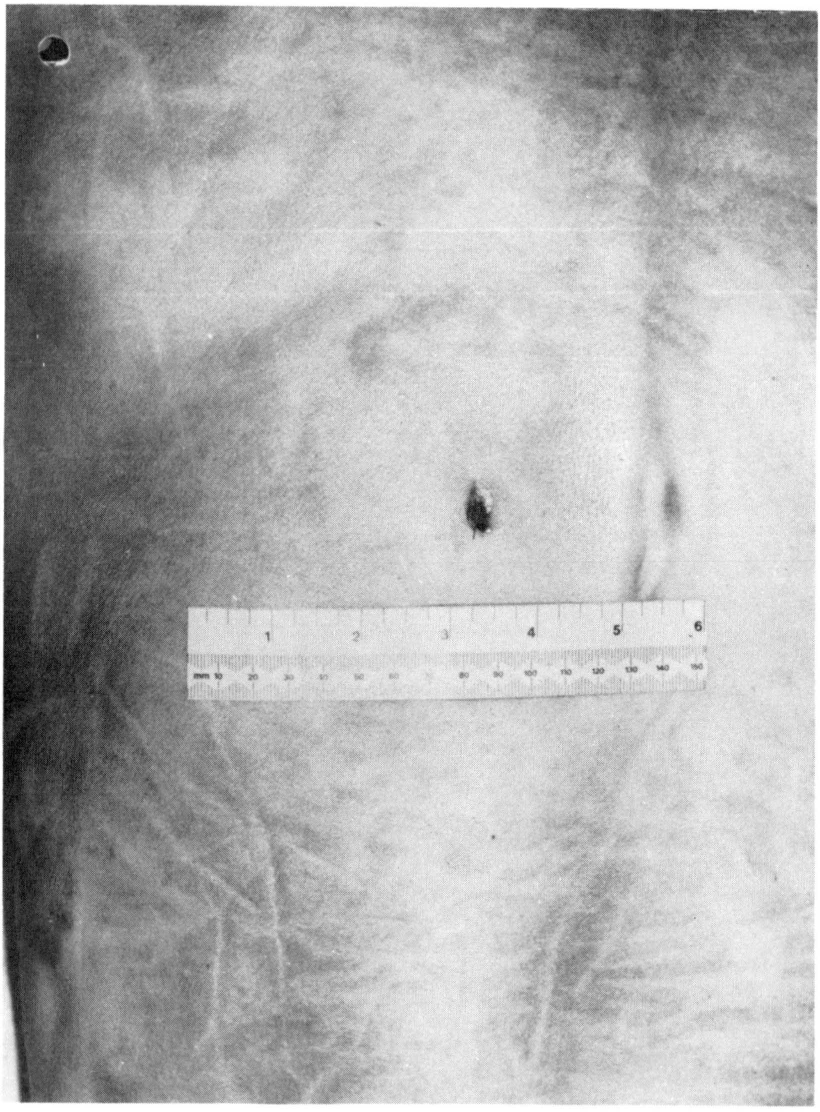

Fig. 1.18. Same case as Fig. 1.16: exit wound in back from 0.38 revolver

material are blown out as well as the projectile; for example, the back of the head may be blown into pieces by a shot-gun inserted into the mouth and fired. The track of a missile may be very difficult to establish, as it may ricochet off bone or even enter a blood vessel and be swept along by the blood flow.

Gunshot Wounds

1.58 (1) Shot-gun cartridges contain multiple portions of shot graded either by their size and weight or by the diameter of the barrel (see Fig. 1.19). At close range the shot will usually enter as a mass, causing a large ragged entry hole with a scalloped edge (Fig. 1.20), the shot separating on impact and being distributed throughout the part of the body

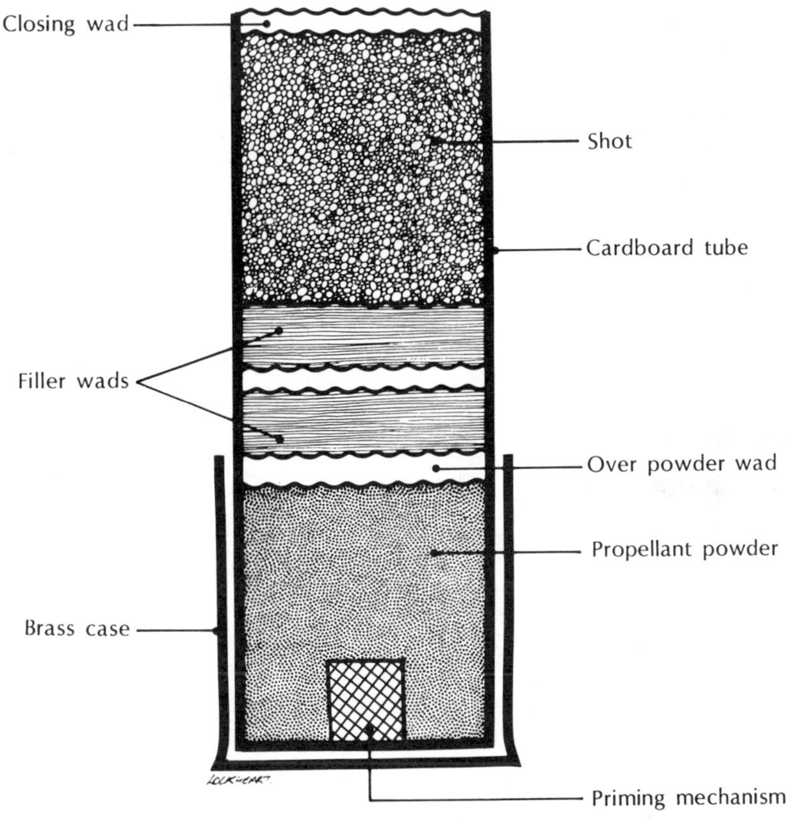

CROSS SECTION OF SHOTGUN CARTRIDGE

Fig. 1.19.

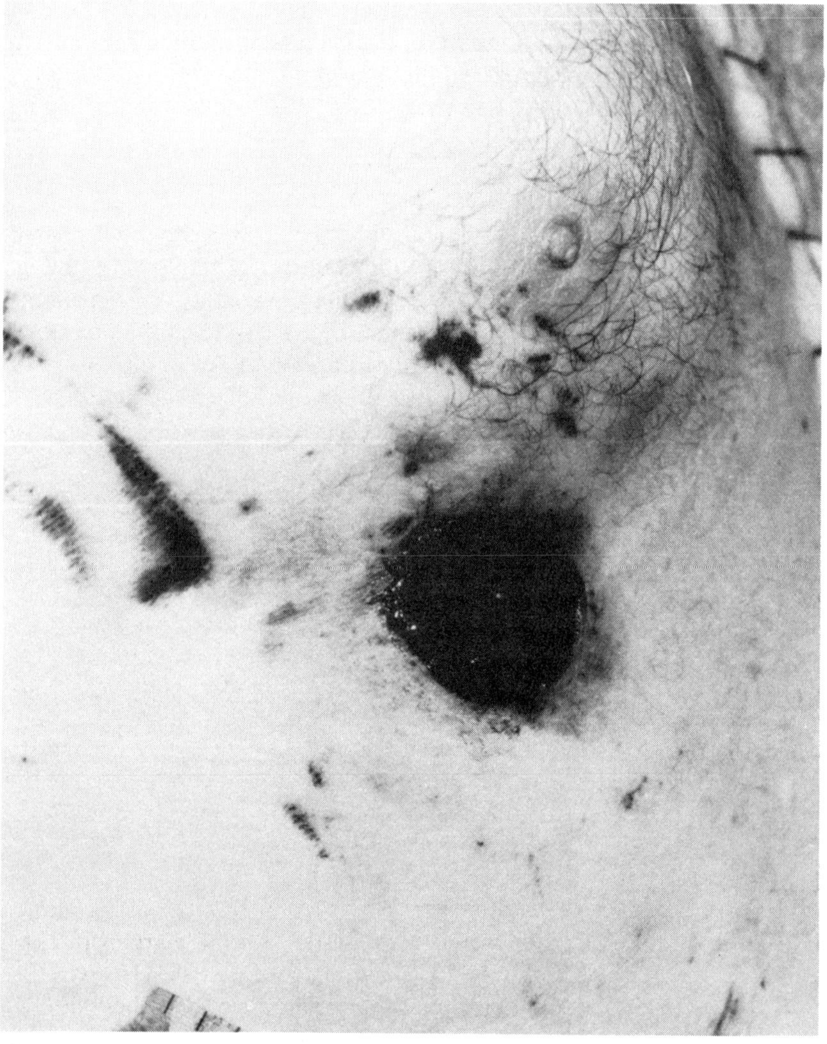

Fig. 1.20. Close range discharge of sawn-off shotgun. Linear abrasions made by barrel of gun pushed against chest prior to discharge

concerned over a considerable area and causing great destruction; the bigger the shot, the more the damage. Very large shot as used for hunting big game may prenetrate through the body and exit from it, but the majority of the shot of the type used in rabbit or game-bird shooting will be retained in the tissues. Shot-guns are fairly short-range weapons. In some models the barrel narrows towards the muzzle, the so called "choke", which increases the range.

(2) Not only will the shot be distributed in the body but so also will be the fibrous or plastic discs or wads or plastic cups which are incorporated into the shot-gun cartridge to keep the shot in position and propel it from the barrel. At close range such wads will also be found within the body cavities and must be searched for by the surgeon or pathologist.

Examination

1.59 In examining a case of homicide by shooting or explosives it is imperative that the pathologist and scenes of crime officer work together, particularly as regards the clothing. This may be extremely informative to the forensic scientist, as it may have portions of powder or explosive material embedded in its fabric. Each item of clothing should be carefully removed by the pathologist and the scientist together, photographed and measured and retained for laboratory examination. Even in a case of explosive devices where the clothing is very badly burned or soiled, it is important to retain all that can be rescued.

1.60 All cases of gunshot wounds must be X-rayed prior to autopsy in order to establish the number and position of the missile or missiles within the body; without X-rays it may be impossible to locate bullets or shot. The pathologist will have to adapt his post mortem technique so as to approach the missiles and recover them without making score marks or other artefacts upon them. This process can be tedious and take many hours. The surgeon removing missiles from a living patient should observe the same care in recovering them. If an entry wound or wounds are excised by the surgeon, he should retain them for examination by the ballistics expert.

1.61 In the same way that the surgeon excises the wound margins in a living patient prior to repairing defects, so the pathologist should excise entry wounds from deceased victims and hand these over together with the bullets or shot and wads to the ballistics expert for examination in the laboratory. The ballistics expert will test-fire any weapon allegedly used to commit a crime by firing it into a large box packed with wadding from which the bullet can be recovered. The rifling marks on the bullet are compared with bullets found in the victim or at the scene by comparison microscopy. He will also test-fire the gun into portions of uncooked pork, the consistency of which is the nearest equivalent to human flesh. A series of shots are fired from different ranges and the appearances of the test firing in the pork are compared with the excised wound from the victim. In this way the identity of the gun can be confirmed and the range of firing assessed.

1.62 Persons committing or attempting suicide by firearms nearly always use sites of election wihch are characteristically in the temple (the right side in a right-handed person and vice-versa in a left), the centre of the forehead, the roof of the mouth, the front of the neck below the chin, and over the heart. Obviously such wounds are contact or near contact and the gun will still be present, either grapsed in the hand by cadaveric spasm or more likely lying beside the body. Occasionally bizarre arrangements are made by the would-be victim such as fixing the gun in a clamp and firing it by means of a string pulling the trigger at a distance. Such elaborate equipment will be found intact at the scene. In addition there may be evidence of other self-inflicted injuries such as cut wrists, or autopsy may show that drugs or posions have been ingested in quantity. There may also be supporting evidence such as suicide notes, locked doors and the like.

1.63 Accidental shootings occur during the careless handling of guns during demonstrations or cleaning or in the field such as during game-bird shoots. There is nearly always a single discharge of the gun which may affect any part of the body and there may well be witnesses who can describe events.

1.64 In homicidal shooting there may be several shots fired into different parts of the body and there may be obvious injuries to the hands and arms suggestive of the victim having put an arm up in a futile attempt to shield himself from the discharge of the weapon. Multiplicity of shots is almost pathognomonic of homicide. Close-range discharge of sawn-off shot-guns is unfortunately a present-day feature of armed robbery. The victim usually has a solitary large entry wound in the front of the body with massive destruction of the internal organs from spread of the shot.

BOMBS AND EXPLOSIVES

1.65 (1) The victims of bombing and other terrorist outrages involving explosives are often severely mutilated and if the victim is carrying a device which explodes prematurely, he may be literally blown to pieces. Persons at a greater distance show a classical triad of burns, lacerations and abrasions with tattooing. There is burning from the explosive, laceration from portions of the device and grazing and tattooing with particles of explosive from the device itself and surrounding material.

(2) Apart from the injuries from the explosive device, victims may well be further injured by being crushed by falling debris if buildings collapse

or by being hurled against walls. They may also be penetrated by wood or other foreign matter from furniture where a bomb has gone off, for example, in a crowded bar.

(3) There may be extensive blast injuries within the body, particularly to the lungs, which are rapidly overdistended, with rupture of the air sacs and haemorrhage into the lung tissue from torn blood vessles.

1.66 (1) Where large numbers of people have crowded together in a confined area where there has been a major explosion, identification may be a very real problem. The pathologist asked to examine the victims of a bomb outrage has two tasks. The first is to identify the victims and as far as possible reconstruct them so that relatives can carry out funeral arrangements on each of their loved ones in the knowledge that he or she has been restored as far as possible. Secondly he must recover fragments of the device so that the bomb itself can either be reconstructed or its components identified so that the origins of the device may be traced or the device linked with others in a series of explosions. There may be material in the body, carrying tool marks or other artefacts, enabling individual bomb factories to be identified and those persons involved in the terrorism to be arrested and charged.

(2) In the same way that the ballistics expert should be present at or consulted about the autopsy in the case of a homicidal shooting, so the explosives expert should be present or consulted about the autopsies on victims of bomb outrages and the pathologist and the explosives expert should work together.

(3) It is essential that all the human remains are collected, however macabre the task may prove to be. If the reason for the collection is explained to those carrying it out and if the pathologist is one of the team concerned, then it is likely that the bulk of the tissue will be recovered and be available for examination. Once all the tissue has been collected, the pathologist should try as far as possible to establish how many victims have been involved in the explosion and try to re-assemble the body or bodies as far as he can. This reconstruction may give some idea of the relation of the victims to the blast; for example it may be possible to show that a driver and a passenger in a car destroyed by a bomb had been sitting side by side with the bomb between them, the pattern of injury being predominantly left-sided in the driver and right-sided in the passenger. All the injuries should be photographed to show the distribution of the injuries rather than close-up views of the wounds themselves unless they have some unusual or individual features which need to be recorded.

1.67 (1) Once the re-assembly and photography has been completed, the whole of the remains, however small, should be X-rayed. The X-rays should be examined and all radio-opaque material should be noted and searched for by the pathologist. This can be a very laborious exercise and may take hours or days. The pathologist should constantly refer to the X-ray plates, and as each fragment is found, its identity should be confirmed with the X-ray appearances and then handed to the exhibits officer. Even the smallest screw or piece of wire may be of very great importance.

(2) Where portions of tissue are embedded in other material or mixed with debris, then it may be worth using a metal detector to see if there are any fragments in the material concerned.

1.68 The forensic scientist and explosives expert may be able to obtain a very large amount of information from what seems to the pathologist to be very unrewarding material, so it is worth the latter's while to carry on until he has found as much as he possibily can of material shown on the X-ray plates. It is possible sometimes to digest portions of flesh with enzymes to soften and break down muscle and other soft tissues in order to reveal small metal fragments that cannot otherwise be detected. As a matter of practical detail several biological washing powders have been used for this purpose with success. All the fragments and portions of device which are recovered from the victim should be numbered and photographed for purposes of continuity of evidence and reconstruction of the device.

STAB AND INCISED WOUNDS

Stab wounds

1.69 Stab wounds are penetrating injuries made by blunt or sharp-pointed weapons which may have single or double cutting edges. They may be enlarged by the partial withdrawal of the weapon and its being driven in again, or notched by twisting of the victim or by the assailant having driven in the weapon in one direction and pulled it out at another angle (Fig. 1.23). Stab wounds may be single or multiple, the latter being a common feature of homosexual assualts. Such wounds often cause rapid death from bleeding or air embolism or sometimes lead to delayed death, often from infection or from thrombosis of leg veins with subsequent pulmonary embolism following recumbency during treatment.

1.70 Stab wounds vary in size and depth according to the configuration of the weapon used and the wounds may often gape and bleed. A double-edged weapon, such as a dagger, usually causes a clean cut wound with two sharp ends (Fig. 1.21), whereas a single-edged weapon, such as an ordinary kitchen knife, will cause a wound which has one clean-cut end

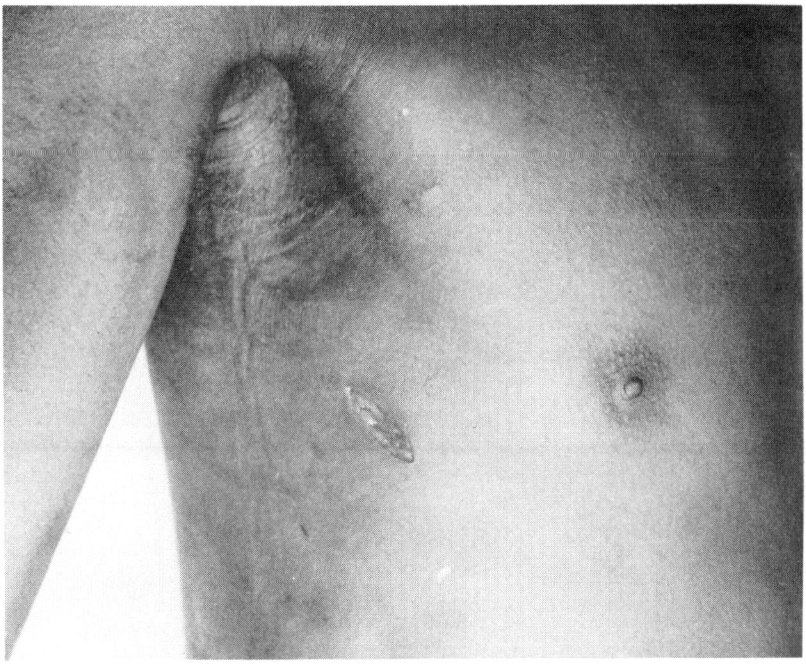

Fig. 1.21. Stabbing: double-edged knife

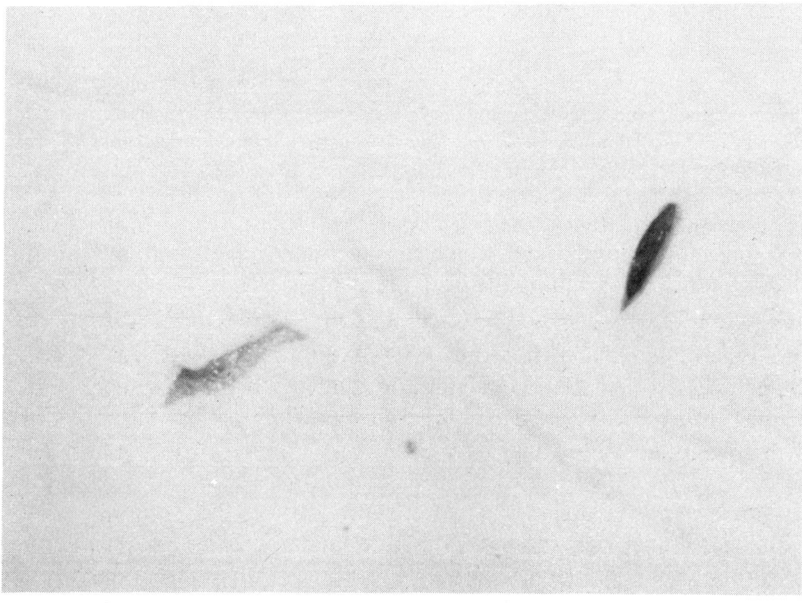

Fig. 1.22. Notched stab wound (left) and single-edged blade stab wound (right). The notched stab wound is shelved on one side and undercut on the other

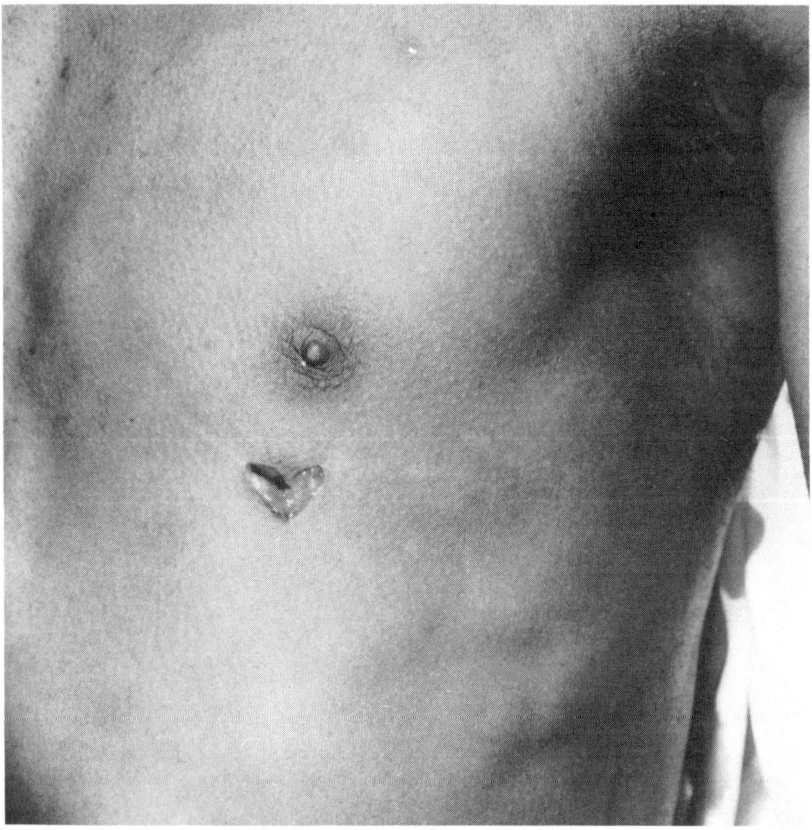

Fig. 1.23. Notched stab wound. The knife was driven in at one angle and pulled out at another

and one more blunted end which may actually have small splits in the skin, so called "fish-tailing" (Fig. 1.22).

Blunt weapons such as a closed pair of scissors will cause an "S"-shaped type of injury (Fig. 1.24), whereas a chisel or other square-ended implement will cause rectangular wounds. Other tools may cause characteristic injuries which may be difficult to identify in the first instance.

Examination

1.71 (1) When stab wounds are measured the sides of the wounds should be brought closely together so that each wound resembles a linear cut before it is measured, as the elasticity of the skin will tend to make any stab wound rounded or even circular. Photography of such a wound

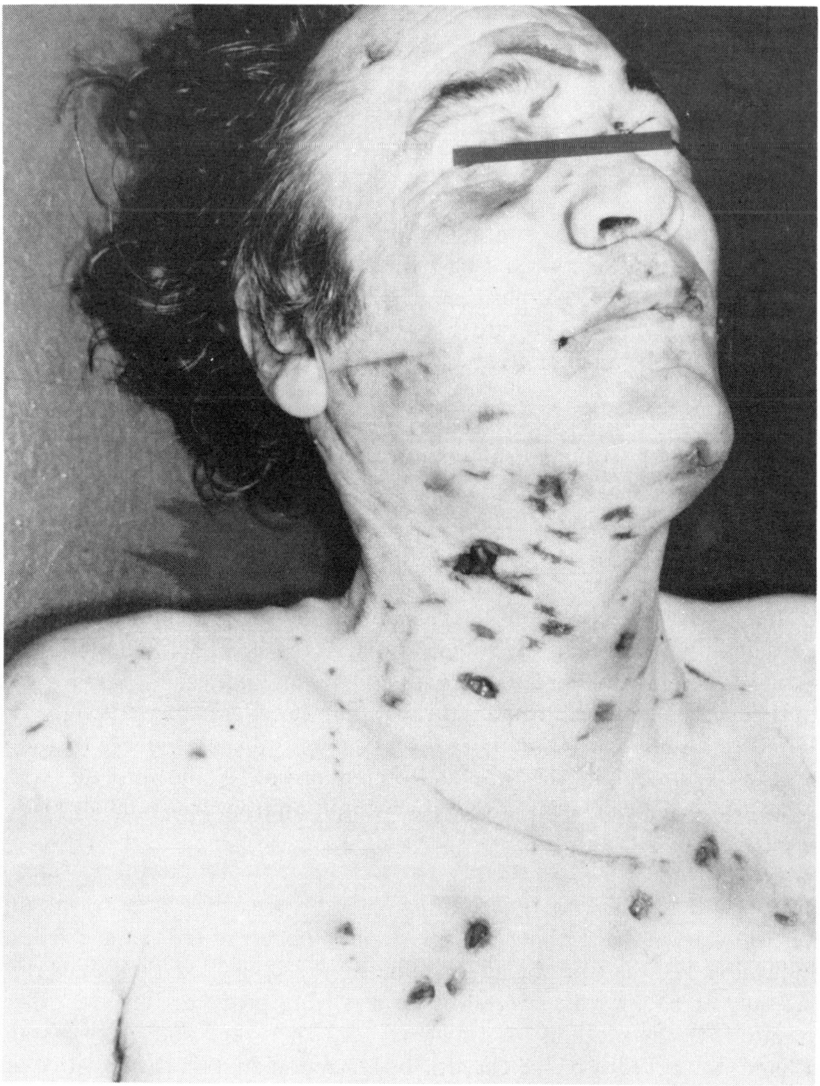

Fig. 1.24. Stab wounds from scissors

with measuring tape stuck alongside it may be frankly misleading when it comes to estimating measurements. The length of the wound is the length on the surface of the skin and the depth is the depth of penetration of the wound into the tissues.

(2) Besides examining the wounds in the victim, the doctor should, if possible, examine the clothing worn by the victim at the time of the

wounding, as this may provide useful information. It may be there are more wounds on the clothing than there are in the victim. The explanation is often that layers of clothing get folded or superimposed prior to being run through with the knife and if subsequently the fabric is stretched out and unfolded, perhaps during transportation of the victim to hospital or mortuary, there then appears to be a series of holes in the clothing overlying a single wound in the victim himself.

(3) Sometimes these multiple holes in clothing may be grouped together and represent would-be suicidal or self-inflicted wounds which have only penetrated the clothing and not the underlying skin, perhaps because the would-be suicide had not pressed firmly enough or the weapon was not sharp or else he was apprehensive of causing pain.

1.72 It is important to see whether the positions of holes in the clothing correspond with wounds in the body. If not, it may be an indication of the position of the victim at the time of the stabbing. If for example there is a hole in the clothing which appears not to overlie a wound in the back of the body, it may be that the victim's arm was raised, pulling up his clothing with it. When the arm is placed by the side of the body the clothing will slip down the back and the hole in the clothing will be considerably lower than the actual wound in the skin itself. Similarly the skin wound may not correspond with underlying injuries. A wound track in the back may appear to pass through the shoulder blade although the bone itself is not obviously injured. This again is further evidence that the arm was raised and the scapula rotated upwards, allowing the stab wound to penetrate between the ribs without injuring the shoulder blade itself.

1.73 (1) To return to the clothing, blood stains may appear to run vertically down the clothing and splash on to uppers of the victim's shoes, indicating he was upright at the time of the injury, or they may run laterally or backwards, suggesting he was lying prone or in some other position. If the clothing is drawn up and there are one or two stab wounds in the front of the chest or upper abdomen, this is suggestive of suicide. In hospital practice clothing is very often cut away and discarded by nursing staff anxious to resuscitate the victim, and this is understandable but sometimes unfortunate from a forensic point of view. Examination of the clothing may be of great assistance when the victim has been subjected to extensive surgery in an effort to save life or repair injuries, with the incorporating of stab wounds into surgical incisions or their conversion into drainage holes. In such cases examination of the clothing may reveal the number and sites of the original injuries.

(2) When the doctor comes to measure the stab wounds in the clothing

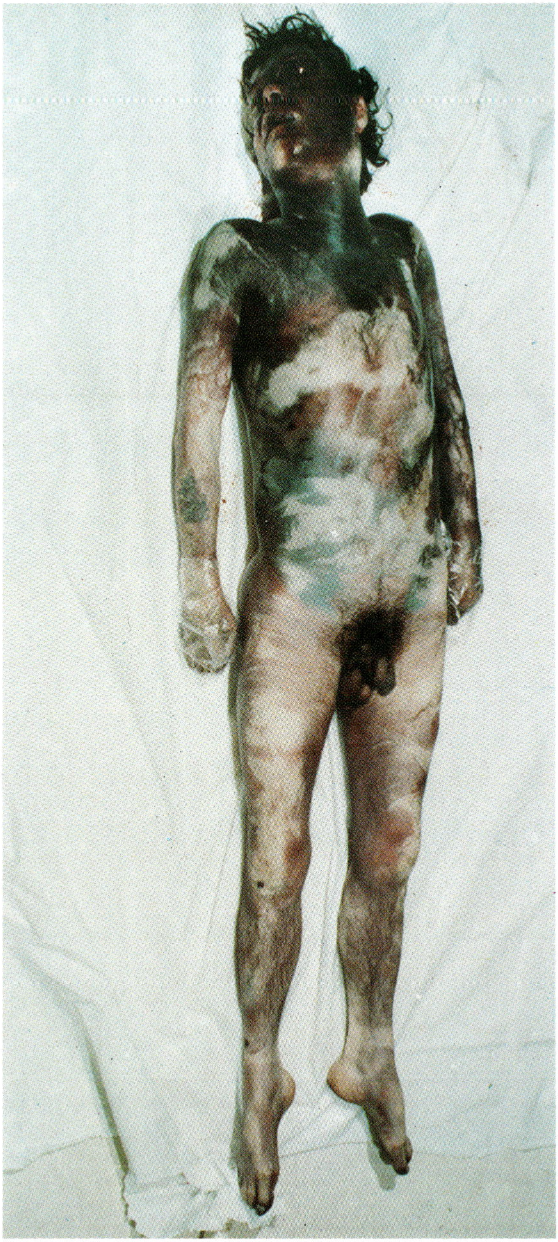

Plate 1. Post mortem decomposition

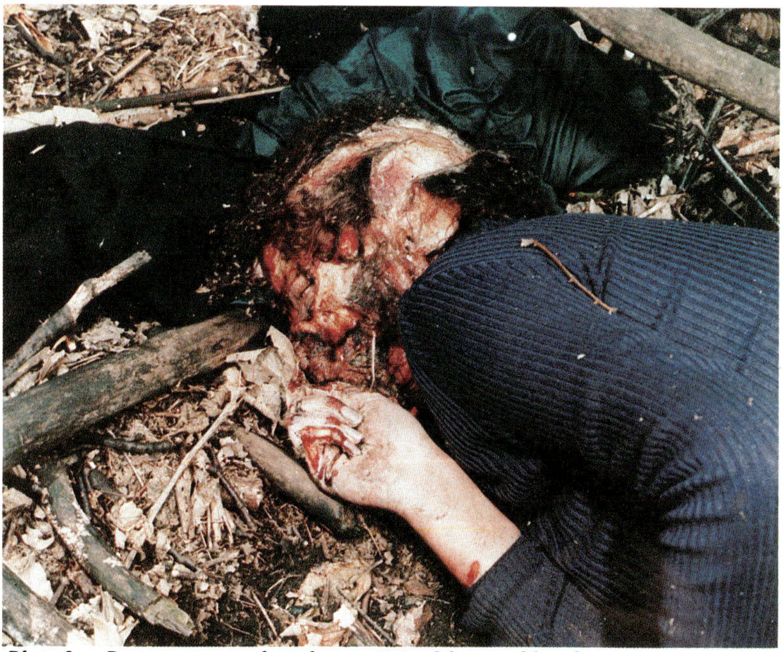

Plate 2. Post mortem rodent destruction of face and hand

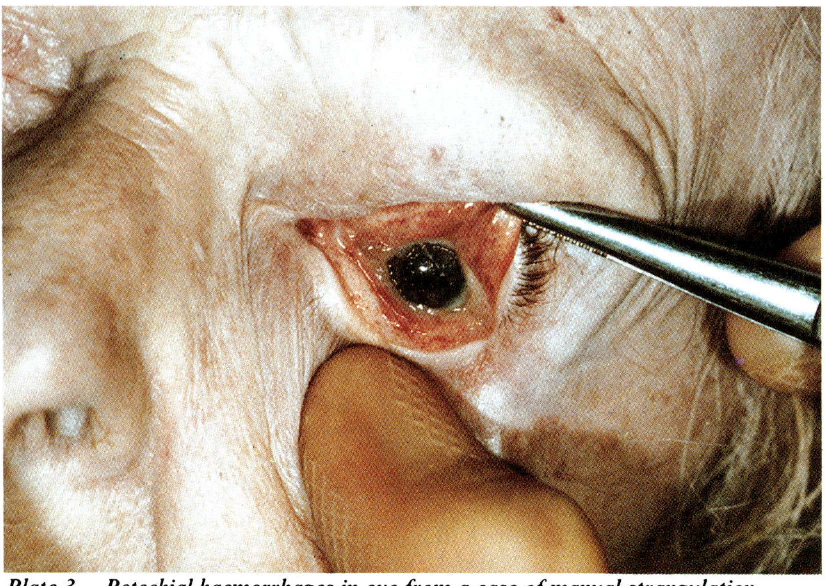

Plate 3. Petechial haemorrhages in eye from a case of manual strangulation

and compare them with the wounds allegedly causing the cuts, it is sometimes disconcerting to find in some fabrics such as a shirt that the actual cuts in the material are smaller than the width of the blade as indicated by the length of the wound. This is particularly so if the weapon is blunt. If such a weapon is pushed through the supported fabric in a test to reproduce the cuts, one finds that the fibres are not all cut through but some are stretched around the edges of the blade, so that when the blade is withdrawn the actual hole is smaller than one expects. One finds that cuts made in the fabric with a sharp knife of identical dimensions may in fact be wider than the ones made by the blunt knife.

1.74 Stab wounds may rarely be caused accidentally, for example by the butcher with a boning knife when preparing meat who inadvertenly stabs himself in the lower abdomen or groin, or a person falling on railing spikes and becoming impaled.

1.75 Suicidal stabbing is not as uncommon as is usually believed. The sites of election are in the left chest or epigastrium, characteristically with the clothing drawn up or removed completely (see Fig. 1.25). Such stab wounds may be multiple, many being superficial or tentative in nature and they may be associated with cuts on the wrists or on the throat. The surrounding circumstances of the finding of a suspected suicide victim may often help to confirm or refute the suggestion—the locked door, the suicide note, the weapon, empty tablet containers and so on setting the scene.

1.76 Examination of a stab wound or stab wounds must of necessity be careful and painstakingly carried out as it may not always be easy to differentiate between suicide and homicide. The doctor should consider a number of features in his examination. The number of wounds may be one or many. A single wound, in many ways the easiest to describe, is often the most difficult to interpret. The position of every stab wound should be recorded with drawings and if possible photographs, the position being related to fixed anatomical points which can be shown in photographs and easily understood by lay persons such as a jury. The height of the victim and the height of the wound above heel should be recorded. The shape of the wound should be recorded graphically. Bruising around the wound may suggest that the weapon has been driven in up to the hilt. The more wounds there are, the easier it is to assess the width of the weapon that has caused them.

1.77 (1) The depth of penetration can be difficult to assess even by dissection at autopsy. If there is no bruising around the external wound,

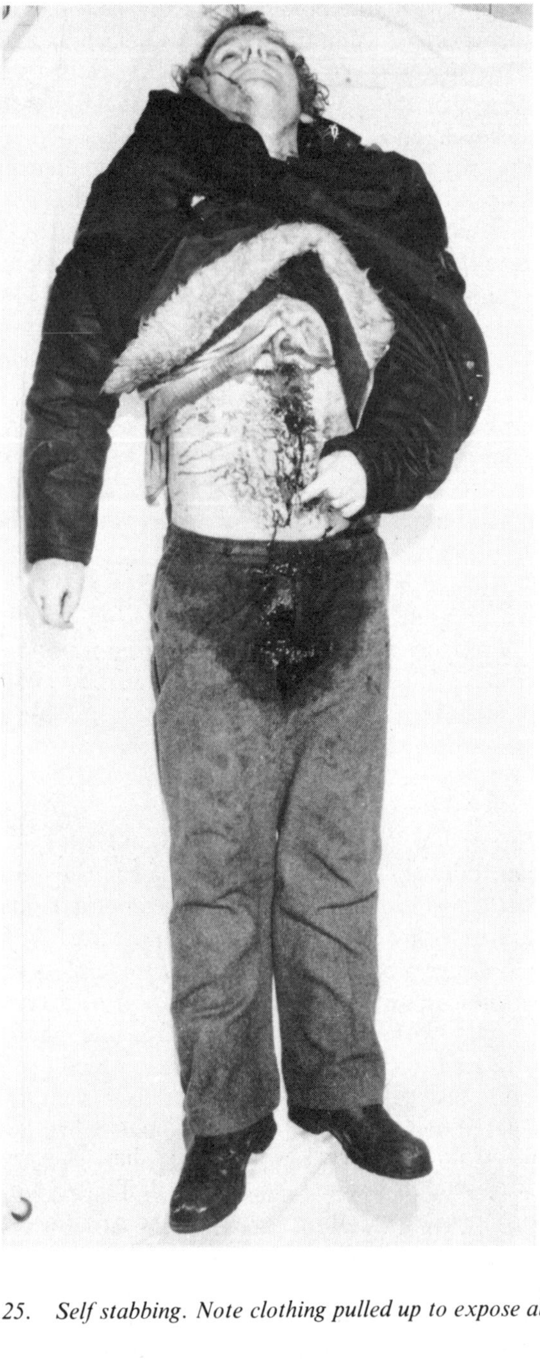

Fig. 1.25. Self stabbing. Note clothing pulled up to expose abdomen

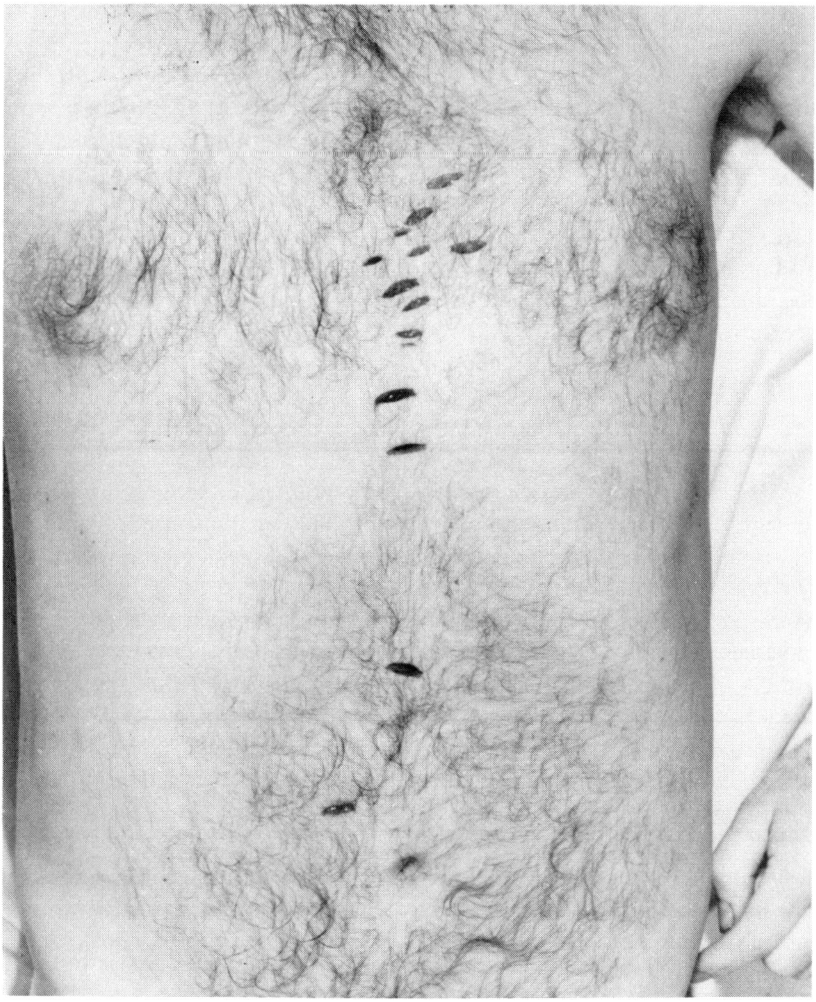

Fig. 1.26. Same case as Fig. 1.25. Multiple parallel stab wounds of varying depth, some being superficial

then it is always possible that the weapon has not been driven into its fullest extent. A small external wound may have a very long track, particularly if a weapon like a stiletto is used. Tracks radiating from a single wound, particularly with bruising of the soft tissues beneath the skin, are suggestive of self-infliction, the wound having been made by the victim withdrawing the knife and pushing it in again slowly at different angles through the same external injury. The external wound may be undercut and slightly flap-like, giving a clue as to the direction of the thrust, and this may be confirmed by dissection (see Fig. 1.22 above). It is important for the doctor to remember while assessing the depth of penetration that the organs in the cadaver lying supine on a mortuary table are in completely different positions from those in an upright person in life, with the heart immediately behind the sternum and left ribs, the lungs filling the chest cavity and the diaphragm and abdominal organs being set much lower.

(2) Because the abdominal wall is soft, a thrust into the yielding abdomen may compress all the tissues, and the depth of penetration when the weapon is withdrawn and the tissues relaxed may appear to be far greater than it actually is.

1.78 The correlation of the length and characteristics of the wound in the skin, the length of the wound track and its cross-section at various levels will give a profile of the weapon responsible and a minimum length for its blade. It may be wide and sharply pointed or long and tapering and it should be possible to describe the weapon used from the information gained from dissection and measurement of the wound or wounds. When a weapon is subsequently produced for the doctor to examine, he should be able to decide whether or not such a weapon could have been used to produce the injuries noted in the victim. Care should always be taken during dissection when using a probe that the wound track is not enlarged or a false passage made by instrumentation, and any suspect weapon should *never* be inserted in the wound "to see if it fits" for fear of ruining any scientific evidence present on the knife itself or of enlarging or distorting the wound track in the victim.

1.80 The force used to cause injury with a stab wound is often less than one imagines. Once the skin is penetrated the weapon slips easily through underlying tissues and viscera; even the sternum and ribs do not require great force for their penetration or severance, especially if the knife is sharp. The force required will be influenced by the victim's clothing if he be wearing any; multiple layers of tough cloth may render penetration more difficult than a single layer of fabric such as a shirt. The skin itself is often the most resistant tissue to penetration.

1.81 The effects of the stabbing will vary with the direction and depth of penetration of structures involved. Death may rapidly supervene if the aorta is penetrated, but it is important to realise how much a person with a potentially fatal stab wound can do prior to collapsing and dying. Many cases are on record where a victim with a penetrating wound of the heart or a great vessel has continued to grapple with his assailant, chased him, gone to fetch a weapon to retaliate or made some other considerable exertion before succumbing from fatal blood loss. It pays the doctor to be guarded as to an opinion of how long it took a victim to die; it may be a surprisingly long time. Many potentially fatal stabbing victims have had their lives saved by rapid major surgery.

1.81A Homicidal stabbing may cause single or multiple wounds, the latter varying in size, shape and depth. The more wounds there are the better the chance of assessing the profile of the weapon responsible, although the dissection for the pathologist may be extremely tedious and time-consuming. Multiple wounds, for example 40, 50, 60 or more stab wounds in a male victim, suggest a homosexual killing, especially if it is associated with sexual mutilation. One difficulty with multiple injuries is that more than one knife may have been used to inflict the wounds on the deceased, as may occur in a gang fight. Here careful measurements and dissection of the wound tracks may clarify the issue.

1.82 The presence or absence of defence wounds is of crucial importance. They may be serious in their own right, particularly a penetrating wound of an arm severing an artery. Great care should be taken to examine the palms of the hands and the palmar aspects of the fingers and thumbs. This may be very difficult in a case affected by rigor mortis. Bending of the wrist to a right angle may facilitate the extending of the fingers in such cases. The classical defence wounds seen in a homicidal stabbing or wounding are cuts in the web between the finger and thumb and across the palmar aspects of the fingers where the blade has been clasped in the victim's hand while he tries to turn the weapon aside (see Plate 4). They may be more easily found when rigor mortis has passed off and the pathologist should check the victim's hands again the day after his original autopsy.

Inaccessible stab wounds rule out self-infliction. There may be considerable disparity between the heights of the assailant and the victim accounting for an apparently unlikely injury.

1.83 The interpretation of the single stab wound in the front of the body can be difficult. In the majority of cases the accused person will say "the deceased ran on to the knife". There is no doubt that the momentum of the forward moving body is more than sufficient to cause fatal injury when it is impaled on a knife held rigidly. However, the knife must be held firmly and be sharply pointed so as to penetrate easily, as a blunt knife held loosely will be turned aside by the approaching body. If there is an element of moving forward by the victim as well as a stabbing thrust by the assailant, then the combination is very likely to cause penetration and serious injury or death. Often the doctor must concede in the witness box at a trial that the same injury could be caused with the weapon held rigidly by the assailant and the victim running on it as by the assailant stabbing the motionless victim. However, the presence of defence injuries may give the lie to the running on the knife story. The appearances and sites of wounds on the clothing may help to explain the posture of the victim, as has been described earlier.[14] The track of the wound may not match up with the explanation offered. Wounds that travel downwards or inwards on the body or upwards are usually caused by deliberate thrusts. A wound caused by running on a knife tends to be more horizontal in direction. Multiple wounds may well be indicative of a frenzied assault, especially if they are associated with genital mutilation, but the pathologist should beware of reading too much into such injuries and usurping the functions of the psychiatrist and the jury.

Incised Wounds

1.84 Incised wounds are made by sharp instruments. They have clean-cut edges and gape and bleed a lot. Such wounds may be caused by knives, razors or broken glass. In the latter case many of these wounds appear to be almost triangular and may be very mutilating (Fig. 1.27). Incised wounds are usually suicidal or homicidal.

1.85 Suicidal incised wounds are more often found in men than in woman and for practical purposes never on the face. The classical sites of self-injury are the throat, wrist, elbows and groins. Such cuts do not pass through clothing, which may have been removed or pulled up out of the way. Cuts themselves are marked by multiplicity and the presence of tentative cuts, through partial thickness of the skin, often superimposed one upon another as though the person was not sure how hard to cut or was frightened of causing pain. In many cases such would-be suicidal attempts are unsuccessful as major vessels are not divided; at the wrist tendons and nerves may be cut across but not the arteries to the hand (see Fig. 1.28).

1.86 Similarly in the neck the skin and soft tissues of the throat and the windpipe may be severed by the victim when tilting his head back, allowing the great vessels on either side of the neck to and from the brain to slide backwards out of reach of the knife he is wielding. Death may result from haemorrhage or from asphyxia where blood has filled the air passages which have been cut across or opened, or from air embolism where a cut has partially severed a major vein such as the jugular vein in the neck, allowing air to be sucked into the circulation and into the heart.

14 At para. 1.72.

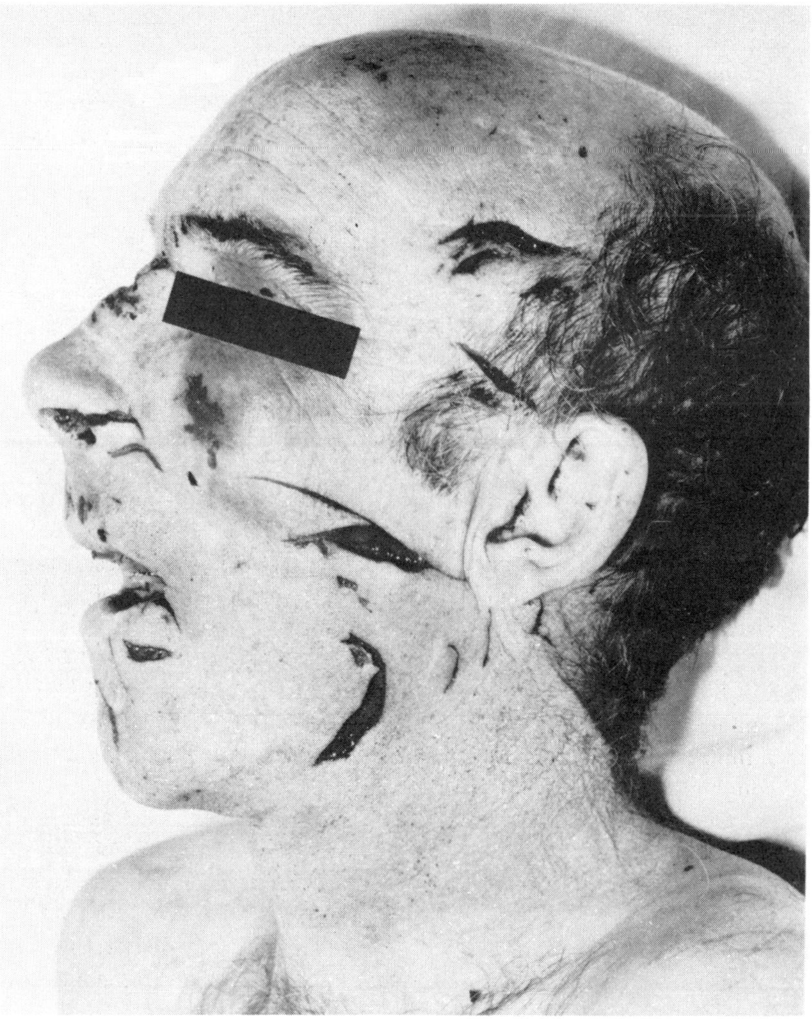

Fig. 1.27. Incised and penetrating wounds from broken bottle

In such circumstances death usually occurs in two or three minutes but there are cases on record where patients have survived several hours, only to die subsequently when the neck structures are disturbed during attempts to treat or sew up the injury.

1.87 In homicidal incised wounds the injuries may be anywhere on the body with no constant pattern and no tentative incisions and no signs of

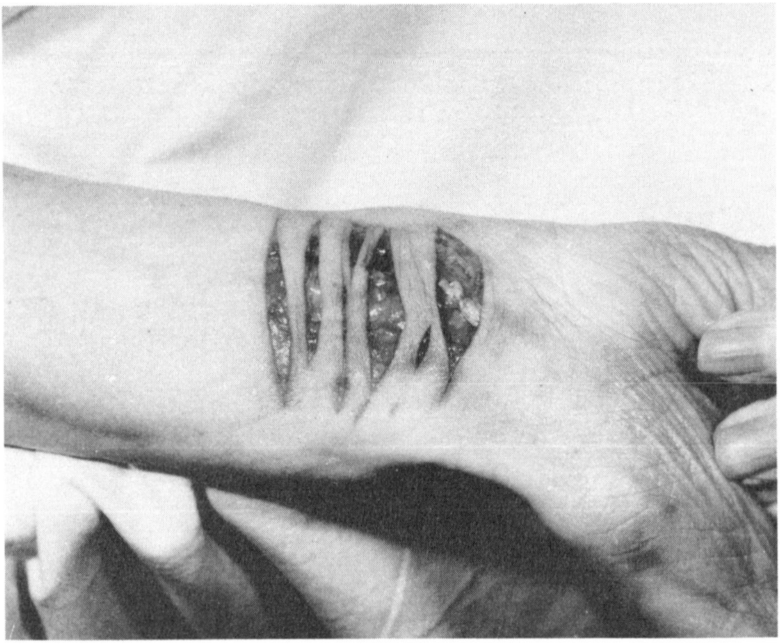

Fig. 1.28. Self-inflicted incised wounds on wrist by left-handed person

hesitancy. They may run across the face and are often associated with defence wounds on the hands, particularly on the palm, across the thumb or fingers or on the outer side of the forearm or hand. They may be associated with mutilating sexual injuries. Wounds of the neck are most likely to result in death from the causes listed above.

Self Inflicted Wounds

1.88 Occasionally persons deliberately inflict incised wounds on themselves either because they are psychiatrically ill and wish to draw attention to themselves or to support an untrue story of assault. A murderer may falsely say that he or she was attacked by an assailant with a knife and received wounds in a struggle between them which ended with him or her stabbing the supposed assailant in self defence. Such wounds are invariably superficial, in accessible sites such as the neck, arms or chest and never involve the face or back. They often comprise multiple parallel linear cuts, sometimes running across each other in groups and seldom penetrate the full thickness of the skin.

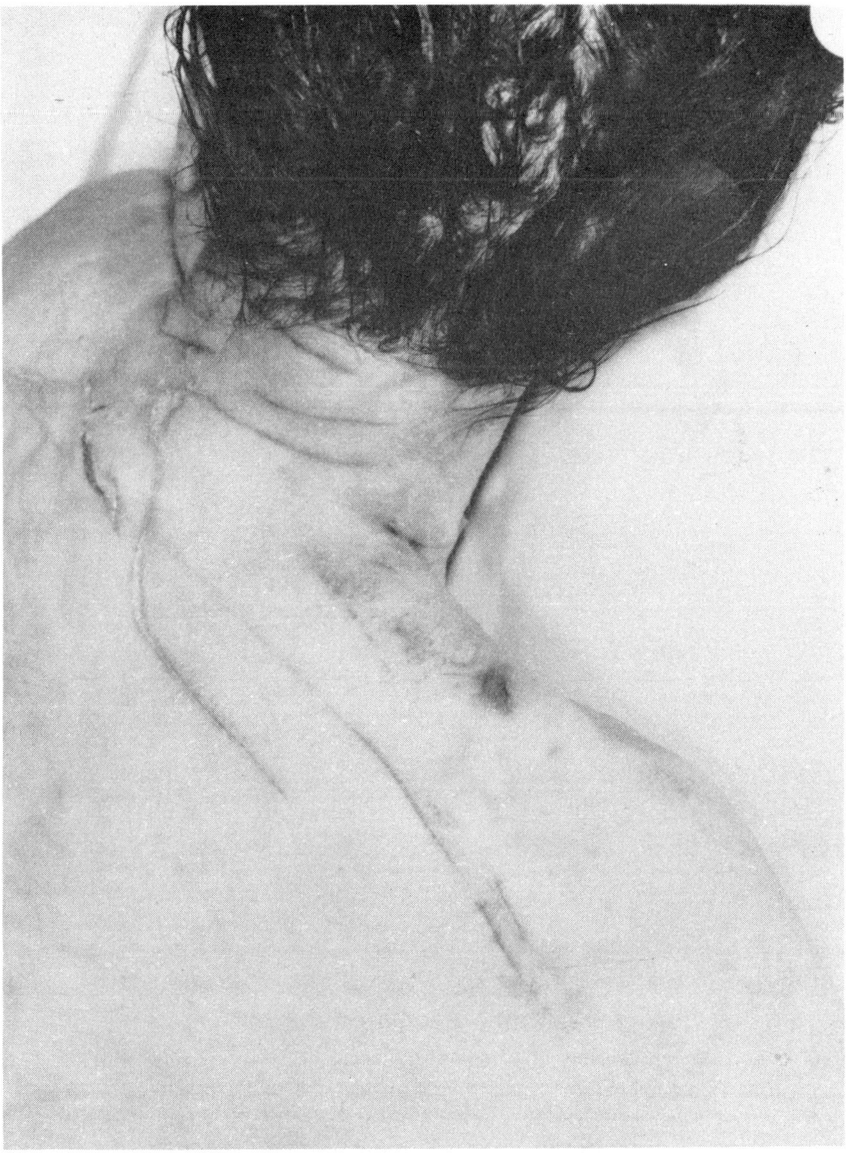

Fig. 1.29. Homicide: incised wounds from point of knife

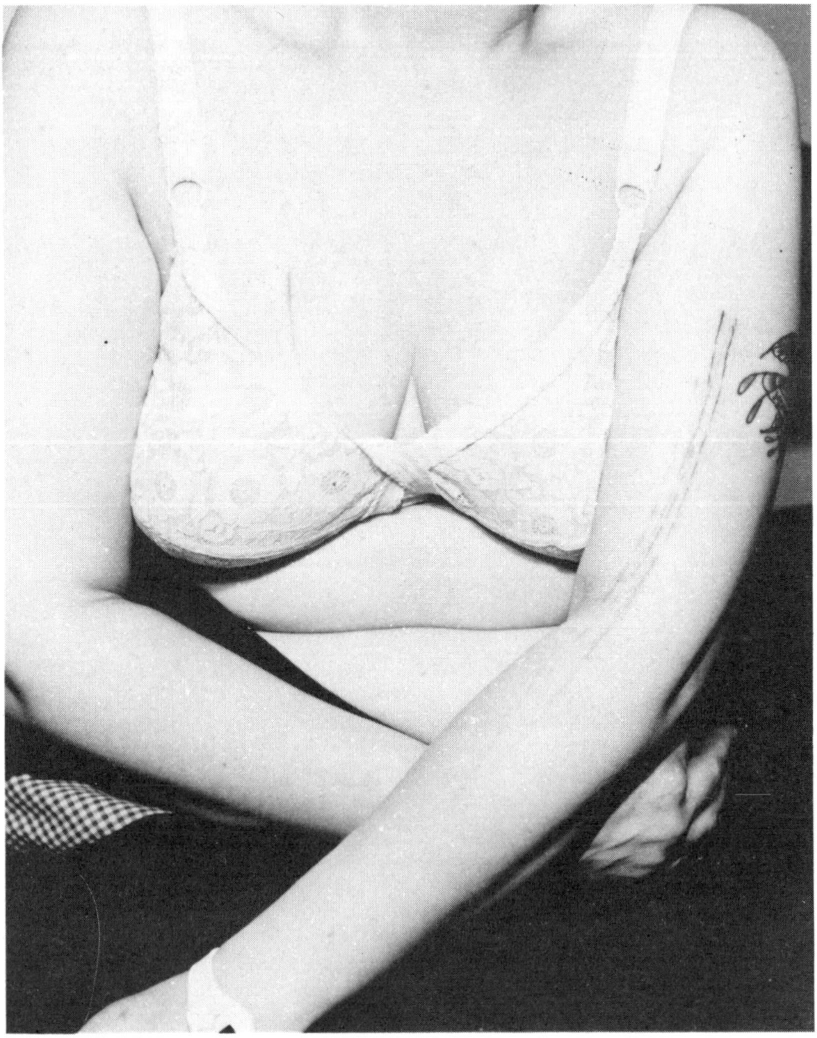

Fig. 1.30. Self-inflicted incised wounds

HEAD INJURIES DUE TO ASSAULT

1.89 Head injuries due to assault can damage to varying degrees the scalp, the underlying skull and the brain and its covering membranes within the skull. There may be direct injury, for example from a blow from a fist, and there may be secondary injuries caused by the person being knocked down by the blow and injuring, say, the back of the head on a hard surface such as the roadway.

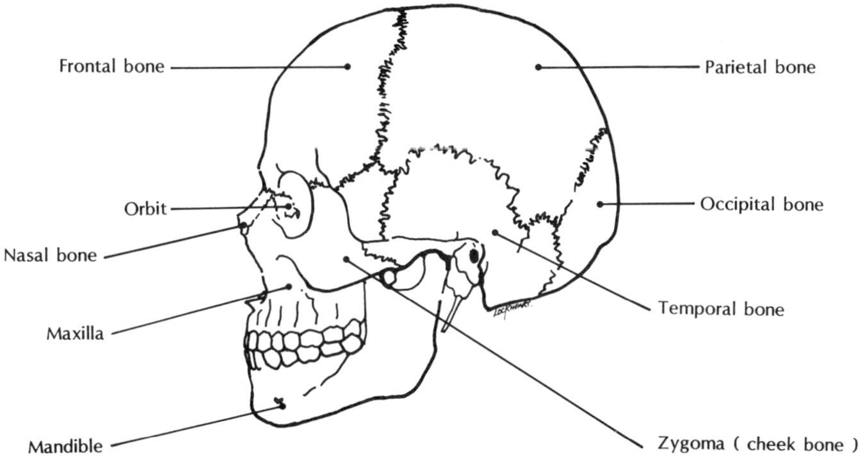

HUMAN SKULL SIDE VIEW

Fig. 1.31.

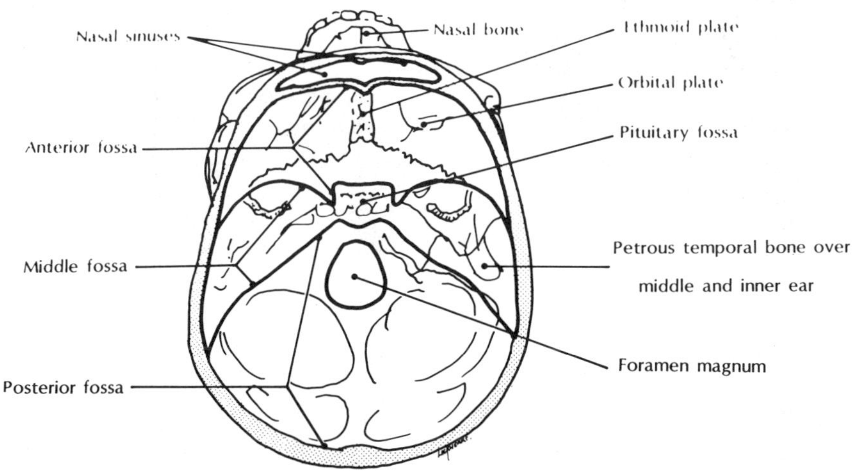

HUMAN SKULL BASE LOOKED AT FROM ABOVE

Fig. 1.32.

1.90 The majority of head injuries are closed head injuries, that is, there is no communication made between the outside environment and the brain itself. A small proportion are open head injuries with compound fractures exposing the brain to the air; the majority of these are caused by gross destructive forces such as firearm wounds or bomb explosions or occasionally by savage assaults with heavy weapons, repeated blows shattering the skull and exposing the brain with severe injury to the latter.

1.91 There is no relation between the damage to the brain and fractures of the skull. There are many cases where blows are struck to the head causing irreparable brain damage that do not fracture the skull. Obviously the thickness of the skull bone is of importance; where the skull bone is thin a simple blow even from a fist may cause a fracture, whereas a person having a thick skull may receive a violent blow or blows which cause massive cerebral damage without fracture.

1.92 All the findings at autopsy must be correlated and attention not confined to the head and neck alone. It may be that the person who has been knocked to the ground and kicked and stamped on may have received multiple internal chest and abdominal injuries as well as head injuries.

1.93 The presence of defence wounds should be looked for carefully and the part played by alcohol must be considered. Alcohol slows the reactions of the victim so that he may not protect himself in time from an assault and be struck down with a minimum of defence injuries to indicate resistance. Alcohol also increases the tendency to bleed by causing dilation and congestion of blood vessels. If there is chronic alcoholic liver disease which impairs the clotting of the blood, then the tendency for bleeding inside the head to be more extensive is increased.

1.94 Another hazard of head injury is that irritation of the brain causes vomiting. Such vomit may be inhaled into the air passages, cutting off the oxygen supply to the lungs and bloodstream and hence to the brain with increasing hypoxia leading to swelling and further irreparable damage. Similar asphyxia may result from the air passages filling with blood following blows to the nose or mouth, the victim then being left lying on his back while the blood trickles down the airway causing obstruction and hypoxia as before. To a certain extent hair protects as a padding for the underlying soft tissues and it also may mask lacerated wounds from blunt injury unless they are carefully sought for. A good head of hair can cushion the effects of a series of blows which may show little injury externally or even on dissection but the underlying brain may be severely damaged. The presence of bruising around the eyes without obvious injury to the eye itself is suggestive of fractures of the anterior fossae in the front of the skull above the orbits, just as cerebro-spinal fluid running from the nose suggests a similar injury to the front of the base of the skull. Blood coming from the ears suggests fractures through the middle fossae of the skull and is of very sinsister import.

1.95 The external injuries caused by assault may be very revealing and the pathologist must carefully examine each and every one. The majority of such injuries are lacerated wounds with ragged abraded edges, with

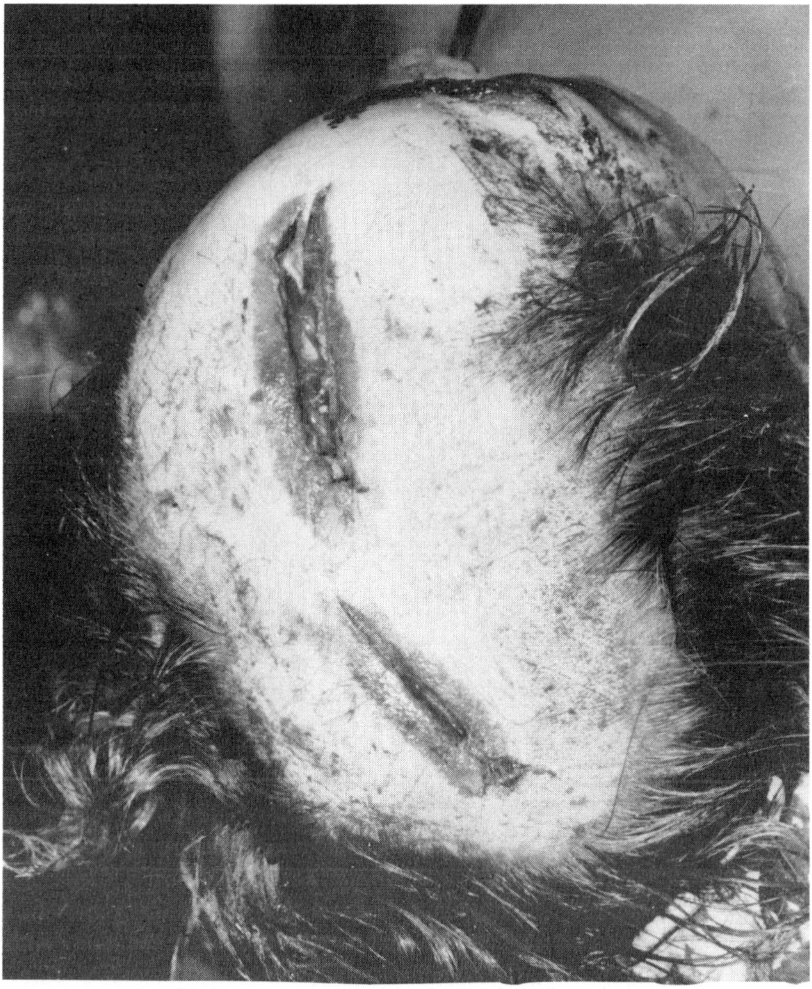

Fig. 1.33. Scalp lacerations inflicted by iron bar

surrounding bruising and hair driven into the base of the wounds (see Fig. 1.33). There may also be foreign particles such as brick dust, paint from gas piping or splinters of wood from a pickaxe handle embedded in the depths of the wound which may be vital trace evidence to connect a weapon and an assailant with the injuries. Punches with a clenched fist usually cause bruising around the eye and splitting of the eyebrow, bruising and fracturing of the nose with haemorrhage, and bruising and splitting of the lips, particularly on the inner aspect where the lips are driven against the teeth, some of which may be loosened or even dislodged.

1.96 Kicking, on the other hand, will cause splitting and tearing of the soft tissues over bony prominences, particularly around the eyes, over the cheek bones, around the temple and ear and along the line of the jaw. Where a victim has been stamped on by his assailant there may be considerable crushing and fracturing of the facial bones and imprints of the sole of the shoe may be seen on the soft tissues. The pattern of such an injury should be photographed with scales alongside it and at right angles to it for comparison with suspect footwear. (See the photograph, Fig. 1.5 in para. 1.42 above). It must be remembered that not only the ridges of the soles may be imprinted but also the grooving of the sole from the effects of suction of the soft tissues.

1.97 Blunt implements such as iron bars and hammers cause longitudinal lacerated split wounds with crushing of soft tissues and fracturing of the underlying skull and brain damage (see Fig. 1.34). Axes and similar sharp implements cause deep cleaving wounds usually compound involving the scalp, the skull and the brain (see Fig. 1.35).

1.98 People who are attacked with broken glass such as broken bottles, beer mugs or wine glasses usually have jagged, rather triangular-shaped facial injuries multiple in nature, often cutting arteries where they run in front of the ear or across the angle of the lower jaw on each side. (See photograph Fig. 1.27 and para. 1.84 above).

1.99 Occasionally stab wounds are delivered to the head. They usually do not penetrate the bone of the skull or face but may cause mutilating injury. On occasion, though, a knife may penetrate alongside the eye through the back of the orbit where the nerves and blood vessels to the eye pass and into the brain.

1.100 (1) It must be remembered that each assault will cause a different pattern of injury, and the various structures of the head may be involved

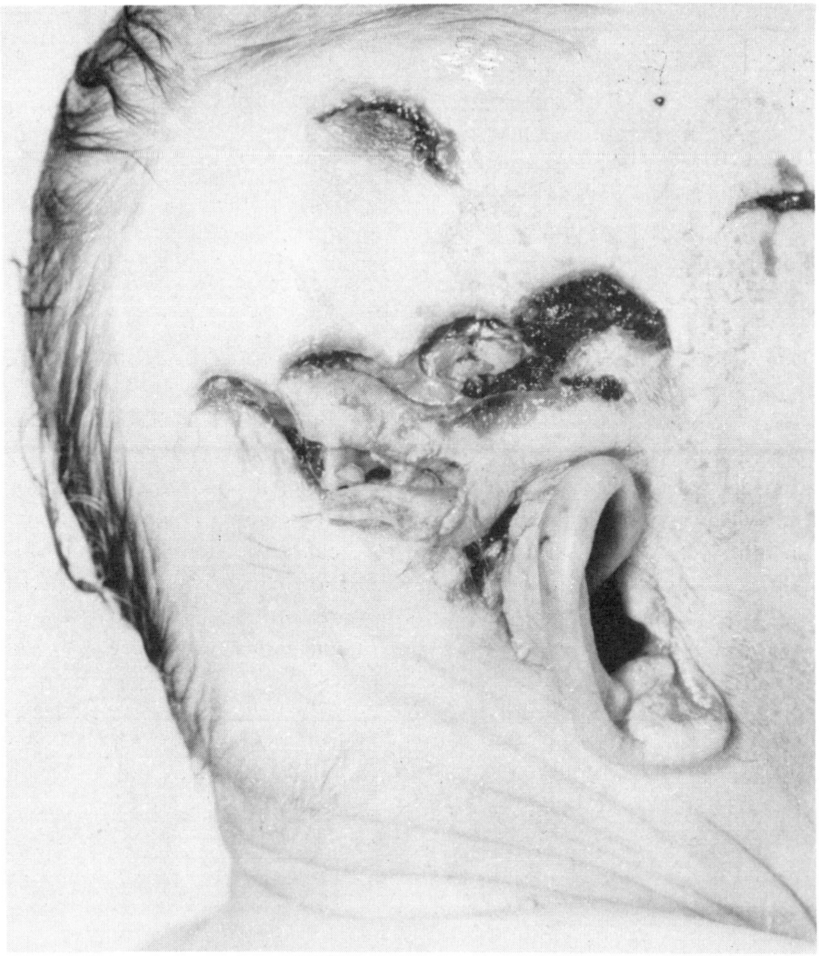

Fig. 1.34. Hammer wounds to the head (the hair has been partly shaved)

to varying degrees. However, the interpretation of head injuries due to assault may be assisted by considering the various tissues and structures involved individually and the different sort of injury and its result relating to each particular structure or part of the head.

(2) *Scalp*. Scalp wounds bleed copiously and multiple superficial wounds may cause torrential haemorrhage while there may be little in the way of significant underlying head injury to the brain, the extent of blood loss being the only significant feature pathologically. Following injury the scalp will swell and blood may track beneath the scalp over the surface of the skull where there may be very extensive bruising.

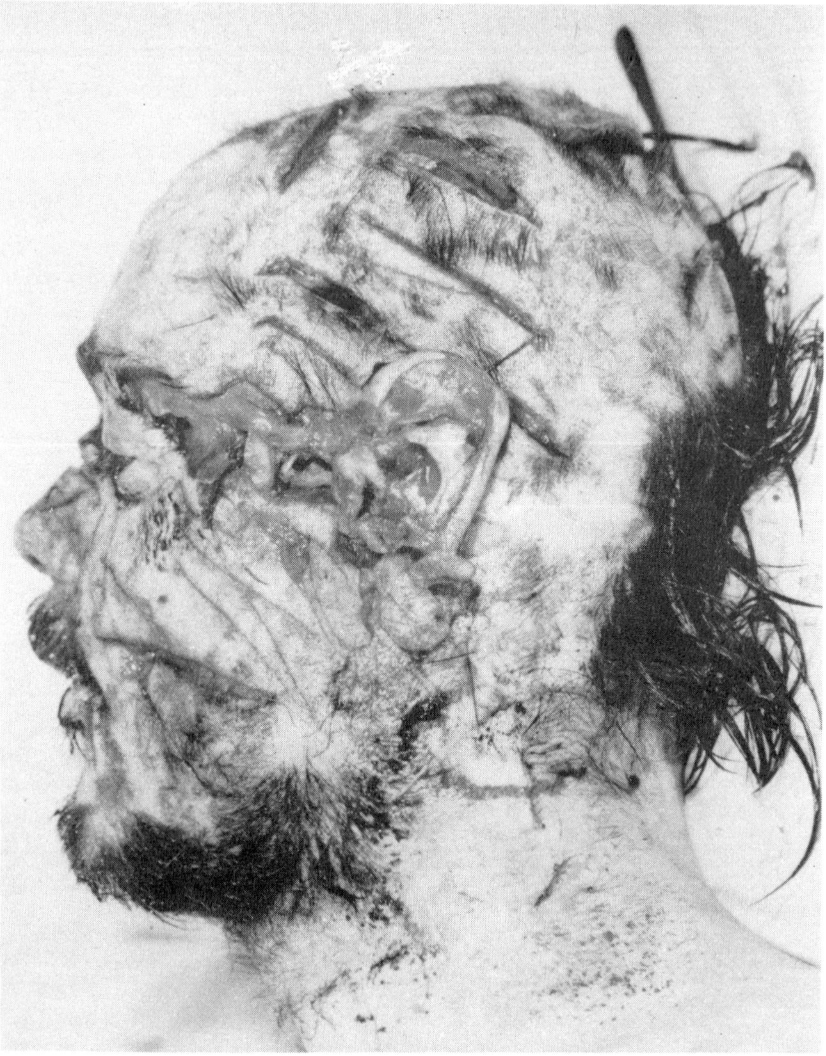

Fig. 1.35. Axe wounds to the head

(3) *Face.* Facial wounds bleed copiously because of the very generous blood supply to the facial tissues. The nose is vulnerable to injury, particularly when it is fractured, and there is haemorrhage and its attendant dangers of asphyxia if the person is left on his or her back, as described at para. 1.94 above. The mouth is similarly vulnerable and all the soft tissues of the mouth will swell considerably following injury and there will be an attendant haemorrhage. The facial bones may be

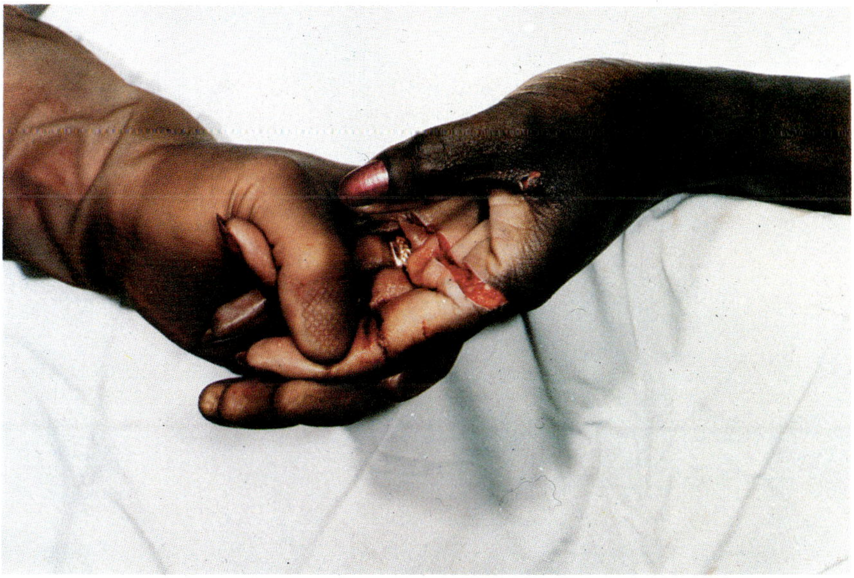

Plate 4. Defence wound. The victim clutched the knife blade in her hand, cutting the palm and between the thumb and index finger

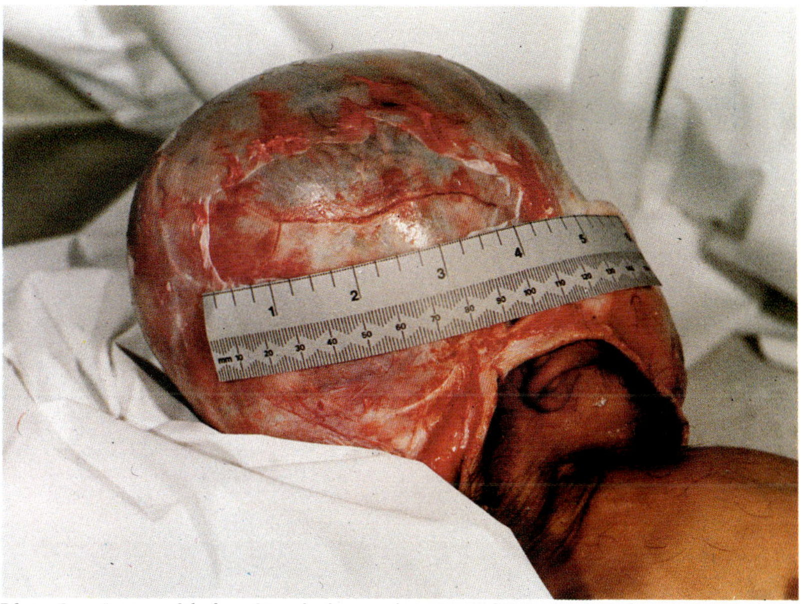

Plate 5. Battered baby. Simple linear fracture of temporal and parietal bones of skull

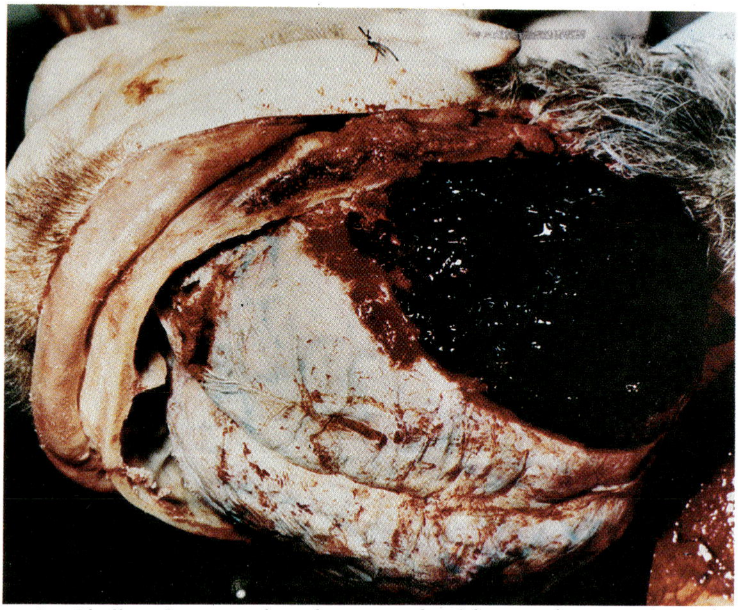

Plate 6. Skull vault removed to show extradural haemorrhage overlying dura on right side of brain

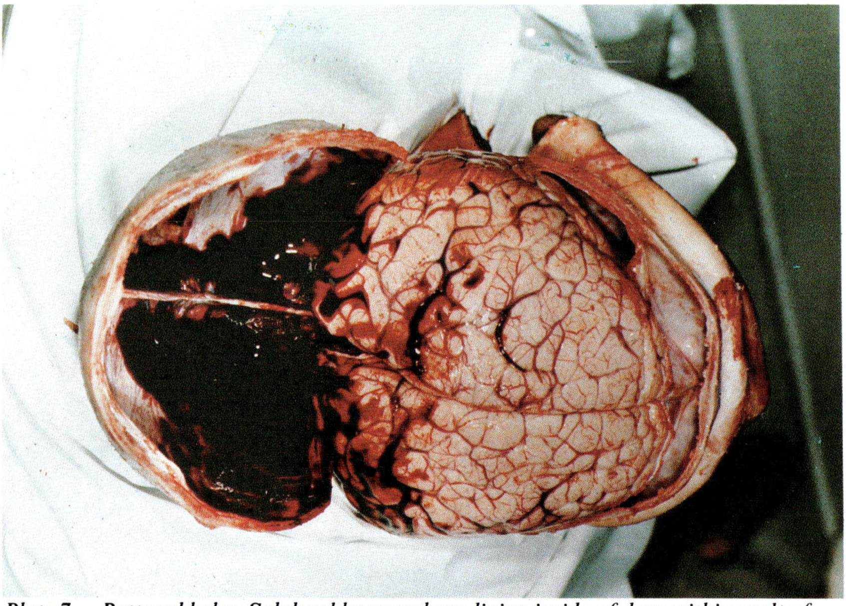

Plate 7. Battered baby. Subdural haemorrhage lining inside of dura within vault of skull

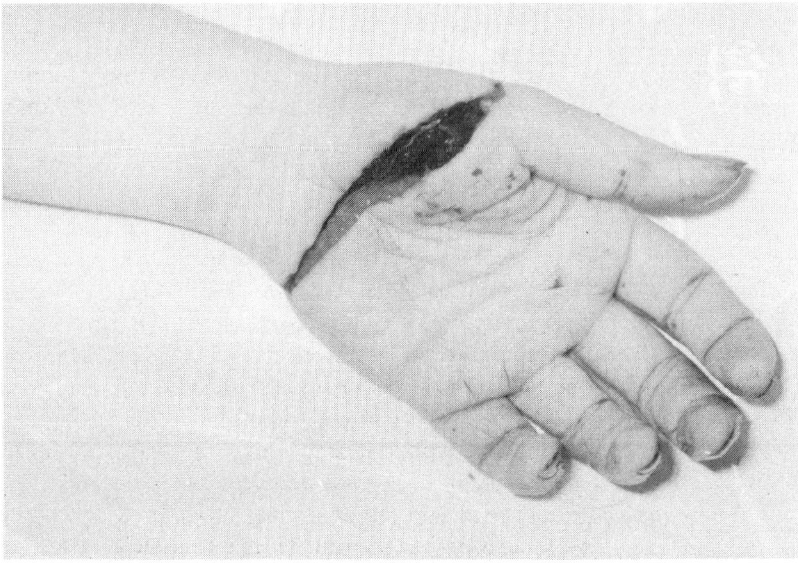

Fig. 1.36. Defence wounds from axe

fractured, particularly by kicking or stamping, and the lower jaw may be fractured.

(4) *Neck*. Kicking and stamping on the neck may cause damage to the larynx with fracturing of the laryngeal cartilages and hyoid bone, bruising of the soft tissues of the neck and very severe swelling around the back of the throat and upper airway (glottic oedema), which may obstruct the airway and lead to death from asphyxia very rapidly (see para. 1.41(5) above).

(5) *Skull*. (i) In all fatal cases of head injury the scalp should be reflected completely from the front, back and sides of the skull to expose possible underlying fractures and in cases of facial injury the face can be dissected forward off the facial bones towards the midline of the face to expose fractures of the upper and lower jaws or around the eyes which would not otherwise be detectable. Although this sounds a very mutilating procedure, it is in fact not so and the face is easily reconstructed following dissection.

(ii) When the top of the skull is removed to expose the brain prior to its removal, the thickness of the skull bone in the front, sides and back of the head should be measured and recorded. The extent of fracturing both of the top and base of the skull should be noted. To this end it is important to strip off the adherent membranes covering the brain (dura), as skull fractures may be very fine and fissured, particularly where the bone is thin over the front of the base of the skull above the eyes (orbital plates).

(iii) Blows to the back of the head cause fractures of the posterior fossae at the back of the base of the skull running towards the foramen magnum, the opening through which the spinal cord passes. Such impacts at the back of the skull may also cause fractures of the orbital plates by transmitted force. (See diagram Fig. 1.32 above.)

(iv) Blows to the front of the head will cause fracturing of the bone of the forehead and of the anterior fossae of the skull. Blows to the side of the head will cause fractures of the temporal bone which is usually thinner than that of the front or back of the skull (see Plate 5). Such impacts are extremely important because a major artery, the middle meningeal artery, spreads out to supply the inside of the skull on the inner aspect of the temporal bone and such fractures may cause damage to one or more branches of the artery, leading to extradural haemorrhage.

(v) Impacts on the top of the head may cause simple fissure fractures radiating from the point of impact, while more heavy blows may cause a depressed fracture where bone is driven inwards, with radiating fractures extending in a stellate manner from the edges of the depressed area. Repeated heavy blows may cause fragmentations of the skull bone, some being driven into the underlying brain. Linear fractures show the direction of the force applied to the skull.

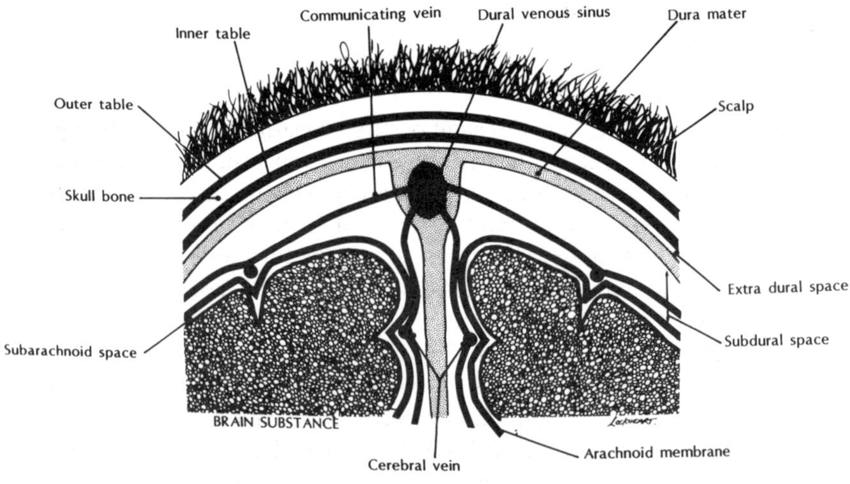

Diagramatic cross section through centre of human skull to show relationship of scalp, skull, membranes and surface of brain.

Fig. 1.37.

(6) *The Membranes.* Within the skull the brain is covered by thin sheets of tissue or membranes, the outer, thicker one being known as the dura and the thinner superficial one covering the brain itself as the arachnoid. They are in fact double-layered structures but for the purpose of description will be referred to as though they were single layers. Bleeding may occur between the skull and the dura (extradural haemorrhage), beneath the dura between the dura and the surface of the brain (subdural haemorrhage), or over the surface of the brain itself beneath the second membrane (subarachnoid haemorrhage). See Fig. 1.37.

Extradural Haemorrhage

1.101 Extradural haemorrhage as described above usually occurs following a blow to the side of the head fracturing the skull and tearing a branch of the middle meningeal artery. Following the assault the victim is usually dazed but appears to recover; however, after a latent period of perhaps half an hour or an hour or at most two hours, the victim rapidly becomes confused, unconscious and comatose and may die unless the blood that has accumulated from the torn vessel is swiftly evacuated surgically. As the blood comes from an artery, it quickly accumulates between the inner aspect of the skull and the dura beneath it, compressing the brain sideways and downwards and distorting the vital structures of the mid brain at the base of the skull which control respiration and heart beat. (See Plate 6.) The victims of such assaults are usually young people and the whole time-scale from assault to death may be a matter of a few hours at most, if no surgical treatment is provided

Subdural Haemorrhage

1.102 (1) Subdural haemorrhage occurs beneath the dura covering the brain and the brain itself. It arises from torn veins that pass between the surfaces of the brain and the collecting channels or sinuses in the dura; these cross the dural space and are known as communicating veins; see Fig. 1.37 above. One or more of these may be torn and blood seeps out over a period of many hours, unlike the rapid arterial collection described above in extradural haemorrhage.

(2) Such bleeding is seen in child abuse, where children are violently shaken and blood accumulates following the tearing of these communicating veins over the ensuing hours because the child's brain is relatively large as compared with the skull surrounding it. The subdural space in an infant is small and it does not take very long for a fatal collection, perhaps as little as 20 or 30 ml of blood, to accumulate and cause death. (See Plate 7.) This matter is further dealt with in the section on non-accidental injury to children (see paras 3.14ff).

(3) The other victims of assault who develop subdural haemorrhages

are the elderly, where comparatively trivial injury may cause tearing of the veins. This is because the brain in an old person shrinks with age, stretching the communicating veins and making them more vulnerable to rotational stresses if the brain moves within the skull, causing tearing and leaking of venous blood. There may be no external sign of injury in either a battered child or an elderly person receiving a diffuse blow to the head.

(4) As in extradural haemorrhage, subdural haemorrhage causes compression and displacement of the brain sideways and downwards, but this is more gradual and the victim may not develop incapacitating symptoms for hours or even days following. In fact the bleeding may stop as the pressure of accumulated blood compresses the source of the haemorrhage but further injury or disturbance of the brain may cause bleeding to recommence.

(5) As a result of the displacement and pressure of extradural or subdural haemorrhage the brain may swell (cerebral oedema) and secondary haemorrhages may occur in the brain stem in the part known as the pons, causing rapid death.

Subarachnoid Haemorrhage

1.103 (1) Subarachnoid haemorrhage usually occurs as a result of natural disease following rupture of a developmental "berry" aneurysm.

(2) It also occurs as a result of trauma. There may be localised areas of haemorrhage over sites of contusion of the brain from blows or impact with hard surfaces. In the latter, if the person is struck and falls to the ground, injury occurs both to the back of the brain and to the front of the brain on the frontal and temporal poles when the brain is displaced within the skull by the decelerating forces of impact over the rough surfaces of the base of the skull. Such haemorrhages may be very extensive.

(3) Fatal traumatic subarachnoid haemorrhage has been recognised as a separate entity in recent years. It usually follows a blow or kick below and behind the ear. The two vertebral arteries running up the back of the spine and entering the base of the skull to supply the back of the brain run in bony canals within the vertebrae of the spine as far as the second cervical vertebra. They then emerge and run in an "S"-shaped manner across the transverse processes of the first cervical vertebra to enter the foramen magnum at the base of the skull. Here they are vulnerable to trauma as they are not protected by bone, and a violent kick or blow on the back and side of the neck behind the angle of the jaw and below the ear lobe may crush the vertebral artery against the plate of bone of the transverse process and tear it, causing massive bleeding around the upper spinal cord and over the base of the brain, usually causing death in about 10 or 15 minutes.

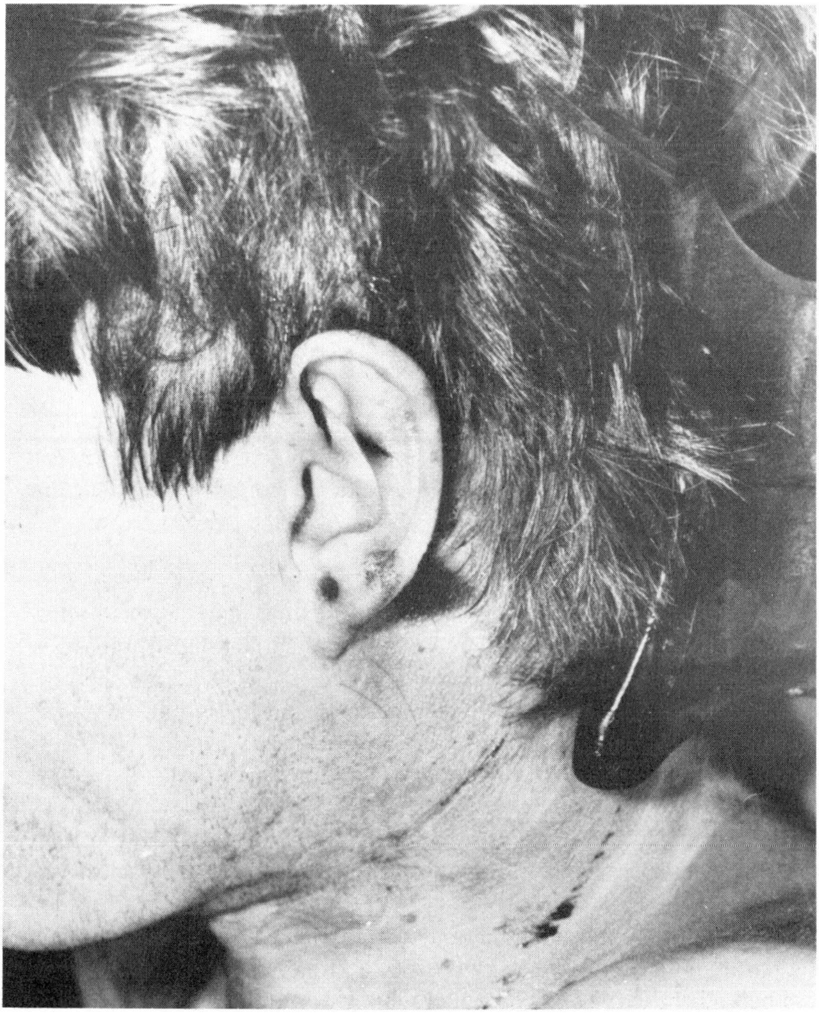

Fig. 1.38. Kick behind ear causing traumatic subarachnoid haemorrhage at base of brain

The Brain

1.104 (1) As the brain is free to move beneath the membranes inside the skull, cushioned by the cerebro-spinal fluid, any excessive or violent movement will cause shear strains and tearing of the brain itself, and injuries caused to the moving brain are much more severe in their effect than those of a fixed head injury. Blows to the moving head or deceleration (as in impact falls) cause injuries to the brain immediately at

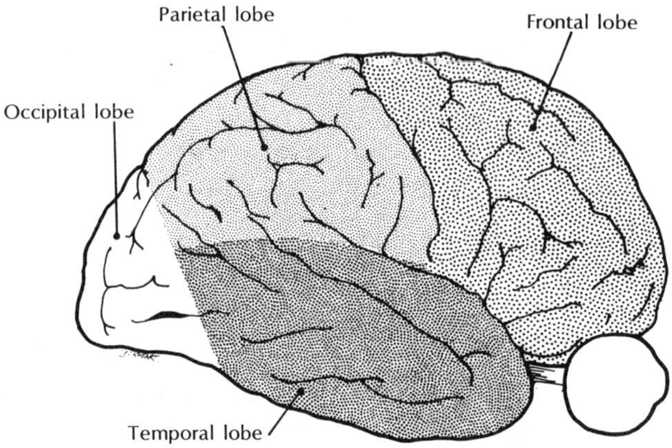

SIDE VIEW OF BRAIN

Fig. 1.39.

the point of impact, the so-called coup injury, and injury to the opposite side of the brain, or contre-coup injury, which is often more severe. Microscopic examination of the brain in such cases will show tearing of many of the nerves and their processes throughout much of the brain so that the naked eye findings are rather like the tip of an iceberg in that the underlying injury is very much more extensive than is apparent macroscopically.

(2) In addition to the tearing of nerve fibres, there may be frank destruction of cerebral tissue and areas of haemorrhage in the brain substance. Such haemorrhages may be primary in the cerebral hemispheres or secondary due to displacement and swelling in the pons.

(3) Any significant brain injury nearly always causes swelling of the brain (cerebral oedema), leading to further compression and displacement of vital structures. The brain may be pressed against the edges of membranes in the base of the skull and blood vessels trapped and squeezed and flattened against the hard edges of the membrane covering the bone of the skull, cutting off the blood supply to part or parts of the brain, leading to death of brain tissue or infarction. This in turn will lead to more swelling and the vicious circle will continue until death supervenes unless the situation can be relieved surgically, and this is only possible in a minority of cases. If the whole brain is swollen, then it is compressed downwards into the base of the skull and the cerebellum and vital mid-brain structures may be trapped in the foramen magnum, leading to death.

(4) It is difficult to correlate pathological findings at autopsy with clinical signs and symptoms in life and the pathologist should beware of trying to paint a clinical picture from what he finds at his post mortem examination. He may be induced if he is incautious into suggesting that somebody was unconscious because of the extent of the injuries he found at autopsy when in fact this was not so. Contrariwise he might be led to believe that the person was able to carry out extensive activity after an assault when in fact the opposite was true.

Penetrating Head Injuries

1.105 (1) These are rare compared with closed head injuries. They may follow violent assaults with axes or similar implements, firearm wounds or explosive injury where breaches are made in the scalp and skull exposing the brain to the air. Such compound fractures of the skull may occur involving a frontal sinus in the skull above the bridge of the nose, or fracture of the base of the skull involving the nose itself, both of which may lead to the possibility of infection and meningitis (inflammation of the coverings of the brain) developing. Foreign material may be driven into the brain and abscesses may form around such material particularly if it is infected. (See diagram Fig. 1.32 above.)

(2) The effects of a penetrating head injury depend obviously on the part of the brain that is involved. Injuries involving the brain stem and base of the brain are nearly always fatal, whereas penetrating wounds involving the frontal lobes may cause surprisingly little disability.

Late Effects

1.106 Patients who are unconscious from head injuries are liable to develop a well recognised series of complications, all of which are potentially fatal. They include pulmonary embolism from thrombosis of the leg veins, pneumonia, kidney and bladder infections and bed sores with supra-added infection.

BURNS AND SCALDS

Burns

1.107 (1) There are different classifications of burns described in medical text books but for simplicity's sake they are best divided into superficial burns, deep burns and those with charring of tissue.

(2) Burns are due to dry heat, scalds to wet heat; the latter are usually found in children under the age of three years.

(3) People particularly at risk from burning are children and old people, those who are drunk, disabled or epileptic and those who smoke in bed.

(4) Fires involving young children are particularly seen where there are families using paraffin heaters; without supervison of the children such heaters are frequently overturned, leading to conflagrations in the home.

(5) Approximately 750 people die in fires in England and Wales in a year, nearly all of them due to accidents. The elderly are particularly at risk, as they may set clothing alight when they brush against electric or gas heaters or open fires when they are dressed in long nightdresses. Efforts have been made in recent years to make such garments of non-flammable material.

(6) The prognosis of a case of burning depends on the age, the health of the patient, the area burnt, the complications and the treatment available. The complications include shock, fluid and protein loss, toxaemia, infection, loss of salts and upsets of body metabolism, kidney failure, thrombosis of leg veins with consequent pulmonary embolism, and rarely peptic ulceration in the second and third week leading to fatal haemorrhage, the so-called Curling's ulcer.

(7) Estimating the extent of body burning is usually carried out using the so-called rule of nine (see diagram Fig. 1.40). The head and neck and both arms rate 9% each, the front and back of the body 18% each, the genitalia 1%, and the legs 18% each, a total of 100%.

(8) It is said that burning over a third of the body surface is potentially fatal in an average adult; much less may cause death in infants and old people and those who are ill already.

(9) The distribution of the burns may help to show the sequence of events. A person whose clothing catches alight will have severe burning, usually of the front of the body more than the back, with particularly severe burning of the hands, where the victim has tried to extinguish the fire by beating out the flames, severe burning of the undersurface of the chin and upper chest where the flames have burnt upwards, and facial injuries with singeing of the hair. The feet and ankles are usually spared. This is in contrast with a case of self-immolation, for example by pouring paraffin over oneself and setting it alight. Here there will be much more extensive burning over nearly the whole of the body, only skin folds such as the axillae and the perineum being spared.

(10) In a badly charred body the problem of identification may cause difficulty. Jewellery is often recognisable despite severe burning. The teeth are nearly always relatively undamaged and the services of a forensic odontologist may be required to assist in the identification of a burnt body, partihcularly where there are several fatalities in one conflagration. Even in severely charred bodies it may be possible to recognise and

RULE OF NINES FOR ASSESSING EXTENT OF BODY BURNING

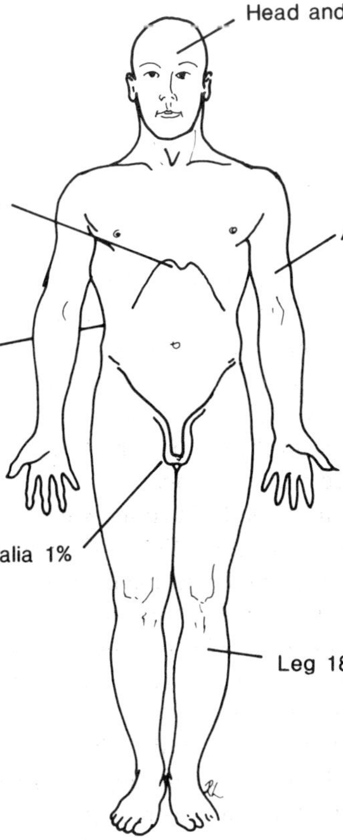

Fig. 1.40.

identify pieces of clothing caught up around the back of the neck or in the axillae or groins, and such material should always be retained by the pathologist in case there is any question of arson or inflammable materials being involved. A forensic scientist can usually identify the agents used.

(11) The body in fire deaths often assumes a pugilistic attitude from heat contraction of the muscles, particularly of the flexor groups in the legs and arms (see Fig. 1.41) and there may be deep splits in the skin exposing subcutaneous fat and muscle simulating wounds (see Fig. 1.42). There may even be heat fractures of the skull with an extradural heat

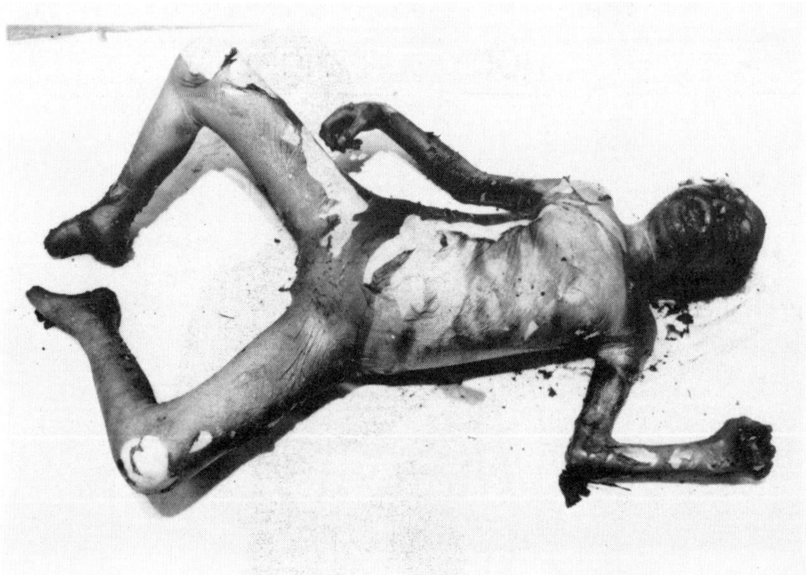

Fig. 1.41. Burning: pugilistic attitude from heat contractures

haematoma, which the pathologist must be careful not to ascribe to ante mortem trauma, as it is a well recognised pathological artefact in fire deaths.

(12) The majority of people dying in fires die not from burns but from the inhalation of fire fumes, a mixture of carbon monoxide, carbon dioxide and cyanide (if there is polypropylene (plastic foam) furniture involved, which when on fire gives off this toxic gas), together with smoke and an almost total lack of oxygen which has been used up in the combustion of the fire itself. All the air passages will be found to be lined with soot as far as can be dissected into the lungs, and the blood and tissues of the body assume a cherry-pink colour due to the presence of carboxyhaemoglobin from the inhaled carbon monoxide. Cyanide also causes another pink pigment in the blood, cyanhaemoglobin, to form. If the person has inhaled flames as well as smoke, there will be scorching and burning of the back of the throat involving the epiglottis and larynx, with oedema of the glottis obstructing the airway.

(13) The inhalation of carbon monoxide often leads to severe muscular inco-ordination and weakness so that the victim in a fire may be not only blinded by smoke but weakened and confused by the carbon monoxide and be unable to escape, dying of asphyxia as a result, the body then being burnt after death.

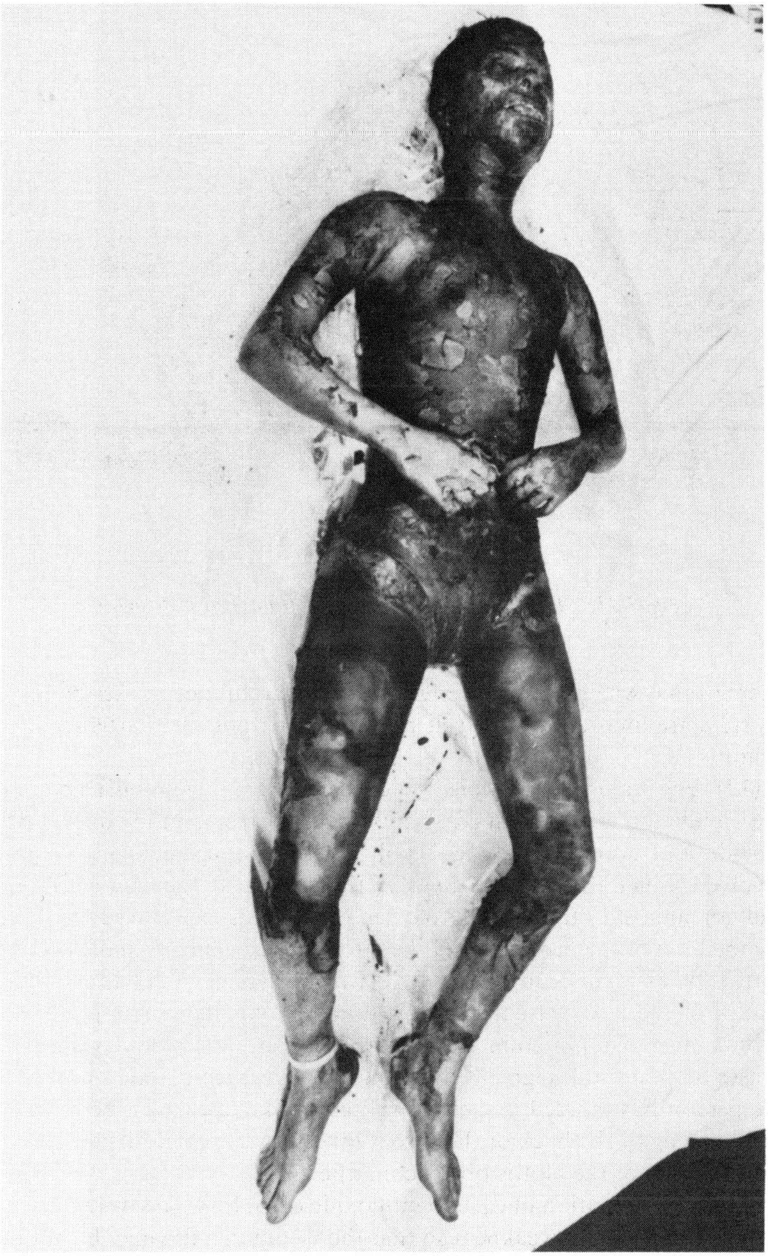

Fig. 1.42. Almost total body surface burning with heat splitting in groins

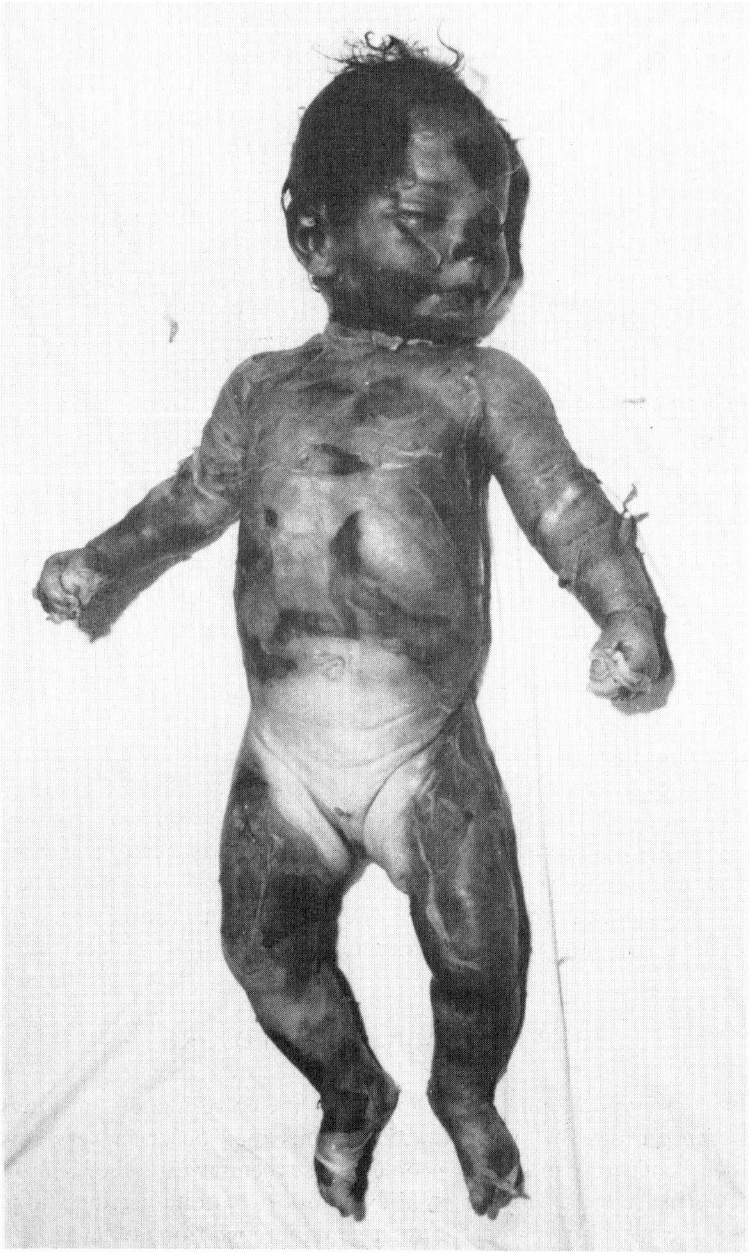

Fig. 1.43. Scalded baby. Lower abdomen and perineum protected by nappy

(14) In all fire deaths analysis should be carried out, not only for the toxic gases described above, but also for alcohol, as many fire victims are found to be intoxicated at post mortem, which often accounts for their inability to escape.

Scalds

1.108 The same criteria apply to cases of scalding regarding the prognosis and complications. Young children may be deliberately scalded by being placed in too hot water or inadvertently scalded by pulling kettles or pans of hot water over themselves while unsupervised. Clothing may protect the skin to an extent by absorbing the hot water under such circumstances (see Fig. 1.43), but it is important that it should be removed rapidly and not left in contact with the skin or else scalding will be inevitable.

Chemical Burns

1.109 Chemical burns are often deep and localised and severe and may have a characteristic smell or colour. They may occur in accidents in school or industrial laboratories or in chemical plants, and occasionally as the result of acid-throwing. Rarely nowadays are chemical agents used as a form of suicide, strong acids or alkalis being imbibed and resulting in burning of the lips and chin and severe corrosion of the mouth, oesophagus and stomach. Occasionally corrosive substances may be drunk inadvertently, having been stored in wrongly labelled bottles, the victim innocently taking a swig from such a bottle. Swallowing corrosives carries a very high mortality, even when rapidly treated. Acid-throwing leads to chemical burns, usually of the face and hands, which may be put up by the victim to protect himself. They may well heal with considerable residual scarring and may need skin grafting.

HYPOTHERMIA AND EXPOSURE

1.110 (1) Hypothermia by definition is the lowering of the internal body temperature below 35°C (95°F). This may occur in very severe weather conditions and where people expose themselves to the hazards of cold, during such activities as polar exploration, mountaineering and pot-holing. People ill-prepared for such climatic conditions or even severe winter weather may die if they are not adequately clothed and warmed. Not only is the actual ambient temperature important but also what is called the "wind chill" factor. Where there is high wind and moisture as well as cold, then the effects of the cold are magnified. Cold injury in its extreme form takes the form of frostbite with gangrene of the extremities and loss of the fingers and toes. In more severe cases the victim dies once the point of no return has been reached.

(2) The work of Keatinge and his colleagues mentioned in the section on drowning[15] demonstrated that the core temperature of the body registered internally only fell slowly in the first instance even if the external body temperature was apparently very low, but then it fell very sharply and rapidly. If the victim is not rapidly warmed, such low temperature becomes irreversible and the person dies.

(3) Hypothermia may be much more insidious and is undoubtedly commoner than is appreciated by the general public. It particularly affects those in the extremes of life, the very old and the very young. Fatigue, alcohol excess and debility predispose to the condition and the mortality in untreated cases is very high. It may be associated with chronic thyroid deficiency such as is seen in myxoedema, and it may be precipitated by drugs, particularly in the elderly who take benzodiazepine sleeping tablets or phenothiazine anti-depressants.

(4) The elderly victim often lives alone with inadequate heating. She, for the victim is often a woman, may fall and injure herself and lie unattended in the cold for many hours. Even a person in bed may be found to be hypothermic despite the presence of bedclothes, as the temperature control mechanisms in the brain may be adversely affected by drugs or disease such as arteriosclerosis.

(5) Patients with hypothermia are often mentally confused and may show the features of paradoxical undressing. They are often found with their clothing in disarray, often with skirt and pants removed, all highly suggestive of a sexual assault. The doctor and lawyer must be aware of this phenomenon, originally described by Gormsen[16] and others in Scandinavia. It has been suggested that the victim no longer appreciates the difference between hot and cold, and in the degree of mental confusion brought on by hypothermia may take off clothing rather than put more on, which logic would dictate.

(6) Infants also have poor temperature control due to immaturity. They may be left in draughty rooms insufficiently heated, poorly clad or inadequately nourished with no warm food. Such infants often look misleadingly healthy although they are in fact extremely cold.

(7) The post mortem appearances of hypothermia are few but characteristic. The classical features include multiple acute gastric erosions in the lining of the stomach, fat necrosis involving the pancreas,

15 See para. 1.46 above.

16 Gormsen, H. (1972) *Med. Sci. and Law*, *12*, 200–2, "Why have some victims of death from cold undressed?"

sometimes adrenal infarction and haemorrhage and pulmonary haemorrhage in infants. The body is often pink due to the lack of dissociation of oxygen and haemoglobin in the blood and the sludging of blood in the capillaries leads to pink patches on the skin. This pink discolouration of the post mortem lividity is very characteristic. Other causes of such pink discolouration are carbon monoxide and cyanide poisoning.

(8) Hypothermia is diagnosed in life by taking the rectal temperature of the patient, which may be astonishingly low; such cases constitute grave emergencies and will need to be energetically treated. Even if warmed to normal body heat, they may well die of complications, such as pneumonia or kidney failure. After death taking the rectal temperature is not of any diagnostic importance except when it is known when somebody was definitely alive and the rectal body temperature taken very shortly after death shows it to be exceptionally low. The post mortem findings in infants are often minimal. The gastric erosions and pancreatitis seen in adults are not usually apparent.

STARVATION AND NEGLECT IN ADULTS

1.111 (1) Starvation on a mass scale is seen in earthquakes, famines and other acts of God where whole communities or even nations may be involved, such as has been seen in recent times in Ethiopia and the Sudan. Under such conditions the mortality can be very high, particularly from dehydration and epidemics of natural disease, such as typhoid fever and cholera, where water or such foodstuffs that are available are contaminated.

(2) Individuals may be deliberately starved and neglected, especially political and other prisoners held in jails or other confinement where there is severe privation. Some prisoners may deliberately go on hunger strike in order to better their conditions or draw attention to a cause. In such cases, if the prisoner refuses all food and fluid, he usually succumbs after approximately sixty days, assuming he was fit at the onset of his hunger strike. If fluid is taken then it is possible for survival to be extended for many weeks, be it with extreme emaciation and weakness on the part of the person concerned.

(3) The elderly are particularly at risk from neglect; sometimes this is through their own inadequacies, due to immobility from arthritis or other rheumatic conditions, weak mindedness from cerebral arteriosclerosis and strokes or from heart failure or other long-standing medical disability. They are also at risk from those looking after them and may be neglected by their own kin at home, being confined to bed deliberately or to a room, or inadequately fed or cared for so that they develop bed sores

and pneumonia. They may be deliberately neglected or inadequately treated in an institution, particularly in a so-called nursing home where there are no proper nursing or medical facilities available. This is especially likely where the patient has no regular visitors or caring famiy or friends to ensure that her interests are being looked after by those having care of her and the true state of affairs may only be discovered by chance or following the death of the person concerned.

(4) Alcoholics and drug addicts may also suffer considerably from self-neglect as their life-style becomes totally orientated around the necessity to obtain and consume alcohol or to obtain and ingest drugs.

(5) From the pathological point of view, all these cases of neglect listed above show much the same pattern. The neglected patient is emaciated, dirty, unkempt, inadequately clothed and often with body or head lice. Men have matted beards. Toenails are uncut and often have a ram's horn appearance, so-called onychogryphosis. There may be skin ulceration and pigmentation, particularly in both folds and creases.

(6) There may be evidence of vitamin deficiency. Vitamin A deficiency causes blindness if prolonged and is seen in the malnourished in Africa and India. Vitamin B deficiency will result in anaemia, sores around the lips and mouth and a raw tongue with skin rashes, diarrhoea and mental disturbance. Vitamin C deficiency leads to scurvy, with bleeding gums, loss of teeth, anaemia and failure of wounds to heal. Lack of vitamin D, which leads to rickets in children, causes bone softening with pathological fractures in adults and intestinal disturbances.

(7) One group of people particularly at risk in the United Kingdom are Asian immigrants who do not have enough milk in their diet and do not go out in the sunshine, confining themselves to their houses and their own communities' diets.

(8) The external emaciation is mirrored in the internal organs, which are often wasted, particularly vital structures such as the heart and liver, whose function may fail or be irreversibly damaged so that even the belated administration of fluid, salts and food comes too late to save them. In such cases the abdomen is often swollen with fluid (ascites) and there is swelling of the legs from oedema. This is particularly seen where there is loss of protein and lack of salt.

(9) A deliberate form of self-neglect, seen in young women particularly, is anorexia nervosa. Here a young girl, usually in her teens or early twenties, becomes obsessed with the idea that she is overweight and deliberately starves herself to the point of extreme emaciation (see Fig. 1.44). If she is forced to eat, she will subsequently put her fingers down her throat to make herself vomit. Often the affected person will take laxative drugs and diuretic pills in order to lose weight, particularly fluid, and she may also resort to herbal remedies or other drugs she thinks may

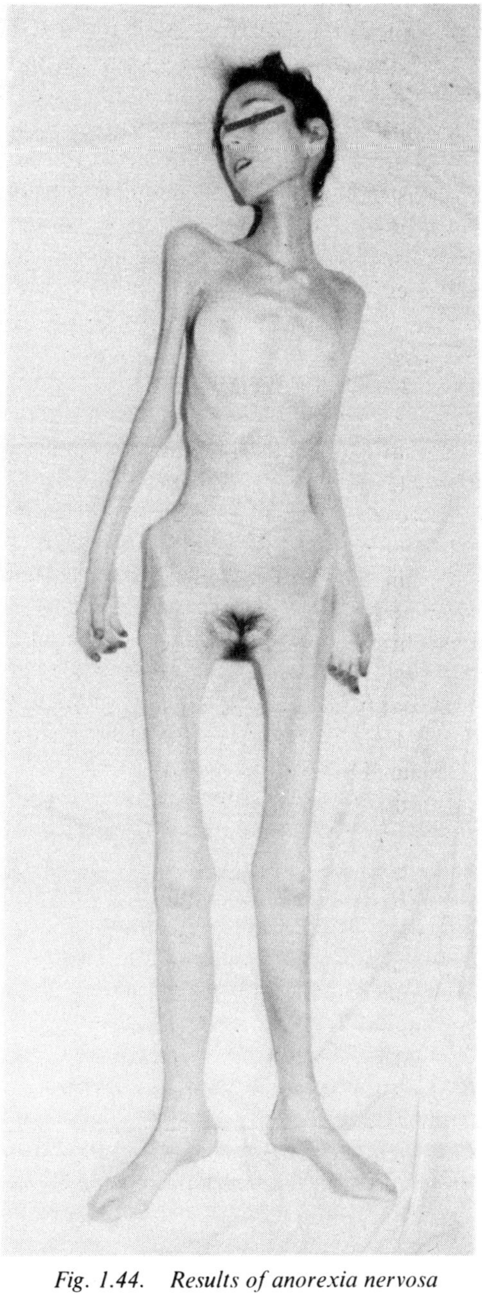

Fig. 1.44. Results of anorexia nervosa

aid her in this course. Rarely, a victim of this disorder may die, usually from heart failure. At autopsy the body is extremely emanicated with internal wasting of organs and possibily terminal infection, such as pneumonia.

(10) Certain diseases may mimic neglect, the persons concerned being too ill to care for their appearance and too apathetic or ill to eat. Such diseases include carcinoma (cancer) of the oesophagus or stomach, rampant tuberculosis and diabetes mellitus. Allegations of neglect may well be made under such circumstances and only autopsy will reveal the true state of afairs.

POISONING

Ethyl Alcohol

1.112 (1) Alcohol affects both the mental and physical functions of the body. Mentally it leads to loss of judgement and control so that an assailant may resort to excessive violence or even cruelty with sadism and mutilation which he may afterwards say he regrets or cannot remember.

(2) The physical effects are both acute and chronic. A person who is intoxicated by alcohol will have congested blood vessels, so that injuries will result in greater haemorrhage than if the person had been sober, and such bleeding may be more prolonged. This is of particular importance where head injuries are involved with intracerebral bleeding, as the excessive haemorrhage may lead to a fatal outcome in the confined space within the skull. If a victim is severely intoxicated, he is likely to die from the inhalation of vomit or of blood while lying on his back following injury, particularly head or facial injury. Facial injuries will cause bleeding into the back of the nose and throat which may become excessive with the dilatation and congestion of the blood vessels seen with alcohol excess. Head injuries are liable to cause vomiting in their own right and a combination of head injury and alcohol is particularly likely to produce emesis and inhalation.

(3) Those with chronic alcoholic liver disease, particularly the vagrant community, have impaired coagulation of the blood. They bruise easily following even minor trauma, and more serious injury may lead to fatal uncontrolled haemorrhage, a picture similar to that seen in persons on anticoagulant treatment following heart attacks.

(4) Intoxication in a victim may impair his ability to put up a struggle or defend himself when he is assaulted, particularly if he is severely intoxicated, and such cases of homicidal assault will be marked by a relative absence of defence type wounds. Alcohol and its effects are dealt with in more detail in Chapter 6.

Drugs in Children

1.113 (1) Drugs may be given to infants and young children with intent to sedate them so that they do not interfere with the activities of their parents and friends. It is not uncommon for an infant to be sedated with alcohol or sleeping tablets, thus allowing the mother to engage in illicit sexual activities without interruption. Occasionally such sedation may be overdone and the child succumbs, particularly if he vomits and chokes.

(2) Drugs may be given to infants who are teething or who are otherwise fractious or difficult and exasperation may lead to deliberate drug overdosage and possible death.

(3) From time to time children are killed by a demented parent and one or more small children in a family may be persuaded to drink a cocktail of soft drinks laced with cyanide or some other lethal drug prior to the homicidal parent commiting suicide or attempting to do so.

Drugs in Adults

1.114 (1) Homicidal poisoning in adults is comparatively rare and such cases tend to be remembered and become *causes célèbres*, particularly if some bizarre drug is used, for example the case of *R. v. Young*,[17] the thallium poisoner. It is difficult to administer a poison to an unco-operative conscious victim, as he or she will nearly always detect the unusual taste or colouring in the food or drink offered.

(2) Prolonged deliberate poisoning may occur but is usually detected thanks to modern toxicological analyses. Occasionally successful homicidal poisoning is achieved by persuading the victim to swallow excessive doses of medicine prescribed or obtained for another person or a properly prescribed drug is given in excess. This is more likely to occur when the victim is elderly and either in a nursing home or similar institution or at the mercy of a younger vindictive family.

(3) The other main form of homicidal poisoning occurs in drug addicts, who often make up cocktails of drugs which are administered by a group of persons, often in a squat, each in turn giving an injection of drugs to another. Those who have lost their tolerance or not developed it are very liable to die under such circumstances and from time to time successful prosecutions are undertaken against those procuring and administering the drugs concerned.

It is not intended to go through a list of common or uncommon poisons which may have been used or are likely to be used in homicidal poisoning, as such information is to be found in current textbooks of toxicology and pharmacology.

17 (1972) The Times 20 June.

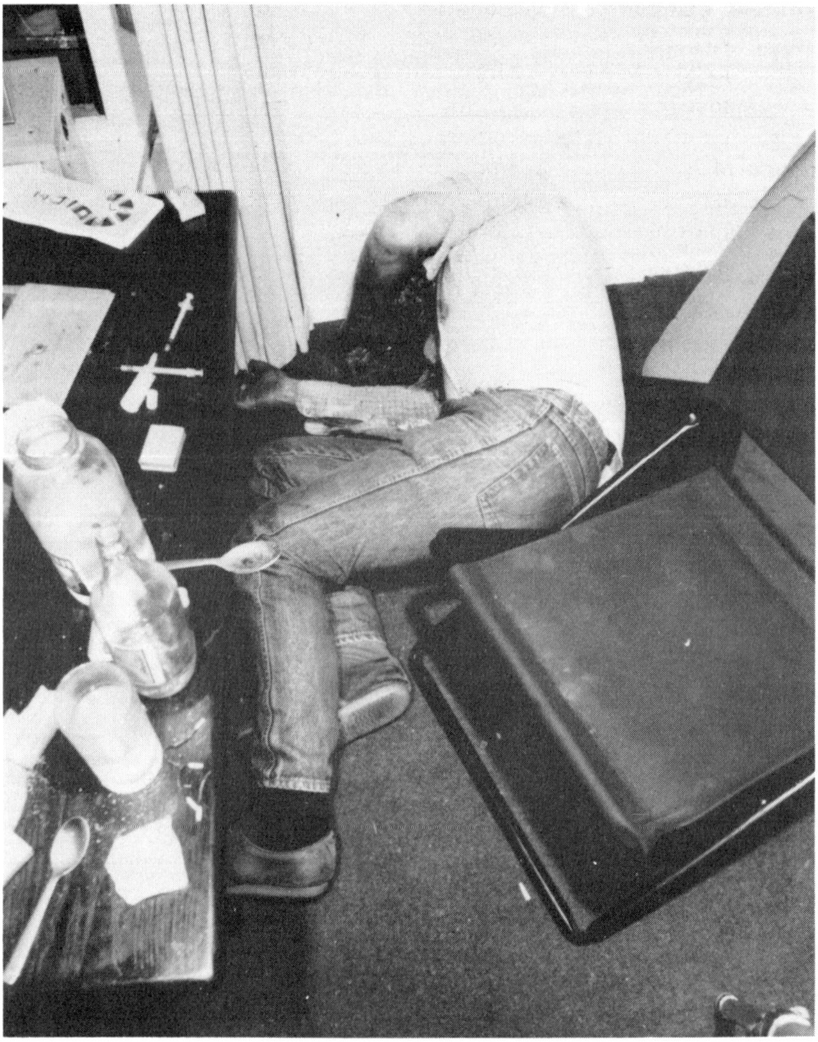

Fig. 1.45. Drug addict dying of postural asphyxia following overdose. Note impedimenta on table

(4)(i) The pathologist who suspects poisoning as being the cause of death in a case of homicide should confer with his toxicological colleague in the forensic laboratory before commencing his autopsy and if practicable the chemist or his representative should be present during the post mortem in order that the correct samples may be collected in suitable quantities and placed in the right containers for analysis. Contaminated samples or inadequate specimens are useless.

(ii) It is usual to collect blood from a major blood vessel in an arm or leg to avoid the danger of contamination by stomach contents. Cavity blood should never be used for analysis. Urine should be collected from the bladder by catheter or syringe, again to avoid contamination. Stomach contents may be very helpful, as will a portion of liver and a sample of bile. More exotic poisons such as the heavy metals including arsenic may require samples of hair, nails and bones. Solvent abuse may call for analysis of body fat, brain and lung.

(iii) Samples that cannot be removed immediately to the laboratory should be stored in a refrigerator at 4°C and transported to the laboratory as soon as feasible or practical. Any samples showing post mortem change may be unsuitable or useless for analysis, although it is always worth doing an analysis, especially of urine, from a decomposed body for alcohol and drugs. This may give some guidance if not an exact figure of the concentration of a drug, thus confirming or eliminating the suspicion of poisoning. Analysis of the vitreous humour, the fluid in the eyeballs, which can be aspirated by needle and syringe, may be useful where the body is decomposing and a blood sample is unsuitable for analysis.

CHAPTER 2

Assaults, Wounding etc.

LAW

2.01 Assault and battery are two different crimes at common law but the word "assault" is often used to include both assault and battery. An assault is any act by which a person intentionally or recklessly causes another to apprehend immediate and unlawful personal violence. Battery is any act by which a person intentionally or recklessly inflicts unlawful personal violence upon another.

Common Assault

2.02 Section 47 of the Offences against the Person Act 1861 provides that any person convicted of common assault on indictment is punishable with one year's imprisonment and may also be, and usually is, tried summarily. The use of the word "assault" in the statute includes "battery" and means a simple assault which is not aggravated and need cause no actual injury to the victim.

Assault Occasioning Actual Bodily Harm

2.03 (1) Section 47 of the Offences against the Person Act 1861 provides that such an assault may be tried either summarily, or on indictment. It has been held that the words "actual bodily harm" need no explanation and mean some actual bodily injury; it need not be an injury of a permanent character nor need it amount to what would be regarded as grievous bodily harm.[1] In *R. v. Miller*[2] Lynskey J. stated with approval that "actual bodily harm includes any hurt or injury calculated to interfere with the health or comfort of the victim," and he held that this included a hysterical and nervous condition resulting from an assault, taking the view that an injury to the state of a victim's mind is actual bodily harm.

(2) The Prohibition of Female Circumcision Act 1985 creates the new offence of female circumcision, subject to a medical defence that such a

1 See para. 2.04 *infra.*
2 [1954] 2 Q.B. 282.

surgical operation is necessary for the physical or mental health of the person and it is performed by a registered medical practitioner, or that it is performed on a person who is in any stage of labour or has just given birth and the operation is performed for purposes connected with that labour or birth and is performed by a registered medical practitioner or registered midwife, or medical student, or student midwife. In determining whether such a surgical operation is necessary for the mental health of a person, no account is to be taken of the effect on that person of any belief that the operation is required as a matter of custom or ritual. It is an offence to excise, infibulate or otherwise mutilate the whole or any part of the labia majora or minora or clitoris of another person.

Wounding with Intent to Cause Grievous Bodily Harm

2.04 Section 18 of the Offences against the Person Act 1861 creates the offence of wounding with intent to cause grievous bodily harm and causing any grievous bodily harm. "Wounding" in this section and also in Section 20 (see 2.5 *infra*) unlawful wounding, includes incised wounds, punctured wounds, lacerated wounds, contused wounds and gunshot wounds.The continuity of the skin must be broken to constitute a wound; it is not enough that the cuticle or outer skin is broken if the inner skin remains intact.[3] In the case of *Wood*[4] the victim was treated with such violence that his collarbone was broken but it was held that there was no wound if the skin was intact. A division of the internal skin within the cheek or lip is sufficient to come within the statute,[5] and in *Waltham*[6] it was held to be a wound where the lining membrane of the urethra was ruptured and bled, evidence being given that the membrane is precisely the same in character as that which lines the cheek and the external and internal skin of the lip. It has also been held that the rupture of blood vessels internally is not a wound.[7]

Provided the skin is broken, the nature of the instrument causing the wound is immaterial and so a wound with a kick from a shoe is within the statute,[8] and under an earlier and now replaced Act,[9] when a hammer was thrown at a person and it struck him on the nose and broke the skin, it was held to be a wound. It was held in *R. v. Sheard*[10] that a defendant was guilty of wounding where he struck the victim, who was wearing a hat, on the head with an air gun and the hard rim of the hat caused a

3 See *Moriarty v. Brooks* (1834) 6 C. & P. 684 and *M'Loughlin* (1838) 8 C. & P. 635.
4 (1830) 1 Mood. C.C. 278.
5 *R.v. Smith* (1837) 8 C. & P. 160.
6 (1849) 3 Cox C.C. 442.
7 See *J.J.C. (a minor) v. Eisenhower* [1983] 3 All E.R. 230 D.C.
8 See *R. v. Briggs* (1831) 1 Mood. C.C. 318.
9 7 Will. 4 & 1 Vict. c. 88 s.4.
10 (1837) 2 Mood. C.C. 13.

wound. "Grievous bodily harm" has the ordinary and natural meaning of really serious bodily harm,[11] and it has been held that it was not necessary that it should either be permanent or dangerous.[12]

Unlawful Wounding

2.05 Section 20 of the Offences against the Person Act 1861 creates the offences of unlawful wounding and inflicting any grievous bodily harm on any person, and the words "wound" and "grievous bodily harm" have the same meaning as in section 18 (see para. 2.04 *supra*). In *R. v. Clarence*[13] a married man knew he had gonorrhoea but his wife did not know. He had intercourse with his wife and gave her the disease. She would not have agreed to intercourse had she known of his condition. It was held that the defendant could not be guilty of an offence under Section 20 (inflicting grievous bodily harm) or of an offence under Section 47 (an assault occasioning actual bodily harm). By analogy, a husband who knew he had AIDS, but whose wife did not, and who had intercourse with her and gave her the disease, would also be not guilty.

Attempting to Choke, Suffocate or Strangle with Intent

2.06 Section 21 of the Offences against the Person Act 1861 creates the offences of attempting to choke, suffocate or strangle any person, or by any means calculated to render any person insensible, unconscious or incapable of resistance with intent to enable himself or any other person to commit any indictable offence. Normally, apart from the evidence of the victim, medical evidence would be appropriate in such cases.

Administering Chloroform etc. to Commit Indictable Offences

2.07 Section 22 of the Offences against the Person Act 1861 creates the offences of applying or administering to, or causing to be taken by or attempting to cause to be administered to or taken by any person, any chloroform, laudanum, or other stupefying or overpowering drug, matter or thing with intent to enable himself or any other person to commit any indictable offence. If the drug is specifically named in the indictment, then its nature will have to be proved and if not specially named, evidence would have to be given to show that it was of a stupefying or overpowering nature calculated to aid the offender in the commission of an indictable offence. It should be noted that section 4 of the Sexual Offences Act 1956 creates the offence of adminstering drugs to any woman with intent to stupefy or overpower her so as to enable any man

11 See *D.P.P. v. Smith* [1961] A.C. 290.
12 See *R. v. Ashman* (1858) 1F. & F. 88.
13 (1888) 22 Q.B.D. 23.

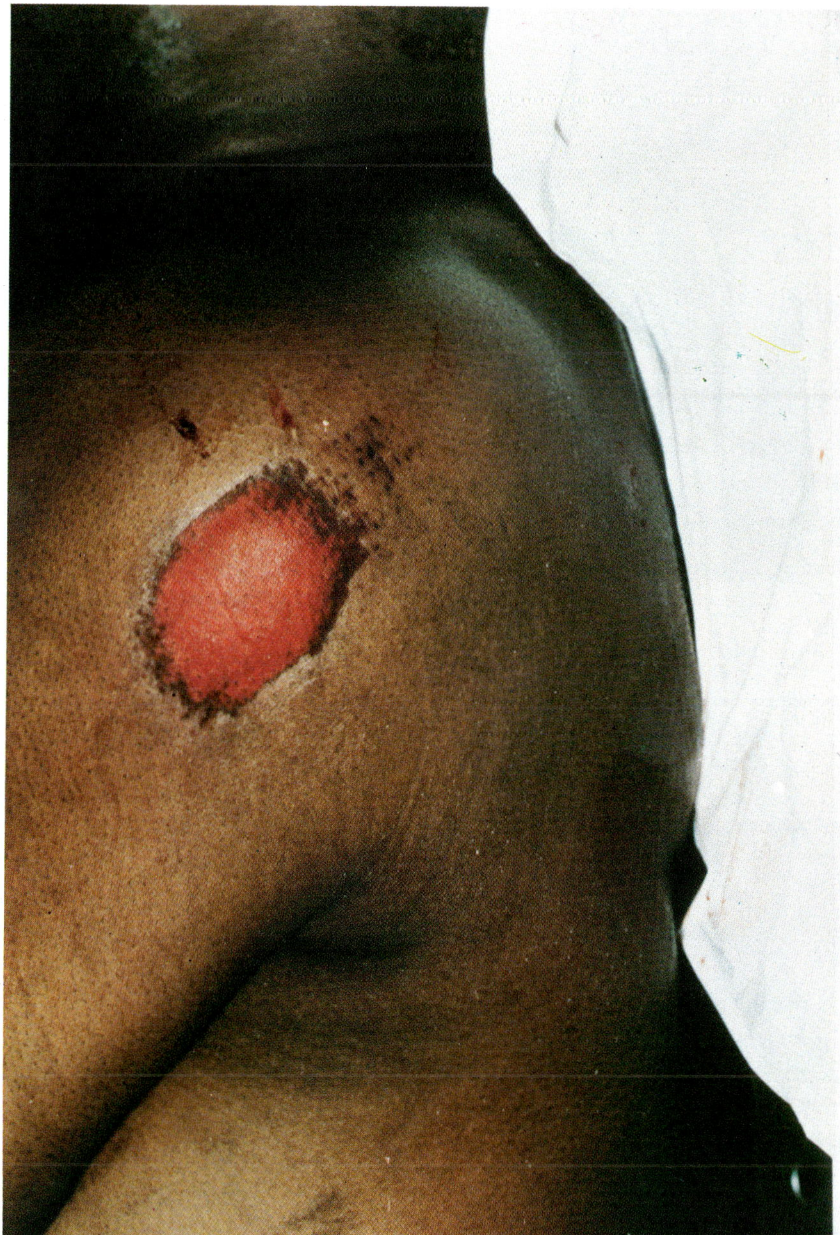

Plate 8. Abrasion on shoulder

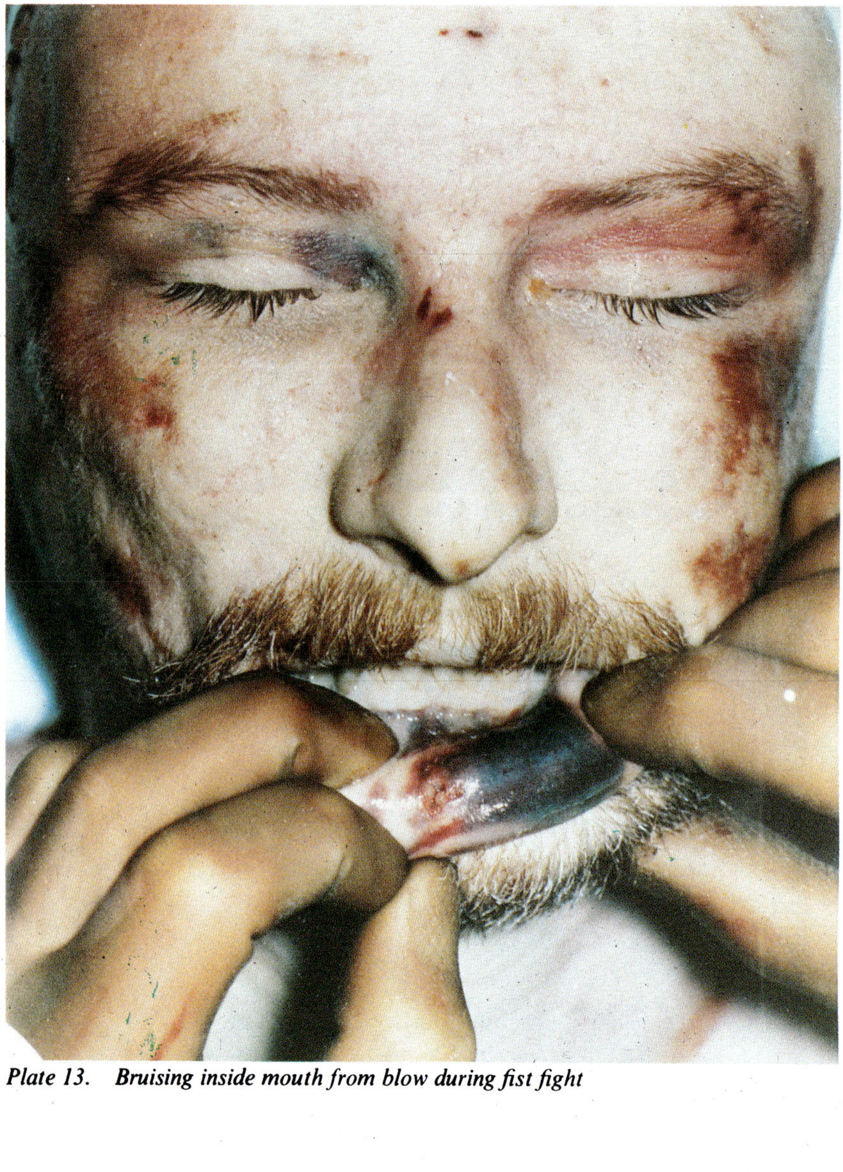

Plate 13.   Bruising inside mouth from blow during fist fight

to have unlawful sexual intercourse with her. The essence of this offence is administering the drug, and where there has been only one administration, there can only be one offence, even though the intention of the administration was to enable more than one man to have intercourse with the woman.[14]

Administering Poison so as to Endanger Life or with Intent to Injure

2.08 Sections 23 and 24 of the Offences against the Person Act 1861 create the offences of unlawfully and maliciously adminstering any poison or other destructive or noxious thing so as thereby to endanger life or as to inflict any grievous bodily harm and similarly with intent to injure, aggrieve or annoy.

Injuring or Attempting to Injure Persons by Explosives or Corrosive Substances

2.09 Section 28 of the Offences against the Person Act 1861 creates the offence of causing bodily injury by explosives, while Section 29 deals with using explosive or corrosive substances with intent to do grievous bodily harm.

TYPES OF WOUNDS AND THEIR INTERPRETATION AND RESULTANT COMPLICATIONS

2.10 (1) The sections below deal with the individual types of wounds separately and in some detail. It must however be remembered that in many homicidal and non-homicidal assaults, particularly where there has been a struggle, with people for example falling to the ground or being thrown down stairs, there may be a multiplicity of injuries of different types. If a gang fight develops, a victim may receive wounds from several weapons wielded by different assailants and the doctor may be faced with considerable difficulty in sorting out how various injuries were caused and by what weapons, and in which order if possible.

(2) Once wounds have healed it may be impossible to say for certain how they were caused, although burn scars are recognisable for the rest of the victim's life, particularly if they are extensive and severe. Simple superficial wounds such as grazes and bruises disappear within days and such injuries should be accurately recorded and if possible photographed as early as possible following their infliction if any useful interpretation is

14 *R. v. Shillingford; R. v. Vanderwall* [1968] 1 W.L.R. 566; 52 Cr.App.R. 188.

to be formed. Wounds that become infected may enlarge and take on a completely different configuration so that the resulting scar once the lesion had healed may bear no relation to the original injury. Occasionally scars become raised up and rubbery, the so-called keloid formation. This is particularly seen after burning. The more generalised complications of wounding are dealt with in paras. 1.34–39 above.

Abrasions

2.11 An abrasion is a superficial grazing of the outer layer of the skin, the epidermis, which is not fully penetrated. Abrasions are most commonly seen where rough trauma has been applied to the skin of the body surface, for example in falls or road traffic accidents, but they may be caused by a multiplicity of other forms of injury such as scratches from fingernails, from weapons or from ligatures, to name but a few. Examination of such abrasions may indicate how the injury was caused. When the skin slides over a rough surface or vice versa, the superficial layers of the skin are dragged and heaped up at the distal margin of the injury indicating the direction in which it was caused. For example fingernail scratches across a face may show heaping up at the bottom end where the nails were dragged down the victim's face.

Contusions

2.12 (1)(a) A contusion is bruising of the superficial skin and underlying tissue with escape of blood from torn blood vessels into the dermis, the deep layer beneath the epidermis or outer skin. It may be associated with swelling of the tissues because of the escape of blood into the fat beneath the skin.

(b) The size of a bruise is no indication of the violence which caused it. It varies with the blood supply to the tissues, the prominence of the part and the type of tissue involved; the slack skin on the back of the hands will allow considerable escape of blood and obvious bruising, whereas the palm of the hand where the skin is tightly applied to the underlying tissues is practically never bruised.

(c) A bruise may appear at a different site from the point of injury. A common example is seen when a person sustains a hip injury resulting in a fracture of the neck of the thigh bone and blood tracks downwards from this injury between the muscles of the thigh and appears subsequently around the knee joint.

(2) The average bruise appears within a few minutes of injury due to escape of blood as a red area which becomes purple or blue and over the course of the next week or ten days this bruise becomes brown, green and

yellow and then disappears. The old bruise very easily and such bruises may persist for weeks or even months. It is said that children bruise more easily than adults. It is more likely that children frequently fall over or expose themselves to much more superficial trauma at play and hence receive more injuries and are more bruised. There is nothing to suggest that their blood or blood vessels are different from those of an adult.

(3)(a) The distribution of bruises can be very informative to the doctor or pathologist. Defence injuries caused by blows from a blunt instrument during an assault are classically found on the outer side of the hands and arms or on the back of the hands when perhaps a victim has put his hands up or over his head to protect it from being injured (see Plates 9–13).

(b) Victims of assault, alive or dead, should always be examined the day following the initial examination if possible, for bruises often take time to develop fully and may become more apparent as the hours pass. This is particularly so in the dead body when the tissues have been drained of blood by the post mortem examination and the residual bruising of the soft tissues is more clearly defined against the white background surrounding them.

(4) Bruising is difficult to assess in coloured people for obvious reasons and in a case of death the pathologist should not be afraid at his examination to cut into the soft tissues where he suspects there may be injury to see if there is bleeding into the fat beneath the skin.

(5) Blunt injury to internal organs will lead to contusions. In such cases there is tearing of blood vessels and escape of blood into the tissues, such injuries being visible at surgery or at post mortem. The brain may also be so injured in a closed head injury.

Lacerations

2.13 (1)(a) A laceration is a splitting or tearing of the whole skin, both epidermis and dermis. Such injuries occur particularly over bony prominences and in the scalp and are frequently seen in road traffic accidents and falls. The edges of a laceration are ragged, the soft tissues are crushed, the hair and skin margin may be turned in and the margins themselves may be bruised or abraded.

(b) There may be foreign matter in the wounds such as paint or wood fragments from a weapon, and these must be diligently searched for, if necessary with a magnifying glass.

(c) In the scalp many lacerations superficially resemble incised wounds because the scalp is tightly stretched over the underlying skull bone and when struck with an implement, the scalp splits and gapes, with severe bleeding. Careful examination of the wound edges will, however, reveal the nature of the injury. (See the photograph Fig. 1.33 and paras. 1.89ff *ante*).

(2) Blows and kicks to the body frequently result in lacerated wounds and the victim of a violent assault will often have a considerable number of injuries, abrasions, contusions and lacerations, some merging one into another. They may be associated with underlying fractures of facial bones or of the skull. Where they occur inside the mouth with dislodgement of the teeth and tearing of the soft tissues there may be severe haemorrhage, as these parts are very well supplied with blood vessels. Such bleeding may cause asphyxia, particularly if the victim of an assault is left unconscious or disabled lying on his back, allowing the blood to flow into the back of the throat and be inhaled down the trachea.

Electrical and Thermal Injuries

Electrocution

2.14 (1) The number of people who die from electrocution in any year in England and Wales is less than 200, of whom about 40 are suicides. The accidental deaths are usually domestic but occasionally may occur in an industrial setting or with scientific equipment. When one considers the extent that electrical appliances are used in the home and at work in modern-day society, the mortality is surprisingly small.

(2) The effects of an electric shock depend on the strength of the current, its amperage and voltage, the duration of the shock, whether the current is a.c. or d.c., (the former being more dangerous) and the body resistance. Television sets are particularly dangerous, and children, especially toddlers, are at risk from such a cause of electrocution as they can insert small fingers through air holes or other gaps in the back of a television set or into the sockets of electric plugs. The body resistance is lowered by moisture, hence the increased risk from electrical appliances employed in bathrooms and kitchens or in gardens. Many fatalaties are due to faulty appliances, inadequate wiring without earthing, or sheer stupidity, such as attempting to service an electrical transformer without turning off the power first.

(3) The normal mechanism of death is interruption of the regular heart beat leading to ventricular fibrillation (a very rapid ineffective heart beat), or total cardiac arrest. Some people die of respiratory paralysis. The lives of such people may be saved by rapid resuscitation, care being taken to turn off the power first or drag the person away by his or her clothing from contact with the electrical supply. Such resuscitation needs to be prolonged before being abandoned as hopeless.

(4) It is said that if the route of the electric current through the body

passes through the heart it is more likely to cause death, for example a current running from a hand to the opposite foot or from one hand to the other across the chest.

(5) At autopsy electric burns, particularly from sources of very high voltage such as power lines or electric rails, will cause deep burns with charring of tissue. Less destructive fatal electrical burns may be deep and are marked by a grey-white centre with a lilac surrounding edge. If the person survives, such a burn will be very slow to heal and may well need grafting. Many cases of electrocution show very little external evidence of burning at all. Injury may be limited to the hands and may not be readily recognised unless carefully looked for. Rigor mortis is always a handicap to the pathologist. He must be sure that he has forced the hand open to look at the palmar surface of the fingers and thumb on each side, as small deep burns on the pads of the fingers and thumb (see Fig. 2.1) may easily be overlooked.

(6) Electrical injury must always be searched for in any person found dead in the bathroom, either in the bath or alongside it.

(7) Internal examination in a case of electrocution usually shows no specific changes and if the significance of small burns on the hands or other parts of the body externally is not appreciated, then the pathologist may well overlook the possibility of electrocution altogether and be faced with a case with no apparent cause of death.

(8) Suicidal electrocution is rare. A person usually winds wires around his fingers or wrists which are then connected to the mains supply by means of a plug; the victim switches the current on and dies almost immediately. The finding of the body under such circumstances is usually self-explanatory, particularly if reinforced by the presence of a suicide note, a locked door and other evidence of self-injury or self-poisoning.

Lightning

2.15 Deaths from lightning are rare; only 14 cases are recorded in the Registrar General's statistics for England and Wales in 1982. The victim may be found in the open with extensive injuries which may mimic an assault. This is because not only is a very high voltage electric current involved but also a blast wave which may cause multiple injuries to the body, and may strip the clothing from it with extensive electric burns as well. Sometimes these take the form of arborescent patterns rather like the imprint of a leaf on the skin (see Fig. 2.2). Such marks are diagnostic, but tend to be transitory and may be missed. Burns may also be located over the position of metallic objects such as buckles on straps or belts, possibly imprinting the pattern of such a device on the skin. The metal itself may become magnetised.

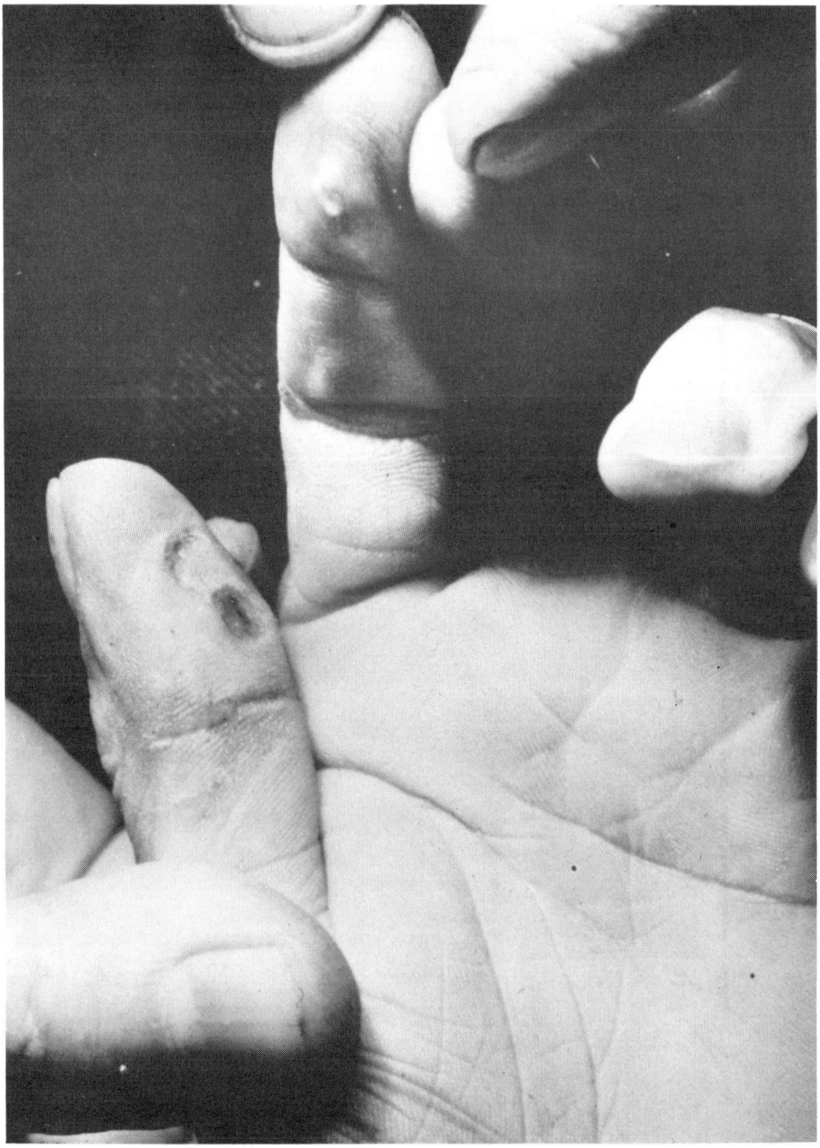

Fig. 2.1. Electric burns on thumb and index finger

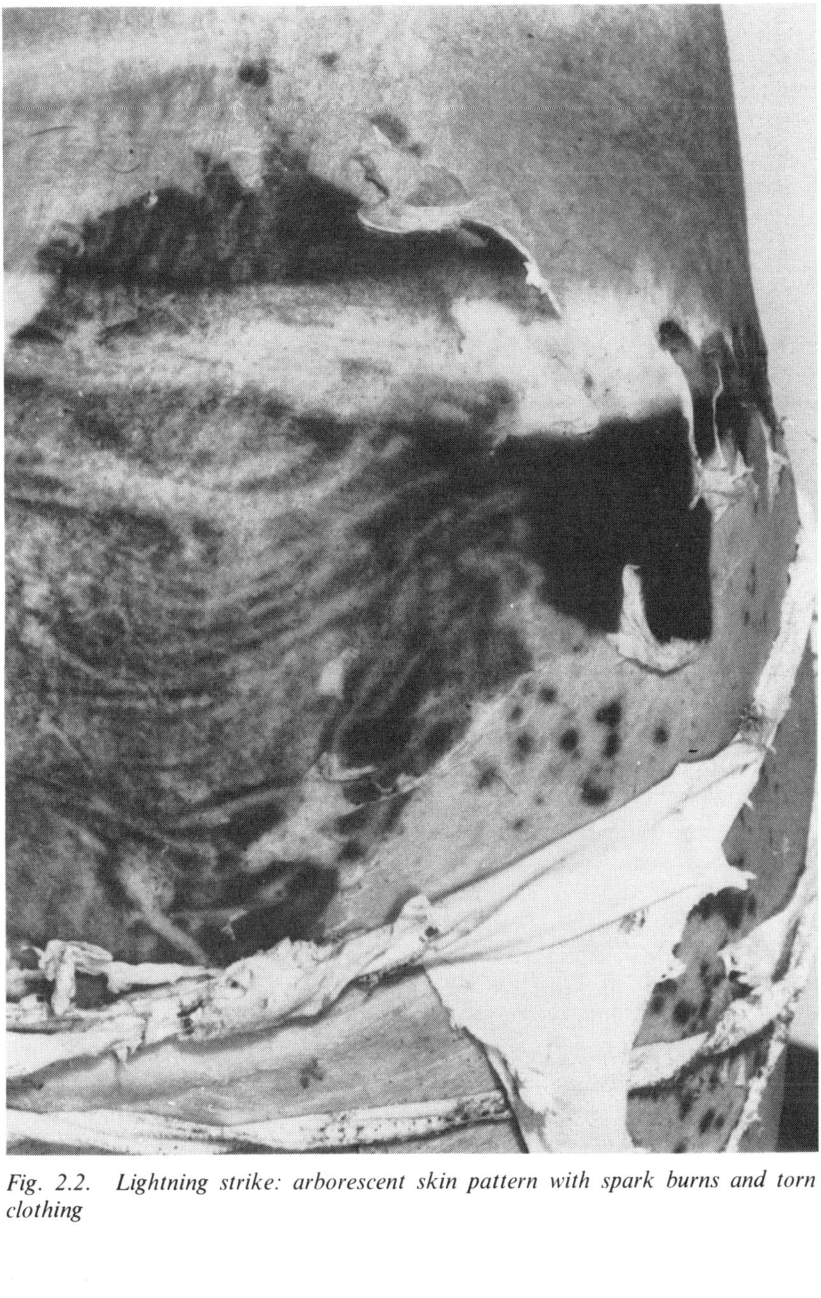

Fig. 2.2. Lightning strike: arborescent skin pattern with spark burns and torn clothing

Radiation Injury

2.16 X-rays and other forms of radiation, such as released by a nuclear explosion, may cause extensive burning, ranging from simple reddening of the skin to extensive destruction resembling burns from a fire. In addition such radiation affects the blood-forming capacity of the bone marrow and people exposed to toxic doses of radiation often die of severe anaemia and bleeding from platelet deficiency. There may also be severe gastro-intestinal disorders with shedding of the lining of much of the stomach and intestines. Such radiation can also cause blindness. The misuse of lasers in recent years has caused similar burns on the skin and eyes and internal organs.

Heatstroke

2.17 (1) This is due to the breakdown of the heat-regulating mechanism of the body, especially where there is a combination of a high temperature and high humidity as in the tropics.

(2) It may also occur in anaesthetic disasters, usually associated with the use of atropine leading to the suppression of sweating. The symptoms of heatstroke are extremely high temperature, up to 40°C or more, delirium, photophobia and possibly fits. A particular form of heatstroke known as malignant hyperpyrexia may rarely complicate anaesthesia. This is due to an inherited biochemical defect and there is usually a family history of anaesthetic problems in parents or siblings. It is particularly associated with the use of suxamethonium (a muscle relaxant) and halothane (an anaesthetic gas). The patient develops a very high body temperature, again of the order of 40°C or more, which may be fatal unless quickly recognised and treated.

Heat Exhaustion

2.18 This must be differentiated from heatstroke; it is due to loss of fluid and salt from prolonged sweating. While it often occurs in hot countries, it is particularly associated in the United Kingdom with boilermen, laundry workers and the like, who work in a very hot enviroment with loss of fluid and chloride depletion. Such workers complain of cramps, giddiness and vomiting and may collapse and die if not treated, although this is unusual. There are no specific post mortem findings in either heatstroke or heat exhaustion, except that sometimes tiny haemorrhages are found in the white matter of the brain in cases of heatstroke.

CHAPTER 3

Death and Injury in Infancy and Childhood

LAW: DEFINITION; ELEMENTS OF THE OFFENCE

Child Destruction

3.01 As has already been noted in para. 1.01 above under murder, the victim must be "a reasonable creature in being", that is, the person must have been born and be still alive before the offence of murder can be committed. If, therefore, the child is still in the womb or in the process of birth, any such killing cannot be murder. By section 58 of the Offences against the Person Act 1861, (see para. 5.29 *infra*) and subject to the Abortion Act 1967, it is an offence to attempt to procure a miscarriage from any time after conception until birth. If the child is capable of being born alive it may also be an offence of child destruction under the Infant Life (Preservation) Act 1929 section 1. If the child is in the process of being born and is killed, it cannot amount to murder or procuring a miscarriage, and can only amount to child destruction. Section 1 of the Infant Life (Preservation) Act 1929 makes it an offence with intent to destroy the life of a child capable of being born alive, to do any wilful act that causes a child to die before it has an existence independent of the mother, provided that no one is guilty of this offence unless it is proved that the act which caused the death of the child was not done in good faith for the purpose only of preserving the life of the mother. Evidence that a woman had been pregnant for a period of eight weeks or more is prima facie proof that she was at that time pregnant of a child capable of being born alive. There is therefore an overlap between attempting to procure a miscarriage under section 58 of the Offences against the Person Act 1861 and the offence of child destruction under section 1 of the Infant Life (Preservation) Act 1929.

Infanticide

3.02 By section 1 of the Infanticide Act 1938 it is an offence called infanticide for a mother to kill her child under the age of 12 months at a time when the balance of her mind was disturbed by reason of her not having fully recovered from the effects of giving birth or by reason of the effect of lactation. This has the effect of reducing what would otherwise be murder to a less serious offence. When such an offence is charged, a jury may find the defendant guilty of manslaughter or guilty but insane.

MEDICAL ASPECTS OF DEATHS IN INFANCY

3.03 It is now extremely rare for a doctor to be called upon to examine the body of a child destroyed in utero after the 28th week of pregnancy. He should examine the child and assess its gestational age particularly by radiography of the ossification centres, a procedure explained in more detail in the section on infanticide (para. 3.04 below). He must also assess the medical possibility of the child having been capable of being born alive and ensure that it has not died naturally in utero with evidence of maceration. He must satisfy himself that there are no congenital abnormalities that might preclude the child being born alive and examine the child's body for evidence of injury. Overall the doctor would do well to follow the procedure described below under infanticide.

Infanticide

3.04 (1) Considering the law of infanticide, as stated at para. 3.02 above, it can be appreciated that the pathologist may be called upon to examine an infant to establish that the child was legally viable, that is must have been born alive, that it must be less than twelve months old and that it must have died by reason of some deliberate act or omission. To this end careful measurements of the child's height and weight must be made and the age of the child checked if necessary by radiography to establish how many ossification centres are present (from these develop the bones of the child's skeleton). They develop in a regular, well recognised order described in all textbooks of anatomy; they are constant, practically speaking, for both sexes and all races. In cases of doubt dental examination of eruption of the milk teeth may help to establish the age of the child, although eruption of teeth is rather more variable than the development of ossification centres.

(2) The mother must be examined psychiatrically to establish the fact that she is mentally ill and she should show symptoms and signs of recognised mental illness.

(3) While the infant may be deliberately killed, often by suffocation or strangulation or by drowning or blunt injury especially to the head, it is as well to remember that many cases of so-called infanticide are in reality deaths due to lack of care and attention at birth. A young teenage girl carrying an illegitimate child in utero, ignorant of pregnancy and delivery, on her own without any help or support, who has received no

ante-natal care, may find herself suddenly going into labour and delivering herself of a child totally unassisted in unsuitable surroundings. When the baby is delivered, she may not know how to resuscitate it by clearing the air passages and establishing respiration and tying off the umbilical cord. She may faint from loss of blood. She may go to the lavatory and deliver the child into the lavatory pan where it drowns. She may deliver the child under bedding so that the child asphyxiates.

(4) Marks on the child's body found by the pathologist may well have been inflicted by the mother herself during delivery. As the child presents at the vulva, head first, she may try and push the child from her body by pressing under the chin on the front of the child's neck to get a purchase along the jaw, and the child may be scratched by fingernails and bruised by fierce gripping by the distraught mother. At autopsy following such circumstances, bruising of the neck and scratch marks may be mistaken for deliberate strangulation. It is important for the pathologist before he begins his examination to try to obtain from those treating the mother the details of the circumstances of the child's delivery as far as possible.

(5) Fluid in the air passages is of no diagnostic import unless it contains foreign material such as soap, indicating deliberate drowning in a bath or basin.

(6) Similarly caution should be exercised over the finding of a fractured skull in case the child has been delivered by forceps as an emergency by someone unskilled in their use, leading to crushing of the soft skull of the child. Again details of the delivery may assist the pathologist to differentiate between deliberate trauma and inadvertant injury.

(7) Sometimes the body, after being delivered, is disposed of by being wrapped and abandoned in a ladies' lavatory (see Fig. 3.1) or in a cupboard, or thrown in a river or left in a ditch.

(8) Often enough when the body is found extensive decomposition has set in, so that the problems of identification and establishing a cause of death may be insurmountable. Identification may be possible from the wrappings in which the baby is found, such as garments, newspaper and the like, but decomposition will make it impossible in many cases for the pathologist to establish whether the child was born alive or not. The presence of post mortem injuries, for example post mortem burning, are indicative of attempts to destroy the body, and although suspicious, are not indicative of infanticide *per se* and the baby's death may have to be dealt with merely as a case of concealment of birth.

(9) Autopsies on new born infants are frequently unrewarding from a pathological point of view. While it may be possible to establish that the child was born alive, in the absence of signs of asphyxia or trauma or obvious congenital or natural disease, it may be very difficult to establish

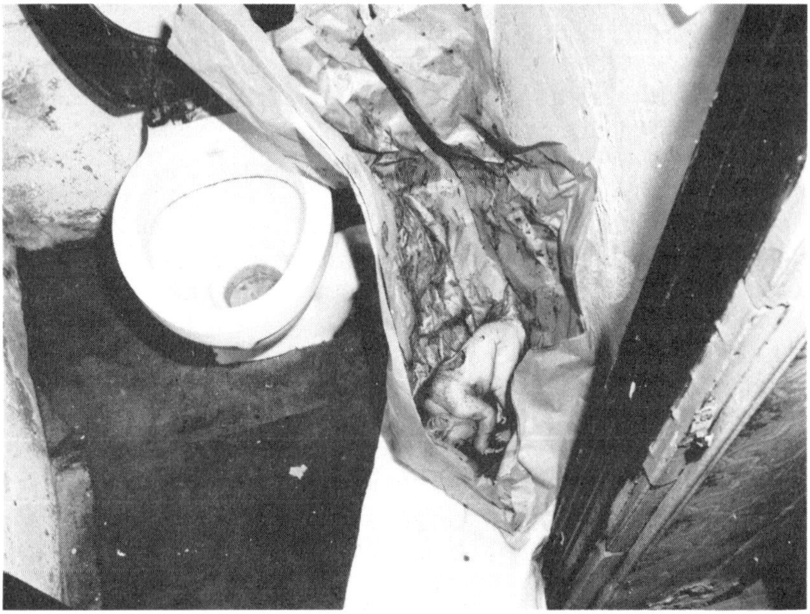

Fig. 3.1. Lack of attention at birth: disposal of body in lavatory

a definite cause of death. The examination should be thorough and include extensive microscopic studies of the tissues as well as their naked eye appearances, together with, if appropriate, bacteriological, virological and chemical studies of the tissues and blood and other body fluids. This problem will be referred to further when sudden infant death syndrome is discussed (see para. 3.05 below).

Sudden Infant Death Syndrome

3.05 (1) Sudden death in infancy has been recognised since Biblical times and over the centuries has been ascribed to a variety of causes from a judgement of God to the more mundane asphyxia due to overlying by an adult or older child with whom the infant was sharing a bed. This latter theory was accepted as the cause of death in many cases during the 19th century and early part of the 20th century. It is only since the early 1950s that research has been undertaken in depth into the causes of death in infancy (see (6) below). Sudden death is infancy occurs world wide. In tropical and under-developed countries it is often the result of infection, especially gastroenteritis, dehydration and malnutrition. In so-called civilised countries in the western world where adequate statistical information of causes of death is recorded, the incidence and causation of infant deaths are tabulated in detail. Different groups of causes can be separated off, e.g. infection, congenital abnormality, trauma etc. This leaves a residual number of infant deaths of undetermined cause which are grouped together under the diagnosis of sudden infant death syndrome. There are approximately 1,500 to 2,000 cases of sudden infant death syndrome, so called "cot deaths" (or "crib deaths" in the United States), in England and Wales in a year. 90% of them occur to babies under the age of 8 months, the majority between 2 and 5 months.

(2) The usual story is of a child who has been a little off colour, with non-specific symptoms such as "snuffles", a cold, loss of appetite, altered cry, sweating or a gastro-intestinal upset, being found dead by a parent in its cot when the time comes to give it a feed, the child having been well a few hours previously.

(3) It is recognised medically that such cases are more prone to occur where the mother is young, is a cigarette smoker, or has too many pregnancies too close to one another, or where the baby was small at birth or one of twins, or has been bottle fed rather than breast fed, the mother often belonging to social classes 4 or 5 in the Registrar General's Classification. That said, cot deaths occur throughout the whole community, no particular group or class being exempt. There is a higher incidence in the winter months in the United Kingdom.

(4) Very extensive research has been carried out in many countries over the last 30 years particularly, to elucidate the cause of this condition, but is must be said that there is no one clear cause of death. Many cases are thought to be due to upper respiratory tract infection, probably viral, with an added element of anoxia from obstruction of the upper air passages by mucus and/or pus, with other causes ascribed to allergy to cow's milk protein, conduction defects in the heart beat, lack of antibodies to protect the child from infection, metabolic disorders particularly associated with hypernatraemia (excessive sodium in the blood) from incorrect making up of milk feeds, disorders of the sleep/wake mechanism in young infants and many more.

(5) At post mortem the child is usually well nourished and well cared for with no marks of asphyxia or injury on the external surface of the body. Internally petechial haemorrhages are frequently found in the thymus gland, on the pleurae of the lungs and pericardial surface of the heart. These changes are indicative of anoxia and not asphyxia. There may be inhaled milk in the air passages, and a milk feed in the stomach.

(6) Microscopical examination of the tissues may show evidence of respiratory infection involving the lungs and air passages, and rarely infection of the brain or heart or kidneys. All such cases need to be examined by an experienced pathologist with a full range of back-up

facilities, including bacteriology, virology, clinical chemistry and histopathology. In a multi-centric survey carried out from 1976 to 1979 and published in 1984 by Knowelden *et al.*[1] where 988 cases of sudden infant deaths were reviewed, one third were found to have definite pathology recognisable at autopsy to account for death, one third had pathological changes which were not in themselves considered sufficient to be lethal, and one third had minimal or no findings at all. Less than 10% of these cases were ascribed to infanticide or trauma or other unnatural causes of death.

(7) It is extremely difficult for the pathologist at autopsy to differentiate between suffocation in an infant, either deliberate or accidental, and so-called "cot death". Unlike asphyxia in adults there may be minimal congestion and cyanosis and sometimes no petechial haemorrhages whatsoever externally. Pressure whitening around the nose and mouth may not be obvious and in the absence of a confession or statements by witnesses it may be impossible for the pathologist to declare beyond a peradventure that the cause of death in a given child was suffocation. However, statements made in the press or on the media that the majority of cot deaths are due to suffocation are clearly totally wrong, as is borne out by the statistics in the Knowelden Report described above.

ENDEAVOURING TO CONCEAL BIRTH

Law

3.06 Section 60 of the Offences against the Person Act 1861 makes it an offence if any woman is delivered of a child, for any person by any secret disposition of the dead body of the child, whether the child died before, at or after its birth, to endeavour to conceal the birth.

Medico-Legal Aspects of Endeavouring to Conceal Birth

3.07 This topic has already been touched on in the section on infanticide (para. 3.04 above). The child's body may be disposed of either simply or in an elaborate manner, sometimes being merely abandoned where it has been born, for example in a public lavatory, and the mother decamping, or it may be parcelled up and left in a public place, or an attempt made to dispose of it through the local refuse collection system. Sometimes attempts are made to burn the body; these are nearly always

1 Knowelden, J., Keeling, J. and Nicholl, J.P. (1984) A multicentric study of post-neonatal mortality. Report by Medical Care Research Unit, University of Sheffield.

unsuccessful. Disposal in rivers, estuaries and lakes are common and sometimes attempts are made to bury the body. This is probably the most successful method of disposal of all.

3.08 (1) The mother herself if she has given birth in a dwelling house will often seek to clear up all the evidence of the birth such as blood stains, amniotic fluid and other secretions, perhaps destroying or disposing of soiled bedding and clothing and seeking to resume her normal lifestyle as rapidly as possible without recourse to medical assistance. In this she is often successful, although she runs the risk of haemorrhage or infection of the genital tract. She may be troubled by her breasts from the unused milk secretion so that she may be driven to seek assistance.

(2) A doctor having to deal with such a patient may find himself in an awkward ethical position. His first duty is to treat the woman concerned and not make statements to the police without her consent. However the doctor may well find himself in a dilemma if he suspects he may become a party to concealment of a crime. In such circumstances he should seek advice from his medical defence organisation.

OFFENCES RELATING TO CHILDREN AND YOUNG PERSONS

Law

3.09 By statutory provisions under the Offences Against the Person Act 1861, and the Children and Young Persons Act 1933 as amended, Parliament has created offences of abandoning or exposing children under two years of age whereby life is endangered, and cruelty to persons under sixteen years of age. In the main the whole subject is now covered by the Children and Young Persons Act 1933. This places an obligation on any person who has attained the age of sixteen and has the custody, charge or care of any child or young person under the age of sixteen not to wilfully assault, ill-treat, neglect, abandon or expose the child, or cause him to be so treated in a manner likely to cause him unnecessary suffering or injury to health, including injury to or loss of sight, or hearing, or any limb or organ of the body, or any mental derangement. The Act makes it clear that a parent or other person legally liable to maintain a child or young person shall be deemed to have neglected him in a manner likely to cause injury to his health if he has failed to provide adequate food, clothing, medical aid or lodging for him, or if having been unable otherwise to provide such food, clothing, medical aid or lodging, he has failed to take steps to procure it to be provided under the Acts relating to the relief of the poor. Where it is proved that the death of an infant under the age of three years of age was caused by suffocation (not being suffocation caused by disease or the presence of any foreign body in the throat or air passages of the infant) while the infant was in bed with some other person who has attained the age of sixteen, if that other person was under the influence of drink when he went to bed, he shall be deemed to have neglected the infant in a manner likely to cause injury to its health.A person may still be convicted under section 1 notwithstanding that actual suffering or injury to health or the likelihood of actual suffering or injury to health, was obviated by the action of another person. He may still be convicted notwithstanding the death of the child or young person.

3.10 Abandoning or exposing children under 2 years of age in a manner whereby their life is endangered is an offence under section 27 of the Offences Against the Person Act 1861.

3.11 Cruelty to persons under 16 years of age is an offence under section 1(3) Children and Young Persons Act 1933, as amended by the Children and Young Persons Act 1963 and the Childrens Act 1975 Schedules 3 and 4. Section 1 of the 1933 Act creates a single wide-ranging offence dealing with various forms of cruelty, e.g. ill treating, wilfully assaulting, neglect, abandonment or exposure in a manner likely to cause unnecessary suffering or injury to health, including injury to or loss of sight or hearing or any limb or organ of the body and any mental derangement.

Neglect in Infancy

3.12 Reference has been made elsewhere to neglect, either inadvertent or deliberate, in adults, particularly the weak-minded and the elderly (see para. 1.111 above).

(1) Neglect in children is predominantly confined to infancy where the child is unable to speak for itself, to gain help or to escape from its environment, although cases are sometimes seen when older children have been confined to locked rooms, chicken houses, dog kennels and the like, sometimes for many years, totally intimidated by those who have incarcerated them.

(2) Neglect in infancy may be due to sheer ignorance, stupidity and incompetence on the part of the mother. She may be young, her partner may have abandoned her or been sent to prison or otherwise be absent from the scene and she may well be left to cope in totally unsuitable conditions without advice, help or supervision. She may not have adequate funds or know of the availability of the Social Services and medical help. As a result the baby may be inadequately clothed, fed and warmed. The infant will fail to gain weight, will become a prey to

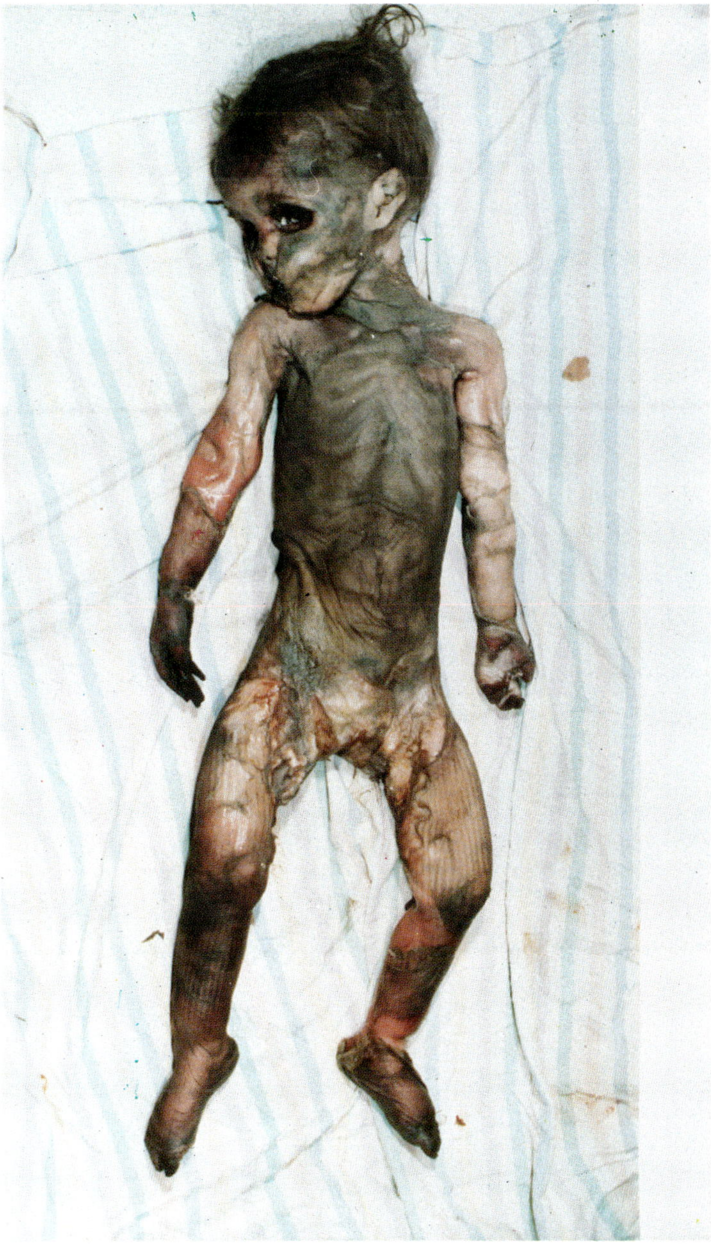

Plate 14. Post mortem decomposition and child neglect. Note body wasting

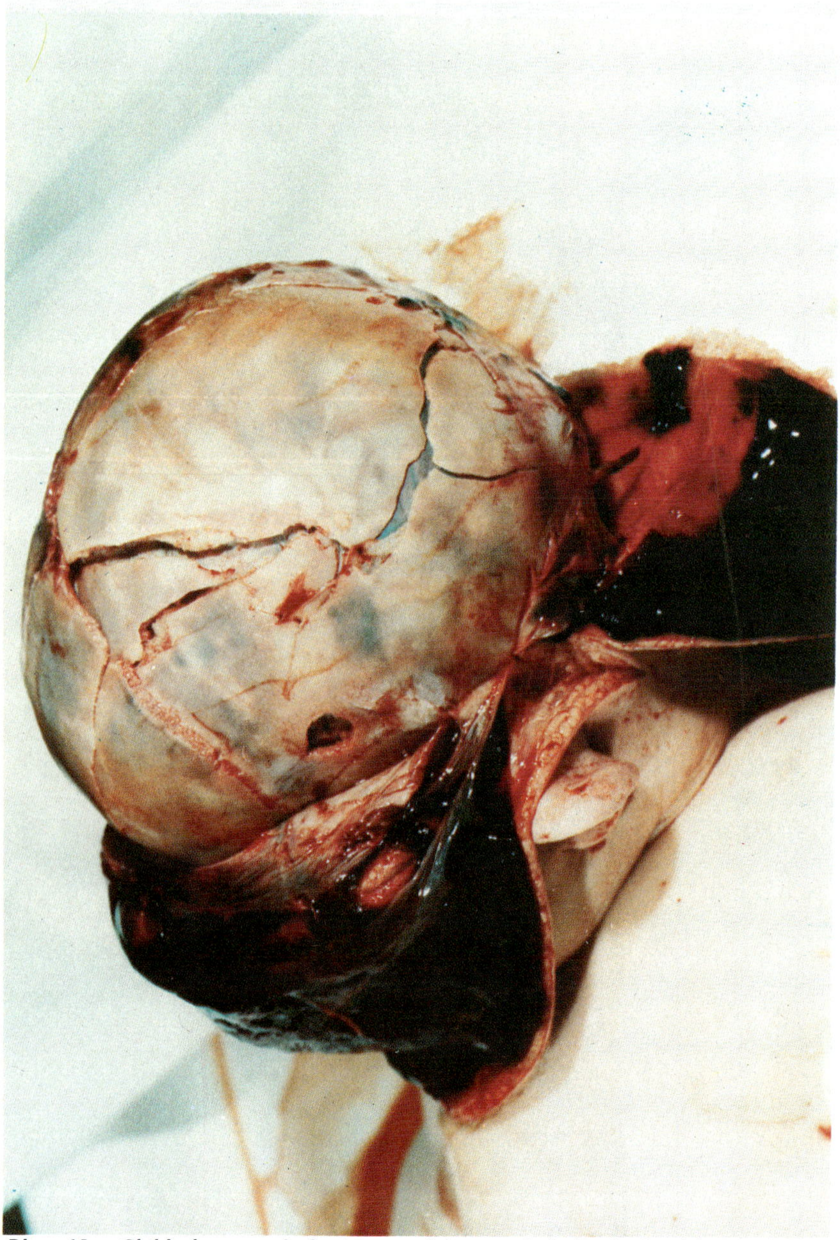

Plate 15. Child abuse: scalp bruising and fractured skull, the head having been struck against a wall

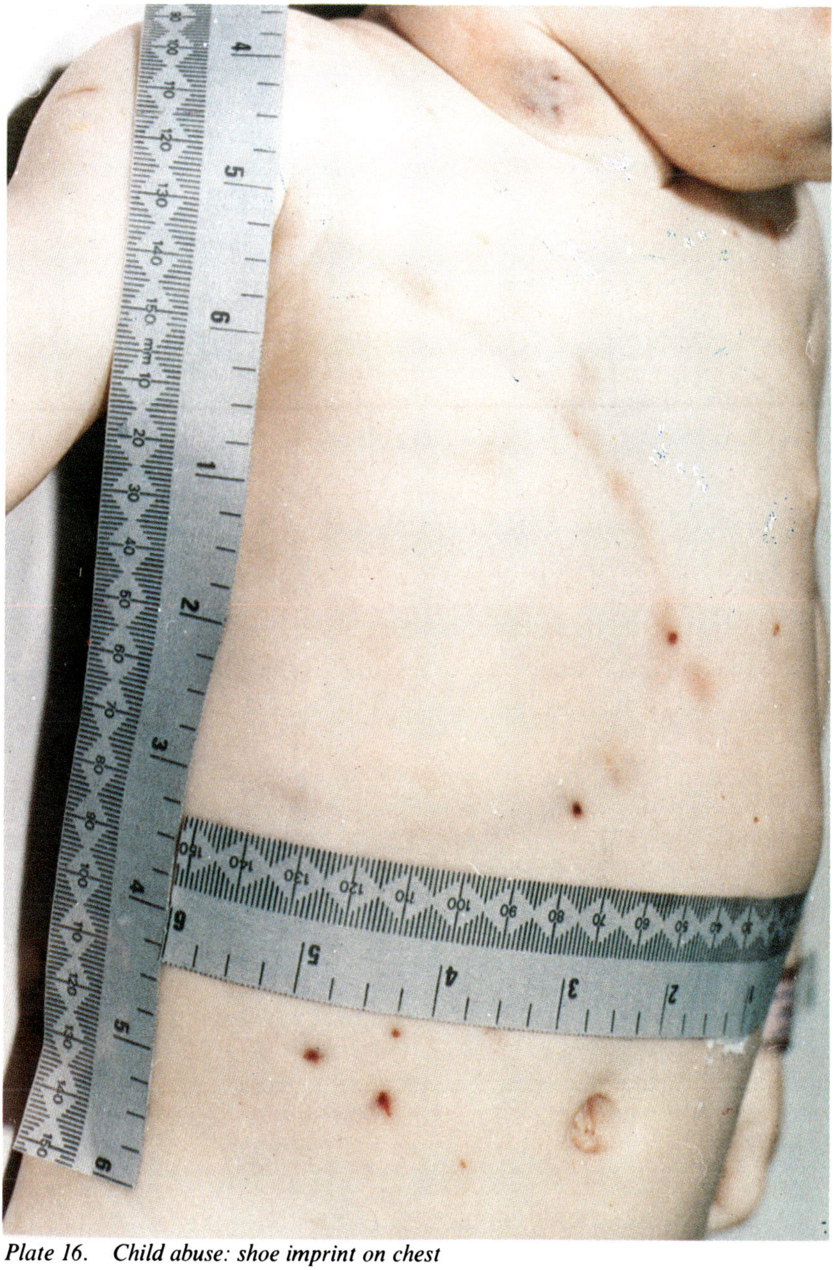

Plate 16. Child abuse: shoe imprint on chest

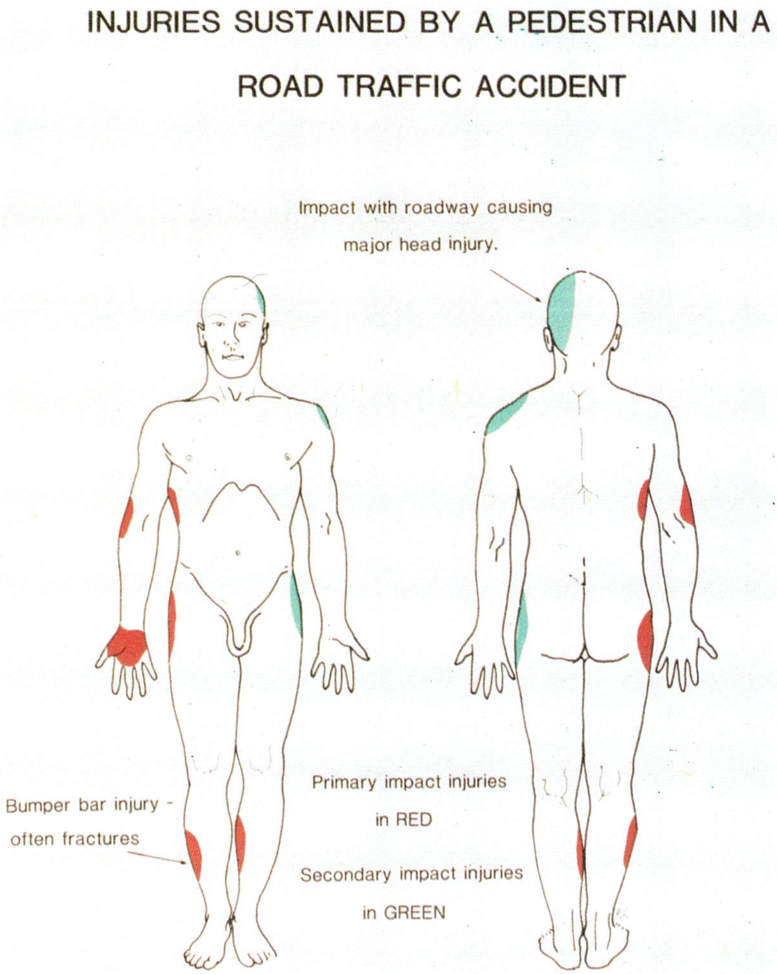

Plate 17. Injuries sustained by a pedestrian in a road traffic accident

infection and may even in extreme circumstances die, usually from pneumonia or gastroenteritis.

(3) At post mortem the infant is found to be dirty, smelly and emaciated, scantily clad and often with a very severe nappy rash, with superficial chemical burns of the skin from overconcentrated urine having been kept in contact with the child's buttocks, perhaps for days on end. There may be in addition faecal soiling of the lower part of the trunk and legs and the whole baby may look wizened and old.

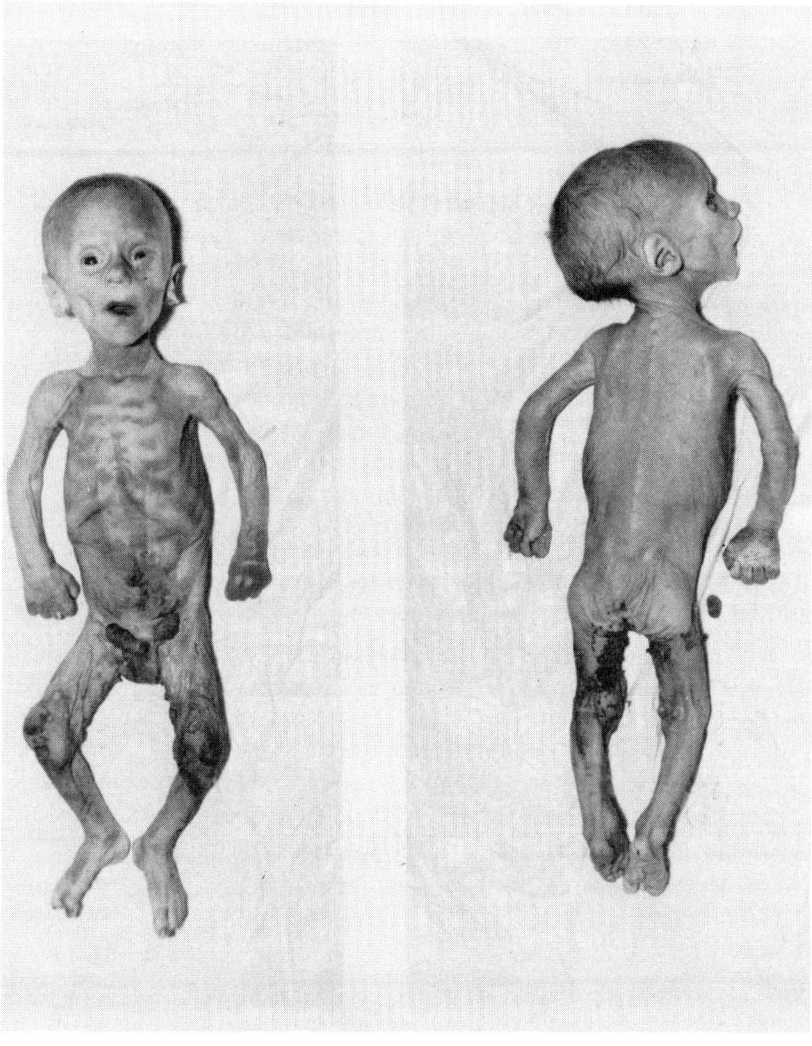

Fig. 3.2. Seven-month-old baby dying from starvation and neglect

(4) Older infants and toddlers may show evidence of vitamin deficiency, with anaemia, sores in the mouth, failure of superficial wounds to heal and bony abnormalities on X-ray from scurvy or rickets. Such extensive evidence of neglect takes weeks to appear and allegations that "it all happened in a few days" should be disregarded. It must however be remembered that an infant with severe gastroenteritis marked by profuse vomiting and diarrhoea may lose an astonishing amount of weight through fluid loss in a remarkably short space of time.

3.13 (1) If such an infant is found alive, he or she should be taken to hospital immediately and placed in the care of a consultant paediatrician, as court proceedings may ensue, for example a care order may be sought, and it is important that someone of standing and experience should be available to assist the court in the aftercare and disposal of the child when he or she has recovered.

(2) If the child is dead, then an experienced pathologist should conduct the autopsy in case criminal proceedings are taken against one or other parent or guardian. The pathologist must take care to exclude natural disease such as infection or congenital abnormality which may have predisposed to the infant's emaciation and failure to thrive.

(3) Deaths in infancy, whether due to neglect or injury, always evoke considerable emotional reaction in those having contact with the case and among the public at large, usually whipped up by the extravagances of the media, so it is as well for the lawyer and doctor to be prepared for the inevitable but unappealing publicity that may attend the case.

NON-ACCIDENTAL INJURY IN CHILDHOOD

3.14 The attention of the medical profession was first drawn to subdural haemorrhage and unexplained fractures in infancy by Caffey in 1946[2] and again in 1957[3], but it was not until Kempe[4] in 1962 in Denver, Colorado, coined the term "battered baby syndrome" that the full extent of the problem of non-accidental injury in childhood began to be appreciated by the medical profession and subsequently by the law and the public at large. Gross cruelty and neglect in infancy had been well recognised for many years and organizations like the National Society

2 Caffey, J. (1946) *Am. J. Roentg.*, *56*, 163-73, "Multiple fractures in long bones of infants suffering from chronic subdural haematoma".

3 Caffey, J. (1957) *Br. J. Radiol.*, *30*, 225-38, "Some traumatic lesions in growing bones other than fractures and dislocations: Clinical and radiological fractures".

4 Kempe, C.H., Silverman, F.N., Steele, B.F., Droegemeller, W. and Silver, H.K. (1962) *J.A.M.A.*, *181*, 17-24, "Battered child syndrome".

for the Prevention of Cruelty to Children and the Church of England Children's Society had been established along with Dr. Barnado's Homes to cope with these unfortunate children. It is a world-wide problem varying in differing parts of the world under different cultures. It is difficult to assess its incidence in the United Kingdom. It has been suggested that among battered children ten to fifteen per cent die and thirty per cent are medically handicapped, usually by brain damage.

3.15 When the child is brought to the doctor, usually with a severe injury such as a skull fracture or a major fracture to a limb bone, the person bringing the child will not give a true history. Examination of the child may reveal older injuries or scars or other superifical injuries elsewhere on the body and the explanations offered by the adult or adults will usually not correspond with the injuries. Such phrases as "he always bruises easily", "he fell out of his cot on to the floor" or "he fell down the stairs when he slipped out of my arms" are offered to explain for example a major head injury with a fractured skull. It must be appreciated that it takes major force and great violence to fracture the skull and bones of an infant or young child.

3.16 Enquiry into the social circumstances usually reveals that the child comes from a liaison where the mother and father are not married or where the man in the house is not the father of the child or there are severe deprivations, either of money or housing, or there is an excess of alcohol consumed. The child is often unwanted or is a nuisance. He may be a bedwetter or be backward as a result of earlier brain injury. Many assaults on such children occur over a period of time and may be precipitated by drink or exhaustion or exasperation; many occur during the hours that television programmes are on in the evenings, the child crying repeatedly and the viewing of the parents being constantly interrupted until tempers snap and injury is caused to the child. The child may be struck with the open hand, shaken vigorously, being held by the arms or gripped round the chest, or struck in the face or abdomen with a clenched fist. The child may be picked up and hurled across a room against a wall, thrown on the floor, through a doorway, down the stairs or even out of a window.

3.17 When the immediate emotional crisis has passed and the extent of the injuries to the child is appreciated, those responsible usually delay seeking medical advice in the hope that the child will recover. When it obviously does not, they then spend more time concocting some story in the hope of confusing the doctor to whom they take the child. It is this delay in seeking medical help that should alert the doctor to the possibility that the injuries are non-accidental, as the natural reaction of a normal parent whose child is injured accidentally is to pick up the child and run for help immediately.

3.18 The medical management of such cases must be rapidly undertaken and be comprehensive. If there is a suspicion of non-accidental injury, the child should be sent to hospital and put under the care of a consultant paediatrician, as his standing and experience will be vital not only for the care of the child but for the subsequent disposal of the child under supervision at home or into care under the local authority. The child should be admitted to hospital and a full history taken including particular enquiries as to previous injury or episodes of medical care. Many of these babies will have been found to have been injured previously and will have been taken to different doctors or medical centres so as not to arouse suspicion of deliberate injury. It may be that enquiry of neighbouring hospitals or doctors will reveal the true state of affairs, or the child may be found to be on an "at risk" register of the local authority following previous episodes elsewhere in the area or in the country.

3.19 There may be obvious discrepancies between the history given by the parents and the clinical findings of the doctor. Not only delay in seeking aid but repeated injuries are very suspicious, and abnormal reaction by a parent is also suspicious. Details should be sought of previous home addresses, illnesses, accidents and doctors' names and addresses and hospital treatment in the past as well as details of accidents to siblings of the child. Child abuse tends to run in families and one of the child's parents may have been battered as a child.

3.20 All injuries should be measured, charted and photographed. Bite marks (Fig. 3.3) and burn and scald marks (Fig. 3.4) should be looked for. The eyes in particular should be examined for evidence of haemorrhage in the retina and other intra-ocular abnormalities; these usually indicate brain damage.

3.21 The whole body should be X-rayed to see if there are fresh or healing fractures or old deformity and to exclude bone disease. The opinion of a consultant radiologist should be sought to report on the X-rays. Suspicious X-ray findings involve multiple bony injuries, especially near the joints, fractures in various stages of healing, displacement of the growing ends of the bones (ephiphyses), fractures of the shafts of long bones, abnormalities of the shape of the bones as compared with the other side of the body and spiral fractures in the limb bones; these latter

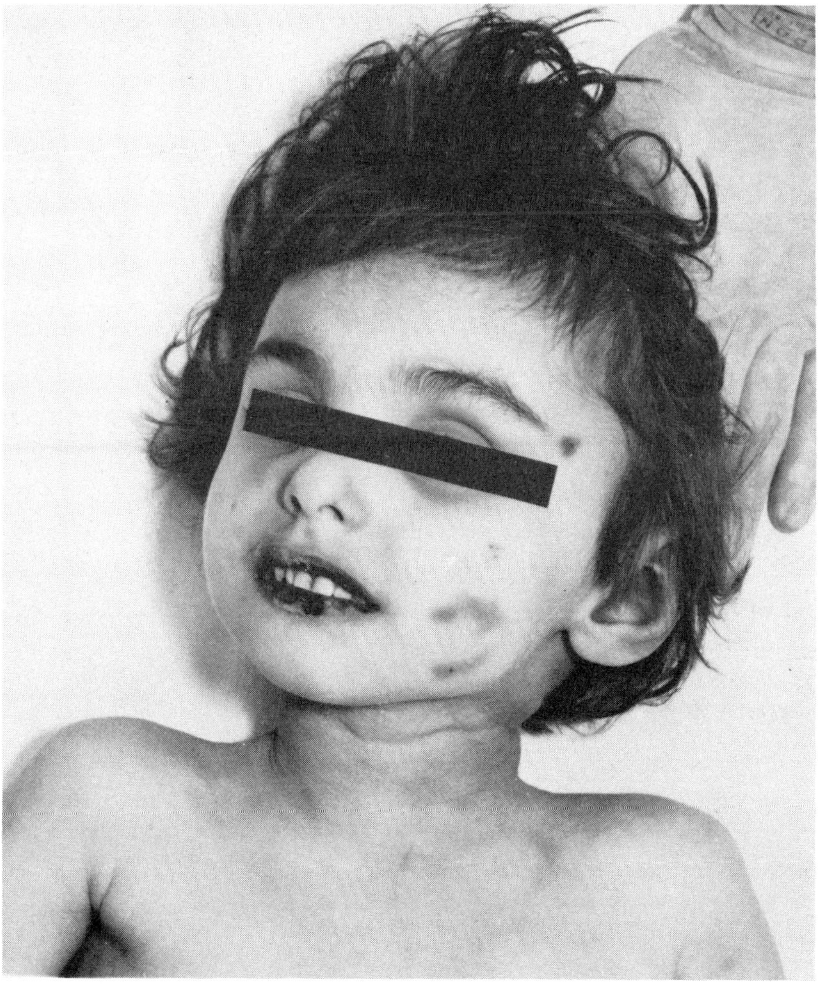

Fig. 3.3. Child abuse: bite mark on cheek

are nearly always caused by the child being seized by a hand or foot which is used as a lever to swing the child and dash it against a hard surface. If there is bleeding or bruising present, defects of blood coagulation should be excluded by haematological examination.

3.22 There should be consultation throughout the child's stay in hospital between the doctors in the various specialities concerned with the treatment of the child, the general practitioner, if there is one, who has seen the child or is likely to be involved in its aftercare, the nursing staff

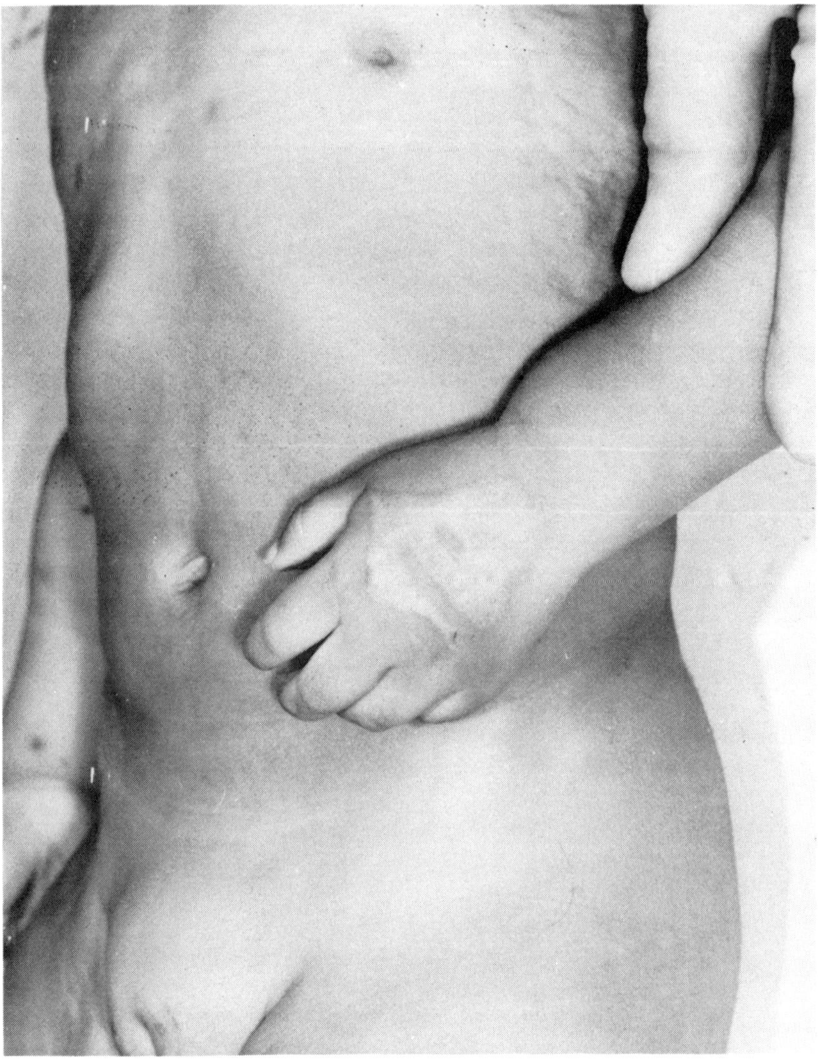

Fig. 3.4. Child abuse: old burn scar on back of hand

and health visitors from the Social Services. The child must not be discharged from the hospital without the agreement of all concerned. The child's progress should be carefully recorded throughout its stay in hospital and the parental attitudes noted by staff members who have contact with them during visiting. Careful examination of the child during visits may show evidence of terror, or subsequent examination may show evidence of fresh injury.

Fig. 3.5. Child abuse: hair pulled out by the roots

3.23 All concerned with the baby's care should consider carefully whether the police should be contacted. Doctors are usually reluctant to involve the police until it is too late. It is much better to make contact early, with senior consultants discussing the case with senior police officers so that responsible decisions can be made in the child's interest. The possibility of psychiatric or social help for the parents and the rest of the family must be considered in the disposal of the child following its recovery. It may be that he or she will be returned to the parents with careful follow-up visits by the general practitioner and social worker or it may be that the child will be better placed with grandparents or other family members. Sometimes the safest course, albeit taken reluctantly, will be to put the child in an institution under a Place of Safety Order after recourse to the courts.

3.24 Nowadays the vast majority of cases of child abuse are recognised clinically and treated swiftly and, thankfully, the mortality is now very much smaller than it was a decade or more ago. However, from time to time a particularly violent assault on a child may result in its death or a child may be brought in to the casualty department of a hospital dead, the parents giving a story suggestive of a "cot death." The case is reported to the Coroner and the hospital pathologist commences an autopsy, only to discover injuries such as a fractured skull or ruptured liver. He should at once stop the autopsy, call for an experienced pathologist and inform the Coroner and the C.I.D.

Post mortem examination

3.25 The pathologist asked to carry out a post mortem examination on a case suspected to be due to non-accidental injury must treat the case as being one of suspected murder. The Coroner's Officer or senior C.I.D. officer should be asked to assemble a full police investigative team, including an identification officer, a photographer and a scenes of crime officer, and have present any doctor or other person who has had care of the child in life prior to its death, either in hospital or at home. The pathologist should appraise himself of all the circumstances relating up to the child's death as far as they are known.

3.26 The child's body must be photographed completely front and back and a full skeletal X-ray survey of the head, trunk and limbs should be carried out if this has not already been done. Often the pathologist will find that some X-rays have been taken, usually of the head and chest, but that the other parts of the body have not been X-rayed. He should make sure that this is done. He should examine all the X-rays for the injuries and abnormalities outlined at para. 3.21 above. If he is uncertain he should ask for a consultant radiologist's opinion. After the child's body has been photographed completely, the pathologist should always commence the examination with the head and neck because the bulk of such infants die from head injury.

The scalp should be reflected to expose the skull and any fractures seen should be photographed (see Plate 15). While the vault of the skull is being removed it is important that the pathologist place a tray or some other collecting bowl under the head, as in many cases the cause of death will be subdural haemorrhage (bleeding beneath the membranes covering the brain—see para. 1.102 above). Such blood will often be fluid and will run out before the skull cap is fully removed and may be lost unless arrangements are made to collect, measure or weigh the blood or blood clot.

Once the skull cap has been removed, if the brain is seen to be damaged or covered with blood it should be photographed prior to its removal. All subdural blood and blood clots should be collected, weighed and measured. Usually a quantity of 20 to 40 ml of blood, something of the order of an ounce, is all that is found. However, it must be appreciated that the child's brain is usually very tightly applied to the membranes of the skull, which in turn are adherent to the skull itself in infancy and that a quantity of 30 ml of blood represents a very large amount of extra material inside the head. Such a quantity of blood clot may press on the brain, displacing it to one side or more often downwards, causing major changes to the circulation of the blood to and from the brain without the brain itself being overtly damaged (see Plate 7 and para. 1.102 above). When the blood clot has been removed and measured and the brain dissected free from the skull, it is often found to be intact to the naked eye or only suffering from minimal damage. However, microscopic examination may reveal deep-seated changes due to cutting off parts of the blood supply, particularly around the base of the brain, or there may be pressure damage around the top of the spinal cord and brain stem, so-called "coning". The brain should be retained by the pathologist for fixation in formalin and subsequent dissection, as infants' brains are remarkably soft and if cut fresh often tend to disintegrate and detail may be obscured or lost during too precipitate an examination. Once the brain has been removed, the base of the skull should be examined for further fractures, thrombosis of the venous sinuses or infection in the middle ears.

3.27 Post mortem examination of the rest of the child's body should be equally careful. Dissection of the chest and abdominal wall may reveal bruising that was not apparent externally, particularly if the child has a deeply pigmented skin, or there may be evidence of old injuries and deformity of the rib cage which did not show up on an X-ray, which may not have been taken at the best angle to demonstrate such abnormalities; these should be photographed whenever they are found. Photography under ultra violet light may help to demonstrate bruising in coloured infants which is not clearly apparent under normal lighting. Apart from thc head injuries described above and the bony injuries to the skeleton, there are often bruises caused by fierce gripping, particularly around the upper arms or the ankles or the front and back of the chest. Such fingertip bruises are usually about 1 cm across; they vary from red when freshly inflicted to blue after some hours and then they fade over the course of the ensuing week. There may also be fresh or old burns on the skin, either caused by cigarettes being extinguished on the child's flesh or by the child being held against a fire. There may be human bite marks. All such injuries should be photographed with a scale beside them.

3.28 (1) If there are bite marks present, then the opinion of a forensic odontologist should be sought before the wound is cut out and distorted by shrinkage, as the odontologist may be able to obtain a pattern of the bite which can be identified with an assailant, for example a parent. It requires very great force to inflict a persistent bite mark on a child and stories that it was only a "love bite" should not be believed (see photograph Fig. 3.3 at para. 3.20 above). It is often worth taking a swab from such bite marks to see if a trace of saliva can be identified and possibly matched with the secretor group of the person inflicting the bite.

(2) There may be evidence of sexual injury, either digital dilation and splitting of the anal margin or of the vulva and vagina or bruising of the penis. All such soft tissue injuries should be carefully photographed.

(3) One very characteristic injury is tearing of the frenulum of the upper lip, the fold of skin attaching the centre of the upper lip to the gum. In many cases of child abuse this is found to be torn. Older children may be found to have teeth knocked out and if the child has teeth, bruising and tearing of the inner aspect of the lips may be found where blows to the mouth to silence screaming have caused the lips to be driven against the teeth (see Fig. 3.6).

3.29 Chest injuries are usually confined to fractured ribs. It takes great force to fracture ribs, usually by fierce gripping or striking the child's back against a projecting surface like the edge of a table. This is because the child's ribs are extremely elastic. There can be extreme compression of the child's chest with the ribs springing back into the normal place without fractures, but internal soft tissue injury particularly to the liver may result from the gripping and compression of the chest. The heart and lungs are not often damaged, although there may be bruising of these structures. The main result of compression of the chest is rupture of the

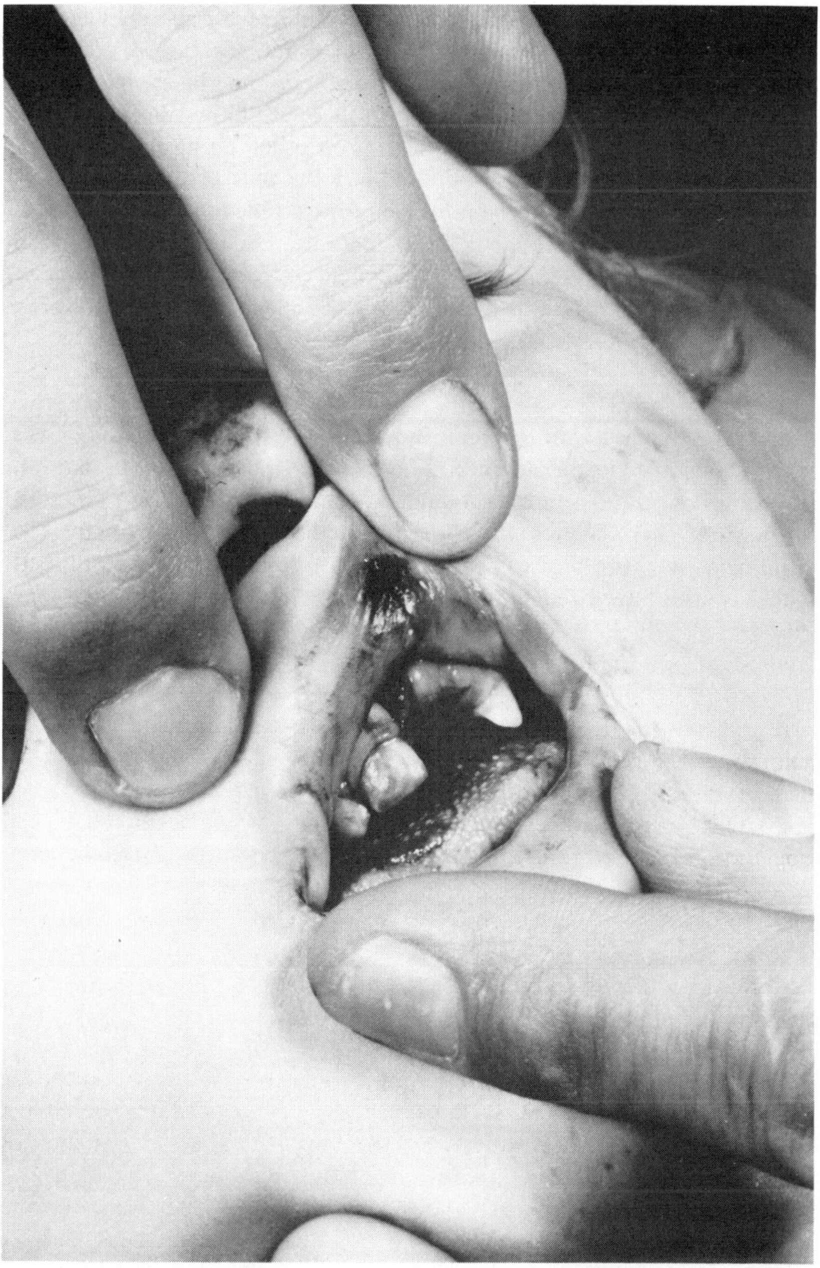

Fig. 3.6. Child abuse: injuries inside mouth from violent blow with fist

liver, more often of the right lobe, without there necessarily being any external sign of bruising on the abdominal wall or lower chest. The liver is a very friable organ and is easily crushed and torn. Less often the spleen below the ribs on the left side of the body may be similarly torn. The kidneys usually escape injury unless there are blows directly struck on the child's loin. Blows with the fist or other blunt injury to the abdomen may not injure the abdominal wall but may result in tearing of the upper small intestine at the junction of the duodenum, which is fixed, and the jejunum, the next part of the small intestine, which is mobile. In addition the mesentery, that is the attachment of the bowel to the back of the abdomen which contains blood vessels to and from the intestine, may be torn by blunt injury, resulting in intra-abdominal haemorrhage.

3.30 Besides a naked eye examination of the entire body, representative portions of tissue should be removed from all the main organs of the body for microscopic examination to exclude the presence of natural disease or congenital abnormality and to confirm the naked eye findings. Twenty-four hours later the body should be re-examined by the pathologist, as often bruises have "come out" following refrigeration. If further bruises have become visible, these should be photographed.

CHAPTER 4

Offences Relating to Motor Vehicles

LAW

Injuries arising from Furious Driving of Carriages or Vehicles

4.01 Section 35 of the Offences Against the Person Act 1861 provides:

> "Whoever having the charge of any carriage or vehicle, shall by wanton or furious driving or racing, or other wilful misconduct, or by wilful neglect, do or cause to be done any bodily harm to any person whatsoever shall be guilty of an offence and being convicted thereof shall be liable, at the discretion of the court to be imprisoned for any term not exceeding two years."

This section applies to all carriages and vehicles, public or private, and includes bicycles and is not restricted to driving on a road.

Causing Death by Reckless Driving

4.02 Section 1 of Road Traffic Act 1972, as amended by the Criminal Law Act 1977, states:

> "A person who causes the death of another person by driving a motor vehicle on a road recklessly shall be guilty of an offence."

The offence of causing death by reckless driving of a motor vehicle on a road still constitutes manslaughter at common law, though it has been a statutory offence since 1956.[1] Evidence of the consumption of drink or drugs (which include toluene, a constituent chemical in "Evo-Stick") is relevant to the issue whether the defendant was driving recklessly.[2] The prosecution must prove that the defendant caused the death of another person, who may be a passenger in the defendant's car. The Court of Appeal in *R. v. Hennigan,*[3] a case of causing death by dangerous driving, reviewed earlier cases and said that the proper way for a jury to be directed with regard to causation is for them to be told to consider whether the defendant's driving is *a* cause, and it no longer has to be a *substantial* cause. Lord Parker C. J. said at p. 135:

1 *Government of U.S.A. v. Jennings* (1982) 75 Cr.App.R. 367 H.L. (an extradition case).
2 *Bradford v. Wilson* (1984) 78 Cr.App.R. 77.
3 [1971] 3 All E.R. 133.

> "The Court would like to emphasise that there is nothing in the statute which requires the manner of the driving to be a substantial cause or a major cause or any other description of cause, of the accident; so long as the dangerous driving is *a* cause and something more than *de minimis*, the statute operates."

For causation generally see para. 1.02 above, but note the case of *R. v. Malcherek*,[4] a murder case, in which the victim was placed on a life support machine because of the danger of brain damage resulting from a period when the heart was not beating. After tests were carried out to confirm that the victim appeared to have suffered irretrievable brain damage, it was decided to disconnect the life support system and the victim was declared dead. At the trial, the judge, after hearing submissions, decided to withdraw from the jury the issue of the cause of the victim's death on the ground that at the time of death, the original injuries inflicted on the victim were an operating cause of death and that it was not open to the jury to conclude that the accused had not caused the death of the victim. The Court of Appeal held that where competent and careful medical treatment given to a victim for an injury inflicted by an assailant included putting the victim on a life support machine, the decision by the medical practitioners concerned to disconnect the machine because by generally accepted medical criteria the victim was dead, could not exonerate the assailant from responsibility for the death if at the time of death the original injury was a continuing and operating cause of the death, for then the disconnection of the machine did not break the chain of causation between the infliction of the original injury and the death. The same principle would undoubtedly apply in cases of causing death by reckless driving. In cases of murder and manslaughter (see Chapter 1) death must occur within a year and a day, and there is no reason to think that the legal position is any different in cases of causing death by reckless driving.

Drunk driving

Driving or attempting to drive a motor vehicle when unfit through drink or drugs, or being in charge of a motor vehicle when unfit to drive through drink or drugs.

4.03 Section 5 Road Traffic Act 1972 states:

> "(1) A person who when driving or attempting to drive a motor vehicle on a road or other public place is unfit to drive through drink or drugs shall be guilty of an offence.

4 [1981] 2 All E.R. 422.

(2) Without prejudice to sub-section (1) above, a person who, when in charge of a motor vehicle which is on a road or other public place, is unfit to drive through drink and drugs shall be guilty of an offence.

(3) For the purposes of this section a person shall be taken to be unfit to drive if his ability to drive properly is for the time being impaired."

These offences are only triable summarily. "Drug" includes insulin. The term drug includes something given to cure or alleviate or assist an ailing body.[5] Section 12 of the Road Traffic Act 1972 as amended defines "drug" as including any intoxicant other than alcohol. "Intoxicant" seems to mean any substance that poisons or affects the body. *Watmore v. Jenkins*[6] is a case in which a diabetic driver collapsed while driving owing to a number of causes including an injection of insulin. He was charged with (1) driving while unfit to drive through drugs, contrary to section 6(1) of the Road Traffic Act 1960; (2) dangerous driving contrary to section 2(1) of the Road Traffic Act 1960; and (3) driving without due care and attention contrary to section 3(1) of the Road Traffic Act 1960. It was held that the acquittal under section 6(1) would be upheld since the Justices were entitled on the special facts of the case to entertain a reasonable doubt whether the injected insulin was more than a predisposing or historical cause comprised in a situation of equilibrium on which the reduction of cortisone operated as an effective cause of the hypoglycaemic episode.

In *R. v. Bailey*[7] the Court of Appeal decided that diabetes (unlike intoxication from alcohol or drugs) could provide a defence not only to crimes of specific intent but also of basic intent. The Court added that the question was whether the Crown had proved the necessary element of recklessness. Similar principles appear to apply in epilepsy cases. It is submitted by Halnan and Spencer[8] that there can be no defence to a charge of reckless or careless driving if the defendant knew of the risks of epilepsy or knew he was a diabectic and was aware of the risks of too much or too little insulin. Where a person commits an offence under the influence of epilepsy, the strict jury verdict should be "not guilty by reason of insanity."[9] Cases concerning epilepsy must be treated accordingly if tried on indictment.

Blood alcohol limits

Driving or being in charge of a motor vehicle with alcohol concentration above prescribed limit.

5 *Armstrong v. Clark* (1957) 41 Cr.App.R. 56.
6 [1962] 2 All E.R. 868.
7 [1983] 2 All E.R. 503.
8 Wilkinson's *Road Traffic Offences*, 12th ed.
9 *R. v. Sullivan* [1983] 2 All E.R. 673.

4.04 Section 6 of the Road Traffic Act 1972 as amended states:

> "(1) If a person:
> (*a*) drives or attempts to drive a motor vehicle on a road or other public place; or
> (*b*) is in charge of a motor vehicle on a road or other public place;
> after consuming so much alcohol that the proportion of it in his breath, blood or urine exceeds the prescribed limit, he shall be guilty of an offence."

These offences are only triable summarily, as are all offences involving drink/driving. The prescribed limit is defined in Section 12 of the Road Traffic Act 1972 as amended as follows:

(a) 35 microgrammes of alcohol in 100 millilitres of breath,
(b) 80 milligrammes of alcohol in 100 millilitres of blood, or
(c) 107 milligrammes of alcohol in 100 millilitres of urine

or such other proportion as may be prescribed by regulation made by the Secretary of State.

Protection for Hospital Patients

4.05 Section 9 of the Road Traffic Act 1972 as amended states:

> "(1) While a person is at a hospital as a patient he shall not be required to provide a specimen of breath for a breath test or to provide a specimen for a laboratory test unless the medical practitioner in immediate charge of his case has been notified of the proposal to make the requirement;
> and
> (a) if the requirement is then made it shall be for the provision of a specimen at the hospital; but
> (b) if the medical practitioner objects on the ground specified in subsection (2) below the requirement shall not be made.
> (2) The ground on which the medical practitioner may object is that the requirement or the provision of a specimen or in the case of a specimen of blood or urine, the warning required under section 8(8), would be prejudicial to the proper care and treatment of the patient.

Section 8(8) states that:

> "On requiring any person to provide a specimen a constable shall warn him that a failure to provide it may render him liable to prosecution."

"Hospital" is defined in Section 12(2), as amended, as an institution which provides medical or surgical treatment for in-patients or out-patients. In *Attorney General's Reference (No. 1 of 1976)*,[10] the Court of Appeal decided that "at a hospital" in this context means anywhere within the hospital precincts, including the car park, and that "patient" means anyone who is at the hospital for the purpose of treatment (as an

10 [1977] 3 All E.R. 577.

in-patient or as an out-patient), but he ceases to be a patient as soon as the treatment contemplated for that visit is over. This would not seem to apply to a person in an ambulance on his way to hospital.[11]

In cases of immediate death the pathologist should collect the blood and urine samples with a view to giving evidence on the results in Court.

Where a patient is admitted to hospital, no sample should be given to the police without the patient's express permission. Any blood samples should be collected by a police surgeon, not the hospital doctor.[12]

ROAD TRAFFIC INJURIES, FATAL AND NON-FATAL

4.06 Every year up to 6,000 people are killed on the roads in England and Wales and about a third of a million injured, many of them seriously. The pathologist carrying out an autopsy on a road traffic accident victim should not merely content himself with finding the exact cause of death. He should be prepared to make a careful note of all the injuries with a view to their interpretation and a possible reconstruction of all the events of the accident leading to the victim's death. He must explore the possibility whether natural disease has caused or contributed to the accident, for example by the sudden rupture of an aneurysm or the presence of a coronary thrombosis, and describe the state of the body and the internal organs, particularly as regards disease with a view to giving an opinion as to the likely expectation of life for possible insurance purposes. He should collect samples of blood and urine and possibly other materials for analysis for the presence or absence of alcohol and/or drugs. Lastly he must try to assess the effects of any treatment that the deceased might have received prior to his or her death.

4.07 Victims' injuries, which are usually multiple, can be fatal or non-fatal. They may be both external and internal.

(1) Examples of *external injuries* include bumper bar wounds to the legs with crushing of the soft tissues and fractures of shin bones, the pattern of a tyre mark on the clothing or skin of a victim who has been run over (see Fig. 4.1), and abrasions and lacerations caused by crushing and pinning under vehicles. External injuries can often be separated off into primary impact injuries, for example in the case of a pedestrian struck by a motor vehicle, the actual impact of the vehicle against the victim causing injuries to the legs, and secondary impact injuries from the victim being thrown down on the roadway, often causing a fatal head

11 *Hollingsworth v. Howard* [1974] R.T.R. 58.
12 See Ministry of Health Circular H.M. (67) 64 quoted in (1967) *Br. Med. J. 4*, 41 (7 October); quoted in full in (1967) *Br. Med. J. Supplement*, *3*, 142.

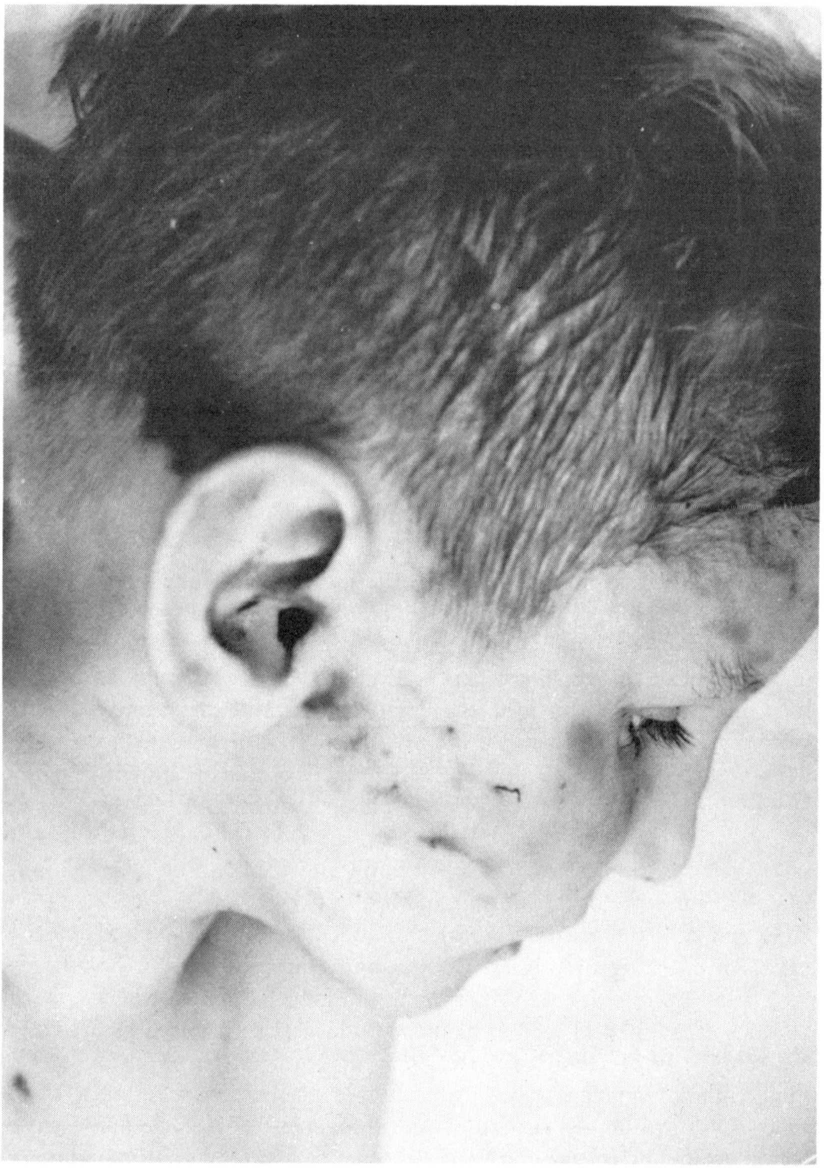

Fig. 4.1. Tyre marks on face

wound on the opposite side of the body. There may be more complicated injuries caused by the victim being run over by a following vehicle or one coming from the opposite direction.

(2) *Internal injuries* are predominantly head injuries, particularly among pedestrians and motor vehicle occupants. There may be very little external sign of injury but very extensive internal damage. Death may result early from shock and haemorrhage or later from complications including infection, embolism, pneumonia, kidney failure and toxaemia from pressure sores.

Pedestrians

4.08 (1) Pedestrians are the most frequently injured of road users, principally because they are the most numerous and are unprotected. Among them the most vulnerable are the elderly and small children. The elderly generally are slow-thinking, often deaf with poor vision and not very mobile because of arthritis and generalised debility. The young are vulnerable because, although they have all the physical attributes that the old lack, they do not have the experience and wisdom that come with age, so that they lack all judgement and may dash out into the road without looking. Small children are often just that, and may be hidden from view by parked vehicles until it is too late for a driver to avoid an accident.

(2) Victims nearly always present to the doctor with primary and secondary impact injuries as outlined above; by far the commonest major injury is bruising of the brain with overlying bleeding and fracturing of the skull on the opposite side of the head to that on which the victim was originally struck by the vehicle (see Plate 17). The victim's head strikes the ground and there is rapid deceleration. The brain, however, is free to move inside the skull and does so sustaining injury both at the site of impact, the so-called coup injury, but even more so on the opposite side of the brain, often described as contre-coup injury. The person may be thrown forwards into the roadway or upwards on to the bonnet and against the windscreen of the vehicle and subsequently fall off on to the roadway, sustaining a different series of injuries at each stage in the process, including possibly being run over. An experienced pathologist should be able to reconstruct the sequence of events from the injuries in the majority of cases.

(3) Prior to examining the body itself at post mortem, the pathologist should, if possible, examine the clothing worn by the deceased. If it has been removed prior to removal of the body to the mortuary, he should ask for it to be brought to him. He should look for marks such as tyre imprints and for foreign material such as paint flakes or glass fragments. All such trace evidence should be collected and preserved in labelled clean

containers and handed to the Coroner's Officer or the police officer responsible for exhibits. This is particularly important in "hit and run" accidents. In such cases the pathologist should retain samples of blood and head hair for grouping and comparing with possible traces found on a suspect vehicle. Any foreign material found in wounds on the victim by the pathologist should be similarly preserved.

Pedal Cyclists

4.09 Pedal cyclists are among the most vulnerable of road users, as they are mixed in among the traffic and not segregated from it on the pavement. The majority are either schoolchildren predominantly boys, or men going to work. They may suffer very extensive injuries from falling under the wheels of lorries and other heavy vehicles. The primary impact injury may be only a glancing blow to a leg and as with the pedestrian thrown down or struck down by a vehicle, so the pedal cyclist who is not required to wear any protective head gear is knocked into the roadway and frequently suffers potentially fatal head injuries.

Motor Cyclists

4.10 Motor cyclists are usually youths or young men aged between 17 and 30. They may contribute to their own destruction by excessive speed and irresponsible riding. Primary impact injuries may be to the leg or to the chest if the victim runs into a stationary vehicle, often causing a ruptured heart or aorta. The impact of a collision or of striking the kerb or other roadside feature combined with the speed of the motor cycle will project the rider into the road or against a wall or some other unyielding surface, so that he will sustain severe or even fatal head injuries despite the obligatory wearing of a crash helmet. However, there is no doubt whatever that the legal obligation to wear crash helmets has considerably reduced the number of fatal head injuries among motor cyclists and their pillion passengers. Broken legs are another characteristic feature of motor cycle accident victims, particularly if the motor cycle is a heavy one and the rider's leg is pinned under it.

Motor Vehicle Occupants

4.11 (1) There are different patterns of injury according to where the victim is sitting in the car. In general terms the bigger the car the better, the back seats are safer than the front seats, and it is much safer to remain in the car following a crash than to be ejected from it. Sometimes the pathologist may be the only person who can tell who was the driver where all the occupants of a car have been ejected following a crash.

(2) The most dangerous seat in the car is the front passenger seat. If the passenger is not restrained by a seatbelt, he or she may be projected against or through the windscreen when the car crashes, sustaining multiple facial cuts which may involve the eyes and primary impact injuries to the knees, which strike the undersurface of the fascia of the dashboard. Such an impact may fracture the patella, cause a fracture dislocation of the knee joint or be transmitted to the hip causing dislocation of the hip joint, particularly if the passenger is sitting with his or her legs crossed prior to impact. Ejection from the vehicle nearly always leads to a fatal head injury as well as further soft tissue injuries. The compulsory wearing of front seatbelts has considerably reduced the number of deaths and serious injuries among front seat passengers (see below).

4.12 (1) The driver, if not restrained by a seatbelt, is similarly likely to be thrown against the windscreen and sustain facial and head injuries, but he is not so likely to be ejected from the vehicle as he will probably be holding the steering wheel at the time of the crash. He will thus receive a violent impact from the steering wheel when he is thrown against it, possibly fracturing his wrists, his sternum or more commonly the ribs on one side of the body or the other, the instinct of the driver being at the

INJURIES SUSTAINED BY UNRESTRAINED MOTOR VEHICLE OCCUPANTS

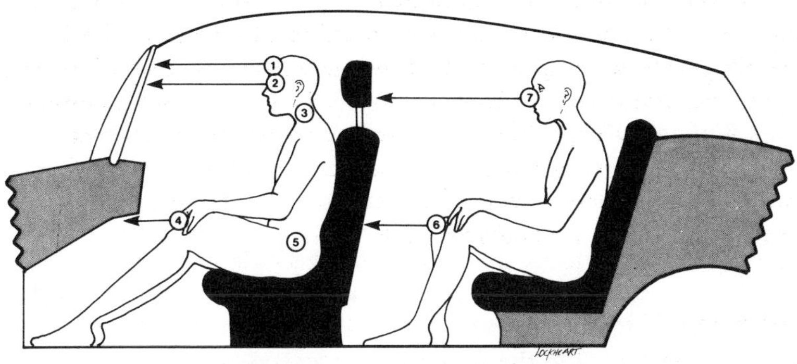

① - Facial cuts
② - Eye injuries
③ - Neck injuries
④ - Knee injury - fractures
⑤ - Hip injury - fracture or dislocation
⑥ - Knee injury - fractures
⑦ - Facial injury

Fig. 4.2.

INJURIES SUSTAINED BY UNRESTRAINED MOTOR VEHICLE OCCUPANTS

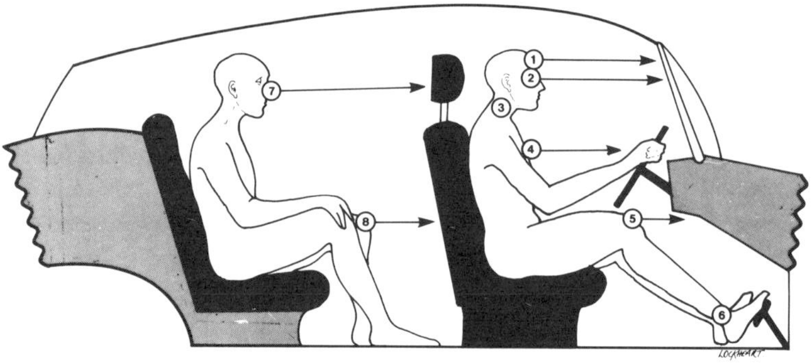

(1) - Facial cuts
(2) - Eye injuries
(3) - Neck injury
(4) - Chest injuries - fractured ribs or sternum
(5) - Knee injury - fractures
(6) - Ankle injury - fractures
(7) - Facial injury
(8) - Knee injury

Fig. 4.3.

last second to turn and put his hand up to prevent personal injury, so that the impact on the chest is not central. The steering wheel injury may cause considerable damage to the heart and aorta or lungs. He may suffer injuries from striking the undersurface of the dashboard or he may sustain fractures of the ankle, particularly if he is pressing the pedals as hard as he can in an attempt to stop the vehicle.

(2) He and his passenger may suffer neck injuries, particularly a fracture dislocation of the cervical spine in its middle or lower part, a so-called whip-lash injury caused by the rapid flexing and extending of the head on impact and immediately following it. The recent introduction of head-rests is designed to prevent this type of injury.

(3) If the driver is thrown from the vehicle, he too, like his passenger, may sustain further head injury. If he has been driving the car with one hand "holding the roof on", the arm outside the window may be badly injured or even amputated in the crash, as it is very difficult for the driver to get his arm back into the car quickly in a sudden emergency.

4.13 (1) It has been estimated that the compulsory wearing of seatbelts, which became law at the end of January 1983, has prevented an estimated 200 deaths and 7,000 injuries each year in the U.K. At the same time there has been a rise in deaths among rear seat passengers and pedestrians and cyclists after the introduction of the regulations. It is possible that the higher death rate may be due to changes of distribution in passengers between the front and rear seats in cars.

(2) At the same time studies of injuries to car occupants restrained by seatbelts has shown an increase in the number of facial injuries among car drivers from their faces striking the hub or boss of the steering column and also chest and abdominal injuries, notably to the clavicle, ribs and sternum. The majority of these cases are probably due to the incorrect fitting and wearing of the seatbelts, although some of the inertia type belts undoubtedly do not react quickly enough in a high-speed collison to restrain the driver adequately and protect him from injury.

(3) The introduction of compulsory rear seatbelts would probably save lives and prevent or reduce injuries not only to rear seat passengers but also to front seat occupants, who may well be injured by the unrestrained impact of those sitting behind them and flung forward during a collision. Powerful lobby groups have so far prevented or delayed the implementation of compulsory seatbelts for all car seats, but it is to be remembered that there was similar reaction to compulsory wearing of crash helmets by motor cycle riders and pillion passengers when legislation was first introduced. Apart from an occasional protest, usually by the Sikh community who wear turbans, there is now little public controversy over the compulsory wearing of such crash helmets. At present anchorage points must be fitted but rear seatbelts themselves are not yet mandatory.

4.14 The back seat passengers are more likely to escape, if not completely uninjured, at least with only superficial wounds, although they may cause further injuries to the front seat occupants if they are projected forward within the confines of the car body following impact, and if they themselves are ejected from the vehicle, they may sustain serious head injuries. They may suffer facial injuries from striking the front seat head rests, particularly if these are not enclosed in padding, or from other projecting features within the car interior. (See earlier diagrams Figs. 4.2 and 4.3).

4.15 Frequently death occurs some days or even weeks following a road traffic accident when some injuries have healed, others may have become infected, operations performed and complications set in. Here the doctor who originally treated the injuries may be in a better position than the pathologist to describe and interpret the injuries in court, although the latter still has an important part to play in evaluating the effects of treatment and the reasons for its non-success. For this reason the hospital notes should be available to the pathologist and the clinicians who looked after the patient in life should, if possible, attend the autopsy.

4.16 (1) The question of the part played by alcohol must always be considered in any road traffic accident involving death or injury, whether the victim be a pedestrian, a pedal or motor cyclist or the occupant of a vehicle. Current English law makes it an offence to be in charge of a vehicle with a breath alcohol level greater than 35 μg per 100 ml, a blood alcohol level above 80 mg per 100 ml or a urine alcohol content greater than 107 mg per 100 ml.[13]

(2) It is not unusual for the pathologist to find that pedestrians, particularly those struck down in the evenings when the light is bad, the weather poor and the pubs are open, often have astonishingly high levels of alcohol in their blood at post mortem. It is always important that analysis is done on *all* victims, not just drivers of motor vehicles, as the finding of high alcohol levels in a pedestrian may explain, for example, an apparently irrational decision to cross a busy road against the lights. Conversely it may add credence to an unlikely statement made by the driver of a vehicle involved in a collision with a pedestrian where he, the driver, makes assertions about the victim's conduct which may sound bizarre in the first instance.

(3) In cases of immediate death the pathologist should collect blood and urine samples with a view to giving evidence on the results in court. Where a patient is admitted to hospital, no sample should be given to the police without the patient's express permission.[14] If the police request permission to take a blood sample, the hospital doctor has the right to allow or refuse the request according to his judgment of the patient's condition. Such samples should be collected by a police surgeon, not the hospital doctor.

13 See para. 4.04 *ante*.
14 S.9 Road Traffic Act 1972 as amended; see para. 4.05 *ante*.

CHAPTER 5

Sexual Offences

RAPE

Law: Definition; Elements of the Offence

5.01 Rape is now a statutory offence by virtue of the Sexual Offences Act 1956 and the Sexual Offences (Amendment) Act 1976 and the meaning of rape for the purpose of the Sexual Offences Act 1956 is as follows:

> "A man commits rape if:
> (a) he has unlawful sexual intercourse with a woman who at the time of the intercourse does not consent to it, and
> (b) at the time he knows that she does not consent to the intercourse or he is reckless as to whether she consents or not."[1]

Sexual intercourse is defined as follows:

> "Where, on the trial of any offence under this Act, it is necessary to prove sexual intercourse (whether natural or unnatural), it shall not be necessary to prove the completion of the intercourse by the emission of seed, but the intercourse shall be deemed complete upon proof of penetration only."[2]

Any degree of penetration, even the slightest, is sufficient, and it is not necessary to prove rupture of the hymen or that penetration was of such a depth as to injure the hymen. It is an irrebuttable presumption that a boy under the age of fourteen is incapable of committing rape or any other crime of which sexual intercourse is an ingredient or buggery.[3]

Medico-Legal Aspects of Rape

5.02 (1) The medical examination of a woman who alleges she has been raped is one of the most important examinations that a doctor may be called upon to undertake. Rape by its very nature is usually carried out without witnesses, the only parties present being the assailant(s) and the victim. A woman may make allegations of rape after she has originally given consent to intercourse for fear of parental or other social retribution, or because she finds she is pregnant, or because of subsequent

1 Sexual Offences (Amendment) Act 1976 s.1(1).
2 Sexual Offences Act 1956 s.44.
3 But he may be convicted of indecent assault: *R. v. Williams* [1983] 1 Q.B. 320.

deterioration in her relationship with the man concerned. Allegations of rape are easily made and difficult for the man to refute. The doctor in a sense has to act as an arbiter and on his examination the outcome of a whole criminal case may depend.

(2) The doctor may find injuries both to the woman generally and in the genital region in particular which will confirm her allegations. On the other hand the woman who has been terrorised and has submitted to sexual intercourse without a struggle may only have minimal signs of injury unless she was *virgo intacta* prior to the rape, and a woman used to intercourse may have no injuries at all. In such cases the confirmation of her story will have to rely on forensic evidence such as demonstrating semen on vaginal swabs. Even so an accused man may claim misidentification or that the woman voluntarily agreed to intercourse, hence the lack of injury, and it may be impossible for the doctor to refute his story.

5.03 Many cases of rape are not reported to the police. Other victims return home, take a bath and change their clothing, discarding or destroying contaminated pants or other garments before complaining to the police, thus making impossible much of the medical and scientific investigation that needs to be carried out in such cases.

Examination of Victim

5.04 The doctor examining a rape victim must carry out the examination in proper medical surroundings in privacy with a female chaperone present. A full medical and gynaecological examination should be carried out, just as with any other gynaecological problem, without criminal overtones. Preferably there should be the minimum of delay between the rape and the medical examination carried out by a person having knowledge and experience in the field such as a gynaecologist or police surgeon. The examination must not be rushed.

5.05 The doctor must get the consent of the victim to the examination preferably in writing. The doctor should begin by taking the details of the name, age and address of the victim, the date and time of her arrival and by whom the examination has been requested. He will listen to the woman's story and make notes thereon adding to it his observations on her appearance, behaviour and demeanour and her apparent age. He will do well to be sceptical. He should take a full medical history, including consumption of food and alcohol, and a gynaecological history including details of the menstrual periods.

5.06 The doctor will note the victim's hair, her face, her clothing, her stockings or tights and her footwear and see if there are any inconsistencies between the girl's account and her general appearance. A woman who is conscious is expected to resist rape to the uttermost and she should therefore appear with her clothing and make-up in disarray, in a state of extreme emotional distress with tears, perhaps to the point of being distraught, and she should have injuries on her person from her assailant. It may be that the woman has been terrified, perhaps by having a knife held at her throat, when she may submit without a struggle, but there still may be marks on the back of the clothing, such as mud stains if rape has occurred in the open or dust or dirt if indoors which may give substance to her story.

5.07 When she is asked to undress she should stand on a sheet of clean brown paper so that any trace evidence in the clothing may fall onto the paper and thus be collected and retained for laboratory examination. All the clothing should be similarly retained, particularly if it is torn or soiled with blood or secretions.

5.08 (1) The doctor must examine the whole body for evidence of disease or injury. In particular he should look for bruises where the assailant has gripped the victim, perhaps by the arms, or forced her legs apart causing fingertip bruising, and bruising around the nose and mouth where the assailant may have tried to silence the victim's screams. There may be bite marks on her body, especially on the breasts, and swabs should be taken from them for saliva traces, and scratches from fingernails.

(2) There may be extensive genital injuries, particularly in a young girl unused to intercourse. There may be bruising and tearing of the labia, the vulval opening, the hymen and the vagina with fresh bleeding. A full examination will include the use of a speculum and the taking of swabs under direct vision with the aid of a surgical lamp.

(3) The doctor should collect duplicate swabs taken from the vulva, the lower part of the vagina and the upper part of the vagina, and pubic hair combings for foreign hairs. If secretion, possibly seminal fluid, is matted and dried on the pubic hair, such hair should be clipped away and preserved. Mouth swabs should be taken if allegations are made of forced oral sex, together with samples of saliva, blood and urine. If allegations of buggery are made, anal swabs must be taken. If the woman alleges she has scratched her assailant, then fingernail scrapings from her may be of value.

(4) All the samples should be collected in suitable containers and labelled clearly with the name of the victim, the time, date and place of

examination and the doctor's name. Most police forces supply a kit for use by the police surgeon which contains the appropriate swabs and containers for specimens.

(5) The doctor must make full notes of his history and examination made at the time and retain them together with such sketches and lists of exhibits as are appropriate. All the samples together with the clothing should be conveyed to the forensic science laboratory for examination, either by the doctor himself or by an exhibits officer from whom the doctor should obtain a receipt.

5.09 It may be difficult for the doctor to determine medically whether the woman has been raped or not. In some cases it is all too clear from the general demeanour of the woman, her clothing, her injuries from the assault and the particular genital injuries of rape all being present, together with positive evidence of seminal fluid in the vagina. In other cases where the victim has been terrorised, examination of the laboratory samples may confirm her story. When the woman has changed her clothing, has bathed or douched, the samples may be uniformly negative and it may be impossible in the absence of specific genital injuries to confirm her allegations or sustain a charge in court.

Examination of a Man Accused of Rape

5.10 Rarely the opportunity occurs for this examination. The only person likely to submit to it is a man who is totally innocent and has been falsely accused. The nature of the examination and its purpose must be made clear to him and his written permission obtained. A true assailant may have fingernail scratches on his hands and face, and bruises and bite marks, particularly on his hands where he has sought to silence his victim's screams. There may be traces of lipstick and other make-up on his person and clothing and there may be blood staining. His clothing should be examined in the laboratory and he himself must be fully examined by the doctor. There may be penile injury and staining, and swabs should be taken together with pubic hair combings for laboratory examination.

SEXUAL INTERCOURSE WITH GIRLS UNDER 13 AND 16 YEARS OF AGE

5.11 The same definitions of sexual intercourse apply in such cases as in rape (see para. 5.01 *supra*).

Medico-Legal Aspects

5.12 The same principles regarding medical examination of such young victims apply as are described in paras 5.04ff above. In addition to the chaperone the child's mother or a close female relative should be present both to give consent to the examination and to provide support for the child. The examination on the child should be performed in exactly the same way as described above. The majority of girls under the age of 16 will not have had sexual experience even in these permissive times and they will have suffered correspondingly more from the mental and physical trauma of sexual assault. The genital injuries in particular are often severe, with splitting and tearing of the tissues around the vulva and perineum, sometimes with substantial or severe haemorrhage, which must be treated urgently. Even where the girl has consented to sexual intercourse there may be injury, particularly if she was *virgo intacta* before the event. The doctor must take the same samples for laboratory examination as listed in para. 5.08 above. If the girl is very small it may be necessary to examine the child under general anaesthesia in order to assess the extent of the injuries and collect the samples and carry out any surgical repair that may be necessary. Obviously the consent of a parent or guardian must be obtained for any examination of the child carried out by the doctor, whether under anaesthesia or not.

INCEST AND INDECENT ASSAULT

Law: Definition; Elements of the Offence

Incest

5.13 By section 10 of the Sexual Offences Act 1956, it is an offence for a man to have sexual intercourse with a woman whom he knows to be his grand-daughter, daughter, sister or mother. Sisters include half-sisters and the relationship between two people applies notwithstanding that the relationship is not traced though lawful wedlock. This offence can be committed both by a man and by a woman over the age of sixteen. The same definitions of sexual intercourse apply in such cases as in rape: see para. 5.01 *supra*.

Indecent Assault on a Woman

5.14 Section 14 of the Sexual Offences Act 1956 creates the offence of indecent assault on a woman. There must be an assault (see para. 2.01 *supra*) accompanied by circumstances of indecency. Kissing a girl against her will accompanied by a suggestion that sexual intercourse or sexual activity should take place between herself and the defendant amounts to an indecent assault.[4]

4 *R. v. Leeson* (1968) 52 Cr.App.R. 185.

Medico-Legal Aspects

Incest

5.15 The examination of a woman or girl who has been having sexual intercourse with a close male relative should follow the procedure described above in a case of rape (see paras 5.04ff). It must be conceded that incest often implies repeated acts of sexual intercourse, usually without the violence or terrorising that marks rape. For this reason the examination of the woman may not show any fresh or significant injury generally or even to the genital area. There may be evidence of much sexual activity, as evidenced by a widely dilated hymen and loss of the rugae or folds of the lining of the vagina. The same swabs should be taken from the woman and submitted to the forensic science laboratory as described in para. 5.08 above.

Indecent Assault on a Woman

5.16 Sexual assault on a woman falling short of rape may result in only slight injury or none at all unless the woman resists and a struggle takes place between the two parties. The assault may consist of fondling the breasts or sucking and biting the nipples or digital interference with the genitalia which may result in vulval, hymenal or vaginal injury. The doctor should adopt the same procedure as described in the rape section (see paras 5.04ff). He should take a full history of the alleged assault from the victim and carry out a full external examination of the woman, including her clothing, to see whether it has been torn or soiled, the external surface of her body for superficial injury and of the breasts and genitalia for evidence of the alleged assault together with the collection of samples. Obviously the nature of the examination and the number of items collected will be dictated by the extent of the alleged assault and the injuries which it has occasioned. In many cases there may be no injury of any significance and the hurt is more to the woman's pride than to her person.

GROSS INDECENCY WITH OR TOWARDS A CHILD UNDER 14 YEARS OF AGE

Law: Definition; Elements of the Offence

5.17 By section 1 of the Indecency with Children Act 1960, any person who commits an act of gross indecency with or towards a child under the age of 14 or who incites a child under 14 to such an act commits an offence. The Act does not define gross indecency and it will be a matter of law whether any particular act is capable of amounting to gross indecency and a question of fact as to whether it does amount to an act of gross indecency. In *R. v. Speck*[5] the Court of Appeal held that an offence under section 1 of the Indecency with Children Act was committed where the defendant possibly permitted a child to keep her hand on his penis for about five minutes, that the defendant's inactivity amounted to an invitation to her to continue the activity, and that if such an invitation could properly be inferred, it would constitute an "act" within the ambit of the section. See also gross indecency at para 5.26 *infra.*

Medico-Legal Aspects

5.18 Sexual assault may be made on young children of both sexes even in infancy as part of the "battered child syndrome".[6]

The Boy

5.19 A small boy may be buggered or penile stimulation and injury may be inflicted on him. He may have been forced to masturbate, fellate or otherwise sexually stimulate his assailant. It may be very difficult for the doctor to obtain an adequate history, as the child will usually be too terrified or distressed to speak. Examination of the child must be carried out in the presence of a parent. It may be necessary to examine the child under general anaesthesia to establish the extent of the injury and to obtain the necessary swabs and samples. Where buggery has been attempted or achieved, there will be severe anal injury with bruising of the surrounding tissues and skin, tearing and splitting of the anal margin and of the mucosa within and it is likely that any attempt to examine this exquisitely tender area will be rejected outright by the child, hence the need for anaesthesia. Penile injury may be visible, perhaps with bruising or bite marks, a torn frenulum or bruising of the scrotum. Such injuries will have to be photographed in black and white and colour for reproduction in court, as a child of such tender years cannot be expected to give evidence, nor should he be subjected to the need to do so unless it is totally unavoidable. Swabs should be taken for seminal fluid and lubricant if buggery has been attempted and swabs for saliva from areas of bite marks. A mouth swab should be taken if suspicions of fellatio exist.

The Girl

5.20 Attempts may have been made to interfere sexually with the girl either vaginally or rectally, either with the penis or with a finger. As described at para. 5.12 above, stretching of the small vulval or soft genital

5 [1977] 2 All E.R. 859.
6 See paras 3.14ff *supra.*

or anal tissues in a young girl may cause severe injury and haemorrhage. She may also have been obliged to submit to fellatio with a man. The same principles of examination of the girl apply as to the boy and in a very young girl once again examination under anaesthesia may be obligatory together with photography. Sometimes it is helpful to use a doll or dolls in obtaining a history from a young victim. She may well be able to indicate on the dolls what she herself experienced. It goes without saying that young children who have been the victims of gross indecency require endless comfort and reassurance and it may be a very long time before they recover from the mental trauma which may result from such hideous sexual experiences.

BUGGERY AND ASSAULT WITH INTENT TO COMMIT BUGGERY

Law: Definition; Elements of the Offence

5.21 By section 12 of the Sexual Offences Act 1956, it is an offence for a person to commit buggery with another person (or with an animal, see para 5.28 *infra*). Buggery consists of sexual intercourse *per anum* by a man with a man, or by a man with a woman. As in rape, any degree of penetration is sufficient and once penetration is proved, both parties, if consenting, are guilty. As in rape, any degree of penetration is sufficient and once penetration is proved, both parties, if consenting, are guilty. As in rape, it is unnecessary to prove emission, and it is also an irrebuttable presumption that a boy under the age of 14 is incapable of committing an act of buggery where he is alleged to be the active party. (See para. 5.01 *supra*.) Section 16(1) of the Sexual Offences Act 1956 makes it an offence for a person to assault another person with intent to commit buggery.

Medico-Legal Aspects

5.22 Of the two people involved in the act of anal intercourse, the active and the passive partner, it is the latter whom the doctor is usually asked to examine. He may be an unwilling participant, a young boy or youth, or he may be an habitual offender of long standing. Occasionally the doctor may be asked to examine the active partner. Each of these situations will be examined in turn.

5.23 The same criteria apply as for the examination of a woman allegedly raped. A full medical examination must be carried out with the person's consent, preferably in writing, with a chaperone of the same sex present during the examination, which should be carried out in conditions of privacy with proper facilities. There must be a minimum of delay between the alleged offence and the medical examination. This will include the taking of a full history from the patient, a full general medical examination and a particular examination of the rectal area.

5.24 (1) In an unwilling partner or a young boy or youth experiencing anal intercourse for the first time, there is nearly always considerable superficial injury around the rectal region. The parts are usually exquisitely tender which may hamper the examiner. The doctor must look for bruising of the anal margins, with splitting of the skin or tearing of the lining within the rectum and stretching of the anus itself. He must look for evidence of seminal stains, because proof of penetration is necessary to confirm the offence. He must take swabs in duplicate from around the anal margin and within the rectum. He must search for foreign hair, semen and lubricants and he must take samples of saliva, blood and urine and a mouth swab for seminal traces if oral intercourse has formed part of the assault. If the victim has been an unwilling partner or been assaulted, then obviously there may be further injuries including bite marks, particularly if the victim is a woman. Such bite marks should be swabbed for evidence of saliva. As in a rape examination, if there are allegations of scratching by the victim then fingernail scrapings must be taken.

(2) If the passive partner is a habitual offender, then the anus will be found to be greatly dilated with thickening (keratinisation) of the skin of the anus. There may be old healed scars from previous stretching and splitting. Swabs must be taken for seminal fluid and lubricants and foreign hair should be collected. A proper rectal examination must be performed to assess the laxity of the anal sphincter.

(3) Examination of the active partner may show evidence of penile injury if the passive partner is inexperienced or has been the victim of assault and there may be faecal staining and evidence of lubricants.

(4) Swabs from these examinations should be properly sealed and labelled and transferred as rapidly as possible to the forensic science laboratory, either directly or through the medium of an exhibits officer from whom the doctor should get a written receipt.

AIDS

5.25 (1) Of recent years it has become apparent that a large number of promiscuous male homosexuals are suffering from acquired immune deficiency syndrome (AIDS), a viral disease transmitted by sexual contact or contamination by blood or body secretions. Infected individuals may themselves be symptom-free, as the incubation period is very long, extending over months or years. The victim loses the power to resist infection and becomes prey to any organism to which he may be exposed, be it bacterial, viral or fungal. As soon as one illness is successfully controlled by appropriate antibiotic therapy, another develops until the patient finally succumbs, usually from pneumonia.

(2)There is no specific treatment for the causal virus, the HIV or LAV. There are tests for the presence of antibodies to the virus in the serum of suspect cases and these should always be performed before an autopsy is commenced on a case of suspected AIDS.

(3) Besides homosexuals, other groups particularly at risk from this infection include intravenous drug abusers and haemophiliacs who need frequent transfusions of pooled blood product clotting factors which may be contaminated with the virus.

(4) It behoves any doctor examining a homosexual male especially one with a history or the external stigmata of drug abuse (see Chapter 6) to take every precaution to avoid contaminating himself or herself with blood or seminal fluid, especially from infected needles and syringes used in taking blood samples.

GROSS INDECENCY

Law: Definition; Elements of the Offence

5.26 Section 13 of the Sexual Offences Act 1956 makes it an offence for a man to commit an act of gross indecency with another man whether in public or private, or to be a party to the commission by a man of an act of gross indecency with another man, or to procure the commission by a man of an act of gross indecency with another man. This is, however, no longer an offence where the act takes place in private and both parties consent and both have attained the age of 21: see sections 1 and 2 of the Sexual Offences Act 1967. Gross indecency is not defined in the Act and there does not appear to be any definition by the Courts, but it has been held that there is no need for actual physical contact; if two men consent to behave in an indecent manner, it is enough that the men put themselves in such a position that it can be said that a grossly indecent exhibition is going on.[7] The Wolfenden Committee [8] was told that "the offence usually takes the form of mutual masturbation or some form of intercourse contact, or oral genital contact with or without emission". The Report continues: "Occasionally the offence may take a more recondite form; techniques in heterosexual relations vary considerably, and the same is true of homosexual relations." See also para. 5.17 *supra.*

7 See *R. v. Hunt* [1950] 2 All E.R. 291.
8 Cmd. 247, p. 38.

Medico-Legal Aspects

5.27 The actual extent of the indecency varies from case to case and may well extend to the borderline of rape. The same principles therefore apply to the medical examination as are described in paras 5.04ff above. The examining doctor must be guided by the account given to him by the victim but he would do well to take all the swabs and specimens listed at para. 5.08 above.

BESTIALITY

Law: Definition; Elements of the Offence

5.28 Section 12 of the Sexual Offences Act 1956 not only creates the offence of buggery with another person, but also with an animal: see para. 5.21 *supra*. So far as sexual intercourse is concerned, any degree of penetration is sufficient, but where an animal is concerned penetration *per anum* is not essential. In *R. v. Bourne* [9] the appellant had been convicted of aiding and abetting his wife to commit buggery with a dog. The evidence proved that the appellant had sexually excited the dog, and compelled his wife by duress to submit to the dog having connection with her *per vaginam*. According to Coke [10] "a great lady had committed buggery with a baboon and conceived by it."

Medico-Legal Aspects

5.29 Intercourse between a man and various animals or birds may occur occasionally in rural life. It is very rarely seen by the practising doctor. The animal concerned should be examined by a veterinary surgeon. The doctor asked to examine the human partner should obtain his permission in writing, having explained the voluntary nature of the examination. The examination should be concentrated on the genitalia with foreign secretions, hair, fur, feathers or other material being collected and sent to the forensic science laboratory together with the clothing worn by the man at the time of the alleged offence.

ATTEMPTS TO PROCURE ABORTION

Law: Definition; Elements of the Offence

5.30 Section 58 of the Offences Against the Person Act 1861 deals with the use of poison or instruments to cause miscarriage, and section 59 of

9 (1952) 36 Cr.App.R. 125.
10 *Institutes* vol. 3, 59.

the same Act deals with supplying or procuring poison or instruments knowing that they are intended to be unlawfully used to procure the miscarriage of any woman, or with such intent, whether she is with child or not. However, the Abortion Act 1967 now legalises abortion in certain circumstances and subject to certain formalities. By section 1(1) a person shall not be guilty of an offence under the law relating to abortion when a pregnancy is terminated by a registered medical practitioner if two registered medical practitioners are of the opinion, formed in good faith:

(a) that the continuance of the pregnancy would involve risk to the life of the pregnant woman or of injury to the physical or mental health of the pregnant woman or any existing children of the family, greater than if the pregnancy were terminated; or

(b) that there is a substantial risk that if the child were born it would suffer from such physical or mental abnormalities as to be seriously handicapped.

Section 1(2) provides that in determining whether the continuance of a pregnancy would involve such risk of injury to health account may be taken of the pregnant woman's actual or reasonably forseeable environment, and section 1(3) provides that any treatment for the termination of pregnancy must be carried out in a hospital vested in the Minister of Health or Secretary of State under the National Health Acts, or in a place for the time being approved by the Minister or Secretary of State. Section 1(4) states that the necessity for the opinion of two registered medical practitioners shall not apply to the termination of a pregnancy by a registered medical practitioner in a case where he is of the opinion, formed in good faith, that the termination is immediately necessary to save the life or to prevent grave permanent injury to the physical or mental health of the pregnant woman. In *Royal College of Nursing v. D.H.S.S.*,[11] the House of Lords by a majority decided that provided a doctor prescribes the treatment for the termination of a pregnancy, remains in charge and accepts responsibility throughout and the treatment is carried out in accordance with his directions, the pregnancy is "terminated by a registered medical practitioner" for the purposes of the Act, and any person taking part in the termination is entitled to the protection of section 1(1) of the Abortion Act 1967.

Medico-Legal Aspects of Abortion

5.31 (1) Criminal abortion outside the confines of licit medical treatment has become very rare since the Abortion Act of 1967 but the doctor would do well to suspect any case of septic abortion admitted to hospital as being criminally induced. The back street abortionist in

11 [1981] 1 All E.R. 545.

England and Wales has become, practically speaking, only a memory. The majority of criminal abortions are carried out under the guise of therapeutic abortions in nursing homes or clinics under a variety of pseudonyms.

(2) Prior to the Abortion Act criminal abortion was usually carried out using drugs or instrumentation which carried a very high morbidity and sometimes led to death. The particular dangers were shock, air and fluid embolism, perforation of the uterus or vagina leading to sepsis or haemorrhage, generalised septicaemia or peritonitis, tubular necrosis of the kidneys, pulmonary embolism from thrombosis of the pelvic veins and often a legacy of sterility and pelvic pain.

(3) Nowadays the majority of illegal abortions are carried out by a person having medical skill and equipment, who may be a doctor, midwife or nurse. The commonest way is for the uterus to be emptied by a dilation and curettage (a "D and C") or by vacuum aspiration. The use of tents and paste has become almost totally outmoded. Prostaglandins, a new group of drugs, may be used for illegal abortion in the form of a vaginal suppository or as an intra-uterine injection.

(4) After the first three months of pregnancy it is often necessary to resort to abdominal surgery, the operation of hysterotomy or opening the uterus and removing the foetus therefrom through the lower abdominal wall. This particular procedure carries a higher mortality than a "D and C" or vacuum aspiration. The introduction of hypertonic sodium chloride or other agents into the uterine cavity is dangerous and such methods have fallen into disuse.

(5) A few women still try and procure their own abortion by taking either drugs such as oestrogenic or pituitary hormones or purgatives which nearly always fail, merely making the patient ill. Self-instrumentation using a Higginson Syringe and douching the vagina, trying to force fluid through the cervical canal into the uterine cavity, the method used by abortionists of old, is rarely successful and only causes the complications described above.

(6) It must be conceded that it is possible in nearly all circumstances in nearly all parts of the United Kingdom to obtain an abortion legally under the present legislation, especially when the obstetrician or gynaecologist has what might be described as a "liberal" approach to the law.

CHAPTER 6

Legal and Medical Aspects of Alcohol and Drug Abuse

LEGAL ASPECTS OF ALCOHOL AND DRUG ABUSE

6.01 From the legal point of view a clear distinction must be drawn between abuses of alcohol or drugs which are offences in themselves, such as being drunk and disorderly, driving when unfit through drink or drugs etc., and those other offences where the use of alcohol or drugs may have an effect on criminal responsibility. We are here concerned principally with the latter category.

(1) The same principles govern alcohol and drug intoxication. It is well known that drunkenness as such is no defence to a crime. Where the amount of drink or drugs taken has caused insanity, albeit temporary insanity, such insanity is just as much a defence to a criminal offence as insanity caused in any other way.[1]

(2) In cases of self-induced intoxication where the prosecution have to prove recklessness as an ingredient of an offence, if an accused was unaware of a risk which would have been obvious to a sober and reasonable man in his position, he cannot rely on his intoxication as a defence and he is to be treated as if he had been aware of the risk. In *Majewski*[2] Lord Elwyn-Jones L.C. stated:

> "If a man of his own volition takes a substance which causes him to cast off the restraints of reason and conscience, no wrong is done to him by holding him answerable criminally for any injury he may do while in that condition. His course of conduct in reducing himself by drugs or drink to that condition in my view supplies the element of *mens rea*, of guilty mind certainly for crimes of basic intent. It is a reckless course of conduct and recklessness is enough to constitute the necessary *mens rea* in such cases."

(3) In the case of *R. v. Hardie*[3] the defendant was charged with criminal damage (arson). The prosecution relied on the alternatives of intent and recklessness. There was no dispute that the defendant must have started the fire, but there was evidence that at the time of and after the fire, he exhibited signs of intoxication and that such signs might have resulted from the taking of valium some hours earlier. The Court of

1 *D.P.P. v. Beard* (1920) 14 Cr.App.R. 600.
2 [1976] 2 All E.R. 142 at 150.
3 [1984] 3 All E.R. 848.

Appeal quashed the conviction, holding that although the jury had been directed in accordance with the rule in *Caldwell*[4] (that self-induced intoxication is no defence to a charge in which recklessness is an ingredient), that did not embrace every drug. The defendant alleged that he took valium to calm his nerves. There was no evidence that he knew, or that it was generally known, that the taking of about five tablets would be liable to render a person aggressive or incapable of appreciating risk to others or have other side effects such that its taking would itself contain an element of recklessness. The Court of Appeal held that the jury should have been directed that if they concluded that as a result of the valium the defendant at the time was unable to appreciate risks to property and persons from his actions, they should consider whether the taking of the valium was itself reckless. In a case of reckless driving, however, the taking of a sedative or soprific drug cannot be a defence .

(4) In the case of *R. v. Bailey*[5] the Court of Appeal decided that diabetes (unlike intoxication from alcohol or drugs) could provide a defence not only to crimes of specific intent but also to crimes of basic intent.

MEDICAL ASPECTS OF ALCOHOL AND DRUG ABUSE

Alcohol

6.02 From a medical point of view alcohol consumption involves the drinking of either methyl alcohol or ethyl alcohol or both, although the drinking of methyl alcohol is nearly always confined to the layabout or vagrant population.

Methyl Alcohol

6.03 (1) Methyl alcohol is a very poisonous drug. It occurs in the pure form of wood spirit or more commonly as methylated spirit (where it is combined with ethyl alcohol), or as surgical spirit (which also contains methyl salicylate and ethyl phthalate). Methylated spirit is coloured with methyl violet and piridine is added to it to discourage its consumption.

(2) Methyl alcohol leads to the symptoms of drunkenness in the same way as ethyl alcohol, but its effects are more prolonged and there is a latent period before they appear. It is broken down mainly to formic acid, leading to the medical condition of acidosis. Methyl alcohol also has a direct toxic effect on the eye, leading to optic atrophy and blindness.

4 [1981] 1 All E.R. 961.
5 [1983] 3 All E.R. 503; see also para. 4.03 *supra*.

Ethyl Alcohol

6.04 The effects of ethyl alcohol may present as acute poisoning, chronic alcoholism or drunkenness. *Acute poisoning* usually follows the consumption of a large quantity of alcohol over a limited period of time. It is particularly seen in those celebrating national holidays or other social events and those working in the licensed trade. Victims usually pass rapidly into coma and die of respiratory failure. They may vomit, inhale stomach contents and suffocate; this is particularly likely if the victim is left lying on his back. A figure of over 250 mg per 100 ml of blood is potentially fatal, especially in the presence of respiratory obstruction.

6.05 The *chronic alcoholic* shows multiple symptoms of mental and physical deterioration. There is brain shrinkage and superficial areas of softening from preceding injuries, usually due to falls while drunk. Fatty and other degenerative changes occur in the heart muscle with cirrhosis of the liver with its attendant complications, especially oesophagal bleeding, peptic ulcers in the stomach and duodenum and chronic pancreatitis.

6.06 *Alcoholic intoxication* is due to the depressant effect of alcohol. The early stages of excitement are due to the suppression of inhibitions, leading to irrational behaviour out of keeping with the person's normal life-style, for example a man making unwelcome sexual advances or exposing himself or urinating in public, etc. As the blood alcohol level rises, so the mental state deteriorates, passing through periods of confusion and stupor before coma supervenes.

6.07 There are different concentrations of alcohol in the various forms of intoxicating liquor, from the 40% of standard gin and whisky to the 3% to 6% found in beer. Most wines contain about 12% alcohol. Fortified wines such as sherry and madeira have had alcohol added to them to strengthen the concentration, as fermentation itself is halted once the alcohol concentration reaches about 13% and the yeast is killed.

6.08 Most alcohol is absorbed within an hour of drinking. This absorption obviously varies with the speed of the drinking, whether food is taken as well as drink, with the dilution of the alcohol itself, the nature of the drink and whether the person is used to drinking. If short drinks and long drinks are mixed, e.g. a pint of beer followed by a tot of whisky, the principle of "chasers", then the person drinking this combination is likely to become intoxicated more rapidly.

6.09 Men appear to be able to tolerate alcohol better than women, probably due to their average larger size absorbing more. The chronic alcoholic often has a stomach lined with mucus which will reduce the speed of absorption. Some people may attempt to slow the absorption of alcohol by taking milk or some other fatty material to mimic this chronic gastritis. The concomitant taking of food to fill the stomach and absorb some of the alcohol, thus delaying its absorption, is probably the most effective way of preventing intoxication.

6.10 Alcohol is excreted in the urine, breath, sweat, saliva and milk. The rate of excretion varies in the same individual on different occasions and with the speed of drinking, but the average person usually metabolises about 13 to 15 mg of alcohol per 100 ml per hour, roughly equivalent to half a pint of beer or a single tot of spirits. Such individual variations make it very difficult to correlate intake of alcohol with subsequent analysis figures produced by the forensic laboratory. A back calculation of levels some hours before based on this rate of breakdown can only be a rough guide at best and may be frankly misleading.

6.11 Certain medical conditions may simulate intoxication. These include head injuries, metabolic disorders such as hypoglycaemia and diabetic precoma in diabetes mellitus, uraemia in those with chronic kidney disease, hyperthyroidism, and in those with liver disorders when the alcohol taken is not broken down in the body. Other conditions that may simulate intoxication include many of the neurological disorders with symptoms of difficulty with speech (dysarthria), tremor, staggering gait (ataxia) and drowsiness. Such neurological disorders include multiple sclerosis, brain tumour, Parkinson's disease, Meniere's disease, cerebral arteriosclerosis and various psychiatric states. Carbon monoxide poisoning may mimic drunkeness and those who are unwell and have taken a drink may appear to be drunk when they are actually ill. The taking of drugs of almost any type with alcohol is fraught with danger, particularly antidepressants and hypnotic drugs, and such drugs may potentiate the effects of alcohol to a remarkable degree.

6.12 Some conditions make a person more susceptible to the effects of alcohol. They include cold, exposure or fatigue, the presence of an empty stomach, previous head injuries, high blood pressure, cerebral arteriosclerosis and the neurological and psychiatric diseases listed above. Previous removal of part or all of the stomach, perhaps for peptic ulceration, will lead to unduly rapid absorption, as the alcohol passes directly into the small intestine where it is absorbed almost immediately. It is a doctor's duty to warn patients of the dangers of taking alcohol while on drug therapy, particularly relating to the driving of motor vehicles.

6.13 It is difficult for the doctor to assess the degree of alcoholic intoxication from clinical examination alone, especially if there is previous disease present. This has led in recent years to road traffic legislation[6] embracing maximum legal levels of alcohol permitted in the body, a blood level of 80 mg per 100 ml, a urine level of 107 mg per 100 ml and a breath level of 35 μg per 100 ml of breath being the upper limits.

Drug Abuse

6.14 Almost any drug in the pharmacopeia may be abused by a patient. A surprisingly large number of the population are dependent on simple drugs obtained over the counter, often analgesic drugs such as aspirin, or prescribed drugs, usually mild sedatives such as diazepam (valium). The prolonged use of these latter drugs may lead to impairing of mental faculties, particularly of intellect and judgment. In the elderly these may lead to disorders of temperature control and hypothermia.

(2) The pharmacopoeia is changing all the time. Drugs go out of favour or become incorporated in statutory legislation, thus restricting their access both by doctors and by patients, and by promotion by manufacturers. Polypharmacy prescribing by doctors is another contributory factor to drug abuse, particularly where cocktails of drugs are prescribed to psychiatric patients. Such patients may have their personalities entirely altered by the therapy prescribed for them. For this reason it is impossible to give a detailed breakdown of the effects of every drug of addiction.

(3) The number of drug addicts is rising world-wide, both from medical and non-medical sources. Drug smuggling is a growth industry and there is big money to be made in it. The effects of drugs are two-fold, firstly on the individual concerned and secondly on society. Generally speaking a person's behaviour is altered, depending on the drug, his reaction times being slowed or quickened, his co-ordination is often impaired and there may well be a synergistic effect with alcohol. A person's personality may change with loss of self-control, self-confidence, mental concentration and disturbance of the sleep/waking pattern and progress to withdrawal from society at large. A person may become so dependent on drugs that his or her whole life revolves around the obtaining and administering of them, to the detriment of his health and life-style, with malnutrition, poverty and degradation marking his downhill progress. The individual loses his job and his income and his family suffers with breakdown of marriage, divorce or separation. He may involve others in his habit and he may cost society a great deal of money supporting him and his dependents.

6 S.12 Road Traffic Act 1972 as amended; see para. 4.04 *supra*.

Types of Dependence

6.15 Drug taking is a very intractable condition and genuine cures are few and far between. The World Health Organisation recognises five types of dependence.

6.16 (1) The first is the *morphine type* and refers to addiction to morphine, heroin, opium or morphine substitutes such as methadone. Addiction to these drugs is characterised by "an overpowering desire or need to continue taking the drug and to obtain it by any means and by a tendency to increase the dose owing to the development of tolerance."[7] Morphine is usually taken by injection, often intravenously, in the addict ("mainlining") or by sniffing up the nose ("snorting"). Withdrawal symptoms occur after deprivation of the drug for more than twelve hours and last about a week. They include anxiety, restlessness, nausea, diarrhoea, running eyes and nose, cramps, weight loss and dehydration. Tolerance is easily developed to this group of drugs and there is cross-tolerance between members of the group. It is not widely recognised by doctors that a standard therapeutic regime involving a morphine type drug for as little as ten days or two weeks is sufficient to cause dependence on the drug in the majority of patients, whether or not they are to be regarded as having a typical predisposition to addiction.

(2) Trafficking in this group of drugs occurs on an international scale, particularly from the Far East and Pakistan to Europe and from South America to the U.S.A. Apart from carrying the drug in hidden compartments in suitcases and other containers, recently couriers have been swallowing the drug in small packets sealed with adhesive tape or in condoms which pass into the intestines. On arrival at his destination the courier takes a laxative, retrieves the packets and passes them on to the "pusher" who distributes the drug. Unfortunately for the courier, from time to time packets become unsealed or burst, allowing massive quantities of the heroin or morphine to escape into the intestinal tract, be absorbed and cause the courier's death from poisoning.

6.17 The second type is the *barbiturate type* of dependence, again to quote the W.H.O. definition, "the continuous use of any barbiturate or similar sedative or hypnotic drug, generally in amounts exceeding a therapeutic dose level, usually up to or in excess of five times the normal dose." In this type of addiction the desire to continue is strong rather than overpowering and the tendency to increase the dose is partly due to tolerance. There is a cross-tolerance between these drugs and alcohol and together they make a powerful and potentially lethal combination. The

7 W.H.O. definition.

withdrawal symptoms reach a maximum in two or three days and subside slowly, and include anxiety, muscle twitching, intention tremor, weakness, dizziness, nausea, vomiting, insomnia, weight loss, postural hypotension and rarely convulsions. 100 tablets of a standard therapeutic dose of barbiturates used as a hypnotic over a period of four weeks is probably the upper limit of safety and it may be potentially dangerous in a person having the appropriate personality defects which might lead to addiction. The above picture applies to most sedatives or hypnotic drugs taken in excess for prolonged periods.

6.18 The third type is the *cocaine type*, where the desire to obtain the drug is overpowering but tolerance is absent. There is psychic but no physical dependence on the drug and no withdrawal symptoms. However, absence of the drug is accompanied by intense craving and the addict may go to extreme lengths including violence to obtain the drug. The use of cocaine has increased in recent years. It may cause progressively intensive toxic reactions including paranoid psychosis and its use may be combined with that of heroin or some other morphine-like compound ("H and C"). Because of a relatively plentiful supply of cocaine in the United Kingdom, the price has come down and it is now more widely abused.

6.19 The fourth type is the *cannabis type*. Here the need or desire is present but there is no tolerance and usually no dose increase. There is psychic dependence only and no abstinence syndrome. The danger of cannabis is not in itself but in the environment in which it may be used, where there may be danger of addiction to other and more dangerous drugs. A person under the influence of cannabis may of course injure himself or cause harm to others.

6.20 The fifth type is the *amphetamine type*, which may be combined with barbiturates in the old-fashioned form of dexedrine. Here the need or desire is present and there is a tolerance to the drug and a tendency to increase the dose. Dependence is psychic and there is no abstinence syndrome, but continuous use of amphetamines may lead to severe toxic psychosis and manic behaviour. Cases of amphetamine dependency are now relatively rare as the use of the drug for treatment has become practically non-existent and it has been replaced by other stimulant drugs such a methedrine, which itself may be abused. The picture of addiction and withdrawal is much the same with this drug as with amphetamine.

6.21 The final group, which is not listed in the W.H.O. classification, include the use of *hallucinogens* such as LSD, "taking a trip". These drugs alter appreciation of images received by the brain through the senses of sight, smell or hearing. There is altered appreciation of time and space which may be pleasurable or terrifying. People who take the drug often think they can fly and may take off their clothes and throw themselves off balconies or high buildings in their mistaken belief and are found gravely injured or dead on the ground beneath. There is psychic dependence only and no abstinence syndrome.

Loss of Tolerance

6.22 One of the problems of the addict is loss of tolerance following withdrawal during hospitalisation or imprisonment. The addict on being released often goes back into his old environment and resumes his addiction, taking the same dose that he did before his incarceration. Such a dose may well prove lethal as the addict needs time to build up his tolerance all over again.

Drug Combination

6.23 The effects of drug combinations are different from each drug taken singly, and mixtures of drugs are particularly liable to lead to tolerance and habituation. Addicts will lie to get as much of a drug as possible in order to be able to sell it to others at a profit. Even the restrictions on prescribing at drug-dependency centres and limited lists of doctors approved by the Home Office have made little difference to the problem in the United Kingdom.

Post Mortem Appearance

6.24 (1) The post mortem appearance of the addict is characteristic. There is often wasting and signs of self-neglect. The body may be extensively tattooed to hide scars. There may be needle puncture marks, old round tissue paper-like scars from previous septic injection sites, particularly on the arms, and thrombosed veins from inflammation following unsuitable or infected injections. Such needle puncture marks must be sought for carefully as they are not necessarily always on the arms or hands, particularly in the long-standing addict in whom many of these accessible veins will have become unsuitable from thrombosis and scarring. Alternative injection sites include the groins and the neck where there are major veins beneath the skin which will often be concealed by clothing. Internally there is often chronic active hepatitis in the liver with enlarged lymph nodes beneath it in the porta hepatis. Foreign body reactive cells in the lung often contain portions of material that can be recognised under the microscope in polarised light; they are starch particles originally used as an adulterant to dilute the drug. There may be evidence of septicaemia, endocarditis (inflammation of the heart valves), internal abscesses and overdosage itself.

(2) Addicts often tend to come to a violent end, from accidents while under the influence of drugs, from suicide or more rarely from homicide. They are often infected with the hepatitis B virus or the AIDS virus and present a health risk to those handling the blood and body fluid samples from them. They are not, however, a risk through casual contact in the ordinary context of everyday life. (For AIDS see para. 5.25 above.)

Solvent Abuse

6.25 (1) A recent form of drug abuse has developed, solvent abuse, so-called "glue-sniffing", although it is by no means confined to glues. The great majority of abusers are young, usually male teenagers who inhale the spray from aerosol cans, often anti-perspirants and deodorants. This is said by abusers to give pleasurable symptoms, dreams, heightened sensation and detachment from reality. To the unaffected observer the sufferer often behaves totally irrationally and may injure or even kill himself while under the influence of the aerosol propellant. Afterwards the abuser will often have complete or almost total amnesia for the period of intoxication and what happened during it.

(2) It is the propellant that has the toxic effects on the abuser. There are several chemical agents used in different aerosols and they cause similar symptoms when inhaled in excess. They may cause death from asphyxia if inhaled with a plastic or paper bag over the person's head and neck due to displacement of oxygen in the air by the propellant.

(3) More commonly, however, death results from some concomitant accident whilst the victim is intoxicated. He may drown if in a bath, fall into water from a canal bank, fall from a balcony or window whilst attempting some feat of bravado or die from suffocation from inhaled vomit, to name some more common examples.

(4) At post mortem there may be reddening or excoriation of the skin around the nose and mouth if the victim is a habitual sniffer, but this is not commonly seen. Toxicological analysis of body fluids and tissues is necessary to establish the diagnosis of solvent intoxication, which should always be suspected in sudden or unnatural deaths in teenagers, especially young boys.

(5) Enquiries among the victim's friends may unmask a story of sniffing among a group of youths who obtained a solvent or aerosol from a supermarket or do-it-yourself shop, inhaled it with varying degrees of toxic effects and found on recovery one of their number missing or dead. Details of what took place are usually lacking due to deliberate or toxic amnesia.

CHAPTER 7

Medical Reports and Conferences

THE LAWYER'S VIEW

7.01 (1) Most medical practitioners in writing reports tend to follow a pattern which may be very helpful when communicating with another doctor about the condition of a particular patient, but may not always be so helpful when the reader is a lawyer. A frequent pattern in medical reports is for them to contain a history of events leading up to the event or events which caused the injuries, indecent assault, rape etc., which may be useful to the lawyer in that it will contain an account of the victim's story to the doctor, which, although probably not a contemporary account and therefore not admissible in evidence, can usefully be compared with any witness statement made by the victim. Normally the medical report will then have a factual account of what was found and noted at examination, and finally an expression of opinion as to the causes of the injuries etc.

(2) It is a common experience that when such reports are seen for the first time by lawyers, the description of the examination, in particular, is couched in highly technical medical terms. Now most practising lawyers have some familiarity with the more common medical terms, but it is not a particularly useful way of spending one's time having to look up various technical terms in a medical dictionary or similar book. It may well be necessary for the lawyer to ask the doctor to make a further report which is expressed in language which is easier for the layman to follow and understand.

(3) It may also happen that although the doctor has expressed an opinion which he considers medically relevant, it may not be legally relevant. In serious cases, therefore, it is often desirable, indeed essential, for the lawyer to have a conference with the doctor. This can be a vital aid to the lawyer in complex matters in understanding the medical points and also enables the doctor to understand the legal points. Frequently the doctor can explain at a conference matters which he did not wish or choose to put in his report or witness statement, and these matters often can and do illuminate the whole matter for the lawyer.

(4) If you have an expert medical witness who is advising, say, on a post mortem report given by another pathologist, it is very helpful to

have a conference with the expert witness, who can tell the lawyer things in conference which he would probably not wish to put in a formal report and who can advise on questions which should be put to the other side's medical witnesses in cross-examination. In serious cases, it is highly desirable to have your expert in court when cross-examining the expert on the other side so that he can advise in court on answers which the expert has given and suggest further lines of questioning.

THE PATHOLOGIST'S VIEW

7.02 The pathologist will have originally been asked to carry out a post mortem examination on a case of suspected homicide by a Coroner and it is to him that his original report should be sent. Copies of this report should not be circulated without the Coroner's consent. If the case proves to be one of murder or manslaughter or some other form of homicide, then the pathologist will be asked to provide a report by the police for the Director of Public Prosecutions.

7.03 Both the report for the coroner and the report for the police should be set out clearly and in detail, avoiding as far as possible the use of medical jargon. If use of technical words proves unavoidable, then some explanation in brackets should be incorporated in the text for the benefit of the lay person reading the report.

7.04 The report itself should be on headed paper with the name, address and telephone number of the pathologist concerned. The police report should normally be typed on a standard printed form supplied by them. It should begin with the time, date and place of examination. The identification procedure of the victim should follow, with a clear statement of the deceased's name and the name and number of the identifying police officer. A list of those persons present and their function should form the next part of the report and be followed by an account of the external examination of the body, incorporating details of clothing and personal effects, the height, weight and build of the deceased and a detailed list of all the injuries. If these are multiple, they are best grouped together under different parts of the body, for example head and neck, chest, right arm, left arm and so on. Details of photography should be incorporated in this section.

7.05 An account of the internal examination should form the next part of the report, again in a logical manner followed by a list of all the exhibits taken during the post mortem, each with an identifying number and a note of to whom it was handed. The pathologist will be expected to sign an exhibit label for each item that he collects. If the pathologist has been shown a weapon or other instrument, then he should identify and describe it.

7.06 The report then finishes with the most important part as far as the police and Coroner are concerned, a set of conclusions. These should be as clear and as unequivocal as possible. It is usually convenient to have a series of numbered short paragraphs beginning with a statement about the deceased's age, height, weight and build and the part, if any, that natural disease has played in his death. The next paragraph should summarise the most important injuries, with a commentary on how they were caused. The third paragraph should deal with the weapon concerned, as to whether the one shown to the pathologist could or could not have caused the injuries described. If there is no weapon, then some description of a likely weapon should be provided. The next paragraph should deal with the presence or absence of defence wounds and other injuries indicative of a fight or struggle. If applicable, a commentary on treatment, be it surgical or medical, that the victim received prior to death should be included. The final paragraph should give the definitive medical cause of death. The pathologist should then sign the report with all his medical degrees and his professional appointments.

7.07 If the pathologist has been asked by the police to attend the scene of death and has done so, the report must incorporate all the details of this visit, with the date, time and place of the examination, who was present, what the pathologist did and what he noted up to the time that he and the accompanying laboratory officers wrapped up and sealed the body prior to its removal to the mortuary. This part of the report will form a preamble to the main autopsy report described above.

Medical Reports for the Defence

7.08 It may be that the pathologist is asked to carry out a second post mortem examination on behalf of the defence of a person accused of murder. Before agreeing to undertake such an examination, the pathologist should obtain all the available documents relating to the case in the possession of the defence solicitor, in particular the post mortem report of the Crown pathologist and a set of photographs taken during that examination, together with any other photographs of the scene of death, of the accused's injuries or other material matters. Having studied all these documents the pathologist should decide whether a second examination is worthwhile or not. It may be that the body is totally decomposed, having been inadequately stored without refrigeration or that far too much time has elapsed from the original autopsy, so that mummification and mould formation has been added to normal decomposition. Alternatively the first pathologist may have removed the relevant tissues and organs, for example the track of a stab wound or the bullet from a case of shooting. This may make a further examination of the whole body pointless and attention need only be given to those particular parts preserved by the original pathologist.

7.09 If, however, the defence pathologist considers a second examination to be worth undertaking, then he should seek the Coroner's permission to carry it out. Having obtained this he must arrange with the police officers concerned and the original pathologist a mutually convenient time for him to carry out his examination, as both the Crown pathologist and a police officer must be present to identify the body formally to the defence pathologist and if necessary to collect further material or note additional injuries that have become apparent since the original examination.

7.10 It is customary for the first pathologist to indicate to his colleague what he has done, pointing out various injuries described in his report and illustrated in the photographs. The second pathologist will carry out a further examination both external and internal. It may be that he will note further injuries because bruising in particular often "comes out" once the blood has drained from the tissues following the first autopsy. Bruises may merge together with blurring of their pattern due to decomposition despite refrigeration. If further important injuries are recognised by the second pathologist, the first pathologist will naturally note them down also and may provide a supplementary report for the Director of Public Prosecutions. If organs or tissues have been preserved, it is customary for the first pathologist to demonstrate them to his colleague. They may dissect, for example, a fixed brain, together noting disease or injury, or examine the neck structures from a case of strangulation.

7.11 In actual practice it is very unusual among experienced pathologists for a second autopsy to reveal any extra major finding or indeed for there to be any real difference of opinion between the two experts on the autopsy findings. The defence pathologist, however, will naturally keep his own counsel as to his interpretation of any injuries and he will prepare a report for his instructing solicitor in detail.

7.12 The report should begin with some such phrase as "Acting on the instructions of Mr. Brown of Brown, Smith and Jones, Solicitors of 15 The Broadway, London NE4, I went to Holborn Mortuary and carried out a second post mortem examination on the body of the deceased John Robinson in the presence of (*names of police officers and the original pathologist*)." He should then describe his findings, referring the while to the original Crown post mortem report and photographs which have been supplied to him.

7.13 He will then comment on the first pathologist's autopsy findings and conclusions, pointing out any differences of fact and interpretation. He will refer to the various police statements and notes of interviews made by the accused as well as the accused's account of events made to his solicitor.

7.14 The pathologist should not be afraid to comment frankly on major discrepancies between the accused's story and the pathological findings. He is giving his opinion in confidence and it is important for the instructing solicitor to know the problems that may beset him in defending his client. The pathologist must remember that even if he is being instructed by the defence, he must not take sides against the prosecution and provide a biased opinion, as he will rapidly come to grief when cross-examined in court.

7.15 It may be, however, that there is some genuinely helpful line of defence or that a real difference of opinion exists as to interpretation of injuries between the two pathologists, and the second pathologist should inform his instructing solicitor accordingly and suggest the possibility of a conference with defending counsel.

The Conference

7.16 This is usually held in counsel's chambers with the pathologist and instructing solicitor present and occasionally a scientific expert in another field if appropriate. It is up to the pathologist to make as clear as humanly possible to the lawyers present the extent of the injuries and how he, the pathologist, thinks they were caused. The lawyers should be encouraged to ask questions, however simple or naive they may appear to be. He is after all only one part of the defence and he does not know the overall concept or plan that counsel and the solicitor are putting together.

7.17 It may be necessary to carry out a little play-acting to demonstrate to the lawyers how injuries could or could not be inflicted and the pathologist should not be afraid to demonstrate on himself or one of those present for fear of looking foolish. Similarly he must curb the more far-fetched flights of fancy put to him if they appear totally unrealistic or impossible and try and present a balanced picture of the probabilities and possibilities from the medical point of view as clearly as he can. He should also comment on the Crown pathologist, if he is known to him, as to his experience and strength and weakness in court, in order to help counsel to handle him during cross-examination.

7.18 Nowadays it is only on rare occasions that a defence pathologist is called upon to give contrary evidence in court on behalf of the defence against the Crown. It is not unusual, however, for the defence pathologist to sit behind counsel when the Crown pathologist is giving his evidence so that he can suggest possible questions to be put to the witness or comment on what he has already said. The presence of the defence pathologist often puts a brake on the Crown pathologist when he sees his colleague across the court, so that he tends to be more careful and guarded in his comments and thus lessen the impact of his evidence.

Conclusion

7.19 This chapter has been written from the viewpoint of the pathologist involved in a case of homicide. The same principles should apply to the clinician, be he police surgeon, hospital doctor or general practitioner, asked to assist the courts as a professional or expert witness, either by the prosecution or the defence, in cases of non-fatal injury and assault prosecuted under the Offences against the Person Act 1861 and other statutes.

APPENDIX 1

Suggested Bibliography for Further Reading

TEXTBOOKS OF FORENSIC MEDICINE, PATHOLOGY AND TOXICOLOGY

A Colour Atlas of Forensic Pathology, G. Austin Gresham (1975) Wolfe Medical Books, London

The Coroner's Autopsy, Bernard Knight (1983) Churchill Livingstone, Edinburgh

The Essentials of Forensic Medicine, C.J. Polson, D.J. Gee and B. Knight, (4th edition 1985) Pergamon Press, Oxford

Forensic Dentistry, J.M. Cameron and B.G. Sims (1974) Churchill Livingstone, Edinburgh

Forensic Medicine, Bernard Knight (1985) Gower Medical Publishing, London

Forensic Medicine, Keith Simpson and Bernard Knight (9th edition 1985) Edward Arnold, London

Forensic Medicine for Lawyers, J.K. Mason (2nd edition 1983) Butterworth, London

Forensic Medicine: A study in trauma and environmental hazards, C.G. Tedeschi, W.G. Eckert, L.G. Tedeschi (1977) W.B. Saunders, Philadelphia

Forensic Radiology, K.T. Evans and B. Knight (1981) Blackwell Scientific Publications, Oxford

Gradwohl's Legal Medicine, 3rd edition, ed. by F.E. Camps, B.G.B. Lucas and A. Robinson (1976) John Wright & Co., Bristol

Legal Aspects of Medical Practice, Bernard Knight (1982) Churchill Livingstone, Edinburgh

Lecture Notes on Forensic Medicine, D.J. Gee (4th edition 1984) Blackwell Scientific Publications, Oxford

The New Police Surgeon, ed. by S.H. Burges (1978) Hutchinson Benham, London

The Pathology of Violent Injury, ed. by J.K. Mason (1978) Edward Arnold, London

Taylor's Principles and Practice of Medical Jurisprudence, ed. by A. Keith Mant (13th edition 1984) Churchill Livingstone, Edinburgh

APPENDIX II

Glossary

adipocere a form of post mortem decomposition (see para. 1.16).
adrenal glands two small glands, one situated above each kidney, which produce hormones including cortisone and adrenaline.
air embolism the entry of air into the circulation, usually via an injury to a large vein in the neck or arm, causing the heart to beat irregularly or stop altogether.
algae microscopic water plants.
amniotic fluid the fluid in which the developing foetus is suspended in the mother's womb during development.
aneurysm a swelling of an artery due to congential weakness or disease of the vessel wall which may rupture with massive bleeding.
anoxia total or almost total lack of oxygen in the blood or body tissues.
aorta the main artery of the body running from the heart down in front of the spine to the pelvis where it divides.
arachnoid the very fine transparent membrane enclosing the brain.
arteriosclerosis hardening, thickening and narrowing of arteries due to increasing age.
artery a muscular blood vessel taking blood from the heart to body tissues and organs.
asphyxia obstruction of the air passages cutting off the oxygen supply to the lungs (see para. 1.40).
ataxia staggering gait due to muscular inco-ordination.
axilla(e) the armpit(s)

barotrauma injury caused by high external pressure as found for example in deep sea divers.
berry aneurysm a swelling of one of the arteries in the brain due to congenital weakness of the arterial wall.
brain stem that part of the brain connecting the spinal cord to the cerebral hemispheres containing vital structures controlling heart action and breathing.
bronchi the air passages to and within each lung.
bronchopneumonia inflammation of the air passages within the lungs and of the lung tissues around them.

cadaveric spasm a rare post mortem phenomenon described in para. 1.10.
caisson disease a disease of deep sea divers and others exposed to an increase in barometric pressure, described in para. 1.53.
carboxyhaemoglobin the pink pigment found in the red blood cells in carbon monoxide poisoning.
carotid arteries the two main arteries from the aorta to the brain running up on each side of the neck.
cerebellum rear and lower part of the brain.

cerebral haemorrhage bleeding into the substance of the brain, which may produce a "stroke".

cerebral oedema swelling of the brain due to fluid excess, often found as a sequel to head injury.

cerebro-spinal fluid the fluid formed in the brain, filling its cavities (ventricles) and bathing its surface and that of the spinal cord.

cervical spine the seven neck vertebrae from the base of the skull to the upper chest.

cirrhosis fibrosis or scarring of the liver, often due to chronic alcoholism.

colon the large intestine.

coma very deep unconsciousness from which a patient cannot be roused or appreciate pain and which may precede death.

conduction defects failure of the electrical communication system in nerves of the heart leading to irregular rhythms or cardiac arrest.

congestion abnormal accumulation of blood.

core temperature the temperature of the internal organs of the body.

coronary artery one of the two arteries arising from the aorta where it leaves the heart, supplying the heart muscle itself with blood.

coronary thrombosis obstruction of a coronary artery by a clot of blood formed in life.

curettage scraping of a body cavity (e.g. the womb) with the surgical instrument the curette

cyanosis blue discolouration of the lips, extremities, blood and internal organs due to lack of oxygen.

diatom microscopic unicellular water plant, described and illustrated in para. 1.50.

dilation expansion, enlargement.

distal margin the further or outer edge of a wound.

diuretic a drug used to increase urine production.

duodenum the first part of the small intestine into which the stomach empties.

dura the fibrous lining of the inside of the skull containing large collecting veins or sinuses.

dysarthria difficulty in speaking.

embolism detachment or throwing off of blood clot, fat, tumour or other material from one part of the body and its carriage by the blood stream to the lung or other organ.

emesis vomiting.

endocarditis inflammation of the internal lining of the heart, particularly the heart valves.

enzyme a biological agent formed in the cells of body tissues or organs carrying out a specific function, e.g. digestion.

epigastrium the upper part of the central abdomen below the ribs.

epiglottis the flap of tissue at the back of the throat which closes off the larynx during swallowing.

excoriation roughening and reddening of the skin surface with skin loss.

exsanguination massive blood loss draining the body of blood.

extradural haemorrhage bleeding between the inner aspect of the skull bone and the dura lining it.

fellatio oral stimulation of the penis.
foramen magnum the opening in the base of the skull through which the spinal cord passes to join the brain.
fossa(e) the depression(s) in the base of the skull on which the base of the brain lies. There are two anterior fossae in the front, two middle, and two posterior fossae at the back. (See diagram in para. 1.89.)
frenulum a bridge of tissue connecting two surfaces together. Such bridges are found inside the centre of the upper lip connecting it to the gum, and on the undersurface of the penis connecting the glans to the shaft.
frontal sinuses cavities in the bone on either side of the forehead above the bridge of the nose.

gastro-enteritis inflammation of the lining of the stomach and intestines due to infection, often found in food poisoning.
glottic oedema swelling of the upper air passages involving the larynx (voice box), vocal cords and soft tissues above them at the back of the throat.
glycogen a carbohydrate substance often found in liver and muscle.

haematoma a bruise or other localised collection of extravasated blood.
haemoglobin the oxygen-carrying pigment present in red blood cells.
haemolysis destruction of red cells releasing blood pigment (haemoglobin).
hepatitis inflammation of the liver.
humerus bone of the upper arm.
hyoid bone a "U"-shaped bone in the upper part of the neck beneath the tongue to which muscles are attached and which may be fractured in cases of manual strangulation.
hypernatraemia excessive concentrations of sodium in the blood and body tissues.
hyperthyroidism excessive activity of the thyroid gland in the neck resulting in over-production of thyroid hormone, characterised by tremor, weight loss, staring eyes, too rapid heart beat and generalised overactivity.
hypoglycaemia abnormally low sugar concentration in the blood, often found in diabetics on insulin.
hypostasis post mortem lividity, the staining of the dependent parts of the body after death by blood settlement due to gravity.
hypothermia lowering of body temperature below 35°C (95°F).
hypoxia reduced oxygen concentration in body tissues.

ileum the main part of the small intestine connecting the jejunum to the colon.
infarction death of tissue or organs due to cutting off their blood supply.
irrespirable gas any gas other than oxygen, usually used to include toxic gases such as methane, sulphur dioxide and other industrial emissions.

jaundice the yellow colouration of the eyes, skin and body tissues found in liver and gall bladder disease due to the presence of excess bile pigment.
jejunum the upper part of the small intestine below the duodenum.
jugular vein the main vein running on each side of the neck taking blood from the brain back to the heart.

lactic acid an acid found in the blood and tissues following the breakdown of carbohydrates such as glycogen (*q.v.*).

lands the spiral ridges running along the inside of a rifle or revolver barrel which impart gyroscopic stability to a bullet by causing it to spin at high speed during flight.

laryngeal stenosis narrowing of the upper airway due to scarring from previous infection or injury.

larynx the voice box (Adam's apple) containing the vocal cords above and leading to the trachea below.

lividity see *hypostasis*.

lymph nodes collections of specialised cells forming glands found in groups under the arms, in the neck, chest, abdomen and groins. They act as a barrier against infection or foreign material and may be involved in the spread of cancer.

maceration wasting away through lack of nourishment.

macroscopic visible with the naked eye.

malignant hyperpyrexia a rare complication of anaesthesia due to an enzyme defect marked by a potentially fatal rise in body temperature.

medulla the nerve centre at the base of the brain connecting it to the spinal cord through which all the nerve fibres to and from it pass and where the centres controlling heart and lung function are situated.

Meniere's disease a disease of the central nervous system involving the inner ear, characterised by loss of balance and deafness.

meningitis inflammation of the coverings of the brain, usually due to infection.

mesentery the fatty attachment of the small intestine to the back wall of the abdominal cavity. It is fan-shaped and contains blood vessels to and from the intestine.

middle meningeal artery an artery arising from a carotid artery near the base of the skull and running in a groove on the inside of the skull in the temple regions, fanning out to supply the skull and dura.

mucous membrane the delicate lining of the body cavities and passages such as the mouth, stomach and intestines.

myxoedema failure of function of the thyroid gland characterised by low body temperature, slowing of all mental and physical processes and loss of hair.

nerve plexuses collection of nerve fibres often acting as junctions or distribution points.

nitrogen narcosis the "bends", a condition found in deep sea divers where an excess of nitrogen dissolved under pressure in the blood and body tissues causes unconsciousness and other toxic effects (see para. 1.53).

oedema pathological swelling of the tissues etc. due to accumulation of fluid.

oesophagus the gullet leading from the back of the throat to the stomach.

orbital plates the bone at the base of the skull behind the forehead forming the roof of the eye sockets (orbits).

pancreatitis inflammation of the pancreas which lies tranversely behind the stomach.

Parkinson's disease a chronic progressive disease of the brain marked by trauma, shambling gait and mask-like features.

pathognomic specifically diagnostic of a particular disease or pathological condition.

pericardial sac/pericardium the heart sac, the bag in which the heart lies.
perineum the lower abdominal area between the anus and the genitalia.
peritoneum the fine membrane covering the external surfaces of the stomach and intestines and the inner aspect of the abdominal cavity.
peritonitis inflammation of the peritoneum.
petechial haemorrhages fine bleeding spots in the eyes, skin and mucous membranes seen in cases of asphyxia due to rupture of small blood vessels (capillaries) from pressure.
photophobia inability to tolerate light.
platelets the small cells in the bloodstream necessary for blood clotting.
pleura(e) the fine membrane(s) covering the external surfaces of the lungs and the inside of the chest wall.
pons the area at the base of the brain connecting the cerebral hemispheres to the cerebellum and medulla which plays a large part in temperature control.
porta hepatis a region in the upper abdomen below the centre of the liver where the bile duct, arteries and veins run and where there is a collection of lymph nodes.
pulmonary embolism the lodging of a blood clot in the lungs following its detachment from the veins of the legs where it has formed, often after injury or due to heart failure or other medical conditions.

rectum (rectal) terminal part of the large intestine; the bowels.
recumbency lying down, usually used to suggest enforced rest following injury or surgery.
reflex cardiac arrest sudden stoppage of the heart due to interference with its nerve supply, often following neck injury or operative trauma.

scapula the shoulder blade.
scrotum the sac containing the testicles.
septicaemia the spread of bacterial infection throughout the body via the blood stream.
serous membranes the lining of the body cavities, for example the pleura and peritoneum.
sternum the breast bone.
strap muscles the muscles running in the front of the neck anchoring the tongue and the larynx and involved in swallowing and moving the head.
subarachnoid haemorrhage bleeding beneath the fine membranes covering the brain, often due to rupture of a berry aneurysm.
subdural haemorrhage bleeding beneath the dura lining the inside of the skull.
suppository medical drug for administration by the rectum.

thrombosis clotting of blood in arteries or veins or in the heart occuring during life.
thymus gland a mass of lymphatic tissue and fat present in childhood lying behind the upper end of the breast bone.
thyroid cartilages two plates of cartilage forming the promontory of the larynx (Adam's apple) shaped like a "V". Each side has an upward extension (the superior cornu or horn) connected to the hyoid bone, which may be fractured in manual strangulation or hanging.
toxaemia the spread of toxic material throughout the body via the blood stream.

trachea the windpipe connecting the larynx to the bronchi.
trauma any form of injury.

uraemia the accumulation of waste products in the blood following kidney failure.
urinary tract infection infection of the bladder or the kidneys which may complicate unconsciousness, paralysis, injury or surgery.

vagal inhibition see *reflex cardiac arrest.*
varicose vein a vein, usually in the leg, that has become dilated and tortuous and in which blood flow is sluggish and liable to clot.
vasovagal attacks sudden short periods of low blood pressure and unconsciousness.
vein (venous) a thin-walled blood vessel carrying blood back to the heart.
ventricular fibrillation very rapid ineffective beating of the heart which, if untreated, is usually fatal.
viscera body organs.
vital reaction changes in body tissues following injury occuring in life and visible to the naked eye or under the microscope.
vulva external orifice of the vagina.

Index